UNIVERSITY CASEBOOK SERIES®

THE LAW OF CONTRACTS

CASES AND MATERIALS

JAMES STEVEN ROGERS
Professor of Law
Boston College Law School

KATHARINE G. YOUNG
Associate Professor
Boston College Law School

FOUNDATION
PRESS

University Casebook Series is a trademark registered in the U.S. Patent and Trademark Office.

© 2017 LEG, Inc. d/b/a West Academic
    444 Cedar Street, Suite 700
    St. Paul, MN 55101
    1-877-888-1330

Printed in the United States of America

ISBN: 978-1-68328-993-7

To
Dorothy, Emma, and Eleanor
and
Vlad, Madeleine, and Alexander

PREFACE

The law of contracts is an evolving field of study, yet it is stable at its core. In the modern period, changes have occurred from the pressures of new case law, updated theories of economic efficiency or individual consent, developments in the broader law of private obligations, and new techniques and domains of commercial practice and dispute resolution. Yet the greatest change to the law of contracts, as a field of teaching and study, has come from the institutional pressure to reduce the study of the subject to a single-semester, less than six-credit course. This requires distilling the core of the subject matter without sacrificing relevance or richness. This book has been designed to offer a sophisticated and challenging course on the law of contracts, within these pressing constraints. It offers a fundamentally different approach from the lengthy compilations and bibliographies that represent the more conventional approach to the teaching and study of contract law.

Our first commitment, therefore, is to pedagogy. We present the following materials in an order that makes most sense from the perspective of students. We follow, primarily, a doctrinal presentation, drawing on the best features of the case method. We also include notes and questions to prompt students to reflect on, and understand, the models of reasoning employed, the policy issues that arise, or the assumptions that are unquestioned, within the unfolding body of caselaw. Using these vehicles, our goal is to introduce the deep-seated topics of concern to the law of contracts, with selective brevity: insights from law and economics, history and philosophy; assumptions about fairness and welfare, the science of cognition or the communication of consent; or newer commentary on the evolving operation of boilerplate or adhesion contracts, or of the effect of arbitration clauses. Although the presentation is primarily of cases, we explore their different implications for contractual counseling and drafting as well as dispute settlement. We include more substantive material on the law of restitution, and on international and comparative developments, than is usual in such a course. In these and other topics, we have sought to include various references without sacrificing the pace or momentum of the course.

Our goal has also been to produce a well-rounded book that opens up the broader jurisprudential issues without favoring any single presentation. While we acknowledge the significance of the rich vein of contract theory—of canonical scholarship and of the literature it has in its turn generated—that has guided the development of Anglo-American contract law, we have drawn on this theory to inform our selection of material, rather than reproduce it. If anything, our main perspective is conceptual. We consider that, like learning the grammar of language, a law student equipped with the conceptual structure of contract law is able to confront the countless legal situations that await him or her. But so, too, must the student understand the basic functions of contract law, its justification, and its consequences. We hope that this text, as one element of a comprehensive private law and public law J.D. curriculum, supplies the basis.

JAMES STEVEN ROGERS
KATHARINE G. YOUNG

December 2016

ACKNOWLEDGMENTS

We are indebted to the American Law Institute for permission to reprint excerpts of copyrighted material, including provisions, comments and illustrations from the following: Restatement of the Law, Contracts (1932); Restatement of the Law (Second) Contracts (1981); Restatement of the Law, Restitution (1937); Restatement of the Law (Third), Restitution and Unjust Enrichment (2011); and the Uniform Commercial Code.

In addition, we gratefully acknowledge the kind permission to reprint material from the following publishers: American Journal of Comparative Law; Associated Press; Columbia Law Review; Greater Boston Real Estate Board; Harvard Law Record Corporation; Harvard Law Review; Oxford University Press; Revista Juridica de la Universidad de Puerto Rico; University of Chicago Law Review; Yale Law Journal.

The authors also acknowledge Sara Almaashoug, Kelsey Rae Brattin and Terence McAllister for their excellent research assistance.

INTRODUCTION

Some Study Tips

Our subject matter in this course is the law of Contracts, but the main task in this and all of your first-year courses is developing skills of legal analysis.

Because the first year of law school is, in some ways, a novel intellectual experience, it is easy for students to become intimidated by it, to feel that "I'll never understand this fully, so I just want to try to get it enough to get by." But stop and think. By the time one gets to the level of entering law school, one has already passed through many tests of mind and character! So have confidence in yourselves—and keep your high ambitions and expectations. There will, inevitably, be times when you just won't have the time to spend on a particular set of topics or readings to feel that you've mastered it; but don't let yourself tell yourself that you can't do it and so needn't try.

Here are a few suggestions on how to approach your task.

Tools you need:

- Casebook
- Source Materials Supplement (containing UCC, Restatement (Second) of Contracts, and other additional materials)[a]
- Legal dictionary
- Brain
- Pencil (or computer etc.)
- Colleagues

In the first few weeks, many of the words in the cases you read will be entirely unfamiliar to you. You should look up each such word in a legal dictionary. The standard legal dictionary, available in the law library, or as a downloadable mobile application, is *Black's Law Dictionary*. There are also adequate legal dictionaries available on-line, e.g., http://dictionary.lp.findlaw.com/.

To fully understand a case, you will probably find that you have to read it three times. First, read though the whole case to get the general idea of what is going on. Second, go back and read it very carefully, trying your best to understand every paragraph. Ask yourself why each paragraph is there, that is, what issue is being discussed in this paragraph, how is it different from the preceding discussion, where is it going next, etc. We often find it useful to number the paragraphs so one

---

[a] While the UCC, Restatement and other materials are available on the internet, you will find it useful to have your own printed materials collected in one place, for study and marking up. We recommend STEVEN J. BURTON AND MELVIN A. EISENBERG, CONTRACT LAW: SELECTED SOURCE MATERIALS ANNOTATED. (As a reproduction of sources, any edition of the last few years will be fine).

can make a little outline of what's going on in each paragraph. Third, after you have gone through the case bit by bit, you should go back and reread it as a whole.

Remember that the point of reading and analyzing cases is not just to learn rules. If the task of learning law were simply a matter of learning rules, there would be no reason to use cases as our basic teaching material. Rather, we'd use some form of textbook that just laid out all the rules. The reason we use cases is that the task of a lawyer is to use rules to solve problems. Application and interpretation of the rules is the key. The goal of a legal education is not to memorize propositions of law; but to learn how to apply legal rules to specific problems. Reading cases gives you an opportunity to follow along as experienced lawyers work through this process. Each case you read is an account of the arguments that the opposing lawyers devised to advance their clients' objectives, and the thought process that the judges went through in assessing those arguments and coming to a conclusion.

Some folks may be able to analyze cases or other legal materials in their heads, but that's pretty uncommon. Together, this casebook's editors have been at this game for more than forty years, and they still can't do it without a pencil. Most of us find that the only way to force ourselves to read carefully and critically is to write out the results of our thinking. That's the whole point of the technique of "briefing cases" that you will hear discussed quite a bit. Think of case briefing as a means, not an end. What's important is not whether your briefs look like anybody else's, but that you go through the task. It's a tried and true technique for forcing ourselves to read cases critically, particularly to identify the most significant facts, to work through the procedural posture of the case, and to form some judgments about the impact of this opinion on other possible cases.

The search for this mystical thing called "the holding" is, in our view, nothing more than the process of figuring out from one opinion what other cases the court is likely to treat as the same as this case. That is, the "holding" of Case A is a description of the decision actually rendered in Case A at a level of generality such that any other case that falls within the same description will (probably) be treated as controlled by Case A. Another way to look at it is to ask, "Could I cite this case for the following proposition . . . " As you learn more and more about the process of common law decision making and the evolution of the law, you'll come to see why it is that there really can't be any single "correct" statement of the holding of a case. The point of trying to state a holding is that it forces us to (i) read carefully to identify exactly what was decided, and (ii) think through the implications of this decision for other cases.

Experience suggests that the best teaching/learning frequently comes from group discussions among yourselves. Another old, tried and true law school technique is the "study group," but again don't get obsessed. The point is simply that most of us find it useful to try out or ideas and reactions in a group.

Tools you probably do NOT need:

- Nutshells
- Commercially published outlines
- Commercially published "case briefs"
- Whatever other clever "study aid" is in vogue—such as Internet sites with case briefs and outlines

We'll repeat the conventional wisdom in urging you not to use these sorts of study aids. Why not? Because chances are that you'll be shooting yourself in the foot by using them. Your main task this year is to learn to read and analyze cases and other legal texts. The only way to do so is to do it; not read the results of somebody else doing it. For that reason, the worst sort of study aids might be the ones that will initially seem most tempting—those that include pre-prepared case briefs or similar discussions of the leading cases. Resist! Using canned briefs, outlines, and the like as principal tools of your law school work is a bit like paying a fortune for a Paris vacation and then spending the whole time in your hotel room watching the visitors' information channel on the TV.

Tools you might, but need not, use:

Secondary sources on the substantive law present a somewhat more subtle problem. Lawyers do use treatises and the like all the time. The best of them can be excellent tools. But you've got to be careful. Your main task this year, and in all of law school, is to learn to read and analyze cases and other legal texts, analyze a new fact pattern to decide what legal doctrines or categories apply, construct persuasive arguments, attempt to draft text to comply with laws etc. You've got to know a fair bit of substantive law to do that, but learning the substantive rules is not the principal objective. We realize that is hard to believe, but as evidence of the point, we can report the results of an empirical survey of what hiring partners at law firms thought about what law students should accomplish in law school. For the category of "Knowledge of Substantive Law," only 30% thought that this should be brought to the job; 70% thought it should be developed in practice. By contrast, for the category of "Ability in Legal Analysis & Reasoning, 81% thought this should be brought to the job; only 19% thought that it should be developed in practice.[b]

---

[b] 1991–1992 American Bar Foundation Survey of Chicago Law Firm Hiring Practices, excerpted in Anne Stein, *Job Hunting? Exude Confidence,* ABA Journal 40 (November 1993). The current Student Learning Outcomes required by the American Bar Association in legal education (in Standard 302) incorporate a number of competencies outside of knowledge of substantive law. These aim to reflect attributes of *knowledge* (general and technical knowledge, and cognitive and analytical skills); *skills* (including those needed to obtain and process information, and those used to transform a situation into a preferred one); *perspective* (such as the ability to consider the historical, political, ethical and moral aspects of a problem); and the *personal attributes* of professionalism: see A.B.A. Section of Legal Educ. & Admissions To The

The problem with misusing or overusing secondary sources like treatises is that doing so may give you the illusion of mastery when you've not yourselves struggled with the material. It's one thing to be able to regurgitate rules; it's another thing entirely to be able to apply rules. In this respect, we don't think that law is all that different from other disciplines. You can't learn how to write a computer program by memorizing the function definitions in a computer coding manual, and you can't learn how to do the electrical wiring of a house by memorizing the National Electrical Code.

Our suggestion is that you at least wait awhile before you seek out any other secondary sources. Later on, you may find it useful to read some of this sort of material, though it's never essential. If you do want to consult some in the library or buy something yourself, at least use your time and/or money wisely. That means that you might be better served by skipping the most simplistic sort of thing, like the nutshells, "black letter on . . . .". Instead, you can bolster your knowledge of the law presented in this book by looking at one of the well-regarded treatises. There are two enormous, multi-volume treatises (Samuel Williston's THE LAW OF CONTRACTS (1920) and Arthur Linton Corbin's CORBIN ON CONTRACT (1950)) that have had multiple new editions and editors, and enjoy a considerable degree of persuasive authority. You could look at either or both of these in the library if you want to go into great detail on a particular topic.

For things of more manageable size, the one volume treatise that we find most useful is FARNSWORTH, CONTRACTS (4th ed. 2004). Professor Farnsworth was the Reporter for the Second Restatement of Contracts, so his book is a good reflection of modern contract law. There are two other one-volume hornbooks, PERILLO, CONTRACTS (7th ed. 2014) and MURRAY ON CONTRACTS (5th ed. 2011) that, on at least some topics, adhere more closely to older concepts. For that reason we find them helpful when considering what lawyers meant by some older concept, such as "mutuality of obligation," that is de-emphasized in modern law. There's also a little paperback, M. CHIRELSTEIN, CONCEPTS AND CASE ANALYSIS IN THE LAW OF CONTRACTS (7th ed. 2013) that some students have liked. It's a bit less of a treatise than it is a discussion of one person's well-considered views on some of the standard cases—and should be treated as such.

If you are interested in collateral reading on contract law and theory, there are thousands of first-rate law review articles: only a fraction are referred to in the notes within this book. Several compilations of excerpts from law review articles are available: P. LINZER, ED., A CONTRACTS ANTHOLOGY (2D ED. 1995), R. BARNETT, ED., PERSPECTIVES ON CONTRACT LAW (4th ed. 2009), and R. CRASWELL & A. SCHWARTZ, FOUNDATIONS OF CONTRACT LAW (1994). There is also a paperback that collects articles

Bar, Report of the Outcome Measures Committee 7 (July 27, 2008); Roy Stuckey et al, Best Practices for Legal Education: A Vision and a Road Map (2007) at 52.

digging into detail on the factual background of several well-known contracts cases, some of which we will study in this course: D. BAIRD, ED., CONTRACTS STORIES (2007). That material is intriguing if you become interested in how these cases came to be contracts classics, although the background facts not discussed in the opinions themselves are not significant to the value of those opinions as precedent. A somewhat similar work is R. DANZIG & G. WATSON, THE CAPABILITY PROBLEM IN CONTRACT LAW (2d ed. 2004).

Finally there are some interesting texts that provide a comparative context to U.S. contract law, which we have found useful to law students, who will graduate into an increasingly globalized world of legal practice. One such introduction is J. SMITS, CONTRACT LAW: A COMPARATIVE INTRODUCTION (2014), or Part II.C of the classic, K. ZWEIGERT & H. KÖTZ, AN INTRODUCTION TO COMPARATIVE LAW (3rd ed., 1998, transl. Tony Weir).

Note on opinion editing:

We have frequently done fairly heavy editing on the cases printed in this book. Our objective is to provide useful teaching materials. Sometimes that requires that discussion of issues that were significant to the court's decision be edited out, often because including the discussion would only add confusion at this early stage of your legal training. That means that you do have to be careful in using this book. It's a teaching tool, not a research tool. If, in other contexts in law school or in practice after law school, you encounter problems related to the cases we have studied, you need to be sure that you consult the full original reports of the decisions, rather than the edited versions printed here.

Conventions used in editing: Footnotes are often omitted without notation, but when they remain in the case excerpt, we have retained the original footnote number. All footnotes written by us are lettered. Within text, deletion of merely citations is indicated by "* * *", while deletion of other textual material is indicated by ". . . ".

SUMMARY OF CONTENTS

TABLE OF CONTENTS

TABLE OF CASES

The principal cases are in bold type.

TABLE OF STATUTES AND RESTATEMENTS

THE LAW OF CONTRACTS

CASES AND MATERIALS

CHAPTER ONE

INTERESTS PROTECTED BY CONTRACT LAW

> The woods are lovely, dark and deep,
> But I have promises to keep,
> And miles to go before I sleep,
> And miles to go before I sleep.
>
> —Robert Frost

A. INTRODUCTION

Restatement (Second) of Contracts § 1. Contract Defined

A contract is a promise or a set of promises for the breach of which the law gives a remedy, or the performance of which the law in some way recognizes as a duty.

Hawkins v. McGee

Supreme Court of New Hampshire, 1929.
84 N.H. 114, 146 A. 641.

H1 Action by George Hawkins against Edward R. B. McGee. Verdict for plaintiff, which was set aside. Transferred on exceptions. New trial.

H2 Assumpsit against a surgeon for breach of an alleged warranty of the success of an operation. Trial by jury. Verdict for the plaintiff. The writ also contained a count in negligence upon which a nonsuit was ordered, without exception.

H3 Defendant's motions for a nonsuit and for a directed verdict on the count in assumpsit were denied, and the defendant excepted. . . . The defendant seasonably moved to set aside the verdict upon the grounds that it was contrary to the evidence . . . and because the damages awarded by the jury were excessive. The court . . . found that the damages were excessive, and made an order that the verdict be set aside, unless the plaintiff elected to remit all in excess of $500. The plaintiff having refused to remit, the verdict was set aside "as excessive and against the weight of the evidence," and the plaintiff excepted.

H4 The foregoing exceptions were transferred by Scammon, J. The facts are stated in the opinion.

■ BRANCH, J.

1 The operation in question consisted in the removal of a considerable quantity of scar tissue from the palm of the plaintiff's right hand and the grafting of skin taken from the plaintiff's chest in place thereof. The scar tissue was the result of a severe burn caused by contact with an electric wire, which the plaintiff received about nine years before the time of the transactions here involved. There was evidence to the effect that before the operation was performed the plaintiff and his father went to the defendant's office, and that the defendant, in answer to the question, "How long will the boy be in the hospital?" replied, "Three or four days, not over four; then the boy can go home and it will be just a few days when he will go back to work with a good hand." Clearly this and other testimony to the same effect would not justify a finding that the doctor contracted to complete the hospital treatment in three or four days or that the plaintiff would be able to go back to work within a few days thereafter. The above statements could only be construed as expressions of opinion or predictions as to the probable duration of the treatment and plaintiff's resulting disability, and the fact that these estimates were exceeded would impose no contractual liability upon the defendant. The only substantial basis for the plaintiff's claim is the testimony that the defendant also said before the operation was decided upon, "I will guarantee to make the hand a hundred per cent perfect hand or a hundred per cent good hand." The plaintiff was present when these words were alleged to have been spoken, and, if they are to be taken at their face value, it seems obvious that proof of their utterance would establish the giving of a warranty in accordance with his contention.

2   The defendant argues, however, that, even if these words were uttered by him, no reasonable man would understand that they were used with the intention of entering "into any contractual relation whatever," and that they could reasonably be understood only "as his expression in strong language that he believed and expected that as a result of the operation he would give the plaintiff a very good hand." It may be conceded, as the defendant contends, that, before the question of the making of a contract should be submitted to a jury, there is a preliminary question of law for the trial court to pass upon, i.e. "whether the words could possibly have the meaning imputed to them by the party who founds his case upon a certain interpretation," but it cannot be held that the trial court decided this question erroneously in the present case. It is unnecessary to determine at this time whether the argument of the defendant, based upon "common knowledge of the uncertainty which attends all surgical operations," and the improbability that a surgeon would ever contract to make a damaged part of the human body "one hundred per cent perfect," would, in the absence of countervailing considerations, be regarded as conclusive, for there were other factors in the present case which tended to support the contention of the plaintiff. There was evidence that the defendant repeatedly solicited from the plaintiff's father the opportunity to perform this operation, and the theory was advanced by plaintiff's counsel in cross-examination of defendant that he sought an opportunity to "experiment on skin grafting," in which he had had little previous experience. If the jury accepted this part of plaintiff's contention, there would be a reasonable

basis for the further conclusion that, if defendant spoke the words attributed to him, he did so with the intention that they should be accepted at their face value, as an inducement for the granting of consent to the operation by the plaintiff and his father, and there was ample evidence that they were so accepted by them. The question of the making of the alleged contract was properly submitted to the jury.

3   The substance of the charge to the jury on the question of damages appears in the following quotation: "If you find the plaintiff entitled to anything, he is entitled to recover for what pain and suffering he has been made to endure and for what injury he has sustained over and above what injury he had before." To this instruction the defendant seasonably excepted. By it, the jury was permitted to consider two elements of damage: (1) Pain and suffering due to the operation; and (2) positive ill effects of the operation upon the plaintiff's hand. Authority for any specific rule of damages in cases of this kind seems to be lacking, but, when tested by general principle and by analogy, it appears that the foregoing instruction was erroneous.

4   "By 'damages,' as that term is used in the law of contracts, is intended compensation for a breach, measured in the terms of the contract." *Davis v. New England Cotton Yarn Co.*, 77 N. H. 403, 404, 92 A. 732, 733. The purpose of the law is "to put the plaintiff in as good a position as he would have been in had the defendant kept his contract." 3 Williston Cont. § 1338; * * * The measure of recovery "is based upon what the defendant should have given the plaintiff, not what the plaintiff has given the defendant or otherwise expended." 3 Williston Cont. § 1341. "The only losses that can be said fairly to come within the terms of a contract are such as the parties must have had in mind when the contract was made, or such as they either knew or ought to have known would probably result from a failure to comply with its terms." *Davis v. New England Cotton Yarn Co.* * * *

5   The present case is closely analogous to one in which a machine is built for a certain purpose and warranted to do certain work. In such cases, the usual rule of damages for breach of warranty in the sale of chattels is applied, and it is held that the measure of damages is the difference between the value of the machine, if it had corresponded with the warranty and its actual value, together with such incidental losses as the parties knew, or ought to have known, would probably result from a failure to comply with its terms. * * *

6   The rule thus applied is well settled in this state. "As a general rule, the measure of the vendee's damages is the difference between the value of the goods as they would have been if the warranty as to quality had been true, and the actual value at the time of the sale, including gains prevented and losses sustained, and such other damages as could be reasonably anticipated by the parties as likely to be caused by the vendor's failure to keep his agreement, and could not by reasonable care on the part of the vendee have been avoided." *Union Bank v. Blanchard,*

65 N. H. 21, 23, 18 A. 90, 91; * * *. We therefore conclude that the true measure of the plaintiff's damage in the present case is the difference between the value to him of a perfect hand or a good hand, such as the jury found the defendant promised him, and the value of his hand in its present condition, including any incidental consequences fairly within the contemplation of the parties when they made their contract. 1 Sutherland, Damages (4th Ed.) § 92. Damages not thus limited, although naturally resulting, are not to be given.

7   The extent of the plaintiff's suffering does not measure this difference in value. The pain necessarily incident to a serious surgical operation was a part of the contribution which the plaintiff was willing to make to his joint undertaking with the defendant to produce a good hand. It was a legal detriment suffered by him which constituted a part of the consideration given by him for the contract. It represented a part of the price which he was willing to pay for a good hand, but it furnished no test of the value of a good hand or the difference between the value of the hand which the defendant promised and the one which resulted from the operation.

8   It was also erroneous and misleading to submit to the jury as a separate element of damage any change for the worse in the condition of the plaintiff's hand resulting from the operation, although this error was probably more prejudicial to the plaintiff than to the defendant. Any such ill effect of the operation would be included under the true rule of damages set forth above, but damages might properly be assessed for the defendant's failure to improve the condition of the hand, even if there were no evidence that its condition was made worse as a result of the operation.

9   It must be assumed that the trial court, in setting aside the verdict, undertook to apply the same rule of damages which he had previously given to the jury, and, since this rule was erroneous, it is unnecessary for us to consider whether there was any evidence to justify his finding that all damages awarded by the jury above $500 were excessive.

10   . . . . New trial.

NOTES

1.   We have added the marginal paragraph numbers (H1, H2, . . .1, 2, 3, . . .) to make it easier for us to refer to specific portions of the opinion.

2.   The first four paragraphs (H1–H4) are what is sometimes called a "headnote." These words were not written by the judge who decided the case, but by the reporter, that is, by the publisher of the volume of case reports. In modern reports, it's usually easy to see what parts were written by the judge and what parts were written by the book publisher. In older cases, that's sometimes a bit harder.

Because these words were written by someone whose job is reporting decisions, they use quite a bit of legal jargon. The reporter is trying to state briefly the results of the litigation that led to the opinion of the New Hampshire Supreme Court, and the reporter is doing so on the assumption that the readers are practicing lawyers already familiar with legal procedure and legal language. The jargon will become more familiar as you become more accustomed to reading opinions. In the early stages of your law school work, you will certainly need to use a legal dictionary to try to make sense of such passages.

As a first effort, try to understand the headnote, looking up the following words in a legal dictionary: assumpsit . . . warranty . . . verdict . . . count . . . nonsuit . . . exception

2. The opinion above doesn't clearly state the amount that the plaintiff sought or the amount of the jury's verdict. A later case involving a dispute between Dr. McGee and his malpractice insurer reveals that Hawkins' complaint sought damages of $10,000, and that the jury verdict—which was set aside in the case above—was for $3000. *McGee v. United States Fidelity & Guar. Co.*, 53 F.2d 953 (1st Cir. 1931).

The headnote in the opinion printed above indicates that on the issue of damages, the trial judge employed a somewhat unusual procedure, known as *remittitur*. See H3. The jury returned a verdict for the plaintiff for $3000. The trial judge thought that the amount of the verdict was not supported by the evidence. He might have refused to enter judgment, and just let the plaintiff appeal. Instead, he did something a bit different. In essence he said to the plaintiff's lawyer "Look, I won't enter judgment for the $3000 full amount of the jury's verdict, but if the jury had returned a verdict for a smaller amount, say $500, I would have entered judgment for that amount. So, I'll give you a choice: take $500 and go home, or refuse that and take your chances on appeal." (Kind of like Monty Hall on Let's Make a Deal: "$500 or Door Number 2"). The plaintiff's lawyer decided not to take the $500, so the trial judge set aside the verdict and plaintiff brought the appeal.

3. The facts call to mind a medical malpractice scenario. Patients sue doctors all the time, contending that the doctors performed surgery in a negligent fashion. In *Hawkins v. McGee*, the patient did allege ordinary negligence in his complaint. But, as the opinion indicates, Dr. McGee also said things that could be construed as a promise that the operation would be successful. So Hawkins' complaint alleged two different causes of action: (1) a tort theory of malpractice ("count in negligence"), and (2) a contract theory of breach of a promise ("assumpsit . . . for breach of warranty").

The basis of the tort theory would have been a contention that Dr. McGee had acted negligently, that is, without the care one would expect of an ordinary physician. The headnote shows that the trial judge dismissed the tort count, and the patient's lawyer dropped the matter. It's not clear from the opinion why the plaintiff did not pursue the negligence theory any further. Perhaps the patient's lawyer could not find any other doctors willing to testify that Dr. McGee had acted negligently. For whatever reason, the plaintiff did not appeal the dismissal of the negligence count. That information is reported, albeit in a kind of secret code, by the statement in H2 that "The writ also contained a count in negligence upon which a nonsuit was ordered, without exception." Since the plaintiff did not bring an appeal on that point, it's essentially irrelevant for purposes of the case that the New Hampshire Supreme Court had to decide.

4.   Broadly speaking, the opinion deals with two issues: (1) did the evidence support a jury verdict for the patient on the theory that the doctor had made an enforceable promise about the outcome of the operation (¶¶ 1–2), and (2) were the trial judge's instructions to the jury correct on the issue of how the award of damages should be computed if the jury did find that the doctor made an enforceable promise (¶¶ 3–8). We will examine those two issues separately.

5.   On the first issue—whether the evidence supported a verdict for the patient on a contract theory—you need to read ¶¶ 1 & 2 very carefully. Identify specifically what facts the evidence would support, and what the Court said about whether that fact alone would suffice to support the jury's verdict. One way of forcing yourself to do that is to suppose that you are the trial judge in a similar case that arose after the *Hawkins* decision. Suppose that the plaintiff proves some, but not all, of the facts akin to those in *Hawkins*. The doctor's lawyer moves for a directed verdict on the grounds that that evidence would not support a verdict for the patient on the contract theory. What ruling do you make on the basis of the *Hawkins* opinion?

6.   On the second issue—how to compute damages in the contract action, you need to consider separately (1) the conceptual issue of what the award of damages is supposed to accomplish, and (2) the evidentiary and computational issue. For the moment, let's ignore the computational issues. In ¶ 4, the Court states that the purpose of contract damages to put the plaintiff in as good a position as he would have been in had the defendant performed the promise. That's a phrase that we will state again and again and again during this course. You'll get sick of hearing your professor say it. But, you'll keep forgetting to think through the implications of the point. That's why we will keep repeating it.

In ¶¶ 5 & 6, the Court takes that general concept and applies it to the setting of an action for breach of a "warranty," that is, a promise by a seller of a machine that the machine will do certain things. In ¶ 5, the Court notes that in such a case the measure of damages would be the "difference between the value of the machine, if it had corresponded with the warranty and its actual value." So, in such a case we would have to figure out how much the machine would have been worth if it had been as promised and how much the machine is worth in the state that it was actually delivered. Now, by analogy, we apply that concept to the somewhat unusual situation of a doctor's promise about the result of an operation. Suppose that the operation caused no pain. Suppose that (somehow) we can conclude:

(a)   that the value of the patient's hand if the operation had been successful would have been $1,700,000;

(b)   that the value of the patient's hand in its original pre-operation state was $1,000,000; and

(c)   that the value of the patient's hand in the condition it was in after the botched operation was $500,000.

What recovery would the plaintiff be entitled to in the contract action for breach of promise? By comparison, consider what recovery the plaintiff would be entitled to in a tort action for malpractice, which is designed to compensate the plaintiff for the harm.

7.   Now think about how, in an actual lawsuit, one would prove what the "value" of the hand in its various conditions would be. What evidence would you want to introduce on the issue of damages if you were representing the patient in *Hawkins*?

8.   The following background facts concerning *Hawkins v. McGee* (based on interviews and correspondence with the Hawkins family and a local lawyer) are reported in Jorie Roberts, Hawkins Case: A Hair-Raising Experience, Harvard Law School Record, March 17, 1978, at 1, 7, 13.

. . . George Hawkins was born in January, 1904—the second of Rose Wilkinson and Charles Augustus Hawkins' six children . . . .

One morning in 1915, 11-year-old George burned his right hand while preparing breakfast for his father on the family's wood-burning stove. At the time, George was trying to turn on the kitchen light to illuminate the stove, but an electrical storm the night before had damaged the wiring so that George received a severe shock. One of George's younger brothers, Howard Hawkins, now an insurance agent in Berlin, described George's initial scar as a "small pencil-size scar" which was between his thumb and index finger and did not substantially affect his use of the hand. Nevertheless, Charles Hawkins took his son George to skin specialists in Montreal after the accident; but there the doctors advised the Hawkinses against doing anything to restore the hand.

During this period, the family physician, Edward McGee, while treating one of George's younger brothers for pneumonia, also became aware of George's scarred hand. Later, in 1919, after returning from several years of medical service in Europe during World War I, McGee requested George and his parents to let him operate on the hand in order to restore it to "perfect" condition.

According to Dorothy St. Hilaire, George's younger sister, McGee claimed to have done a number of similar skin grafts on soldiers in Germany during the war, although he later admitted that he had really only observed such operations.

St. Hilaire recollects that McGee, in persuading George to undergo the surgery, emphasized the social problems which his scarred hand might create. McGee encouraged the Hawkinses to allow him to operate on the hand for three years, until finally George agreed shortly after his 18th birthday . . . .

McGee operated on George's hand in the St. Louis Hospital in Berlin in March of 1922. The skin graft operation was supposed to be quick, simple, and effective, and to require only a few days of hospitalization. Instead, St. Hilaire recalls that her brother bled very badly for several days . . . .

. . . George was, in the words of his brother Howard, "in the throes of death" for quite a while after the operation because of his extensive bleeding and the ensuing infection. Moreover, the post-operation scar covered his thumb and two fingers and was densely covered with hair. Howard Hawkins remembers that George's hand was partially closed up and continued to bleed periodically throughout his life . . . .

The jury only awarded the Hawkinses $3,000 for damages, and the final settlement was for $1,400 and lawyers fees. St. Hilaire believes the jurors, while at heart solidly behind the Hawkinses' cause, were afraid to return heavier damages against McGee because he was one of the more prominent physicians in the area. Charles Hawkins took the $1,400 and his injured son back to Montreal to see if any subsequent operations would alleviate George's deformity, but the doctors there said that the grafted skin was so tough that nothing more could be done . . . .

Hawkins' crippled hand affected his employment and outlook throughout his lifetime. After the operation, George Hawkins never returned to high school, even though, in Howard's opinion, "George was very bright, learned quickly, and had a pleasing personality." He was encouraged by his parents to finish school, but would not because, in his siblings' view, he was embarrassed by his hand.

Karl Llewellyn, The Bramble Bush (1930)

Extracted from pp. 40–45 THE BRAMBLE BUSH by Karl Llewellyn (1930), By permission of Oxford University Press

[The following passage is from a book written for law students by one of the "giants" of twentieth century American law, Karl Llewellyn. It attempts to articulate some of the implicit assumptions that lawyers make when they are "reading cases." You are just starting that process, so you should not expect to master it, or even be more or less proficient at it, for a long time. A good deal of your time in law school will be devoted to the task of learning to read and interpret cases. Right now, the things that Llewellyn says in this passage are likely to strike you as fairly obvious or inconsequential. That is because you have not yet had to wrestle with the problems of trying to figure out how to read and interpret judicial opinions. Here's our suggestion: Read the passage below now, and take from it whatever enlightenment you may find in it. Then, come back and re-read this passage every month or so throughout this year (and even beyond). You will see more and more in this passage as you have more and more experience with the process of reading cases.]

The first thing to do with an opinion, then, is read it. The next thing is to get clear the actual decision, the judgment rendered. Who won, the plaintiff or defendant? And watch your step here. You are after in first instance the plaintiff and defendant *below*, in the trial court. In order to follow through what happened you must therefore first know the outcome *below*; else you do not see what was appealed from, nor by whom. You now follow through in order to see exactly what *further* judgment has been rendered on appeal. The stage is then cleared of form—although of course you do not yet know all that these forms mean, that they imply. You can turn now to what you want peculiarly to know. Given the actual judgments below and above as your indispensable framework—what has the case decided, and what can you derive from it as to what will be decided later?

You will be looking, in the opinion, or in the preliminary matter plus the opinion, for the following: a statement of the facts the court assumes; a statement of the precise way the question has come before the court— which includes what the plaintiff wanted below, and what the defendant did about it, the judgment below, and what the trial court did that is complained of; then the outcome on appeal, the judgment; and finally the reasons this court gives for doing what it did. This does not look so bad. But it is much worse than it looks.

For all our cases are decided, all our opinions are written, all our predictions, all our arguments are made, on four certain assumptions. They are the first presuppositions of our study. They must be rutted into you till you can juggle with them standing on your head and in your sleep.

(1) *The court must decide the dispute that is before it*. It cannot refuse because the job is hard, or dubious, or dangerous.

(2) *The court can decide only the particular dispute which is before it*. When it speaks to that question it speaks ex cathedra, with authority, with finality, with an almost magic power. When it speaks to the question before it, it announces *law*, and if what it announces is new, it legislates, it *makes* the law. But when it speaks to any other question at all, it says mere words, which no man needs to follow. Are such words worthless? They are not. We know them as judicial *dicta*; when they are wholly off the point at issue we call them *obiter dicta*—words dropped along the road, wayside remarks. Yet even wayside remarks shed light on the remarker. They may be very useful in the future to him, or to us. But he will not feel bound to them, as to his ex cathedra utterance. They came not hallowed by a Delphic frenzy. He may be slow to change them; but not so slow as in the other case.

(3) *The court can decide the particular dispute only according to a general rule which covers a whole class of like disputes*. Our legal theory does not admit of single decisions standing

on their own. If judges are free, are indeed forced, to decide new cases for which there is no rule, they must at least make a rule as they decide. So far, good. But how wide, or how narrow, is the general rule in this particular case? That is a troublesome matter. The practice of our case-law, however, is I think fairly stated thus: it pays to be suspicious of general rules which look too wide; it pays to go slow in feeling certain that a wide rule has been laid down at all, or that, if seemingly laid down, it will be followed. For there is a fourth accepted cannon

(4) Everything, everything, everything, big or small, a judge may say in an opinion, is to be read with primary reference to the particular dispute, the particular question before him. You are not to think that the words mean what they might if they stood alone. You are to have your eye on the case in hand, and to learn how to interpret all that has been said merely as a reason for deciding that case that way.

Now why these canons? The first, I take it, goes back to the primary purpose of law. If the job is in first instance to settle disputes which do not otherwise get settled, then the only way to do it is to do it. And it will not matter so much how it is done, in a baffling instance, so long as it is done at all.

The third, that cases must be decided according to a general rule, goes back in origin less to purpose than to superstition. As long as law was felt as something ordained of god, or even as something inherently right in the order of nature, the judge was to be regarded as a mouthpiece, not as a creator; and a mouthpiece of the general, who but made clear an application to the particular. Else he broke faith, else he was arbitrary, and either biased or corrupt. Moreover, justice demands, wherever that concept is found, that like men be treated alike in like conditions. Why, I do not know; the fact is given. That calls for general rules, and for their even application. So, too, the "separation of powers" comes in powerfully to urge that general rules are made by the Legislature or the system, not the judges, and that the judge has but to act *according* to the general rules there are. Finally, a philosophy even of expediency will urge the same. Whatever may be the need of shaping decision to individual cases in the juvenile court, or in the court of domestic relations, or in a business man's tribunal for commercial cases—still, when the supreme court of a state speaks, it speaks first to clear up a point of general interest. And the responsibility for formulating general policy forces a wider survey, a more thorough study of the policies involved. So, too, we gain an added guarantee against either sentimentalism or influence in individual cases. And, what is not to be disregarded, we fit with the common notion of what justice calls for. . . .

Back, if I may now, to the why of the two canons I have left: that the court can decide only the particular dispute before it; that all that is said is to be read with eyes on that dispute. Why these? I do believe that here we have as fine a deposit of slow growing wisdom as ever has been laid down through the centuries by the unthinking social sea. Here, hardened into institutions, carved out and given line by rationale. What is this wisdom? Look to your own discussion, look to any argument. You know where you would go. You reach, at random if hurried, more carefully if not, for a foundation, for a major premise. But never for itself. Its interest lies in leading to the conclusion you are headed for. You shape its words, its content, to an end decreed. More, with your mind upon your object you use words, you bring in illustrations, you deploy and advance and concentrate again. When you have done, you have said much you did not mean. You did not mean, that is, *except* in reference to your point. You have brought generalization after generalization up, and discharged it at your goal; all, in the heat of argument, were over-stated. None would you stand to, if your opponent should urge them to *another* issue.

So with the judge. Nay, more so with the judge. He is not merely human, as are you. He is, as well, a lawyer, . . . and as such skilled in manipulating the resources of persuasion at his hand. A lawyer, and as such prone without thought to twist analogies, and rules, and instances, to his conclusion. A lawyer, and as such peculiarly prone to disregard the implications which do not bear directly on his case.

More, as a practiced campaigner in the art of exposition, he has learned that one must prepare the way for argument. You set the mood, the tone, you lay the intellectual foundation—all with the case in mind, with the conclusion—all, because those who hear you also have the case in mind, without the niggling criticism which may later follow. You wind up, as a pitcher will wind up—and as in the pitcher's case, the wind-up often is superfluous. As in the pitcher's case, it has been known to be intentionally misleading.

With this it should be clear, then, why our canons thunder. Why we create a class of dicta, of unnecessary words, which later readers, their minds now on quite other cases, can mark off as not quite essential to the argument. Why we create a class of *obiter dicta*, the wilder flailings of the pitcher's arms, the wilder motions of his gum-ruminant jaws. Why we set about, as our job, to crack the kernel from the nut, to find the true rule the case in fact decides: *the rule of the case*.

Now for a while I am going to risk confusion for the sake of talking simply. I am going to treat as the rule of the case the *ratio decidendi*, the rule *the court tells you* is the rule of the case, the ground, as the phrase goes, upon which the court itself has rested its decision. For there is where you must begin, and such refinements as are needed may come after.

The court, I will assume, has talked for five pages, only one of which portrayed the facts assumed. The rest has been discussion. And judgment has been given for the party who won below: judgment affirmed. We seek the rule.

The first thing to note is this: no rule can be the *ratio decidendi* from which the actual judgment (here: affirmance) does not follow. Unless affirmance follows from a rule, it cannot be the rule which produced an actual holding of affirmance. But the holding is the decision, and the court speaks ex cathedra only as to the dispute decided, and only as to the decision it has made. At this point, too, I think you begin to see the bearing of the procedural issue. There can be a decision (and so an ex cathedra ratio) only as to a point which is before the court. But points come before a court of review by way of specific complaint about specific action of the court below, and in no other way. Hence nothing can be held which is not thus brought up.

Lucy v. Zehmer

Supreme Court of Appeals of Virginia, 1954.
196 Va. 493, 84 S.E.2d 516.

■ BUCHANAN, J., delivered the opinion of the court.

This suit was instituted by W. O. Lucy and J. C. Lucy, complainants, against A. H. Zehmer and Ida S. Zehmer, his wife, defendants, to have specific performance of a contract by which it was alleged the Zehmers had sold to W. O. Lucy a tract of land owned by A. H. Zehmer in Dinwiddie county containing 471.6 acres, more or less, known as the Ferguson farm, for $50,000. J. C. Lucy, the other complainant, is a brother of W. O. Lucy, to whom W. O. Lucy transferred a half interest in his alleged purchase.

The instrument sought to be enforced was written by A. H. Zehmer on December 20, 1952, in these words: 'We hereby agree to sell to W. O. Lucy the Ferguson Farm complete for $50,000.00, title satisfactory to buyer,' and signed by the defendants, A. H. Zehmer and Ida S. Zehmer.

The answer of A. H. Zehmer admitted that at the time mentioned W. O. Lucy offered him $50,000 cash for the farm, but that he, Zehmer, considered that the offer was made in jest; that so thinking, and both he and Lucy having had several drinks, he wrote out 'the memorandum' quoted above and induced his wife to sign it; that he did not deliver the memorandum to Lucy, but that Lucy picked it up, read it, put it in his pocket, attempted to offer Zehmer $5 to bind the bargain, which Zehmer refused to accept, and realizing for the first time that Lucy was serious, Zehmer assured him that he had no intention of selling the farm and that the whole matter was a joke. Lucy left the premises insisting that he had purchased the farm.

Depositions were taken and the decree appealed from was entered holding that the complainants had failed to establish their right to specific performance, and dismissing their bill. The assignment of error is to this action of the court.

W. O. Lucy, a lumberman and farmer, thus testified in substance: He had known Zehmer for fifteen or twenty years and had been familiar with the Ferguson farm for ten years. Seven or eight years ago he had offered Zehmer $20,000 for the farm which Zehmer had accepted, but the agreement was verbal and Zehmer backed out. On the night of December 20, 1952, around eight o'clock, he took an employee to McKenney, where Zehmer lived and operated a restaurant, filling station and motor court. While there he decided to see Zehmer and again try to buy the Ferguson farm. He entered the restaurant and talked to Mrs. Zehmer until Zehmer came in. He asked Zehmer if he had sold the Ferguson farm. Zehmer replied that he had not. Lucy said, 'I bet you wouldn't take $50,000.00 for that place.' Zehmer replied, 'Yes, I would too; you wouldn't give fifty.' Lucy said he would and told Zehmer to write up an agreement to that effect. Zehmer took a restaurant check and wrote on the back of it, 'I do hereby agree to sell to W. O. Lucy the Ferguson Farm for $50,000 complete.' Lucy told him he had better change it to 'We' because Mrs. Zehmer would have to sign it too. Zehmer then tore up what he had written, wrote the agreement quoted above and asked Mrs. Zehmer, who was at the other end of the counter ten or twelve feet away, to sign it. Mrs. Zehmer said she would for $50,000 and signed it. Zehmer brought it back and gave it to Lucy, who offered him $5 which Zehmer refused, saying, 'You don't need to give me any money, you got the agreement there signed by both of us.'

The discussion leading to the signing of the agreement, said Lucy, lasted thirty or forty minutes, during which Zehmer seemed to doubt that Lucy could raise $50,000. Lucy suggested the provision for having the title examined and Zehmer made the suggestion that he would sell it 'complete, everything there,' and stated that all he had on the farm was three heifers.

Lucy took a partly filled bottle of whiskey into the restaurant with him for the purpose of giving Zehmer a drink if he wanted it. Zehmer did, and he and Lucy had one or two drinks together. Lucy said that while he felt the drinks he took he was not intoxicated, and from the way Zehmer handled the transaction he did not think he was either.

December 20 was on Saturday. Next day Lucy telephoned to J. C. Lucy and arranged with the latter to take a half interest in the purchase and pay half of the consideration. On Monday he engaged an attorney to examine the title. The attorney reported favorably on December 31 and on January 2 Lucy wrote Zehmer stating that the title was satisfactory, that he was ready to pay the purchase price in cash and asking when Zehmer would be ready to close the deal. Zehmer replied by letter, mailed on January 13, asserting that he had never agreed or intended to sell.

Mr. and Mrs. Zehmer were called by the complainants as adverse witnesses. Zehmer testified in substance as follows:

He bought this farm more than ten years ago for $11,000. He had had twenty-five offers, more or less, to buy it, including several from Lucy, who had never offered any specific sum of money. He had given them all the same answer, that he was not interested in selling it. On this Saturday night before Christmas it looked like everybody and his brother came by there to have a drink. He took a good many drinks during the afternoon and had a pint of his own. When he entered the restaurant around eight-thirty Lucy was there and he could see that he was 'pretty high.' He said to Lucy, 'Boy, you got some good liquor, drinking, ain't you?' Lucy then offered him a drink. 'I was already high as a Georgia pine, and didn't have any more better sense than to pour another great big slug out and gulp it down, and he took one too.'

After they had talked a while Lucy asked whether he still had the Ferguson farm. He replied that he had not sold it and Lucy said, 'I bet you wouldn't take $50,000.00 for it.' Zehmer asked him if he would give $50,000 and Lucy said yes. Zehmer replied, 'You haven't got $50,000 in cash.' Lucy said he did and Zehmer replied that he did not believe it. They argued 'pro and con for a long time,' mainly about 'whether he had $50,000 in cash that he could put up right then and buy that farm.'

Finally, said Zehmer, Lucy told him if he didn't believe he had $50,000, 'you sign that piece of paper here and say you will take $50,000.00 for the farm.' He, Zehmer, 'just grabbed the back off of a guest check there' and wrote on the back of it. At that point in his testimony Zehmer asked to see what he had written to 'see if I recognize my own handwriting.' He examined the paper and exclaimed, 'Great balls of fire, I got 'Firgerson' for Ferguson. I have got satisfactory spelled wrong. I don't recognize that writing if I would see it, wouldn't know it was mine.'

After Zehmer had, as he described it, 'scribbled this thing off,' Lucy said, 'Get your wife to sign it.' Zehmer walked over to where she was and she at first refused to sign but did so after he told her that he 'was just needling him [Lucy], and didn't mean a thing in the world, that I was not selling the farm.' Zehmer then 'took it back over there . . . and I was still looking at the dern thing. I had the drink right there by my hand, and I reached over to get a drink, and he said, 'Let me see it.' He reached and picked it up, and when I looked back again he had it in his pocket and he dropped a five dollar bill over there, and he said, 'Here is five dollars payment on it.' . . . I said, 'Hell no, that is beer and liquor talking. I am not going to sell you the farm. I have told you that too many times before."

Mrs. Zehmer testified that when Lucy came into the restaurant he looked as if he had had a drink. When Zehmer came in he took a drink out of a bottle that Lucy handed him. She went back to help the waitress who was getting things ready for next day. Lucy and Zehmer were talking but she did not pay too much attention to what they were saying. She heard Lucy ask Zehmer if he had sold the Ferguson farm, and Zehmer replied that he had not and did not want to sell it. Lucy said, 'I bet you wouldn't take $50,000 cash for that farm,' and Zehmer replied, 'You haven't got $50,000 cash.' Lucy said, 'I can get it.' Zehmer said he might form a company and get it, 'but you haven't got $50,000.00 cash to pay me tonight.' Lucy asked him if he would put it in writing that he would sell him this farm. Zehmer then wrote on the back of a pad, 'I agree to sell the Ferguson Place to W. O. Lucy for $50,000.00 cash.' Lucy said, 'All right, get your wife to sign it.' Zehmer came back to where she was standing and said, 'You want to put your name to this?' She said 'No,' but he said in an undertone, 'It is nothing but a joke,' and she signed it.

She said that only one paper was written and it said: 'I hereby agree to sell,' but the 'I' had been changed to 'We'. However, she said she read what she signed and was then asked, 'When you read 'We hereby agree to sell to W. O. Lucy,' what did you interpret that to mean, that particular phrase?' She said she thought that was a cash sale that night; but she also said that when she read that part about 'title satisfactory to buyer' she understood that if the title was good Lucy would pay $50,000 but if the title was bad he would have a right to reject it, and that that was her understanding at the time she signed her name.

On examination by her own counsel she said that her husband laid this piece of paper down after it was signed; that Lucy said to let him see it, took it, folded it and put it in his wallet, then said to Zehmer, 'Let me give you $5.00,' but Zehmer said, 'No, this is liquor talking. I don't want to sell the farm, I have told you that I want my son to have it. This is all a joke.' Lucy then said at least twice, 'Zehmer, you have sold your farm,' wheeled around and started for the door. He paused at the door and said, 'I will bring you $50,000.00 tomorrow. . . . No, tomorrow is Sunday. I will bring it to you Monday.' She said you could tell definitely that he was drinking and she said to her husband, 'You should have taken him home,' but he said, 'Well, I am just about as bad off as he is.'

The waitress referred to by Mrs. Zehmer testified that when Lucy first came in 'he was mouthy.' When Zehmer came in they were laughing and joking and she thought they took a drink or two. She was sweeping and cleaning up for next day. She said she heard Lucy tell Zehmer, 'I will give you so much for the farm,' and Zehmer said, 'You haven't got that much.' Lucy answered, 'Oh, yes, I will give you that much.' Then 'they jotted down something on paper . . . and Mr. Lucy reached over and took it, said let me see it.' He looked at it, put it in his pocket and in about a minute he left. She was asked whether she saw Lucy offer Zehmer any money and replied, 'He had five dollars laying up there, they didn't take it.' She said Zehmer told Lucy he didn't want his money 'because he didn't have enough money to pay for his property, and wasn't going to sell his farm.' Both of them appeared to be drinking right much, she said.

She repeated on cross-examination that she was busy and paying no attention to what was going on. She was some distance away and did not see either of them sign the paper. She was asked whether she saw Zehmer put the agreement down on the table in front of Lucy, and her answer was this: 'Time he got through writing whatever it was on the paper, Mr. Lucy reached over and said, 'Let's see it.' He took it and put it in his pocket,' before showing it to Mrs. Zehmer. Her version was that Lucy kept raising his offer until it got to $50,000.

The defendants insist that the evidence was ample to support their contention that the writing sought to be enforced was prepared as a bluff or dare to force Lucy to admit that he did not have $50,000; that the whole matter was a joke; that the writing was not delivered to Lucy and no binding contract was ever made between the parties.

It is an unusual, if not bizarre, defense. When made to the writing admittedly prepared by one of the defendants and signed by both, clear evidence is required to sustain it.

In his testimony Zehmer claimed that he 'was high as a Georgia pine,' and that the transaction 'was just a bunch of two doggoned drunks bluffing to see who could talk the biggest and say the most.' That claim is inconsistent with his attempt to testify in great detail as to what was said and what was done. It is contradicted by other evidence as to the condition of both parties, and rendered of no weight by the testimony of his wife that when Lucy left the restaurant she suggested that Zehmer drive him home. The record is convincing that Zehmer was not intoxicated to the extent of being unable to comprehend the nature and consequences of the instrument he executed, and hence that instrument is not to be invalidated on that ground. 17 C.J.S., Contracts, § 133 b., p. 483; *Taliaferro v. Emery,* 124 Va. 674, 98 S.E. 627. It was in fact conceded by defendants' counsel in oral argument that under the evidence Zehmer was not too drunk to make a valid contract.

The evidence is convincing also that Zehmer wrote two agreements, the first one beginning 'I hereby agree to sell.' Zehmer first said he could not remember about that, then that 'I don't think I wrote but one out.' Mrs. Zehmer said that what he wrote was 'I hereby agree,' but that the 'I' was changed to 'We' after that night. The agreement that was written and signed is in the record and indicates no such change. Neither are the mistakes in spelling that Zehmer sought to point out readily apparent.

The appearance of the contract, the fact that it was under discussion for forty minutes or more before it was signed; Lucy's objection to the first draft because it was written in the singular, and he wanted Mrs. Zehmer to sign it also; the rewriting to meet that objection and the signing by Mrs. Zehmer; the discussion of what was to be included in the sale, the provision for the examination of the title, the completeness of the instrument that was executed, the taking possession of it by Lucy with no request or suggestion by either of the defendants that he give it back, are facts which furnish persuasive evidence that the execution of the contract was a serious business transaction rather than a casual, jesting matter as defendants now contend.

On Sunday, the day after the instrument was signed on Saturday night, there was a social gathering in a home in the town of McKenney at which there were general comments that the sale had been made. Mrs. Zehmer testified that on that occasion as she passed by a group of people, including Lucy, who were talking about the transaction, $50,000 was mentioned, whereupon she stepped up and said, 'Well, with the high-price whiskey you were drinking last night you should have paid more. That was cheap.' Lucy testified that at that time Zehmer told him that he did not want to 'stick' him or hold him to the agreement because he, Lucy, was too tight and didn't know what he was doing, to which Lucy replied that he was not too tight; that he had been stuck before and was going through with it. Zehmer's version was that he said to Lucy: 'I am not trying to claim it wasn't a deal on account of the fact the price was too low. If I had wanted to sell $50,000.00 would be a good price, in fact I think you would get stuck at $50,000.00.' A disinterested witness testified that what Zehmer said to Lucy was that 'he was going to let him up off the deal, because he thought he was too tight, didn't know what he was doing. Lucy said something to the effect that 'I have been stuck before and I will go through with it."

If it be assumed, contrary to what we think the evidence shows, that Zehmer was jesting about selling his farm to Lucy and that the transaction was intended by him to be a joke, nevertheless the evidence shows that Lucy did not so understand it but considered it to be a serious business transaction and the contract to be binding on the Zehmers as well as on himself. The very next day he arranged with his brother to put up half the money and take a half interest in the land. The day after that he employed an attorney to examine the title. The next night, Tuesday, he was back at Zehmer's place and there Zehmer told him for the first time, Lucy said, that he wasn't going to sell and he told Zehmer, 'You know you sold that place fair and square.' After receiving the report from his attorney that the title was good he wrote to Zehmer that he was ready to close the deal.

Not only did Lucy actually believe, but the evidence shows he was warranted in believing, that the contract represented a serious business transaction and a good faith sale and purchase of the farm.

In the field of contracts, as generally elsewhere, 'We must look to the outward expression of a person as manifesting his intention rather than to his secret and unexpressed intention. 'The law imputes to a person an intention corresponding to the reasonable meaning of his words and acts." *First Nat. Bank v. Roanoke Oil Co.,* 169 Va. 99, 114, 192 S.E. 764, 770.

At no time prior to the execution of the contract had Zehmer indicated to Lucy by word or act that he was not in earnest about selling the farm. They had argued about it and discussed its terms, as Zehmer admitted, for a long time. Lucy testified that if there was any jesting it was about paying $50,000 that night. The contract and the evidence show that he was not expected to pay the money that night. Zehmer said that after the writing was signed he laid it down on the counter in front of Lucy. Lucy said Zehmer handed it to him. In any event there had been what appeared to be a good faith offer and a good faith acceptance, followed by the execution and apparent delivery of a written contract. Both said that Lucy put the writing in his pocket and then offered

Zehmer $5 to seal the bargain. Not until then, even under the defendants' evidence, was anything said or done to indicate that the matter was a joke. Both of the Zehmers testified that when Zehmer asked his wife to sign he whispered that it was a joke so Lucy wouldn't hear and that it was not intended that he should hear.

The mental assent of the parties is not requisite for the formation of a contract. If the words or other acts of one of the parties have but one reasonable meaning, his undisclosed intention is immaterial except when an unreasonable meaning which he attaches to his manifestations is known to the other party. * * *

An agreement or mutual assent is of course essential to a valid contract but the law imputes to a person an intention corresponding to the reasonable meaning of his words and acts. If his words and acts, judged by a reasonable standard, manifest an intention to agree, it is immaterial what may be the real but unexpressed state of his mind. * * *

So a person cannot set up that he was merely jesting when his conduct and words would warrant a reasonable person in believing that he intended a real agreement, * * *

Whether the writing signed by the defendants and now sought to be enforced by the complainants was the result of a serious offer by Lucy and a serious acceptance by the defendants, or was a serious offer by Lucy and an acceptance in secret jest by the defendants, in either event it constituted a binding contract of sale between the parties.

Defendants contend further, however, that even though a contract was made, equity should decline to enforce it under the circumstances. These circumstances have been set forth in detail above. They disclose some drinking by the two parties but not to an extent that they were unable to understand fully what they were doing. There was no fraud, no misrepresentation, no sharp practice and no dealing between unequal parties. The farm had been bought for $11,000 and was assessed for taxation at $6,300. The purchase price was $50,000. Zehmer admitted that it was a good price. There is in fact present in this case none of the grounds usually urged against specific performance.

. . .

The complainants are entitled to have specific performance of the contracts sued on. The decree appealed from is therefore reversed and the cause is remanded for the entry of a proper decree requiring the defendants to perform the contract in accordance with the prayer of the bill.

Reversed and remanded.

NOTES

1. In *Lucy v. Zehmer*, Buyer sued Seller seeking "specific performance" of Seller's promise to sell the land. What that means is that

the Buyer wanted an order from the court forcing the seller to convey the land. As we will see, that's not the usual form of remedy. Other than in cases to enforce promises to convey real estate, considered below, a successful lawsuit ordinarily ends with the plaintiff obtaining an award of damages, rather than an order to the defendant to do something. For example, in *Hawkins*, the court did not order the doctor to fix the patient's hand, instead, the court said that the patient was entitled to recover from the doctor an amount of money computed to place the patient in the position he would have been in if the promise had been performed.

2.   The plaintiff in *Lucy* was the buyer, and he lost at trial; that is, the trial court ruled that the plaintiff had not proved that the defendant really made a serious promise to sell the land. As you can see from the opinion, deciding whether Zehmer seriously intended to sell or was just joking requires a pretty careful examination of the facts. Ordinarily fact determinations are pretty much left to the fact-finder at trial—either the jury in a case tried to a jury or the trial judge in a case tried without a jury. Ordinarily an appellate court will not disturb the findings made at trial on an issue of fact, unless no reasonable fact-finder could have decided the issue as it was decided at trial. The appellate court in *Lucy v. Zehmer* seems to have been willing to reverse on a largely factual matter. That's a bit surprising, and we really can't give you a convincing explanation of why that happened. For our purposes, the case is useful as an exercise in how one might treat facts at trial. That is, we'll ignore the appellate procedure points and consider how one might have argued the case to the fact-finder (judge or jury) at trial given the evidence that was introduced.

So, look at the opinion carefully to identify what facts support a conclusion that Lucy thought that Zehmer was making a serious promise to sell, and what facts support a conclusion that Lucy should have realized that Zehmer was just joking.

3.   As the opinion notes, intoxication can deprive someone of their capacity to contract (in somewhat the same way as an infant is deemed to lack the capacity to contract). But such intoxication must be so extreme that the person is unable to understand the nature of the business at hand. Section 16 of the Restatement (Second) of Contracts points also to the relevance of the question of whether the other party has reason to know of the extent of the intoxication, or whether that party induced it (see Cmt b). It is rare that someone might escape contractual obligations on this ground.

B. SOURCES OF CONTRACT LAW

For most of the subjects we study in this course, the governing law is found in the rules established by judicial decisions over the centuries. As the phrase goes, this is "common law" as distinguished from rules that are the law by virtue of enactment by the legislature. For example, in *Hawkins v. McGee* and *Lucy v. Zehmer,* the principal authorities cited by the courts were earlier decision of courts in the same state, or other states if there were no cases in that state on the point. One of the principal tasks for you as beginning law students will be to see how to work with judicial opinions in resolving new issues.

Another important goal of the first year of law study is to work toward precision in the use of language. For example, suppose that you were asked to describe the *Hawkins v. McGee* decision in a few sentences. It can be done, but it's not easy. In working toward precision in language it's helpful to see how other lawyers have expressed a point, when they have given the subject careful thought. For that purpose, one of our main tools will be the RESTATEMENT (SECOND) OF CONTRACTS, excerpts of which appear in the Selected Source Materials book that we use in this course.

Restatement (Second) of Contracts

Please read—very carefully—the Editors' Introduction passage explaining the Restatement, and look at the Table of Contents of the Restatement. It's important to understand what the Restatement is, and is not. No body having any governmental power produced or adopted the Restatement. So a certain proposition cannot be the law simply by virtue of the fact that it is written in the Restatement. Rather, the Restatements are the product of a private organization, the American Law Institute ("ALI"), dedicated to working toward improvement of the law. To get a better idea of the ALI's work, look at their website (www.ali.org) especially the "About ALI" tab.

Uniform Commercial Code ("U.C.C")

We will also examine some subjects that are governed by statutes. In some cases, those will simply be statutes adopted by the legislatures of particular states. But there is one statute that we will examine from time to time that has a somewhat different background—the Uniform Commercial Code ("U.C.C"). Article 2 of the U.C.C. deals with the sale of goods. Excerpts from Article 2 also appear in the Selected Source Materials book that we use in this course. Please read—very carefully— the Editors' Introduction passage explaining the Uniform Commercial Code, and look at the table of contents of Article 2. The recommended text of the U.C.C. is produced by a non-governmental organization, the National Conference of Commissioners on Uniform State Law (now called the "Uniform Law Commission"). As with the Restatements, the fact that the sponsoring body has "adopted" something as part of the U.C.C. does not make it law. Rather, the U.C.C. or a part of it is law in a given jurisdiction only if it has been adopted as the law in that jurisdiction. Unlike the Restatements, however, the U.C.C. is a statute. That is, it has force of law not by virtue of action of the courts, but by virtue of enactment by the legislature of the state in question. The idea behind the U.C.C. is to get all of the states to adopt the same statute. That project has been pretty successful, but there is nothing that says that the legislature of a certain state has to adopt precisely the recommended text. Article 2 of the U.C.C. had been enacted by 49 states, plus the District of Columbia and the Virgin Islands.[a] Most states have made some changes when they adopted the statute, so the actual law in a given state is not the U.C.C, but the particular statute based on the U.C.C. that was adopted in that state. In law school, it's convenient to look at the text of "the U.C.C," but in practice you must consult the particular statutory version of the jurisdiction in question.

Students are very frequently confused by the scope of Article 2 of the U.C.C. First, be clear on terminology. The U.C.C. is a very lengthy statute dealing with all kinds of commercial law subjects, such as checks, security interests, etc., etc. Article 2—dealing with the sale of goods—is the only part of the U.C.C. that we will examine in this course. Many of you will take other courses in Commercial Law later in law school and study other parts of the U.C.C.

Second, and perhaps most troublesome, there is a tendency to assume, based on nothing more than the title, that Article 2 of the U.C.C. applies only to transactions among businesses. *That is wrong.* Article 2 applies to any contract for the sale of goods. So if your friend sells you their used bicycle, that's a transaction governed by Article 2 of the U.C.C., even though neither of you is involved in any aspect of the bicycle business. There are some rules in Article 2 that apply only to "merchants," but aside from these rules, U.C.C. Article 2 applies to any sale of goods between anybody.

Third, U.C.C. Article 2 applies only to the *sale* of goods. That means that U.C.C. Article 2 has no application to subjects other than sales. For example, a contract between an advertising agency and a toothpaste company would involve services to design an ad campaign, not the sale of toothpaste. So, that arrangement would not be governed by U.C.C. Article 2. Even if we are dealing with a sale, Article 2 of the U.C.C. applies only to the sale of *goods*. In Anglo-American law there is a very deep divide between "real property"—like land and houses—and "personal property"—like cars and TVs. So a contract for sale of an office building would not be covered by U.C.C. Article 2, but a contract for sale of a photocopy machine would be governed by U.C.C. Article 2.

Later in the course, we will take a brief look at another body of law governing the sale of goods, but this time *international* sales: the United Nations Convention on the International Sale of Goods, or "CISG". We'll see that this body of law deals with import-export contracts, but actually excludes consumer contracts from its reach. Like the U.C.C., the CISG can displace inconsistent rules of state common law when certain conditions are met.

Finally, U.C.C. Article 2 does not attempt to be a complete statement of all of the rules of contract law concerning contracts for the sale of goods. For example, in the next Chapter we will spend a good deal of time

---

[a]   Steven J. Burton & Melvin A. Eisenberg, Contract Law: Selected Source Materials (2014 ed), 2 (law as of May 1, 2012).

on questions of contract formation, some of which turn on the concepts of "offer" and "acceptance." As we will see, there are a few rules on these matters in Article 2, but if there doesn't happen to be a rule on the specific issue in U.C.C. Article 2, then a court would treat it in the same fashion as any other issue of contract law. The court would look to general contract law in the state in question, or might look to some secondary source, like a treatise on contract law or the RESTATEMENT (SECOND) OF CONTRACTS.

The following case and problems provide an opportunity to examine more carefully the relationship between U.C.C. Article 2 and other law. Before reading the case, refer to:

UCC §§ 2–102, 2–106(1), 2–725(1)

Custom Communications Engineering, Inc. v. E.F. Johnson Co.

Superior Court of New Jersey, Appellate Division, 1993.
269 N.J.Super. 531, 636 A.2d 80.

The central issue on appeal is whether the four-year statute of limitations under the Uniform Commercial Code (UCC), *N.J.S.A.* 12A:2–725(1), is applicable to the parties' dealership agreement.

Plaintiff Custom Communications Engineering, Inc. (Custom) appeals from an order for summary judgment dismissing its complaint against defendants E.F. Johnson Company (Johnson). . . . In its complaint, Custom seeks damages against Johnson for economic loss arising from Johnson's termination of its dealership agreement with Custom. . . . The Law Division judge determined that *N.J.S.A.* 12A:2–725(1) applied and therefore Custom's complaint was time-barred because it was filed four years after the accrual of its cause of action. We affirm the summary judgment order . . . .

Johnson is a manufacturer of radio equipment. On June 17, 1978, Custom entered into a Land Mobile Dealer Agreement with Johnson which granted Custom the right to sell and service Johnson's products within a designated "Dealer's Territory" in northern New Jersey. The agreement provides that Custom is required to use its best efforts to promote the sale of Johnson products in the designated area and to maintain an inventory of products, as well as a service facility for the benefit of Johnson customers.

The agreement also restricts Custom to the selling of Johnson products within its designated territory. Although the agreement does not expressly state that Custom's territory was exclusive, Custom claims that Johnson had made oral representations as to its exclusivity. Paragraph 3 of the agreement provides that Custom may sell Johnson products in the territory of other dealers only upon their approval and upon Custom paying them compensation for the sales. Paragraph 11 specifies that the relationship between the parties was "that of buyer and seller." Finally, paragraph 14 provides that either party may terminate the agreement, with or without cause, upon thirty days' written notice.

According to Custom, in 1978 Johnson began making sales in Custom's territory through other dealers without permission and without compensating Custom. Custom also claims that Johnson established other dealers in Custom's "exclusive" territory beginning some time in 1981–82. On March 18, 1985, Johnson terminated the agreement.

. . .

On April 19, 1988, Custom filed the present complaint . . . . [Johnson] moved for summary judgment, arguing that Custom's cause of action accrued no later than 1982, and thus was barred by the four-year statute of limitations under the UCC, *N.J.S.A.* 12A:2–725. Judge D'Ambrosio of the Law Division agreed, reasoning that since the parties were involved in a "sales" agreement, Custom's claim of breach of contract was governed by the UCC time-bar. . . .

N.J.S.A. 12A:2–725(1) provides that an action for breach of any contract for "sale" under the UCC must be commenced within four years after the accrual of the cause of action. *N.J.S.A.* 2A:14–1, the six-year statute of limitation generally governing breach of contract claims, expressly states that its time-bar does not apply to any action governed by *N.J.S.A.* 12A:2–725(1). Article 2 of the UCC applies to "transactions in goods." *N.J.S.A.* 12A:2–102. The term "goods" is defined as "all things (including specially manufactured goods) which are movable at the time of identification to the contract for sale other than the money in which the price is to be paid [.]" *N.J.S.A.* 12A:2–105(1). A "sale" involves "the passing of title from the seller to the buyer for a price." *N.J.S.A.* 12A:2–106(1).

Notwithstanding these narrowly-defined terms, whether *N.J.S.A.* 12A:2–725(1) applies depends on how the contract between the parties may be accurately characterized: as one involving a transaction of goods (*N.J.S.A.* 12A:2–102) plus incidental services, or as one for services plus the incidental sale of goods. * * * The legal analysis most frequently employed when courts are faced with such mixed contracts is that Article 2 of the UCC is applicable "if the sales aspect predominates and is inapplicable if the service aspect predominates." Sonja A. Soehnel, Annotation, Applicability of UCC Article 2 to Mixed Contracts for Sale of Goods and Services, 5 A.L.R. 4th 501, 505 (1981), and see cases annotated therein.

Custom argues that the six-year statute of limitations under *N.J.S.A.* 2A:14–1 applies because its agreement with Johnson was a dealership or distributorship, the predominate purpose of which was not the "sale" of goods, but for Custom to act as Johnson's agent in promoting its products, and to provide a service facility for customers who have purchased those products.

No doubt there are nonsale aspects to the parties' agreement. However, we view the nonsale components as intending to foster the dominant purpose of the agreement: to sell Johnson products through Custom to customers in Custom's distribution area. For example, under the agreement, Custom is required to buy from Johnson and maintain an inventory of Johnson products. Also, Custom's purchase orders are subject to the price, terms and conditions set by Johnson at the time the order was made, and Johnson reserves the right to "alter . . . the credit terms upon which [Custom] *buys* [Johnson's] Products and parts thereof." (Emphasis added). Finally, paragraph 11 of the agreement expressly states that the relationship between the parties shall be "buyer" and "seller." Thus, it is clear that a critical aspect of the agreement is the sale of goods from Johnson to Custom "for a price." *N.J.S.A.* 12A:2–106(1).

We accept Custom's argument that the agreement may be characterized as a dealership or distributorship contract: Custom is an intermediary in the consumer chain whose function is to promote and sell products manufactured by Johnson. Focusing strictly on the definitions under Article 2, one might assume that the UCC does not reach such a relationship because of the hybrid nature of the parties' respective roles.

However, the rule in most out-of-state jurisdictions is that dealerships or distributorships are to be treated as sales of goods contracts under the UCC. * * * [citing numerous cases] The common theme expressed in nearly all of the cases is that, although most dealership or distributorship agreements involve more than a mere sale of goods, the sales aspect of the relationship predominates. * * * Accordingly, courts have not hesitated to conclude that a direct dealership agreement, as here, is subject to the four-year statute of limitations under § 2–725(1) of the UCC. * * *

We adopt the majority rule as sound, since it is entirely consistent with the underlying purposes of the UCC: to foster consistency and predictability in the commercial marketplace. *See N.J.S.A.* 12A:1–102. Indeed, for that reason, our Supreme Court has observed that "the U.C.C. is the more appropriate vehicle for resolving commercial disputes arising out of business transactions between persons in a distributive chain." *Spring Motors Distribs., Inc. v. Ford Motor Company*, 98 N.J. 555, 571, 489 A.2d 660 (1985). This fundamental theme of the UCC is particularly pertinent in applying a statute of limitations to claims arising under Article 2. The purpose of § 2–725(1) is "[t]o introduce a uniform statute of limitations for sales contracts," thus eliminating jurisdictional variations. Comment to *N.J.S.A.* 12A:2–725(1). Application of the UCC time-bar to distributorship and dealership agreements accommodates the interests of both parties: it permits the nationwide merchant-seller to rely on the repose afforded by a uniform statute, and gives notice to the local merchant-dealer that all claims for economic loss under Article 2 must be filed within four years of the accrual of its cause of action.

The order for summary judgment in favor of Johnson is affirmed. . . .

PROBLEM

Here are excerpts from New Jersey's generally applicable statute of limitations:

New Jersey Statutes § 2A:14–1. (6 years)

Every action at law for trespass to real property, for any tortious injury to real or personal property, for taking, detaining, or converting personal property, for replevin of goods or chattels . . . or for recovery upon a contractual claim or liability, express or implied, not under seal . . . shall be commenced within 6 years next after the cause of any such action shall have accrued. This section shall not apply to any action for breach of any contract for sale governed by section 12A:2–725 of the New Jersey Statutes.

New Jersey Statutes § 2A:14–2 (2 years)

Every action at law for an injury to the person caused by the wrongful act neglect or default of any person within this state shall be commenced within 2 years next after the cause of action shall have accrued.

Here is New Jersey's enactment of the statute of limitations suggested in Article 2 of the Uniform Commercial Code:

New Jersey Statutes § 12A:2–725

(1) An action for breach of any contract for sale must be commenced within four years after the cause of action has accrued. By the original agreement the parties may reduce the period of limitation to not less than one year but may not extend it.

Note that the U.C.C. Article 2 statute of limitations (N.J. § 12A:2–725) applies only if the case is otherwise governed by U.C.C. Article 2. That depends on whether the case involves a sale "of goods." See U.C.C. §§ 2–102 & 2–106(1). So, if the case involves a sale "of goods," the statute of limitations is four years. If the case involves some other form of contract, the statute of limitations is six years.

Assume that all of the events below occur in New Jersey.

1. Safeway Stores, Inc. entered into a contract to sell a vacant store to Budget Department Stores, Inc. (For simplicity, please make the somewhat unrealistic assumption that there is no down payment). Safeway refused to perform the contract. Budget found a similar store and bought it, but it cost $350,000 more. Five years after the Safeway-Budget contract, Budget brings a lawsuit against Safeway. Safeway says that the suit is barred by the statute of limitations.

Is the case governed by the general statute of limitations in NJ Statutes § 2A:14–1 or the NJ U.C.C. Article 2 statute of limitations in NJ Statutes § 12A:2–725?

2. Sabeena Consumer entered into a contract to sell her big screen TV to Brie Neighbor for $1200. Sabeena refused to perform the contract. Brie found a similar TV elsewhere and bought it, but it cost $2000.

Five years after the Sabeena-Brie contract, Brie brings a lawsuit against Sabeena. Sabeena says that the suit is barred by the statute of limitations.

Is the case governed by the general statute of limitations in NJ Statutes § 2A:14–1 or the NJ U.C.C. Article 2 statute of limitations in NJ Statutes § 12A:2–725?

3.   Brunswick Auto Parts Co. borrowed $75,000 from First National Bank to pay the price of an inventory of auto parts that Brunswick bought from Secaucus Equipment Inc. Brunswick signed a loan agreement promising to repay the $75,000 to First National Bank in one year. Brunswick failed to repay the loan when it came due.

Five years after Brunswick's default, First National Bank sues Brunswick for the $75,000.

Is the case governed by the general statute of limitations in NJ Statutes § 2A:14–1 or the NJ U.C.C. Article 2 statute of limitations in NJ Statutes § 12A:2–725?

4.   Suppose that the events in *Hawkins v. McGee* occurred in New Jersey, and that Hawkins brought the suit against Dr. McGee three years after the operation.

Would the case be governed by the 6 year statute of limitations in New Jersey Statutes § 2A:14–1 or the 2 year statute of limitations in New Jersey Statutes § 2A:14–2?

C. OBJECTIVES OF CONTRACT REMEDIES

1.   COMPENSATION OR PUNISHMENT?

Oliver Wendell Holmes, The Path of the Law (1897)
10 Harv. L. Rev. 457, at 459, 460–2

I think it desirable at once to point out and dispel a confusion between morality and law, which sometimes rises to the height of conscious theory, and more often and indeed constantly is making trouble in detail without reaching the point of consciousness. You can see very plainly that a bad man has as much reason as a good one for wishing to avoid an encounter with the public force, and therefore you can see the practical importance of the distinction between morality and law. A man who cares nothing for an ethical rule which is believed and practiced by his neighbors is likely nevertheless to care a good deal to avoid being made to pay money, and will want to keep out of jail if he can.

I take it for granted that no hearer of mine will misinterpret what I have to say as the language of cynicism. The law is the witness and external deposit of our moral life. Its history is the history of the moral development of the race. The practice of it, in spite of popular jests, tends to make good citizens and good men. When I emphasize the difference between law and morals I do so with reference to a single end, that of learning and understanding the law. For that purpose you must definitely master its specific marks, and it is for that that I ask you for the moment to imagine yourselves indifferent to other and greater things.

I do not say that there is not a wider point of view from which the distinction between law and morals becomes of secondary or no importance, as all mathematical distinctions vanish in presence of the infinite. But I do say that that distinction is of the first importance for the object which we are here to consider—a right study and mastery of the law as a business with well understood limits, a body of dogma enclosed within definite lines. I have just shown the practical reason for saying so. If you want to know the law and nothing else, you must look at it as a bad man, who cares only for the material consequences which such knowledge enables him to predict, not as a good one, who finds his reasons for conduct, whether inside the law or outside of it, in the vaguer sanctions of conscience. The theoretical importance of the distinction is no less, if you would reason on your subject aright. . . .

. . . .

The confusion with which I am dealing besets confessedly legal conceptions. Take the fundamental question, What constitutes the law? You will find some text writers telling you that it is something different from what is decided by the courts of Massachusetts or England, that it is a system of reason, that it is a deduction from principles of ethics or admitted axioms or what not, which may or may not coincide with the decisions. But if we take the view of our friend the bad man we shall find that he does not care two straws for the axioms or deductions, but that he does want to know what the Massachusetts or English courts are likely to do in fact. I am much of this mind. The prophecies of what the courts will do in fact, and nothing more pretentious, are what I mean by the law.

Take again a notion which as popularly understood is the widest conception which the law contains—the notion of legal duty, to which already I have referred. We fill the word with all the content which we draw from morals. But what does it mean to a bad man? Mainly, and in the first place, a prophecy that if he does certain things he will be subjected to disagreeable consequences by way of imprisonment or compulsory payment of money. . . .

Nowhere is the confusion between legal and moral ideas more manifest than in the law of contract. Among other things, here again the so-called primary rights and duties are invested with a mystic significance beyond what can be assigned and explained. The duty to keep a contract at common law means a prediction that you must pay damages if you do not keep it—and nothing else. If you commit a tort, you are liable to pay a compensatory sum. If you commit a contract, you are liable to pay a compensatory sum unless the promised event comes to pass, and that is all the difference.

NOTES & QUESTIONS

1.   Oliver Wendell Holmes, Jr (1841–1935), exercised a significant influence on the development of American private law. He served as justice and then chief justice of the Massachusetts Supreme Judicial Court for two decades, and then as justice of the U.S. Supreme Court for another three decades, applying a pragmatic jurisprudence that went on to be cited in many foundational cases of contract law. Do you agree that the moral pangs caused by breach of a promise are to be left out of the law of contract? For a skeptical view, see, e.g., Seana Valentine Shiffrin, *The Divergence of Contract and Promise*, 120 HARV. L. REV. 708 (2007).

2.   Suppose that an out-of-work artist agrees to paint a house for $12,000. Before the time for performance, the artist gets an opportunity to paint a portrait for $20,000. The houseowner can get someone else to paint the house for $15,000. If the artist breaches, and pays the houseowner the $3,000 damages, the houseowner gets what she contracted for, but the artist's skills are devoted to a better use. This outcome is sometimes referred to as an "efficient breach", and one doesn't have to be an expert in the law and economics of contract to understand the gains that flow to the artist and, perhaps, to society in general, as a consequence of this breach. State, in your own words, how the breach might be understood to be efficient. How might it understood to be inefficient?

3.   Efficient breach has offered an influential paradigm for explaining why some breaches are worthwhile. Do you think the artist-houseowner type of deal in the above question is representative of contracts in general, or is it better understood as a specific type? How might you describe the fact-specific characteristics of efficient breach?

White v. Benkowski

Supreme Court of Wisconsin, 1967.
37 Wis.2d 285, 155 N.W.2d 74.

This case involves a neighborhood squabble between two adjacent property owners.

Prior to November 28, 1962, Virgil and Gwynneth White, the plaintiffs, were desirous of purchasing a home in Oak Creek. Unfortunately, the particular home that the Whites were interested in was without a water supply. Despite this fact, the Whites purchased the home.

The adjacent home was owned and occupied by Paul and Ruth Benkowski, the defendants. The Benkowskis had a well in their yard which had piping that connected with the Whites' home.

On November 28, 1962, the Whites and Benkowskis entered into a written agreement wherein the Benkowskis promised to supply water to the White home for ten years or until an earlier date when either water was supplied by the municipality, the well became inadequate, or the Whites drilled their own well. The Whites promised to pay $3 a month for the water and one-half the cost of any future repairs or maintenance that the Benkowski well might require. As part of the transaction, but not included in the written agreement, the Whites gave the Benkowskis $400 which was used to purchase and install a new pump and an additional tank that would increase the capacity of the well.

Initially, the relationship between the new neighbors was friendly. With the passing of time, however, their relationship deteriorated and the neighbors actually became hostile. In 1964, the water supply, which was controlled by the Benkowskis, was intermittently shut off. Mrs. White kept a record of the dates and durations that her water supply was not operative. Her record showed that the water was shut off on the following occasions:

(1) March 5, 1964, from 7:10 p.m. to 7:25 p.m.

(2) March 9, 1964, from 3:40 p.m. to 4:00 p.m.

(3) March 11, 1964, from 6:00 p.m. to 6:15 p.m.

(4) June 10, 1964, from 6:20 p.m. to 7:03 p.m.

The record also discloses that the water was shut off completely or partially for varying lengths of time on July 1, 6, 7, and 17, 1964, and on November 25, 1964.

Mr. Benkowski claimed that the water was shut off either to allow accumulated sand in the pipes to settle or to remind the Whites that their use of the water was excessive. Mr. White claimed that the Benkowskis breached their contract by shutting off the water.

Following the date when the water was last shut off (November 25, 1964), the Whites commenced an action to recover compensatory and punitive damages for an alleged violation of the agreement to supply water. A jury trial was held. Apparently it was agreed by counsel that for purposes of the trial 'plaintiffs' case was based upon an alleged deliberate violation of the contract consisting of turning off the water at the times specified in the plaintiffs' complaint.' Accordingly, in the special verdict the jury was asked:

'QUESTION 1:   Did the defendants maliciously, vindictively or wantonly shut off the water supply of the plaintiffs for the purpose of harassing the plaintiffs?'

The jury was also asked:

'QUESTION 2:   If you answered Question 1 'Yes', then answer this question:

'(a) What compensatory damages did the plaintiffs suffer?

'(b) What punitive damages should be assessed?'

Before the case was submitted to the jury, the defendants moved to strike the verdict's punitive-damage question. The court reserved its ruling on the motion. The jury returned a verdict which found that the Benkowskis maliciously shut off the Whites' water supply for harassment purposes. Compensatory damages were set at $10 and punitive damages at $2,000. On motions after verdict, the court reduced the compensatory award to $1 and granted defendants' motion to strike the punitive damage question and answer.

Judgment for plaintiffs of $1 was entered and they appeal.

■ WILKIE, JUSTICE.

Two issues are raised on this appeal.

1. Was the trial court correct in reducing the award of compensatory damages from $10 to $1?

2. Are punitive damages available in actions for breach of contract?

Reduction of Jury Award.

The evidence of damage adduced during the trial here was that the water supply had been shut off during several short periods. Three incidents of inconvenience resulting from these shut-offs were detailed by the plaintiffs. Mrs. White testified that the lack of water in the bathroom on one occasion caused an odor and that on two other occasions she was forced to take her children to a neighbor's home to bathe them. Based on this evidence, the court instructed the jury that:

> '. . . in an action for a breach of contract the plaintiff is entitled to such damages as shall have been sustained by him which resulted naturally and directly from the breach if you find that the defendants did in fact breach the contract. Such damages include pecunitary loss and inconvenience suffered as a natural result of the breach and are called compensatory damages. In this case the plaintiffs have proved no pecuniary damages which you or the Court could compute. In a situation where there has been a breach of contract which you find to have damaged the plaintiff but for which the plaintiffs have proven no actual damages, the plaintiffs may recover nominal damages.
>
> 'By nominal damages is meant trivial—a trivial sum of money.'

Plaintiffs did not object to this instruction. In the trial court's decision on motions after verdict it states that the court so instructed the jury because, based on the fact that the plaintiffs paid for services they did not receive, their loss in proportion to the contract rate was approximately 25 cents. This rationale indicates that the court disregarded or overlooked Mrs. White's testimony of inconvenience. In viewing the evidence most favorable to the plaintiffs, there was some injury. The plaintiffs are not required to ascertain their damages with mathematical precision, but rather the trier of fact must set damages at a reasonable amount. Notwithstanding this instruction, the jury set the plaintiffs' damages at $10. The court was in error in reducing that amount to $1.

The jury finding of $10 in actual damages, though small, takes it out of the mere nominal status. The award is predicated on an actual injury. . . . Here there was credible evidence which showed inconvenience and thus actual injury, and the jury's finding as to compensatory damages should be reinstated.

Punitive Damages.

> 'If a man shall steal an ox, or a sheep, and kill it, or sell it; he shall restore five oxen for an ox, and four sheep for a sheep.' Exodus 22:1.

Over one hundred years ago this court held that, under proper circumstances, a plaintiff was entitled to recover exemplary or punitive damages. . . .

In Wisconsin compensatory damages are given to make whole the damage or injury suffered by the injured party. On the other hand, punitive damages are given

> 'on the basis of punishment to the injured party not because he has been injured, which injury has been compensated with compensatory damages, but to punish the wrongdoer for his malice and to deter others from like conduct.' [Malco, Inc. v. Midwest Alum. Sales, 109 N.W. 2d 516, 521 (Wis. 1961)]

Thus we reach the question of whether the plaintiffs are entitled to punitive damages for a breach of the water agreement.

The overwhelming weight of authority supports the proposition that punitive damages are not recoverable in actions for breach of contract. * * * In Chitty on Contracts, the author states that the right to receive punitive damages for breach of contract is now confined to the single case of damages for breach of a promise to marry. 1 Chitty, Contracts (22d ed. 1961), p. 1339.

Simpson states:

> 'Although damages in excess of compensation for loss are in some instances permitted in tort actions by way of punishment . . . in contract actions the damages recoverable are limited to compensation for pecunitary loss sustained by the breach.' Simpson, Contracts (2d ed. hornbook series), p. 394, sec. 195.

Corbin states that as a general rule punitive damages are not recoverable for breach of contract. 5 Corbin, Contracts, p. 438, sec. 1077.

In Wisconsin, the early case of *Gordon v. Brewster* (7 Wis 309 (1858)) involved the breach of an employment contract. The trial court instructed the jury that if the nonperformance of the contract was attributable to the defendant's wrongful act of discharging the plaintiff, then that would go to increase the damages sustained. On appeal, this court said that the instruction was unfortunate and might have led the jurors to suppose that they could give something more than actual compensation in a breach of contract case. We find no Wisconsin case in which breach of contract (other than breach of promise to marry) has led to the award of punitive damages.

Persuasive authority from other jurisdictions supports the proposition (without exception) that punitive damages are not available in breach of contract actions. * * * This is true even if the breach, as in the instant case, is willful. * * *

. . . .

Reversed in part by reinstating the jury verdict relating to compensatory damages and otherwise affirmed. Costs to appellant.

NOTES

1.   Did it make a difference here that the facts involved a deliberate, rather than inadvertent, violation of the contract? Should it?

2.   We will consider the overlap between contract and tort law in Chapter 2.B. One possible tort claim might be the intentional infliction of emotional distress. It might be early days in your study of tort, but would you have brought such a claim, if you were the White's lawyer? What types of issues do you think might influence your answer?

2.   DAMAGES OR SPECIFIC PERFORMANCE?

McCallister v. Patton

Supreme Court of Arkansas, 1948.
214 Ark. 293, 215 S.W. 2d 701.

■ MILLWEE, JUSTICE.

A. J. McCallister was plaintiff in the chancery court in a suit for specific performance of an alleged contract for the sale and purchase of a new Ford automobile from the defendant, R. H. Patton. The complaint alleges:

> 'That on or about the 15th day of September, 1945, the Plaintiff entered into a contract with the Defendant, whereby the Plaintiff contracted to purchase and the Defendant to sell, one Ford super deluxe tudor sedan and radio.

> 'That the Defendant is an automobile dealer and sells Ford automobiles and trucks within the city of Jonesboro, Craighead County, Arkansas and that at the time this Plaintiff entered into this contract the Defendant had no new Ford automobiles in stock of any kind and was engaged in taking orders by contract, numbering the contracts in the order that they were executed and delivered to him. As the cars were received the Defendant would fill the orders as he had previously received the contracts. The Plaintiff's number was number 37.

> 'As consideration and as part of the purchase price the Plaintiff paid to this Defendant the sum of $25.00 and at all

times stood ready, able and willing to pay the balance upon the purchase price in accordance with the terms of the contract. . . .

'The Plaintiff is informed and verily believes and the Defendant has admitted to this Plaintiff that he has received more than 37 cars since the execution of this contract. The Defendant refuses to sell an automobile of the above make and description to this Plaintiff.

'Since the execution of this contract and to the present date, new Ford automobiles have been hard to obtain and this Plaintiff is unable to purchase an automobile at any other place or upon the open market of the description named in this contract and there is not an adequate remedy at law and the Court should direct specific performance of this contract.'

The prayer of the complaint was that the defendant be ordered to sell the automobile to plaintiff in compliance with the contract, and for all other proper relief. Under the terms of the 'New Car Order' attached to the complaint as Exhibit 'A,' delivery of the car was to be made 'as soon as possible out of current or future production' at defendant's regularly established price. Plaintiff was not required to trade in a used car but might do so, if the price of such car could be agreed upon and, if not, plaintiff was entitled to cancel the order and to the return of his deposit. The deposit of $25 was to be held in trust for the plaintiff and returned to him at his option on surrender of his rights under the agreement. There was no provision for forfeiture of the deposit in the event plaintiff refused to accept delivery of the car.

Defendant demurred to the complaint on the grounds that it did not state facts sufficient to entitle plaintiff to the relief of specific performance . . . . There were further allegations . . . to the effect that plaintiff was engaged in the sale of used cars and had contracted to resell whatever vehicle he obtained from the defendant; and that upon being so informed, defendant tendered and plaintiff refused to accept return of the $25 deposit. . . .

The chancellor sustained the demurrer to the complaint and overruled the motion to strike. . . . This appeal follows.

In testing the correctness of the trial court's ruling in sustaining the demurrer we first determine whether the allegations of the complaint are sufficient to bring plaintiff within the rule that equity will not grant specific performance of a contract for the sale of personal property if damages in an action at law afford a complete and adequate remedy. Our cases on the question are in harmony with the rule recognized generally that, while equity will not ordinarily decree specific performance of a contract for the sale of chattels, it will do so where special and peculiar reasons exist such as render it impossible for the injured party to obtain adequate relief by way of damages in an action at law. . . .

. . .

Among the various exceptions to the general rule are those cases involving contracts relating to personal property which has a peculiar, unique or sentimental value to the buyer not measurable in money damages. In *Chamber of Commerce v. Barton*, 195 Ark. 274, 112 S.W.2d 619, 625, this court held that the purchaser, Barton, was entitled to specific performance of a contract for the sale of Radio Station KTHS as an organized business. Justice Baker, speaking for the court, said:

> 'A judgment for a bit of lumber from which a picture frame might be made and also for a small lot of tube paint and a yard of canvas would not compensate one who had purchased a great painting.

> 'By the same token Barton would not be adequately compensated by a judgment for a bit of wire, a steel tower or two, more or less, as the mere instrumentalities of KTHS when he has purchased an organized business including these instrumentalities, worth perhaps not more than one-third of the purchase price. Moreover, he has also contracted for the good will of KTHS, which is so intangible as to be incapable of delivery or estimation of value. So the property is unique in character and, so far as the contract is capable of enforcement, the vendee is entitled to relief.'

. . .

Plaintiff says we will take judicial knowledge of the scarcity of new automobiles as a result of the recent world war. If so, we would also take judicial notice of the fact that large numbers of cars of the type mentioned in the alleged contract have been produced since 1945, and sold through both new and used car dealers in the open market. Although the complaint alleges inadequacy of the remedy at law, it does not set forth facts sufficient to demonstrate such conclusion. It is neither alleged nor contended that the car ordered has any special or peculiar qualities not commonly possessed by others of the same make so as to make it practically impossible to replace it in the market. While it is alleged that new Ford automobiles have been hard to obtain, no harm or inconvenience of a kind which could not be fully compensated by an award of damages in a law action is set forth in the complaint.

We conclude that the allegations of the complaint are insufficient to entitle plaintiff to equitable relief and that his remedy at law is adequate. . . .

The decree is affirmed.

Morris v. Sparrow

Supreme Court of Arkansas, 1956.
225 Ark. 1019, 287 S.W.2d 583.

■ ROBINSON, JUSTICE.

Appellee Archie Sparrow filed this suit for specific performance, seeking to compel appellant Morris to deliver possession of a certain horse, which Sparrow claims Morris agreed to give him as part consideration for work done by Sparrow. The appeal is from a decree requiring the delivery of the horse.

Morris owns a cattle ranch near Mountain View, Arkansas, and he also participates in rodeos. Sparrow is a cowboy, and is experienced in training horses; occasionally he takes part in rodeos. He lives in Florida; while at a rodeo in that state, he and Morris made an agreement that they would go to Morris' ranch in Arkansas and, later, the two would go to Canada. After arriving at the Morris ranch, they changed their plans and decided that, while Morris went to Canada, Sparrow would stay at the ranch and do the necessary work. The parties are in accord that Sparrow was to work 16 weeks for a money consideration of $400. But, Sparrow says that as an additional consideration he was to receive a brown horse called Keno, owned by Morris. However, Morris states that Sparrow was to get the horse only on condition that his work at the ranch was satisfactory, and that Sparrow failed to do a good job. Morris paid Sparrow the amount of money they agreed was due, but did not deliver the horse.

At the time Sparrow went to Morris' ranch, the horse in question was practically unbroken; but during his spare time, Sparrow trained the horse and, with a little additional training, he will be a first class roping horse.

First there is the issue of whether Sparrow can maintain, in equity, a suit to enforce, by specific performance, a contract for the delivery of personal property. Although it has been held that equity will not ordinarily enforce, by specific performance, a contract for the sale of chattels, it will do so where special and peculiar reasons exist which render it impossible for the injured party to obtain relief by way of damages in an action at law. *McCallister v. Patton*, 214 Ark. 293, 215 S.W.2d 701. . . . Certainly when one has made a roping horse out of a green, unbroken pony, such a horse would have a peculiar and unique value; if Sparrow is entitled to prevail, he has a right to the horse instead of its market value in dollars and cents.

Morris claims that the part of the agreement whereby Sparrow was to receive the horse was conditional, depending on Sparrow doing a good job, and that he did not do such a job. Both parties were in Chancery Court and the Chancellor had a better opportunity than this court to evaluate the testimony of the witnesses; we cannot say the Chancellor's finding in favor of Sparrow is against the preponderance of the evidence.

[handwritten: → deferring to lower court]

. . .

Kitchen v. Herring

Supreme Court of North Carolina, 1851.
7 Ired.Eq. 190, 42 N.C. 190.

■ PEARSON, J.

In December 1846, the defendant, Herring, executed a contract in writing in these words, "Rec'd. of John L. Kitchen payment in full for a certain tract of land lying on the South west side of Black River, adjoining the lands of William Haffland and Martial, for which I am to give him a good deed &c." . . .

The prayer of the Bill is for a specific performance, . . .[b]

The defendant's Counsel insisted, that the contract was void, because of its vagueness and uncertainty. This position is untenable. The description is sufficiently certain to identify the land—"that is certain which can be made certain," and for this purpose an enquiry would be ordered if necessary. But the parties seem to have had no difficulty in this respect; for, it is admitted, that the tract of land which was the subject of the contract, has been conveyed by deed to Pridgen, and in that way its identity is established. . . .

It was further insisted, that, as it appears by the plaintiff's own showing, that "the land is chiefly valuable on account of the timber," this case does not come within the principle, on which a specific performance is decreed.

The position is new, and the Counsel admitted, that there was no authority to sustain it, but he contended with earnestness, that it was so fully sustained by "the reason of the thing," as to justify a departure from a well settled rule of this Court, under the maxim, *cessante ratione cessat lex.*[c]

The argument failed wholly to prove, that "the reason of the thing" called for an exception. The principle in regard to land was adopted, not because it was fertile or rich in minerals, or *valuable for timber,* but simply because it was *land*—a favorite and favored subject in England, and every country of Anglo Saxon origin. Our constitution gives to land pre-eminence over every other species of property; and our law, whether administered in Courts of law or of equity, gives to it the same preference. Land, whether rich or poor, cannot be taken to pay debts until the personal property is exhausted. Contracts concerning land must be in writing. Land must be sold at the Court House, must be conveyed by deeds duly registered, and other instances "too tedious to mention." The

---

[b]   Eds. Because of the age of the case, the exact procedure is hard to follow. For our purposes we can treat this as if this were an opinion by the trial court.

[c]   Eds. The Latin "cessante ratione legis cessat ipsa lex" can be translated as "when the reason for the law ceases, the law itself ceases".

principle is, that land is *assumed* to have a peculiar value, so as to give an equity for a specific performance, without reference to its quality or quantity. . . . [I]n regard to other property, less favored, a specific performance will not be decreed, unless there be peculiar circumstances; for, if with the money, an article of the same description can be bought in market—corn, cotton, &c., the remedy at law is adequate.

Kalinowski v. Yeh

Intermediate Court of Appeals of Hawaii, 1993.
9 Haw.App. 473, 847 P.2d 673.

■ WATANABE, JUDGE.

Plaintiffs Harry and Adelaine Kalinowski (Kalinowskis) brought the instant action, seeking specific performance of a contract to purchase a condominium unit from Defendants Jim and Lisa Yeh (Yehs). The trial court held for the Kalinowskis, and we affirm.

[The Court concluded that the sellers, the Yehs, were bound by a contract to sell the condo unit, and that they had breached that contract.]

Specific Performance

The Yehs insist that specific performance is an extraordinary remedy that should not have been awarded the Kalinowskis by the trial court.

However, it is a well-accepted principle that "where the parties have fairly and understandingly entered into a valid contract for the sale of *real property*,[d] specific performance of the contract is a matter of right and equity will enforce it, absent circumstances of oppression and fraud." *Giannini v. First Nat'l Bank of Des Plaines,* 136 Ill.App.3d 971, 981, 91 Ill.Dec. 438, 447, 483 N.E.2d 924, 933 (1985). * * * The rationale for this principle is explained in the *Restatement (Second) of Contracts* as follows:

> Contracts for the sale of land have traditionally been accorded a special place in the law of specific performance. A specific tract of land has long been regarded as unique and impossible of duplication by the use of any amount of money. Furthermore, the value of land is to some extent speculative. Damages have therefore been regarded as inadequate to enforce a duty to transfer an interest in land[.]

Restatement (Second) of Contracts § 360, comment e, at 174 (1981).

Whether this principle applies to a contract for the sale of a specific condominium unit has never previously been addressed by the Hawaii appellate courts. However, courts in other jurisdictions have generally concluded that the remedy of specific performance is available to a

---

[d]   Eds. Note carefully that the opinion here refers to real property, that is, real estate, as distinguished from personal property (goods, securities, money, etc.)

purchaser of a specific condominium unit. In *Giannini, supra,* for example, the Illinois Appellate Court held that where there was no evidence that other condominium units were available for purchase by the buyer at the same price, terms, or conditions, the buyer of a specific condominium unit was entitled to the remedy of specific performance. 136 Ill.App.3d at 981, 91 Ill.Dec. at 447, 483 N.E.2d at 933. The New Jersey Superior Court more broadly held in *Pruitt v. Graziano,* 215 N.J.Super. 330, 521 A.2d 1313 (1987), that "a contract of sale of a designated condominium unit like any real property is specifically enforceable by the purchaser irrespective of any special proof of its uniqueness." 215 N.J.Super. at 332, 521 A.2d at 1314–15.

In the instant case, there is no evidence that the Kalinowskis would have been able to buy an identical unit in the same condominium project at no more than the same price, terms, and conditions. Instead, the evidence reveals that market prices for the Yehs' unit had rapidly escalated between the time of the Kalinowskis' offer and the termination of the agreement by the Yehs, rendering it unlikely that the Kalinowskis could obtain a condominium unit in the same project at no more than the price agreed upon in the Salt Lake DROA. Moreover, the Kalinowskis were entirely blameless in their own transactional conduct and expectations, and we see no reason to deprive them of the benefit of their bargain.

Accordingly, we affirm the judgment of the trial court granting the Kalinowskis specific performance of their agreement to purchase the Yehs' condominium unit.

QUESTIONS

1.   Consider how the above four cases treat the issue of damages or specific performance. Do you think specific performance would be available for breach by the seller in a contract to purchase, in our contemporary setting, a (1) 1945 Ford motorcar, (2) 2001 Tesla electric car, and (3) standard 1 Bedroom apartment in a hi-rise development in downtown Las Vegas? What further issues of law or fact would you need to consider for each?

2.   The order of specific performance is one which requires the party who has breached the contract to perform, on penalty of being held in contempt of court if she or he does not. If you had sympathy for the idea of "efficient breach", expressed in C.1 above, what misgivings do you have about the availability of this remedy? See further RICHARD A. POSNER, ECONOMIC ANALYSIS OF LAW 130–132 (1992).

D. CONTRACT INTERESTS—IN GENERAL

Restatement (Second) of Contracts §§ 344, 347, 349, 371

One of the most influential modern law review articles on contracts is a work principally authored by a leading figure in jurisprudence, Lon Fuller. The article, which Fuller co-authored with one of his students, is L. Fuller & W. Perdue, *The Reliance Interest in Contract Damages I & II*, 46 YALE L.J. 52, 373 (1936, 1937).

When we studied *Hawkins v. McGee* at the beginning of the course, we saw that the classical concept of contract law is that the objective of contract law is to place the non-breaching party in the position she would have been in if the promised had been performed. Lon Fuller described that objective as the "expectation interest." The main theme of Fuller's article is that while protection of the expectation interest may be the usual approach of contract law, there are many situations in which it doesn't really seem right either to award the full expectation measure of recovery or to deny any relief altogether. Fuller coined the term "reliance interest" to describe another possible objective, that of returning the non-breaching party to the situation she was in before the agreement was made. A third interest described by Fuller was the "restitution interest," that is, the interest in restoring to the non-breaching party any benefit that she has conferred on the other party.

Fuller's article, and the description he worked out of the three contract interests, has been enormously influential in a variety of areas. We shall examine some of them later on. For the nonce, our goal is only to develop some familiarity with these three concepts, so that we can use them later on in working through various contract law problems.

To become familiar with these concepts, begin by studying the Restatement sections cited above, and working through the following problem.

PROBLEM—CONTRACT INTERESTS

Facts:

- Artist & Promoter agree as follows:
  - Artist will play piano recital
  - Promoter will pay Artist $10,000
    - $2000 up front
    - $8000 after performance
- Promoter pays Artist $2000.
- Promoter incurs $3000 non-recoverable costs in
  - hiring recital hall,
  - printing ads,

o   etc.

- Artist cancels, without justification
- Promoter sues Artist for breach of contract

QUESTIONS

1.   If the law of contract protected only the Restitution interest, what would you expect the measure of damages to be?

2.   If the law of contract protected only the Reliance interest, what would you expect the measure of damages to be?

3.   If the law of contract protected only the Expectation interest, what would you expect the measure of damages to be, assuming that Promoter can prove that if Artist had performed:

(a)   Promoter's revenues from ticket sales would have been $20,000

(b)   Promoter's additional costs of the performance would have been $1500

1.   EXPECTATION INTEREST

Bolin Farms v. American Cotton Shippers Ass'n

United States District Court, Western District of Louisiana, 1974.
370 F.Supp. 1353.

■ EDWIN F. HUNTER, JR., CHIEF JUDGE.

This litigation arises out of the attempts by eleven (11) cotton farmers to test the contracts by which they concededly obligated themselves to sell and deliver their cotton. In essence, defendants agreed to purchase whatever was planted by these farmers on specific acreage at a price agreed upon between January and March of 1973, irrespective of what the price might be at harvest time. Meanwhile, the price of cotton unexpectedly skyrocketed to at least double the price agreed upon. The complaints seek a declaration that the contracts are null and void, so that plaintiffs may achieve a better price than they bargained for.[e] The fundamental question in each action involves the enforceability vel non of contracts for the advance or forward sale of cotton grown for the 1973 crop.

. . .

The record is a morass of pleadings which can best be unraveled by proceeding to the very core of the case—that is, the validity and enforceability of a contract for the purchase and sale of cotton, entered into between a willing buyer and a willing seller, both adult (experienced

---

[e]   [Eds. The farmers brought an action for a "declaratory judgment" that the contracts were not enforceable. You'll study declaratory judgments in your civil procedure class. For present purposes, the case would be no different if the cotton buyers had sued the farmers seeking to enforce the contracts.]

Profit — costs + what you already spent

cotton farmers on the one hand and experienced cotton buyers on the other hand) on an open and competitive market.

. . .

It is a matter of public record and public knowledge that as a result of the sudden and spectacular rise in the price of cotton in the latter part of 1973, literally scores of suits have been filed, either to enforce or rescind these advance or forward contracts. Defendants have cited thirteen (13) cases that arose between September 18 and November 9, 1973. In each, the validity of the contracts has been upheld by either summary judgment, declaratory judgment, preliminary injunction, and/or permanent injunction. These affirmations of the contracts have emanated from the United States District Courts for the Middle District of Georgia, the Northern District of Mississippi, the Western District of Tennessee, the Northern District of Alabama, The District of South Carolina, the Northern District of Georgia, and from the state courts of Arkansas, Georgia, Alabama and Mississippi. * * *

The contracts are in evidence. They speak for themselves. No useful purpose would be served by detailing each provision. They were entered into between January 9, 1973 and March 29, 1973. In each, plaintiffs obligated themselves to sell and deliver to the defendant cotton buyers all of the cotton raised and harvested on designated acreage. The price ranged from 29 cents to 41 cents per pound. The actual cotton produced was physically to be delivered to the buyers, to be by them physically received and paid for on delivery. These contracts were negotiated prior to planting. We call them "forward" sales contracts. Each plaintiff cotton farmer was experienced, having been a cotton producer for several years, and each was familiar with the forward sale contract procedure.

The depositions reveal that during the period of time from January 9th through March 29, 1973, the competitive open market range ran from 28 cents to 32 cents per pound. On the basis of the record it would be difficult to quarrel with the proposition that the sales were for a fair market price at the time they were made, and as a matter of law we conclude that the price and circumstances prevailing at the time are determinative.

From April through September, the cotton market rose spectacularly. The price of 29 cents or 30 cents a pound, which looked so good to the farmers in February, no longer looked so good against 80 cents in September.

These farmers certainly have every right to contest the validity of their contracts. Likewise, the buyer has every right to assert the validity of their bargain. To quote the Honorable Wilbur D. Owens, Jr., U. S. District Judge, Middle District of Georgia (see Mitchell-Huntley Cotton Co. v. Fulton Benson, Civil Action 2902): "Ladies and Gentlemen, this case illustrates about as well as any case that will ever be in a court room that life is a two way street, that when we make bargains that turn out to be good for us that we keep them and then when we make bargains that turn out to be bad for us that we also keep them. That seems to be the essence of what this case is about. The defendants, naturally, don't want to sell cotton because the price has gone up and if I were one of those defendants I would feel the same way. I would be sick as an old hound dog who ate a rotten skunk, but unfortunately—well, not unfortunately—fortunately we all abide by contracts and that (is) the foundation of which all of the business that you have heard about here today is done."

What caused the upward price spiral of April to September? There were many causes. We are unable to pin down any one. Be that as it may, the cause has no relevance to the validity of the contracts. Some of the deponents point to such factors as large export shipments to China, high water and flood conditions in the cotton belt; late plantings forced by heavy rains, and the devaluation of the dollar. These elements and others are reasonable causes, but whatever causes the market to go up and down after the date of a contract has no relevancy to its validity. One facet of plaintiffs' attack is that the cotton buyers had inside information at the time they contracted with plaintiffs, and that these factors would coincide and drive the price of cotton to the level that it had never before reached. The record does not reveal this to be true. The record will reveal that Dallas Thomason sold his cotton at 30 cents; Frank Jones, Jr., Executive Vice-President of Cook Industries, Inc., sold his cotton at 30 cents; Conner Morscheimer, cotton buyer for W. K. Kennedy Co., Inc., sold his cotton at 29 ½ cents.

Plaintiffs emphasize that the cotton farmer has always been at the mercy of the weather and the boll weevil. This may be true, but by firm forward selling, the farmer shifts many of his risks to the buyer. The farmer guarantees neither quality nor quantity. He obligates himself to sell and the buyer obligates himself to buy all the cotton the farmer harvests from identifiable acreage. He sells it at a price at which he figures at the time of the contract he can make a profit in relation to his expectable costs. Against that firm contract he can arrange his crop financing. The depositions reveal the system used, and there can be no argument that it does give the grower a very real limitation of risk.

. . .

NOTES & QUESTIONS

1.   We'll often have occasion to refer to this case—or, actually, this and similar cases—under the shorthand description the "Cotton Futures Cases." Be sure that you understand how one goes from the general concept of expectation damages—an award of money sufficient to place the non-breaching party in the position she would have been in if the promise had been performed—to a specific award in a situation such as that in the Cotton Futures Cases. If the farmers had performed, how much would the buyers pay to receive the cotton? If, as in the case itself, the farmers did not perform

their promises and the buyers had to buy the cotton in the open market, how much would the buyers have to pay?

2.   Why should the farmers be obligated to sell their cotton for only about 30¢ per pound when the market price had—for reasons nobody expected—gone up to 80¢ per pound? Are the arguments for that result the same as in *Hawkins v. McGee*? To put the point in a slightly different way, assume that we conclude that the right result in the Cotton Futures Cases is that the farmers do have to sell their cotton for 30¢ per pound. Do the reasons for reaching that conclusion also lead us to the conclusion that the patient in *Hawkins* should be entitled to a sum of money that will place him in the position he would have been in if the promise had been performed?

2.   RELIANCE INTEREST

[handwritten: Stove company originally sought expectation damages]

Security Stove & Mfg. Co. v. American Ry. Express Co.

Kansas City Court of Appeals, Missouri, 1932.
227 Mo.App. 175, 51 S.W.2d 572.

[handwritten: Restitution → wouldn't cover all the expenses incurred by the plaintiff ↓ reliance!]

■ BLAND, J.

This is an action for damages for the failure of defendant to transport, from Kansas City to Atlantic City, New Jersey, within a reasonable time, a furnace equipped with a combination oil and gas burner. The cause was tried before the court without the aid of a jury, resulting in a judgment in favor of plaintiff in the sum of $801.50 and interest, or in a total sum of $1,000.00. Defendant has appealed.

The facts show that plaintiff manufactured a furnace equipped with a special combination oil and gas burner it desired to exhibit at the American Gas Association Convention held in Atlantic City in October, 1926. The president of plaintiff testified that . . . "the thing wasn't sent there for sale but primarily to show"; that at the time the space was engaged it was too late to ship the furnace by freight so plaintiff decided to ship it by express, and, on September 18th, 1926, wrote the office of the defendant in Kansas City, stating that it had engaged a booth for exhibition purposes at Atlantic City, New Jersey, from the American Gas Association, for the week beginning October 11th; that its exhibit consisted of an oil burning furnace, together with two oil burners which weighed at least 1,500 pounds; that, "In order to get this exhibit in place on time it should be in Atlantic City not later than October the 8th. What we want you to do is to tell us how much time you will require to assure the delivery of the exhibit on time."

Mr. Bangs, chief clerk in charge of the local office of the defendant, upon receipt of the letter, sent Mr. Johnson, a commercial representative of the defendant, to see plaintiff. Johnson called upon plaintiff taking its letter with him. Johnson made a notation on the bottom of the letter giving October 4th, as the day that defendant was required to have the exhibit in order for it to reach Atlantic City on October 8th.

On October 1st, plaintiff wrote the defendant at Kansas City, referring to its letter of September 18th, concerning the fact that the furnace must be in Atlantic City not later than October 8th, and stating what Johnson had told it, saying: "Now Mr. Bangs, we want to make doubly sure that this shipment is in Atlantic City not later than October 8th and the purpose of this letter is to tell you that you can *have your truck call for the shipment between 12 and 1 o'clock on Saturday, October 2nd for this.*" (Italics plaintiff's.) On October 2d, plaintiff called the office of the express company in Kansas City and told it that the shipment was ready. Defendant came for the shipment on the last mentioned day, received it and delivered the express receipt to plaintiff. The shipment contained 21 packages. Each package was marked with stickers backed with glue and covered with silica of soda, to prevent the stickers being torn off in shipping. Each package was given a number. They ran from 1 to 21.

Plaintiff's president made arrangements to go to Atlantic City to attend the convention and install the exhibit, arriving there about October 11th. When he reached Atlantic City he found the shipment had been placed in the booth that had been assigned to plaintiff. The exhibit was set up, but it was found that one of the packages shipped was not there. This missing package contained the gas manifold, or that part of the oil and gas burner that controlled the flow of gas in the burner. This was the most important part of the exhibit and a like burner could not be obtained in Atlantic City.

Wires were sent and it was found that the stray package was at the "over and short bureau" of defendant in St. Louis. Defendant reported that the package would be forwarded to Atlantic City and would be there by Wednesday, the 13th. Plaintiff's president waited until Thursday, the day the convention closed, but the package had not arrived at the time, so he closed up the exhibit and left. About a week after he arrived in Kansas City, the package was returned by the defendant.

Bangs testified that the reasonable time for a shipment of this kind to reach Atlantic City from Kansas City would be four days; that if the shipment was received on October 4th, it would reach Atlantic City by October 8th; that plaintiff did not ask defendant for any special rate; that the rate charged was the regular one; that plaintiff asked no special advantage in the shipment; that all defendant, under its agreement with plaintiff was required to do was to deliver the shipment at Atlantic City in the ordinary course of events; that the shipment was found in St. Louis about Monday afternoon or Tuesday morning; that it was delivered at Atlantic City at the Ritz Carlton Hotel, on the 16th of the month. There was evidence on plaintiff's part that the reasonable time for a shipment of this character to reach Atlantic City from Kansas City was not more than three or four days. . . .

. . .

Defendant contends that . . . the only damages, if any, that can be recovered in cases of this kind, are for loss of profits and that plaintiff's evidence is not sufficient to base any recovery on this ground.

. . .

We think, under the circumstances in this case, that it was proper to allow plaintiff's expenses as its damages. Ordinarily the measure of damages where the carrier fails to deliver a shipment at destination within a reasonable time is the difference between the market value of the goods at the time of the delivery and the time when they should have been delivered. But where the carrier has notice of peculiar circumstances under which the shipment is made, which will result in an unusual loss by the shipper in case of delay in delivery, the carrier is responsible for the real damage sustained from such delay if the notice given is of such character, and goes to such extent, in informing the carrier of the shipper's situation, that the carrier will be presumed to have contracted with reference thereto. * * *

In the case at bar defendant was advised of the necessity of prompt delivery of the shipment. Plaintiff explained to Johnson the "importance of getting the exhibit there on time." . . .

. . .

Defendant contends that plaintiff "is endeavoring to achieve a return of the status quo in a suit based on a breach of contract. Instead of seeking to recover what he would have had, had the contract not been broken, plaintiff is trying to recover what he would have had, had there never been any contract of shipment"; that the expenses sued for would have been incurred in any event. It is no doubt, the general rule that where there is a breach of contract the party suffering the loss can recover only that which he would have had, had the contract not been broken . . . . But this is merely a general statement of the rule and is not inconsistent with the holdings that, in some instances, the injured party may recover expenses incurred in relying upon the contract, although such expenses would have been incurred had the contract not been breached. * * *

In *Sperry et al. v. O'Neill-Adams Co.* (C. C. A.) 185 F. 231, the court held that the advantages resulting from the use of trading stamps as a means of increasing trade are so contingent that they cannot form a basis on which to rest a recovery for a breach of contract to supply them. In lieu of compensation based thereon the court directed a recovery in the sum expended in preparation for carrying on business in connection with the use of the stamps. The court said, loc. cit. 239:

> "Plaintiff in its complaint had made a claim for lost profits, but, finding it impossible to marshal any evidence which would support a finding of exact figures, abandoned that claim. Any attempt to reach a precise sum would be mere blind guesswork.

Nevertheless a contract, which both sides conceded would prove a valuable one, had been broken and the party who broke it was responsible for resultant damage. In order to carry out this contract, the plaintiff made expenditures which otherwise it would not have made. . . . The trial judge held, as we think rightly, that plaintiff was entitled at least to recover these expenses to which it had been put in order to secure the benefits of a contract of which defendant's conduct deprived it."

. . .

The case at bar was to recover damages for loss of profits by reason of the failure of the defendant to transport the shipment within a reasonable time, so that it would arrive in Atlantic City for the exhibit. There were no profits contemplated. The furnace was to be shown and shipped back to Kansas City. There was no money loss, except the expenses, that was of such a nature as any court would allow as being sufficiently definite or lacking in pure speculation. Therefore, unless plaintiff is permitted to recover the expenses that it went to, which were a total loss to it by reason of its inability to exhibit the furnace and equipment, it will be deprived of any substantial compensation for its loss. The law does not contemplate any such injustice. It ought to allow plaintiff, as damages, the loss in the way of expenses that it sustained, and which it would not have been put to if it had not been for its reliance upon the defendant to perform its contract. There is no contention that the exhibit would have been entirely valueless and whatever it might have accomplished defendant knew of the circumstances and ought to respond for whatever damages plaintiff suffered. In cases of this kind the method of estimating the damages should be adopted which is the most definite and certain and which best achieves the fundamental purpose of compensation. * * * Had the exhibit been shipped in order to realize a profit on sales and such profits could have been realized, or to be entered in competition for a prize, and plaintiff failed to show loss of profits with sufficient definiteness, or that he would have won the prize, defendant's cases might be in point. But as before stated, no such situation exists here.

While, it is true that plaintiff already had incurred some of these expenses, in that it had rented space at the exhibit before entering into the contract with defendant for the shipment of the exhibit and this part of plaintiff's damages, in a sense, arose out of a circumstance which transpired before the contract was even entered into, yet, plaintiff arranged for the exhibit knowing that it could call upon defendant to perform its common law duty to accept and transport the shipment with reasonable dispatch. The whole damage, therefore, was suffered in contemplation of defendant performing its contract, which it failed to do, and would not have been sustained except for the reliance by plaintiff upon defendant to perform it. It can, therefore, be fairly said that the damages or loss suffered by plaintiff grew out of the breach of the contract, for had the shipment arrived on time, plaintiff would have had the benefit of the contract, which was contemplated by all parties, defendant being advised of the purpose of the shipment.

The judgment is affirmed.

NOTES

1. The plaintiffs in *Security Stove* were awarded their reliance interest. Why did they not receive expectation? What about restitution? What would their restitution interest have been had it been awarded?

2. Freight transportation is a risky business, and risk allocation is a long-standing feature of contract in this area. Both statute and case law now reflect that fact, as carriers now routinely limit their liability (within certain parameters). We will encounter such limitations of liability in our focus on remedies in Chapter 7.

Sullivan v. O'Connor

Supreme Judicial Court of Massachusetts, Suffolk, 1973.
363 Mass. 579, 296 N.E.2d 183.

■ KAPLAN, JUSTICE.

The plaintiff patient secured a jury verdict of $13,500 against the defendant surgeon for breach of contract in respect to an operation upon the plaintiff's nose. The substituted consolidated bill of exceptions presents questions about the correctness of the judge's instructions on the issue of damages.

The declaration was in two counts. In the first count, the plaintiff alleged that she, as patient, entered into a contract with the defendant, a surgeon, wherein the defendant promised to perform plastic surgery on her nose and thereby to enhance her beauty and improve her appearance; that he performed the surgery but failed to achieve the promised result; rather the result of the surgery was to disfigure and deform her nose, to cause her pain in body and mind, and to subject her to other damage and expense. The second count, based on the same transaction, was in the conventional form for malpractice, charging that the defendant had been guilty of negligence in performing the surgery. Answering, the defendant entered a general denial.

On the plaintiff's demand, the case was tried by jury. At the close of the evidence, the judge put to the jury, as special questions, the issues of liability under the two counts, and instructed them accordingly. The jury returned a verdict for the plaintiff on the contract count, and for the defendant on the negligence count. The judge then instructed the jury on the issue of damages.

As background to the instructions and the parties' exceptions, we mention certain facts as the jury could find them. The plaintiff was a professional entertainer, and this was known to the defendant. The agreement was as alleged in the declaration. More particularly, judging from exhibits, the plaintiff's nose had been straight, but long and prominent; the defendant undertook by two operations to reduce its prominence and somewhat to shorten it, thus making it more pleasing in relation to the plaintiff's other features. Actually the plaintiff was obliged to undergo three operations, and her appearance was worsened. Her nose now had a concave line to about the midpoint, at which it became bulbous; viewed frontally, the nose from bridge to midpoint was flattened and broadened, and the two sides of the tip had lost symmetry. This configuration evidently could not be improved by further surgery. The plaintiff did not demonstrate, however, that her change of appearance had resulted in loss of employment. Payments by the plaintiff covering the defendant's fee and hospital expenses were stipulated at $622.65.

. . .

It has been suggested on occasion that agreements between patients and physicians by which the physician undertakes to effect a cure or to bring about a given result should be declared unenforceable on grounds of public policy. See *Guilmet v. Campbell*, 385 Mich. 57, 76, 188 N.W.2d 601 (dissenting opinion). But there are many decisions recognizing and enforcing such contracts, see annotation, 43 A.L.R.3d 1221, 1225, 1229–1233, and the law of Massachusetts has treated them as valid, although we have had no decision meeting head on the contention that they should be denied legal sanction. * * * These causes of action are, however, considered a little suspect, and thus we find courts straining sometimes to read the pleadings as sounding only in tort for negligence, and not in contract for breach of promise, despite sedulous efforts by the pleaders to pursue the latter theory. * * *

It is not hard to see why the courts should be unenthusiastic or skeptical about the contract theory. Considering the uncertainties of medical science and the variations in the physical and psychological conditions of individual patients, doctors can seldom in good faith promise specific results. Therefore it is unlikely that physicians of even average integrity will in fact make such promises. Statements of opinion by the physician with some optimistic coloring are a different thing, and may indeed have therapeutic value. But patients may transform such statements into firm promises in their own minds, especially when they have been disappointed in the event, and testify in that sense to sympathetic juries. If actions for breach of promise can be readily maintained, doctors, so it is said, will be frightened into practising 'defensive medicine.' On the other hand, if these actions were outlawed, leaving only the possibility of suits for malpractice, there is fear that the public might be exposed to the enticements of charlatans, and confidence in the profession might ultimately be shaken. See Miller, The Contractual Liability of Physicians and Surgeons, 1953 Wash.L.Q. 413, 416–423. The law has taken the middle of the road position of allowing actions based on alleged contract, but insisting on clear proof.

Instructions to the jury may well stress this requirement and point to tests of truth, such as the complexity or difficulty of an operation as bearing on the probability that a given result was promised. See annotation, 43 A.L.R.3d 1225, 1225–1227.

If an action on the basis of contract is allowed, we have next the question of the measure of damages to be applied where liability is found. Some cases have taken the simple view that the promise by the physician is to be treated like an ordinary commercial promise, and accordingly that the successful plaintiff is entitled to a standard measure of recovery for breach of contract—'compensatory' ('expectancy') damages, an amount intended to put the plaintiff in the position he would be in if the contract had been performed, or, presumably, at the plaintiff's election, 'restitution' damages, an amount corresponding to any benefit conferred by the plaintiff upon the defendant in the performance of the contract disrupted by the defendant's breach. See *Restatement: Contracts* § 329 and comment a, §§ 347, 384(1). Thus in *Hawkins v. McGee*, 84 N.H. 114 * * *, the defendant doctor was taken to have promised the plaintiff to convert his damaged hand by means of an operation into a good or perfect hand, but the doctor so operated as to damage the hand still further. The court, following the usual expectancy formula, would have asked the jury to estimate and award to the plaintiff the difference between the value of a good or perfect hand, as promised, and the value of the hand after the operation. (The same formula would apply, although the dollar result would be less, if the operation had neither worsened nor improved the condition of the hand.) If the plaintiff had not yet paid the doctor his fee, that amount would be deducted from the recovery. There could be no recovery for the pain and suffering of the operation, since that detriment would have been incurred even if the operation had been successful; one can say that this detriment was not 'caused' by the breach. But where the plaintiff by reason of the operation was put to more pain that he would have had to endure, had the doctor performed as promised, he should be compensated for that difference as a proper part of his expectancy recovery. It may be noted that on an alternative count for malpractice the plaintiff in the Hawkins case had been nonsuited; but on ordinary principles this could not affect the contract claim, for it is hardly a defence to a breach of contract that the promisor acted innocently and without negligence. . . .

Other cases, including a number in New York, without distinctly repudiating the *Hawkins* type of analysis, have indicated that a different and generally more lenient measure of damages is to be applied in patient-physician actions based on breach of alleged special agreements to effect a cure, attain a stated result, or employ a given medical method. This measure is expressed in somewhat variant ways, but the substance is that the plaintiff is to recover any expenditures made by him and for other detriment (usually not specifically described in the opinions) following proximately and foreseeably upon the defendant's failure to carry out his promise. * * * This, be it noted, is not a 'restitution' measure, for it is not limited to restoration of the benefit conferred on the defendant (the fee paid) but includes other expenditures, for example, amounts paid for medicine and nurses; so also it would seem according to its logic to take in damages for any worsening of the plaintiff's condition due to the breach. Nor is it an 'expectancy' measure, for it does not appear to contemplate recovery of the whole difference in value between the condition as promised and the condition actually resulting from the treatment. Rather the tendency of the formulation is to put the plaintiff back in the position he occupied just before the parties entered upon the agreement, to compensate him for the detriments he suffered in reliance upon the agreement. This kind of intermediate pattern of recovery for breach of contract is discussed in the suggestive article by Fuller and Perdue, *The Reliance Interest in Contract Damages*, 46 Yale L.J. 52, 373, where the authors show that, although not attaining the currency of the standard measures, a 'reliance' measure has for special reasons been applied by the courts in a variety of settings, including noncommercial settings. See 46 Yale L.J. at 396–401.

For breach of the patient-physician agreements under consideration, a recovery limited to restitution seems plainly too meager, if the agreements are to be enforced at all. On the other hand, an expectancy recovery may well be excessive. The factors, already mentioned, which have made the cause of action somewhat suspect, also suggest moderation as to the breadth of the recovery that should be permitted. Where, as in the case at bar and in a number of the reported cases, the doctor has been absolved of negligence by the trier, an expectancy measure may be thought harsh. We should recall here that the fee paid by the patient to the doctor for the alleged promise would usually be quite disproportionate to the putative expectancy recovery. To attempt, moreover, to put a value on the condition that would or might have resulted, had the treatment succeeded as promised, may sometimes put an exceptional strain on the imagination of the fact finder. As a general consideration, Fuller and Perdue argue that the reasons for granting damages for broken promises to the extent of the expectancy are at their strongest when the promises are made in a business context, when they have to do with the production or distribution of goods or the allocation of functions in the market place; they become weaker as the context shifts from a commercial to a noncommercial field. 46 Yale L.J. at 60–63.

There is much to be said, then, for applying a reliance measure to the present facts, and we have only to add that our cases are not unreceptive to the use of that formula in special situations. . . .

The question of recovery on a reliance basis for pain and suffering or mental distress requires further attention. We find expressions in the decisions that pain and suffering (or the like) are simply not compensable in actions for breach of contract. The defendant seemingly espouses this proposition in the present case. True, if the buyer under a contract for the purchase of a lot of merchandise, in suing for the seller's breach, should claim damages for mental anguish caused by his disappointment in the transaction, he would not succeed; he would be told, perhaps, that the asserted psychological injury was not fairly foreseeable by the defendant as a probable consequence of the breach of such a business contract. See *Restatement: Contracts,* § 341, and comment a. But there is no general rule barring such items of damage in actions for breach of contract. It is all a question of the subject matter and background of the contract, and when the contract calls for an operation on the person of the plaintiff, psychological as well as physical injury may be expected to figure somewhere in the recovery, depending on the particular circumstances. * * * Suffering or distress resulting from the breach going beyond that which was envisaged by the treatment as agreed, should be compensable on the same ground as the worsening of the patient's condition because of the breach. Indeed it can be argued that the very suffering or distress 'contracted for'—that which would have been incurred if the treatment achieved the promised result—should also be compensable on the theory underlying the New York cases. For that suffering is 'wasted' if the treatment fails. Otherwise stated, compensation for this waste is arguably required in order to complete the restoration of the status quo ante.

In the light of the foregoing discussion, all the defendant's exceptions fail: the plaintiff was not confined to the recovery of her out-of-pocket expenditures; she was entitled to recover also for the worsening of her condition, and for the pain and suffering and mental distress involved in the third operation. These items were compensable on either an expectancy or a reliance view. We might have been required to elect between the two views if the pain and suffering connected with the first two operations contemplated by the agreement, or the whole difference in value between the present and the promised conditions, were being claimed as elements of damage. But the plaintiff waives her possible claim to the former element, and to so much of the latter as represents the difference in value between the promised condition and the condition before the operations. . . .

NOTES & QUESTIONS

1.   The court in *Sullivan v. O'Connor* note that, while awarding the expectation interest might be more typical, there may be "special reasons . . . applied by courts in a variety of settings, including noncommercial settings" for awarding the reliance interest. Can you suggest a list of such "special reasons"? What might be the policy behind keeping such a list small?

2.   In Restatement (Second), it is now § 353 that excludes recovery for emotional disturbance "unless the breach also caused bodily harm or the contract or the breach is of such a kind that serious emotional disturbance was a particularly likely result". These are limited. Consider whether you think such a contract is likely to be open to such recovery in: (a) a childcare

arrangement; (b) an arrangement with a funeral home on correct burial procedures of a relative; (c) the rental of an Airbnb room; (d) the purchase of a wedding ring.

3.   RESTITUTION INTEREST

Yurchak v. Jack Boiman Construction Co.

Court of Appeals of Ohio, First District, 1981.
3 Ohio App.3d 15, 443 N.E.2d 526.

■ PER CURIAM.

This contract action arose out of a transaction between Michael Yurchak, plaintiff-appellee, and Jack Boiman Construction Company and Jack Boiman, defendants-appellants. On May 7, 1977, the parties entered into a written agreement whereby defendants undertook to waterproof plaintiff's basement. Central to the contract was defendants' guaranty that the basement would be waterproof for ten years. Plaintiff paid defendants $2,400, leaving a balance of $800 to be paid upon the job's completion. After defendants had finished their work, but before plaintiff could make final payment, it rained, and water leaked into plaintiff's basement much as it did before defendants attempted to waterproof it. Defendants endeavored several times to repair the leaks but were unable to do so. Plaintiff sued defendants on the breach of the guaranty and sought recovery of the $2,400 paid to defendants under the contract, and defendants counterclaimed for the outstanding $800. The evidence indicated that plaintiff received some minimal benefit from defendants' services. The jury found for plaintiff awarding him $2,000. Defendants appeal raising four assignments of error, none of which have merit.

In their first assignment of error defendants state that the trial court erred in overruling their motion for a directed verdict where the evidence showed that whereas the defendants had performed the contract, plaintiff had failed to perform his obligations thereunder (by withholding payment of the $800). We find this assignment unconvincing because it assumes that defendants had fully performed but the evidence showed that defendants' performance failed to achieve the ultimate object of the contract (the waterproofing of the basement). Final payment by plaintiff was clearly conditioned upon defendants' satisfactory completion of the task, and plaintiff was justified in withholding payment until the waterproofing of the basement was fully performed. Defendants' first assignment of error is overruled.

Defendants' second assignment of error is that the trial court erred in awarding a judgment to plaintiff in the absence of evidence indicating that the job was done in an unworkmanlike fashion or contrary to the contract specifications. This assignment is similar to the first in that it assumes that defendants fully complied with the contract specifications

[handwritten margin note: Rule: Restitution is an appropriate remedy if the party who breached the contract failed to perform.]

Company → Should give $$ back → didn't perform, defending

when the evidence, as well as the jury's verdict, clearly indicate the contrary. Defendants' failure to waterproof the basement was a material breach of the contract and entitled plaintiff to sue for an appropriate remedy.

This brings us to the third assignment of error that it was improper for the court to award judgment to the plaintiff when there was no evidence as to the amount of damages. The controlling fact is that plaintiff bargained and paid for a watertight basement which he did not receive. Defendants failed to render the consideration due under the contract and the plaintiff was entitled to recover the money he had paid for that promise.

The right to restitution[1] from a party who has substantially failed to perform[2] his part of the bargain is firmly established. * * *. "Once it is determined that a substantial breach has occurred, the non-breaching party has several options about what measures of recovery to pursue." Dobbs, The Law of Remedies, Section 12.1. He may pursue his expectancy interest and sue for damages or, "[i]f it is easier for him to show his restitution measure, then so be it, for that measure will certainly not be an unfair one to the defendant in the usual case." Id. at 793. When a contract is breached, the innocent party may recover either his expectancy or the benefits he has conferred upon the breaching party by his performance under the contract. 3 Restatement of Contracts 2d 208, Section 373.

In a case strikingly similar to this one, *Economy Swimming Pool Co. v. Freeling* (1963), 236 Ark. 888, 370 S.W.2d 438, defendant contracted with plaintiff to build a watertight fallout shelter on plaintiff's property. The shelter leaked and defendant unsuccessfully attempted for three months to prevent the seepage. Plaintiff sued for restitution of his payments made under the contract to which the court, at page 891, 370 S.W.2d 438, stated: "It seems to be basic contract law—apparently so

---

[1]   The term "restitution," as it applies in breach of contract cases, refers only to the remedy of placing plaintiff in the position where he was before the contract was made; that is, to return him to the status quo ante (as opposed to damages, or his expectancy, which are to place him in the position he would be in if the contract were performed). It should not be confused with the equitable action, restitution, which is used in situations involving unjust enrichment where the existence of a contract is immaterial.

[2]   In order to obtain restitution as a measure of damages, the breach must be substantial, not minor. Professor Corbin explains:

"In the case of a breach by non-performance, however, assuming that there has been no repudiation, the injured party's alternative remedy by way of restitution depends upon the extent of the non-performance by the defendant. The defendant's breach may be nothing but a failure to perform some minor part of his contractual duty. Such a minor non-performance is a breach of contract and an action for damages can be maintained. The injured party, however, can not maintain an action for restitution of what he has given the defendant unless the defendant's non-performance is so material that it is held to go to the 'essence'; it must be such a breach as would discharge the injured party from any further contractual duty on his own part. Such a vital breach by the defendant operates, with respect to the right of restitution, in the same way that a repudiation of the contractual obligation would operate." 5 Corbin on Contracts 561–564, Section 1104.

basic that there is little case law on the point—that where there is a material breach of contract, substantial nonperformance and entire or substantial failure of consideration, the injured party is entitled to rescission of the contract and restitution and recovery back of money paid." See, also, *Bause v. Anthony Pools, Inc.* (1962), 205 Cal.App.2d 606, 23 Cal.Rptr. 265.[3]

Defendants' fourth assignment of error is that plaintiff prevented defendants from performing their part of the contract. We find no evidence in the record that plaintiff refused to permit defendants to complete the job. The jury properly weighed the evidence and found for the plaintiff.

We affirm.

NOTES & QUESTIONS

1.   What might Mr. Yurchak's expectation interest have been in this case? Why might he have favoured the recovery of the restitution interest?

2.   Think through the different rationales for expectation, reliance, and the restitution interest. Expectation is the more usual remedy, and we will explore it further in Chapter 7. It has been said that "Reliance is often difficult to prove . . . and when proved it may be difficult to measure": Sharp, *Promissory Liability*, 7 U. Chi. L. Rev. 1, 20–21 (1939). As against restitution:

> [I]t is sometimes said that a credit economy depends, to a peculiar extent, on the keeping of promises, or at least of contracts, and so the equivalent of performance should be given in a case of breach. It is to be noted that if one understands credit in a limited sense, the force of this observation is likely to be lost. Credit in the sense of relations analogous to those of lender and borrower, could be taken care of by restitution. A more exact statement of the relations between our economy and expectation damages, seem to depend on the observation that it is not only an industrial and credit economy, but also a risk taking, profit making, more or less gambling economy. *Id*.

---

[3]   The restitution sought by plaintiff in this case was the payment he made on the contract ($2,400). However if defendants' services resulted in any benefit to the plaintiff, the plaintiff's restitution must be offset by the value of that benefit. 5 Corbin on Contracts 573, Section 1107. The jury apparently gave credit to testimony that defendants' work had stopped some of the mud that had previously oozed into plaintiff's basement and offset plaintiff's award by $400. We do not rule on the propriety of this aspect of the verdict because plaintiff, apparently satisfied with the verdict, chose not to cross-appeal and raise this issue.

CHAPTER TWO

RESTITUTION

> In one word, the gist of this kind of action is
> that the defendant, upon the circumstances
> of the case, is obliged by the ties of natural
> justice and equity to refund the money.

—Lord Mansfield, in Moses v. Macferlan (1760) 2 Bur, 1005

A. RESTITUTION AS A SEPARATE BODY OF SUBSTANTIVE LAW

George E. Palmer, The Law of Restitution § 1.1 (1978)

It has been traditional to regard tort and contract as the two principal sources of civil liability at common law . . . . There is another category that must be separated from all of these; this is liability based in unjust enrichment. . . . Restitution based upon unjust enrichment cuts across many branches of the law, including contract [and] tort . . . but it also occupies much territory that is its sole preserve.

Bank of Naperville v. Catalano

Appellate Court of Illinois, Second District, 1980.
86 Ill.App.3d 1005, 408 N.E.2d 441.

■ LINDBERG, JUSTICE.

Defendants, Robert and Beth J. Catalano, appeal from a judgment of the Circuit Court of DuPage County ordering them to make restitution to plaintiff, the Bank of Naperville. Restitution was ordered to be made by the Catalanos jointly in the amount of $2,780.94, by Robert Catalano individually in the amount of $1,825.45 and by Beth J. Catalano, individually in the amount of $35.97. The bank cross-appeals the trial court's denial of its claim for interest and attorney's fees.

The business relationship between the parties began on April 3, 1975, when the Catalanos took up residence on real estate in Naperville and retained the former owner's real estate trust with the bank. The Catalanos thereafter conducted various transactions with the bank, including the maintenance of a checking account and a commercial loan account. Mr. Catalano testified at trial to instances where the bank had paid checks over stop payment orders and failed to honor checks when sufficient funds to cover them were on deposit.

On September 13, 1975, Mrs. Catalano took out a $4,000 loan from the bank, secured by a note on which Mr. Catalano was guarantor. The note was renewed seven times and was due following the last renewal on July 5, 1977. As of August 3, 1977, the note was approximately 30 days past due, and Mrs. Catalano's checking account was overdrawn in the amount of $35.95. Mr. Stearns, the bank's president, determined that the loan was a "troublesome credit" which had been renewed too many times and that there was considerable difficulty with the checking account. Accordingly, he instructed that the checking account be closed and that the loan be paid off.

On August 4, 1977, Mr. Catalano went to the bank's drive-in window to make a deposit. The teller asked him to step inside, at which time an employee told him that his deposit could not be accepted and that his account had been closed. The employee tendered to Mr. Catalano a group of documents, including a paid-up loan statement, a cashier's check drawn on the bank for $1,825.45 and the documents which had accompanied the attempted deposit. Mr. Catalano refused to accept these papers and asked to see the bank president. He was shown into Mr. Stearns' office shortly thereafter. Mr. Stearns testified that he told Mr. Catalano that the bank would charge his savings account for the principal and interest due on the note and for the overdraft, with the balance being returned to him in the form of a cashier's check. Mr. Catalano admitted at one point that Stearns had said the money came from a savings account, but elsewhere denied having been so informed. Mr. Catalano stated that his money was "scattered all over," implying that he was uncertain as to which accounts had been used by the bank to produce the cashier's check.

Mr. Stearns testified that Catalano had thereafter made a telephone call from the bank lobby and cashed the check. According to Mr. Stearns, Catalano then threatened Stearns' life and Stearns called the police. Following arrival of the police, Catalano left the premises. Mr. Catalano, on the other hand, denied threatening Stearns' life. Catalano testified that Stearns had said that the bank did not choose to do business with people of Catalano's character, and that Stearns had called the police when he had refused to accept the various papers given to him. The police advised Catalano to accept the documents, so Catalano, not trusting the bank, had cashed the cashier's check and departed.

Subsequent to these events, it was discovered that defendants did not maintain a savings account at the Bank of Naperville, and that the money which the bank had applied to the overdraft, the loan and the cashier's check had been inadvertently taken from the savings account of a third party who coincidentally was also named Robert Catalano. Mr. Stearns admitted that preparation of the cashier's check had been done in "a less than careful manner."

This lawsuit followed.

. . .

As a general rule, where money is paid under a mistake of fact, and payment would not have been made had the facts been known to the payor, such money may be recovered. The fact that the person to whom the money was paid under a mistake of fact was not guilty of deceit or unfairness, and acted in good faith, does not prevent recovery of the sum paid, nor does the negligence of the payor preclude recovery. * * *

. . .

The next question presented is whether the payment to the Catalanos was actually made in consequence of a mistake of fact. The Catalanos reply in the negative, contending that there can be no recognized mistake of fact where facts were readily ascertainable, where the channels of information were open, where there was a failure to investigate known facts or where there was carelessness, indifference or inattention. They cite *John J. Calnan Co. v. Talsma Builders, Inc.* (1977), 67 Ill.2d 213, 10 Ill.Dec. 242, 367 N.E.2d 695 and *Steinmeyer v. Schroeppel* (1907), 226 Ill. 9, 80 N.E. 564, for the proposition that a mistake of fact must not be due to negligence, but both of those cases involved discussions of the conditions necessary before a contract will be rescinded for a mistake by one of the parties. While it has been held that a court of equity will not relieve a party from a mistake which was the result of his own negligence when the channels of information are open to him and no fraud or deception is practiced upon him (*National Union Fire Ins. Co. v. John Spry Lumber Co.* (1908), 235 Ill. 98, 85 N.E. 256), that holding came in the course of an action by certain insurance companies to reform their policies because of mistakes made in the descriptions of the location of the property intending to be covered, such actions coming after the property was destroyed. These cases do not stand for the proposition that a party erroneously receiving money may keep it simply because the payment was negligently made.

The Catalanos contend that inasmuch as the bank knows what its agents know, the instant plaintiff had actual knowledge that its payment was in error. This overlooks that, despite apparent negligence, there is no evidence that any of the bank's agents actually knew of the error. In our view, the bank's good faith misidentification of its depositor is a mistake of fact, entitling the bank to restitution of amounts erroneously paid to the erroneously identified party. The Catalanos characterize the bank's conduct as reckless and vengeful, but the record does not reveal any deliberate misconduct on its part. The bank may have been negligent in debiting the wrong account. However, as noted above, restitution will generally not be precluded because an overpayment was made negligently.

The Catalanos, referring to the trial court's citation of the Restatement of Restitution, § 59 (1937), further contend that restitution may not be ordered in the instant case because they have made a change of position in reliance on the mistaken payment, thereby defeating the bank's claim. The change of position to which defendants refer was their alleged failure to bring suit against the bank for wrongfully paying an $8,400 check over defendant's stop payment order.

It is true that when one party is misled by the representations or conduct of another and acts on these representations to his injury, the party making the representation may be "estopped" from asserting a legal right. (*Moline I.F.C. Finance, Inc. v. Soucinek* (1968), 91 Ill.App.2d 257, 234 N.E.2d 57.) However, in the instant case, there is no evidence that the Catalanos changed their position or suffered any permanent injury as a result of their alleged failure to sue the bank on their unrelated claim. We can see no reason why this failure to stop-payment claim could not have been brought as a counterclaim in the instant action. (See Section 38 of the Civil Practice Act, Ill.Rev.Stat.1977, ch. 110, par. 38.) Also, there has been no allegation that this claim has been barred by any statute of limitations and thus we must assume that it could be prosecuted in the future. In sum, we find that even if the Catalanos had deferred bringing suit against the bank as some sort of extra-judicial set-off, such a deferral was not a change of position under § 59 of the Restatement of Restitution. Accordingly, the trial court's award of restitution is affirmed.

Cotnam v. Wisdom

Supreme Court of Arkansas, 1907.
83 Ark. 601, 104 S.W. 164.

Action by F. L. Wisdom and another against T. T. Cotnam, administrator of A. M. Harrison, deceased, for services rendered by plaintiffs as surgeons to defendant's intestate. Judgment for plaintiffs. Defendant appeals. . . . .

Instructions 1 and 2, given at the instance of plaintiffs, are as follows: "(1) If you find from the evidence that plaintiffs rendered professional services as physicians and surgeons to the deceased, A. M. Harrison, in a sudden emergency following the deceased's injury in a street car wreck, in an endeavor to save his life, then you are instructed that plaintiffs are entitled to recover from the estate of the said A. M. Harrison such sum as you may find from the evidence is a reasonable compensation for the services rendered. (2) The character and importance of the operation, the responsibility resting upon the surgeon performing the operation, his experience and professional training, and the ability to pay of the person operated upon, are elements to be considered by you in determining what is a reasonable charge for the services performed by plaintiffs in the particular case."

■ HILL, C. J. (after stating the facts).

The reporter will state the issues and substance of the testimony and set out instructions 1 and 2 given at instance of appellee, and it will be seen therefrom that instruction 1 amounted to a peremptory instruction to find for the plaintiff in some amount.

The first question is as to the correctness of this instruction. As indicated therein the facts are that Mr. Harrison, appellant's intestate, was thrown from a street car, receiving serious injuries which rendered him unconscious, and while in that condition the appellees were notified of the accident and summoned to his assistance by some spectator, and performed a difficult operation in an effort to save his life, but they were unsuccessful, and he died without regaining consciousness. The appellant says: "Harrison was never conscious after his head struck the pavement. He did not and could not, expressly or impliedly, assent to the action of the appellees. He was without knowledge or will power. However merciful or benevolent may have been the intention of the appellees, a new rule of law, of contract by implication of law, will have to be established by this court in order to sustain the recovery." Appellant is right in saying that the recovery must be sustained by a contract by implication of law, but is not right in saying that it is a new rule of law, for such contracts are almost as old as the English system of jurisprudence. They are usually called "implied contracts." More properly they should be called "quasi contracts" or "constructive contracts." See 1 Page on Contracts, § 14; also 2 Page on Contracts, § 771.

The following excerpts from *Sceva v. True*, 53 N. H. 627, are peculiarly applicable here: "We regard it as well settled . . . that an insane person, an idiot, or a person utterly bereft of all sense and reason by the sudden stroke of an accident or disease may be held liable, in assumpsit, for necessaries furnished to him in good faith while in that unfortunate and helpless condition. And the reasons upon which this rest are too broad, as well as too sensible and humane, to be overborne by any deductions which a refined logic may make from the circumstances that in such cases there can be no contract or promise, in fact, no meeting of the minds of the parties. The cases put it on the ground of an implied contract; and by this is not meant, as the defendant's counsel seems to suppose, an actual contract—that is, an actual meeting of the minds of the parties, an actual, mutual understanding, to be inferred from language, acts, and circumstances by the jury—but a contract and promise, said to be implied by the law, where, in point of fact, there was no contract, no mutual understanding, and so no promise. The defendant's counsel says it is usurpation for the court to hold, as a matter of law, that there is a contract and a promise, when all the evidence in the case shows that there was not a contract, nor the semblance of one. It is doubtless a legal fiction, invented and used for the sake of the remedy. If it was originally usurpation, certainly it has now become very inveterate, and firmly fixed in the body of the law. Illustrations might be multiplied, but enough has been said to show that when a contract or promise implied by law is spoken of, a very different thing is meant from a contract in fact, whether express or tacit. The evidence of an actual contract is generally to be found either in some writing made by the parties, or in verbal communications which passed between them, or in their acts and conduct considered in the light of the circumstances of each particular case. A contract implied by law, on the contrary, rests upon no evidence. It has no actual existence. It is simply a mythical creation of the law. The law says it shall be taken that there was a promise, when in point of fact, there was none. Of course this is not good logic, for the obvious and sufficient reason that it is not true. It is a legal fiction, resting wholly for its support on a plain legal obligation, and a plain legal right. If it were true, it would not be a fiction. There is a class of legal rights, with their correlative legal duties, analogous to the obligationes quasi ex contractu of the civil law, which seem to lie in the region between contracts on the one hand, and torts on the other, and to call for the application of a remedy not strictly furnished either by actions ex contractu or actions ex delicto. The common law supplies no action of duty, as it does of assumpsit and trespass; and hence the somewhat awkward contrivance of this fiction to apply the remedy of assumpsit where there is no true contract and no promise to support it."

. . . .

The defendant sought to require the plaintiff to prove, in addition to the value of the services, the benefit, if any, derived by the deceased from the operation, and alleges error in the court refusing to so instruct the jury. The court was right in refusing to place this burden upon the physicians. The same question was considered in *Ladd v. Witte*, 116 Wis. 35, 92 N. W. 365, where the court said: "That is not at all the test. So that a surgical operation be conceived and performed with due skill and care, the price to be paid therefor does not depend upon the result. The event so generally lies with the forces of nature that all intelligent men know and understand that the surgeon is not responsible therefor. In absence of express agreement, the surgeon, who brings to such a service due skill and care, earns the reasonable and customary price therefor, whether the outcome be beneficial to the patient or the reverse."

. . . .

[Although the Arkansas Supreme Court agreed that the doctor was entitled to recover from the decedent's estate, the case was remanded because the Supreme Court concluded that there was an error in the precise manner that the jury had been instructed to calculate the amount of recovery. That portion of the opinion is omitted.]

NOTES & QUESTIONS

1.   Would the outcome have been different if Mr. Harrison had suddenly regained consciousness, told the doctors to leave him alone, and passed out again, still in dire need of assistance?

2.   The reasoning in *Cotnam v. Wisdom* is pretty clear, even if the terminology of 1907 appears outdated. Compare it to the language used in the following case, from 1982.

Cablevision of Breckenridge, Inc. v. Tannhauser Condominium Assn.

Supreme Court of Colorado, 1982.
649 P.2d 1093.

■ LOHR, JUSTICE.

We granted certiorari to review the decision of the Colorado Court of Appeals in Cablevision of Breckenridge, Inc. v. Tannhauser Condominium Association (Colo.App.No. 79CA0924, * * *), which reversed the judgment of the Summit County District Court awarding the plaintiff, Cablevision of Breckenridge, Inc. (Cablevision), damages for the wrongful conversion of its subscription cable service. We reverse the decision of the court of appeals and remand for reinstatement of the district court judgment.

. . . Cablevision is a corporation engaged in providing cable television and FM radio to its subscribers in areas where the television signals are weak or nonexistent. This is a frequently encountered problem in the vicinity of Breckenridge, Colorado, because the topography of the community and its distance from the originating broadcast stations generally result in an inability to receive a useful broadcast signal when using only the traditional antennas normally employed by individual households.

In order to provide its service, Cablevision constructed several antennas on a mountain peak near Breckenridge, by which it receives six television stations as well as FM radio. At the point of reception, the television signals are strong enough to reproduce a black and white picture, but are too weak to allow color reproduction. Consequently, the signals are fed into a "pre-amp," which magnifies their strength. The signals are then transmitted to a "head-end" building, located near the receiving antennas, where they are passed through a channel processor and mixer for the purpose of improving the clarity of the picture produced by the transmission. From this building, the signals are sent by coaxial cable to the "hub" facility in Breckenridge, and thence through distribution lines to the individual subscribers. Additional amplification of the signals is necessary as they are transmitted through the system, so amplifiers are installed along the distribution lines. Cablevision's capital investment in the transmission system is approximately $450,000.

. . . [I]n October 1972 Cablevision entered into an oral agreement for the provision of subscription cable services with Judy Keller, who was acting on behalf of the owners of the condominium units comprising the Tannhauser I development in Breckenridge. The Tannhauser I building consisted of 33 condominium units, and each was to receive the Cablevision service. Pursuant to this agreement Cablevision installed the equipment necessary to provide its service to each of the units. This was accomplished by running a connecting line from the distribution system to an amplifier located inside Tannhauser I. The signals were then transmitted from this amplifier to individual wall plates serving each of the units. From January 1, 1972, through March 1974, Tannhauser I paid for the service to these 33 units at a specified rate per unit.

Effective May 1974, Cablevision ceased billing for service to 33 units and began billing for service to only three units. This was done at the request of Jerry White, whose status is not described in the stipulation but who apparently acted as a representative for the Tannhauser I owners. The stipulation reflects disagreement over the exact events leading to this change in service, but it is undisputed that the Cablevision amplifier inside Tannhauser I was removed; that White then substituted his own amplifier and connected it to the Cablevision line; and that, following May 1, television and FM radio service was still provided to all 33 units of Tannhauser I despite the payment to Cablevision for service to only three of those units. This state of affairs continued from May 1, 1974, to approximately December 1, 1976.

In the fall of 1974 a second building, known as Tannhauser II and comprised of 25 condominium units, was constructed near Tannhauser I. Cablevision was never requested to supply service to Tannhauser II. However, the new building was wired internally for cable television and FM radio, and in November 1974 White supervised and assisted in the installation of a cable between Tannhauser I and Tannhauser II enabling extension of the Cablevision service to each of the 25 units in Tannhauser II. Tannhauser II began receiving the Cablevision transmission approximately November 30, 1974. Cablevision subsequently discovered the unauthorized use of its transmission by Tannhauser I and II and terminated all service to the condominiums about December 1, 1976.

Thereafter, Cablevision brought the present action, naming the condominium associations for Tannhausers I and II and the owners of the individual condominium units as defendants. Cablevision's amended complaint contained eight claims for relief, including breach of contract, concealment, conversion, various claims of unjust enrichment, and a request for injunctive relief.

However, as part of the pre-trial stipulation of facts summarized above, the parties submitted for judicial resolution the following single stipulated issue:

> Have the Defendants, or any of them, breached any contract with Plaintiff, written or oral, in fact or implied, for which Plaintiff is entitled for damages, actual or punitive?

After a hearing, the trial court entered an oral ruling incorporating the parties' stipulated facts, and holding that the defendants were liable for conversion of Cablevision's service. . . . The court . . . concluded:

> [T]he plaintiff's property and services in the furnishing of cable television is a legally protected interest for which it is

entitled to charge an appropriate and lawful rate to its subscribers. The defendants, through the actions stated in the Stipulation, have converted those protected interests without fully paying for them.

Based upon the damages hearing, the court entered judgment for actual damages of $11,597.50 plus statutory interest and court costs, and denied the prayer for punitive damages. The defendants then appealed.

The court of appeals reversed. It held that the trial court erred in ruling that the defendants were liable on the basis that they converted Cablevision's property interests because, pursuant to the parties' stipulation, "the only issue before the trial court was whether any defendant breached any contract with (Cablevision)." It further held that, because the stipulation did not establish the essential elements of a contract, Cablevision had not proved its breach of contract claim. Therefore, it directed the trial court to enter judgment for the defendants.

We accepted certiorari to review the court of appeals' decision. Cablevision contends that the propriety of the trial court's departure from the stipulated issue was not properly before the court of appeals because it was not raised in the defendants' motion for a new trial. It further argues that, in any case, the trial court did not err in considering the liability of the defendants under a theory of conversion and that the court was correct on the merits of this issue. However, we do not address these arguments because we conclude that the judgment of the trial court is supported by an alternative basis of liability raised by the stipulated issue submitted by the parties.

As stipulated by the parties, the issue for decision was whether "the Defendants, or any of them, breached any contract with Plaintiff, written or oral, in fact or implied." (Emphasis added.) We read the mention of "implied" contracts as a reference to the doctrine of quasi-contract or unjust enrichment, under which courts imply a contract as a matter of law where necessary to avoid unjust enrichment. This interpretation is based in part upon the apparent intent of parties in distinguishing "implied contracts" and contracts "in fact," and draws further support from the inclusion of unjust enrichment claims in the complaint.

In addressing only the issue of whether the stipulated evidence established a contract in fact, the court of appeals did not consider this alternative basis of liability. We conclude that the facts of this case present an appropriate basis for application of the doctrine of unjust enrichment, and reverse the decision of the court of appeals for that reason.

To recover under a theory of quasi-contract or unjust enrichment, a plaintiff must show (1) that a benefit was conferred on the defendant by the plaintiff, (2) that the benefit was appreciated by the defendant, and (3) that the benefit was accepted by the defendant under such circumstances that it would be inequitable for it to be retained without payment of its value. * * * Application of the doctrine does not depend upon the existence of a contract, express or implied in fact, but on the need to avoid unjust enrichment of the defendant notwithstanding the absence of an actual agreement to pay for the benefit conferred. * * * The scope of this remedy is broad, cutting across both contract and tort law, with its application guided by the underlying principle of avoiding the unjust enrichment of one party at the expense of another. 1 G. Palmer, The Law of Restitution § 1.1 (1978) * * *.

In the present case, we conclude that a benefit was conferred upon the defendants by Cablevision and that the defendants appreciated this benefit. The defendants' initial payment for this service in connection with the 33 Tannhauser I condominium units and their continued payment for service to three of those units amply demonstrate both the beneficial service provided by Cablevision and the appreciation of that service by the defendants. Instructive in this regard is the broad definition of benefit contained in the Restatement of Restitution § 1, comment b (1937):

> A person confers a benefit upon another if he gives to the other possession of or some other interest in money, land, chattels, or choses in action, performs services beneficial to or at the request of the other, satisfies a debt or a duty of the other, or in any way adds to the other's security or advantage. He confers a benefit not only where he adds to the property of another, but also where he saves the other from expense or loss. The word "benefit," therefore, denotes any form of advantage.

We also conclude that the defendants have retained this service under such circumstances that it would be inequitable to allow its use without payment for its value. The stipulated facts demonstrate that Cablevision never intended to provide its service to all of Tannhausers I and II in exchange for payment in connection with only three units. Indeed, upon discovery of the unauthorized use of its signals, Cablevision terminated all service to the defendants. Further, the defendants were not innocent or unwilling recipients of this benefit, but actively facilitated its provision.

The defendants contend that Cablevision was not harmed by the use made of its signal because it received compensation for the three signals delivered to the three Tannhauser I units pursuant to oral agreement; additional signals were not appropriated by the defendants; and the amplification and use of these signals within Tannhausers I and II did not impair Cablevision's ability to serve its other subscribers. However, this argument ignores the substance and effect of the defendants' conduct and the nature of the harm suffered by Cablevision. The ability of Cablevision to charge for its service is necessary to its economic viability. "Subscription stations rely upon fees paid by viewers rather than upon advertising proceeds for their support. Continued existence of the subscription television industry therefore depends upon the stations' ability to charge fees by limiting reception of their message to subscribers." Note, Decoding Section 605 of The Federal Communications Act: A Cause of Action for Unauthorized Reception of Subscription Television, 50 U.Cin.L.Rev. 362 (1981). By retransmission of the signals purchased in connection with three Tannhauser I units to non-subscribers, the defendants have undercut Cablevision's ability to sell its signal to these other potential customers. These business realities highlight the inequity of permitting the defendants to retain the benefits of Cablevision's service without payment of its value.

For similar reasons we reject the defendants' contention that their conduct is analogous to a subscriber moving his television set from room to room within his house or to a subscriber recording Cablevision's transmission by means of a video tape recorder. Such devices or activities merely increase the utility of the signals to the paying subscriber. In contrast, the defendants' conduct in the present case impairs the ability of Cablevision to sell its service to other potential subscribers.

The defendants also point to the fact that Cablevision acquires its signals free of charge and contends that, because Cablevision merely intercepts broadcast signals originated by others, it has no legally protected interest in those images and transmissions. Again, we find this argument unpersuasive. Although Cablevision does not acquire an exclusive right in the broadcast signals it receives, in the sense that it could prohibit others from independently receiving those signals by use of a home antenna or a competing, properly licensed subscription service, see *Intermountain Electronics, Inc. v. Tintic School District*, 14 Utah 2d 86, 377 P.2d 783 (1963), Cablevision does have a legally protected interest in the reception, processing and distribution system it has installed and in the service that this system enables Cablevision to provide. . .

The defendants have accepted a service from Cablevision that is customarily paid for and, in fact, was initially paid for by these defendants. The defendants were active participants in obtaining this benefit from Cablevision, and, based on the initial agreement to serve Tannhauser I, their representatives must have acted with the knowledge that Cablevision expected compensation for each Tannhauser unit receiving the Cablevision transmission. Under these facts, restitution is appropriate to avoid unjust enrichment to the defendants. * * *.

The damages awarded were based upon the rate prescribed in Cablevision's franchise from Breckenridge, which correspond to the rate paid for the three Tannhauser I units during the period of unauthorized use of the Cablevision signals. This was an appropriate measure of the benefit conferred upon the defendants and the amount of restitution due. * * *.

Although we do not reach the correctness of the grounds relied upon by the trial court . . . , we conclude that the judgment was proper based upon a theory of quasi-contract or unjust enrichment, and that the court of appeals therefore erred in reversing that judgment. * * *

We reverse the decision of the court of appeals and return the case to that court for remand to the trial court with directions to enter judgment in accordance with the views expressed in this opinion.

B. RELATIONSHIP AMONG RESTITUTION, CONTRACT, AND TORT[a]

The law of restitution—in the sense of a separate body of substantive law—has long been overshadowed by the law of tort and contract. There was a Restatement of Restitution back in the 1930s, and a few law schools have at times offered separate upper-year courses on the law of restitution, but the area has been largely underdeveloped in the United States in recent years, with the important exception of an excellent four volume treatise, GEORGE E. PALMER, THE LAW OF RESTITUTION (1978). That neglect may be changing. In 2011, the American Law Institute produced a new, two volume, Restatement (Third) of Restitution and Unjust Enrichment, which supercedes the Restatement of the Law of Restitution: Quasi Contracts and Constructive Trusts, 1937–1988. The fact that there never was and never will be a Restatement (Second) is a pretty good illustration of the fact that the subject was neglected for much of the twentieth century.

Perhaps once the profession has become more familiar with the Restatement (3d) of Restitution and Unjust Enrichment, it will be possible to discuss a specific topic within the law of restitution without an introduction explaining terminology. However, we are still far from that point. Cases are still filled with passages such as:

> As stipulated by the parties, the issue for decision was whether "the Defendants, or any of them, breached any contract with Plaintiff, written or oral, in fact or implied." We read the mention of "implied" contracts as a reference to the doctrine of quasi-contract or unjust enrichment, under which courts imply a contract as a matter of law where necessary to avoid unjust enrichment. This interpretation is based in part upon the apparent intent of parties in distinguishing "implied contracts" and contracts "in fact," and draws further support from the inclusion of unjust enrichment claims in the complaint.[b]

Or:

> Finally, plaintiff assigns error to the trial court's denial of its motion to conform the pleadings to the evidence it presented at trial. The motion did not supply the proposed pleadings, but

---

[a]   This passage is adapted from James Steven Rogers, *Restitution for Wrongs and the Restatement (Third) of the Law of Restitution and Unjust Enrichment*, 42 WAKE FOREST L. REV. 55 (2007)

[b]   *Cablevision of Breckenridge, Inc. v. Tannhauser*, 649 P.2d 1093, 1096 (Colo. 1982).

we infer, based on plaintiff's brief, that it sought to add a specification seeking to recover $298.78 for parts and labor that it supplied and that defendant did not pay for. That specification, presumably, would have been in equity based on some theory such as unjust enrichment or *quantum meruit.* . . . Here, granting plaintiff's motion would have injected an equitable claim based in quasi-contract into a legal action based on statutory law.[c]

There is no reason to mince words. These passages are little short of gibberish. "Quantum meruit?" "Contract implied in law?" "Quasi contract?" "Equitable claim?" These are nifty sounding lawyer words. But it is rare to encounter a lawyer who can use them with any precision. That is mostly because law professors have not done a competent job of training law students in the law of restitution.

The key to understanding the relationships among tort, contract, and restitution is to think about the central organizing principles of each body of law:

Tort. The central substantive notion is that one must not (unjustifiably) harm another. The correlative remedial principle might be expressed as "a party who unjustifiably harms another owes a duty to pay a sum of money that will compensate the other for the harm."

Contract. The central substantive notion is that one must not (unjustifiably) fail to perform one's promise to another. The correlative remedial principle might be expressed as "a party who unjustifiably fails to perform a promise to another owes a duty to pay a sum of money that will place the non-breaching party where she would have been if the promise had been performed."

Restitution. The central substantive notion is that one must not (unjustifiably) enrich oneself at the expense of another. The correlative remedial principle might be expressed as "a party who unjustifiably enriches himself at the expense of another owes a duty to pay a sum of money that will disgorge the enrichment."

If we imagine the range of conduct that might give rise to litigation, we can easily see that these three bodies of substantive law overlap, in more or less the sense of those Venn Diagrams that we all remember with dread from junior high school math classes:

---

 c *Pro Car Care, Inc. v. Johnson*, 118 P.3d 815, 820 (Or. Ct. App. 2005).

One can easily imagine some scenarios that can only be captured by one of these three bodies of substantive law.

Consider these three hypothetical scenarios:

Case One. Debbie hits Paul with a baseball bat, causing him great injury. Paul sues Debbie.

Case Two. Debbie owns the baseball bat that Babe Ruth used to hit his last home run. She promises to sell that bat to Paul. Later, she regrets the agreement and refuses to sell. Paul sues Debbie.

Case Three. Paul owns the baseball bat that Babe Ruth used to hit his last home run. He sells it for $250,000 and decides to donate the money to the Baseball Hall of Fame. He packages up $250,000 in currency[d] and sends it, along with a letter saying "Here's a donation. It's the money I received from selling the Babe's bat," to "B-ball Hall of Fame, Springfield MA." Later he realizes that he mistakenly sent it to the Basketball Hall of Fame in Springfield Massachusetts instead of the Baseball Hall of Fame in Cooperstown New York. Paul sues the Basketball Hall of Fame seeking return of the money.

Each of Cases One, Two, and Three falls only within one of the established branches of substantive private law.

Case One falls squarely and solely within the substantive law of tort. Debbie unjustifiably caused injury to Paul, and Paul seeks compensation for that injury. No one would be confused into thinking that Paul's action against Debbie had anything to do with any promise nor with any notion of unjust enrichment.

Case Two falls squarely and solely within the substantive law of contract. Debbie made a promise to Paul and unjustifiably refused to perform that promise. Paul sues seeking a remedy that will place him in the position he would have been in if Debbie had performed her promise. No one would be confused into thinking that Paul's action against Debbie had anything to do with harm suffered by Paul nor with any notion of unjust enrichment.

Case Three falls squarely and solely within the substantive law of restitution. Paul conferred a benefit upon the Basketball Hall of Fame

---

[d]   We use currency in the example because if we used a more plausible example of donation by check, the issues would be complicated by the possibility of actions based on the law of the check system.

and did so simply as a result of a mistake. There is no reason that the Basketball Hall of Fame should retain that benefit. Now, in fact, lawyers are likely to be confused about this; but no well-trained lawyer should be confused about it. Paul is entitled to judgment for $250,000 from the Basketball Hall of Fame. That's been settled law since at least the middle of the seventeenth century.[e] For some reason, however, there never cease to be news stories on some version of this scenario, presenting it as though it were some novel problem.[f] It's not. It's about as simple a case as one can imagine for the substantive law of restitution. Paul's right to recover has nothing to do with any bad action by the Basketball Hall of Fame. It doesn't make any difference that Paul may have been sloppy— "negligent" if one likes fancy lawyer talk.[g] Nor does Paul's right against the Basketball Hall of Fame have anything to do with any promise, explicit or implied, made by the Basketball Hall of Fame.

Now consider three further scenarios, where the substantive law of restitution overlaps with one or more of the other two branches.

Case Four. Debbie goes to Dr. Paul for dental treatment. Nothing is said about the charge. Dr. Paul sends Debbie a bill for $75, his customary charge for the work. Debbie refuses to pay. Dr. Paul sues Debbie.

Case Five. Debbie steals $1000 from Paul. Paul sues Debbie for $1000.

Case Six. Debbie goes to Chez Paul, a fancy restaurant. She orders a meal from the menu and eats it. After dessert, she looks around the dining room carefully, discovers that none of the waiters are present, and

---

[e] *E.g., Bonnel v Foulke*, 82 Eng. Rep. 1224 (K.B. 1657)

[f] *E.g., Battle over Money Deposited in Wrong Account*, Associated Press, Sept. 10, 2004:

MIDDLETOWN, Conn.—The company that owns the Chicago Cubs and The Hartford Courant are battling a former newspaper carrier to get back the last of $301,000 it accidentally gave to him instead of a baseball player with the same name.

The Tribune Co. money that was meant for Mark Guthrie, the relief pitcher, was sent to the bank account of Mark Guthrie, the Courant deliveryman, in three payments, the final one made last October. Five weeks later, the Cubs realized the error, and the team took back $275,000 before Guthrie froze his account.

The Cubs sued in February but last month filed legal documents offering to drop the suit if he handed over the final $26,000.

"We have no desire to embarrass Mr. Guthrie or bring undue attention to his actions—we just want the money back," said attorney Paul Guggina, who is representing the Cubs.

Guthrie, 43, said the matter is more complicated than that.

"I need them to open the books to me and show me I don't have any tax liabilities," he said. "It's mind-boggling. They never should have made the mistake to begin with."

The carrier said he had waited for the team to call him as his bank account ballooned.

Guthrie the pitcher, 38, is now a free agent."

Copyrighted 2017. Associated Press. 128541:0417PF.

[g] *E.g., Bank of Naperville v. Catalano*, 408 N.E.2d 441, 444 (Ill. App. Ct. 1980) ("As a general rule, where money is paid under a mistake of fact, and payment would not have been made had the facts been known to the payor, such money may be recovered. The fact that the person to whom the money was paid under a mistake of fact was not guilty of deceit or unfairness, and acted in good faith, does not prevent recovery of the sum paid, nor does the negligence of the payor preclude recovery.")

runs out of the restaurant without paying the bill. Chez Paul sues Debbie for the price of the meal.

Each of Cases Four, Five, and Six falls within more than one of the established branches of substantive private law.

Case Four illustrates the overlap of contract and restitution. The case might be regarded as falling within the law of contract, in the usual sense of enforcing promises. Debbie's action of going to Dr. Paul's office and requesting and receiving treatment can be treated as a manifestation of assent to pay Dr. Paul the $75 customary charge for the work. Suppose Debbie was an odd sort of person—perhaps a lawyer—and went to Dr. Paul and said "I offer to pay you $75 if you clean my teeth. You may signify your acceptance of this offer by performing the work." We could then say that Dr. Paul has an action against Debbie on the grounds that she made offer, that the offer was accepted, that performance was rendered, and that she thereby became obligated to place Dr. Paul in the position he would have been in if she had performed her promise to pay him the $75. Or, suppose the same facts, except that Debbie says "I offer to pay you your usual fee if you clean my teeth." Again, we could say that her liability is based on her promise. But, there really is no need to haul out all the cumbersome conceptual machinery of contract law for this simple case. She got her teeth cleaned, so she has to pay. The substantive law of restitution provides an easy way to describe her obligation. Dr. Paul conferred a benefit upon Debbie by performing the work. Dr. Paul did so in circumstances where payment is routinely required. Accordingly it would be inappropriate for Debbie to retain the benefit of the services with paying for them.

To see the restitution perspective on Case Four, one need only change the facts slightly to suppose that Dr. Paul is a physician who performs emergency services for Debbie when she is lying unconscious after an accident. Though the services are competently performed, Debbie does not survive. Dr. Paul seeks payment for his customary charge from Debbie's estate. It has been settled for years that the doctor would win the case.[h] The simple explanation is provided by the substantive law of restitution. The doctor is entitled to recover for the reasonable value of the benefit he conferred by providing the services. It makes no difference whether one could find some basis for construing any action by Debbie as tantamount to making a promise. Nonetheless, confusion about the relationship between contract and restitution has sometimes led lawyers representing the patient's estate in such cases to waste their client's money by trying to show that the patient never regained consciousness and so could not have manifested assent.[i]

---

[h]   *E.g., Cotnam v. Wisdom*, 104 S.W. 164 (Ark. 1907).

[i]   *Id.* at 165 (Court dismisses as silly the argument of the patient's lawyer that the patient "was never conscious after his head struck the pavement. He did not and could not, expressly or impliedly, assent to the action of the appellees. He was without knowledge or will power.")

Case Five illustrates the overlap of tort and restitution. One might think this as a case where Debbie inflicted a harm on Paul by depriving him of $1000, and so must compensate him for the harm he suffered. Or, one might think of this as a case where Debbie inappropriately obtained a benefit from Paul by taking the $1000 from him, and so owes a duty to disgorge the enrichment she obtained. In a simple case, it really doesn't matter which way we describe the case. We get into troubles only if we get caught up in arcane lawyer's jargon and start talking about the restitution action as one in which Paul "waives the tort and sues in assumpsit."

Case Six illustrates the overlap of tort, contract, and restitution. There is no question that Debbie is obligated to Chez Paul for the cost of the meal. We can describe that obligation in various ways. We might say that by sitting down in the restaurant, ordering from the menu, and eating the meal, Debbie manifested that she promised to pay Chez Paul the price of the meal. Or, we could say that what Debbie did was equivalent to stealing from Chez Paul, and she is obligated to pay damages for the harm she inflicted. Or, we could say that Debbie inappropriately enriched herself by eating the meal and not paying for it, so she is obligated to disgorge the enrichment she received.

The irony is that despite the fact that this is all very simple, many, if not most, lawyers thinking about these six examples will feel entirely comfortable with the simple tort and contract cases, and will feel comfortable with the overlap cases, so long as they are described from the perspective of tort or contract. By contrast, the restitution approach, either in the case of payment by mistake where restitution is the only plausible approach, or in any of the overlap cases, is likely to leave lawyers feeling a bit uneasy. It's pretty common to hear law students and lawyers say something along the lines of "I more or less understood contracts and torts, but I never really understood that stuff about quasi-contract or restitution." That, we suspect, is the product of little more than the way that we organize the first year curriculum in law school. Suppose that in the first year of law school we taught tort and restitution, but not contracts. Or, contracts and restitution, but not tort. Students would emerge saying that they more or less understood the subjects they took, but never felt comfortable about that odd other subject.

C. BORDERLINE OF RESTITUTION AND CONTRACT

Kellum v. Browning's Adm'r.

Court of Appeals of Kentucky, 1929.
231 Ky. 308, 21 S.W.2d 459.

■ STANLEY, C.

Mrs. Lena Browning died in August, 1925, possessed of an estate of about $30,000. She bequeathed $3,000 to each of her four nieces and nephews, including the appellant, Mrs. Emma F. Kellum. A certain house and lot was devised to Georgetown College, at Georgetown, Ky., and the residue to the Baptist Church at Grayson, Ky. Mrs. Browning had no children, and her next of kin were Mrs. Kellum and the other nieces and nephews, her sisters, who resided at remote points.

Mrs. Kellum filed a claim with the administrator with the will annexed for $4,680 for nursing and care of the decedent and for furnishing her a room, fuel, laundry, etc., for a period of five years next preceding her death. This was allowed first by the administrator and then by the master commissioner, to whom the case was referred. The claimant filed a response to exceptions filed to the allowance, which was also denominated as an answer and cross-petition. It alleged an express contract to pay for the services, and stated that during all the time the claimant conducted a rooming and boarding house, furnishing accommodations for hire to those desiring them. The claim presented with this pleading covered a period of more than nine years and was on the basis of $25 a week, the aggregate being $12,000. She acknowledged payment of approximately $900.

Upon a trial before a jury on an issue out of chancery, at the close of evidence introduced in behalf of the claimant, the jury was peremptorily instructed to find for the estate. The court thereupon entered judgment sustaining the exceptions and denying the claim. From that judgment this appeal is prosecuted.

No election having been required as between the allegations of an implied and an express contract, the claimant had the right to rely upon both, or either contract, as she might be able to sustain. * * *

So far as the claim for board is concerned, ever since the establishment of the commonwealth, and in Virginia before us as far back as 1663, the statutes have required an express contract for payment of compensation without regard to kinship. The same rule was early adopted by the courts for nursing, and other personal services where the relationship was such as to raise the presumption of gratuity or mutuality of benefit. The rule in this respect has been many times stated in substantially the same language. In *Lucius' Adm'r v. Owens*, 198 Ky. 114, 248 S. W. 495, 496, it is thus given: "So it appears the doctrine is well established in this jurisdiction that, where the relation of the parties is sufficient to raise the presumption that they live together as a matter of mutual convenience, or as members of the same family, no presumption will be raised by the law that one member, though sick, has promised or agreed to pay the other members of the family, or any one of them, for services rendered to the sick person. On the contrary, the presumption is that the services, being natural, were rendered without hope or expectation of pay, and before a recovery can be had an express contract must be proved; and to establish such a contract stricter proof is required than in a case of an ordinary contract. This rule applies not only to cases between parent and child, but between uncles and aunts on the one side, and nephews and nieces on the other, and between cousins and other near relatives."

There was no evidence in this case tending to prove a contract arising from a definite offer and a definite acceptance, the claimant resting her case on evidence of conditions, circumstances, and statements of the deceased recipient of the services shown to have been rendered. The court has before it, therefore, the duty of determining her right to a recovery, or rather her right to have had the case submitted to the jury, under such evidence.

There is a paucity of early cases of this character, which bears silent testimony to the traditional hospitality of Kentuckians. But the scarcity is fully made up in recent years, in which claims of this nature have been prolific of litigation. And while the principles of law have become pretty well established, there have crept into the opinions of the court what are apparently inharmonious and inconsistent expressions, but which are really but general statements or a confusion of terms. We have concluded, therefore, to review the law and consider the subject at some length in order to clarify the situation. Cases not involving the presumption of gratuity, however, are not included within the scope of the review.

The "Restatement of the Law of Contracts," by the American Law Institute, thus defines a contract (section 1): "A contract is a promise or a set of promises for the breach of which the law gives a remedy, or the performance of which the law in some way recognizes as a duty."

We are not here concerned with a simple, formal promise and acceptance, clearly established from spoken or written words. And we pass for the present a consideration of contracts which arise by implication of law, that is, obligations created by law for reasons of equity and justice, which are generally denominated implied contracts, but which are more accurately designated as quasi contracts. Unlike true contracts, these are not based on the apparent intention of the parties to undertake the performance in question nor to promise anything. We are interested here in the law as it relates to a contract based on a promise which may be inferred from the conduct of the parties. As declared in section 5 of the Restatement above referred to, a promise in a contract may be inferred wholly or partly from such conduct as justifies the promisee in understanding that the promisor intended to make a promise. To constitute such a contract there must, of course, be a mutual assent by the parties—a meeting of minds—and also an intentional manifestation of such assent. *Springfield Fire & Marine Ins. Co. v. Snowden*, 173 Ky. 664, 191 S. W. 439. Such manifestation may consist wholly or partly of acts, other than written or spoken words. Section 21, "Restatement of Law of Contracts." Commenting on this declaration, that authority says: "Words are not the only medium of expression. Conduct may often convey as clearly as words a promise or an assent to a proposed promise, and where no particular requirement of form is made by the law a condition of the validity or enforceability of a contract, there is no distinction in the effect of a promise whether it is expressed (1) in writing, (2) orally, (3) in acts, or (4) partly in one of these ways and partly in others."

It is often difficult to determine whether the conduct of the parties as disclosed by the evidence is a manifestation of an agreement, promise, or understanding that (in this class of cases) compensation would be paid and accepted for services shown to have been rendered; that is to say, whether from the relation and operative acts of the parties the existence of a contract may logically and reasonably be inferred or implied. There is no difference in the legal effect of an express contract formally executed and of an inferred contract of this character, or, indeed, of a quasi contract. But there is a vast difference in the character and quantum of proof necessary to establish them. In establishing a contract by inference, the facts and circumstances must be sufficient to clearly and convincingly manifest or prove a mutual assent of minds to enter into the contract sought to be implied or established. In determining this sufficiency we frequently encounter conflicting presumptions. Thus, where one performs labor or services for another with his knowledge and assent and under circumstances which ordinarily call for payment, there is a presumption that the beneficiary intended payment and that there was an assent of minds as to this. On the other hand is the presumption of gratuitous service where there was a duty, moral obligation, or natural affection, or mutuality of benefit (*Nicely v. Howard*, 195 Ky. 327, 242 S. W. 602), by reason of which it has been often declared there can be no recovery under an implied contract. However, when these conflicting presumptions do arise, the latter presumption of gratuity is considered the stronger and is conclusive unless overcome by affirmative proof that there was an express contract. And the degree of the relationship may strengthen or diminish the presumption according to its proximity or remoteness.

. . . .

Although not hitherto so denominated by this court, what we have been considering is often called a "contract implied in fact." It requires an actual agreement or meeting of minds although not expressed. It is implied or presumed from acts or circumstances which, according to the ordinary course of dealing and the common understanding of men, a mutual intent to contract is shown. 6 R. C. L. 587. In this class of cases, death has silenced the voice of one of the parties to the transaction, and the law seals the lips of the other. But as guilt of crime may be established by proof of circumstances, and a tort be inferred from conditions, so may the existence of an agreement or contract, as we have shown, be deduced from proven facts. Thus it is said in *Peters v. Poro*, 96 Vt. 95, 117 A. 244, 246, 25 A. L. R. 615: "The terms 'express contract' and 'contract implied in fact' indicate a difference only in the mode of proof. A contract implied in fact is implied only in that it is to be inferred from the circumstances, the conduct, acts, or relation of the parties, rather than from their spoken words."

In other words, from the facts disclosed the court concludes that the parties themselves had entered into an agreement respecting them, although there is no evidence of an express offer and a definite acceptance.

The term "contract implied in law" is applied to a class of obligations created by law without regard to the assent of the parties upon whom the obligation is imposed-one which is not a contract obligation in the true sense, but a quasi contract, constructively imported by law, as where one has received money or its equivalent under such circumstances that in equity and in good conscience he ought not to retain it, in which case the owner may recover in an action in form ex contractu. *People v. Dummer*, 274 Ill. 637, 113 N. E. 934. As stated in 6 R. C. L. 588: "The liability exists from an implication of law that arises from the facts and circumstances independent of agreement or presumed intention. The intention of the parties in such case is entirely disregarded, while in cases of express contracts and contracts implied in fact the intention is of the essence of the transaction. As has been well said, in the case of consensual contracts the agreement defines the duty, while in the case of quasi-contracts the duty defines the contract. The duty which thus forms the foundation of a quasi-contractual obligation is frequently based on the doctrine of unjust enrichment."

. . . .

Coming now to consider the facts in the case before the court and to a determination of the right of appellant to recover compensation under the uncontradicted evidence, or rather to have the question submitted to the jury: it was proved that shortly after the death of her husband in 1916, the deceased, Mrs. Browning, came to appellant's home in Falmouth and remained there continuously until her death nine years later, with the exception of a few weeks now and then when she would return to her own house, about a half mile distant, in which she had retained a room. When there Mrs. Kellum went every day, and sometimes oftener, to look after her aunt's wants and to care for her, even though at the time Mrs. Browning had a servant employed. During her absence from Mrs. Kellum's, it was shown that Mrs. Browning objected to having her room occupied by any one else, and that it was retained for her. During all the time the appellant was conducting a rooming and boarding house. After occupying an upstairs room for awhile when she first came, it was testified that the best room in the house was turned over to Mrs. Browning and a door was cut directly into the dining room for her convenience. She was crippled and partially paralyzed, necessitating the use of crutches, and oftentimes ill and bedridden, requiring much attention. Her room was attended to, fires kept burning when needed, and there were performed by Mrs. Kellum all kinds of menial services, such as are required by an old, crippled lady confined to her room. On occasion she would take her aunt out in a wheel chair. She was critical of the food and in all things rather exacting in her demands.

Mrs. Browning's physician testified the character of attention given by Mrs. Kellum as a nurse was of the reasonable value of $15 to $20 a week. The reasonable worth of the board and lodging was also proven. Numerous checks for different small sums, and given at irregular times and marked as being for board, were offered in evidence by the claimant. For the year 1916 these aggregated $35. There was none for 1917, and the total for each year was anywhere from $35 to a maximum of $266 in 1923. It was explained that during the early part of the period Mrs. Browning owned a farm and her tobacco crop was pledged, so that her ready income and cash was limited. Another niece stayed with her in her own house awhile in 1923, and Mrs. Browning gave her a check for $50 bearing the notation, "for staying with me and making garden."

While there was no evidence introduced showing a "categorical promise by the recipient to pay for and a like agreement by the performer to render the services upon that promise," and no verbal expression on the part of the decedent except to the effect that she was paying her way, the conduct and the respective situations of the parties (financial and otherwise), the exacting demands of the aunt, the degree of kinship, and the significant indication of the intention of the parties as evidenced by payments for board from time to time. . . , all taken together were sufficient, we think, to take the case to the jury on both the claim for board and nursing on the theory of a contract implied in fact, that is to say, on the issue as to the existence of an express contract. . . .

. . . .

The pleadings and facts of the instant case also make applicable the law of quasi contracts, or contracts implied in law. The evidence showed the claimant here was conducting a boarding or lodging house, and engaged in the business of supplying for pay those accommodations which the aunt accepted. The general rule which denies a recovery on a contract implied in law ought not to be applied where the claim arises out of commercial relationships. There is no more reason for concluding or presuming that the niece rendered these services gratuitously, or by reason of her affection, or in recognition of a moral obligation, than there would be had she been conducting a mercantile establishment and her aunt during the years had obtained her clothing and food in her store. The facts do not bring the case within that class where the presumption of gratuity is raised by reason of mutual convenience or benefits, for the benefit all inured to Mrs. Browning. . . . .

. . . .

Our conclusion in the case is this: That in the absence of an election, the case should have been submitted to the jury as to the right of recovery for both board and nursing under a contract implied in fact, as stated, and also under a contract implied in law.

. . . .

The administrator may, of course, show if he can that all these services were rendered by the claimant gratuitously and without any purpose to charge for them. As to proving the rendition of service and establishing the express contract to compensate therefor, the burden is on the claimant. As to the contract implied in law, the burden is on the administrator to show compensation was not contemplated.

. . . .

The judgment of the lower court is reversed for proceedings consistent with this opinion.

D. RESTITUTION OF BENEFIT CONFERRED UNDER AGREEMENT WHERE PLAINTIFF CANNOT SUE FOR BREACH

Stark v. Parker
Supreme Judicial Court of Massachusetts, 1824.
2 Pick. 267, 19 Mass. 267.

This was an action of *indebitatus assumpsit* brought to recover the sum of 27 dollars, 33 cents, as a balance due for services rendered by the plaintiff on the defendant's farm. Plea, the general issue.

At the trial, in the Court of Common Pleas, before *Strong* J., the defendant admitted that the plaintiff had performed the service set forth in the declaration, and for the price therein stated, and that he, the defendant, had paid him from time to time, before he left the defendant's service, money amounting in the whole to about 36 dollars, and on account of his labor, but the defendant proved that the plaintiff agreed to work for him a year, for the sum of 120 dollars, and that he, the defendant, agreed to pay him that sum for his labor. He also proved that the plaintiff voluntarily left his service before the expiration of the year, and without any fault on the part of the defendant, and against his consent.

The judge thereupon instructed the jury, that the plaintiff would be entitled to recover in this action a sum in proportion to the time he had served, deducting therefrom such sum, if any, as the jury might think the defendant had suffered by having his service deserted; and if such sum should exceed the sum claimed by the plaintiff, they might find a verdict for the defendant.

The jury having returned a verdict for the plaintiff, the defendant filed his exceptions to this instruction.

. . . .

■ LINCOLN J. delivered the opinion of the Court.

This case comes before us upon exceptions filed, pursuant to the statute, to the opinion, in matter of law, of a judge of the Court of Common Pleas, before whom the action was tried by a jury; and we are thus called upon to revise the judgment which was there rendered. The exceptions present a precise abstract question of law for consideration, namely, whether upon an entire contract for a term of service for a stipulated sum, and a part-performance, without any excuse for neglect of its completion, the party guilty of the neglect can maintain an action against the party contracted with, for an apportionment of the price, or a *quantum meruit,* for the services actually performed. . . .

It cannot but seem strange to those who are in any degree familiar with the fundamental principles of law, that doubts should ever have been entertained upon a question of this nature. Courts of justice are eminently characterized by their obligation and office to enforce the performance of contracts, and to withhold aid and countenance from those who seek, through their instrumentality, impunity or excuse for the violation of them. And it is no less repugnant to the well established rules of civil jurisprudence, than to the dictates of moral sense, that a party who deliberately and understandingly enters into an engagement and voluntarily breaks it, should be permitted to make that very engagement the foundation of a claim to compensation for services under it. The true ground of legal demand in all cases of contracts between parties is, that the party claiming has done all which on his part was to be performed *by the terms of the contract,* to entitle him to enforce the obligation of the other party. . . .

. . . .

The law indeed is most reasonable in itself. It denies only to a party an advantage from his own wrong. It requires him to act justly by a faithful performance of his own engagements, before he exacts the fulfilment of dependent obligations on the part of others. It will not admit of the monstrous absurdity, that a man may voluntarily and without cause violate his agreement, and make the very breach of that agreement the foundation of an action which he could not maintain under it. Any apprehension that this rule may be abused to the purposes of oppression, by holding out an inducement to the employer, by unkind treatment near the close of a term of service, to drive the laborer from his engagement, to the sacrifice of his wages, is wholly groundless. It is only in cases where the desertion is voluntary and without cause on the part of the laborer, or fault or consent on the part of the employer, that the principle applies. Wherever there is a reasonable excuse, the law allows a recovery. To say that this is not sufficient protection, that an excuse may in fact exist in countless secret and indescribable circumstances, which from their very nature are not susceptible of proof, or which, if proved, the law does not recognise as adequate, is to require no less than that the law should *presume* what can never legally be established, or should admit that as *competent,* which by positive rules is held to be wholly *immaterial.* We think well established principles are not thus to be shaken, and that in this commonwealth more especially, where the important business of husbandry leads to multiplied engagements of precisely this description, it should least of all be questioned, that the laborer is worthy of his hire, only upon the performance of his contract, and as the reward of fidelity.

The judgment of the Court of Common Pleas is reversed.

. . .

Britton v. Turner

Superior Court of Judicature of New Hampshire, 1834.
6 N.H. 481.

Assumpsit for work and labour, performed by the plaintiff, in the service of the defendant, from March 9th, 1831, to December 27, 1831.

The declaration contained the common counts, and among them a count in *quantum meruit,* for the labor, averring it to be worth one hundred dollars.

At the trial in the C. C. Pleas, the plaintiff proved the performance of the labor as set forth in the declaration.

The defence was that it was performed under a special contract— that the plaintiff agreed to work one year, from some time in March, 1831, to March 1832, and that the defendant was to pay him for said year's labor the sum of one hundred and twenty dollars; and the defendant offered evidence tending to show that such was the contract under which the work was done.

Evidence was also offered to show that the plaintiff left the defendant's service without his consent, and it was contended by the defendant that the plaintiff had no good cause for not continuing in his employment.

There was no evidence offered of any damage arising from the plaintiffs departure, farther than was to be inferred from his non fulfilment of the entire contract.

The court instructed the jury, that if they were satisfied from the evidence that the labor was performed, under a contract to labor a year, for the sum of one hundred and twenty dollars, and if they were satisfied that the plaintiff labored only the time specified in the declaration, and then left the defendant's service, against his consent, and without any good cause, yet the plaintiff was entitled to recover, under his *quantum meruit* count, as much as the labor he performed was reasonably worth, and under this direction the jury gave a verdict for the plaintiff for the sum of $95.

The defendant excepted to the instructions thus given to the jury.

. . . .

■ PARKER, J. delivered the opinion of the court.

It may be assumed, that the labor performed by the plaintiff, and for which he seeks to recover a compensation in this action, was commenced under a special contract to labor for the defendant the term of one year, for the sum of one hundred and twenty dollars, and that the plaintiff has labored but a portion of that time, and has voluntarily failed to complete the entire contract.

It is clear, then, that he is not entitled to recover upon the contract itself, because the service, which was to entitle him to the sum agreed upon, has never been performed.

But the question arises, can the plaintiff, under these circumstances, recover a reasonable sum for the service he has actually performed, under the count in *quantum meruit*.

Upon this, and questions of a similar nature, the decisions to be found in the books are not easily reconciled.

It has been held, upon contracts of this kind for labor to be performed at a specified price, that the party who voluntarily fails to fulfil the contract by performing the whole labor contracted for, is not entitled to recover any thing for the labor actually performed, however much he may have done towards the performance . . . . Stark v. Parker, 19 Mass 267 (1824) * * * That such rule in its operation may be very unequal, not to say unjust, is apparent.

A party who contracts to perform certain specified labor, and who breaks his contract in the first instance, without any attempt to perform it, can only be made liable to pay the damages which the other party has sustained by reason of such non performance, which in many instances may be trifling—whereas a party who in good faith has entered upon the performance of his contract, and nearly completed it, and then abandoned the further performance—although the other party has had the full benefit of all that has been done, and has purhaps sustained no actual damage—is in fact subjected to a loss of all which has been performed, in the nature of damages for the non fulfilment of the remainder, upon the technical rule, that the contract must be fully performed in order to a recovery of any part of the compensation.

By the operation of this rule, then, the party who attempts performance may be placed in a much worse situation than he who wholly disregards his contract, and the other party may receive much more, by the breach of the contract, than the injury which he has sustained by such breach, and more than he could be entitled to were he seeking to recover damages by an action.

The case before us presents an illustration. Had the plaintiff in this case never entered upon the performance of his contract, the damage could not probably have been greater than some small expense and trouble incurred in procuring another to do the labor which he had contracted to perform. But having entered upon the performance, and labored nine and a half months, the value of which labor to the defendant as found by the jury is $95, if the defendant can succeed in this defence, he in fact receives nearly five sixths of the value of a whole year's labor, by reason of the breach of contract by the plaintiff a sum not only utterly disproportionate to any probable, not to say possible damage which could have resulted from the neglect of the plaintiff to continue the remaining two and an half months, but altogether beyond any damage which could have been recovered by the defendant, had the plaintiff done nothing towards the fulfilment of his contract.

. . . .

We hold then, that where a party undertakes to pay upon a special contract for the performance of labor, or the furnishing of materials, he is not to be charged upon such special agreement until the money is earned according to the terms of it, and where the parties have made an express contract the law will not imply and raise a contract different from that which the parties have entered into, except upon some farther transaction between the parties.

In case of a failure to perform such special contract, by the default of the party contracting to do the service, if the money is not due by the terms of the special agreement he is not entitled to recover for his labor, or for the materials furnished, unless the other party receives what has been done, or furnished, and upon the whole case derives a benefit from it. * * *

But if, where a contract is made of such a character, a party actually receives labor, or materials, and thereby derives a benefit and advantage, over and above the damage which has resulted from the breach of the contract by the other party, the labor actually done, and the value received, furnish a new consideration, and the law thereupon raises a promise to pay to the extent of the reasonable worth of such excess. . . .

If on such failure to perform the whole, the nature of the contract be such that the employer can reject what has been done, and refuse to receive any benefit from the part performance, he is entitled so to do, and in such case is not liable to be charged, unless he has before assented to and accepted of what has been done, however much the other party may have done towards the performance. He has in such case received nothing, and having contracted to receive nothing but the entire matter contracted for, he is not bound to pay, because his express promise was only to pay on receiving the whole, and having actually received nothing the law cannot and ought not to raise an implied promise to pay. But where the party receives value—takes and uses the materials, or has advantage from the labor, he is liable to pay the reasonable worth of what he has received.* * *. And the rule is the same whether it was received and accepted by the assent of the party prior to the breach, under a contract by which, from its nature, he was to receive labor, from time to time until the completion of the whole contract; or whether it was received and accepted by an assent subsequent to the performance of all which was in fact done. If he received it under such circumstances as precluded him from rejecting it afterwards, that does not alter the case—it has still been received by his assent.

. . .

The amount, however, for which the employer ought to be charged, where the laborer abandons his contract, is only the reasonable worth, or the amount of advantage he receives upon the whole transaction, * * * and, in estimating the value of the labor, the contract price for the service cannot be exceeded. * * *.

If a person makes a contract fairly he is entitled to have it fully performed, and if this is not done he is entitled to damages. He may maintain a suit to recover the amount of damage sustained by the non performance.

The benefit and advantage which the party takes by the labor, therefore, is the amount of value which he receives, if any, after deducting the amount of damage; and if he elects to put this in defence he is entitled so to do, and the implied promise which the law will raise, in such case, is to pay such amount of the stipulated price for the whole labor, as remains after deducting what it would cost to procure a completion of the residue of the service, and also any damage which has been sustained by reason of the non fulfilment of the contract.

If in such case it be found that the damages are equal to, or greater than the amount of the labor performed, so that the employer, having a right to the full performance of the contract, has not upon the whole case received a beneficial service, the plaintiff cannot recover.

This rule, by binding the employer to pay the value of the service he actually receives, and the laborer to answer in damages where he does not complete the entire contract, will leave no temptation to the former to drive the laborer from his service, near the close of his term, by ill treatment, in order to escape from payment; nor to the latter to desert his service before the stipulated time, without a sufficient reason; and it will in most instances settle the whole controversy in one action, and prevent a multiplicity of suits and cross actions.

. . .

Applying the principles thus laid down, to this case, the plaintiff is entitled to judgment on the verdict.

. . .

Judgment on the verdict.

Restatement (Second) of Contracts § 374(1)

[I]f a party justifiably refuses to perform on the ground that his remaining duties of performance have been discharged by the other party's breach, the party in breach is entitled to restitution for any benefit that he has conferred by way of part performance or reliance in excess of the loss that he has caused by his own breach.

Comment:

a. *Restitution in spite of breach.* The rule stated in this Section applies where a party, after having rendered part performance, commits a breach by either non-performance or repudiation that justifies the other party in refusing further performance. It is often unjust to allow the injured party to retain the entire benefit of the part performance rendered by the party in breach without paying anything in return. The party in breach is, in any case, liable for the loss caused by his breach. If the benefit received by the injured party does not exceed that loss, he owes nothing to the party in breach. If the benefit received exceeds that loss, the rule stated in this Section generally gives the party in breach the right to recover the excess in restitution. . . .

The rule stated in this Section is of particular importance in connection with breach by the buyer under a land sale contract . . . and breach by the builder under a construction contract . . . It is less important in the case of the defaulting employee, who has the protection afforded by statutes that require salary payments at relatively short intervals. The case of defaulting buyer of goods is governed by Uniform Commercial Code § 2–718(2), which generally allows restitution of all but an amount fixed by that section. . . .

b. *Measurement of benefit.* If the party in breach seeks restitution of money that he has paid, no problem arises in measuring the benefit to the other party. . . . If, however, he seeks to recover a sum of money that represents the benefit of services rendered to the other party, measurement of the benefit is more difficult. Since the party seeking restitution is responsible for posing the problem of measurement of benefit, doubts will be resolved against him and his recovery will not exceed the . . . other party's increase in wealth. . . . Although the contract price is evidence of the benefit, it is not conclusive. However, in no case will the party in breach be allowed to recover more than a ratable portion of the total contract price where such a portion can be determined.

NOTES

1. Consider how the judges writing in the *Stark v. Parker* and *Britton v. Turner* cases use particular techniques to create implied contract terms. Go back to each case and find arguments from (1) precedent, (2) custom and convention, (3) policy, (4) rules, (5) standards, and (6) basic principle. See further Robert W. Gordon, Britton *v.* Turner: *A Signpost on the Crooked Road to "Freedom" in the Employment Contract*, in CONTRACTS STORIES 186, 217–9 (D. Baird ed., 2007). A legal historian, Professor Gordon uses this case to demonstrate how law constructs the boundaries between "free contract" and "free labor". See further at 224ff.

2.   As the Restatement excerpt above indicates, the approach taken in *Britton v. Turner*, rather than that in *Stark v. Parker*, would commonly be followed today. In the setting of those cases, however, the problem is unlikely to arise today, because statutes commonly require that employees be paid their wages on a regular periodic basis, such as every two weeks.

PROBLEMS

1.   Suppose the facts were as in *Britton*—that is, the employee promised to work for 12 months for $120, but quit after 9 ½ months. Suppose that the employer is able to find someone else to work for the remaining part of the year, but has to pay $40 for that work. Would the employee be entitled to $95 or some other amount? Remember, the employee's claim is based on the notion that the employer would be unjustly enriched if the employer gets the benefit of the work done but does not pay for it. By what amount is the employer enriched in this variant?

2.   Suppose the facts were as in *Britton*—that is, the employee promised to work for 12 months for $120, but quit after 9 ½ months. Suppose, however, that the employer is able to prove that the going rate for work of that sort was only $60. Would the employee be entitled to $95 or some other amount?

CHAPTER THREE

CONTRACT FORMATION INCLUDING OFFER & ACCEPTANCE

> I'm gonna make him an offer he can't refuse.
>
> –Vito Corleone

A. FORMATION IN GENERAL

Restatement (Second) of Contracts § 17(1), 18, 22

U.C.C. § 2–204

Gregory and Appel, Inc. v. Duck

Court of Appeals of Indiana, Second District, 1984.
459 N.E.2d 46.

. . .

The action before the trial court concerned whether or not a contract existed for the sale of certain property known as the Colonial Apartments in downtown Indianapolis. The property is owned by defendants, Donald Duck and members of his family. Plaintiff, Gregory and Appel, brought an action for declaratory judgment that a contract existed, and for specific performance to cause the Ducks to convey the property. The contractual dispute arose from a letter sent by Donald Duck in his capacity as attorney for the Ducks, to Gregory and Appel in which he set forth the terms of an offer that would be acceptable to the Ducks. The letter in question is characterized by the Ducks as a "solicitation of an offer", an "agreement to agree", and in the letter itself, as an invitation for a "proposal . . . for the purchase . . . of property. . . ." Gregory and Appel contends that the letter constitutes an offer to sell. It purports to have accepted the offer by submitting to the Ducks a contract for the sale of real estate which, it argues, contains the terms specified in Duck's letter, thereby creating a binding contract.

. . .

In order for a contract to exist, there must be an offer and an acceptance of the offer which meets the terms of the offer in every respect. * * * An acceptance which varies the terms of an offer is a rejection and operates as a counter-offer which may be accepted by the original offeror. * * * A binding agreement also requires a meeting of the minds or mutual assent. * * * Where the expression of two parties purported to be acts of offer and acceptance are materially different in meaning or if the expressions fail to show agreement on essential terms, there is no mutual assent and thus no contract. * * * Furthermore, a mere request for an offer is not an offer, and an agreement to make an agreement is not enforceable unless all the conditions of the contemplated agreement are specified. * * *

With regard to whether a contract exists, the record discloses the following facts:

(1) The Ducks sent a letter to Gregory and Appel which set forth the terms of an offer which the Ducks would find acceptable.

(2) Gregory and Appel, in response to the letter, submitted its first proposed contract, the title and first paragraph of which is as follows:

> "CONTRACT FOR PURCHASE OF REAL ESTATE
> OFFER TO PURCHASE REAL ESTATE
>
> Gregory and Appel, Inc. (hereinafter referred to as 'Purchaser'), *offers to purchase* from Donald C. Duck, Berkley W. Duck and Thomas Duck d.b.a. Colonial Apartments (hereinafter referred to as 'Vendor'), the following described real estate and other property located in Marion County, Indiana, commonly known as: Colonial Apartment Building, 402 N. Delaware Street . . ." (Emphasis supplied)

(3) The Ducks rejected the above proposed contract, whereupon Gregory and Appel made a few minor changes and submitted its otherwise identical second proposed contract, the title and first paragraph of which is:

> "CONTRACT FOR PURCHASE OF REAL ESTATE
> OFFER TO PURCHASE REAL ESTATE
>
> Gregory and Appel, Inc. (hereinafter referred to as 'Purchaser') *offers to purchase* from Donald C. Duck and Jane K. Duck, Thomas S. Duck and Junia Duck, and Berkley W. Duck d/b/a Colonial Apartments (hereinafter referred to as 'Vendor'), the following described real estate and other property located in Marion County, Indiana, commonly known as: Colonial Apartment Building, 402 N. Delaware Street . . ." (Emphasis supplied)

(4) Gregory and Appel tendered a check for $10,000 to the Ducks as earnest money which was returned after the rejection of Gregory's second proposed contract.

(5) The proposed contracts submitted by Gregory and Appel contain a number of terms which are not identical to those specified in the Ducks' letter.

(6) The proposed contracts submitted by Gregory and Appel contain a number of additional terms not specified in the Ducks' letter.

(7)   Neither of the proposed contracts are signed or dated by either party.

Given these facts, Ducks' letter, on its face, appears to constitute a solicitation of an offer. Its phraseology is such that it was clearly not intended to be mistaken for an offer. More significant, however, is the fact that the proposed contract submitted by Gregory and Appel states plainly on its face in bold face print that it is an offer to purchase. Gregory and Appel's characterization of the document as an acceptance is manifestly refuted upon an initial inspection of the first page alone. Furthermore, the document bears no signature and no date, and is therefore unexecuted.

Finally, even if the Ducks' letter were properly characterized as an offer, a meticulous examination of its terms and those contained in Gregory and Appel's second proposed contract reveals a number of divergent and additional terms. An acceptance must meet and correspond with the offer in every respect, point for point. Where the acceptance varies the terms from the offer, it is a rejection and amounts to a counteroffer. * * * Thus Gregory and Appel's proposed contract could not have been an acceptance.

In summation, the true offer in this case was Gregory and Appel's. It was not accepted by the Ducks, and therefore, no contract was formed between the parties. We conclude that upon the Ducks' motion, the trial court properly found that no genuine issue of material fact existed, and correctly applied the law to find no contract.

We affirm that ruling.

NOTES

1.   *Gregory and Appel, Inc. v. Duck* illustrates the common setting in which disputes about offer and acceptance arise: The prospective sellers and prospective buyers were negotiating about a sale. Something happened—not really described in the opinion—and the deal did not go through. The buyers thought that the negotiations had reached the stage of a binding agreement; the sellers thought not. So, the issue in the case was whether the parties had or had not reached a binding agreement. For better or worse, the way that our legal system commonly resolves such disputes is by parsing the communications one by one under the concepts of "offer" and "acceptance."

2.   An offer is a communication that the recipient could reasonably understand as proposing an agreement and signifying that the person making the offer ("offeror") understands that an agreement can be formed simply by the other party ("offeree") assenting to the proposal. RESTATEMENT (SECOND) OF CONTRACTS § 24. An acceptance is a communication in response to an offer that signifies assent. RESTATEMENT (SECOND) OF CONTRACTS § 50(1). Can you count how many offers were made in *Gregory & AppelEds?*

3.   It's common to find statements to the effect that "in every contract there must be an offer and an acceptance."[a] *That's wrong.* In fact, in a carefully planned transaction, one of the key objectives of the lawyers representing each side is to make absolutely sure that there are never any offers. The *Reprosystem* case illustrates that fact. To see why, think about the consequences of concluding that a communication is an offer.

Reprosystem, B.V. v. SCM Corp.
United States Court of Appeals, Second Circuit, 1984.
727 F.2d 257.

■ GEORGE C. PRATT, CIRCUIT JUDGE.

Defendant SCM Corporation appeals from a judgment of the United States District Court for the Southern District of New York, Robert W. Sweet, *Judge,* awarding $1,062,000 in damages to plaintiffs Reprosystem, B.V., a Netherlands corporation, and N. Norman Muller, a New York resident. * * * The trial court found that SCM was contractually obligated to sell its six foreign subsidiaries to plaintiffs, that SCM breached the claimed contract of sale . . . . On appeal, SCM contends that there was no contract because the parties intended not to be bound unless and until a formal written contract was executed, and that none ever was. . . . [W]e reverse the district court's conclusions that the parties were bound by a contract . . . .

Defendant SCM is a multinational enterprise that manufactures and distributes a variety of products. In 1976 the part of its business that consisted of marketing, leasing, and servicing copy machines in Europe, Africa, and the Middle East, was conducted by SCM's International Business Equipment Division through six wholly owned subsidiaries incorporated under the laws of five foreign countries. During fiscal year 1976, the six subsidiaries together generated annual sales exceeding $40 million and profits exceeding $4 million, and had approximately one thousand employees.

In late 1975 Paul Elicker, who was president, chief executive officer, and chairman of the board of SCM, and Herbert Elgi, the vice president of finance, decided that SCM should dispose of its European copier subsidiaries. At Elicker's direction, Frank De Maio, who was vice president and general manager of the International Division, began to seek out potential purchasers. . . .

In a letter prepared without assistance of counsel, Muller, on May 7, 1976, offered to pay $9 million for the SCM subsidiaries, subject to two conditions: (1) a satisfactory audit by Muller's accountants, and (2) execution of a formal agreement, satisfactory to both SCM and Muller. Rodich informed Muller that the letter provided a basis for negotiations,

[a]   For example in *Gregory & Appel*, the court says "In order for a contract to exist, there must be an offer and an acceptance of the offer which meets the terms of the offer in every respect."

but that discussions would have to be suspended during a securities offering by SCM.

When negotiations resumed in August 1976, Rodich presented Muller with a list of nine points that SCM considered to be nonnegotiable. These nine points, supplemented by four more in September, became the basis for an "agreement in principle" between Muller and SCM. One provision of the "agreement in principle" was that during negotiations the companies would be operated by SCM for the benefit of Muller, so that any profits or losses occurring after August 1, 1976 would be used to adjust the purchase price. SCM issued a press release on September 28, 1976 announcing the "agreement in principle", but stating also that "[t]he proposed sale is subject to a definitive agreement expected to be reached soon." SCM's 10-K report, filed with the SEC on September 30, 1976, also stated that SCM made "no assurance that the transaction would be completed."

The parties contemplated that the transaction would be developed in a "Global Agreement" setting out the general terms of the transaction, plus six separate agreements covering the respective details for the sales of the six subsidiary corporations. Using the "agreement in principle" as a starting point, general counsel for SCM prepared a draft model agreement for sale of one of the subsidiaries. After Muller's attorneys, Hardee, Barovick, Konecky & Braun, reviewed the draft and found it incomplete, SCM retained the firm of Sullivan & Cromwell to assist in negotiating and drafting all of the agreements.

Concentrating on the Global Agreement and a model agreement for one of the subsidiaries, Sullivan & Cromwell generated more than fifteen drafts by mid-December, each of which was reviewed by the Hardee, Barovick firm and returned for revision. Consistent with the proviso in Muller's initial offer that conditioned the contemplated transaction on execution of a formal agreement, each draft of the Global Agreement prepared by Sullivan & Cromwell provided that the obligations of each party were subject to a condition precedent that it shall have been provided with an opinion from counsel for the other party that "this [Global] Agreement and each of the Purchase Agreements has been duly authorized, executed and delivered by [the other party]".

On December 15 and 16, 1976 the parties and their attorneys met to resolve all outstanding issues. At this meeting the drafts prepared by Sullivan & Cromwell were reviewed paragraph by paragraph, including the paragraphs that required formal execution as a prerequisite to binding effect. After two days of negotiations no problems remained, the parties exchanged congratulations, and Rodich took Muller to De Maio's office where he acknowledged that the meetings had been successfully completed.

On December 17, 1976 Rodich sent telexes to the general managers of the subsidiaries: "we now feel that the problems are resolved and that the deal is made subject to approval by various government agencies."

On December 27, 1976 and January 5, 1977, "final drafts" of the Global Agreement and six separate agreements were circulated by Sullivan & Cromwell. Because Rodich was being reassigned to a new post, Elgi took over the negotiations on behalf of SCM. At year's end, Elgi reviewed the proposed transaction, discovered that the subsidiaries were operating more profitably than expected, and decided that the sale was a better deal for Muller than for SCM. Elgi proposed alternatives to Elicker in a meeting on January 4, including the alternative of killing the deal with Muller and selling the subsidiaries individually. Elicker instructed Elgi to attempt to close the proposed transaction with Muller.

In January the negotiations stalled. SCM introduced new items for negotiation, fired the New York management that was supposed to be transferred to Muller intact, and discovered an accounting error which led to a substantial increase in the purchase price. Muller continued to avoid SCM's requests that he document his ability to provide the purchase price on closing. On January 20, 1977 SCM issued a press release stating that it felt free to pursue other alternatives.

On January 31 Muller wrote SCM claiming that the "final drafts" constituted binding contracts for the purchase and sale of the subsidiaries. SCM responded on February 2 by terminating the negotiations. At no time was any of the draft contracts signed by either side.

Although "[c]ontract law has progressed and evolved sounder principles since the days of ritualistic and formalistic sealed instrument requirements", *V'Soske v. Barwick,* 404 F.2d 495, 499 (2d Cir.1968), *cert. denied,* 394 U.S. 921, 89 S.Ct. 1197, 22 L.Ed.2d 454 (1969), there are still situations where the absence of a signed, formal agreement is fatal to an argument that a contract exists. This court summarized the alternative New York rules on this subject in *V'Soske:*

First, if the parties intend not to be bound until they have executed a formal document embodying their agreement, they will not be bound until then; and second, the mere fact that the parties contemplate memorializing their agreement in a formal document does not prevent their informal agreement from taking effect prior to that event. * * * These rules, placing the emphasis on intention rather than form, are sensible and reasonable.

Id. at 499 (citations omitted).

In *V'Soske* we held that the party invoking the first rule of New York contract law described above must prove either that both parties understood they were not to be bound until the executed contract was delivered, or that the other party should have known that the disclaiming party did not intend to be bound before the contract was signed. In *V'Soske* the defendant buyer failed to prove either proposition.

Thus, the primary question on this appeal is one of intent. *Banking & Trading Corp. v. Floete,* 257 F.2d 765, 769 (2d Cir.1958). Did the parties intend not to be bound prior to execution of a formal contract? Or, did they merely contemplate that their informal agreement would be reduced to a formal writing at some later time?

In this case the trial judge determined that the parties intended to be bound by the unexecuted "final drafts" and did not intend their contractual obligations to be contingent upon their signing formal contractual documents. He wrote:

> [I]t has been determined as a matter of fact that eventually both parties intended to be bound by the Final Drafts. Taking into account the totality of the parties' objective manifestations of intent as the transaction progressed and the circumstances surrounding the negotiations, I reject SCM's contention that a final signing would be required to constitute a binding agreement. In the circumstances at bar, SCM's—indeed, both parties'—contemplation of subsequent formal signed agreements did not overcome the objective facts which established an agreement.

Thus the district judge, relying upon the second rule of *V'Soske,* concluded that the parties merely contemplated memorializing their informal agreement in a signed, formal document. This finding of fact is subject to the clearly erroneous standard of review embodied in Federal Rule of Civil Procedure 52(a). * * * Therefore, the district court's finding that the parties intended to be contractually bound prior to execution of the formal contracts must be upheld unless it was made without adequate evidentiary support, is against the clear weight of the evidence, or was induced by an erroneous view of the law. * * *

Our review of the entire record leaves us with the definite and firm conviction that a mistake was made by the district court, *United States v. United States Gypsum,* 333 U.S. 364, 395, 68 S.Ct. 525, 542, 92 L.Ed. 746 (1948), because the documents and testimony clearly showed that the intent of both parties was not to be bound prior to the execution of a formal, written contract. Therefore, the first rule summarized in *V'Soske* applies, and SCM was not bound by the "agreement in principle", by the "final drafts", or by any claimed oral understanding reached in the course of the extended negotiations.

The uncontested evidence clearly establishes the parties' intent not to be bound prior to execution of formal contracts. Muller's initial purchase offer was made on the expressed condition that "a formal agreement, which is satisfactory to SCM and [plaintiffs] be entered into." Muller testified that Rodich "had no problem with that." Additionally, the September press release, prepared by SCM and reviewed by Muller, stated: "The proposed sale of the European copier business is subject to a definitive agreement expected to be reached soon." SCM's 10-K report, filed with the SEC in September 1976, also stated: "[SCM] makes no assurance that this transaction will be completed."

Finally, the numerous drafts of the "Global Agreement" conditioned the parties' obligations on the receipt of opinions from counsel of both buyer and seller confirming that the "[Global] Agreement and each of the Purchase Agreements have been duly authorized, executed and delivered". Draft agreements for the sale of several of the subsidiaries had similar provisions. Additionally, the drafts of the Global Agreement provided "when executed and delivered, this [Global] Agreement and each of the Purchase Agreements will be a valid and binding agreement * * * in accordance with its terms." Despite their many other differences over the proposed contracts, neither party took exception to these provisions that conditioned their binding effect on formal execution and delivery. Thus, the contract drafts, combined with the parties' other written communications, conclusively establish a mutual intent not to be bound prior to execution of the formal documents, and the district court's finding to the contrary is clearly erroneous. Its conclusion that a contract existed must, therefore, be reversed.

The result we reach is supported by prior decisions applying New York law . . .[citing cases]

Our conclusion that no contract existed eliminates the only basis on which Judge Sweet awarded damages to plaintiffs. Nevertheless, the plaintiffs argue on this appeal that the award can be sustained on alternative theories of unjust enrichment and breach of a duty to negotiate in good faith. We disagree.

NOTES

1.   Think about a large complex deal, such as the purchase of a company or a large office building. There are lots of details to be worked out before either side is willing to be bound to an agreement. The negotiation commonly begins with the business people working toward agreement on the major financial terms, and then bringing in the lawyers to continue the process, refining the financial terms and working out all kinds of other issues. It's not uncommon for the deal to blow up during that process. Something that at first seemed like a matter of minor detail comes to take on greater significance, and the parties just can't reach agreement on that point. Suppose that when the negotiations break down, one side still wants the deal and the other side doesn't. The side that wants the deal might look through the communications, using the lawyer's lens of "offer and acceptance." If any of the many communications that went back and forth could be construed as an "offer," then there is the possibility that the next communication could be construed as an "acceptance." If that characterization is plausible, then the parties are legally bound. No competent lawyer would ever subject her client to that sort of risk.

2.   A competent lawyer wants to be sure that there is a clear divide between two stages: (1) negotiation about the terms that the parties might agree to, and (2) actually reaching agreement. That's commonly done by including explicit language in all of the negotiation documents such as the following: "This [communication] does not constitute a binding offer on behalf

of the Tenant; and Tenant, without prior notice, may cease negotiations at any time prior to a lease being fully executed and delivered." *Javit v. Marshalls, Inc.*, 1994 WL 86360 (Conn. Super. Ct. 1994). Then, if the parties do settle all their differences, there will be a formal meeting arranged by the lawyers—commonly called the "closing"—at which both parties will appear and simultaneously sign the definitive agreement. Then, and only then, will both sides be bound to the agreement. None of the documents or other communications could be described as the "offer"; none could be described as the "acceptance."

3.   All well drafted legal texts recognize this basic point. For example, the Restatement explicitly states that "A manifestation of mutual assent may be made even though neither offer nor acceptance can be identified and even though the moment of formation cannot be determined." RESTATEMENT (SECOND) OF CONTRACTS § 22(2). *See also* U.C.C. § 2–204.

4.   The *Reprosystem* opinion cites the concurring opinion of the very well-known and highly-regarded judge, Henry Friendly, in *International Telemeter Corp. v. Teleprompter Corp.* 592 F.2d 49 (2d Cir. 1979). Applying New York law, the court held that parties had reached a binding agreement to settle a patent dispute, even though the parties had not yet signed a definitive written agreement. Judge Friendly's concurring opinion, at 592 F.2d 57–58, has a good discussion of the general problem:

> FRIENDLY, Circuit Judge, concurring: The difficulty in deciding this case comes from the gap between the realities of the formation of complex business agreements and traditional contract formulation. The nature of the gap is well described in a passage in 2 Schlesinger (ed.), Formation of Contracts: A Study of the Common Core of Legal Systems 1584–86 (1968), reprinted in Farnsworth, Young and Jones, Cases and Materials on Contracts (2d ed. 1972) at 99–100, which is reproduced in the margin.[b] Under a view conforming to the realities of business life, there would be no contract in such cases until the document is signed and delivered; until then either party would be free to bring up new points of form or substance, or even to withdraw altogether. However, I cannot conscientiously assert that the courts of New York or, to the extent

[b] "Especially when large deals are concluded among corporations and individuals of substance, the usual sequence of events is not that of offer and acceptance; on the contrary, the businessmen who originally conduct the negotiations, often will consciously refrain from ever making a binding offer, realizing as they do that a large deal tends to be complex and that its terms have to be formulated by lawyers before it can be permitted to become a legally enforceable transaction. Thus the original negotiators will merely attempt to ascertain whether they see eye to eye concerning those aspects of the deal which seem to be most important from a business point of view. Once they do, or think they do, the negotiation is then turned over to the lawyers, usually with instructions to produce a document which all participants will be willing to sign. . . . When the lawyers take over, again there is no sequence of offer and acceptance, but rather a sequence of successive drafts. These drafts usually will not be regarded as offers, for the reason, among others, that the lawyers acting as draftsmen have no authority to make offers on behalf of their clients. After a number of drafts have been exchanged and discussed, the lawyers may finally come up with a draft which meets the approval of all of them, and of their clients. It is only then that the parties will proceed to the actual formation of the contract, and often this will be done by way of a formal 'closing' . . . or in any event by simultaneous execution or delivery in the course of a more or less ceremonial meeting, of the document or documents prepared by the lawyers."

they have not spoken, the Restatement of Contracts 2d s 26 and comment C (Tent. Drafts 1–7 Revised and Edited) have gone that far, nor can I find a fair basis for predicting that the New York Court of Appeals is yet prepared to do so.

On the other hand, it does seem to me that the New York cases cited by the majority can be read as holding, or at least as affording a fair basis for predicting a holding, that when the parties have manifested an intention that their relations should be embodied in an elaborate signed contract, clear and convincing proof is required to show that they meant to be bound before the contract is signed and delivered. Such a principle would accord with what I believe to be the intention of most such potential contractors; they view the signed written instrument that is in prospect as "the contract", not as a memorialization of an oral agreement previously reached. Also, from an instrumental standpoint, such a rule would save the courts from a certain amount of vexing litigation. The clear and convincing proof could consist in one party's allowing the other to begin performance, as in *Viacom International, Inc. v. Tandem Productions, Inc.*, 526 F.2d 593 (2d Cir. 1975) and *V'Soske v. Barwick*, 404 F.2d 495 (2 Cir. 1968), Cert. denied, 394 U.S. 921, 89 S.Ct. 1197, 22 L.Ed.2d 454 (1969),or in unequivocal statements by the principals or authorized agents that a complete agreement had been reached and the writing was considered to be of merely evidentiary significance

. . . .

5. Although the reasoning is not excerpted here, you can see from the final paragraph that the plaintiffs in *Reprosystem* argued on appeal that they should recover on alternative theories of (1) unjust enrichment and (2) breach of a duty to negotiate in good faith. For (1), recall our discussion of restitution in Chapter 2, and restate, in your own words, what the argument would be. Did Reprosystem confer a benefit on SCM Corp? Was a benefit appreciated by SMC Corp? For (2), note that the duty to negotiate in good faith would rely on an agreement between the parties to do so, which might prevent one party from unilaterally withdrawing from negotiations, or from insisting on blatantly unreasonable terms, but which would not prevent mutual abandonment of the deal. As we will see in Chapter 8.F, a general good faith requirement is one of performance, not negotiation. We will consider another alternative basis of liability for investments made during negotiations, when we canvas promissory estoppel in Chapter 5. The basic dilemma has produced a rich literature. For one illustration, amongst many, see Alan Schwartz & Robert E. Scott, *Precontractual Liability and Preliminary Agreements*, 120 Harv. L. Rev. 661 (2007).

6. In summary, when we study offer and acceptance, we are not really looking at the typical process by which contracts are formed. Rather, we are looking at the legal problems that arise in those cases where something went seriously wrong in the contract formation process. Even in that setting, it is not unusual to see cases in which one can conclude that an agreement was

formed, even though one cannot decide exactly when or how the agreement was formed. Consider the following case:

Ingrassia Constr. Co. v. Walsh

Superior Court of Pennsylvania, 1984.
337 Pa.Super. 58, 486 A.2d 478.

■ CAVANAUGH, JUDGE.

This is an appeal from the Judgment entered in the Court of Common Pleas of Monroe County denying defendant's Motion for Judgment N.O.V. Appellant [contends] that the court below erred in denying his Motion for Judgment N.O.V.: . . . [because] there was no "meeting of the minds" to support the jury's finding of a contract. For the reasons stated below, we affirm.

Appellant . . . contends that a Judgment N.O.V. should have been granted because there was no "meeting of the minds" between the parties on material provisions thus preventing formation of a contract. The pertinent facts involved in the instant appeal may be summarized as follows. Ingrassia Construction Company, Inc., appellee, was general contractor for the construction of a library building at East Stroudsburg State College. With respect to this job, it obtained a telephone bid on March 16, 1977 from Walsh Steel Service Company pertaining to steel and wire mesh work. A price was quoted in the bid for both the reinforcing steel and for the wire mesh and it delineated certain of the subcontractor's duties. Ingrassia's agent, Herbert Johnson, was in communication with appellant Walsh between March and June of 1977 concerning the pending job. Mr. Johnson attempted to have the price lowered, but to no avail. Mr. Johnson testified that an agreement was reached during this period in accordance with the terms of the verbal telephoned bid of March 16.

The appellant, Mr. Walsh, testified that an agreement was reached as to some, but not all, matters. Two matters not agreed upon were the terms of payment, and the issue of which party was to supply certain equipment and tools. It is undisputed that although both parties sent writings containing proposals to the other, neither party signed the other's writing. These proposals exchanged by the parties contained differing terms as to terms of payment and as to which party was to supply certain equipment, among other things. Mr. Johnson, Ingrassia's agent, testified that an agreement was reached prior to the exchange of proposals. At Walsh's behest, Mr. Lou Fallon visited the construction site on July 12, 1977, for the purpose of commencing work. Mr. Fallon was informed by the superintendent on the job that Ingrassia would not provide certain equipment called "standees" needed for the job Mr. Fallon was to perform. As a result of this controversy, Walsh refused to perform. Disputed evidence at trial showed that the custom of the industry was for the subcontractor to provide this equipment. Ingrassia contends that

Walsh's refusal to perform put Walsh in breach of contract. Walsh, on the other hand, maintains that a binding contract was never formed. At trial, the jury returned a verdict for Ingrassia, for $12,750.00. Walsh's motion for a Judgment N.O.V. was denied and this appeal followed.

Where the facts are in dispute, the question of whether a contract was formed is for the jury to decide. * * * "People do business in a very informal fashion, using abbreviated and elliptical language. A transaction is complete when the parties mean it to be complete. It is a mere matter of interpretation of their expressions to each other, a question of fact." 1 A. Corbin, *Corbin on Contracts* § 29 (1963).

The appellant contends that because there was no "meeting of the minds", contractual formation never occurred. A true and actual meeting of the minds is not necessary to form a contract. 1 S. Williston, *Williston on Contracts* §§ 66, 94 (3d ed.1957); 1 A. Corbin, *Corbin on Contracts* § 107 (1963). In ascertaining the intent of the parties to a contract, it is their outward and objective manifestations of assent, as opposed to their undisclosed and subjective intentions, that matter. * * * In the instant case, it matters not whether Walsh truly believed a contract did not exist *if* his manifested intent reasonably suggested the contrary to Ingrassia. Furthermore, a contract could be formed even if Walsh did not contemplate that legal consequences would attach to the transaction. A party's subjective intent will form the basis of a contract only if the other party knows or has reason to know of the intent. 1 A. Corbin, Corbin on Contracts, § 107 (1963).

In the instant case, a reasonable jury could find the existence of . . . a contract . . . based on the evidence admitted. . . . The surrounding facts of the transaction in question—including the original telephone bid, the telephoned negotiations, appellant's July 12th attempt to commence work, and Ingrassia's apparent forebearance from contracting with another company to do the work—could indicate to a reasonable jury Walsh's intent to commit himself to perform the job. A contract implied in fact can be found by looking to the surrounding facts of the parties' dealings.[7] Offer and acceptance need not be identifiable and the moment of formation need not be pinpointed. Restatement (Second) of Contracts § 22(2) (1981). "Implied contracts . . . arise under circumstances which, according to the ordinary course of dealing and the common understanding of men, show a mutual intention to contract." *Pollock Industries, Inc. v. General Steel Castings Corp.,* 203 Pa.Super. 453, 201 A.2d 606, 610 (1964). (Citation omitted).

Appellant alleges, however, that the parties did not intend to be bound to a contract absent a signed writing. If a party wishes to withhold

---

[7]   A contract implied in fact has the same legal effect as any other contract. It differs from an express contract only in the manner of its formation. An express contract is formed by either written or verbal communication. The intent of the parties to an implied in fact contract "is inferred from their acts in light of the surrounding circumstances." *Cameron v. Eynon,* 332 Pa. 529, 532, 3 A.2d 423, 424 (1939).

his assent upon the condition that a contract be signed, it is surely within his province to do so. However, there exists a presumption that the parties intend their contract to be operative absent a signed writing unless one of them indicates to the contrary. *See* 1 S. Williston, *Williston on Contracts* § 28 (1957). Our review of the record discloses no such indication by either party.

Walsh next argues that the "missing" terms prevent contractual formation. We disagree. Walsh argues that the parties never reached agreement over who was to supply "standees"—equipment necessary to the job. "A court cannot enforce a contract unless it can determine what it is." I A. Corbin, *Corbin on Contracts* § 95 (1963). If a court is unable, due to indefiniteness or incompleteness in contracting, to determine whether the contract has been performed then it must find that no contract existed in the first place. *See Columbian Rope Co. v. Rinek Cordage Co.,* 314 Pa.Super. 585, 592, 461 A.2d 312, 316 (1983). However, there was disputed testimony showing a usage in the trade that the subcontractor is to supply the standees. A usage of trade or industry custom may give precision to an otherwise indefinite contract. *See* E.A. Farnsworth, *Contracts* § 713 (1982). The jury was free to believe or disbelieve the evidence as to trade usage, and this court will not interfere with the jury's factfinding function.

As to the absence of agreement over the terms of payment, there is an implied condition that absent contractual terms to the contrary, payment is to occur upon completion of the job. *Commonwealth General State Authority v. Loffredo,* 16 Pa. Commonwealth Ct. 237, 247, 328 A.2d 886, 893 (1974).

Judgment affirmed.

B. OFFER

Restatement (Second) of Contracts §§ 24, 26, 35(1)

Note on terminology: "Offer" and "Promise"

It's not uncommon, even among people who are generally pretty careful with language, to describe an offer as a "promise." For example, take the simple real estate sale setting. The prospective buyer sends an offer and the prospective seller assents. It's common to describe the buyer's offer as a "promise" to pay for the house. E.g., E. ALLAN FARNSWORTH, CONTRACTS § 3.4 (4th ed. 2004):

> What is an "offer"? It can be defined as a manifestation to another of assent to enter into a contract if the other manifests assent in return by some action, often a promise but sometimes a performance. By making an offer, the offeror thus confers upon the offeree the power to create a contract. An offer is nearly always a promise and, in a sense, the action (promise or performance) on which the offeror conditions the promise is the

'price' of its becoming enforceable. Offer, then, is the legal name given to a promise that is conditional on some action by the promisee if the legal effect of the promisee's taking that action is to make the promise enforceable.

As we will soon see, the power of acceptance created by an offer can be terminated by all kinds of things, including "revocation," that is, a communication received by the offeree before acceptance indicating that the offeror has changed her mind. So, if we describe the offer itself as a "promise" then we have to pack in a lot of qualifications, to the effect that the promise will be enforceable only if accepted before something happens that will terminate the power of acceptance. That's why Farnsworth describes the "promise" made in an offer as "conditional."

Describing an offer as a "promise," is, however, a bit odd. Suppose your friend says to you "I'll take you to lunch next Tuesday, unless I change my mind before then." It would be odd to say that your friend made any "promise." They promise to do something unless they change my mind?? Huh??

There is another way to describe an offer that does not present that difficulty. We could say that an offer is a *proposal* to enter into an agreement, and that the *agreement*, if entered into, will consist of an exchange of promises.[c] So, when the prospective buyer in the real estate setting sends an "offer" she is saying "I propose that we enter into an agreement in which I will promise to pay money and you will promise to convey the real estate." An agreement will be formed only if that offer is "accepted" before anything happens that would terminate the power of acceptance. Only when the agreement is formed will the parties be bound to any promises. Precision in use of the terms "offer" and "promise" will become important latter on, when we examine situations in which the usual power to revoke is limited. So, please come back and re-read this passage in connection with the well-known case of *Drennan v. Star Paving* that we will study in detail in Chapter 5.

Offer or Preliminary Negotiation?

Here is a standard form of an offer for the purchase of real estate, produced by the Greater Boston Real Estate Board. Suppose that the prospective buyer fills in the blanks in the form and gives it to the prospective seller. Suppose that the prospective seller signs the form in the place indicated following the words "This Offer is hereby accepted . . . ." Are the parties bound to a contract? What is the significance of the language in paragraph 3?

---

[c] This way of describing an offer comes from Peter M. Tiersma, *Reassessing Unilateral Contracts: The Role of Offer, Acceptance, and Promise*, 26 U.C. DAVIS L. REV. 1 (1992).

G R E A T E R   B O S T O N   R E A L   E S T A T E   B O A R D

OFFER TO PURCHASE REAL ESTATE

TO _____   Date: _____
            (Seller and Spouse)   From the Office of : _____

The property herein referred to is identified as follows: _____

Special provisions (if any) re fixtures, appliances, etc. _____

hereby offer to buy said property, which has been offered to me by _____
_____ as the Broker(s) under the following terms and conditions:

                                                CHECK ONE:

1. I will pay therefore $_____, of which   ❑ Check, subject to collection

    (a) $ _____ is paid herewith as a deposit to bind this Offer   ❑ Cash

    (b) $ _____ is to be paid as an additional deposit upon the execution of the Purchase and Sale Agreement provided for below.

    (c) $ _____ is to be paid at the time of delivery of the Deed in cash, or by certified, cashier's, treasurer's or bank check(s).

    (d) $ _____

    (e) $ _____ Total Purchase Price

2. This Offer is good until _____ A.M. P.M. on _____, 20____ at or before which time a copy hereof shall be signed by you, the Seller and your (husband) (wife), signifying acceptance of this Offer, and returned to me forthwith, otherwise this Offer shall be considered as rejected and the money deposited herewith shall be returned to me forthwith.

3. The parties hereto shall, on or before _____ A.M. P.M. _____, 20____ execute the applicable Standard Form Purchase and Sale Agreement recommended by the Greater Boston Real Estate Board or any form substantially similar thereto, which, when executed, shall be the agreement between the parties hereto.

4. A good and sufficient Deed, conveying a good and clear record and marketable title shall be delivered at 12:00 Noon on _____, 20____ at the appropriate Registry of Deeds, unless some other time and place are mutually agreed upon in writing.

5. If I do not fulfill my obligations under this Offer, the above mentioned deposit shall forthwith become your property without recourse to either party. Said deposit shall be held by _____ as escrow agent subject to the terms hereof provided however that in the event of any disagreement between the parties, the escrow agent may retain said deposit pending instructions mutually given in writing by the parties. A similar provision shall be included in the Purchase and Sale Agreement with respect to any deposit held under its terms.

6. Time is of the essence hereof.

7. Disclosures: For one to four family residences, the Buyer hereby acknowledges receipt of the Home Inspectors: Facts for Consumers brochure produced by the Office of Consumer Affairs. For residential property constructed prior to 1978, Buyer must also sign Lead Paint "Property Transfer Notification."

8. The initialed riders, if any, attached hereto are incorporated herein by reference. Additional terms and conditions, if any:

_____
_____

NOTICE: This is a legal document that creates binding obligations. If not understood, consult an attorney. WITNESS MY HAND AND SEAL

_____   _____
Buyer   Buyer

_____   _____
Address/City/State/Zip   Phone Numbers (Work & Home)

Receipt of deposit check for transmittal by: (Agent/Facilitator) _____
Check shall not be deposited unless offer is accepted.

This Offer is hereby accepted upon the foregoing terms and conditions at _____ A.M. / P.M. on _____, 20____
WITNESS my (our) hand(s) and seal(s)

_____   _____
Seller (or spouse)   Seller

Date _____   RECEIPT FOR DEPOSIT

Received from _____ Buyer the sum of $_____ as deposit under the terms
and conditions of above Offer, to be held by _____ as escrow agent.

Under regulations adopted pursuant to the Massachusetts license law: All offers submitted to brokers or salespeople to purchase real property that they have a right to sell shall be conveyed forthwith to the owner of such real property.

_____
Agent for Seller

McCarthy v. Tobin

Supreme Judicial Court of Massachusetts, Suffolk, 1999.
429 Mass. 84, 706 N.E.2d 629.

■ ABRAMS, J.

We granted the interveners' application for further appellate review following the Appeals Court's opinion in McCarthy v. Tobin, 44 Mass.App.Ct. 274, 279, 690 N.E.2d 460 (1998), concluding that the plaintiff was entitled to specific performance of a real estate purchase. The plaintiff, John J. McCarthy, Jr., claims that the defendant, Ann G. Tobin, agreed to sell certain real estate to him. He asserts that they created a binding agreement when they signed a standard Offer to Purchase (OTP) form. The DiMinicos intervened because they later agreed to purchase the property in question from Tobin. McCarthy and Tobin each moved for summary judgment and the DiMinicos for partial summary judgment. The motion judge allowed Tobin's and the DiMinicos' motions, declaring that Tobin had no obligation to sell to McCarthy and therefore McCarthy had no right to the specific performance of the real estate agreement. The Appeals Court vacated the judgment in favor of Tobin and the DiMinicos and remanded for entry of judgment in favor of McCarthy. The Appeals Court reasoned that the OTP was a firm offer that became a contract binding on the parties when it was accepted. Id. at 278–279, 690 N.E.2d 460.

The facts, which are undisputed, are as follows. On August 9, 1995, McCarthy executed an offer to purchase real estate on a pre-printed form generated by the Greater Boston Real Estate Board. The OTP contained, among other provisions, a description of the property, the price to be paid, deposit requirements, limited title requirements, and the time and place for closing. The OTP also included several provisions that are the basis of this dispute. The OTP required that the parties "shall, on or before 5 P.M. August 16, 1995, execute the applicable Standard Form Purchase and Sale Agreement recommended by the Greater Boston Real Estate Board . . . which, when executed, shall be the agreement between the parties hereto." In the section containing additional terms and conditions, a typewritten insertion states, "Subject to a Purchase and Sale Agreement satisfactory to Buyer and Seller." The OTP provided, "Time is of the essence hereof." Finally, an unnumbered paragraph immediately above the signature line states: "NOTICE: This is a legal document that creates binding obligations. If not understood, consult an attorney." Tobin signed the OTP on August 11, 1995.

On August 16, 1995, sometime after 5 P.M., Tobin's lawyer sent a first draft of the purchase and sale agreement by facsimile transmission to McCarthy's lawyer. On August 21, McCarthy's lawyer sent a letter by facsimile transmission containing his comments and proposing several changes to Tobin's lawyer. The changes laid out the requirements for good title; imposed on Tobin the risk of casualty to the premises before sale; solicited indemnification, for title insurance purposes, regarding mechanics' liens, parties in possession, and hazardous materials; and sought an acknowledgment that the premises' systems were operational. The next day, the two lawyers discussed the proposed revisions. They did not discuss an extension of the deadline for signing the purchase and sale agreement, and Tobin's lawyer did not object to the fact that the deadline had already passed. On August 23, Tobin's lawyer sent a second draft of the agreement to McCarthy's lawyer. On August 25, a Friday, McCarthy's lawyer informed Tobin's lawyer that the agreement was acceptable, McCarthy would sign it, and it would be delivered the following Monday.[2] On Saturday, August 26, McCarthy signed the purchase and sale agreement. On the same day, Tobin accepted the DiMinicos' offer to purchase the property.

On August 28, McCarthy delivered the executed agreement and a deposit to Tobin's broker. The next day, Tobin's lawyer told McCarthy's lawyer that the agreement was late and that Tobin had already accepted the DiMinicos' offer. In September, 1995, Tobin and the DiMinicos executed a purchase and sale agreement. Before the deal closed, McCarthy filed this action for specific performance and damages.

1. *Firm offer.* The primary issue is whether the OTP executed by McCarthy and Tobin was a binding contract. Tobin and the DiMinicos argue that it was not because of the provision requiring the execution of a purchase and sale agreement. McCarthy urges that he and Tobin intended to be bound by the OTP and that execution of the purchase and sale agreement was merely a formality.

McCarthy argues that the OTP adequately described the property to be sold and the price to be paid. The remaining terms covered by the purchase and sale agreement were subsidiary matters which did not preclude the formation of a binding contract. Lafayette Place Assocs. v. Boston Redevelopment Auth., 427 Mass. 509, 516, 694 N.E.2d 820 (1998); * * * We agree.

The controlling fact is the intention of the parties. See Schwanbeck v. Federal-Mogul Corp., 412 Mass. 703, 706, 592 N.E.2d 1289 (1992), quoting Kuzmeskus v. Pickup Motor Co., 330 Mass. 490, 493, 115 N.E.2d 461 (1953) ("It is a settled principle of contract law that '[a] promise made with an understood intention that it is not to be legally binding, but only expressive of a present intention, is not a contract' "); Levenson v. L.M.I. Realty Corp., 31 Mass.App.Ct. 127, 130, 575 N.E.2d 370 (1991).

Tobin argues that language contemplating the execution of a final written agreement gives rise to a strong inference that she and McCarthy have not agreed to all material aspects of a transaction and thus that they do not intend to be bound. See Rosenfield v. United States Trust Co., 290 Mass. 210, 216, 195 N.E. 323 (1935); Goren v. Royal Invs., Inc., 25

---

[2] McCarthy and Tobin disagree about the content of this conversation. McCarthy claims that Tobin's lawyer agreed to the Monday delivery date. Tobin's lawyer says that the agreement was to be signed on Friday. Because this is not a dispute of material fact, it is irrelevant to our inquiry.

Mass.App.Ct. 137, 140, 516 N.E.2d 173 (1987). "If, however, the parties have agreed upon all material terms, it may be inferred that the purpose of a final document which the parties agree to execute is to serve as a polished memorandum of an already binding contract." Id., supra. See Coan v. Holbrook, 327 Mass. 221, 224, 97 N.E.2d 649 (1951) ("Mutual manifestations of assent that are in themselves sufficient to make a contract will not be prevented from so operating by the mere fact that the parties also manifest an intention to prepare and adopt a written memorial thereof . . .").

Although the provisions of the purchase and sale agreement can be the subject of negotiation, "norms exist for their customary resolution." Goren, supra at 141, 516 N.E.2d 173. "If parties specify formulae and procedures that, although contingent on future events, provide mechanisms to narrow present uncertainties to rights and obligations, their agreement is binding." Lafayette Place Assocs., supra at 518, 694 N.E.2d 820.

The interveners argue that McCarthy departed from the customary resolution of any open issues, and therefore manifested his intent not to be bound, by requesting several additions to the purchase and sale agreement. We agree with the Appeals Court, however, that McCarthy's revisions were "ministerial and nonessential terms of the bargain." McCarthy, supra at 276, 690 N.E.2d 460, quoting Goren, supra at 139, 516 N.E.2d 173. . . .

The inference that the OTP was binding is bolstered by the notice printed on the form. McCarthy and Tobin were alerted to the fact that the OTP "create[d] binding obligations." The question is what those obligations were. The DiMinicos argue that the OTP merely obligated the parties to negotiate the purchase and sale agreement in good faith. We disagree. The OTP employs familiar contractual language. It states that McCarthy "hereby offer[s] to buy" the property, and Tobin's signature indicates that "[t]his Offer is hereby accepted." The OTP also details the amount to be paid and when, describes the property bought, and specifies for how long the offer was open. This was a firm offer, the acceptance of which bound Tobin to sell and McCarthy to buy the subject property. We conclude that the OTP reflects the parties' intention to be bound.

2.   Waiver. Even though the purchase and sale agreement was not necessary to bind the parties, its execution was required by the OTP. The agreement is unambiguous in this regard and thus must be enforced. * * * Courts hold parties to deadlines they have imposed on themselves when they agree that time is of the essence. * * * The DiMinicos argue that McCarthy violated his obligations by failing to execute the purchase and sale agreement by the August 16 deadline.

The August 16 date is a condition subsequent. Without an executed purchase and sale agreement by that date, the OTP provides that the parties' obligations to each other are extinguished.[d] 3A A. Corbin, Contracts § 739, at 442 (1960) ("A fact is a condition subsequent to the legal relation that it extinguishes"). Conditions, however, may be waived. Church of God in Christ, Inc. v. Congregation Kehillath Jacob, 370 Mass. 828, 834, 353 N.E.2d 669 (1976); 3A A. Corbin, supra at § 757.

We are persuaded that Tobin waived the August 16 deadline. Tobin's lawyer, acting as her agent, voluntarily undertook the task of drafting the purchase and sale agreement. He did not produce the first draft until it was impossible for McCarthy to sign it before the deadline. He also did not object to the passage of the deadline in the telephone calls and facsimile transmissions that followed. Instead, he continued to deal with McCarthy's lawyer in an effort to craft a mutually satisfactory agreement. In the only express communication concerning the execution of the agreement, Tobin's lawyer implied that a date later than August 16 was satisfactory. Words and conduct attributable to Tobin signified her waiver of the August 16 deadline. * * * Once there was a waiver, time was no longer of the essence. McCarthy's subsequent tender of the signed agreement and a deposit was timely and within reason. * * * We conclude that there is no issue of material fact and that McCarthy was entitled to a judgment as a matter of law. * * *

3.   Specific performance. On remand, the issue of the appropriate remedy will arise. A judge generally has considerable discretion with respect to granting specific performance, but it is usually granted in disputes involving the conveyance of land. * * *"It is well-settled law in this Commonwealth that real property is unique and that money damages will often be inadequate to redress a deprivation of an interest in land." Greenfield Country Estates Tenants Ass'n, Inc. v. Deep, 423 Mass. 81, 88, 666 N.E.2d 988 (1996). It is therefore proper to allow McCarthy specific relief.

McCarthy's right to specific performance is unaltered by Tobin's execution of a purchase and sale agreement with the DiMinicos. McCarthy filed this action prior to the execution of that agreement. The DiMinicos had actual notice of McCarthy's claim to the property and assumed the risk of a result favorable to McCarthy. Cf. Greenfield, supra at 89, 666 N.E.2d 988 (specific performance was proper remedy to enforce option to purchase real property; right not extinguished by sale to third party with notice).

The judgment is vacated. The case is remanded to the Superior Court for the entry of a judgment in favor of McCarthy's claim for specific performance.

So ordered.

---

[d]   [Eds. We will address express conditions in Chapter 9.]

NOTES

1.   The court uses the phrase "firm offer", as did the court below, to signal an offer rather than a preliminary negotiation towards a later, formal agreement: McCarthy v. Tobin, 44 Mass. App. Ct. 274, 277, 690 N.E.2d 460, 462 (1998), citing Schwanbeck v. Federal-Mogul Corp., 412 Mass. 703, 707 n. 4, 592 N.E.2d 1289 (1992) (a "firm offer" is one that would be enforceable on the offeree's manifestation of acceptance of the terms of the offer). Note that a "firm offer" is defined in the U.C.C. § 2–205 as one that cannot be revoked for a stated period, or, if none stated, for a reasonable period of time. This applies to sale of goods contracts. (We will encounter the law governing revocable and non-revocable offers in the next Part).

2.   Why is McCarthy claiming specific performance, rather than damages?

Germagian v. Berrini

Appeals Court of Massachusetts, Worcester, 2004.
60 Mass.App.Ct. 456, 803 N.E.2d 354.

■ SMITH, J.

The plaintiff, Jeffrey Germagian, appeals from a judgment entered in the Superior Court granting the defendants' motions for summary judgment and dismissing the complaint.

Facts. The undisputed record before the motion judge . . . establishes the following material facts.

In 1997, the defendant James Berrini owned a parcel of commercial real estate in Milford (property). Berrini listed the property for sale with a broker, the defendant David Consigli. In September of 1997, the plaintiff contacted Consigli and expressed an interest in purchasing the property. The plaintiff was an experienced real estate broker, having owned a real estate company since the mid-1970's.

On September 23, 1997, the plaintiff prepared and sent to Berrini a standard, preprinted offer to purchase form wherein he offered to purchase the property for $219,000 (offer). The offer called for a purchase and sale agreement to be executed by October 21, 1997, and indicated a closing date of "December 31, 1997 . . . or 30 days from the expiration of the appeal period." The appeal period referred to the period following necessary zoning approvals, as the offer was "[s]ubject to the following variances: Area, frontage, width and access to property from RT 85." It was also "[s]ubject to 50% of the purchase price in financing." The offer further provided that "[t]ime is of the essence hereof."

When Berrini returned the offer to the plaintiff two or three weeks after he received it, it contained his signature, and the words "on or before" had been added to the closing date. Berrini had initialed the addition; the plaintiff did not initial the change. The plaintiff knew that

Berrini wanted to close the deal as soon as possible because Berrini was ill and "wanted to get rid of [the property]."

Although Berrini had signed and returned the offer to the plaintiff, the plaintiff did not begin the process of applying for a mortgage, variances, and a curb cut permit, because those "processes [would] cost thousands of dollars" and he was waiting for a signed purchase and sale agreement before he proceeded.

In mid-October, the plaintiff's attorney began discussions with Berrini's attorney and Consigli regarding a purchase and sale agreement. After it was clear that a purchase and sale agreement would not be executed by October 21, 1997 (the date specified in the offer), the parties negotiated beyond that date in an attempt to finalize such an agreement. Despite the plaintiff's request, Berrini refused to extend the closing date to three months beyond December 31, 1997.

By early November, 1997, Berrini and the plaintiff still had not signed a purchase and sale agreement. Berrini believed the deal was "all over." Accordingly, he put the property back on the market. On November 10, 1997, the defendants John F. Silva and James M. Silva, as trustees of Whitewood Realty Trust, submitted an offer to buy the property for $180,000, with no contingencies. Berrini accepted the offer, and the sale of the property occurred on December 29, 1997, two days before the deadline contained in the plaintiff's offer.

On December 29, 1997, the plaintiff filed a complaint in Superior Court seeking specific performance of his offer and monetary damages against Berrini for breach of contract . . .

The parties filed cross motions for summary judgment. The judge below ruled that the offer constituted a valid, enforceable contract once Berrini had accepted it. He also ruled that the parties had agreed that time was of the essence and that the deadline was waived as to the date for execution of a purchase and sale agreement but not waived as to the closing date. The judge further ruled that Berrini did not violate the offer because as of the proposed date of the closing (December 31, 1997), the plaintiff was not able to perform because he had not sought financing or commenced the process of obtaining the variances and curb cut permit required by the offer.

The judge therefore concluded that Berrini was entitled to summary judgment on the counts seeking specific performance and breach of contract. . . .

Analysis. Summary judgment is appropriate "if the pleadings, depositions, answers to interrogatories, and admissions on file, together with the affidavits, if any, show that there is no genuine issue as to any material fact and that the moving party is entitled to a judgment as a matter of law." Mass.R.Civ.P. 56(c), 365 Mass. 824 (1974). . . .

We have examined the materials before the judge, including the depositions of the plaintiff, Berrini, and Consigli. We agree with the result reached by the judge but on a different ground. See *Greeley v. Zoning Bd. of Appeals of Framingham,* 350 Mass. 549, 551, 215 N.E.2d 791 (1966), quoting from *Weidman v. Weidman*, 274 Mass. 118, 125, 174 N.E. 206 (1931) ("A correct decision will be sustained even though the ground stated for it may be unsound"); . . . Rather, we conclude that the offer was not a valid, enforceable contract and that the parties intended that the purchase and sale agreement would fill that role.

In *McCarthy v. Tobin*, 429 Mass. 84, 87, 706 N.E.2d 629 (1999), the Supreme Judicial Court considered the question whether an offer to purchase agreement can constitute a valid enforceable contract. The court ruled that the intent of the parties controls, and if the parties agreed upon all of the essential terms of the transaction in an offer to purchase agreement, it reflected the parties' intention to be bound by that agreement. *Ibid.*

The language in the offer to purchase agreement at issue is similar to the language in the offer to purchase in *McCarthy v. Tobin*. However, there are important differences between that case and the case at bar. Here, the plaintiff's conduct after he received the signed offer back from Berrini demonstrates his intent with regard to the offer. Prior to the closing date, the plaintiff made no attempt to commence the processes leading to the financing of the purchase or obtaining the variances and curb cut permit described in the offer. In his deposition, the plaintiff stated that those processes cost "thousands of dollars," and that before he spent the money, he was expecting, and waiting for, a signed purchase and sale agreement. Thus, the plaintiff's conduct demonstrates that he did not intend that the offer be a binding contract—only the signed purchase and sale agreement would fill that role. Furthermore, Berrini's addition of the words "on or before" to the closing date contained in the offer, the clause stating that time was of the essence, and the plaintiff's subsequent request to extend the closing date by three months demonstrate that the parties did not, in fact, agree in the offer upon an essential term—the closing date.

Thus, it is clear from the record that the parties intended the offer to be merely a preliminary step and the purchase and sale agreement to serve as the binding contract. Therefore, the offer was not a valid, enforceable contract, and Berrini was free to sell the property to others. The judge properly granted summary judgment for the defendants.

Judgment affirmed.

PROBLEM

In 2010, there was an IRS provision that gave a tax credit to a first time home buyer, provided that the buyer had "bought—or entered into a binding agreement to buy—a principal residence on or before April 30, 2010." Suppose documents like those in McCarthy and Germagian were signed on April 27, 2010, with the contemplation that a final P&S would be signed by May 10, 2010.

Imagine you are the buyers' lawyer, and your clients, first time home buyers, want to be assured that they will be eligible for the tax credit. If the Offer and Acceptance were signed on Friday, April 27, would you take the weekend off, as you had planned, or would you scramble to get the P&S signed by the end of the day on Monday April 30?

Are Advertisements Offers?

O'Keefe v. Lee Calan Imports, Inc.
Appellate Court of Illinois, First District, Third Division, 1970.
128 Ill.App.2d 410, 262 N.E.2d 758.

■ McNamara, Justice.

Christopher D. O'Brien brought suit against defendant for an alleged breach of contract. O'Brien died subsequent to the filing of the lawsuit, and the administrator of his estate was substituted in his stead. Field Enterprises, Inc., was joined as a third party defendant, but was dismissed from the suit, and that order of dismissal is not involved in this appeal. Plaintiff and defendant filed cross-motions for summary judgment. The court denied plaintiff's motion for summary judgment and granted defendant's motion. This appeal follows. The facts as set forth in the pleadings and cross—motions for summary judgment are not in dispute.

On July 31, 1966, defendant advertised a 1964 Volvo Station Wagon for sale in the Chicago Sun-Times. Defendant had instructed the newspaper to advertise the price of the automobile at $1,795. However, through an error of the newspaper and without fault on part of defendant, the newspaper inserted a price of $1,095 for said automobile in the advertisement. O'Brien visited defendant's place of business, examined the automobile and stated that he wished to purchase it for $1.095. . . .[Defendant] refused to sell the car for the erroneous price listed in the advertisement.

Plaintiff appeals, contending that the advertisement constituted an offer on the part of defendant, which O'Brien duly accepted and thus the parties formed a binding contract. . . .

It is elementary that in order to form a contract there must be an offer and an acceptance. A contract requires the mutual assent of the parties. *Calo, Inc. v. AMF Pinspotters, Inc.*, 31 Ill.App.2d 2, 176 N.E.2d 1 (1961).

The precise issue of whether a newspaper advertisement constitutes an offer which can be accepted to form a contract or whether such an advertisement is merely an invitation to make an offer, has not been determined by the Illinois courts. Most jurisdictions which have dealt with the issue have considered such an advertisement as a mere invitation to make an offer, unless the circumstances indicate otherwise. * * * As was stated in Corbin on Contracts § 25 (1963):

'It is quite possible to make a definite and operative offer to buy or to sell goods by advertisement, in a newspaper, by a handbill, or on a placard in a store window. It is not customary to do this, however; and the presumption is the other way. Neither the advertiser nor the reader of his notice understands that the latter is empowered to close the deal without further expression by the former. Such advertisements are understood to be mere requests to consider and examine and negotiate; and no one can reasonably regard them otherwise unless the circumstances are exceptional and the words used are very plain and clear.'

In *Craft v. Elder & Johnston Co.,* 38 N.E.2d 416 (Ohio App.1941), defendant advertised in a local newspaper that a sewing machine was for sale at a stated price. Plaintiff visited the store, attempted to purchase the sewing machine at that price, but defendant refused. In holding that the newspaper advertisement did not constitute a binding offer, the court held that an ordinary newspaper advertisement was merely an offer to negotiate. In *Ehrlich v. Willis Music Co.,* 93 Ohio App. 246, 113 N.E.2d 252 (1952), defendant advertised in a newspaper that a television set was for sale at a mistaken price. The actual price was ten times the advertised price. The court found that no offer had been made, but rather an invitation to patronize defendant's store. The court also held that defendant should have known that the price was a mistake. In *Lovett v. Frederick Loeser & Co.,* 124 Misc. 81, 207 N.Y.S. 753 (1924), a newspaper advertisement offering radios for sale at 25% To 50% Reductions was held to be an invitation to make an offer. *Accord, People v. Gimbel Bros.,* 202 Misc. 229, 115 N.Y.S.2d 857 (1952).

We find that in the absence of special circumstances, a newspaper advertisement which contains an erroneous purchase price through no fault of the defendant advertiser and which contains no other terms, is not an offer which can be accepted so as to form a contract. We hold that such an advertisement amounts only to an invitation to make an offer. . . .

The judgment of the Circuit Court is affirmed.

Lefkowitz v. Great Minneapolis Surplus Store, Inc.

Supreme Court of Minnesota, 1957.
251 Minn. 188, 86 N.W.2d 689.

■ MURPHY, JUSTICE.

This is an appeal from an order of the Municipal Court of Minneapolis denying the motion of the defendant for amended findings of fact, or, in the alternative, for a new trial. The order for judgment awarded the plaintiff the sum of $138.50 as damages for breach of contract.

This case grows out of the alleged refusal of the defendant to sell to the plaintiff a certain fur piece which it had offered for sale in a newspaper advertisement. It appears from the record that on April 6, 1956, the defendant published the following advertisement in a Minneapolis newspaper:

'Saturday 9 A.M. Sharp 3 Brand New Fur Coats Worth to $100.00

First Come First Served $1 Each'

On April 13, the defendant again published an advertisement in the same newspaper as follows:

'Saturday 9 A.M. 2 Brand New Pastel Mink 3-Skin Scarfs

Selling for.$89.50

Out they go Saturday. Each . . . $1.00

1 Black Lapin Stole Beautiful, worth $139.50 . . . $1.00

First Come First Served'

The record supports the findings of the court that on each of the Saturdays following the publication of the above-described ads the plaintiff was the first to present himself at the appropriate counter in the defendant's store and on each occasion demanded the coat and the stole so advertised and indicated his readiness to pay the sale price of $1. On both occasions, the defendant refused to sell the merchandise to the plaintiff, stating on the first occasion that by a 'house rule' the offer was intended for women only and sales would not be made to men, and on the second visit that plaintiff knew defendant's house rules.

The trial court properly disallowed plaintiff's claim for the value of the fur coats since the value of these articles was speculative and uncertain. The only evidence of value was the advertisement itself to the effect that the coats were 'Worth to $100.00,' how much less being speculative especially in view of the price for which they were offered for sale. With reference to the offer of the defendant on April 13, 1956, to sell the '1 Black Lapin Stole . . . worth $139.50 . . .' the trial court held that the value of this article was established and granted judgment in favor of the plaintiff for that amount less the $1 quoted purchase price.

The defendant contends that a newspaper advertisement offering items of merchandise for sale at a named price is a 'unilateral offer' which may be withdrawn without notice. He relies upon authorities which hold that, where an advertiser publishes in a newspaper that he has a certain quantity or quality of goods which he wants to dispose of at certain prices and on certain terms, such advertisements are not offers which become contracts as soon as any person to whose notice they may come signifies his acceptance by notifying the other that he will take a certain quantity of them. Such advertisements have been construed as an invitation for an offer of sale on the terms stated, which offer, when received, may be accepted or rejected and which therefore does not become a contract of sale until accepted by the seller; and until a contract has been so made, the seller may modify or revoke such prices or terms. * * *

There are numerous authorities which hold that a particular advertisement in a newspaper or circular letter relating to a sale of articles may be construed by the court as constituting an offer, acceptance of which would complete a contract. * * *

The test of whether a binding obligation may originate in advertisements addressed to the general public is 'whether the facts show that some performance was promised in positive terms in return for something requested.' 1 Williston, Contracts (Rev. ed.) § 27.

The authorities above cited emphasize that, where the offer is clear, definite, and explicit, and leaves nothing open for negotiation, it constitutes an offer, acceptance of which will complete the contract. The most recent case on the subject is *Johnson v. Capital City Ford Co.*, La.App., 85 So.2d 75, in which the court pointed out that a newspaper advertisement relating to the purchase and sale of automobiles may constitute an offer, acceptance of which will consummate a contract and create an obligation in the offer or to perform according to the terms of the published offer.

Whether in any individual instance a newspaper advertisement is an offer rather than an invitation to make an offer depends on the legal intention of the parties and the surrounding circumstances. Annotation, 157 A.L.R. 744, 751; 77 C.J.S., Sales, § 25b; 17 C.J.S., Contracts, § 389. We are of the view on the facts before us that the offer by the defendant of the sale of the Lapin fur was clear, definite, and explicit, and left nothing open for negotiation. The plaintiff having successful managed to be the first one to appear at the seller's place of business to be served, as requested by the advertisement, and having offered the stated purchase price of the article, he was entitled to performance on the part of the defendant. We think the trial court was correct in holding that there was in the conduct of the parties a sufficient mutuality of obligation to constitute a contract of sale.

The defendant contends that the offer was modified by a 'house rule' to the effect that only women were qualified to receive the bargains advertised. The advertisement contained no such restriction. This objection may be disposed of briefly by stating that, while an advertiser has the right at any time before acceptance to modify his offer, he does not have the right, after acceptance, to impose new or arbitrary conditions not contained in the published offer. * * *

Affirmed.

NOTES & QUESTIONS

1.   Is the problem presented by scenarios of the sort involved in the *O'Keefe* and *Lefkowitz* cases that someone made a contract but refused to perform it? Or, is the problem that someone refused to make a contract?

Consider various ways that the legal system might respond to these sorts of problems.

2.   One approach, illustrated by the *Lefkowitz* case, is to conclude that a contract was formed so that the seller is liable for breach of contract. Another approach is to adopt a statute, or a regulation administered by an agency, prohibiting deceptive advertising. The Federal Trade Act, 15 U.S.C. §§ 41–58, creates a federal administrative agency, the Federal Trade Commission ("FTC") and empowers it to bring actions against companies that engage in "unfair or deceptive acts or practices in or affecting commerce." The FTC has power to adopt regulations specifying what counts as an unfair or deceptive practice. Set out below is the FTC regulation dealing with "bait advertising."

FTC Guides Against Bait Advertising
16 CFR PART 238.

§ 238.0   Bait advertising defined.

Bait advertising is an alluring but insincere offer to sell a product or service which the advertiser in truth does not intend or want to sell. Its purpose is to switch consumers from buying the advertised merchandise, in order to sell something else, usually at a higher price or on a basis more advantageous to the advertiser. The primary aim of a bait advertisement is to obtain leads as to persons interested in buying merchandise of the type so advertised.

§ 238.1   Bait advertisement.

No advertisement containing an offer to sell a product should be published when the offer is not a bona fide effort to sell the advertised product.

§ 238.2   Initial offer.

(a) No statement or illustration should be used in any advertisement which creates a false impression of the grade, quality, make, value, currency of model, size, color, usability, or origin of the product offered, or which may otherwise misrepresent the product in such a manner that later, on disclosure of the true facts, the purchaser may be switched from the advertised product to another.

(b) Even though the true facts are subsequently made known to the buyer, the law is violated if the first contact or interview is secured by deception.

§ 238.3   Discouragement of purchase of advertised merchandise.

No act or practice should be engaged in by an advertiser to discourage the purchase of the advertised merchandise as part of a bait scheme to sell other merchandise. Among acts or practices which will be considered in determining if an advertisement is a bona fide offer are:

(a)   The refusal to show, demonstrate, or sell the product offered in accordance with the terms of the offer,

(b)   The disparagement by acts or words of the advertised product or the disparagement of the guarantee, credit terms, availability of service, repairs or parts, or in any other respect, in connection with it,

(c)   The failure to have available at all outlets listed in the advertisement a sufficient quantity of the advertised product to meet reasonably anticipated demands, unless the advertisement clearly and adequately discloses that supply is limited and/or the merchandise is available only at designated outlets,

(d)   The refusal to take orders for the advertised merchandise to be delivered within a reasonable period of time,

(e)   The showing or demonstrating of a product which is defective, unusable or impractical for the purpose represented or implied in the advertisement,

(f)   Use of a sales plan or method of compensation for salesmen or penalizing salesmen, designed to prevent or discourage them from selling the advertised product.

§ 238.4   Switch after sale.

No practice should be pursued by an advertiser, in the event of sale of the advertised product, of "unselling" with the intent and purpose of selling other merchandise in its stead. Among acts or practices which will be considered in determining if the initial sale was in good faith, and not a stratagem to sell other merchandise, are:

(a)   Accepting a deposit for the advertised product, then switching the purchaser to a higher-priced product,

(b)   Failure to make delivery of the advertised product within a reasonable time or to make a refund,

(c)   Disparagement by acts or words of the advertised product, or the disparagement of the guarantee, credit terms, availability of service, repairs, or in any other respect, in connection with it,

(d)   The delivery of the advertised product which is defective, unusable or impractical for the purpose represented or implied in the advertisement.

Note: Sales of advertised merchandise. Sales of the advertised merchandise do not preclude the existence of a bait and switch scheme. It has been determined that, on occasions, this is a mere incidental byproduct of the fundamental plan and is intended to provide an aura of legitimacy to the overall operation.

C. TERMINATION OF POWER OF ACCEPTANCE

Restatement (Second) of Contracts §§ 35, 36, 38, 39, 41, 42

The making of an offer creates a power of acceptance, that is, the offeree can complete the contract formation process by accepting. Various things could terminate this power of acceptance. There is a useful catalog in RESTATEMENT 2D § 36. If the power of acceptance has been terminated, then it's too late for the offeree to complete the contract formation process by accepting.

The two cases in this section, *Akers v. Sedberry* and *Ardente v. Horan*, involve various scenarios of possible termination of the power of acceptance. As you work with law school casebooks, you will find that the cases are used for various purposes. Sometimes a case will be included because it has both a good illustration of a problem and a good treatment of the problem by the lawyers and judges. Sometimes, however, a case is a good teaching vehicle because the lawyers and judges did a terrible job. In those situations, your task as a student is to try to recognize what was done badly and think about how it could have been done better. The two cases in this section are of the latter sort. *Akers* is not too bad; it just has some sloppy language and a somewhat puzzling way of resolving the matter. *Ardente* is a disaster. The lawyers bungled the case, and the court's language is very sloppy.

Akers and *Ardente* also illustrate a common problem that you will confront in law school. Litigated cases rarely, if ever, involve simple situations. The simple scenarios don't produce litigation, because the proper legal analysis is so obvious that there is no need for litigation. So, you'll almost always be reading about oddball scenarios. One of the challenges in doing that is to think through what the rules would be in the simple cases. Then you can consider how to treat the complex cases. Termination of power of acceptance provides a good illustration. To understand the issues in *Akers* and *Ardente* you first need to work through simple scenarios in which a power of acceptance created by an offer is terminated by rejection, by passage of time, by revocation, by death, or by counter-offer. The following simple problem tracks through these matters.

PROBLEMS

In all cases Seller has listed a house for sale. The asking price was $250,000. Buyer has looked at it and is interested.

1   Buyer delivers to Seller a signed letter saying "I'll buy for $225,000."

    Seller delivers to Buyer a signed letter saying "I'm not interested in selling for $225,000."

A day later, Seller delivers to Buyer a signed letter saying "I've changed my mind, and I accept your $225,000 offer."

Buyer delivers to Seller a signed letter saying "Sorry, I've changed my mind too, I don't want to buy."

See Restatement (Second) of Contracts § 38.

2   On October 1, Buyer delivers to Seller a signed letter saying "I'll buy for $225,000." Buyer gets no immediate response from Seller

On November 15, Seller delivers to Buyer a signed letter saying "I accept your $225,000 offer."

See Restatement (Second) of Contracts § 41

3   Buyer delivers to Seller a signed letter saying "I'll buy for $225,000."

Later that same day, before Seller makes any response, Buyer delivers to Seller a second signed letter saying "I've changed my mind. I don't want to buy."

The next day, Seller delivers to Buyer a signed letter saying "I accept your $225,000 offer."

See Restatement (Second) of Contracts § 42.

4   Buyer delivers to Seller a signed letter saying "I'll buy for $225,000."

Later that same day, before Seller makes any response, Buyer dies.

The next day, Seller delivers to Buyer's house a signed letter saying "I accept your $225,000 offer."

See Restatement (Second) of Contracts § 48.

5   Buyer delivers to Seller a signed letter saying "I'll buy for $225,000."

A day later, Seller delivers to Buyer a signed letter saying "I'll sell for $235,000."

A day later, Seller delivers to Buyer a signed letter saying "I've changed my mind, and I accept your $225,000 offer."

Buyer delivers to Seller a signed letter saying "Sorry, I've changed my mind too, I don't want to buy."

See Restatement (Second) of Contracts § 39.

Akers v. J. B. Sedberry, Inc.

Court of Appeals of Tennessee, 1955.
39 Tenn.App. 633, 286 S.W.2d 617.

■ FELTS, JUDGE.

These two consolidated causes are before us upon a writ of error sued out by J. B. Sedberry, Inc., and Mrs. M. B. Sedberry, defendants below, to review a decree of the Chancery Court, awarding a recovery against them in favor of each of the complainants, Charles William Akers and William Gambill Whitsitt, for damages for breach of a contract of employment. . . .

On July 1, 1947, J. B. Sedberry, Inc., by written contract, employed complainant Akers as Chief Engineer for a term of five years at a salary of $12,000 per year, payable $1,000 per month, plus 1% of its net profits for the first year, 2% the second, 3% the third, 4% the fourth, and 5% the fifth year. His duties were to carry on research for his employer, and to see that the Jay Bee Manufacturing Company, Tyler, Texas, manufactured the mills and parts according to proper specifications. Mrs. M. B. Sedberry guaranteed the employer's performance of this contract.

On August 1, 1947, J. B. Sedberry, Inc., by written contract, employed complainant Whitsitt as Assistant Chief Engineer for a term of five years at a salary of $7,200 per year, payable $600 per month, plus 1% of the corporation's net profits for the first year, 2% for the second, 3% for the third, 4% for the fourth, and 5% for the fifth year. His duties were to assist in the work done by the Chief Engineer. Mrs. M. B. Sedberry guaranteed the employer's performance of this contract.

Under Mrs. Sedberry's instructions, Akers and Whitsitt moved to Tyler, Texas, began performing their contract duties in the plant of the Jay Bee Manufacturing Company, continued working there, and were paid under the contracts until October 1, 1950, when they ceased work, under circumstances hereafter stated.

In 1947, when these employment contracts were made, Mrs. Sedberry owned no stock in the Jay Bee Manufacturing Company. In 1948 she purchased the shares of stock in this company which were owned by the Glasgow interests, and in 1949 she purchased the 750 shares owned by her brother, B. G. Byars. . . .

Glasgow had been general manager of the Jay Bee Manufacturing Company, but when he sold his stock, he was succeeded by A. M. Sorenson as manager. There soon developed considerable friction between Sorenson and complainants Akers and Whitsitt. The Jay Bee Manufacturing Company owed large sums to the Tyler State Bank & Trust Co.; and the bank's officers, fearing the company might fail under Sorenson's management, began talking to Akers and Whitsitt about the company's financial difficulties.

One of the bank's vice-presidents, J. Harold Stringer, made a trip to Franklin to see Mrs. Sedberry about the company's indebtedness to the bank. He told her that they could not get along with Sorenson and did not agree with the way he was managing the company's affairs. Mrs. Sedberry asked Stringer as soon as he got back to Tyler to see Akers and Whitsitt and discuss with them plans for the refinancing and the operation of the company; and thereafter the bank's officers had a number of conferences with Akers and Whitsitt about these matters.

While these matters were pending, Akers and Whitsitt flew to Nashville and went to Franklin to talk with Mrs. Sedberry about them. They had a conference with her at her office on Friday, September 29, 1950, lasting from 9:30 a. m. until 4:30 p. m. As they had come unannounced, and unknown to Sorenson, they felt Mrs. Sedberry might mistrust them; and at the outset, to show their good faith, they offered to resign, but she did not accept their offer. Instead, she proceeded with them in discussing the operation and refinancing of the business.

Testifying about this conference, Akers said that, at the very beginning, to show their good faith, he told Mrs. Sedberry that they would offer their resignations on a ninety-day notice, provided they were paid according to the contract for that period; that she pushed the offers aside—'would not accept them', but went into a full discussion of the business; that nothing was thereafter said about the offers to resign; and that they spent the whole day discussing the business, Akers making notes of things she instructed him to do when he got back to Texas.

Whitsitt testified that . . . Mrs. Sedberry. . . did not accept the offer, but proceeded with the business, and nothing further was said about resigning.

Mrs. Sedberry testified that Akers and Whitsitt came in and 'offered their resignations'; that they said they could not work with Sorenson and did not believe the bank would go along with him; and that 'they said if it would be of any help to the organization they would be glad to tender their resignation and pay them what was due them.' She further said that she 'did not accept the resignation', that she 'felt it necessary to contact Mr. Sorenson and give consideration to the resignation offer.' But she said nothing to complainants about taking the offer under consideration.

On cross-examination she said that in the offer to resign 'no mention was made of any ninety-day notice'. Asked what response she made to the offer she said, 'I treated it rather casually because I had to give it some thought and had to contact Mr. Sorenson.' She further said she excused herself from the conference with complainants, went to another room, tried to telephone Sorenson in Tyler, Texas, but was unable to locate him.

She then resumed the conference, nothing further was said about the offers to resign, nothing was said by her to indicate that she thought the offers were left open or held under consideration by her. But the discussion proceeded as if the offers had not been made. She discussed with complainants future plans for refinancing and operating the business, giving them instructions, and Akers making notes of them.

Following the conference, complainants, upon Mrs. Sedberry's request, flew back to Texas to proceed to carry out her instructions. On the way back, and while in Nashville, Friday evening, Akers telephoned her in Franklin to tell her that he had just learned that the bank had sued both the companies and process had been served that day. On the next morning, September 30, Akers had a conference with the bank officials about the refinancing of the company, the results of which he reported to Mrs. Sedberry by long-distance telephone conversation that day.

On Monday, October 2, 1950, Mrs. Sedberry sent to complainants similar telegrams, signed by 'J. B. Sedberry, Inc., by M. B. Sedberry, President', stating that their resignations were accepted, effective immediately. We quote the telegram to Akers, omitting the formal parts:

'Account present unsettled conditions which you so fully are aware we accept your kind offer of resignation effective immediately. Please discontinue as of today with everyone employed in Sedberry, Inc., Engineering Department, discontinuing all expenses in this department writing.'

While this said she was 'writing', she did not write. Akers wrote her, but held up sending his letter, at the request of her brother, Mr. Byars, who was one of the officers of the bank in Tyler, Texas. Akers later rewrote practically the same letter and mailed it to her on October 16, 1950. Whitsitt also sent her a similar letter on the same day.

In his letter, Akers said that he was amazed to get her telegram, and called her attention to the fact that no offer to resign by him was open or outstanding when she sent the telegram; that while he had made a conditional offer to resign at their conference on September 29, she had immediately rejected the offer, and had discussed plans for the business and had instructed him and Whitsitt as to things she wanted them to do in the business on their return to Tyler.

This letter further stated that Akers was expecting to be paid according to the terms of his contract until he could find other employment that would pay him as much income as that provided in his contract, and that if he had to accept a position with less income, he would expect to be paid the difference, or whatever losses he suffered by her breach of the contract. Whitsitt's letter contained a similar statement of his position. . . .

An employee's tender of his resignation, being a mere offer is, of course, not binding until it has been accepted by the employer. Such offer must be accepted according to its terms and within the time fixed. The matter is governed by the same rules as govern the formation of contracts. * * *

An offer may be terminated in a number of ways, as, for example, where it is rejected by the offeree, or where it is not accepted by him within the time fixed, or, if no time is fixed, within a reasonable time. An offer terminated in either of these ways ceases to exist and cannot thereafter be accepted. 1 Williston on Contracts (1936), secs. 50A, 51, 53, 54; 1 Corbin on Contracts (1950), secs. 35, 36; 1 Rest., Contracts, secs. 35, 40.

The question what is a reasonable time, where no time is fixed, is a question of fact, depending on the nature of the contract proposed, the usages of business and other circumstances of the case. Ordinarily, an offer made by one to another in a face to face conversation is deemed to continue only to the close of their conversation, and cannot be accepted thereafter.

The rule is illustrated by Restatement of Contracts, section 40, Illustration 2, as follows:

'2. While A and B are engaged in conversation, A makes B an offer to which B then makes no reply, but a few hours later meeting A again, B states that he accepts the offer. There is no contract unless the offer or the surrounding circumstances indicate that the offer is intended to continue beyond the immediate conversation.'

. . .

Professor Williston says:

'A reasonable time for the acceptance of most offers made in conversation will not extend beyond the time of the conversation unless special words or circumstances indicate an intention on the part of the offer or that it shall do so.' Williston on Contracts (1938), section 54.

Professor Corbin says:

'When two negotiating parties are in each other's presence, and one makes an offer to the other without indicating any time for acceptance, the inference that will ordinarily be drawn by the other party is that an answer is expected at once. * * * If, when the first reply is not an acceptance, the offeror turns away in silence, the proper inference is that the offer is no longer open to acceptance.' 1 Corbin on Contracts (1950), section 36, p. 111.

The only offer by Akers and Whitsitt to resign was the offer made by them in their conversation with Mrs. Sedberry. They made that offer at the outset, and on the evidence it seems clear that they expected an answer at once. Certainly, there is nothing in the evidence to show that they intended the offer to continue beyond that conversation; and on the above authorities, we think the offer did not continue beyond that meeting.

Indeed, it did not last that long, in our opinion, but was terminated by Mrs. Sedberry's rejection of it very early in that meeting. While she did not expressly reject it, and while she may have intended, as she says, to take the offer under consideration, she did not disclose such an intent to complainants; but, by her conduct, led them to believe she rejected the offer, brushed it aside, and proceeded with the discussion as if it had not been made.

'An offer is rejected when the offeror is justified in inferring from the words or conduct of the offeree that the offeree intends not to accept the offer or to take it under further advisement (Rest. Contracts sec. 36).' 1 Williston on Contracts, section 51.

So, we agree with the Trial Judge that when defendants sent the telegrams, undertaking to accept offers of complainants to resign, there was no such offer in existence; and that this attempt of defendants to terminate their contract was unlawful and constituted a breach for which they are liable to complainants. * * *

NOTES & QUESTIONS

1.   This is one of the cases that we will examine in considerable detail in class. So, before class you should try to figure out exactly what the basis of the decision was. As part of that process consider this variant: Suppose that late in the morning of Friday September 29, Mrs. Sedberry stepped out of the meeting with Akers and Whitsitt and succeeded in reaching Sorenson by phone. After talking with Sorenson, Mrs. Sedberry came back into the meeting and told Akers and Whitsitt "I accept your offer to resign." How would that difference in the facts affect the opinion?

2.   What is the exact basis of the court's decision? Was the power of acceptance terminated by rejection or by lapse of time?

Restatement (Second) of Contracts §§ 59, 60, 61

Ardente v. Horan
Supreme Court of Rhode Island, 1976.
117 R.I. 254, 366 A.2d 162.

■ DORIS, JUSTICE.

Ernest P. Ardente, the plaintiff, brought this civil action in Superior Court to specifically enforce an agreement between himself and William A. and Katherine L. Horan, the defendants, to sell certain real property. The defendants filed an answer together with a motion for summary judgment pursuant to Super.R.Civ.P. 56. Following the submission of affidavits by both the plaintiff and the defendants and a hearing on the motion, judgment was entered by a Superior Court justice for the defendants. The plaintiff now appeals.

In August 1975, certain residential property in the city of Newport was offered for sale by defendants. The plaintiff made a bid of $250,000 for the property which was communicated to defendants by their attorney. After defendants' attorney advised plaintiff that the bid was acceptable to defendants, he prepared a purchase and sale agreement at the direction of defendants and forwarded it to plaintiff's attorney for plaintiff's signature. After investigating certain title conditions, plaintiff executed the agreement. Thereafter plaintiff's attorney returned the document to defendants along with a check in the amount of $20,000 and a letter dated September 8, 1975, which read in relevant part as follows:

'My clients are concerned that the following items remain with the real estate: a) dining room set and tapestry wall covering in dining room; b) fireplace fixtures throughout; c) the sun parlor furniture. I would appreciate your confirming that these items are a part of the transaction, as they would be difficult to replace.'

The defendants refused to agree to sell the enumerated items and did not sign the purchase and sale agreement. They directed their attorney to return the agreement and the deposit check to plaintiff and subsequently refused to sell the property to plaintiff. This action for specific performance followed.

In Superior Court, defendants moved for summary judgment on the ground that the facts were not in dispute and no contract had been formed as a matter of law.[1] The trial justice ruled that the letter quoted above constituted a conditional acceptance of defendants' offer to sell the property and consequently must be construed as a counteroffer. Since defendants never accepted the counteroffer, it followed that no contract was formed, and summary judgment was granted.

Summary judgment is a drastic remedy and should be cautiously applied; nevertheless, where there is no genuine issue as to any material fact and the moving party is entitled to judgment as a matter of law, summary judgment properly issues. . . .

The plaintiff assigns several grounds for appeal in his brief. He urges first that summary judgment was improper because there existed a genuine issue of fact. The factual question, according to plaintiff, was whether the oral agreement which preceded the drafting of the purchase and sale agreement was intended by the parties to take effect immediately to create a binding oral contract for the sale of the property.

We cannot agree with plaintiff's position. A review of the record shows that the issue was never raised before the trial justice. The plaintiff did not, in his affidavit in opposition to summary judgment or by any other means, bring to the attention of the trial court any facts which established the existence of a relevant factual dispute. Indeed, at the hearing on the motion plaintiff did not even mention the alleged factual dispute which he now claims the trial justice erred in overlooking. The only issue plaintiff addressed was the proper interpretation of the language used in plaintiff's letter of acceptance. This was solely a question of law. . . .

---

[1] Although the contract would appear to be within the statute of frauds, defendants did not raise this defense in the trial court, nor do they raise it here. Where a party makes no claim to the benefit of the statute, the court sua sponte will not interpose it for him. *Conti v. Fisher*, 48 R.I. 33, 36, 134 A. 849, 850 (1926).

The trial justice proceeded on the theory that the delivery of the purchase and sale agreement to plaintiff constituted an offer by defendants to sell the property. Because we must view the evidence in the light most favorable to the party against whom summary judgment was entered, in this case plaintiff, we assume as the trial justice did that the delivery of the agreement was in fact an offer.[3]

The question we must answer next is whether there was an acceptance of that offer. The general rule is that where, as here, there is an offer to form a bilateral contract, the offeree must communicate his acceptance to the offeror before any contractual obligation can come into being. A mere mental intent to accept the offer, no matter how carefully formed, is not sufficient. The acceptance must be transmitted to the offeror in some overt manner. * * * A review of the record shows that the only expression of acceptance which was communicated to defendants was the delivery of the executed purchase and sale agreement accompanied by the letter of September 8. Therefore it is solely on the basis of the language used in these two documents that we must determine whether there was a valid acceptance. Whatever plaintiff's unexpressed intention may have been in sending the documents is irrelevant. We must be concerned only with the language actually used, not the language plaintiff thought he was using or intended to use.

There is no doubt that the execution and delivery of the purchase and sale agreement by plaintiff, without more, would have operated as an acceptance. The terms of the accompanying letter, however, apparently conditioned the acceptance upon the inclusion of various items of personalty. In assessing the effect of the terms of that letter we must keep in mind certain generally accepted rules. To be effective, an acceptance must be definite and unequivocal. 'An offeror is entitled to know in clear terms whether the offeree accepts his proposal. It is not enough that the words of a reply justify a probable inference of assent.' 1 Restatement Contracts § 58, comment a (1932). The acceptance may not impose additional conditions on the offer, nor may it add limitations. 'An acceptance which is equivocal or upon condition or with a limitation is a counteroffer and requires acceptance by the original offeror before a contractual relationship can exist.' *John Hancock Mut. Life Ins. Co. v. Dietlin*, 97 R.I. 515, 518, 199 A.2d 311, 313 (1964). Accord, *Cavanaugh v. Conway*, 36 R.I. 571, 587, 90 A. 1080, 1086 (1914).

However, an acceptance may be valid despite conditional language if the acceptance is clearly independent of the condition. Many cases have so held. Williston states the rule as follows:

---

[3]   The conclusion that the delivery of the agreement was an offer is not unassailable in view of the fact that defendants did not sign the agreement before sending it to plaintiff, and the fact that plaintiff told defendants' attorney after the agreement was received that he would have to investigate certain conditions of title before signing the agreement. If it was not an offer, plaintiff's execution of the agreement could itself be no more than an offer, which defendants never accepted.

'Frequently an offeree, while making a positive acceptance of the offer, also makes a request or suggestion that some addition or modification be made. So long as it is clear that the meaning of the acceptance is positively and unequivocally to accept the offer whether such request is granted or not, a contract is formed.' 1 Williston, Contracts § 79 at 261–62 (3d ed. 1957).

Corbin is in agreement with the above view. 1 Corbin, supra, § 84 at 363–65. Thus our task is to decide whether plaintiff's letter is more reasonably interpreted as a qualified acceptance or as an absolute acceptance together with a mere inquiry concerning a collateral matter.

In making our decision we recognize that, as one text states, 'The question whether a communication by an offeree is a conditional acceptance or counter-offer is not always easy to answer. It must be determind by the same common-sense process of interpretation that must be applied in so many other cases.' 1 Corbin, supra § 82 at 353. In our opinion the language used in plaintiff's letter of September 8 is not consistent with an absolute acceptance accompanied by a request for a gratuitous benefit. We interpret the letter to impose a condition on plaintiff's acceptance of defendants' offer. The letter does not unequivocally state that even without the enumerated items plaintiff is willing to complete the contract. In fact, the letter seeks 'confirmation' that the listed items 'are a part of the transaction'. Thus, far from being an independent, collateral request, the sale of the items in question is explicitly referred to as a part of the real estate transaction. Moreover, the letter goes on to stress the difficulty of finding replacements for these items. This is a further indication that plaintiff did not view the inclusion of the listed items as merely collateral or incidental to the real estate transaction.

. . .

Accordingly, we hold that since the plaintiff's letter of acceptance dated September 8 was conditional, it operated as a rejection of the defendants' offer and no contractual obligation was created.

NOTES

1.   This is another case that we will examine in considerable detail in class. The first step in working through the issues in *Ardente* is to identify exactly what act was treated as the making of the offer. Read the second paragraph of the opinion carefully, and analyze each step in the dealings between the prospective buyer and seller.

2.   *Ardente* is a good illustration of the point that an appellate court generally takes the case as the lawyers presented it, even if the lawyers made assumptions that were not sound. Look carefully at the footnotes.

D. ACCEPTANCE

Restatement (Second) of Contracts §§ 50, 58

Town of Lindsay v. Cooke County Elec. Coop. Ass'n

Supreme Court of Texas, 1973.
502 S.W.2d 117.

■ WALKER, JUSTICE.

The controlling question in this case is whether the Cooke County Electric Cooperative Association properly accepted a franchise ordinance entitling it to operate in the Town of Lindsay. Suit was brought by the Town, petitioner here, to require the Association, respondent, to remove its lines and equipment from the streets and alleys within the corporate limits. The trial court rendered judgment on the verdict for respondent, and the Court of Civil Appeals affirmed. 497 S.W.2d 406.

[Cooke County Elec. Coop. Ass'n had been providing electricity to an area of Texas since 1938. At that time, the area served by Cooke County Elec. Coop. Ass'n was unincorporated, that is, it was not part of any established municipality. The area was incorporated as a town in 1959. A Texas statute provided that when an area was incorporated as a town, any existing utility company was to apply to the town for a franchise to continue operating. If such a franchise was not obtained, the utility could continue serving the area for ten years, but then had to stop and remove all of its poles and lines. When the town of Lindsay was incorporated, Cooke County Elec. Coop. Ass'n applied to the town for a franchise to continue serving the area. The Town adopted an ordinance to grant the franchise to Cooke County Elec. Coop. Ass'n.]

The ordinance was enacted by the council on March 24, 1960, but was not immediately effective. The final section provided:

Section 8: The Electric Cooperative Association shall file its written acceptance of this franchise within thirty (30) days after the passage of this ordinance, and this ordinance shall take effect and be enforced from and after its passage, approval and acceptance.

The ordinance further provided that the franchise was conditioned upon payment by respondent on April 1, 1960, and annually thereafter, of two per cent of the gross receipts from the sale of electric energy within the corporate limits during the preceding calendar year. Within a few days after March 25, 1960, [Cooke County Elec. Coop. Ass'n] mailed its check for $12.45 to [the Town]. The check was accompanied by a statement of the 1959 receipts from inhabitants of the town and by a voucher showing that the check was in payment of '2% Gross Receipts Tax for the Year 1960.' The check was endorsed by [the Town's] Secretary-Treasurer and deposited in [the Town's] bank account. It was paid by the drawee bank on April 4, 1960. On April 20, 1960, the ordinance was considered at a meeting of [Cooke County Elec. Coop. Ass'n's] Board of Directors, which unanimously approved the franchise agreement. The attorney retained by [Cooke County Elec. Coop. Ass'n] at that time was instructed to file a formal written acceptance of the ordinance with [the Town], but there is no evidence that this was ever done.

On June 9, 1960, after expiration of the 30-day acceptance period, respondent's manager appeared before the Council and requested that the ordinance be allowed to stay in effect. No action on the matter was taken on that meeting. On June 30, 1960, the franchise ordinance was repealed and the Council at the same time ordered that the franchise tax be refunded to respondent. Petitioner thereupon issued its check for $12.45 to respondent, and the check was accepted by respondent and deposited in its bank account. In July or August, 1960, and again in 1963 and in 1970, respondent's manager appeared before the Council and requested a franchise, but the request was denied.

Under the provisions of Art. 1436a, Vernon's Ann.Tex.Civ.St., respondent was entitled to continue operating within the corporate limits and without a franchise for ten years after the date of the petitioner's incorporation. In 1970, after the expiration of the 10-year period, petitioner requested respondent to remove its poles and lines from the streets and alleys of the Town. Respondent declined to do so, and this suit followed.

In response to the two special issues that were submitted, the jury found: (1) that the cooperative filed its written acceptance of the franchise within 30 days after March 24, 1960, and (2) respondent's payment of the gross receipts tax by writing its check with the accompanying voucher and statement was intended by both parties as an acceptance of the franchise. It was on the basis of these findings that the trial court rendered judgment for respondent. Petitioner appealed to the Court of Civil Appeals, contending that there is no evidence to support the jury's findings. The Court of Civil Appeals concluded that the issues were raised by the evidence. We do not agree.

Where, as here, an offer prescribes the time and manner of acceptance, its terms in this respect must be complied with to create a contract. The use of a different method of acceptance by the offeree will not be effectual unless the original offeror thereafter manifests his assent to the other party. See Restatement, Contracts, § 61; 1 Williston on Contracts, 3rd ed. 1957, § 76; 17 Am.Jur.2d, Contracts, § 44. Petitioner's Mayor and Secretary-Treasurer testified that there had never been a written acceptance of the franchise. While their testimony may not be conclusive, there is no evidence to the contrary. If the manner of acceptance had not been specified in the ordinance, respondent's act in paying the gross receipts tax might constitute an implied acceptance of the franchise. Its conduct in this respect was not, however, a written acceptance within the meaning of the ordinance, and the record does not suggest that petitioner assented to an implied acceptance. In our opinion there is no evidence to support the jury's findings, and the trial court erred in overruling petitioner's motion for judgment non obstante veredicto.

The judgments of the courts below are reversed, and the cause is remanded to the district court with instructions to render judgment for petitioner [town].

PROBLEM

Seller had a house for sale. Buyer looked at it.

On Friday, Sept. 1, 2017, Buyer delivered a signed letter to Seller, offering to buy the house for $250,000. The letter said "If you wish to accept this proposal, you must deliver your signed acceptance to me by 10:00 am on September 4, 2017."

On Monday, Sept. 4, 2017 at 9:30 am, Seller's car broke down as Seller was driving to Buyer to deliver signed assent. At 9:45 am, Seller telephoned Buyer, and said "I accept." At 10:15 am, Seller arrived at Buyer's place, and delivered the written letter signifying assent.

As it happens, Buyer found a cheaper house elsewhere over the weekend, and would prefer not to do the deal with Seller.

Is Buyer legally obligated to Seller?

E. ACCEPTANCE BY CONDUCT

Restatement (Second) of Contracts § 69

The principle involved in the following case is often described as "acceptance by silence." That's not really a good description. The only situations in which "silence" would operate as an acceptance are those where, by virtue of prior dealings or some other circumstances, a failure explicitly to reject can appropriately be interpreted by the offeror as a manifestation of assent. Hence, we think it more useful to describe the topic as "acceptance by conduct."

Cole-McIntyre-Norfleet Co. v. Holloway

Supreme Court of Tennessee, 1919.
141 Tenn. 679, 214 S.W. 817.

■ LANSDEN, C. J.

This case presents a question of law, which . . . has not been decided by this court. . . . March 26, 1917, a traveling salesman of plaintiff in error solicited and received from defendant in error, at his country store in Shelby county, Tenn., an order for certain goods, which he was authorized to sell. Among these goods were 50 barrels of meal. The meal was to be ordered out by defendant by the 31st day of July, and afterwards 5 cents per barrel per month was to be charged him for storage.

After the order was given, the defendant heard nothing from it until the 26th of May, 1917, when he was in the place of business of plaintiff in error, and told it to begin shipment of the meal on his contract. He was informed by plaintiff in error that it did not accept the order of March 26th, and for that reason the defendant had no contract for meal.

The defendant in error never received confirmation or rejection from plaintiff in error, or other refusal to fill the order. The same traveling salesman of plaintiff in error called on defendant as often as once each week, and this order was not mentioned to defendant, either by him or by his principals, in any way. Between the day of the order and the 26th of May, the day of its alleged rejection, prices on all of the articles in the contract greatly advanced. All of the goods advanced about 50 per cent. in value. Some jobbers at Memphis received orders from their drummers, and filled the orders or notified the purchaser that the orders were rejected; but this method was not followed by plaintiff in error.

The contract provided that it was not binding until accepted by the seller at its office in Memphis, and that the salesman had no authority to sign the contract for either the seller or buyer. It was further stipulated that the order should not be subject to countermand.

It will be observed that plaintiff in error was silent upon both the acceptance and rejection of the contract. It sent forth its salesman to solicit this and other orders. The defendant in error did not have the right to countermand orders and the contract was closed, if and when it was accepted by plaintiff in error. . . .

The circuit court and the court of civil appeals were both of opinion that the contract was completed because of the lapse of time before plaintiff in error rejected it. The time intervening between the giving of the order by defendant and its alleged repudiation by plaintiff in error was about 60 days. Weekly opportunities were afforded the salesman of plaintiff in error to notify the defendant in error of the rejection of the contract, and, of course, daily occasions were afforded plaintiff in error to notify him by mail or wire. The defendant believed the contract was in force on the 26th of May, because he directed plaintiff in error to begin shipment of the meal on that day. Such shipments were to have been completed by July 31st, or defendant to pay storage charges. From this evidence the Circuit Court found as an inference of fact that plaintiff in error had not acted within a reasonable time, and therefore its silence would be construed as an acceptance of the contract. The question of whether the delay of plaintiff in error was reasonable or unreasonable was one of fact, and the circuit court was justified from the evidence in finding that the delay was unreasonable. Hence the case, as it comes to us, is whether delay upon the part of plaintiff in error for an unreasonable time in notifying the defendant in error of its action upon the contract is an acceptance of its terms.

We think such delay was unreasonable, and effected an acceptance of the contract. . . . Plaintiff's agent in this case was authorized to do precisely that which he did do, both as to time and substance. The only thing which was left open by the contract was the acceptance or rejection of its terms by plaintiff in error. It will not do to say that a seller of goods like these could wait indefinitely to decide whether or not he will accept the offer of the proposed buyer. This was all done in the usual course of business, and the articles embraced within the contract were consumable in the use, and some of them would become unfitted for the market within a short time.

It is undoubtedly true that an offer to buy or sell is not binding until its acceptance is communicated to the other party. The acceptance, however, of such an offer, may be communicated by the other party either by a formal acceptance, or acts amounting to an acceptance. Delay in communicating action as to the acceptance may amount to an acceptance itself. When the subject of a contract, either in its nature or by virtue of conditions of the market, will become unmarketable by delay, delay in notifying the other party of his decision will amount to an acceptance by the offerer. Otherwise, the offerer could place his goods upon the market, and solicit orders, and yet hold the other party to the contract, while he reserves time to himself to see if the contract will be profitable.

Writ denied.

39 U.S.C. § 3009 Mailing of Unordered Merchandise

(a) Except for (1) free samples clearly and conspicuously marked as such, and (2) merchandise mailed by a charitable organization soliciting contributions, the mailing of unordered merchandise or of communications prohibited by subsection (c) of this section constitutes an unfair method of competition and an unfair trade practice in violation of section 45(a)(1) of title 15 [Federal Trade Commission Act]"

(b) Any merchandise mailed in violation of subsection (a) of this section, or within the exceptions contained therein, may be treated as a gift by the recipient, who shall have the right to retain, use, discard, or dispose of it in any manner he sees fit without any obligation whatsoever to the sender. All such merchandise shall have attached to it a clear and conspicuous statement informing the recipient that he may treat the merchandise as a gift to him and has the right to retain, use, discard, or dispose of it in any manner he sees fit without any obligation whatsoever to the sender

(c) No mailer of any merchandise mailed in violation of subsection (a) of this section, or within the exceptions contained therein, shall mail to any recipient of such merchandise a bill for such merchandise or any dunning communications.

(d) For the purposes of this section, "unordered merchandise" means merchandise mailed without the prior expressed request or consent of the recipient.

F. THE "UNILATERAL CONTRACT" PROBLEM

All contracts are either ovine or non-ovine.[e]

That's undoubtedly true. Contracts are either about sheep, or they are not about sheep. But, it's pretty unlikely that anyone (except maybe somebody in the sheep business) would think that's a very important fact. If virtually no legal rules turn on the difference between contracts about sheep and other contracts, then there isn't much point in making the distinction.

All contracts are either bilateral or unilateral.

Cool!!

That sounds really impressive and lawyerly. It gets even more impressive when one fills in the details. A bilateral contract is one where both sides make promises, that is a promise is exchanged for another promise. For example, a real estate sales contract would be bilateral: the seller promises to convey the real estate and the buyer promises to pay the purchase price. A unilateral contract is one in which only side makes a promise, that is, a promise is exchanged for an act. Some lending contracts would be unilateral: the borrower promises to repay but the lender simply lends the money.

Our intuition is that it's silly to worry about the difference between ovine and non-ovine contracts, because it seems incredibly unlikely that any legal rules make that difference important. The same thought is the key to avoiding the confusion that can come from getting caught up in a nifty-sounding notion like the difference between "bilateral" and "unilateral" contracts. The distinction is important only if there is some legal rule that makes that distinction important. So, there is no reason to talk about "bilateral" and "unilateral" contracts unless we are dealing with some setting in which that difference matters.

In the nineteenth and early twentieth centuries, lawyers and law professors—for some reason—decided that it was fun to talk about "bilateral" and "unilateral" contracts. Careful lawyers and law professors, however, have always realized that almost nothing of any significance turned on that distinction. As Karl Llewellyn observed over a half-century ago, "that great dichotomy of the first year class-room, the division of Contract into two major categories of formation, the bilateral and the pure 'unilateral,' . . . represents doctrine divorced from life . . . and therefore is misleading.": Karl Llewellyn, *On Our Case-Law of Contract: Offer and Acceptance*, 48 YALE L.J. 1, 36 (1938). The Second Restatement avoids any use of the terms. "[T]he original Restatement

---

[e]   "Ovine . . . of, relating to, or resembling sheep." Webster's New Collegiate Dictionary.

defined unilateral and bilateral contracts. It has not been carried forward because of doubt as to the utility of the distinction." RESTATEMENT (SECOND) OF CONTRACTS § 1, Comment f. So, the only real reason to talk about the distinction is to explain why it is not very important.

Maybe one of the reasons that the distinction caught on is that some of the cases one might use to illustrate it are so much fun. One of the old Contracts classics is an English case, *Carlill v. Carbolic Smoke Ball Company* [1893] 1 Q.B. 256 (C.A. 1892). A company published an advertisement promising to pay £100 to anyone who caught the flu despite using their influenza prevention device—the carbolic smoke ball. Someone who did just that sued, and won. The buyer never made any promise, so the arrangement could be described as one in which the company made a promise and in exchange the buyer performed an act. For further enlightenment, including a copy of the ad and a portrait of Mrs. Carlill, see www.carbolicsmokeball.co.uk. One supposes that the real concern in such cases is how to treat the possibility of misleading advertising.

If one presses for an answer to the question why it matters whether a contract is bilateral or unilateral, one must turn to a rather obscure corner of the law of offer and acceptance. As we saw above, the offeror is generally free to revoke the offer, so long as the revocation is made before acceptance. Ordinarily, that poses no significant hardship, because all that the offeree will have lost is the hope of getting the deal. If, however, one is very inventive, one can come up with a scenario where the offeree might be harmed by revocation.

Suppose your friend says to you, "If you walk across the Brooklyn Bridge, I'll pay you $100." Suppose you say "OK, it's a deal." Has a contract been formed? That depends on how we construe the offer. Was your friend saying "I propose that we enter into an agreement in which I will promise to pay $100, and you will promise to walk across the Brooklyn Bridge"? If so, then we could say that your friend's offer was accepted when you said "OK, it's a deal." But, suppose your friend says very clearly that they are not interested in being bound if all you have done is promise to walk across the Brooklyn Bridge. Rather, they say explicitly "I offer to pay you $100 if you walk across the Brooklyn Bridge, but the only thing that I will count as acceptance of this offer is your act of walking across the Brooklyn Bridge—promises are of no interest to me." As the old saw goes, the offeror is the master of the offer.

If you actually do walk across the Brooklyn Bridge, then you will have accepted, and your friend will be contractually bound to pay you the $100. That's the *Carbolic Smoke Ball* case. But, suppose that you start walking across the bridge, but after you get nine tenths of the way across, your friend zooms up in a car and shouts out the window: "I hereby revoke my offer to pay you $100 if you cross the Brooklyn Bridge." Your friend had made an offer, but you had not yet accepted. Their offer was revocable at any time before acceptance. They revoked, so you're left 9/10 of the way across the bridge with no remedy. Awwwww.[f]

We are not making this up. The Brooklyn Bridge hypo is the classic "unilateral contract" scenario. *See* Wormser, *The True Conception of Unilateral Contracts*, 26 YALE L.J. 136 (1916). The others are at least as weird, e.g., "I promise to pay you $100 if you climb that greased flag pole outside the school."

If one thinks this is a real problem, the solution is actually pretty simple. We just need a minor modification of the rule on revocability of offers. We just want to say that in this sort of weird case, the offeror cannot revoke once the offeree has begun performance. That is a common way of resolving the problem. For example, the Restatement provides that in those unusual cases where an offeror makes it clear that only a performance, not a return promise, will count as acceptance, the offeror cannot revoke once the offeree begins the requested performance. RESTATEMENT (SECOND) OF CONTRACTS § 45.

Unfortunately, however, the Restatement expresses that rule in a somewhat confusing way, using the concept of an "option contract" in a very counter-intuitive way:

Restatement (Second) of Contracts § 45

Option Contract Created by Part Performance or Tender

(1)   Where an offer invites an offeree to accept by rendering a performance and does not invite a promissory acceptance, an

---

[f]   Note that the problem arises only because the statement is interpreted as making an offer and making it clear that only your act of crossing the bridge will count as acceptance. If we were dealing with the usual case of an offer for a "bilateral contract" then acceptance would occur as soon as you promised to cross the bridge, hence the offeror would not have the power to revoke.

In one of the casebook classic cases, the problem was eliminated by construing the offeror communication as inviting acceptance by a return promise. *Davis v. Jacoby*, 34 P.2d 1026 (Cal. 1934). An elderly man living in California wrote to his wife's niece in Canada telling her that they were not well and promising that if the niece and her husband came to California and took care of them, they would leave her all their property in their will. The niece and her husband wrote back that they were coming, uprooted themselves from Canada, and set out for California. As it happened, however, the elderly man who had written the letter passed away before the niece got to California. The niece and her husband arrived in California and took care of the aunt until she too passed away. Then it was discovered that the elderly couple had not changed their will as promised. The niece sued the couple's estate seeking to enforce the uncle's promise.

The estate argued that the uncle's letter should be treated as an offer for a unilateral contract, that is, the offer could be accepted only by the niece's act of coming to California. That argument would work for the estate because of another quirk of the rules of offer and acceptance—that the power of acceptance created by an offer is automatically terminated by the death of the offeror. RESTATEMENT (SECOND) OF CONTRACTS § 48. Since the uncle died before the niece got to California, the offer—so construed—would not have been accepted.

The court avoided that result by construing the offer as inviting acceptance by a return promise, rather than only by an act. The uncle's letter had said "so if you can come, [niece] will inherit everything . . . will you let me hear from you as soon as possible . . . ." So, the court could say that the uncle really wanted the niece to promise to come, and therefore acceptance occurred when the niece wrote back that they were coming. On that interpretation, the offer was accepted before the uncle died.

option contract is created when the offeree tenders or begins the invited performance or tenders a beginning of it.

We will examine true option contracts later on. As we shall see, an option contract means an offer coupled with an enforceable promise not to revoke the offer. The only reason that Restatement § 45 speaks of "option contract" is that under a true option contract, the offeror cannot revoke, because the offeror has made an enforceable promise not to do so.[g] Hence, as the Restatement puts it:

Restatement (Second) of Contracts § 37

Termination of Power of Acceptance under Option Contract

> Notwithstanding sections 38–49, the power of acceptance under an option contract is not terminated by rejection or counter-offer, by revocation, or by the death or incapacity of the offeror . . . .

If we take the rule stated in Section 45, take out the confusing phrase "option contract" and plug in the rule on non-revocability stated in Section 37, then we get the following:

> Where an offer invites an offeree to accept by rendering a performance and does not invite a promissory acceptance, ~~an option contract is created~~ *the [offeree's] power of acceptance . . . is not terminated by . . . revocation . . . .* when the offeree tenders or begins the invited performance or tenders a beginning of it.

So, once you begin crossing the Brooklyn Bridge ("begins the invited performance") your power of acceptance is not terminated by my effort to revoke. Hurrah!!

Some Remaining Applications of a Unilateral Contract

There are, of course, many settings in which a promise is made in exchange for an act. Think of simple sales. Buyer pays money, Seller delivers goods. Suppose that Seller also make warranties about the qualities of the goods, either implied or express. We could describe this as a "unilateral contract" in that Buyer performs an act (paying the price) and Seller makes a promise (the warranty). But, nothing turns on that description. Remember, the distinction really matters only because of the usual rule that an offer can be revoked any time before acceptance. In the simple sales setting, we would never have a case in which the Seller made an offer for that unilateral contract and then sought to revoke that offer after the Buyer had done something.

There are, to be sure, a few settings in which unilateral contract discussion does figure into the analysis of some issue of genuine importance. There are, for example, some cases in which the owner of

---

[g]   As we shall see when we study the concept of consideration, there are some significant issues about what is required to make the promise not to revoke in a true option contract an enforceable promise.

real estate engages a broker to sell the property, the broker finds a suitable buyer, but the owner then refuses to go through with the deal. The owner will have no obligation to the *prospective buyer*, because at most the prospective buyer made an offer to buy, but the prospective seller never accepted. A different question is whether the prospective seller has any obligation to the *broker*. In some of the cases where an affirmative answer has been given to that question, the contract analysis has drawn on the notion of limitations on the revocability of offers for unilateral contracts. The idea is that the prospective seller made an offer to the broker, and while that offer could be accepted only by performance of an act (producing a ready, willing, and able buyer), the prospective seller's freedom to revoke that offer was limited once the broker had taken substantial steps toward performance.

Another setting in which unilateral contract concepts have been used involves employment. Suppose that an employee handbook or the like says that if an employee works for a certain period of time, the employee will be entitled to certain rights. The employee does so, but the employer then changes its policy. Does the employee have any legal rights against the employer? In many such cases the significant legal issue is not a matter of contract law but of special statutory law concerning labor and employment. For example, unionized employees' rights may turn on a collective bargaining agreement between the employer and the employees' union. Or, in the setting of retirement benefit plans, the employees' rights may be governed by federal statutory law, the Employee Retirement Income Security Act of 1974 (ERISA), 29 U.S.C. § 1001 et seq. In situations not governed by any such special law, there is a rather confusing body of case law about whether the employer is precluded from changing its policies once employees have worked for a significant period of time on the assumption that the benefits would be provided in accordance with the announced plan. Some of that case law uses the concept that the usual freedom to revoke an offer may be limited in the setting of an offer for unilateral contract. But, the case law is by no means consistent, and other issues are at least as significant as the revocation of offer point, for example, issues about the effect of the customary disclaimer in any employee manual to the effect that the employer reserves the right to change policies. Such issues are examined in courses dealing with the employment relationship.

G. Timing Issues in Offer & Acceptance; The "Mailbox Rule"; Comparative Contract Law and an Introduction to the CISG

1. The Mailbox Rule in the U.S.

In our offer and acceptance problems we have tried to eliminate messy timing issues by assuming that no communications crossed in the mail or other means of communication. When communications cross, one may encounter timing issues. Consider the following scenario:

Day 1   Buyer receives from Seller a letter saying "I'll sell my house for $300,000, you may accept by writing"

Day 2   Buyer mails a letter to Seller saying "I accept"

Day 3   Buyer receives a fax from Seller saying "I've changed my mind; I will not sell"

Day 4   Seller receives the letter that Buyer mailed on Day 2.

If Buyer's assent was effective as an acceptance when it was *dispatched*, then a contract was formed on Day 2. On that view, the fax that Seller sent on Day 3 came too late to operate as a revocation, even if it was received before the letter.

By contrast, if Buyer's assent was not effective as an acceptance until it was *received* then no contract was formed, because the power of acceptance was terminated by revocation on Day 3.

U.S. contract law follows the first rule, that an acceptance is effective "as soon as put out of the offeree's possession", i.e. when transmitted or dispatched. RESTATEMENT (SECOND) OF CONTRACTS § 63. That's the result of an old English case, *Adams v. Lindsell*, 106 Eng Rep 250 (K.B. 1818). That rule is often described as the "mailbox rule," that is, the acceptance is effective when deposited in the mail, even if it is overtaken by other communications, and even if it never reaches the offeror. Karl Llewellyn defended this rule in the following terms:

> As between hardship on the offeror which is really tough, and hardship on the offeree which would be even tougher, the vital reason for throwing the hardship of an odd delayed or lost letter upon the offeror remains this: the offeree is already relying, with the best reason in the world, on the deal being on; the offeror is only holding things open; and, in view of the efficiency of communication facilities, we can protect the offerees in all these deals at the price of hardship on offerors in very few of them: Karl N. Llewellyn, *Our Case-Law of Contract, Offer and Acceptance (pt.2)*, 48 Yale L. J. 779, 795 (1939).

Of course, as "master of the offer", the offeror is free to insist upon acceptance being effective only upon receipt, and therefore contract out of the mailbox rule.

The "mailbox rule" governs only acceptances: it is important to note that many other communications are effective only when received. For example, an offer can only be effective when received, because, by definition, a communication operates as an offer only if made in circumstances that justify the offeree as understanding that his assent will conclude the deal. RESTATEMENT (SECOND) OF CONTRACTS § 24. A revocation is effective to terminate the offeree's power of acceptance only when the revocation is received by the offeree. RESTATEMENT (SECOND)

OF CONTRACTS § 42. A rejection or counteroffer is (generally) effective to terminate the offeree's power of acceptance only when the communication is received by the offeror. RESTATEMENT (SECOND) OF CONTRACTS § 40.

So, it would be wrong to say that there is some general "mailbox rule" saying that communications, in general, are effective when transmitted. Rather the U.S. contract rule that goes under the name of "the mailbox rule" is limited to the specific setting of when a communication assenting to an offer is effective.

2. THE MAILBOX RULE AND COMPARATIVE LAW

The "mailbox rule" serves as an interesting point of comparison with the law of contract in countries outside of the U.S. For example, in European legal systems, a general rule that communications are effective only when *received* is also applied to acceptances. In the German Civil Code, for instance, acceptance is only effective on receipt. This creates legal, as well as business, differences, for American and non-American based contractors, and for their lawyers.

What follows from the fact that the common law system of the U.S., and the civil law system of Europe, do not follow the same rule? Of course, the practical import of this distinction is reduced as modern techniques of data transmission such as email and texting enable almost instantaneous dispatch and arrival. And yet, the difference points to broader underlying distinctions between the different legal systems. In Germany, for example, offers may not be revoked for a certain period of time, which departs strongly from the U.S. system, where offers may always be revoked (unless consideration has been exchanged for the offeror not to withdraw the offer (option contract), or the offeree has incurred expenditure in reliance of its continuation, both discussed in the next Chapter). In short, the binding nature of the offer is different depending upon jurisdiction: "the offeror is least bound in the Anglo-Saxon legal family and most strongly bound in the German systems, the Romanistic legal family adopting an intermediate position": KONRAD ZWEIGERT & HEIN KÖTZ, INTRODUCTION TO COMPARATIVE LAW 357 (3rd rev. ed., trans. Tony Weir, 1996).

To appreciate these differences, consider the ways in which legal systems are understood to resemble different "legal families", or "legal traditions", which represent the different histories of legal systems, their different sources of law and their different reasoning "mentalities". Recall that the U.S. belongs to the "common law" tradition, along with much of the English-speaking world. The other major legal tradition is the "civil law" tradition, which includes much of Europe, Africa and South America. Other traditions include so-called "mixed jurisdictions", such as South Africa, as well as, for historical reasons, Louisiana and Puerto Rico within the U.S. And yet another tradition belongs to those countries that declare Islamic law to be the law of the State, such as

Saudi Arabia and Iran. We can imagine, therefore, many different versions of contractual obligations, which the modern lawyer may have to address.

3. The Aims of International and Comparative Contract Law

These distinctions help to demonstrate the various uses of comparative study: to help us understand how similar problems are handled in different ways, for example, or how different approaches can lead to similar outcomes, or even, sometimes, how comparing contract law can lead "to a better understanding of one's own regime and provides ideas for law reform": E. Allan Farnsworth, *Comparative Contract Law*, in The Oxford Handbook of Comparative Law 904 (Mathias Reimann & Reinhard Zimmermann, eds., 2006).

Indeed, of all the legal areas analyzed with a comparative lens, contract law has for a long time been the most prominent. This is so for a number of reasons. First, comparative contract law reveals the similarities and differences between the common law system, at work in the U.S., and civil law systems, at work in continental Europe and elsewhere. Yet despite different institutional backdrops, common law and civil law systems of contract often deal with similar topics, including the offer and acceptance doctrines studied in this Chapter, as well as the topics we present later, such as how to interpret a contract, what happens when circumstances change, and what remedies are available for breach. Within these topics, each system may pursue different resolutions, distinct emphases, and internal idiosyncrasies that comparative contract law usefully highlights.

Secondly, comparative law is historically revealing: modern comparative law came into its own just as contract law did, in the late nineteenth and twentieth centuries' celebration of liberalism, individual autonomy and market freedom, and the epochal move in the West, in the famous phrase of Sir Henry Maine (1822–88), "from Status to Contract": Henry Sumner Maine, Ancient Law (1861) 100. This was a prodigious shift, and although it was made up of many parts, the value of free exchange was of central importance. This value finds a home in the famous contribution of Adam Smith (1723–1790):

> It is not from the benevolence of the butcher, the brewer, or the baker that we expect our dinner, but from their regard to their own interest. We address ourselves, not to their humanity but to their self-love, and never talk to them of our own necessities but of their advantages: An Inquiry into the Nature and Causes of the Wealth of Nations (1776) bk. 1, ch. 2.

And third, the economic significance of global commerce makes similarities and differences practically relevant to law and policy makers, the bench and the bar, and the international business community. It is this third reason that probably explains the massive boost in efforts to unify certain areas of contract law, especially the law of sales. The biggest success of this latter effort has been the United Nations Convention on Contracts for the International Sale of Goods ("CISG").

4. THE CISG AND ACCEPTANCE RULES

The CISG was adopted by the United Nations Commission on International Trade Law ("UNCITRAL") in 1980 and applies to contracts for the sale of goods across borders, apart from consumer goods. It appears in your Statutory Supplement, along with other examples of international contract law, such as the UNIDROIT Principles. The CISG was drafted to facilitate global commerce, and avoids difficult choice-of-law problems by advancing its own law of sales. Much of it is very close to U.S. contract law, but some of departs from it. The United States ratified the treaty in 1986 and UNCITRAL reports that 85 States have adopted the CISG (as of December 2016), including the big trading partners of Canada, Mexico, France, Germany, China and Singapore: http://www.uncitral.org/uncitral/en/uncitral_texts/sale_goods/1980CISG _status.html. It is therefore important to note that in dealing with contracts for sale between parties in different countries, a lawyer must check whether the CISG applies.

When addressing the law of offer and acceptance, the CISG is closer to civil law systems, as the following excerpt indicates:

United Nations Convention on Contracts for the International Sale of Goods

Vienna, 1980

Article 1

(1) This Convention applies to contracts of sale of goods between parties whose places of business are in different States:

(a) When the States are Contracting States . . .

Article 2

This Convention does not apply to sales:

(a) of goods bought for personal, family or household use

. . .

Article 6

The parties may exclude the application of this Convention, or . . . derogate from or vary the effect of any of its provisions.

Article 16

(1) Until a contract is concluded an offer may be revoked if the revocation reaches the offeree before he has dispatched an acceptance. . . .

Article 18

(1) A statement made by or other conduct of the offeree indicating assent to an offer is an acceptance. . . . .

(2) An acceptance of an offer becomes effective at the moment the indication of assent reaches the offeror. An acceptance is not effective if the indication of assent does not reach the offeror within the time he has fixed or, if no time is fixed, within a reasonable time, due account being taken of the circumstances of the transaction, including the rapidity of the means of communication employed by the offeror. . . .

Notice how Articles 16 and 18 differ from the common law mailbox rule. On the one hand, Article 18(2) of the CISG adopts an acceptance-on-receipt rule, in contrast to the mailbox acceptance-on-dispatch. But Article 16(1) also removes the power to revoke after the dispatch of an acceptance. Thus, the CISG and the common law both protect the offeree against the possibility of a revocation once the acceptance is dispatched, but the CISG places the risk of a lost communication on the offeree rather than the offeror. This may be an improvement over the common law, since it places the risks of a lost communication on the party who is in the best position to prevent that loss, by choosing a more reliable means of communication.

PROBLEMS

1. On Sept. 2, a sales representative of World Wide Widgets Inc. in Kentucky wrote to Bakti Enterprises in New York offering to sell them 1000 widgets for $10,000. After experiencing difficulties in securing their electronic systems, World Wide Widgets Inc. indicated that an answer was required in the course of post. Bakti Enterprises received the letter on Sept. 5, and posted their acceptance on the same day. Due to a mail strike, Bakti's letter was not received until Sept. 10. Meanwhile, on Sept. 9, the sales representative sold the widgets to someone else, and sent a fax to Bakti Enterprises revoking the offer. Do World Wide Widgets and Bakti Enterprises have a contract? Do the examples at the end of Chapter 3 (termination of the power of acceptance) have any impact on your answer?

2. Would your answer to the question above change if World Wide Widgets Inc. was located in Germany? What further questions would you need to ask?

NOTES & QUESTIONS

1. Alongside the CISG, other international efforts have focused on non-binding, but persuasive, approaches, intended to operate much like a

restatement. Thus, for example, the UNIDROIT Principles of International Commercial Contracts (1994, amended 2004, 2010), operate to harmonize and modernize particular commercial law principles. These principles have been endorsed by the United Nations Commission on International Trade Law (in 2007), and are increasingly used in international commercial arbitration. Contracting parties can choose to agree to these principles, or, if they have not agreed on governing law, the principles can be applied. The UNIDROIT Principles are available in your Statutory Supplement. Read articles 2.1.4 (revocation of offer), 2.1.6 (mode of acceptance). Is this a statement of U.S. law, German law, or a blend between the two?

2.   How does the following feature of the civil law resemble the project of the CISG? Can you think of a U.S. analogy? Would the U.C.C. or the Restatement 2d be a better candidate?

> [T]he Civil Law has been centered around a book and a set of universities. The book is the Corpus Iuris Civilis, the codification, or, better, the compilation, of the Roman Law undertaken in the days of the very decomposition of the Roman Empire by its very latest protagonist, the Byzantine emperor Justinian (527–565). Long forgotten, the Corpus Iuris was rediscovered in the 12th century by the legal scholars of the University of Bologna. . . . With the consolidation of the national states the demand for national legal unification was satisfied with those great national codifications whose line begins with the Prussian Code of 1794 and whose high points are marked by the French Civil Code of 1804, the German Civil Code of 1896 and the Swiss Civil Code of 1907: Max Rheinstein, *Common Law and Civil Law: An Elementary Comparison* 22 REVISTA JURIDICA DE LA UNIVERSIDAD DE PUERTO RICO 90, 92–93 (1953).

3.   Consider this description of the civil law mentality by Schlesinger, below, and compare it with your earlier readings from Oliver Wendell Holmes (*The Path of the Law*) and Karl Llewellyn (*The Bramble Bush*). Now articulate, in your own words, how the civil law and common law mentalities can be said to differ:

> The very idea of codification rests on the . . . belief that the human mind could use reason to project the solution of future controversies in a systematic and comprehensive manner. . . . [A] true code [is] a systematic, authoritative and direction-giving statute of broad coverage: Ugo A. Mattei et al, *Schlesinger's Comparative Law* (7th ed., 2006).

4.   As comparative scholars have noted, American interest in comparative law has waxed and waned over the more than 200 years of the U.S. republic. In the earliest years, many who contributed to legal development were trained in English common law, but were also surprisingly informed about European political philosophy and Roman or civil law. And indeed, some leading participants in the development of English common law (such as Lord Mansfield, chief of the English King's Bench from 1756–1788, see Chapter 10), were themselves influenced by

Roman and civil sources. American interest again increased from the input of émigré lawyers from Europe after World War II. The latest impetus for comparative study has occurred since the 1990s, with the acceleration of economic, social and cultural globalization, in many parts of the world, in the wake of the collapse of the Soviet Union. American lawyers have been influential in providing transnational legal services in this new setting, which occur primary in English and build on different legal traditions.

5.   Can one say that the common law system, including the particular way in which contractual obligations are enforced, is the best legal system available? A large and provocative literature has developed which explicitly evaluates the strengths and weaknesses of different systems: e.g. Rafael La Porta et al, *The Economic Consequences of Legal Origins*, 46 J. ECON. LITERATURE 285 (2008) (suggesting the greater efficiency in the common law as against civil law systems). Consider how one might go about approaching this question, and what obstacles present themselves.

6.   Islamic law stands apart by its emphasis on the religious laws of Islam (the *Shari'a* or *Shar'*). In systems adopting Islamic law, the *fiqh* (often translated as substantive law) constitutes a system of legal and ethical norms that jurists seek to develop by deriving rules from the texts of the revelation (the *Qur'an*), the normative practice of the Prophet (the *Sunna*), and the consensus of scholars (*ijmā*), through varied forms of legal reasoning. The implications for comparative contract law are notable: in commercial agreements, for example, Islamic banking and finance institutions have developed rapidly in recent decades, and seek to promote trade and investment supported by credit practices that avoid interest (*ribā*), gambling, and other activities considered unethical. Excessive uncertainty in transactions (*gharar*) is also prohibited. See further JAN M. SMITS, CONTRACT LAW: A COMPARATIVE INTRODUCTION 35 (2014); MAHMOUD A. EL-GAMAL, ISLAMIC FINANCE: LAW, ECONOMICS, AND PRACTICE (2006). We will consider the broader issues of the scope of U.S. contract law in Chapter 13, and you might keep this comparative feature of contracts and public policy in mind.

CHAPTER FOUR

CONSIDERATION

> I'd gladly pay you Tuesday
> for a hamburger today
>
> —J. Wellington Wimpy

A. INTRODUCTION: USAGE OF THE TERM "CONSIDERATION"

In this Chapter we explore the traditional basis for enforcing promises—"consideration." The basic rule is easy to state. A promise is enforceable if it is supported by "consideration"; a promise is not enforceable if it is not supported by "consideration." Unfortunately, that statement (1) obscures lots of confusion and (2) is oversimplified.

First, there is the problem of usage.

The term "consideration" might be used in a colloquial sense to mean something like "motive." For example, in the first case in this Chapter, *Dougherty v. Salt*, an aunt promised to pay $3000 to her nephew because she thought highly of him. As we will see, the court held that the promise was not enforceable because it was not supported by "consideration." If the aunt was fond of legalistic speech, she might have said something along the lines of "In consideration of the high regard that I have for my nephew, I promise to pay him $3000." That would mean only that her motive for making the promise was the high regard that she had for her nephew. Saying words like that would not have changed the result. The court would still have held that the promise was not supported by "consideration," using that word as a term of legal art.

As we will see, the rules on which promises are and are not enforceable have become pretty complicated. There are several ways of describing the outcomes. The most useful is to use the term "consideration" only to mean something specific. For example, the Restatement uses the word "consideration" to mean something that the promisor sought in exchange for making the promise, or, as it is often expressed, a "bargained for exchange." RESTATEMENT (SECOND) OF CONTRACTS § 71.

If we use the term consideration in that sense, then our general rule would be that if the promise was made in exchange for something, then it is enforceable. We would not ask any questions about why the promisor wanted whatever she sought, nor how valuable the exchange was. As we will see in *Hamer v. Sidway* and *Batsakis v. Demotsis*, that is generally the case. In a few contexts, however, largely for historical reasons, the law has developed the approach that certain promises are not enforceable, even though they were made in exchange for something that the promisor wanted, unless the return had some real value. See Section D *infra*. If we are going to be consistent with our use of the term "consideration," we would have to describe those settings as exceptions to the general rule that any promise supported by consideration (bargained for exchange) is enforceable. That's what the Restatement does. RESTATEMENT (SECOND) OF CONTRACTS § 72 says that *"except as stated in §§ 73 and 74,* any performance which is bargained for is consideration." Then, in section 73 and 74, the Restatement describes several situations in which the cases have developed rules that something more than a mere "bargained for exchange" is required to make a promise enforceable. We'll examine those issues below.

The flip side of that usage point would be that if a promise is not supported by consideration, in the sense of "bargained for exchange" then the promise is not enforceable. But, as we shall see in this Chapter and the next, the cases have developed rules to the effect that in some situations a promise will be enforceable even though it is not supported by consideration in the sense of a bargained for exchange. If we are going to stick with our general concept of "consideration" as any bargained for exchange, then we would have to describe these situations as exceptions to the general rule that consideration is required for a promise to be enforceable. That's what the Restatement does. Topic 2 of Chapter 4 of the Restatement, covering Sections 82–100, is entitled "Contracts Without Consideration," that is, the rules in those sections describe situations where the cases have said that a promise is enforceable even though it is not supported by consideration in the sense of any bargained for exchange.

The result of this terminological convention is coherent, if untidy. We start with the general rule that a promise is enforceable if and only if it is supported by "consideration," meaning any bargained for exchange. RESTATEMENT (SECOND) OF CONTRACTS §§ 71, 72, 79. Then we have exceptions to that general rule, covering cases where something in addition to consideration (in the sense of bargained for exchange) is required for a promise to be enforceable. RESTATEMENT (SECOND) OF CONTRACTS §§ 73 & 74. Then we have another set of exceptions, covering cases where a promise is enforceable even though not supported by consideration (in the sense of bargained for exchange). RESTATEMENT (SECOND) OF CONTRACTS §§ 82–100.

Unfortunately, usage by lawyers and judges is not always as tidy as the drafters of the Restatement would like. You are all going to be really good lawyers, which means that you will use language carefully. But, everyone else will not necessarily be a good lawyer. Or, he or she will have lived at a time before the usage crystallized in the fashion reflected in the Restatement. So, you will often encounter usage of the term "consideration" that is not consistent with the usage rules just laid done. At the worst, the term will be used in a completely conclusory fashion.

That is, if the result is that the promise is enforceable, then one will say that the promise is supported by "consideration"—or, as it is often phrased, the situation "imports a consideration." If the result is that the promise is not enforceable, then one will say that the promise is not supported by "consideration." If one uses the word in that way, then it really doesn't have any meaning. We're left with the rule that a promise is enforceable if it is enforceable, but is not enforceable if it is not enforceable. That's true, but it's not very helpful. So, if you plan to be a good lawyer, you will avoid that sort of conclusory use of the term, and watch out for older cases, and sloppier lawyers, who do not use the term carefully.

B. GRATUITOUS PROMISES

Dougherty v. Salt

Court of Appeals of New York, 1919.
227 N.Y. 200, 125 N.E. 94.

■ CARDOZO, J.

The plaintiff, a boy of eight years, received from his aunt, the defendant's testatrix, a promissory note for $3,000 payable at her death or before. Use was made of a printed form, which contains the words 'value received.' How the note came to be given, was explained by the boy's guardian, who was a witness for his ward. The aunt was visiting her nephew. 'When she saw Charley coming in, she said 'Isn't he a nice boy?' I answered her, yes, that he is getting along very nice, and getting along nice in school, and I showed where he had progressed in school, having good reports, and so forth, and she told me that she was going to take care of that child, that she loved him very much. I said, 'I know you do, Tillie, but your taking care of the child will be done probably like your brother and sister done, take it out in talk.' She said: 'I don't intend to take it out in talk, I would like to take care of him now.' I said, 'Well, that is up to you.' She said, 'Why can't I make out a note to him?' I said, 'You can, if you wish to.' She said, 'Would that be right?' And I said, 'I do not know, but I guess it would; I do not know why it would not.' And she said, 'Well, will you make out a note for me?' I said, 'Yes, if you wish me to,' and she said, 'Well, I wish you would." A blank was then produced, filled out, and signed. The aunt handed the note to her nephew with these words, 'You have always done for me, and I have signed this note for you. Now, do not lose it. Some day it will be valuable.'

The trial judge submitted to the jury the question whether there was any consideration for the promised payment. Afterwards, he set aside the verdict in favor of the plaintiff, and dismissed the complaint. The Appellate Division, by a divided court, reversed the judgment of dismissal, and reinstated the verdict on the ground that the note was sufficient evidence of consideration.

We reach a different conclusion. The inference of consideration to be drawn from the form of the note has been so overcome and rebutted as to leave no question for a jury. This is not a case where witnesses summoned by the defendant and friendly to the defendant's cause, supply the testimony in disproof of value. * * * This is a case where the testimony in disproof of value comes from the plaintiff's own witness, speaking at the plaintiff's instance. The transaction thus revealed admits of one interpretation, and one only. The note was the voluntary and unenforceable promise of an executory gift. * * * This child of eight was not a creditor, nor dealt with as one. The aunt was not paying a debt. She was conferring a bounty. * * * The promise was neither offered nor accepted with any other purpose. 'Nothing is consideration that is not regarded as such by both parties' * * *. A note so given is not made for 'value received,' however its maker may have labeled it. The formula of the printed blank becomes, in the light of the conceded facts, a mere erroneous conclusion, which cannot overcome the inconsistent conclusion of the law. * * * The plaintiff, through his own witness, has explained the genesis of the promise, and consideration has been disproved. * * *.

We hold, therefore, that the verdict of the jury was contrary to law, and that the trial judge was right in setting it aside. . . .

    . . .

NOTES

In *Dougherty* the aunt wrote out a "promissory note" using a standard form, and gave it to the nephew. That did not make any difference. The result would be the same whether the aunt expressed her promise in the special form of a promissory note or just wrote out on a sheet of paper "I promise to pay Charley $3000 /s/ Aunt Hellena." Some of you may take a course in Commercial Law: if it covers payment systems, you will study the law of promissory notes in more detail. For our purposes it is enough to know that even if a promise to pay money is written in the special form of a promissory note that qualifies as a "negotiable instrument" under Article 3 of the U.C.C., lack of consideration is still a defense. U.C.C. § 3–303(b). The only difference in that regard between a simple contract and a promissory note that qualifies as a negotiable instrument is that under U.C.C. Article 3 there is a presumption of consideration. U.C.C. § 3–308(b). But, if, as in *Dougherty*, the maker proves that the note was not given for consideration, the note is not enforceable.

C. CONSIDERATION AS "BARGAINED FOR EXCHANGE"

Restatement (Second) of Contracts §§ 71, 72, and 79

Hamer v. Sidway

Court of Appeals of New York, Second Division, 1891.
79 Sickels 538, 27 N.E. 256.

APPEAL from order of the General Term of the Supreme Court in the fourth judicial department, made July 1, 1890, which reversed a judgment in favor of plaintiff entered upon a decision of the court on trial at Special Term and granted a new trial.

This action was brought upon an alleged contract.

The plaintiff presented a claim to the executor of William E. Story, Sr., for $5,000 and interest from the 6th day of February, 1875. She acquired it through several mesne assignments from William E. Story, 2d. The claim being rejected by the executor, this action was brought. It appears that William E. Story, Sr., was the uncle of William E. Story, 2d; that at the celebration of the golden wedding of Samuel Story and wife, father and mother of William E. Story, Sr., on the 20th day of March, 1869, in the presence of the family and invited guests he promised his nephew that if he would refrain from drinking, using tobacco, swearing and playing cards or billiards for money until he became twenty-one years of age he would pay him a sum of $5,000. The nephew assented thereto and fully performed the conditions inducing the promise. When the nephew arrived at the age of twenty-one years and on the 31st day of January, 1875, he wrote to his uncle informing him that he had performed his part of the agreement and had thereby become entitled to the sum of $5,000. The uncle received the letter and a few days later and on the sixth of February, he wrote and mailed to his nephew the following letter:

'BUFFALO, Feb. 6, 1875.

'W. E. STORY, Jr.:

'DEAR NEPHEW—Your letter of the 31st ult. came to hand all right, saying that you had lived up to the promise made to me several years ago. I have no doubt but you have, for which you shall have five thousand dollars as I promised you. I had the money in the bank the day you was 21 years old that I intend for you, and you shall have the money certain. Now, Willie I do not intend to interfere with this money in any way till I think you are capable of taking care of it and the sooner that time comes the better it will please me. I would hate very much to have you start out in some adventure that you thought all right and lose this money in one year. The first five thousand dollars that I got together cost me a heap of hard work. You would hardly believe me when I tell you that to obtain this I shoved a jackplane many a day, butchered three or four years, then came to this city, and after three months' perseverance I obtained a situation in a grocery store. I opened this store early, closed late, slept in the fourth story of the building in a room 30 by 40 feet and not a human being in the building but myself. All this I done to live as cheap as I could to save something. I don't want you to take up with this kind of fare. I was here in the cholera season '49 and '52 and the deaths averaged 80 to 125 daily and plenty of small-pox. I wanted to go home, but Mr. Fisk, the gentleman I was working for, told me if I left then, after it got healthy he probably would not want me. I stayed. All the money I have saved I know just how I got it. It did not come to me in any mysterious way, and the reason I speak of this is that money got in this way stops longer with a fellow that gets it with hard knocks than it does when he finds it. Willie, you are 21 and you have many a thing to learn yet. This money you have earned much easier than I did besides acquiring good habits at the same time and you are quite welcome to the money; hope you will make good use of it. I was ten long years getting this together after I was your age. Now, hoping this will be satisfactory, I stop. One thing more. Twenty-one years ago I bought you 15 sheep. These sheep were put out to double every four years. I kept track of them the first eight years; I have not heard much about them since. Your father and grandfather promised me that they would look after them till you were of age. Have they done so? I hope they have. By this time you have between five and six hundred sheep, worth a nice little income this spring. Willie, I have said much more than I expected to; hope you can make out what I have written. To-day is the seventeenth day that I have not been out of my room, and have had the doctor as many days. Am a little better to-day; think I will get out next week. You need not mention to father, as he always worries about small matters.

Truly Yours,

'W. E. STORY.

'P. S.—You can consider this money on interest.'

The nephew received the letter and thereafter consented that the money should remain with his uncle in accordance with the terms and conditions of the letters. The uncle died on the 29th day of January, 1887, without having paid over to his nephew any portion of the said $5,000 and interest.

■ PARKER, J.

The question which provoked the most discussion by counsel on this appeal, and which lies at the foundation of plaintiff's asserted right of recovery, is whether by virtue of a contract defendant's testator William E. Story became indebted to his nephew William E. Story, 2d, on his twenty-first birthday in the sum of five thousand dollars. The trial court found as a fact that 'on the 20th day of March, 1869, . . . William E. Story agreed to and with William E. Story, 2d, that if he would refrain from drinking liquor, using tobacco, swearing, and playing cards or billiards for money until he should become 21 years of age then he, the said William E. Story, would at that time pay him, the said William E. Story, 2d, the sum of $5,000 for such refraining, to which the said William E. Story, 2d, agreed,' and that he 'in all things fully performed his part of said agreement.'

The defendant contends that the contract was without consideration to support it, and, therefore, invalid. He asserts that the promisee by refraining from the use of liquor and tobacco was not harmed but benefited; that that which he did was best for him to do independently of his uncle's promise, and insists that it follows that unless the promisor was benefited, the contract was without consideration. A contention, which if well founded, would seem to leave open for controversy in many cases whether that which the promisee did or omitted to do was, in fact, of such benefit to him as to leave no consideration to support the enforcement of the promisor's agreement. Such a rule could not be tolerated, and is without foundation in the law. The Exchequer Chamber, in 1875, defined consideration as follows: 'A valuable consideration in the sense of the law may consist either in some right, interest, profit or benefit accruing to the one party, or some forbearance, detriment, loss or responsibility given, suffered or undertaken by the other.' Courts 'will not ask whether the thing which forms the consideration does in fact benefit the promisee or a third party, or is of any substantial value to anyone. It is enough that something is promised, done, forborne or suffered by the party to whom the promise is made as consideration for the promise made to him.' (Anson's Prin. of Con. 63.)

'In general a waiver of any legal right at the request of another party is a sufficient consideration for a promise.' (Parsons on Contracts, 444.)

'Any damage, or suspension, or forbearance of a right will be sufficient to sustain a promise.' (Kent, vol. 2, 465, 12th ed.)

Pollock, in his work on contracts, page 166, after citing the definition given by the Exchequer Chamber already quoted, says: 'The second branch of this judicial description is really the most important one. Consideration means not so much that one party is profiting as that the other abandons some legal right in the present or limits his legal freedom of action in the future as an inducement for the promise of the first.'

Now, applying this rule to the facts before us, the promisee used tobacco, occasionally drank liquor, and he had a legal right to do so. That right he abandoned for a period of years upon the strength of the promise of the testator that for such forbearance he would give him $5,000. We need not speculate on the effort which may have been required to give up the use of those stimulants. It is sufficient that he restricted his lawful freedom of action within certain prescribed limits upon the faith of his uncle's agreement, and now having fully performed the conditions imposed, it is of no moment whether such performance actually proved a benefit to the promisor, and the court will not inquire into it, but were it a proper subject of inquiry, we see nothing in this record that would permit a determination that the uncle was not benefited in a legal sense. . . .

. . .

The order appealed from should be reversed and the judgment of the Special Term affirmed, with costs payable out of the estate.

NOTES & QUESTIONS

1. Uncle Willie made the promise to Nephew Willie at the family gathering in March 1869. In 1875, when Nephew Willie had turned 21, he wrote to Uncle Willie and said that he had performed his side of the bargain, that is, he had refrained from vice. Uncle Willie did not immediately pay Nephew Willie the $5000. Rather, in 1875 he wrote him the long avuncular letter indicating that he did plan to pay the money. Note that Uncle Willie did not actually pay the money in 1875. Rather, he just reaffirmed his promise to do so. Hence the lawsuit was based on the promise that Uncle Willie made to Nephew Willie at the family gathering in March 1869; the 1875 letter really doesn't change anything.

2. The lawsuit was not actually brought by Nephew Willie. Nephew Willie had assigned his right to collect from Uncle to someone else, and that someone had further assigned it. But, again, this really doesn't matter. The assignee could enforce Uncle's promise only if Nephew (the assignor) could have enforced it.

3. As is not uncommon in decisions about consideration, particularly opinions written way back at the time of the case, the opinion in *Hamer* uses the words like "benefit," "detriment," "forbearance," "legal right," etc. Think about how the ruling in *Hamer* might be expressed without such fancy talk.

How is the result in *Hamer* expressed in the Restatement? See RESTATEMENT (SECOND) OF CONTRACTS §§ 71, 72, and 79. Think very hard about what is said in RESTATEMENT (SECOND) OF CONTRACTS § 79(a).

4. Compare the situation with gifts that have conditions attached. Williston explained the distinction with the following "tramp" hypo from 1922. A benevolent man says to a person asking for charity: "If you go around the corner to the clothing shop there, then you may purchase an overcoat on my credit." As Williston writes, no reasonable person would understand that the short walk was requested as consideration for the promise. Rather, in the event that the person asking for charity goes to the shop, the promisor would donate the coat. 1 Samuel Williston, The Law of Contracts § 112 (1922). Can you explain why this would not be consideration? What facts might change the situation to one involving consideration?

Schnell v. Nell

Supreme Court of Indiana, 1861.
17 Ind. 29.

■ PERKINS, J.

Action by *J. B. Nell* against *Zacharias Schnell,* upon the following instrument:

"This agreement, entered into this 13th day of *February,* 1856, between *Zach. Schnell,* of *Indianapolis, Marion* county, State of *Indiana,* as party of the first part, and *J. B. Nell,* of the same place, *Wendelin Lorenz,* of *Stilesville, Hendricks* county, State of *Indiana,* and *Donata Lorenz,* of *Frickinger, Grand Duchy of Baden, Germany,* as parties of the second part, witnesseth: The said *Zacharias Schnell* agrees as follows: whereas his wife, *Theresa Schnell,* now deceased, has made a last will and testament, in which, among other provisions, it was ordained that every one of the above named second parties, should receive the sum of $200; and whereas the said provisions of the will must remain a nullity, for the reason that no property, real or personal, was in the possession of the said *Theresa Schnell,* deceased, in her own name, at the time of her death, and all property held by *Zacharias* and *Theresa Schnell* jointly, therefore reverts to her husband; and whereas the said *Theresa Schnell* has also been a dutiful and loving wife to the said *Zach. Schnell,* and has materially aided him in the acquisition of all property, real and personal, now possessed by him; for, and in consideration of all this, and the love and respect he bears to his wife; and, furthermore, in consideration of one cent, received by him of the second parties, he, the said *Zach, Schnell,* agrees to pay the above named sums of money to the parties of the second part, to wit: $200 to the said *J. B. Nell;* $200 to the said *Wendelin Lorenz;* and $200 to the said *Donata Lorenz,* in the following installments, viz., $200 in one year from the date of these presents; $200 in two years, and $200 in three years; to be divided between the parties in equal portions of $66 2/3 each year, or as they may agree, till each one has received his full sum of $200.

. . . .

In witness whereof, the said parties have, on this 13th day of *February,* 1856, set hereunto their hands and seals.

ZACHARIAS SCHNELL, [SEAL.]

J. B. NELL, [SEAL.]

WEN. LORENZ." [SEAL.]

The complaint contained no averment of a consideration for the instrument, outside of those expressed in it; and did not aver that the one cent agreed to be paid, had been paid or tendered.

. . .

The defendant answered, that the instrument sued on was given for no consideration whatever. He further answered, that it was given for no consideration, because his said wife, *Theresa,* at the time she made the will mentioned, and at the time of her death, owned, neither separately, nor jointly with her husband, or any one else (except so far as the law gave her an interest in her husband's property), any property, real or personal, &c.

[The trial court ruled for the plaintiff, saying that the allegations of the complaint were sufficient to withstand a motion to dismiss.]. . .

The case turned below, and must turn here, upon the question whether the instrument sued on does express a consideration sufficient to give it legal obligation, as against *Zacharias Schnell*. It specifies three distinct considerations for his promise to pay $600:

1. A promise, on the part of the plaintiffs, to pay him one cent.

2. The love and affection he bore his deceased wife, and the fact that she had done her part, as his wife, in the acquisition of property.

3. The fact that she had expressed her desire, in the form of an inoperative will, that the persons named therein should have the sums of money specified.

The consideration of one cent will not support the promise of *Schnell*. It is true, that as a general proposition, inadequacy of consideration will not vitiate an agreement. * * * But this doctrine does not apply to a mere exchange of sums of money, of coin, whose value is exactly fixed, but to the exchange of something of, in itself, indeterminate value, for money, or, perhaps, for some other thing of indeterminate value. In this case, had the one cent mentioned, been some particular one cent, a family piece, or ancient, remarkable coin, possessing an indeterminate value, extrinsic from its simple money value, a different view might be taken. . . . The consideration of one cent is, plainly, in this case, merely nominal, and intended to be so. . . . The promise was simply one to make a gift. The past services of his wife, and the love and affection he had borne her, are objectionable as legal considerations for *Schnell's* promise, on two grounds: 1. They are past considerations. * * * 2. The fact that *Schnell* loved his wife, and that she had been industrious, constituted no consideration for his promise to pay *J. B. Nell,* and the *Lorenzes,* a sum of money. Whether, if his wife, in her lifetime, had made a bargain with *Schnell,* that, in consideration of his promising to pay, after her death, to the persons named, a sum of money, she would be industrious, and worthy of his affection, such a promise would have been valid and consistent with public policy, we need not decide. Nor is the fact that

Schnell now venerates the memory of his deceased wife, a legal consideration for a promise to pay any third person money.

The instrument sued on, interpreted in the light of the facts alleged in the second paragraph of the answer, will not support an action. . . . [Hence the Indiana Supreme Court ruled for the defendant.]

NOTES

1.   In *Schnell v. Nell*, the widow, Theresa, had written a will in which she devised $200 to each of the three children. But, that will had no effect. As it turned out, Theresa owned no property in her own name. All property owned by Theresa and her husband, Zacharias, was held by them jointly. As a result, when Theresa died all of her interest in property passed automatically to her husband Zacharias, that is, Zacharias got the property as the surviving joint tenant rather than receiving it by virtue of the will. There was no property to pass under the will, so the children received nothing under Theresa's will.

Apparently the reason that Zacharias made the promise to pay $200 to each of the three children was that, at the time, he thought that they should get the money that Theresa had wanted them to have, as shown by her will. But, for whatever reason, Zacharias changed his mind and refused to pay the three children the money he had promised to pay them. Hence the lawsuit.

2.   In the *Dougherty v. Salt* and *Hamer v. Sidway* the promises might have been regarded as spur of the moment gestures that the promisor might or might not have taken very seriously. It's pretty hard to imagine the same in *Schnell v. Nell*. Normal people do not write out instruments of the sort involved in *Schnell v. Nell*. Rather you end up with writings like that only if people are sufficiently serious about what they are doing that they go to a lawyer to write the document. But *Schnell v. Nell* shows that even if a promisor is very serious about making the promise, the promise may not be not enforceable if it is not supported by consideration.

3.   One of the devices used by the person who drafted the document in *Schnell v. Nell*—presumably a lawyer—was to have the promisor, Zacharias, sign the writing "**under seal**." That is a vestige of a very old legal formality. In the era before widespread literacy, it was common for the wealthy to have a seal that they would use in executing legal documents. The seal was a die that was used to make an impression in a drop of molten wax placed on the document. In very old English law, a promise made under seal was enforceable without proof that there was actually any consideration for the promise. Over time, however, the device of seals ceased to have the significance that it once carried. Often an instrument would be signed without the actual formality of the hot wax, but the document would recite that it was signed "as if under seal." That's presumably what happened in *Schnell v. Nell*. Sometimes the instrument would simply have the letters "L.S." next to the signature line, an abbreviation for the Latin phrase "locus sigilli" or place of the seal. With the decline of the elaborate formal ceremony, the seal lost its practical significance of really calling to someone's attention the fact that they were performing a legally significant act. As a result, the

seal ceased to play as important a role as it once did. In many jurisdictions, there are now statutes eliminating any difference between sealed writings and writings having only ordinary signatures. In some states, however, the statute of limitations is longer for a writing signed under seal than for a writing with only an ordinary signature. For our purposes we can simply assume that placing a seal on a document has no significant legal effect.

4.   The plaintiff in *Schnell v. Nell* made three different consideration arguments:

(1)   that the consideration for Zacharias' promise to pay $200 was the fact that she had expressed her desire that each of the children receive $200.

(2)   that the consideration for Zacharias' promise to pay $200 was that each of the three children paid (or promised to pay) one cent to Zacharias.

(3)   that the consideration for Zacharias' promise to pay $200 was that Teresa had been industrious and the love and affection that he had for his wife Theresa.

Consider carefully exactly why none of those arguments worked. Start with the meaning of the concept of consideration that we can derive from *Hamer v. Sidway*. Using that concept think about whether any of the three arguments above would work to show that there was consideration for Zacharias' promise.

Batsakis v. Demotsis

Court of Civil Appeals of Texas, El Paso, 1949.
226 S.W.2d 673.

■ McGILL, JUSTICE.

This is an appeal from a judgment of the 57th judicial District Court of Bexar County. Appellant was plaintiff and appellee was defendant in the trial court. The parties will be so designated.

Plaintiff sued defendant to recover $2,000 with interest at the rate of 8% per annum from April 2, 1942, alleged to be due on the following instrument, being a translation from the original, which is written in the Greek language:

Peiraeus

April 2, 1942

Mr. George Batsakis

Konstantinou Diadohou #7

Peiraeus

Mr. Batsakis:

I state by my present (letter) that I received today from you the amount of two thousand dollars ($2,000.00) of United States of America money, which I borrowed from you for the support of my family during these difficult days and because it is impossible for me to transfer dollars of my own from America.

The above amount I accept with the expressed promise that I will return to you again in American dollars either at the end of the present war or even before in the event that you might be able to find a way to collect them (dollars) from my representative in America to whom I shall write and give him an order relative to this. You understand until the final execution (payment) to the above amount an eight per cent interest will be added and paid together with the principal.

I thank you and I remain yours with respects.

The recipient,

(Signed) Eugenia The. Demotsis.

Trial to the court without the intervention of a jury resulted in a judgment in favor of plaintiff for $750.00 principal, and interest at the rate of 8% per annum from April 2, 1942 to the date of judgment, totaling $1163.83, with interest thereon at the rate of 8% per annum until paid. Plaintiff has perfected his appeal.

The court sustained certain special exceptions of plaintiff to defendant's first amended original answer on which the case was tried, and struck therefrom paragraphs II, III and V. Defendant excepted to such action of the court, but has not cross-assigned error here. The answer, stripped of such paragraphs, consisted of a general denial contained in paragraph I thereof, and of paragraph IV, which is as follows:

'IV. That under the circumstances alleged in Paragraph II of this answer, the consideration upon which said written instrument sued upon by plaintiff herein is founded, is wanting and has failed to the extent of $1975.00, and defendant pleads specially under the verification hereinafter made the want and failure of consideration stated, and now tenders, as defendant has heretofore tendered to plaintiff, $25.00 as the value of the loan of money received by defendant from plaintiff, together with interest thereon.

'Further, in connection with this plea of want and failure of consideration defendant alleges that she at no time received from plaintiff himself or from anyone for plaintiff any money or thing of value other than, as hereinbefore alleged, the original loan of 500,000 drachmae. That at the time of the loan by plaintiff to defendant of said 500,000 drachmae the value of 500,000 drachmae in the Kingdom of Greece in dollars of money of the United States of America, was $25.00, and also at said time the value of 500,000 drachmae of Greek money in the United States of America in dollars was $25.00 of money of the

United States of America. The plea of want and failure of consideration is verified by defendant as follows.'

The allegations in paragraph II which were stricken, referred to in paragraph IV, were that the instrument sued on was signed and delivered in the Kingdom of Greece on or about April 2, 1942, at which time both plaintiff and defendant were residents of and residing in the Kingdom of Greece, and

> [Defendant] avers that on or about April 2, 1942 she owned money and had credit in the United States of America, but was then and there in the Kingdom of Greece in straitened financial circumstances due to the conditions produced by World War II and could not make use of her money and property and credit existing in the United States of America. That in the circumstances the plaintiff agreed to and did lend to defendant the sum of 500,000 drachmae, which at that time, on or about April 2, 1942, had the value of $25.00 in money of the United States of America. That the said plaintiff, knowing defendant's financial distress and desire to return to the United States of America, exacted of her the written instrument plaintiff sues upon, which was a promise by her to pay to him the sum of $2,000.00 of United States of America money.'

Plaintiff specially excepted to paragraph IV because the allegations thereof were insufficient to allege either want of consideration or failure of consideration, in that it affirmatively appears therefrom that defendant received what was agreed to be delivered to her, and that plaintiff breached no agreement. The court overruled this exception, and such action is assigned as error. Error is also assigned because of the court's failure to enter judgment for the whole unpaid balance of the principal of the instrument with interest as therein provided.

Defendant testified that she did receive 500,000 drachmas from plaintiff. It is not clear whether she received all the 500,000 drachmas or only a portion of them before she signed the instrument in question. Her testimony clearly shows that the understanding of the parties was that plaintiff would give her the 500,000 drachmas if she would sign the instrument. She testified:

> Q. . . . . . who suggested the figure of $2,000.00?
>
> A.   That was how he asked me from the beginning. He said he will give me five hundred thousand drachmas provided I signed that I would pay him $2,000.00 American money.

The transaction amounted to a sale by plaintiff of the 500,000 drachmas in consideration of the execution of the instrument sued on, by defendant. It is not contended that the drachmas had no value. Indeed, the judgment indicates that the trial court placed a value of $750.00 on them or on the other consideration which plaintiff gave defendant for the instrument if he believed plaintiff's testimony. Therefore the plea of want of consideration was unavailing. . . .

Mere inadequacy of consideration will not void a contract. * * *

Nor was the plea of failure of consideration availing. Defendant got exactly what she contracted for according to her own testimony. The court should have rendered judgment in favor of plaintiff against defendant for the principal sum of $2,000.00 evidenced by the instrument sued on, with interest as therein provided. We construe the provision relating to interest as providing for interest at the rate of 8% per annum. The judgment is reformed so as to award appellant a recovery against appellee of $2,000.00 with interest thereon at the rate of 8% per annum from April 2, 1942. . . . As so reformed, the judgment is affirmed.

Reformed and affirmed.

NOTES

1.   The *Batsakis* opinion refers to two concepts "want of consideration" and "failure of consideration." "Want of consideration" is the real issue. All that phrase means is "no consideration." Thus, the defendant's argument was that receipt of the 500,000 drachmae was not consideration for the promise to pay $2000.

The phrase "failure of consideration" is a bit confusing. What it means is that a promise was made in exchange for a promise, but that the return promise was not performed. Suppose, for example, that we have an ordinary real estate sales contract. Seller promises to convey; Buyer promises to pay. The consideration for Seller's promise to convey is Buyer's promise to pay. The consideration for Buyer's promise to pay is Seller's promise to convey. So, each promise is supported by consideration. Now, suppose that something happens so that Seller does not perform the promise to convey. It's pretty obvious that if Seller doesn't convey, then Buyer doesn't have to pay. That's really got nothing to do with consideration. As we will see in Chapter 10, the relevant concept is that each party's duty to perform is constructively conditioned on the other party's performance of its promise.

In older cases, and in sloppy lawyer talk, this fairly simple notion is sometimes expressed by saying that if Seller doesn't convey, then there has been a "failure of consideration" and that is why Buyer is not obligated to pay. That's a confusing way of expressing the point, since it suggests that the issue has something to do with consideration. It doesn't. For that reason, the Restatement is careful to avoid any use of the phrase "failure of consideration." See RESTATEMENT (SECOND) OF CONTRACTS § 237 cmt a.

So, in *Batsakis*, there would be an argument of "failure of consideration" only if Batsakis had not actually paid the 500,000 drachmae that he promised to pay to Demotsis. Apparently Batsakis did pay the 500,000 drachmae, so there's no issue on that score.

2.   Note two different issues:

   (1)   Should it matter whether $2000 was a fair amount to pay in exchange for the 500,000 drachmae?

   (2)   Should that question be addressed under the concept of consideration?

As we will see later, even if a promise is supported by consideration, a court might refuse to enforce the promise if it concludes that doing so would be "unconscionable." See Chapter 11.E.

D. SHOULD A WORTHLESS OR ILLUSORY PROMISE COUNT AS CONSIDERATION?

Newman & Snell's State Bank v. Hunter

Supreme Court of Michigan, 1928.
243 Mich. 331, 220 N.W. 665.

■ FELLOWS, J.

Defendant is the widow of Lee C. Hunter, who died intestate January 25, 1926. His estate was insufficient to pay his funeral expenses and the widow's allowance. At the time of his death, plaintiff bank held his note for $3,700 . . . . The facts were agreed upon on the trial in the court below. We quote from the agreed statement of facts:

   'On March 1, 1926, the defendant gave the plaintiff the note described in the plaintiff's declaration in this cause, and the plaintiff surrendered to her therefor, and, in consideration thereof, the note of said Lee C. Hunter. The defendant also paid the plaintiff the earned interest due on the deceased's note.'

Defendant pleaded want of consideration. [The trial court entered judgment for plaintiff (the bank) and the widow appealed.]

We . . . consider whether the surrender of the note of her deceased husband who left no estate was a sufficient consideration for the note sued upon. Counsel for both parties have furnished able briefs, and their arguments have been helpful. They have doubtless brought to our attention all the cases which would be of assistance to us in reaching a conclusion. While all the authorities cited have been examined, we shall not take up each one of them and discuss them, nor shall we cite them all, nor shall we attempt a reconciliation of the decisions of those states whose own decisions are claimed to be out of accord with each other. There is a definite conflict in the decisions from other states, and it is possible there is a conflict between cases from the same court.

Nowlin v. Wesson, 93 Ala. 509, 8 So. 800, unequivocally sustains the plaintiff's contention. It was there held (quoting the syllabus):

   'The surrender to a widow of a claim against the estate of her deceased husband, treating it as no longer binding on his estate, is a sufficient consideration to support her promissory note for the amount, although the husband's estate is in fact insolvent.'

We likewise quote the syllabus of *Wilton v. Eaton,* 127 Mass. 174:

'The surrender to an administrator of a promissory note made by his intestate, whether the note, at the time of the surrender, is capable or incapable of being enforced at law, is a sufficient consideration for the giving of a new note by the administrator, and he is personally liable thereon; although, when the new note is given, his final account has been allowed, and no new assets have since come into his hands.'

. . .

We now take up some of the cases relied upon by defendant. In *Paxson v. Nields*, 137 Pa. 385, 20 A. 1016, 21 Am. St. Rep. 888, it was held (quoting the syllabus):

'A note given by a widow for the payment of a debt due from her deceased husband's estate, which estate is insolvent, is void in law without a new consideration; and such consideration will not be raised by an agreement on the part of the creditor that the note will be renewed from time to time after maturity.'

We quote from the syllabus in *Ferrell v. Scott,* 2 Speers (S. C.) 344, 42 Am. Dec. 371:

'It is no sufficient consideration to support the promise of the surviving widow of a pauper in a promissory note, given by her shortly after her husband's death, to one of his creditors, that such demand should be discharged against the estate of her husband by virtue of her undertaking to pay it.'

. . .

Here we have the widow's note given to take up the note of her insolvent husband, a worthless piece of paper. When plaintiff surrendered this worthless piece of paper to the defendant, it parted with nothing of value, and defendant received nothing of value, the plaintiff suffered no loss or inconvenience, and defendant received no benefit. The weight of authority sustains defendant's contention, but, going back to fundamentals, it seems clear to me that the transaction was without consideration. It is urged that plaintiff's right as a creditor to administer the estate was valuable, and was waived. Had there been assets or prospective undisclosed assets, there might be some force to this contention. But the agreed statements of facts negative any such situation. Under the agreement of facts, there was not enough in the estate to pay the funeral expenses or the widow's support.

. . . [The appellate court ruled that the bank's complaint should have been dismissed.]

NOTES

Mr. Hunter had borrowed money from the bank and had signed a promissory note promising to repay the loan. Mrs. Hunter was not obligated on that note. The fact that she was married to Mr. Hunter does not, without more, make her liable for his debts. After Mr. Hunter died, Mrs. Hunter promised to pay the bank that amount that Mr. Hunter owed to the bank. The issue in the case is whether there is consideration for Mrs. Hunter's promise to pay the debt of her deceased husband.

Wood v. Lucy, Lady Duff Gordon

Court of Appeals of New York, 1917.
222 N.Y. 88, 118 N.E. 214.

■ CARDOZO, J.

The defendant styles herself 'a creator of fashions.' Her favor helps a sale. Manufacturers of dresses, millinery and like articles are glad to pay for a certificate of her approval. The things which she designs, fabrics, parasols and what not, have a new value in the public mind when issued in her name. She employed the plaintiff to help her to turn this vogue into money. He was to have the exclusive right, subject always to her approval, to place her indorsements on the designs of others. He was also to have the exclusive right to place her own designs on sale, or to license others to market them. In return, she was to have one-half of 'all profits and revenues' derived from any contracts he might make. The exclusive right was to last at least one year from April 1, 1915, and thereafter from year to year unless terminated by notice of ninety days. The plaintiff says that he kept the contract on his part, and that the defendant broke it. She placed her indorsement on fabrics, dresses and millinery without his knowledge, and withheld the profits. He sues her for the damages . . . .

The agreement of employment is signed by both parties. It has a wealth of recitals. The defendant insists, however, that it lacks the elements of a contract. She says that the plaintiff does not bind himself to anything. It is true that he does not promise in so many words that he will use reasonable efforts to place the defendant's indorsements and market her designs. We think, however, that such a promise is fairly to be implied. The law has outgrown its primitive stage of formalism when the precise word was the sovereign talisman, and every slip was fatal. It takes a broader view to-day. A promise may be lacking, and yet the whole writing may be 'instinct with an obligation,' imperfectly expressed * * *. If that is so, there is a contract.

The implication of a promise here finds support in many circumstances. The defendant gave an exclusive privilege. She was to have no right for at least a year to place her own indorsements or market her own designs except through the agency of the plaintiff. The acceptance of the exclusive agency was an assumption of its duties * * *.

We are not to suppose that one party was to be placed at the mercy of the other * * *. Many other terms of the agreement point the same way. We are told at the outset by way of recital that 'the said Otis F. Wood possesses a business organization adapted to the placing of such indorsements as the said Lucy, Lady Duff-Gordon has approved.' The implication is that the plaintiff's business organization will be used for the purpose for which it is adapted. But the terms of the defendant's compensation are even more significant. Her sole compensation for the grant of an exclusive agency is to be one-half of all the profits resulting from the plaintiff's efforts. Unless he gave his efforts, she could never get anything. Without an implied promise, the transaction cannot have such business 'efficacy as both parties must have intended that at all events it should have' * * *. But the contract does not stop there. The plaintiff goes on to promise that he will account monthly for all moneys received by him, and that he will take out all such patents and copyrights and trademarks as may in his judgment be necessary to protect the rights and articles affected by the agreement. It is true, of course, as the Appellate Division has said, that if he was under no duty to try to market designs or to place certificates of indorsement, his promise to account for profits or take out copyrights would be valueless. But in determining the intention of the parties, the promise has a value. It helps to enforce the conclusion that the plaintiff had some duties. His promise to pay the defendant one-half of the profits and revenues resulting from the exclusive agency and to render accounts monthly, was a promise to use reasonable efforts to bring profits and revenues into existence. For this conclusion, the authorities are ample * * *.

The judgment of the [intermediate appellate court] should be reversed, and the order of the [trial court for plaintiff is] affirmed . . . .

E. CONSIDERATION AND SETTLEMENTS

Restatement (Second) of Contracts § 74

Dyer v. National By-Products, Inc.

Supreme Court of Iowa, 1986.
380 N.W. 2d 732.

■ SCHULTZ, JUSTICE.

The determinative issue in this appeal is whether good faith forbearance to litigate a claim, which proves to be invalid and unfounded, is sufficient consideration to uphold a contract of settlement. The district court determined, as a matter of law, that consideration for the alleged settlement was lacking because the forborne claim was not a viable cause of action. We reverse and remand.

On October 29, 1981, Dale Dyer, an employee of National By-Products, lost his right foot in a job-related accident. Thereafter, the employer placed Dyer on a leave of absence at full pay from the date of his injury until August 16, 1982. At that time he returned to work as a foreman, the job he held prior to his injury. On March 11, 1983, the employer indefinitely laid off Dyer.

Dyer then filed the present lawsuit against his employer claiming that his discharge was a breach of an oral contract. He alleged that he in good faith believed that he had a valid claim against his employer for his personal injury. Further, Dyer claimed that his forbearance from litigating his claim was made in exchange for a promise from his employer that he would have lifetime employment. The employer specifically denied that it had offered a lifetime job to Dyer after his injury. . . .

The employer, on the other hand, maintains that workers' compensation[1] benefits are Dyer's sole remedy for his injury and that his claim for damages is unfounded. It then urges that forbearance from asserting an unfounded claim cannot serve as consideration for a contract. For the purpose of this discussion, we shall assume that Dyer's tort action is clearly invalid and he had no basis for a tort suit against either his employer or his fellow employees. We recognize that the fact issue, as to whether Dyer in good faith believed that he had a cause of action based in tort against the employer, remains unresolved. The determinative issue before the district court and now on appeal is whether the lack of consideration for the alleged promise of lifetime employment has been established as a matter of law.

Preliminarily, we observe that the law favors the adjustment and settlement of controversies without resorting to court action. * * * Compromise of a doubtful right asserted in good faith is sufficient consideration for a promise. * * *

The more difficult problem is whether the settlement of an unfounded claim asserted in good faith is consideration for a contract of settlement. Professor Corbin presents a view favorable to Dyer's argument when he states:

> [F]orbearance to press a claim, or a promise of such forbearance, may be a sufficient consideration even though the claim is wholly ill-founded. It may be ill-founded because the facts are not what he supposes them to be, or because the existing facts do not have the legal operation that he supposes them to have. In either case, his forbearance may be a sufficient

---

[1] It is undisputed that the employee was covered under workers' compensation. The Iowa workers' compensation act states in pertinent part that:

"The rights and remedies provided in this chapter . . . for an employee on account of injury . . . for which benefits under this chapter . . . are recoverable, *shall be the exclusive and only rights and remedies of such employee* . . . at common law or otherwise, on account of such injury . . . against:

(1) his or her employer. . . ."

Iowa Code § 85.20 (1983) (emphasis added).

consideration, although under certain circumstances it is not. The fact that the claim is ill-founded is not in itself enough to prevent forbearance from being a sufficient consideration for a promise.

1 *Corbin on Contracts* § 140, at 595 (1963). Further, in the same section, it is noted that:

> The most generally prevailing, and probably the most satisfactory view is that forbearance is sufficient if there is any reasonable ground for the claimant's belief that it is just to try to enforce his claim. He must be asserting his claim "in good faith"; but this does not mean he must believe that his suit can be won. It means that he must not be making his claim or threatening suit for purposes of vexation, or in order to realize on its "nuisance value."

Id. § 140, at 602 (emphasis added). Indeed, we find support for the Corbin view in language contained in our cases. * * *

The Restatement (Second) of Contracts section 74 (1979), supports the Corbin view and states:

Settlement of Claims

> (1) Forbearance to assert or the surrender of a claim or defense which proves to be invalid is not consideration unless

>> (a) the claim or defense is in fact doubtful because of uncertainty as to the facts or the law, or

>> (b) *the forbearing or surrendering party believes that the claim or defense may be fairly determined to be valid.*

> . . .

Comment: . . .

> b. *Requirement of good faith.* The policy favoring compromise of disputed claims is clearest, perhaps, where a claim is surrendered at a time when it is uncertain whether it is valid or not. Even though the invalidity later becomes clear, *the bargain is to be judged as it appeared to the parties at the time*; if the claim was then doubtful, no inquiry is necessary as to their good faith. Even though the invalidity should have been clear at the time, the settlement of an honest dispute is upheld. But a mere assertion or denial of liability does not make a claim doubtful, and *the fact that invalidity is obvious may indicate that it was known.* In such cases Subsection (1)(b) requires a showing of *good faith.* (Emphasis added.) * * *

However, not all jurisdictions adhere to this view. Some courts require that the claim forborne must have some merit in fact or at law before it can provide consideration and these jurisdictions reject those claims that are obviously invalid. * * *

In fact, we find language in our own case law that supports the view which is favorable to the employer in this case. * * *

We believe, however, that the better reasoned approach is that expressed in the Restatement (Second) of Contracts section 74. . . . As noted before, as a matter of policy the law favors compromise and such policy would be defeated if a party could second guess his settlement and litigate the validity of the compromise. The requirement that the forbearing party assert the claim in good faith sufficiently protects the policy of law that favors the settlement of controversies. Our holdings which are to the contrary to this view are overruled.

In the present case, the invalidity of Dyer's claim against the employer does not foreclose him, as a matter of law, from asserting that his forbearance was consideration for the alleged contract of settlement. However, the issue of Dyer's good faith must still be examined. In so doing, the issue of the validity of Dyer's claim should not be entirely overlooked:

> Although the courts will not inquire into the validity of a claim which was compromised in good faith, there must generally be reasonable grounds for a belief in order for the court to be convinced that the belief was honestly entertained by the person who asserted it. Sufficient consideration requires more than the bald ascertion [sic] by a claimant who has a claim, and to the extent that the validity or invalidity of a claim has a bearing upon whether there were reasonable grounds for believing in its possible validity, evidence of the validity or invalidity of a claim may be relevant to the issue of good faith.

15A Am.Jur.2d Compromise and Settlement § 17, at 790. We conclude that the evidence of the invalidity of the claim is relevant to show a lack of honest belief in the validity of the claim asserted or forborne.

Under the present state of the record, there remains a material fact as to whether Dyer's forbearance to assert his claim was in good faith. Summary judgment should not have been rendered against him. Accordingly, the case is reversed and remanded for further proceedings consistent with this opinion.

Reversed and remanded.

NOTES

1.   Using the concept of consideration derived from *Hamer v. Sidway*, was there consideration for National By-Products' promise to pay money to Dyer? Did National By-Products want something? Did National By-Products get what it wanted?

Is the result in *Dyer v. National By-Products* consistent with the general approach to consideration derived from *Hamer v. Sidway*?

2.   Look carefully at how the drafters of the Restatement expressed the result of cases such as *Dyer v. National By-Products*. RESTATEMENT (SECOND) OF CONTRACTS §§ 72 and 74. Note that § 74(1) might be rephrased more or less as follows:

> Forbearance to assert or the surrender of a claim or defense which proves to be invalid is not consideration *(even though that forebearance was bargained for)* **unless**:
>
> (a)   the claim or defense is in fact doubtful because of uncertainty as to the facts or the law, or
>
> (b)   the forbearing or surrendering party believes that the claim or defense may be fairly determined to be valid.

F. CASES WHERE A PROMISE IS ENFORCEABLE EVEN THOUGH THERE REALLY ISN'T ANY "BARGAINED FOR EXCHANGE"

Restatement (Second) of Contracts §§ 82, 83, 85

Suppose that Lender lends $500 to Borrower, and Borrower promises to repay that amount. Years go by, but Lender does not ask for repayment. If enough time has gone by, Lender might find that it has lost the ability to sue Borrower as a result of the running of the statute of limitations. Suppose, for example that the statute of limitations for an action to collect a debt is six years. Borrower borrows the money and makes the promise to repay in 1995. In 2003, the lender realizes that it has not been paid and asks Borrower to repay. Borrower might say "Tough Luck! The statute of limitations has run, so you cannot enforce the promise that I made in 1995." Borrower would be legally correct. Lender's delay in bringing suit would preclude Lender from enforcing the promise.

Suppose, though, that in 2003 the Borrower says "Yes, I realize that I still owe you $500. I just can't afford to pay now, but I promise that I will pay by Dec 31, 2004."

Dec 31, 2004 goes by, but Borrower does not repay. On Jan 15, 2005 Lender sues Borrower for the $500.

If we think of Lender's action as based on the 1995 promise, Lender loses because of the running of the statute of limitations.

If we think of the Lender's action as based on the 2003 promise, there is a consideration problem. Did Borrower receive anything for the promise that Borrower made in 2003? Pretty clearly not. Even if we use the expansive concept of consideration that we can derive from *Hamer v. Sidway*, we'd probably be forced to say that there was no consideration for the 2003 promise. So, if we apply the general rule that a promise is not enforceable unless supported by consideration, we'd have to say that the 2003 promise is not enforceable.

The cases, however, quite uniformly hold that a new promise to pay a debt that has become unenforceable merely because of the running of the statute of limitations is enforceable. Lots of the cases express that point by tortured language about consideration. For example, it is sometimes said that "a moral obligation is sufficient consideration to support an express promise." See *Mills v. Wyman*, 20 Mass. (3 Pick.) (1825). But such statements can't be taken literally. Any coherent moral theory would say that the father in *Schnell v. Nell* should have performed his promise—after all he got the property that his wife thought was going to the children—but the conclusion in that case was that the father's promise was not enforceable because not supported by consideration.

A simpler way of expressing the point is to say that in cases of new promises to pay debts barred by the statute of limitations, the new promise is enforceable even though it is *not* supported by consideration. That's the way the problem is treated in the Restatement. See RESTATEMENT (SECOND) OF CONTRACTS § 82. Note that Section 82 is part of the part of the Restatement entitled "Contracts Without Consideration."

There are several similar special rules. For example, suppose that debtor owes money and files a bankruptcy case. The result of the bankruptcy case is that the debtor is discharged, that is, the creditors can no longer sue for the debts. Suppose that after the bankruptcy case, the debtor makes a new promise to one of the old creditors, saying that he will repay the debt despite the bankruptcy discharge. Suppose, though, that the debtor later changes his mind and refuses to pay. If the creditor sues on the old debt, the debtor can defend on the basis of the bankruptcy discharge. If the creditor sues on the post-bankruptcy promise, the debtor can argue that there was no consideration for the post-bankruptcy promise. As in the case of a new promise to pay a debt that has become unenforceable by virtue of the statute of limitations, the cases pretty uniformly do enforce a new promise to pay a debt discharged in bankruptcy. The Restatement treats that as another example of a promise that is enforceable even though *not* supported by consideration. See RESTATEMENT (SECOND) OF CONTRACTS § 83. Though state cases in the early and mid-twentieth century generally would enforce promises to pay debts discharged in bankruptcy contract law, the Federal bankruptcy statute adopted in 1986 imposes significant limits on the enforceability of such reaffirmation agreements. 15 U.S.C. § 524(c).

Another example. Suppose that when Betty is only fourteen years old, Clara (who is 35 years old) sells Betty a collection of Pokémon cards in exchange for Betty's promise to pay $500 for the cards. If Betty fails to pay and Clara sues her, Betty will have a complete defense of "infancy," that is, no promise she makes before she reaches the legal age of maturity can be enforced against her. Suppose that in the relevant jurisdiction the age of majority is eighteen, and, after her eighteenth birthday, Betty makes a new promise to Clara to pay her the $500 for the cards. Then,

Betty changes her mind and refuses to pay. If Clara sues on the promise Betty made when she was fourteen, Betty can defend on grounds of infancy. If Clara sues on the promise that Betty made after her eighteenth birthday, Betty could argue that there was no consideration for her promise. That argument would be sound under the general concept of consideration we have been working with, but, as in the previous examples, the cases pretty uniformly do enforce a new promise to pay a debt that was previously unenforceable because of infancy. The Restatement treats that as another example of a promise that is enforceable even though *not* supported by consideration. See RESTATEMENT (SECOND) OF CONTRACTS § 85.

There is a somewhat related special rule illustrated by two old Contracts casebook classics: *Mills v. Wyman*, 20 Mass. (3 Pick.) (1825) and *Webb v. McGowin*, 168 So. 196 (Ala. Civ. App. 1935). In *Mills* a twenty-five year old man became sick. Mills ran a boarding home and took care of him until he passed away. After Mills had provided the care, the man's father wrote a letter promising to pay for the care provided to the son. The father, though, apparently changed his mind and refused to pay. Mills brought suit against the father. The court held that the father's promise was not enforceable because not supported by consideration. If the father had made the promise *before* the care was provided, then we'd have an easy case: Mills would have done what the father wanted Mills to do, so the father's promise would have been enforceable. But, the father made the promise *after* the care had been provided. So, if we view the case through the lens of the consideration concept derived from *Hamer v. Sidway*, we'd have to say that the promise was not supported by consideration. That was the result in the case itself.

Webb v. McGowin involved a legally analogous situation, but reached the opposite result. An employee working in a lumber mill saw that a block of wood was about to fall on the owner of the mill and jumped in to push the block away. His action saved the owner from harm, but the employee suffered serious injuries that prevented him from working. In gratitude, the owner promised to pay the employee a modest monthly amount. The owner did so until he died, but then the executors of his estate refused to make any further payments. The employee sued to enforce the promise. Under a strict application of consideration concepts, one would have to say that there was no consideration for the promise. As in *Mills v. Wyman*, one can't say that the owner made the promise because he wanted the employee to do something. The employee acted before there was any promise, and the owner promised to pay him in gratitude for something the employee had already done. But, the court enforced the promise in *Webb v. McGowin*, in an opinion notable for its lack of clarity. There are relatively few other cases applying the approach taken in *Webb*, but the principal of the case is stated in the Restatement. See RESTATEMENT (SECOND) OF CONTRACTS § 86.

The problems discussed above are often described under the heading of "past consideration." That's a somewhat misleading phrase. The point is that under our general concept of consideration, a promise made in exchange for something that was received in the past cannot be regarded as supported by consideration. We can't say that the promise was made because the promisor wanted something in exchange for the promise. The promisor had already received something in the past. In gratitude, the promisor made the promise, but we can't say that the promise was made in order to get something. In this universe, time flows only in one direction. Nonetheless, in these situations the cases have ruled that promise is enforceable, even though it was made in exchange for something received in the past. As the Restatement puts it, these are cases where promises are enforceable even though the promise is not supported by consideration.

We'll now look at another situation in which a promise may be enforced, even though it would be hard to say that it was supported by consideration, in the sense of bargained-for exchange.

Restatement (Second) of Contracts § 89

Angel v. Murray
Supreme Court of Rhode Island, 1974.
113 R.I. 482, 322 A.2d 630.

■ ROBERTS, CHIEF JUSTICE.

[The case was brought under a statute permitting taxpayers to sue asserting that the City was not legally obligated to pay certain money. The named defendants were John E. Murray, Jr., Director of Finance of the City of Newport, the city of Newport, and James L. Maher. The complaint alleges] that Maher had illegally been paid the sum of $20,000 by the Director of Finance and pray[s] that the defendant Maher be ordered to repay the city such sum. The case was heard by a justice of the Superior Court, sitting without a jury, who entered a judgment ordering Maher to repay the sum of $20,000 to the city of Newport. Maher is now before this court prosecuting an appeal.

The record discloses that Maher has provided the city of Newport with a refuse-collection service under a series of five-year contracts beginning in 1946. On March 12, 1964, Maher and the city entered into another such contract for a period of five years commencing on July 1, 1964, and terminating on June 30, 1969. The contract provided, among other things, that Maher would receive $137,000 per year in return for collecting and removing all combustible and noncombustible waste materials generated within the city.

In June of 1967 Maher requested an additional $10,000 per year from the city council because there had been a substantial increase in the cost of collection due to an unexpected and unanticipated increase of 400 new dwelling units. Maher's testimony, which is uncontradicted, indicates the 1964 contract had been predicated on the fact that since 1946 there had been an average increase of 20 to 25 new dwelling units per year. After a public meeting of the city council where Maher explained in detail the reasons for his request and was questioned by members of the city council, the city council agreed to pay him an additional $10,000 for the year ending on June 30, 1968. Maher made a similar request again in June of 1968 for the same reasons, and the city council again agreed to pay an additional $10,000 for the year ending on June 30, 1969.

The trial justice found that each such $10,000 payment was made in violation of law. . . . [H]e found that Maher was not entitled to extra compensation because the original contract already required him to collect all refuse generated within the city and, therefore, included the 400 additional units. The trial justice further found that these 400 additional units were within the contemplation of the parties when they entered into the contract. It appears that he based this portion of the decision upon the rule that Maher had a preexisting duty to collect the refuse generated by the 400 additional units, and thus there was no consideration for the two additional payments.

. . .

Rose is a perfect example of the preexisting duty rule. Under this rule an agreement modifying a contract is not supported by consideration if one of the parties to the agreement does or promises to do something that he is legally obligated to do or refrains or promises to refrain from doing something he is not legally privileged to do. * * * In *Rose* there was no consideration for the new agreement because the debtor was already legally obligated to repay the full amount of the debt.

. . .

The primary purpose of the preexisting duty rule is to prevent what has been referred to as the 'hold-up game.' See 1A Corbin, supra, § 171. A classic example of the 'hold-up game' is found in *Alaska Packers' Ass'n v. Domenico*, 117 F. 99 (9th Cir. 1902). There 21 seamen entered into a written contract with Domenico to sail from San Francisco to Pyramid Harbor, Alaska. They were to work as sailors and fishermen out of Pyramid Harbor during the fishing season of 1900. The contract specified that each man would be paid $50 plus two cents for each red salmon he caught. Subsequent to their arrival at Pyramid Harbor, the men stopped work and demanded an additional $50. They threatened to return to San Francisco if Domenico did not agree to their demand. Since it was impossible for Domenico to find other men, he agreed to pay the men an additional $50. After they returned to San Francisco, Domenico refused to pay the men an additional $50. The court found that the subsequent agreement to pay the men an additional $50 was not supported by consideration because the men had a preexisting duty to work on the ship under the original contract, and thus the subsequent agreement was unenforceable.

Another example of the 'hold-up game' is found in the area of construction contracts. Frequently, a contractor will refuse to complete work under an unprofitable contract unless he is awarded additional compensation. The courts have generally held that a subsequent agreement to award additional compensation is unenforceable if the contractor is only performing work which would have been required of him under the original contract. See, e.g., *Lingenfelder v. Wainwright Brewing Co.*, 103 Mo. 578, 15 S.W. 844 (1891), which is a leading case in this area. * * *

These examples clearly illustrate that the courts will not enforce an agreement that has been procured by coercion or duress and will hold the parties to their original contract regardless of whether it is profitable or unprofitable. However, the courts have been reluctant to apply the preexisting duty rule when a party to a contract encounters unanticipated difficulties and the other party, not influenced by coercion or duress, voluntarily agrees to pay additional compensation for work already required to be performed under the contract. . . .

Although the preexisting duty rule has served a useful purpose insofar as it deters parties from using coercion and duress to obtain additional compensation, it has been widely criticized as a general rule of law. With regard to the preexisting duty rule, one legal scholar has stated:

> 'There has been a growing doubt as to the soundness of this doctrine as a matter of social policy. . . . In certain classes of cases, this doubt has influenced courts to refuse to apply the rule, or to ignore it, in their actual decisions. Like other legal rules, this rule is in process of growth and change, the process being more active here than in most instances. The result of this is that a court should no longer accept this rule as fully established. It should never use it as the major premise of a decision, at least without giving careful thought to the circumstances of the particular case, to the moral deserts of the parties, and to the social feelings and interests that are involved. It is certain that the rule, stated in general and all-inclusive terms, is no longer so well-settled that a court must apply it though the heavens fall.'

1A Corbin, supra, § 171; see also Calamari & Perillo, supra, § 61.

The modern trend appears to recognize the necessity that courts should enforce agreements modifying contracts when unexpected or unanticipated difficulties arise during the course of the performance of a contract, even though there is no consideration for the modification, as long as the parties agree voluntarily.

Under the Uniform Commercial Code, § 2–209(1), which has been adopted by 49 states, '(a)n agreement modifying a contract (for the sale of goods) needs no consideration to be binding.' * * * Although at first blush this section appears to validate modifications obtained by coercion and duress, the comments to this section indicate that a modification under this section must meet the test of good faith imposed by the Code, and a modification obtained by extortion without a legitimate commercial reason is unenforceable.

The modern trend away from a rigid application of the preexisting duty rule is reflected by § 89 of the American Law Institute's Restatement Second of the Law of Contracts, which provides: 'A promise modifying a duty under a contract not fully performed on either side is binding (a) if the modification is fair and equitable in view of circumstances not anticipated by the parties when the contract was made . . . .'

We believe that § 89 is the proper rule of law and find it applicable to the facts of this case. It not only prohibits modifications obtained by coercion, duress, or extortion but also fulfills society's expectation that agreements entered into voluntarily will be enforced by the courts. * * * Section 89, of course, does not compel a modification of an unprofitable or unfair contract; it only enforces a modification if the parties voluntarily agree and if (1) the promise modifying the original contract was made before the contract was fully performed on either side, (2) the underlying circumstances which prompted the modification were unanticipated by the parties, and (3) the modification is fair and equitable. . . .

The evidence, which is uncontradicted, reveals that in June of 1968 Maher requested the city council to pay him an additional $10,000 for the year beginning on July 1, 1968, and ending on June 30, 1969. This request was made at a public meeting of the city council, where Maher explained in detail his reasons for making the request. Thereafter, the city council voted to authorize the Mayor to sign an amendment to the 1964 contract which provided that Maher would receive an additional $10,000 per year for the duration of the contract. Under such circumstances we have no doubt that the city voluntarily agreed to modify the 1964 contract.

Having determined the voluntariness of this agreement, we turn our attention to the three criteria delineated above. First, the modification was made in June of 1968 at a time when the five-year contract which was made in 1964 had not been fully performed by either party. Second, although the 1964 contract provided that Maher collect all refuse generated within the city, it appears this contract was premised on Maher's past experience that the number of refuse-generating units would increase at a rate of 20 to 25 per year. Furthermore, the evidence is uncontradicted that the 1967–1968 increase of 400 units 'went beyond any previous expectation.' Clearly, the circumstances which prompted the city council to modify the 1964 contract were unanticipated. Third, although the evidence does not indicate what proportion of the total this increase comprised, the evidence does indicate that it was a 'substantial' increase. In light of this, we cannot say that the council's agreement to pay Maher the $10,000 increase was not fair and equitable in the circumstances.

The judgment appealed from is reversed, and the cause is remanded to the Superior Court for entry of judgment for the defendants.

G. CONSIDERATION AND OPTION CONTRACTS

Restatement (Second) of Contracts § 87(1)

U.C.C. § 2–205

The concept of an "option contract" can be a little tricky. Suppose that Developer is interested in building a shopping center in an area that is currently divided into 10 parcels of land, each owned by a different person. The deal will not be feasible unless Developer can reach agreement with each of the 10 owners to buy their land. It would not make sense for Developer to sign a sales contract with any of the 10 owners until Developer can reach agreement will all of them, since Developer does not want to be stuck having to buy some of the parcels if Developer can't buy all of them.

Developer can solve the problem by negotiating for "options" with the owners, one by one. Suppose Developer and Owner 1 reach agreement that $1,250,000 is a fair price for Owner 1's land, if it turns out that Developer does want to buy it. They can sign an "option contract" giving Developer the right to buy the property for $1,250,000 at any time within, say, the next four months, but not imposing on Developer the duty to buy the property. When asked to grant such an option, Owner 1 would realize that she is giving up something of value—the right to sell to others—and is incurring the obligation to sell the property for the agreed price if Developer decides to exercise the option. Owner 1 may not be willing to incur that obligation without getting something in return. So, Owner 1 might say, I will grant the option only in exchange for your payment to me of $10,000. Developer agrees, and pays the $10,000 for the option.

Note that the option combines two different deals.

(1)   In exchange for $10,000, Developer has obtained the right, but not the duty, to buy the land for the agreed price.

(2)   If Developer does decide to buy the land ("exercise the option") Developer can do so, paying $1,250,000 in exchange for the land.

If Developer decides not to buy the land, Developer will have lost the $10,000 paid for the option, but that was the price of getting the right, but not duty, to buy the land. Developer thought it was worthwhile to pay that amount to get things lined up on that parcel, so that Developer could move on to negotiating with the other nine owners. If Developer decides to exercise the option, Developer will pay the agreed $1,250,000 price for the land, in addition to the $10,000 paid for the option.

Now, let's take that business arrangement and apply the concepts of contract law to it. It would not make any sense for the parties to enter into an ordinary sales contract at the beginning. If they did so, Developer would get the right to buy the land, but would also have the duty to do so.

How about having Owner 1 make an offer to sell the land for $1,250,000, and give Developer four months to decide whether to accept or not. Sounds good, but there is a problem. Under ordinary offer and acceptance principles, an offer can be revoked at any time before acceptance. That's no good for Developer, because Developer wants to get to right to buy the land from Owner.

Suppose Owner says:

> "I offer to sell the land for $1,250,000. This offer will be irrevocable for a period of four months."

Sounds good, but what does "irrevocable" mean? Presumably it means "I promise not to revoke this offer for a period of four months." OK, but is that promise *legally enforceable*? Remember our basic consideration concept. In *Dougherty v. Salt*, Aunt Hellena promised to pay Charley $3000. In *Schnell v. Nell,* Zacharias promised to pay $200 to each of the three children. The promises were not enforceable in either case because they were not supported by consideration. So even though Owner promised not to revoke the offer, Developer would not be safe in relying on that promise, unless that promise is supported by consideration.

But, remember our business deal. Owner 1 was not willing to commit to sell for $1,250,000 unless Developer paid $10,000 as the price of that commitment. So, we have two contractual arrangements:

(1)   Owner offers to sell the land for $1,250,000. Developer does not then actually accept that offer. But, Owner promises not to revoke that offer. In exchange, for Owner's promise not to revoke, Developer pays Owner $10,000.

(2)   If Developer does decide to "exercise the option," Developer will accept Owner's offer to sell for $1,250,000. At that point Owner will be contractually obligated to convey the land, and Developer will be contractually obligated to pay $1,250,000.

The messy legal issue is how rigorously the concept of consideration should be applied in the setting of options—that is, promises not to revoke. Suppose that in our hypo, Owner 1 had been trying to sell the land for some time, without any success. Then, Owner 1 came up with the shopping center idea. Owner 1 had no experience developing shopping centers and went to Developer to try to persuade Developer to pursue the project. Developer had some interest, but was concerned about the cost of lining up all of the options that it would need with the other nine owners. Owner 1 really wanted Developer to pursue the project. Accordingly, Owner 1 said "In exchange for $10, I'll grant you an option to buy to my land for $1,250,000." If Developer agrees, would Owner 1's promise be enforceable? Would it be supported by consideration? What about *Hamer v. Sidway*? The following two cases explore that problem. Note that both are Michigan decisions. *Sulzberger* says that the option is enforceable. *Burgess* says that the option is not enforceable. Note that *Burgess* even cites *Sulzberger*. Are you convinced by *Burgess* court's explanation of the different outcomes?

Sulzberger v. Steinhauer

Supreme Court of Michigan, 1926.
235 Mich. 253, 209 N.W. 68.

■ WIEST, J.

Defendants appealed from a decree granting plaintiff specific performance of the following option agreement: 'Detroit, Michigan, October 10, 1924. 'In consideration of the sum of one ($1.00) dollar and other valuable considerations to us in hand paid, the receipt of which is hereby acknowledged, we hereby agree to sell, within 90 days from the date hereof, the property located as follows, to wit: About 20 acres on the S. E. corner of Telegraph road and Wick road in Taylor township (excepting a strip with house thereon bounded by the southerly boundary of said 20 acres, by Telegraph road on the west, by a line at right angles to Telegraph road and running north of present well, and extending 200 feet in depth)—to M. B. Sulzberger or his assigns, for the sum of $1,500 per acre, terms of sale to be as follows: $1 herewith paid, $200 within 90 days above specified, and the balance of $1,800 to be paid when the sale is closed, and the balance of money on or before ten years, with interest on unpaid balance at 6 per cent. per annum, from closing, payable semiannually. 'The sellers agree to join in the plat of the above-described property, and shall release out and give free and clear deed to such lots as purchasers designate upon a payment of $300 for each lot so released, and such sums shall be applied to next payment due. The sale shall be closed within sixty (60) days after the delivery to purchaser of a Burton or Union Trust Company abstract written to date of closing, showing a good and merchantable title in the sellers free and clear of all liens and incumbrances. * * * It is understood that J. Dodatko and M. B. Sulzberger are acting as brokers, and are to receive commission on the purchase price of said land only over and above $1,500 per acre above specified.'

At the time this agreement was signed by defendants, the $1 specified was tendered them, and Mr. Steinhauer stated he did not want it. Three days later Mr. Steinhauer wrote plaintiff that he wanted to reserve an acre of land, instead of the parcel designated in the option. In response to the letter, plaintiff visited defendants and indorsed upon their copy of the option his consent to the requested modification, and described by metes and bounds the acre reserved.

December 30, 1924, plaintiff gave defendants his check for $200. January 2, 1925, defendants returned the check in a letter, stating they had decided not to sell the farm. Plaintiff then visited defendants and placed $200 in money on the lap of Mr. Steinhauer. January 6, 1925, defendants, by money orders, returned the $200, with a request not to be molested any more. Thereupon plaintiff filed the bill herein and made profert of performance.

We find no fraudulent misrepresentations. Defendants knew the option gave plaintiff the right to purchase the premises on the terms fixed, or, if sold by plaintiff within 90 days, he would be entitled to all above $1,500 per acre as his commission. The modification of the option fixing the reserved parcel as an acre of land did not annul the option, or release defendants from performance, except as to the one-acre parcel.

Three days after signing the option, defendants wrote plaintiff, stating: 'I did not get satisfied. I want to keep one full acre of land, and then I will be satisfied. * * * Mr. Sulzberger, if you will not let me keep that one acre, then I will be against you. If people come here and ask me what I'm selling the land for, I will tell them for $1,500 the acre. Then you won't get any commission that way. But if you will be good, and let me keep my one acre now, then I will help you all I can, and, if you did not sell it in 90 days, then I will give you longer time to sell it.'

Responding to this desire of defendants, the plaintiff indorsed the wished reservation on the duplicate copy of the option possessed by defendants.

The option was accompanied by a listing for sale on commission. Under the option, plaintiff had a right to accept the terms specified, and purchase under land contract. Under the listing, plaintiff had a right to find a purchaser, and have for his services all above $1,500 per acre. It was not necessary for plaintiff to sign the option.

There is no merit in the point that the consideration was inadequate. Consideration for an option may be nominal. The consideration for the sale, in the event of acceptance, is entirely apart from the consideration for the option, and such consideration must be specified. It was specified, was certain in amount at $1,500 per acre of land, and such price was adequate.

We think the tender of $1, together with recital of its payment, stated in the option over the signatures of defendants, estops them from disputing such payment for the purpose of destroying the effect and operation of their option. * * *

We also think the description of the land and its location sufficiently definite to meet requirements of the law. Surely no man with the option in hand would have the least difficulty in going straightway to the premises and recognizing the same without any other aid. This is all the law requires, and it is useless refinement to suppose the existence of another township of Taylor, either in or out of the state; for, if actually found, there would not also be found therein 20 acres of land at the southeast corner of the Wick and Telegraph roads, owned by defendants.

Decree affirmed, with costs to plaintiff.

Board of Control of Eastern Michigan University v. Burgess

Court of Appeals of Michigan, Division No. 2, 1973.
45 Mich.App. 183, 206 N.W.2d 256.

■ R. B. BURNS, JUDGE.

On February 15, 1966, defendant signed a document which purported to grant to plaintiff a 60-day option to purchase defendant's home. That document, which was drafted by plaintiff's agent, acknowledged receipt by defendant of 'One and no/100 ($1.00) Dollar and other valuable consideration.' Plaintiff concedes that neither the one dollar nor any other consideration was ever paid or even tendered to defendant. On April 14, 1966, plaintiff delivered to defendant written notice of its intention to exercise the option. On the closing date defendant rejected plaintiff's tender of the purchase price. Thereupon, plaintiff commenced this action for specific performance.

At trial defendant claimed that the purported option was void for want of consideration, that any underlying offer by defendant had been revoked prior to acceptance by plaintiff . . . . The trial judge . . . held that defendant's acknowledgment of receipt of consideration bars any subsequent contention to the contrary. Accordingly, the trial judge entered judgment for plaintiff.

Defendant appeals. She claims that acknowledgment of receipt of consideration does not bar the defense of failure of consideration. She further claims that the trial judge's findings of fact as to the absence of fraud and material mistake are in error, and that the record supports a finding that defendant was the victim of plaintiff's coercion.

Options for the purchase of land, if based on valid consideration, are contracts which may be specifically enforced. * * * Conversely, that which purports to be an option, but which is not based on valid consideration, is not a contract and will not be enforced. * * * One dollar is valid consideration for an option to purchase land, provided the dollar is paid or at least tendered. * * * Sulzberger v. Steinhauer, 235 Mich. 253, 257, 209 N.W. 68 (1926). In the instant case defendant received no consideration for the purported option of February 15, 1966.

A written acknowledgment of receipt of consideration merely creates a rebuttable presumption that consideration has, in fact, passed. Neither the parol evidence rule nor the doctrine of estoppel bars the presentation of evidence to contradict any such acknowledgment. * * *

It is our opinion that the document signed by defendant on February 15, 1966, is not an enforceable option, and that defendant is not barred from so asserting.

The trial court premised its holding to the contrary on Lawrence v. McCalmont, 43 U.S. (2 How.) 426, 452, 11 L.Ed. 326, 336 (1844). That case is significantly distinguishable from the instant case. Mr. Justice Story held that '(t)he guarantor acknowledged the receipt of one dollar, and is now estopped to deny it.' However, in reliance upon the guaranty substantial credit had been extended to the guarantor's sons. The guarantor had received everything she bargained for, save one dollar. Cf. Fischer v. Union Trust Co., 138 Mich. 612, 616, 101 N.W. 852 (1904). In the instant case defendant claims that she never received any of the consideration promised her.

That which purports to be an option for the purchase of land, but which is not based on valid consideration, is a simple offer to sell the same land. * * * An option is a contract collateral to an offer to sell whereby the offer is made irrevocable for a specified period. * * * Ordinarily, an offer is revocable at the will of the offeror. Accordingly, a failure of consideration affects only the collateral contract to keep the offer open, not the underlying offer.

A simple offer may be revoked for any reason or for no reason by the offeror at any time prior to its acceptance by the offeree. * * * Thus, the question in this case becomes, 'Did defendant effectively revoke her offer to sell before plaintiff accepted that offer?'

. . .

Defendant testified that within hours of signing the purported option she telephoned plaintiff's agent and informed him that she would not abide by the option unless the purchase price was increased. Defendant also testified that when plaintiff's agent delivered to her on April 14, 1966, plaintiff's notice of its intention to exercise the purported option, she told him that 'the option was off'.

Plaintiff's agent testified that defendant did not communicate to him any dissatisfaction until sometime in July, 1966.

If defendant is telling the truth, she effectively revoked her offer several weeks before plaintiff accepted that offer, and no contract of sale was created. If plaintiff's agent is telling the truth, defendant's offer was still open when plaintiff accepted that offer, and an enforceable contract was created. The trial judge thought it unnecessary to resolve this particular dispute. In light of our holding the dispute must be resolved.

An appellate court cannot assess the credibility of witnesses. We have neither seen nor heard them testify. * * * Accordingly, we remand this case to the trial court for additional findings of fact based on the record already before the court.

NOTES

Taken literally, the difference between the *Sulzberger* case and the *Eastern Michigan University* case seems to be only that the $1 was at least tendered in *Sulzberger*, but was neither paid nor tendered in *Eastern Michigan University*. One is reminded of Dickens's remark in Oliver Twist that "If the law supposes that . . . the law is an ass—an idiot." There must be something else going on. Consider how the Restatement addresses the issue:

Restatement (Second) of Contracts § 87

Chapter 4.   Formation of Contracts—Consideration

Topic 2.   Contracts Without Consideration

Section 87. Option Contract

(1)   An offer is binding as an option contract if it

(a)   is in writing and signed by the offeror, recites a purported consideration for the making of the offer, and proposes an exchange on fair terms within a reasonable time; or

. . .

Comment:

a.   *Consideration and form.* The traditional common-law devices for making a firm offer or option contract are the giving of consideration and the affixing of a seal. See §§ 25, 95. But the firm offer serves a useful purpose even though no preliminary bargain is made: it is often a necessary step in the making of the main bargain proposed, and it partakes of the natural formalities inherent in business transactions. The erosion of the formality of the seal has made it less and less satisfactory as a universal formality. As literacy has spread, the personal signature has become the natural formality and the seal has become more and more anachronistic. The rules stated in this section reflect the judicial and legislative response to this situation. . . .

b.   *Nominal consideration.* Offers made in consideration of one dollar paid or promised are often irrevocable under Subsection (1)(a). The irrevocability of an offer may be worth much or little to the offeree, and the courts do not ordinarily inquire into the adequacy of the consideration bargained for. See § 79. Hence a comparatively small payment may furnish consideration for the irrevocability of an offer proposing a transaction involving much larger sums. But gross disproportion between the payment and the value of the option commonly indicates that the payment was not in fact bargained for but was a mere formality or pretense. In such a case there is no consideration as that term is defined in § 71.

Nevertheless, such a nominal consideration is regularly held sufficient to support a short-time option proposing an exchange on fair terms. The fact that the option is an appropriate preliminary step in the conclusion of a socially useful transaction provides a sufficient substantive basis for enforcement, and a signed writing taking a form appropriate to a bargain satisfies the desiderata of form. In the absence of statute, however, the bargaining form is essential: a payment of one dollar by each party to the other is so obviously not a bargaining transaction that it does not provide even the form of an exchange.

Illustrations:

1.   In consideration of twenty-five cents paid by B, A executes and delivers to B a written option agreement giving B the right to buy a piece of land for $100,000 if B gives notice of intention to buy within 120 days. The price and terms of sale are fair. A has made an irrevocable offer.

2.   In consideration of one dollar paid by B, A, a widow who owns land worth $25,000 as a farm, gives B a ten-year option to take phosphate rock from the land on paying a royalty of twenty-five cents per ton. As B knows but A does not, the prevailing royalty in such transactions ranges from $1.00 to $1.10 per ton. The offer is not made irrevocable by the one-dollar payment.

c.   *False recital of nominal consideration.* A recital in a written agreement that a stated consideration has been given is evidence of that fact as against a party to the agreement, but such a recital may ordinarily be contradicted by evidence that no such consideration was given or expected. See § 218. In cases within Subsection (1)(a), however, the giving and recital of nominal consideration performs a formal function only. The signed writing has vital significance as a formality, while the ceremonial manual delivery of a dollar or a peppercorn is an inconsequential formality. In view of the dangers of permitting a solemn written agreement to be invalidated by oral testimony which is easily fabricated, therefore, the option agreement is not invalidated by proof that the recited consideration was not in fact given. A fictitious rationalization has sometimes been used for this rule: acceptance of delivery of the written instrument conclusively imports a promise to make good the recital, it is said, and that promise furnishes consideration. Compare § 218. But the sound basis for the rule is that stated above.

Illustration:

3.   A executes and delivers to B a written agreement "in consideration of one dollar in hand paid" giving B an option to buy described land belonging to A for $15,000, the option to expire at noon six days later. The fact that the dollar is not in fact paid does not prevent the offer from being irrevocable.

PROBLEM A

Salma owns a rather unusual home in Massachusetts. In June, Salma learned that she was to be transferred to Los Angeles the following December. Salma listed her home for sale at an asking price of $775,000, but no interested buyers appeared through the summer. In late September, Barney looked at the house and expressed some interest. On Oct 1, Salma and Barney made arrangements as described in the following hypos. In each case, analyze whether Salma is contractually obligated to sell the house to Barney for $700,000.

Hypo 1

Oct 1   Salma notifies Barney in writing that she is willing to sell the house to Barney for $700,000 and that Barney may signify his assent by notifying her in writing.

Oct 5   Salma learns that she is not going to be transferred to L.A. after all. She immediately notifies Barney in writing that she will not be able to sell her house.

Oct 6   Barney notifies Salma in writing that he assents to the proposal in her 1 Oct letter, and will expect Salma to convey the house to him for $700,000.

Hypo 2

Oct 1   Barney and Salma sign an agreement providing that in return for $7500 paid by Barney to Salma, Salma agrees that Barney will have the option to purchase the house from Salma for $700,000. The option is to expire on 1 Nov. Barney pays Salma the $7500.

Oct 5   Salma learns that she is not going to be transferred to L.A. after all. She immediately notifies Barney in writing that she will not be able to sell her house, and says that she is willing to return Barney's $7500.

Oct 6   Barney notifies Salma in writing that he is exercising his option and will expect Salma to convey the house to him for $700,000.

Hypo 3

Same facts as in Hypo 2, except that the Oct 1 agreement provides for a payment by Barney to Salma of $1.00 rather than $7500.

PROBLEM B

Our firm represents Ben.

On 1 Oct, Ben and Sally signed an agreement providing that in return for $2500 paid by Ben to Sally, Sally agreed that Ben would have the option to purchase certain described real estate from Sally for $300,000. The option was to expire on 1 Nov. Ben paid Sally the $2500.

On 5 Oct, Sally learned that the market value of the real estate is actually at least $450,000. Sally told Ben, "Sorry I won't sell to you for $300,000; I'll return your $2500."

On 6 Oct, Ben notified Sally that he would exercise the option to buy for $300,000; Sally refused.

One of the other associates in the firm was handling the matter for Ben. Our firm has filed suit against Sally seeking specific performance, and has moved for summary judgment in favor of Ben. That motion is coming up for a hearing next week. The lawyer who was handling the case was recently injured in an auto accident, so the partner has asked you to look over the matter. You have gotten the file, and found in the file a hand-written note from the associate who had been handling the case saying:

"Ooops!! Restatement 87(1)—fair exchange??—testimony??"

Partner wants your advice on Ben's prospects of success in the summary judgment motion.

Note that the issue is whether buyer can prevail *in a motion for summary judgment.* You have probably only briefly touched on summary judgment in your civil procedure class. You'll study it in detail later in that class. The relevant portion of the Federal Rules of Civil Procedure reads as follows:

> Rule 56. Summary Judgment
>
> (a) MOTION FOR SUMMARY JUDGMENT OR PARTIAL SUMMARY JUDGMENT. A party may move for summary judgment, identifying each claim or defense—or the part of each claim or defense—on which summary judgment is sought. The court shall grant summary judgment if the movant shows that *there is no genuine dispute as to any material fact* and the movant is entitled to judgment as a matter of law. (emphasis added).

Summary judgment is a way of disposing of a case without any trial. A party cannot win a summary judgment motion if resolution of the case would require determination of disputed factual issues. Summary judgment is appropriate only if the moving party can say "Even if the facts are as my opponent contends, I still win." It's quite common for parties to conclude that if they can win on summary judgment, then it is worth bringing a lawsuit. On the other hand, if summary judgment would not be available, then the expenses of a full trial may be so large that it's not worth bothering with the lawsuit. In other words, the big difference is not "will I ultimately win?" but "can I win without trial."

So, you have to consider whether it's necessary to resolve fact issues. One could imagine folks arguing about whether $300,000 is or is not a "fair exchange" for property said to be worth $450,000. But, if one has to resolve that factual question, then the buyer cannot win on summary judgment; rather, we'd need a trial.

CHAPTER FIVE

PROMISSORY ESTOPPEL

But you promised . . .

A. INTRODUCTION—HISTORICAL DEVELOPMENT OF PROMISSORY ESTOPPEL

Restatement (Second) of Contracts § 90(1)

The principle stated in Section 90(1) of the Restatement 2d was regarded as a novel break with classical contract doctrine when it was first proposed in the first Restatement in the 1920s. Our first task in understanding the concept is to look at some old cases that can be regarded as precursors of the concept. Of course, in these cases the courts do not talk explicitly about promissory estoppel or Restatement 2d § 90, for the simple reason that these cases predate Restatement 2d § 90 or the legal profession's development of the concept of "promissory estoppel."

Devecmon v. Shaw

Court of Appeals of Maryland, 1888.
69 Md. 199, 14 A. 464.

■ BRYAN, J

John Semmes Devecmon brought suit against the executors of John S. Combs, deceased. He declared on the common counts, and also filed a bill of particulars. After judgment by default, a jury was sworn to assess the damages sustained by the plaintiff. The evidence consisted of . . . testimony that the plaintiff was a nephew of the deceased, and lived for several years in his family, and was in his service as clerk for several years. The plaintiff then made an offer of testimony which is thus stated in the bill of exceptions:

> "That the plaintiff took a trip to Europe in 1878, and that said trip was taken by said plaintiff, and the money spent on said trip was spent by the said plaintiff, at the instance and request of said Combs, and upon a promise from him that he would reimburse and repay to the plaintiff all money expended by him in said trip; and that the trip was so taken, and the money so expended, by the said plaintiff, but that the said trip had no connection with the business of said Combs; and that said Combs spoke to the witness of his conduct, in being thus willing to pay his nephew's expenses, as liberal and generous on his part."

On objection the court refused to permit the evidence to be given, and the plaintiff excepted.

It might very well be, and probably was the case, that the plaintiff would not have taken a trip to Europe at his own expense. But, whether this be so or not, the testimony would have tended to show that the plaintiff incurred expense at the instance and request of the deceased, and upon an express promise by him that he would repay the money spent. It was a burden incurred at the request of the other party, and was certainly a sufficient consideration for a promise to pay. Great injury might be done by inducing persons to make expenditures beyond their means, on express promise of repayment, if the law were otherwise. It is an entirely different case from a promise to make another a present, or render him a gratuitous service. It is nothing to the purpose that the plaintiff was benefited by the expenditure of his own money. He was induced by this promise to spend it in this way, instead of some other mode.

. . .

Judgment reversed, and new trial ordered.

NOTES → *bargained for exchange*

1.   Suppose that Uncle operated a business and was interested in developing business opportunities in Europe. Uncle, however, did not have the time to go there himself. Uncle asked Nephew to travel around Europe, scout around for business opportunities, and report back. Uncle told Nephew "If you go the Europe, I'll pay your expenses." Nephew went on the trip, but Uncle died before making payment. Nephew sued the executor of Uncle's estate. Would Uncle's promise be supported by consideration?

2.   Suppose that Uncle did not operate a business, but was merely a gentleman of leisure, living off his capital. Uncle thought that all proper young gentlemen should take a Grand Tour of Europe as part of their education. At a family gathering, Uncle asked Nephew when he was planning to take the Grand Tour. Nephew said had no plans to take a European tour, because he thought it was stupid to waste time wandering around old countries, looking at cathedrals and castles. Uncle was horrified. Uncle told Nephew "If you go the Europe, I'll pay your expenses." Nephew went on the trip, but Uncle died before making payment. Nephew sued the executor of Uncle's estate. Would Uncle's promise be supported by consideration?

3.   Suppose that a family gathering, Nephew told Uncle that he wanted to take a Grand Tour of Europe as part of his education, but was afraid that he couldn't do so because he couldn't afford it. Uncle—a hard headed business man—told Nephew that he thought it was stupid to waste time wandering around old countries, looking at cathedrals and castles. But, Nephew was unpersuaded. Uncle said, "All right, if you go the Europe, I'll pay your expenses." Nephew went on the trip, but Uncle died before making

payment. Nephew sued the executor of Uncle's estate. Would Uncle's promise be supported by consideration?

Kirksey v. Kirksey

Supreme Court of Alabama, 1845.
8 Ala. 131.

Assumpsit by the defendant, against the plaintiff in error. The question is presented in this Court, upon a case agreed, which shows the following facts:

The plaintiff was the wife of defendant's brother, but had for some time been a widow, and had several children. In 1840, the plaintiff resided on public land, under a contract of lease, she had held over, and was comfortably settled, and would have attempted to secure the land she lived on. The defendant resided in Talladega county, some sixty, or seventy miles off. On the 10th October, 1840, he wrote to her the following letter:

> "Dear sister Antillico,
>
> Much to my mortification, I heard, that brother Henry was dead, and one of his children. I know that your situation is one of grief, and difficulty. You had a bad chance before, but great deal worse now. I should like to come and see you, but cannot with convenience at present. . . .
>
> I do not know whether you have a preference on the place you live on, or not, If you had, I would advise you to obtain your preference, and sell the land and quit the country, as I understand it is very unhealthy, and I know society is very bad.
>
> If you will come down and see me, I will let you have a place to raise your family, and I have more open land than I can tend; and on the account of your situation, and that of your family, I feel like I want you and the children to do well."

Within a month or two after the receipt of this letter, the plaintiff abandoned her possession, without disposing of it, and removed with her family, to the residence of the defendant, who put her in comfortable houses, and gave her land to cultivate for two years, at the end of which time he notified her to remove, and put her in a house, not comfortable, in the woods, which he afterwards required her to leave.

A verdict being found for the plaintiff, for two hundred dollars, the above facts were agreed and if they will sustain the action, the judgment is to be affirmed, otherwise it is to be reversed.

■ ORMOND, J.

The inclination of *my mind*, is, that the loss and convenience, which the plaintiff sustained in breaking up, and moving to the defendant's, a distance of sixty miles, is a **sufficient consideration** to support the promise, to furnish her with a house, and land to cultivate, until she could raise her family. *My brothers*, however think, that the promise on the part of the defendant, was a mere gratuity, and that an action will not lie for its breach. The judgment of the Court below must therefore be reversed, pursuant to the agreement of the parties.

NOTES & QUESTIONS

1.   We've added the italics in the opinion. Note that Judge Ormond was announcing the decision in the case, even though he himself thought that the case should be decided the other way. That is, although Judge Ormond personally thought that the promise should be enforceable, a majority of the court thought it was not. So, the plaintiff lost the case. In modern times, one of the other judges would have written the opinion for the majority, and Judge Ormond would have written a dissenting opinion.

2.   Judge Ormond expresses the thought that the promise should be enforced by using the word "consideration" in a conclusory sense. He says that Antillico's act of moving "is a sufficient consideration to support the promise." All that really meant is that Judge Ormond thought that the promise should be enforced. It doesn't really tell us *why* Judge Ormond thought that the promise should be enforced.

3.   Was there consideration for the brother-in-law's promise, using the term "consideration" in the sense derived from *Hamer v. Sidway*? Did brother-in-law make the promise because he wanted something in exchange?

B. REMEDY IN PROMISSORY ESTOPPEL CASES

The issue of the proper remedy in promissory estoppel cases was discussed at the meeting of the American Law Institute in 1926 when Section 90 was first considered. The issue is captured in a famous exchange between Samuel Williston, Reporter for the RESTATEMENT (FIRST) OF CONTRACTS, and the distinguished practicing lawyer Frederick Coudert, concerning a hypothetical case in which an uncle promises $1000 to his nephew Johnny, knowing that Johnny will use the money to buy a new car.

MR. COUDERT: Would you say, Mr. Reporter, in your case of Johnny and the uncle, the uncle promising the $1000 and Johnny buying the car—say, he goes out and buys the car for $500—that uncle would be liable for $1000 or would he be liable for $500?

MR. WILLISTON: If Johnny had done what he was expected to do, or is acting within the limits of his uncle's expectation, I think the uncle would be liable for $1000; but not otherwise.

MR. COUDERT: In other words, substantial justice would require that uncle should be penalized in the sum of $500.

MR. WILLISTON: Why do you say "penalized"?

. . .

MR. COUDERT: Because substantial justice there would require, it seems to me, that Johnny get his money for his car, but should he get his car and $500 more? I don't see.

. . .

MR. WILLISTON: Either the promise is binding or it is not. If the promise is binding it has to be enforced as it is made . . . . [I]t seems to me you have to take one leg or the other. You have either to say the promise is binding or you have to go on the theory of restoring the status quo

Proceedings at Fourth Annual Meeting, 4 A.L.I. PROC. APP. 98–99, 103–04 (1926)

The RESTATEMENT (SECOND) OF CONTRACTS takes a different view on the issue, adopting the position that Coudert suggested and Williston rejected. Compare the two versions of § 90:

Restatement (First) Of Contracts § 90 (1932)

A promise which the promisor should reasonably expect to induce action or forbearance of a definite and substantial character on the part of the promisee and which does induce such action or forbearance is binding if injustice can be avoided only by enforcement of the promise.

Restatement (Second) Of Contracts

(1) A promise which the promisor should reasonably expect to induce action or forbearance on the part of the promisee or a third person and which does induce such action or forbearance is binding if injustice can be avoided only by enforcement of the promise. The remedy granted for breach may be limited as justice requires.

. . .

REPORTER'S NOTE

The principal change from former § 90 is the recognition of the possibility of partial enforcement. See Fuller & Perdue, The Reliance Interest in Contract Damages: 1, 46 Yale L.J. 52, 63–65 (1936); id.: 2, 46 Yale L.J. 373, 401–06 (1937); Shattuck, Gratuitous Promises—A New Writ? 35 Mich.L.Rev. 908 (1937); 1A Corbin, Contracts § 205 (1963 & Supp.1980). Partly because of that change, the requirement that the action or forbearance have "a definite and substantial character" is deleted; and provision is added for reliance by beneficiaries. See Boyer, Promissory Estoppel: Requirements and Limitations of the Doctrine, 98 U.Pa.L.Rev. 459 (1950); 1A Corbin, Contracts § 200 (1963 & Supp.1980)

It's easy to see that a sensible result in the Uncle-Nephew situation discussed by Williston and Coudert would be to limit the award to the actual amount that the nephew spent ($500) as a consequence of the Uncle's promise. The alternative position, taken by Williston, seems unduly rigid in its insistence that promise was to pay $1000 and that promise either is or is not enforceable. In modern terminology, we'd say that under Section 90 of the RESTATEMENT (SECOND) OF CONTRACTS, the remedy might be limited to "reliance damages," just as the reason for enforcing is reliance on a promise not supported by consideration. In actual cases, it's a good deal harder to decide what the appropriate remedy should be. The following two cases deal with that problem.

Goodman v. Dicker

United States Court of Appeals, District of Columbia, 1948.
169 F.2d 684.

■ PROCTOR, ASSOCIATE JUSTICE.

This appeal is from a judgment of the District Court in a suit by appellees for breach of contract.

Appellants are local distributors for Emerson Radio and Phonograph Corporation in the District of Columbia. Appellees, with the knowledge and encouragement of appellants, applied for a 'dealer franchise' to sell Emerson's products. The trial court found that appellants by their representations and conduct induced appellees to incur expenses in preparing to do business under the franchise, including employment of salesmen and solicitation of orders for radios. Among other things, appellants represented that the application had been accepted; that the franchise would be granted, and that appellees would receive an initial delivery of thirty to forty radios. Yet, no radios were delivered, and notice was finally given that the franchise would not be granted.

The case was tried without a jury. The court held that a contract had not been proven but that appellants were estopped from denying the same by reason of their statements and conduct upon which appellees relied to their detriment. Judgment was entered for $1500, covering cash outlays of $1150 and loss of $350, anticipated profits on sale of thirty radios.

The main contention of appellants is that no liability would have arisen under the dealer franchise had it been granted because, as understood by appellees, it would have been terminable at will and would have imposed no duty upon the manufacturer to sell or appellees to buy any fixed number of radios. From this it is argued that the franchise agreement would not have been enforceable (except as to acts performed thereunder) and cancellation by the manufacturer would have created no liability for expenses incurred by the dealer in preparing to do business. Further, it is argued that as the dealer franchise would have been unenforceable for failure of the manufacturer to supply radios appellants would not be liable to fulfill their assurance that radios would be supplied.

We think these contentions miss the real point of this case. We are not concerned directly with the terms of the franchise. We are dealing with a promise by appellants that a franchise would be granted and radios supplied, on the faith of which appellees with the knowledge and encouragement of appellants incurred expenses in making preparations to do business. Under these circumstances we think that appellants cannot now advance any defense inconsistent with their assurance that the franchise would be granted. Justice and fair dealing require that one who acts to his detriment on the faith of conduct of the kind revealed here should be protected by estopping the party who has brought about the situation from alleging anything in opposition to the natural consequences of his own course of conduct. . . .

In our opinion the trial court was correct in holding defendants liable for moneys which appellees expended in preparation to do business under the promised dealer franchise. These items aggregated $1150. We think, though, the court erred in adding the item of $350 for loss of profits on radios promised under an initial order. The true measure of damage is the loss sustained by expenditures made in reliance upon the assurance of a dealer franchise. As thus modified, the judgment is [a]ffirmed.

NOTES & QUESTIONS

1.   What is the relevant promise in *Goodman v. Dicker*?

2.   Recall our discussion of the overlap between contract, tort, and restitution in Chapter 2. Is the availability of different measures of remedy in § 90 helpful, in light of possible overlaps in certain factual situations?

3.   The following case shows that courts remain divided on what should be the appropriate recovery, whether expectation or reliance damages, on a claim of promissory estoppel. Why might this issue be controversial when the claim is for lost-profits damages?

Walters v. Marathon Oil Co.

United States Court of Appeals, Seventh Circuit, 1981.
642 F.2d 1098.

■ SPEARS, DISTRICT JUDGE. This action arose as a result of the Iranian revolution and the uncertainty of oil supplies. Marathon Oil Company, the appellant, is engaged in the business of reselling and distributing petroleum products. The appellee, Dennis E. Walters, contacted appellant in late December, 1978, about the possibility of locating a combination foodstore and service station on a vacant gasoline service station site in Indianapolis. Appellees (husband and wife) purchased the service station in February, 1979, and continued to make improvements upon it, based upon promises made, and the continuing negotiations with representatives from appellant. Paper work apparently proceeded normally, and appellees' proposal was delivered to appellant along with a three-party agreement, signed by appellees and Time Oil Company, the previous supplier to the service station site appellees had purchased. Before appellees' proposal was accepted by appellant, but after it was received at the office, appellant placed a moratorium on the consideration of new applications for dealerships and seller arrangements, and refused to sign the three-party agreement.

After a bench trial, the court found for appellees and against appellant on the theory of promissory estoppel. This finding has not been challenged. The two issues presented for review in this appeal pertain only to the award of damages in the form of lost profits, and the alleged failure of appellees to take reasonable steps to mitigate their damages. We affirm the judgment of the district court.

. . .

The appellant next argues that the trial court's computation of damages is clearly erroneous and contrary to the law. The trial court found that appellees lost anticipated profits of six cents per gallon for the 370,000 gallons they were entitled to receive under their allocation for the first year's gasoline sales, totalling $22,200.00, and awarded this amount in damages. The appellant insists that since appellees succeeded at trial solely on a promissory estoppel theory, and the district court so found, loss of profits is not a proper measure of damages. It contends that appellees' damages should have been the amount of their expenditures in reliance on the promise, measured by the difference between their expenditures and the present value of the property. Using this measure of damages, appellees would have received no award, for the present value of the real estate and its improvements is slightly more than the amount expended by appellees in reliance upon the promise. As a consequence, the appellant says that because appellees can recoup all they spent in reliance on appellant's promise, they would be in the same position they would have been in had the promise not been made.

However, in reliance upon appellant's promise to supply gasoline supplies to them, appellees purchased the station, and invested their funds and their time. It is unreasonable to assume that they did not anticipate a return of profits from this investment of time and funds, but, in reliance upon appellant's promise, they had foregone the opportunity to make the investment elsewhere. As indicated, the record reflects that had appellant performed according to its promise, appellees would have received the anticipated net profit of $22,200.00. The findings of the trial court in this regard were fully supported by the evidence. For example, it was shown that the 19 77/78 base period for this particular station was 375,450 gallons. The appellant's own exhibit reflected the same amount. The testimony of the previous owner showed that the location pumped 620,000 gallons in 1972, and that he pumped 375,450 gallons in 1978. Furthermore, an expert witness testified that the site would pump 360,000 gallons a year. Appellant's own witness testified that all of its dealers received 100% of their base period allocation for the time in question. Thus, the trial court was not clearly erroneous in its finding that appellees would have sold 370,000 gallons of gasoline had appellant's promise been performed.

An equity court possesses some discretionary power to award damages in order to do complete justice. *Albemarle Paper Co. v. Moody*, 422 U.S. 405, 95 S.Ct. 2362, 45 L.Ed.2d 280 (1975); *Minnis v. International Union, United Automobile, Aerospace and Agricultural Workers of America, UAW*, 531 F.2d 850 (8th Cir. 1975). Furthermore, since it is the historic purpose of equity to secure complete justice, the courts are able to adjust the remedies so as to grant the necessary relief, *Equal Employment Opportunity Commission v. General Tel. Co. of Northwest, Inc.*, 599 F.2d 322 (9th Cir. 1979), *affirmed*, 446 U.S. 318, 100 S.Ct. 1698, 64 L.Ed.2d 319 (1980), and a district court sitting in equity may even devise a remedy which extends or exceeds the terms of a prior agreement between the parties, if it is necessary to make the injured party whole. *Levitt Corp. v. Levitt*, 593 F.2d 463 (2nd Cir. 1979).

Since promissory estoppel is an equitable matter, the trial court has broad power in its choice of a remedy, and it is significant that the ancient maxim that "equity will not suffer a wrong to be without a remedy" has long been the law in the State of Indiana. *King v. City of Bloomington*, 239 Ind. 548, 159 N.E.2d 563 (Ind.1959); Ritter v. Ritter, 219 Ind. 487, 38 N.E.2d 997 (Ind.1942); *Dodd v. Reese*, 216 Ind. 449, 24 N.E.2d 995 (Ind.1940); and *Department of Insurance v. Motors Insurance Corporation*, 236 Ind. 1, 138 N.E.2d 157 (Ind.1966).

In this case the promissory estoppel finding of the district court is not challenged. Moreover, it is apparent that the appellees suffered a loss of profits as a direct result of their reliance upon the promise made by appellant, and the amount of the lost profits was ascertained with reasonable certainty.[1] In addition, appellees took reasonable steps to mitigate their damages, and an award of damages based upon lost profits was appropriate in order to do complete justice.

Under the circumstances, and concluding, as we do, that the findings of the district court are not clearly erroneous, we affirm the judgment which awards damages to appellees based upon lost profits.

---

[1] In *Goodman v. Dicker*, 169 F.2d 684 (D.C.Cir.1948), relied upon by appellant, the court held that the true measure of damages in that . . . case was the loss in the sum of $1150 sustained by expenditures made in reliance on assurances given to the injured parties, and that the trial court had erred in adding the item of $350 for lost profits. No reasons were assigned or authorities cited by the court for the action it took, and there was no suggestion that in an appropriate case loss of profits could not be a true measure of damages. In any event, it is apparent that the award of double damages was rejected and the higher figure of $1150 was chosen in order to do complete justice. In this connection, it is interesting to note that in *National Savings and Trust Company v. Kahn*, 300 F.2d 910 (D.C.Cir.1962), the same circuit commented that "(T)he cost of performance may be the proper measure of damages where plaintiff renders part performance and it is impossible to estimate the profits he would have received but for defendant's breach. (Citing authorities). That is not this case." (Emphasis supplied). See id. at 914 n. 7.

NOTES

1.   The discussion of "equity" and "equitable" in *Walters* is a common, but regrettable, phenomenon of, to put it bluntly, sloppiness. As we saw toward the beginning of the course, the word "equity" in legal parlance refers to the historically separate court system of the courts of chancery in England and the United States. We considered, for example, whether a party suing for breach of contract would be entitled to sue "in equity" for the "equitable" remedy of specific performance, or is limited to suing "at law" for the usual remedy of damages.

Suppose that the *Walters* case had arisen before the merger of the separate court systems of law and equity. Plaintiff was seeking money damages for breach of a promise. That's an ordinary action "at law." It would have been brought in the ordinary "law" courts, not the special "equity" courts. A long time ago, say in the middle of the nineteenth century, the plaintiff would probably have lost. Recall *Kirksey v. Kirksey*. After the development of the promissory estoppel concept, plaintiff would win. That's just a change in the governing law. It's got nothing to do with "law" and "equity."

Courts—at law—in promissory estoppel cases need to decide what remedy is "fair." That's the issue in the Williston-Coudert conversation, or in *Goodman v. Dicker*, or in *Walters v. Marathon Oil Co.* That's got nothing to do with "equity" in the sense of the courts of chancery. So, the fourth paragraph of the *Walters* opinion ("An equity court possesses some discretionary power to award damages in order to do complete justice") is just silliness. Of course the court has to reach a fair result. There's nothing surprising about that. Nor does that have anything to do with courts "of equity." Suppose Judge Spear had an ordinary tort or a contract case where the promise was enforceable because supported by consideration. Would he say "This is an action at law, not in equity, so there is no need for us to reach a fair result"?

2.   Liability based on a specific promise intersects with the law of pre-contractual liability. Although we are presently dealing with the issue of remedy for promissory estoppel, recall our discussion of pre-contractual liability in Chapter 3.A. Many cases of promissory estoppel have developed in the context of negotiations between franchisors and prospective franchisees. Why do you think prospective franchisees might be more likely to recover at least reliance damages?

Think about how the claimant must show that a promise was made and reliance on the promise was justified in the context of the negotiations. That represents a considerable burden. In *Walters*, the terms of the ultimate franchise agreement were known. In *Hoffman v. Red Owl Stores, Inc.*, 26 Wis.2d 683, 133 N.W.2d 267 (1965), a supermarket franchisor was held liable for its promise to a prospective franchisee that his $18,000 cash contribution would suffice to obtain a franchise. We will return to the issue of pre-contractual liability in *Drennan v. Star Paving*, below.

C. MODERN APPLICATIONS OF PROMISSORY ESTOPPEL

Feinberg v. Pfeiffer Co.

St. Louis Court of Appeals, Missouri, 1959.
322 S.W.2d 163.

This is a suit brought in the Circuit Court of the City of St. Louis by plaintiff, a former employee of the defendant corporation, on an alleged contract whereby **defendant agreed to pay plaintiff the sum of $200 per month for life upon her retirement.** A jury being waived, the case was tried by the court alone. Judgment below was for plaintiff for $5,100, the amount of the pension claimed to be due as of the date of the trial, together with interest thereon, and defendant duly appealed.

The parties are in substantial agreement on the essential facts. Plaintiff began working for the defendant, a manufacturer of pharmaceuticals, in 1910, when she was but 17 years of age. By 1947 she had attained the position of bookkeeper, office manager, and assistant treasurer of the defendant, and owned 70 shares of its stock out of a total of 6,503 shares issued and outstanding. Twenty shares had been given to her by the defendant or its then president, she had purchased 20, and the remaining 30 she had acquired by a stock split or stock dividend. Over the years she received substantial dividends on the stock she owned, as did all of the other stockholders. Also, in addition to her salary, plaintiff from 1937 to 1949, inclusive, received each year a bonus varying in amount from $300 in the beginning to $2,000 in the later years.

On December 27, 1947, the annual meeting of the defendant's Board of Directors was held at the Company's offices in St. Louis, presided over by Max Lippman, its then president and largest individual stockholder. The other directors present were George L. Marcus, Sidney Harris, Sol Flammer, and Walter Weinstock, who, with Max Lippman, owned 5,007 of the 6,503 shares then issued and outstanding. At that meeting the Board of Directors adopted the following resolution, which, because it is the crux of the case, we quote in full:

'The Chairman thereupon pointed out that the Assistant Treasurer, Mrs. Anna Sacks Feinberg, has given the corporation many years of long and faithful service. Not only has she served the corporation devotedly, but with exceptional ability and skill. The President pointed out that although all of the officers and directors sincerely hoped and desired that Mrs. Feinberg would continue in her present position for as long as she felt able, nevertheless, in view of the length of service which she has contributed provision should be made to **afford her retirement privileges and benefits which should become a firm obligation of the corporation to be available to her whenever she should see fit to retire from active duty,** however many years in the future such retirement may become effective. It was, accordingly, proposed that Mrs. Feinberg's salary which is presently $350.00 per month, be increased to $400.00 per month, and that Mrs. Feinberg would be given the privilege of retiring from active duty at any time she may elect to see fit so to do upon a retirement pay of $200.00 per month for life, with the distinct understanding that the retirement plan is merely being adopted at the present time in order to afford Mrs. Feinberg security for the future and in the hope that her active services will continue with the corporation for many years to come. After due discussion and consideration, and upon motion duly made and seconded, it was—

'Resolved, that the salary of Anna Sacks Feinberg be increased from $350.00 to $400.00 per month and that she be afforded the privilege of retiring from active duty in the corporation at any time she may elect to see fit so to do upon retirement pay of $200.00 per month, for the remainder of her life.'

At the request of Mr. Lippman his sons-in-law, Messrs. Harris and Flammer, called upon the plaintiff at her apartment on the same day to advise her of the passage of the resolution. Plaintiff testified on cross-examination that she had no prior information that such a pension plan was contemplated, that it came as a surprise to her, and that she would have continued in her employment whether or not such a resolution had been adopted. It is clear from the evidence that there was no contract, oral or written, as to plaintiff's length of employment, and that she was free to quit, and the defendant to discharge her, at any time.

Plaintiff did continue to work for the defendant through June 30, 1949, on which date she retired. In accordance with the foregoing resolution, the defendant began paying her the sum of $200 on the first of each month. Mr. Lippman died on November 18, 1949, and was succeeded as president of the company by his widow. Because of an illness, she retired from that office and was succeeded in October, 1953, by her son-in-law, Sidney M. Harris. Mr. Harris testified that while Mrs. Lippman had been president she signed the monthly pension check paid plaintiff, but fussed about doing so, and considered the payments as gifts. After his election, he stated, a new accounting firm employed by the defendant questioned the validity of the payments to plaintiff on several occasions, and in the Spring of 1956, upon its recommendation, he consulted the Company's then attorney, Mr. Ralph Kalish. Harris testified that both Ernst and Ernst, the accounting firm, and Kalish told him there was no need of giving plaintiff the money. He also stated that he had concurred in the view that the payments to plaintiff were mere gratuities rather than amounts due under a contractual obligation, and that following his discussion with the Company's attorney plaintiff was sent a check for $100 on April 1, 1956. Plaintiff declined to accept the reduced amount, and this action followed. Additional facts will be referred to later in this opinion.

Appellant's first assignment of error relates to the admission in evidence of plaintiff's testimony over its objection, that at the time of trial she was sixty-five and a half years old, and that she was no longer able to engage in gainful employment because of the removal of a cancer and the performance of a colocholecystostomy operation on November 25, 1957. Its complaint is not so much that such evidence was irrelevant and immaterial, as it is that the trial court erroneously made it one basis for its decision in favor of plaintiff. As defendant concedes, the error (if it was error) in the admission of such evidence would not be a ground for reversal, since, this being a jury-waived case, we are constrained by the statutes to review it upon both the law and the evidence, * * * and to render such judgment as the court below ought to have given. * * * We consider only such evidence as is admissible, and need not pass upon questions of error in the admission and exclusion of evidence. * * * However, in fairness to the trial court it should be stated that while he briefly referred to the state of plaintiff's health as of the time of the trial in his amended findings of fact, it is obvious from his amended grounds for decision and judgment that it was not, as will be seen, the basis for his decision.

Appellant's next complaint is that there was insufficient evidence to support the court's findings that plaintiff would not have quit defendant's employ had she not known and relied upon the promise of defendant to pay her $200 a month for life, and the finding that, from her voluntary retirement until April 1, 1956, plaintiff relied upon the continued receipt of the pension installments. The trial court so found, and, in our opinion, justifiably so. Plaintiff testified, and was corroborated by Harris, defendant's witness, that knowledge of the passage of the resolution was communicated to her on December 27, 1947, the very day it was adopted. She was told at that time by Harris and Flammer, she stated, that she could take the pension as of that day, if she wished. She testified further that she continued to work for another year and a half, through June 30, 1949; that at that time her health was good and she could have continued to work, but that after working for almost forty years she thought she would take a rest. Her testimony continued:

> 'Q. Now, what was the reason—I'm sorry. Did you then quit the employment of the company after you—after this year and a half?
>
> A.   Yes.
>
> 'Q.   What was the reason that you left?
>
> A.   Well, I thought almost forty years, it was a long time and I thought I would take a little rest.
>
> 'Q.   Yes.

A.   And with the pension and what earnings my husband had, we figured we could get along.

'Q.   Did you rely upon this pension?

A.   We certainly did.

'Q.   Being paid?

A.   Very much so. We relied upon it because I was positive that I was going to get it as long as I lived.

'Q.   Would you have left the employment of the company at that time had it not been for this pension?

A.   No.

'Mr. Allen: Just a minute, I object to that as calling for a conclusion and conjecture on the part of this witness.

'The Court: It will be overruled.

'Q.   (Mr. Agatstein continuing): Go ahead, now. The question is whether you would have quit the employment of the company at that time had you not relied upon this pension plan?

A.   No, I wouldn't.

'Q.   You would not have. Did you ever seek employment while this pension was being paid to you—

A.   (interrupting): No.

'Q.   Wait a minute, at any time prior—at any other place?

A.   No, sir.

'Q.   Were you able to hold any other employment during that time?

A.   Yes, I think so.

'Q.   Was your health good?

A.   My health was good.'

It is obvious from the foregoing that there was ample evidence to support the findings of fact made by the court below.

We come, then, to the basic issue in the case. While otherwise defined in defendant's third and fourth assignments of error, it is thus succinctly stated in the argument in its brief: 'whether plaintiff has proved that she has a right to recover from defendant based upon a legally binding contractual obligation to pay her $200 per month for life.'

It is defendant's contention, in essence, that the resolution adopted by its Board of Directors was a mere promise to make a gift, and that no contract resulted either thereby, or when plaintiff retired, because there was no consideration given or paid by the plaintiff. It urges that a promise to make a gift is not binding unless supported by a legal consideration; that the only apparent consideration for the adoption of the foregoing resolution was the 'many years of long and faithful service' expressed therein; and that past services are not a valid consideration for a promise. Defendant argues further that there is nothing in the resolution which made its effectiveness conditional upon plaintiff's continued employment, that she was not under contract to work for any length of time but was free to quit whenever she wished, and that she had no contractual right to her position and could have been discharged at any time.

Plaintiff concedes that a promise based upon past services would be without consideration, but contends that there were two other elements which supplied the required element: First, the continuation by plaintiff in the employ of the defendant for the period from December 27, 1947, the date when the resolution was adopted, until the date of her retirement on June 30, 1949. And, second, her change of position, i.e., her retirement, and the abandonment by her of her opportunity to continue in gainful employment, made in reliance on defendant's promise to pay her $200 per month for life.

We must agree with the defendant that the evidence does not support the first of these contentions. There is no language in the resolution predicating plaintiff's right to a pension upon her continued employment. She was not required to work for the defendant for any period of time as a condition to gaining such retirement benefits. She was told that she could quit the day upon which the resolution was adopted, as she herself testified, and it is clear from her own testimony that she made no promise or agreement to continue in the employ of the defendant in return for its promise to pay her a pension. . . .

But as to the second of these contentions we must agree with plaintiff . . . Section 90 of the Restatement of the Law of Contracts states that:

> 'A promise which the promisor should reasonably expect to induce action or forbearance of a definite and substantial character on the part of the promisee and which does induce such action or forbearance is binding if injustice can be avoided only by enforcement of the promise.'

> This doctrine has been described as that of 'promissory estoppel" . . . .

. . .

Was there such an act on the part of plaintiff, in reliance upon the promise contained in the resolution, as will estop the defendant, and therefore create an enforceable contract under the doctrine of promissory estoppel? We think there was. One of the illustrations cited under Section 90 of the Restatement is:

> '2.   A promises B to pay him an annuity during B's life. B thereupon resigns a profitable employment, as A expected that he might. B receives the annuity for some years, in the

meantime becoming disqualified from again obtaining good employment. A's promise is binding.'

This illustration is objected to by defendant as not being applicable to the case at hand. The reason advanced by it is that in the illustration B became 'disqualified' from obtaining other employment *before* A discontinued the payments, whereas in this case the plaintiff did not discover that she had cancer and thereby became unemployable until *after* the defendant had discontinued the payments of $200 per month. We think the distinction is immaterial. The only reason for the reference in the illustration to the disqualification of A is in connection with that part of Section 90 regarding the prevention of injustice. The injustice would occur regardless of when the disability occurred. Would defendant contend that the contract would be enforceable if the plaintiff's illness had been discovered on March 31, 1956, the day before it discontinued the payment of the $200 a month, but not if it occurred on April 2nd, the day after? Furthermore, there are more ways to become disqualified for work, or unemployable, than as the result of illness. At the time she retired plaintiff was 57 years of age. At the time the payments were discontinued she was over 63 years of age. It is a matter of common knowledge that it is virtually impossible for a woman of that age to find satisfactory employment, much less a position comparable to that which plaintiff enjoyed at the time of her retirement.

The fact of the matter is that plaintiff's subsequent illness was not the 'action or forbearance' which was induced by the promise contained in the resolution. As the trial court correctly decided, such action on plaintiff's part was her retirement from a lucrative position in reliance upon defendant's promise to pay her an annuity or pension. In a very similar case, *Ricketts v. Scothorn*, 57 Neb. 51, 77 N.W. 365, 367, 42 L.R.A. 794, the Supreme Court of Nebraska said:

> 'According to the undisputed proof, as shown by the record before us, the plaintiff was a working girl, holding a position in which she earned a salary of $10 per week. Her grandfather, desiring to put her in a position of independence, gave her the note accompanying it with the remark that his other grandchildren did not work, and that she would not be obliged to work any longer. In effect, he suggested that she might abandon her employment, and rely in the future upon the bounty which he promised. He doubtless desired that she should give up her occupation, but, whether he did or not, it is entirely certain that he contemplated such action on her part as a reasonable and probable consequence of his gift. Having intentionally influenced the plaintiff to alter her position for the worse on the faith of the note being paid when due, it would be grossly inequitable to permit the maker, or his executor, to resist payment on the ground that the promise was given without consideration.'

[F]or the reasons stated, . . . the judgment [should] be affirmed.

Hayes v. Plantations Steel

Supreme Court of Rhode Island, 1982.
438 A.2d 1091.

■ SHEA, JUSTICE.

The defendant employer, Plantations Steel Company (Plantations), appeals from a Superior Court judgment for the plaintiff employee, Edward J. Hayes (Hayes). The trial justice, sitting without a jury, found that Plantations was obligated to Hayes on the basis of an implied-in-fact contract to pay him a yearly pension of $5,000. The award covered three years in which payment had not been made. . . .

We reverse the findings of the trial justice regarding Plantations's contractual obligation to pay Hayes a pension. . . .

Plantations is a closely held Rhode Island corporation engaged in the manufacture of steel reinforcing rods for use in concrete construction. The company was founded by Hugo R. Mainelli, Sr., and Alexander A. DiMartino. A dispute between their two families in 1976 and 1977 left the DiMartinos in full control of the corporation. Hayes was an employee of the corporation from 1947 until his retirement in 1972 at age of sixty-five. He began with Plantations as an "estimator and draftsman" and ended his career as general manager, a position of considerable responsibility. Starting in January 1973 and continuing until January 1976, Hayes received the annual sum of $5,000 from Plantations. Hayes instituted this action in December 1977, after the then company management refused to make any further payments.

Hayes testified that in January 1972 he announced his intention to retire the following July, after twenty-five years of continuous service. He decided to retire because he had worked continuously for fifty-one years. He stated, however, that he would not have retired had he not expected to receive a pension. After he stopped working for Plantations, he sought no other employment.

Approximately one week before his actual retirement Hayes spoke with Hugo R. Mainelli, Jr., who was then an officer and a stockholder of Plantations. This conversation was the first and only one concerning payments of a pension to Hayes during retirement. Mainelli said that the company "would take care" of him. There was no mention of a sum of money or a percentage of salary that Hayes would receive. There was no formal authorization for payments by Plantations's shareholders and/or board of directors. Indeed, there was never any formal provision for a pension plan for any employee other than for unionized employees, who benefit from an arrangement through their union. The plaintiff was not a union member.

Mr. Mainelli, Jr., testified that his father, Hugo R. Mainelli, Sr., had authorized the first payment "as a token of appreciation for the many years of (Hayes's) service." Furthermore, "it was implied that that check would continue on an annual basis." Mainelli also testified that it was his "personal intention" that the payments would continue for "as long as I was around."

Mainelli testified that after Hayes's retirement, he would visit the premises each year to say hello and renew old acquaintances. During the course of his visits, Hayes would thank Mainelli for the previous check and ask how long it would continue so that he could plan an orderly retirement.

The payments were discontinued after 1976. At that time a succession of several poor business years plus the stockholders' dispute, resulting in the takeover by the DiMartino family, contributed to the decision to stop the payments.

The trial justice ruled that Plantations owed Hayes his annual sum of $5,000 for the years 1977 through 1979. The ruling implied that barring bankruptcy or the cessation of business for any other reason, Hayes had a right to expect continued annual payments.

. . .

Assuming for the purpose of this discussion that Plantations in legal effect made a promise to Hayes, we must ask whether Hayes did supply the required consideration that would make the promise binding? And, if Hayes did not supply consideration, was his alleged reliance sufficiently induced by the promise to estop defendant from denying its obligation to him? We answer both questions in the negative.

We turn first to the problem of consideration. The facts at bar do not present the case of an express contract. As the trial justice stated, the existence of a contract in this case must be determined from all the circumstances of the parties' conduct and words. Although words were expressed initially in the remark that Hayes "would be taken care of," any contract in this case would be more in the nature of an implied contract. Certainly the statement of Hugo Mainelli, Jr., standing alone is not an expression of a direct and definite promise to pay Hayes a pension. Though we are analyzing an implied contract, nevertheless we must address the question of consideration.

Contracts implied in fact require the element of consideration to support them as is required in express contracts. The only difference between the two is the manner in which the parties manifest their assent. * * * In this jurisdiction, consideration consists either in some right, interest, or benefit accruing to one party or some forbearance, detriment, or responsibility given, suffered, or undertaken by the other. * * * Valid consideration furthermore must be bargained for. It must induce the return act or promise. To be valid, therefore, the purported consideration must not have been delivered before a promise is executed, that is, given without reference to the promise. * * * Consideration is therefore a test of the enforceability of executory promises, * * * and has no legal effect when rendered in the past and apart from an alleged exchange in the present. * * *

In the case before us, Plantations's promise to pay Hayes a pension is quite clearly not supported by any consideration supplied by Hayes. Hayes had announced his intent to retire well in advance of any promise, and therefore the intention to retire was arrived at without regard to any promise by Plantations. Although Hayes may have had in mind the receipt of a pension when he first informed Plantations, his expectation was not based on any statement made to him or on any conduct of the company officer relative to him in January 1972. In deciding to retire, Hayes acted on his own initiative. Hayes's long years of dedicated service also is legally insufficient because his service too was rendered without being induced by Plantations's promise. * * *

Clearly then this is not a case in which Plantations's promise was meant to induce Hayes to refrain from retiring when he could have chosen to do so in return for further service. * * * Nor was the promise made to encourage long service from the start of his employment. * * * Instead, the testimony establishes that Plantations's promise was intended "as a token of appreciation for (Hayes's) many years of service." As such it was in the nature of a gratuity paid to Hayes for as long as the company chose. * * *

The plaintiff's most relevant citations are still inapposite to the present case. *Bredemann v. Vaughan Mfg. Co.,* 40 Ill.App.2d 232, 188 N.E.2d 746 (1963), presents similar yet distinguishable facts. . . . As in the present case, the employer made the promise one week prior to the employee's retirement, and in almost the same words. However, Bredemann is distinguishable because the court characterized that promise as a concrete offer to pay if she would retire immediately. In fact, the defendant wanted her to retire. *Id.* 188 N.E.2d at 749. On the contrary, Plantations in this case did not actively seek Hayes's retirement. . . . Unlike *Bredemann,* here Hayes announced his unsolicited intent to retire.

Hayes also argues that the work he performed during the week between the promise and the date of his retirement constituted sufficient consideration to support the promise. He relies on *Ulmann v. Sunset-McKee Co.,* 221 F.2d 128 (9th Cir. 1955), in which the court ruled that work performed during the one-week period of the employee's notice of impending retirement constituted consideration for the employer's offer of a pension that the employee had solicited some months previously. But there the court stated that its prime reason for upholding the agreement was that sufficient consideration existed in the employee's consent not to compete with his employer. These circumstances do not appear in our case. . . .

Hayes argues in the alternative that even if Plantations's promise was not the product of an exchange, its duty is grounded properly in the theory of promissory estoppel. This court adopted the theory of promissory estoppel in *East Providence Credit Union v. Geremia*, 103 R.I. 597, 601, 239 A.2d 725, 727 (1968) (quoting 1 Restatement Contracts § 90 at 110 (1932)) stating:

> "A promise which the promisor should reasonably expect to induce action or forbearance of a definite and substantial character on the part of the promisee and which does induce such action or forbearance is binding if injustice can be avoided only by enforcement of its promise."

In *East Providence Credit Union* this court said that the doctrine of promissory estoppel is invoked "as a substitute for a consideration, rendering a gratuitous promise enforceable as a contract." *Id.* To restate the matter differently, "the acts of reliance by the promisee to his detriment (provide) a substitute for consideration." *Id.*

Hayes urges that in the absence of a bargained-for promise the facts require application of the doctrine of promissory estoppel. He stresses that he retired voluntarily while expecting to receive a pension. He would not have otherwise retired. Nor did he seek other employment.

We disagree with this contention largely for the reasons already stated. One of the essential elements of the doctrine of promissory estoppel is that the promise must induce the promisee's action or forbearance. The particular act in this regard is plaintiff's decision whether or not to retire. As we stated earlier, the record indicates that he made the decision on his own initiative. In other words, the conversation between Hayes and Mainelli which occurred a week before Hayes left his employment cannot be said to have induced his decision to leave. He had reached that decision long before.

An example taken from the Restatement provides a meaningful contrast:

> "2. A promises B to pay him an annuity during B's life. B thereupon resigns profitable employment, as A expected that he might. B receives the annuity for some years, in the meantime becoming disqualified from again obtaining good employment. A's promise is binding." (Emphasis added.) 1 Restatement Contracts § 90 at 111 (1932).

. . .

It is not reasonable to infer from the facts that Hugo R. Mainelli, Jr., expected retirement to result from his conversation with Hayes. Hayes had given notice of his intention seven months previously. Here there was thus no inducement to retire which would satisfy the demands of § 90 of the Restatement. Nor can it be said that Hayes's refraining from other employment was "action or forbearance of a definite and substantial character." The underlying assumption of Hayes's initial decision to retire was that upon leaving the defendant's employ, he would no longer work. It is impossible to say that he changed his position any more so because of what Mainelli had told him in light of his own initial decision. These circumstances do not lead to a conclusion that injustice can be avoided only by enforcement of Plantations's promise. Hayes received $20,000 over the course of four years. He inquired each year about whether he could expect a check for the following year. Obviously, there was no absolute certainty on his part that the pension would continue. Furthermore, in the face of his uncertainty, the mere fact that payment for several years did occur is insufficient by itself to meet the requirements of reliance under the doctrine of promissory estoppel.

For the foregoing reasons, the defendant's appeal is sustained and the judgment of the Superior Court is reversed. The papers of the case are remanded to the Superior Court.

NOTE

State, in your own words, the critical difference between the plaintiffs' situations in *Feinberg* and *Hayes*.

D. PROMISSORY ESTOPPEL IN CONTRACT FORMATION

James Baird Co. v. Gimbel Bros., Inc.
United States Circuit Court of Appeals, Second Circuit, 1933.
64 F.2d 344.

■ L. HAND, CIRCUIT JUDGE.

The plaintiff sued the defendant for breach of a contract to deliver linoleum under a contract of sale; the defendant denied the making of the contract; the parties tried the case to the judge under a written stipulation and he directed judgment for the defendant. The facts . . . were as follows: The defendant, a New York merchant, knew that the Department of Highways in Pennsylvania had asked for bids for the construction of a public building. It sent an employee to the office of a contractor in Philadelphia, who had possession of the specifications, and the employee there computed the amount of the linoleum which would be required on the job, underestimating the total yardage by about one-half the proper amount. In ignorance of this mistake, on December twenty-fourth the defendant sent to some twenty or thirty contractors, likely to bid on the job, an offer to supply all the linoleum required by the specifications at two different lump sums, depending upon the quality used. These offers concluded as follows: "If successful in being awarded this contract, it will be absolutely guaranteed, * * * and * * * we are offering these prices for reasonable" (sic), "prompt acceptance after the general contract has been awarded." The plaintiff, a contractor in Washington, got one of these on the twenty-eighth, and on the same day the defendant learned its mistake and telegraphed all the contractors to whom it had sent the offer, that it withdrew it and would substitute a new one at about double the amount of the old. This withdrawal reached the plaintiff at Washington on the afternoon of the same day, but not until after it had put in a bid at Harrisburg at a lump sum, based as to linoleum upon the prices quoted by the defendant. The public authorities accepted the plaintiff's bid on December thirtieth, the defendant having meanwhile written a letter of confirmation of its withdrawal, received on the thirty-first. The plaintiff formally accepted the offer on January second, and, as the defendant persisted in declining to recognize the existence of a contract, sued it for damages on a breach.

Unless there are circumstances to take it out of the ordinary doctrine, since the offer was withdrawn before it was accepted, the acceptance was too late. Restatement of Contracts, § 35. To meet this the plaintiff argues as follows: It was a reasonable implication from the defendant's offer that it should be irrevocable in case the plaintiff acted upon it, that is to say, used the prices quoted in making its bid, thus putting itself in a position from which it could not withdraw without great loss. While it might have withdrawn its bid after receiving the revocation, the time had passed to submit another, and as the item of linoleum was a very trifling part of the cost of the whole building, it would have been an unreasonable hardship to expect it to lose the contract on that account, and probably forfeit its deposit. While it is true that the plaintiff might in advance have secured a contract conditional upon the success of its bid, this was not what the defendant suggested. It understood that the contractors would use its offer in their bids, and would thus in fact commit themselves to supplying the linoleum at the proposed prices. The inevitable implication from all this was that when the contractors acted upon it, they accepted the offer and promised to pay for the linoleum, in case their bid were accepted.

It was of course possible for the parties to make such a contract, and the question is merely as to what they meant; that is, what is to be imputed to the words they used. Whatever plausibility there is in the argument, is in the fact that the defendant must have known the predicament in which the contractors would be put if it withdrew its offer after the bids went in. However, it seems entirely clear that the contractors did not suppose that they accepted the offer merely by putting in their bids. If, for example, the successful one had repudiated the contract with the public authorities after it had been awarded to him, certainly the defendant could not have sued him for a breach. If he had become bankrupt, the defendant could not prove against his estate. It seems plain therefore that there was no contract between them. And if there be any doubt as to this, the language of the offer sets it at rest. The phrase, "if successful in being awarded this contract," is scarcely met by the mere use of the prices in the bids. Surely such a use was not an "award" of the contract to the defendant. Again, the phrase, "we are offering these prices for * * * prompt acceptance after the general contract has been awarded," looks to the usual communication of an acceptance, and precludes the idea that the use of the offer in the bidding shall be the equivalent. It may indeed be argued that this last language contemplated no more then an early notice that the offer had been accepted, the actual acceptance being the bid, but that would wrench its natural meaning too far, especially in the light of the preceding phrase. The contractors had a ready escape from their difficulty by insisting upon a contract before they used the figures; and in commercial transactions it does not in the end promote justice to seek strained interpretations in aid of those who do not protect themselves.

But the plaintiff says that even though no bilateral contract was made, the defendant should be held under the doctrine of "promissory estoppel." This is to be chiefly found in those cases where persons subscribe to a venture, usually charitable, and are held to their promises after it has been completed. It has been applied much more broadly, however, and has now been generalized in section 90, of the Restatement of Contracts. We may arguendo accept it as it there reads, for it does not apply to the case at bar. Offers are ordinarily made in exchange for a consideration, either a counter-promise or some other act which the promisor wishes to secure. In such cases they propose bargains; they presuppose that each promise or performance is an inducement to the other. * * * But a man may make a promise without expecting an equivalent; a donative promise, conditional or absolute. The common law provided for such by sealed instruments, and it is unfortunate that these are no longer generally available. The doctrine of 'promissory estoppel' is to avoid the harsh results of allowing the promisor in such a case to repudiate, when the promisee has acted in reliance upon the promise. * * * But an offer for an exchange is not meant to become a promise until a consideration has been received, either a counter-promise or whatever else is stipulated. To extend it would be to hold the offeror regardless of the stipulated condition of his offer. In the case at bar the defendant offered to deliver the linoleum in exchange for the plaintiff's acceptance, not for its bid, which was a matter of indifference to it. That offer could become a promise to deliver only when the equivalent was received; that is, when the plaintiff promised to take and pay for it. There is no room in such a situation for the doctrine of "promissory estoppel."

Nor can the offer be regarded as of an option, giving the plaintiff the right seasonably to accept the linoleum at the quoted prices if its bid was accepted, but not binding it to take and pay, if it could get a better bargain elsewhere. There is not the least reason to suppose that the defendant meant to subject itself to such one-sided obligation. True, if so construed, the doctrine of 'promissory estoppel' might apply, the plaintiff having acted in reliance upon it, though, so far as we have found, the decisions are otherwise. * * * As to that, however, we need not declare ourselves.

Judgment affirmed.

Drennan v. Star Paving Co.
Supreme Court of California, 1958.
51 Cal.2d 409, 333 P.2d 757.

■ TRAYNOR, JUSTICE.

1 Defendant appeals from a judgment for plaintiff in an action to recover damages caused by defendant's refusal to perform certain paving work according to a bid it submitted to plaintiff.

2 On July 28, 1955, plaintiff, a licensed general contractor, was preparing a bid on the 'Monte Vista School Job' in the Lancaster school district. Bids had to be submitted before 8:00 p. m. Plaintiff testified that it was customary in that area for general contractors to receive the bids of subcontractors by telephone on the day set for bidding and to rely on them in computing their own bids. Thus on that day plaintiff's secretary, Mrs. Johnson, received by telephone between fifty and seventy-five subcontractors' bids for various parts of the school job. As each bid came in, she wrote it on a special form, which she brought into plaintiff's office. He then posted it on a master cost sheet setting forth the names and bids of all subcontractors. His own bid had to include the names of subcontractors who were to perform one-half of one per cent or more of the construction work, and he had also to provide a bidder's bond of ten per cent of his total bid of $317,385 as a guarantee that he would enter the contract if awarded the work.

3 Late in the afternoon, Mrs. Johnson had a telephone conversation with Kenneth R. Hoon, an estimator for defendant. He gave his name and telephone number and stated that he was bidding for defendant for the paving work at the Monte Vista School according to plans and specifications and that his bid was $7,131.60. At Mrs. Johnson's request he repeated his bid. Plaintiff listened to the bid over an extension telephone in his office and posted it on the master sheet after receiving the bid form from Mrs. Johnson. Defendant's was the lowest bid for the paving. Plaintiff computed his own bid accordingly and submitted it with the name of defendant as the subcontractor for the paving. When the bids were opened on July 28th, plaintiff's proved to be the lowest, and he was awarded the contract.

4 On his way to Los Angeles the next morning plaintiff stopped at defendant's office. The first person he met was defendant's construction engineer, Mr. Oppenheimer. Plaintiff testified: 'I introduced myself and he immediately told me that they had made a mistake in their bid to me the night before, they couldn't do it for the price they had bid, and I told him I would expect him to carry through with their original bid because I had used it in compiling my bid and the job was being awarded them. And I would have to go and do the job according to my bid and I would expect them to do the same.'

5 Defendant refused to do the paving work for less than $15,000. Plaintiff testified that he 'got figures from other people' and after trying for several months to get as low a bid as possible engaged L & H Paving Company, a firm in Lancaster, to do the work for $10,948.60.

6   The trial court found on substantial evidence that defendant made a definite offer to do the paving on the Monte Vista job according to the plans and specifications for $7,131.60, and that plaintiff relied on defendant's bid in computing his own bid for the school job and naming defendant therein as the subcontractor for the paving work. Accordingly, it entered judgment for plaintiff in the amount of $3,817.00 (the difference between defendant's bid and the cost of the paving to plaintiff) plus costs.

7   Defendant contends that there was no enforceable contract between the parties on the ground that it made a revocable offer and revoked it before plaintiff communicated his acceptance to defendant.

8   There is no evidence that defendant offered to make its bid irrevocable in exchange for plaintiff's use of its figures in computing his bid. Nor is there evidence that would warrant interpreting plaintiff's use of defendant's bid as the acceptance thereof, binding plaintiff, on condition he received the main contract, to award the subcontract to defendant. In sum, there was neither an option supported by consideration nor a bilateral contract binding on both parties.

9   Plaintiff contends, however, that he relied to his detriment on defendant's offer and that defendant must therefore answer in damages for its refusal to perform. Thus the question is squarely presented: Did plaintiff's reliance make defendant's offer irrevocable?

10   Section 90 of the Restatement of Contracts states: 'A promise which the promisor should reasonably expect to induce action or forbearance of a definite and substantial character on the part of the promisee and which does induce such action or forbearance is binding if injustice can be avoided only by enforcement of the promise.' This rule applies in this state. * * *

11   Defendant's offer constituted a promise to perform on such conditions as were stated expressly or by implication therein or annexed thereto by operation of law. (See 1 Williston, Contracts (3rd. ed.), § 24A, p. 56, § 61, p. 196.) Defendant had reason to expect that if its bid proved the lowest it would be used by plaintiff. It induced 'action . . . of a definite and substantial character on the part of the promisee.'

12   Had defendant's bid expressly stated or clearly implied that it was revocable at any time before acceptance we would treat it accordingly. It was silent on revocation, however, and we must therefore determine whether there are conditions to the right of revocation imposed by law or reasonably inferable in fact. In the analogous problem of an offer for a unilateral contract, the theory is now obsolete that the offer is revocable at any time before complete performance. Thus section 45 of the Restatement of Contracts provides: 'If an offer for a unilateral contract is made, and part of the consideration requested in the offer is given or tendered by the offeree in response thereto, the offeror is bound by a contract, the duty of immediate performance of which is conditional on the full consideration being given or tendered within the time stated in the offer, or, if no time is stated therein, within a reasonable time.' In explanation, comment b states that the 'main offer includes as a subsidiary promise, necessarily implied, that if part of the requested performance is given, the offeror will not revoke his offer, and that if tender is made it will be accepted. Part performance or tender may thus furnish consideration for the subsidiary promise. Moreover, merely acting in justifiable reliance on an offer may in some cases serve as sufficient reason for making a promise binding (see § 90).'

13 Whether implied in fact or law, the subsidiary promise serves to preclude the injustice that would result if the offer could be revoked after the offeree had acted in detrimental reliance thereon. Reasonable reliance resulting in a foreseeable prejudicial change in position affords a compelling basis also for implying a subsidiary promise not to revoke an offer for a bilateral contract.

14 The absence of consideration is not fatal to the enforcement of such a promise. It is true that in the case of unilateral contracts the Restatement finds consideration for the implied subsidiary promise in the part performance of the bargained-for exchange, but its reference to section 90 makes clear that consideration for such a promise is not always necessary. The very purpose of section 90 is to make a promise binding even though there was no consideration 'in the sense of something that is bargained for and given in exchange.' (See 1 Corbin, Contracts 634 et seq.) Reasonable reliance serves to hold the offeror in lieu of the consideration ordinarily required to make the offer binding. In a case involving similar facts the Supreme Court of South Dakota stated that 'we believe that reason and justice demand that the doctrine (of section 90) be applied to the present facts. We cannot believe that by accepting this doctrine as controlling in the state of facts before us we will abolish the requirement of a consideration in contract cases, in any different sense than an ordinary estoppel abolishes some legal requirement in its application. We are of the opinion, therefore, that the defendants in executing the agreement (which was not supported by consideration) made a promise which they should have reasonably expected would induce the plaintiff to submit a bid based thereon to the Government, that such promise did induce this action, and that injustice can be avoided only by enforcement of the promise.' *Northwestern Engineering Co. v. Ellman*, 69 S.D. 397, 408, 10 N.W.2d 879, 888; * * * c. *James Baird Co. v. Gimbel Bros.*, 2 Cir., 64 F.2d 344.

15 When plaintiff used defendant's offer in computing his own bid, he bound himself to perform in reliance on defendant's terms. Though defendant did not bargain for this use of its bid neither did defendant make it idly, indifferent to whether it would be used or not. On the contrary it is reasonable to suppose that defendant submitted its bid to obtain the subcontract. It was bound to realize the substantial possibility that its bid would be the lowest, and that it would be included by plaintiff in his bid. It was to its own interest that the contractor be awarded the general contract; the lower the subcontract bid, the lower the general contractor's bid was likely to be and the greater its chance of acceptance and hence the greater defendant's chance of getting the paving subcontract. Defendant had reason not only to expect plaintiff to rely on its bid but to want him to. Clearly defendant had a stake in plaintiff's reliance on its bid. Given this interest and the fact that plaintiff is bound by his own bid, it is only fair that plaintiff should have at least an opportunity to accept defendant's bid after the general contract has been awarded to him.

16 It bears noting that a general contractor is not free to delay acceptance after he has been awarded the general contract in the hope of getting a better price. Nor can he reopen bargaining with the subcontractor and at the same time claim a continuing right to accept the original offer. See, *R. J. Daum Const. Co. v. Child, Utah*, 247 P.2d 817, 823. In the present case plaintiff promptly informed defendant that plaintiff was being awarded the job and that the subcontract was being awarded to defendant.

17 Defendant contends, however, that its bid was the result of mistake and that it was therefore entitled to revoke it. It relies on the rescission cases of *M. F. Kemper Const. Co. v. City of Los Angeles*, 37 Cal.2d 696, 235 P.2d 7, and *Brunzell Const. Co. v. G. J. Weisbrod, Inc.*, 134 Cal.App.2d 278, 285 P.2d 989. * * *. In those cases, however, the bidder's mistake was known or should have been known to the offeree, and the offeree could be placed in status quo. Of course, if plaintiff had reason to believe that defendant's bid was in error, he could not justifiably rely on it, and section 90 would afford no basis for enforcing it. *Robert Gordon, Inc., v. Ingersoll-Rand, Inc.*, 7 Cir., 117 F.2d 654, 660. Plaintiff, however, had no reason to know that defendant had made a mistake in submitting its bid, since there was usually a variance of 160 per cent between the highest and lowest bids for paving in the desert around Lancaster. He committed himself to performing the main contract in reliance on defendant's figures. Under these circumstances defendant's mistake, far from relieving it of its obligation, constitutes an additional reason for enforcing it, for it misled plaintiff as to the cost of doing the paving. . . .

. . .

The judgment is affirmed.

NOTES

1. In *Baird v. Gimbel*, Judge Learned Hand ruled for the subcontractor in a case essentially indistinguishable from *Drennan*. Judge Hand explicitly considered the argument based on Section 90 of the

Restatement but rejected it. In *Drennan*, Justice Traynor reached the opposite result. Both decisions come from highly skillful judges, and their direct comparison is worthwhile.

Learned Hand served on the U.S. District Court for the Southern District of New York from 1909 to 1924 and on the U.S. Court of Appeals for the Second Circuit from 1924–1951, serving as Chief Judge from 1948–1951. Judge Hand has been quoted more often by legal scholars and by the Supreme Court of the United States than any other lower-court judge. Roger Traynor was a Justice of the California Supreme Court from 1940 until 1970, and served as Chief Justice from 1964–1970. Prior to becoming a judge, he taught at the University of California Berkeley law school from 1929–1940. In departing from *Baird v. Gimbel,* he was no doubt aware of the significance of his decision.

We have added the marginal paragraph numbers (1, 2, 3, . . .) to *Drennan* to make it easier to refer to specific portions of the opinion.

2.   Section 87(2) of the Restatement is the way that the Restatement drafters expressed the result of the *Drennan* case. There was nothing like Section 87(2) in the first Restatement, the one that had been written at the time of the *Baird v. Gimbel* and *Drennan* cases. In other words, there is no point in looking at Section 87(2) of the Restatement in trying to understand the *Drennan* case.

3.   We will examine the *Drennan* case in great detail, because it is an excellent vehicle for practicing the technique of very careful case reading. First, a word is warranted on the general situation. The school district wanted to enter into a contract for construction of the school building. The mechanism used for that contract formation process was for the school district to solicit bids from general contractors and then open the bids and award the job to the lowest qualified bidder. Someone who wants a building constructed might do that as a matter of general business practice. Public bodies, like the school district, are often required by statutes to use the bidding process as the manner of entering into contracts, largely as a result of concerns that the public body might otherwise give the job to a builder favored for other illicit reasons. But, our concerns are not affected by such statutes. Rather, we look at the situation from the standpoint of general contract concepts.

4.   There are two different levels of contracting involved in a situation like that in *Drennan*:

(1)   The owner (School District) enters into a contract with the general contractor (Drennan). Under that contract, the general promises to build the building; the owner promises to pay the agreed price.

(2)   The general contractor (Drennan) enters into contracts with sub-contractors (Star Paving). Under those contracts, the subs make a promise to the general that they will do certain work, e.g., the paving, and the general promises to pay them for that work.

There is no direct contractual relationship between the subs and the owner. The owner receives a promise *from the general* that the general will do whatever is necessary to get the building constructed. The general receives a promise *from the sub* that the sub will do some of the work. The owner does not have any contract with the subs. But, once the owner and the general contractor have entered into the contract for construction of the project as a whole, the general is contractually obligated to cause the work to be done for the price set in the agreement between the owner and the general.

Hence the problem that the general faced in the case. Drennan computed its bid for the entire job on the assumption that Star would do the paving work for the $7000 amount of Star's bid. When Star discovered its mistake and refused to do the work for the $7000 price, Drennan had to get another company to do the paving work, and the substitute paver charged about $11,000. So, Drennan had to pay about $4000 more than it expected, and Drennan had no right to recover that extra amount from the school district.

5.   The case poses a genuine issue of policy: Should subcontractors be held liable to a general contractor if they submit an erroneous bid? There are good arguments that can be made either way, which sheds a different light on the comparison between *Baird v. Gimbel* and *Drennan*. One might wonder whether subs or generals are, on the whole, better able to absorb the costs of mistakes of the sort involved in the case.

The case also poses issues about the relationship between legal obligations and practical business judgments. Someone in Star Paving's position might well decide that it should go ahead and do the work for the original $7000 bid price, even though it submitted that bid as a result of a mistake, and even though it is going to take a loss on that job. Star might be worried that if it refuses to do the job, then word will get around that you can't rely on Star's bids. That might have a significant impact on Star's business reputation. So, Star might decide that in the long run, it is better off if it goes ahead and does the job for the mistakenly low price. Star might make that decision whatever the legal rules are. Some of you may have encountered bidding situations of this sort in your pre-law school life, and, based on that business experience, you might assume that it's always been tough luck for a sub if it submits a mistaken bid. That may be correct as a matter of ordinary business practice, but that's different from the question of legal obligation.

Think about the way the two cases resolve these concerns of policy and of the relationship between law and practice.

6.   Now, suppose that one has decided that the appropriate outcome is that the sub should be held to the mistaken bid, i.e. one sides with *Drennan*. How do we reach that result given our existing concepts of offer and acceptance?

The first step in unpacking the *Drennan* opinion is to work through the exact sequence of offer and acceptance. Examine the facts in ¶¶ 2–4 of the opinion very carefully. Write out the significant steps in temporal order. Then consider what the parties' legal rights were step by step.

As part of that analysis, consider the following variant. Suppose that on the evening of July 28, Drennan sent a fax to Star saying "We have been awarded the Monte Vista School contract. We want you to do the paving work." How would that change have affected the parties' legal obligations?

Suppose that: (a) that such a fax had been sent, (b) Star refused to do the work for $7000, (c) Drennan got someone else to do the work but had to pay $11,000, and (d) Drennan sued Star for the $4000. You are the law clerk to the judge hearing the case. Drennan moves for summary judgment. The judge wants you to draft an opinion. What does your draft look like?

7.   When was the offer made by Star's bid accepted? Did Drennan's use of Star's bid constitute acceptance? If so, what would happen if Drennan had been awarded the general contract, but Drennan decided to have someone else to the paving work? In that connection, consider the case of *Southern California Acoustics Co v. C. V. Holder, Inc.*, printed below, and note that the case was decided by the same court as *Drennan*.

8.   Look carefully at ¶ 9 of the *Drennan* opinion:

Plaintiff contends, however, that he relied to his detriment on defendant's offer and that defendant must therefore answer in damages for its refusal to perform. Thus the question is squarely presented: Did plaintiff's reliance make defendant's offer irrevocable?

The *Drennan* case was decided in 1958, and by then the general principle in Restatement § 90 was widely accepted. Paragraphs 9 & 10 of the opinion show that the Court regarded the § 90 principle as law. But, note that it is not until ¶ 15 that Justice Traynor starts talking about the specific facts bearing on Drennan's argument that it reasonably relied on Star's bid and got hurt as a result. So, what's going on in ¶¶ 11–14? Justice Traynor was a very skillful and careful judge. He didn't write things just for the heck of it. Paragraphs 11–14 would not be in the opinion unless there was some reason for them to be there.

Section 90 says that in some cases a promise is enforceable even though not supported by consideration. Did Star make a promise to Drennan to do the work? Try very hard to understand the difference between an *offer* and a *promise*. That point is probably the most important thing in trying to get a precise understanding of what Justice Traynor is doing in the *Drennan* case. Go back and re-read the text note on offers and promises in Chapter 3B, *supra*.

9.   Why is ¶ 16 of the opinion included? Note the somewhat odd opening phrase: "It bears noting . . . ." Why is Traynor noting that?

Southern California Acoustics
Co. v. C. V. Holder, Inc.

Supreme Court of California, 1969.
71 Cal.2d 719, 456 P.2d 975.

■ TRAYNOR, CHIEF JUSTICE.

Plaintiff appeals from a judgment of dismissal entered after a demurrer to its second amended complaint was sustained without leave to amend.

Plaintiff alleged this it is a licensed specialty subcontractor. On November 24, 1965, it submitted by telephone to defendant C. V. Holder, Inc., a general contractor, a subcontract bid in the amount of $83,400 for the furnishing and installation of acoustical tile on a public construction job. Later that day Holder submitted a bid for the prime contract to codefendant Los Angeles Unified School District. As required by law, Holder listed the subcontractors who would perform work on the project of a value in excess of one-half of one percent of the total bid. Holder listed plaintiff as the acoustical tile subcontractor. Holder was subsequently awarded the prime contract for construction of the facility and executed a written contract with the school district on December 9, 1965. A local trade newspaper widely circulated among subcontractors reported that Holder had been awarded the contract and included in its report the names of the subcontractors listed in Holder's bid. Plaintiff read the report and, acting on the assumption that its bid had been accepted, refrained from bidding on other construction jobs in order to remain within its bonding limits.

Sometime between December 27, 1965, and January 10, 1966, Holder requested permission from the school district to substitute another subcontractor for plaintiff, apparently on the ground that plaintiff had been inadvertently listed in the bid in place of the intended subcontractor. The school district consented, and the substitution was made. Plaintiff then sought a writ of mandamus to compel the school district to rescind its consent to the change in subcontractors. The trial court sustained the district's demurrer and thereafter dismissed the proceeding. Plaintiff did not appeal. Plaintiff then brought this action for damages against Holder and the school district.

Plaintiff contends that the trial court erred in sustaining the demurrer on the ground that the facts alleged in its complaint would support recovery of damages for breach of contract, breach of a statutory duty, and for negligence. . . .

There was no contract between plaintiff and Holder, for Holder did not accept plaintiff's offer. Silence in the face of an offer is not an acceptance, unless there is a relationship between the parties or a previous course of dealing pursuant to which silence would be understood as acceptance. * * * No such relationship or course of dealing is alleged. Nor did Holder accept the bid by using it in presenting its own bid. In the absence of an agreement to the contrary, listing of the subcontractor in the prime bid is not an implied acceptance of the subcontractor's bid by the general contractor. * * * The listing by the general contractor of the subcontractors he intends to retain is in response to statutory command * * * and cannot reasonably be construed as an expression of acceptance. * * *

Plaintiff contends, however, that its reliance on Holder's use of its bid and Holder's failure to reject its offer promptly after Holder's bid was accepted constitute acceptance of plaintiff's bid by operation of law under the doctrine of promissory estoppel. Section 90 of the Restatement of Contracts states: 'A promise which the promisor should reasonably expect to induce action or forbearance of a definite and substantial character on the part of the promisee and which does induce such action or forbearance is binding if injustice can be avoided only by enforcement of the promise.' This rule applies in this state. *Drennan v. Star Paving Co.* (1958) 51 Cal.2d 409, 413, 333 P.2d 757. Before it can be invoked, however, there must be a promise that was relied upon. * * *

In *Drennan*, we held that implicit in the subcontractor's bid was a subsidiary promise to keep his bid open for a reasonable time after award of the prime contract to give the general contractor an opportunity to accept the offer on which he relied in computing the prime bid. The subsidiary promise was implied 'to preclude the injustice that would result if the offer could be revoked after the offeree had acted in detrimental reliance thereon.' * * *

Plaintiff urges us to find an analogous subsidiary promise not to reject its bid in this case, but it fails to allege facts showing the existence of any promise by Holder to it upon which it detrimentally relied. Plaintiff did not rely on any promise by Holder, but only on the listing of subcontractors required by section 4104 of the Government Code and on the statutory restriction on Holder's right to change its listed subcontractors without the consent of the school district. * * * Holder neither accepted plaintiff's offer, nor made any promise or offer to plaintiff intended to 'induce action or forbearance of a definite and substantial character.'

. . . [The portion of the opinion dealing with the specific California statutes concerning the public construction bidding process is omitted.]

CHAPTER SIX

REQUIREMENT OF WRITING: "STATUTE OF FRAUDS"

> An oral contract isn't worth
> the paper it's written on.
>
> —Attributed to Samuel Goldwyn

A. INTRODUCTION

In this Chapter we examine what difference it makes whether an agreement is in writing or is oral. As a first step, let's be careful with language. In particular, let's agree that we will not use the word "verbal" when we mean "oral." The word "verbal" has at least two meanings: (1) consisting of words, and (2) spoken (rather than written). Given that ambiguity, it's pretty unhelpful to talk about "verbal agreements" in this context. Maybe Marcel Marceau or other mimes can enter into "non-verbal" contracts, but the rest of us are going to use words. So the issue is whether it matters whether an agreement is "oral" or "written."

If you Google the phrase "get it in writing" you'll get thousands of hits, most of them being some sort of advice that one should always have a written agreement for any significant contractual arrangement. That's usually good advice, but it's not directly relevant to the issues we have here. Suppose there were no legal rules that ever required written evidence as a condition to the enforceability of agreements. Would people still have written agreements? Of course. If the parties to an agreement do not put it in writing, then it's going to be difficult and expensive to prove that there was oral agreement and to prove the terms of an oral agreement. So, careful people are going to get written agreements no matter what the law is.

One consequence of this fairly obvious point is often overlooked by lawyers. As we will soon see, the rules on whether a writing is required for various forms of agreements have become pretty complex. So it's not uncommon to have a dispute about whether a writing was required, or whether there was an adequate writing. A lawyer arguing that the agreement should not be enforceable will sometimes end up saying something along the lines of "Your Honor, we should be rigorous here. If we don't require writings, or don't require more complete writings, then all kinds of terrible consequences will follow. People will get sloppy, and courts will be swamped with cases where people assert oral agreements. More harm than good will result from allowing parties to sue on oral agreements when they have neglected the simple formality of getting written agreements." That's at least a little odd. If the parties thought about the problem, they would have gotten a written agreement no matter what the legal rules are. The problem is what to do in the cases where the parties did not get a clear writing.

While common sense suggests that one should get a written agreement for any significant business agreement, the applicable legal rule is not that simple. The requirement of a writing is imposed by statute, typically a statute known as the "Statute of Frauds." But, the word "fraud" is misleading in this context. The "Statute of Frauds" doesn't have much of anything to do with "fraud" in the sense of misrepresentation. Rather the "Statute of Frauds" is the common lawyer's jargon for those statutes that impose a requirement of a writing as a condition to legal enforceability of certain promises.

Anglo-American law on this subject can be traced back to a statute enacted in England in 1677. Stat. 29 Car. 2, c.3. All American jurisdictions have statutes derived from the old English statute, as well as other statutes requiring writings for various other types of contracts. Many of these statutes are very old, using language that has not changed very much since the seventeenth century. Most of the elements of the Statute of Frauds have been the subject of centuries of judicial construction and interpretation. Quite a bit of that case law is rather quirky. So, though the source of law on this subject is, in theory, a statute, the mode of interpretation is much more like the model of law development by judicial decision that we have been working with in other areas.

B. SCOPE OF WRITING REQUIREMENT

Restatement (Second) of Contracts § 110

It's a little odd to have a Restatement provision describing a statute. Why not just look at the statute? We don't have Restatement provisions describing other statutes, like the statute of limitations or Article 2 of the U.C.C. But, as noted above, judicial decisions in this area are at least as important as the text of any actual statute. So, it's useful to have a general description in the Restatement.

Look carefully at Restatement § 110, and think about whether it imposes a requirement of a writing for all significant business transactions.

PROBLEM

Owner owns land on which he is interested in building a house. Owner has Architect draw up plans for the house.

Owner shows the plans to Builder, and asks how much it will cost to build the house in accordance with the plans. Builder says he will think it over and get back to Owner.

Builder sends an e-mail to Owner offering to build house, per plans, for $400,000.

Owner telephones Builder, and says "I accept."

The next week, Owner hears a bad report about Builder. Also, Owner is told by another builder that the cost for that job shouldn't be any more than $375,000.

Owner sends a telegram to Builder, saying that the deal is off.

Builder sues Owner.

Owner moves to dismiss on the grounds that there was no written agreement.

What result?

C. SUFFICIENCY OF WRITING

Restatement (Second) of Contracts §§ 131–137

Chomicky v. Buttolph

Supreme Court of Vermont, 1986.
147 Vt. 128, 513 A.2d 1174.

■ HILL, JUSTICE.

Defendants, Edward and Barbara Buttolph, appeal from the lower court's order granting specific performance of an alleged oral agreement for the sale of property. . . . We reverse the court's decree of specific performance on the basis that this dispute is properly resolved under the Statute of Frauds . . . .

Defendants are landowners of lakeside property on Lake Dunmore. Their property is divided by a road. Intending to retain title to the undeveloped back lot together with a 50-foot strip leading to the lake, defendants offered the front lakeside lot and summer cottage for sale.

Plaintiffs inspected the property, and entered into negotiations with defendants. The parties eventually reached an understanding, and plaintiffs' attorney drew up a purchase and sale contract that reflected the terms of their agreement. Both parties signed the contract in August, 1985; the closing was to occur in mid-October. The contract, however, was made contingent on the defendants obtaining a subdivision permit from the Leicester Planning Commission.

While defendants' subdivision petition was pending, plaintiff Eugene Chomicky telephoned defendants to discuss an alternative that would allow them to proceed with the sale in the event that the permit was denied. Plaintiff proposed that defendants retain an easement granting them a 50-foot right-of-way in lieu of outright ownership. Mr. Buttolph told Mr. Chomicky that they had considered that option, but that his wife was opposed to it. He agreed to discuss it with her again.

On October 1, Mr. Buttolph called the plaintiffs, and indicated that the right-of-way arrangement previously discussed was acceptable in the event that the Leicester Planning Commission did not approve their subdivision permit.

The Commission met on October 12, 1985, and denied defendants' permit application. On October 13, defendants called plaintiffs and advised them that "the deal was off." They now wanted to sell the whole parcel or nothing. Plaintiffs sued for specific performance on the oral contract allegedly concluded over the phone.

A contract involving the sale of land or interests therein is controlled by the Statute of Frauds. See 12 V.S.A. § 181(5). As a general rule, such contracts must be in writing to be enforceable. * * * Moreover, any proposed changes or modifications "are subjected to the same requirements of form as the original provisions." * * *

According to plaintiffs, defendants have admitted to the existence of the oral contract in question, and are thus precluded from setting up the Statute of Frauds as a defense to this action. Plaintiffs cite a footnote in *Bryant v. Strong*, 141 Vt. 244, 245 n. 1, 448 A.2d 142, 143 n. 1 (1982), as controlling precedent on this issue. Even if we accept plaintiffs' characterization of the facts, a characterization which is very much contested by the defendants, we do not believe that such an admission takes the contract outside the Statute of Frauds.

First, the statement relied on by plaintiffs is dicta. The Court in *Bryant* ruled that the plaintiff, not being a party to the contract, had no standing to challenge its validity. *Bryant*, supra, 141 Vt. at 245 n. 1, 448 A.2d at 143 n. 1. Thus, it had no occasion to pass on the validity of the underlying oral contract granting a would-be purchaser a right of first refusal.

Second, while the writing requirement is imposed primarily as a shield against possible fraud, *see Couture* [*v. Lowery*, 122 Vt. 239, 243, 168 A.2d 295, 298 (1961)], it also "promotes deliberation, seriousness, certainty, and shows that the act was a genuine act of volition." Rabel, *The Statute of Frauds and Comparative Legal History*, 63 L.Q. Rev. 174, 178 (1947). In short, it helps to ensure that contracts for the sale of land or interests therein are not entered into improvidently. Thus, in *Couture*, supra, 122 Vt. at 243, 168 A.2d at 298, we expressly stated that "[o]ne may admit the sale of land by a verbal contract, and yet defend an action for specific performance by pleading the statute." *See also Radke v. Brenon*, 271 Minn. 35, 37–38, 134 N.W.2d 887, 889–90 (1965) (fact that defendant admits parol contract sued upon does not preclude him from setting up and insisting upon the Statute of Frauds as a defense to the action).

. . .

Radke v. Brenon

Supreme Court of Minnesota, 1965.
271 Minn. 35, 134 N.W. 2d 887.

■ ROGOSHESKE, JUSTICE.

Defendants appeal from a judgment of the district court decreeing specific performance of a contract for the sale of real estate.

The judgment was entered upon findings made after trial that 'subsequent to the Defendant acquiring' the property in question they 'did offer to sell the property to the Plaintiff for the sum of Two Hundred Sixty-two ($262.00) Dollars, which offer the Plaintiff did accept' . . . The court concluded that defendants 'have wrongfully and improperly failed and refused' to deliver a deed of the property to plaintiff.

Resolving the conflicts in the evidence in plaintiff's favor, as we must, these appear to be the facts. Plaintiff and defendants are neighbors owning adjoining lots in Wakefield Park addition in Ramsey County. At the times each acquired ownership, their lots and eight neighboring lots did not extend to the west shoreline of Wakefield Lake, located nearby. The strip of land between the shoreline of the lake and the east boundary of the platted lots was owned by Dr. Gulden, the developer of the addition, and his brother. They had been hopeful of selling the entire strip to the county for use of a park, but when the county finally declined the offer in 1956, Dr. Gulden attempted to sell to the several owners separated from the lake. These attempts were unsuccessful until December 1, 1959, when defendants acquired ownership of the entire strip. Preston Brenon, hereinafter referred to as defendant, was a licensed real estate agent. Following his purchase, he had the property surveyed, and on June 28, 1960, he sent an identical letter to plaintiff and the eight other neighbors offering to sell them the irregular parcels that separated their lots from the lake. In the letter he explained that since he was interested only in that part of the strip adjoining his property, he had no desire to retain the remainder. He stated he had 'no desire to make any profit on this transaction if everyone owning adjoining property is willing to buy their portion' and divide the cost 'equally among all 10 including (him)self.' He itemized the total cost at $2,120 and offered to sell each lot for $212 on any terms agreeable. This letter was not signed by defendant but his name was typewritten thereon, he having authorized this and considered such to be tantamount to his signature. Previous to the receipt of this letter, plaintiff and defendant had discussed the latter's intent of acquiring the property for the neighborhood on at least two occasions. About 2 weeks after plaintiff received this offer, he orally accepted it. Sometime later, plaintiff learned from a neighbor that two neighbors declined to purchase, and thus the divided cost of each lot was increased to $262. Although he was agreeable to pay the increase, he did not immediately so inform defendant. Despite defendant's progress in completing sales to other interested neighbors, plaintiff, for reasons not explained except that he believed he was waiting for defendant to furnish him a copy of the survey and an abstract, delayed making a request for the abstract until May 7, 1961. On cross-examination, he admitted that the survey was received by him with the June 28 letter. In any event, it is clear that plaintiff accepted defendant's offer on May 7, at which time plaintiff knew of the price increase. Defendant testified:

> 'Q. And did he agree to buy that time?
>
> 'A. At that time he did.'

Later in May, defendant delivered to plaintiff a stub abstract covering entries from July 2, 1947, to May 9, 1961. At that time plaintiff offered 'some money' but was told by defendant to 'wait till it's all settled.' There was a further delay before a title opinion could be given, made necessary when plaintiff's attorney insisted on procuring a complete abstract. On August 14, plaintiff delivered to his attorney a check for $262 payable to defendants for the purpose of completing the sale. On August 16, plaintiff's attorney wrote defendant informing him that he held the check for payment of the sale price to be delivered on receipt of a deed. Sometime after August 16, plaintiff received a letter from defendant dated August 16 informing him that the offer to sell was revoked.

. . .

As admitted by defendant, an oral contract to sell the land was made, and the trial court was clearly justified in so finding. There being no formal, integrated, written contract, however, the problem is whether the oral contract is unenforceable because it comes within * * * the statute of frauds. Briefly, that provision decrees void any contract for the sale of lands unless the contract or some memorandum of the contract is in writing. The precise issue in this case is whether, under the circumstances, the letter written by defendant offering the land to plaintiff is a memorandum sufficient to satisfy the requirements of the statute.

The statute expresses a public policy of preventing the enforcement by means of fraud and perjury of contracts that were never in fact made. To inhibit perversion of this policy by those who would deny an oral contract actually made, the statute itself permits enforcement of an oral contract if there exists a note or memorandum as evidence of the contract. To the courts, then, is left promotion of the policy of the statute, either by denying enforcement urged by defrauders or by granting enforcement against wrongful repudiators. As an aid in this objective, the statute itself lists some requisites of a memorandum and this court has added others, so that we have some indication of what content a memorandum normally must have in order to be sufficient evidence of the contract.

The statute requires that the writing . . . be subscribed by the party by whom the sale is to be made or by his lawful agent authorized in writing. This court has stated that the memorandum is sufficient when, in addition to the above requirements, it states expressly or by necessary implication the parties to the contract, the lands involved, and the general terms and conditions upon which the sale will be made.

These latter elements are clearly present in the letter written by defendant. Plaintiff's name is included in the inside address heading the letter, and Brenon's name is typewritten at the bottom. The land to be sold is positively delineated. The letter offers 'their portion' to 'everyone owning adjoining property,' and the survey map accompanying the letter depicts each tract. Considering the conversation both before and after the letter was sent, it is inconceivable that the parties could be uncertain concerning the land to be sold. As to other terms of the contract, such as manner of payment, Brenon merely held himself ready 'to work out any kind of terms' with the purchasers.

. . .

The necessity of a subscription presents the final problem. A 'subscription' is the same as a 'signing,' and it is clear that Brenon's typewritten name, which according to his testimony was typed with the intent that it be tantamount to a written signature, is a sufficient subscription. A problem here is that his wife, who owned the property with him in joint tenancy, apparently neither signed the letter nor authorized him in writing to sell her share. But this deficiency was at no time claimed or asserted before the trial court or in defendants' brief to this court. It was suggested for the first time upon oral argument. If it is a fact, it was not a part of the theory upon which the case was tried and submitted. We must therefore adhere to our well-settled rule that an unlitigated issue may not be asserted for the first time on appeal.

We by no means intend to hold that Brenon's letter would be a sufficient memorandum in every case. We will overlook technical requirements only if proof of the oral contract is clear and uncontradicted as in this case where defendant admitted that a contract had been made. But those technical requirements are only aids to discern where the truth lies in a given case, and we will not blindly apply those technicalities if they lead to a conclusion repugnant to commonsense. As Professor Williston has said:

> 'In brief, the Statute 'was intended to guard against the perils of perjury and error in the spoken word.' Therefore, if after a consideration of the surrounding circumstances, the pertinent facts and all the evidence in a particular care, the court concludes that enforcement of the agreement will not subject the defendant to fraudulent claims, the purpose of the Statute will best be served by holding the note or memorandum sufficient even though it be ambiguous or incomplete.'—4 Williston, Contracts (3 ed.) § 567A; 2 Corbin, Contracts, § 498.

Most persuasive is defendant's admission during trial that a contract was in fact made between plaintiff and himself. Although we have followed the majority rule that admission of the contract does not preclude assertion of the statute of frauds, an admission that a contract was made certainly cannot be ignored when all other evidence submitted supports the same conclusion. Even though it may be argued that the formal requirements contemplated by the statute are lacking, when all the evidence is taken into account we are of the opinion that the letter should be held a sufficient memorandum in this case. The policy of the statute of frauds would be perverted if the admitted contract were not enforced. The judgment of the trial court is therefore affirmed.

NOTES & QUESTIONS

1.   *Chomicky* cites *Radke* in the last sentence of the opinion. Do you agree with the Supreme Court of Vermont's treatment of the case?

2.   The Statute of Frauds has been assigned various functions. Consider this summary: "(1) the Statute still serves an evidentiary function thereby lessening the danger of perjured testimony (the original rationale); (2) the requirement of a writing has a cautionary effect which causes reflection by the parties on the importance of the agreement; and (3) the writing is an easy way to distinguish enforceable contracts from those which are not, thus channeling certain transactions into written form." (*McIntosh v. Murphy*, below, citing Fuller, *Consideration and Form*, 41 COLUM. L. REV. 799, 800–03 (1941)). Does it matter what the purpose of the statute is? What flows from this?

PROBLEM

On Sept 1, Sally Smith and Bob Brown orally agreed that Sally would sell Bob her condo unit, #123 at 2334 Main St., Enfield MA, for $225,000, with the closing to take place on Nov 1.

On Oct. 1, Sally sent Bob an e-mail note saying:

"Dear Bob,

I'm sorry to have to inform you that due to unforeseen circumstances, I will not be able to sell you my condo unit. I had expected to be moving to California, but my job offer there has now fallen through and I will not be moving.

Sally Smith"

On Nov 1, Bob bought an essentially identical condo unit in the same building, but due to general price rise, it cost him $250,000.

Bob sues Sally for $25,000 damages. Sally defends on the basis of Statute of Frauds.

What result?

D. ELECTRONIC COMMERCE & STATUTE OF FRAUDS

Electronic Signatures in Global and National Commerce Act of 2000, 15 U.S.C. §§ 7001(a) & 7006(5)

In the past decade or so, quite a bit of attention has been devoted to formulating rules on what sort of electronic records should suffice for satisfaction of the "writing" requirement of the Statute of Frauds.

In one sense, the issue is very old. Since the middle of the nineteenth century, people have been communicating electronically. Remember that fancy new machine Samuel F. B. Morse developed in the 1830s? What was it called—"telegraph"—or something? Can an electronic communication by telegram satisfy the writing requirement of the Statute of Frauds? Here's what a court said on that "new" issue over a century ago:

> So when a contract is made by telegraph, which must be in writing by the statute of frauds, if the parties authorize their agents either in writing or by parol, to make a proposition on one side and the other party accepts it through the telegraph, that constitutes a contract in writing under the statute of frauds; because each party authorizes his agents, the company or the company's operator, to write for him; and it makes no difference whether that operator writes the offer or the acceptance in the presence of his principal and by his express direction, with a steel pen an inch long attached to an ordinary penholder, or whether his pen be a copper wire a thousand miles long. In either case the thought is communicated to the paper by the use of the finger resting upon the pen; nor does it make any difference that in one case common record ink is used, while in the other case a more subtle fluid, known as electricity, performs the same office.

Howley v. Whipple, 48 N.H. 487 (1869).

For a variety of reasons, however, companies interested in doing commerce by electronic means, such as banks, felt uncomfortable relying solely on potential case law developments. So, various efforts were launched in the 1980s and 1990s to provide greater certainty for electronic commerce. After lengthy discussion in various settings, the issue of treatment of electronic communications eventually became the subject of a federal statute, the Electronic Signatures in Global and National Commerce Act of 2000, commonly referred to as "E-Sign." You should look through the E-Sign act, which appears in the Statutory Supplement to get a general idea of how it operates. The provisions to examine with care are §§ 7001(a) & 7006(5).

E. RESTITUTION OF BENEFITS CONFERRED UNDER ORAL AGREEMENTS

Restatement (Second) of Contracts § 375

Rule: If someone [one party] has given $ as consideration (down payment) & the other party fails to perform the party is entitled to a refund of that & even if the contract is unenforceable.

Gilton v. Chapman
Supreme Court of Arkansas, 1950.
217 Ark. 390, 230 S.W.2d 37.

■ LEFLAR, JUSTICE.

Appellee Chapman brought this action to recover a $1,000 down payment which he had made to appellants on an oral contract for the purchase of a farm and equipment for a total price of $16,500. Appellants gave testimony tending to show that they were at all times willing to convey the land to appellee had he produced 'cash on the barrelhead' for payment of the balance agreed upon, which they say appellee never offered them. Appellee claimed that he did offer to pay cash, in the form of a check that would have been honored, but that appellants refused to go on with the deal and he finally took back his check on the theory that appellants had refused to perform the oral contract. Contradictory evidence was presented to the jury on the issue thus formed, and a verdict for plaintiff for $1,000 resulted. Judgment was duly entered according to the verdict, and defendant appeals.

The contract for sale of land being oral, it was unenforceable under the Statute of Frauds. Ark. Stats. § 38–101. It is well established, however, that a defendant who refuses to perform a contract unenforceable because of the Statute of Frauds, the plaintiff being willing to perform, must repay to the plaintiff any amounts in good faith paid to the withdrawing defendant. . . . '* * * when one who has given his performance in return for a promise of a specific exchange does not receive that exchange, there is failure of consideration on the one side and unjust enrichment on the other; and his knowledge beforehand that he may not receive that exchange does not alter the case. It would be as unfortunate in law as in morals if one who had paid a thousand dollars for an absolute promise of a piece of land believing that the vendor's word was as good as his bond, though knowing the oral agreement was legally unenforceable, should be without remedy if the vendor or his representatives failed to perform. In fact, without regard to the plaintiff's knowledge, or lack of knowledge, of the invalidity of the oral contract, he is allowed to recover the fair value of what he has given when the defendant fails or refuses to perform on his part. It is immaterial whether the plaintiff has parted with money, property, or services.' 2 Williston, Contracts (Rev.Ed., 1936) § 534.

. . . .

The testimony at the trial was in sharp conflict as to whether appellee had or could immediately procure enough cash to compete the payment called for by the oral contract, whether he made to appellant a tender of payment conditioned only on delivery of a good deed to the land, and whether appellant refused to perform the contract after such tender. The trial court submitted these issues to the jury under instructions which correctly stated the law, and the jury found for the plaintiff appellee. We have concluded that there was sufficient evidence before the jury to sustain its verdict. There was testimony by the plaintiff, supported by corroborating testimony of other witnesses, that he had secured the money so that the check he posted with a third party would have been honored, and that appellants nevertheless refused to proceed with delivery of the deed unless other conditions clearly not included in the original contract were also complied with by plaintiff. In view of this evidence we are not free to supersede the jury's verdict.

The judgment of the Circuit Court is affirmed.

F. EFFECT OF RELIANCE ON ORAL AGREEMENTS

1. SPECIFIC PERFORMANCE OF ORAL AGREEMENTS FOR SALE OF LAND

Restatement (Second) of Contracts § 129

Gleason v. Gleason

Court of Appeals of Ohio, Fourth District, 1991.
64 Ohio App.3d 667, 582 N.E.2d 657.

■ STEPHENSON, PRESIDING JUDGE.

This is an appeal from a judgment entered by the Scioto County Court of Common Pleas following a jury trial granting Walter Gleason, plaintiff below and appellee herein, an undivided one-half interest in a ninety-acre farm located in rural Scioto County and owned by James Gleason, a defendant below and appellant herein, in which Hilda Gleason, a defendant below and appellant herein, had a life estate.

. . . .

The following facts are pertinent to this appeal. On October 7, 1988, appellee filed a complaint in the Scioto County Court of Common Pleas. In the complaint, he averred that in the fall of 1979, appellee's parents, Murray Gleason, deceased, and appellant Hilda Gleason, orally promised they would transfer a one-half interest in the ninety-acre family farm if appellee would maintain and pay expenses relating to the farm. Appellee claimed that he agreed to terms of the agreement. Murray Gleason died in 1981 and, following probate of his estate, appellant Hilda Gleason became the sole owner of the property on January 29, 1982. Appellee further averred that Hilda reassured him at that time that the agreement to transfer to him a one-half interest in the farm was still in effect. Appellee claims from 1979 through 1986 he fulfilled his duties pursuant to the agreement and expended approximately $27,250 for the maintenance and care of the farm.

Appellee averred that on or about September 9, 1988, appellant Hilda Gleason transferred the farm to appellant James Gleason, one of appellee's brothers. Appellee claimed that he was reassured that he would still receive his one-half interest in the farm; however, on September 7, 1988, James Gleason, through his attorney, sent appellee a letter ordering him to vacate the farm. Appellee prayed for reimbursement of his expenditures or specific performance of the promise. Appellee's complaint contained a jury demand.

On November 22, 1988, appellants answered and denied that any agreement existed. They further filed a counterclaim seeking reasonable value for appellee's use of the land after October 8, 1988. Appellants also demanded a jury trial on all issues.

A four-day jury trial commenced on February 22, 1988. The majority of the testimony presented involved whether an agreement existed and the amount of money and time appellee expended in working the farm. After both parties rested, the jury returned a verdict in favor of appellee awarding him a one-half interest in the farm.

. . . .

[A]ppellants' argue, the statute of frauds should have prevented appellee from seeking enforcement of the agreement.

The statute of frauds is codified in Ohio in R.C. Chapter 1335. In particular, R.C. 1335.05 reads, in pertinent part as follows:

> "No action shall be brought whereby to charge the defendant, upon a special promise, to answer for the debt, default, or miscarriage of another person; nor to charge an executor or administrator upon a special promise to answer damages out of his own estate; nor to charge a person upon an agreement made upon consideration of marriage, *or upon a contract or sale of lands, tenements, or hereditaments, or interest in or concerning them*, or upon an agreement that is not to be performed within one year from the making thereof; unless the agreement upon which such action is brought, or some memorandum or note thereof, is in writing and signed by the party to be charged therewith or some other person thereunto by him or her lawfully authorized." (Emphasis added.)

Basically, in part, the statute requires that any agreement involving the transfer of an interest in land must be in writing. In the case at bar, there was no writing which contained the alleged agreement between appellee and his parents wherein appellee's parents promised to convey a one-half interest in the property if appellee took care of the property.

Under ordinary circumstances, appellee would be barred from asserting the existence of such an agreement. However, there is an exception which would take the agreement out of the statute of frauds, to wit: the doctrine of part performance.

Part performance is a doctrine in equity to prevent an injustice to the party seeking enforcement of the contract. The leading case in Ohio on the issue of part performance is *Delfino v. Paul Davis Chevrolet, Inc.* (1965), * * * 209 N.E.2d 194, where the following is stated * * *:

"The doctrine of part performance is based in equity. It is applied in situations where it would be inequitable to permit the statute to operate and where the acts done sufficiently establish the alleged agreement to provide a safeguard against fraud in lieu of the statutory requirements.

"Part performance to be sufficient to remove the agreement from the operation of the statute of conveyances (Section 5301.01, Revised Code) must consist of unequivocal acts by the party relying upon the agreement, which are exclusively referable to the agreement and which have changed his position to his detriment and make it impossible or impractical to place the parties *in statu quo.* * * * If the performance can reasonably be accounted for in any other manner or if plaintiff has not altered his position in reliance on the agreement, the case remains within the operation of the statute.

"In *Tier v. Singrey*, * * * 97 N.E.2d at 23, it is stated: 'Possession alone is not sufficient to remove the sale from the operation of the statute of frauds. . . .

" 'In an action for specific enforcement of an oral contract for the sale of land, equity intervenes to render the statute of frauds inoperative only when a failure to enforce the contract will result in fraud and injury. To entitle one claiming to have purchased land to enforce an oral contract for the conveyance thereof, he must, in reliance on the promise, have performed acts which changed his position to his prejudice. 37 Corpus Juris Secundum 764, 766, Section 252.

" 'The rule in such cases is well stated in 49 American Jurisprudence 886, 887, Section 580, as follows: "In order to escape the effect of the statute upon the theory of fraud, one must establish that he acted in reliance on the contract and on the acts or acquiescence of the other party thereto in such way as to have changed his position or prejudiced himself. The fraud against which the courts grant relief, notwithstanding the statute of frauds, consists in a refusal to perform an agreement upon the faith of which the plaintiff has been misled to his injury or made some irretrievable change of position, especially where the defendant has secured an unconscionable advantage, and not in the mere moral wrong involved in the refusal to perform a contract which by reason of the statute cannot be enforced. When one party induces another, on the faith of a parol contract, to place himself, in a worse situation than he could have been if no agreement existed, and especially if the former derives a benefit therefrom at the expense of the latter, and avails himself of his legal advantage, he is guilty of fraud, and uses the statute for a purpose not intended—the injury of another—for his own profit. In such cases, equity regards the case as being removed from the statute of frauds and will in proper cases enforce the contract or otherwise interfere to prevent the application of the statute.'

"The rule particularly applicable here is well stated in 49 American Jurisprudence 732, Section 427, as follows: 'Since the doctrine of part performance is based upon the prevention of fraud, and its application to permit specific performance of an oral contract is dependent upon the existence of the general prerequisites to equitable relief, nothing can be regarded as a part performance to take a verbal [oral] contract out of the operation of the statute which does not place the party in a situation whereby he will be defrauded unless the contract is executed. The acts relied upon as part performance of a parol contract for the sale of land must be such as change the plaintiff's position and would result in a fraud, injustice, or hardship upon him, if the contract were not executed or enforced. * * * 'Equity has no concern in cases of part performance except to prevent the perpetration of a fraud. That is the only ground which can justify its interference. Otherwise, the exercise of its jurisdiction for the practical annulment of the statute would be merely bare usurpation. * * * '

. . . .

The majority of appellants' argument concerning part performance is that there was not sufficient performance shown to take the agreement out of the statute of frauds. In essence, appellee was required to show that he partially performed in reliance and to his detriment upon the promise that if he so performed, he would receive a one-half interest in the farm and that the only remedy which would prevent him from being defrauded would be enforcement of the agreement. Incumbent in appellee's burden was to show that he would not have performed in the absence of the agreement.

At trial, appellee presented evidence that from 1979–1986 he paid the taxes and insurance on the farm, he grew tobacco all but two years, and made improvements on the farm which included liming the fields, clearing the fields and building fences. He also built a house on the farm. However, it should be noted that the piece of property upon which he built the house was part of a two and one-half acre tract of land which had already been deeded to him.

From this evidence, the jury could have concluded that his performance was induced from the promise to convey to him a one-half interest in the land. Even the act of building the house on the farm could be so interpreted. If he had not been promised the interest in the farm, he may have decided to locate elsewhere. Some of the actions, such as building the fences and liming the fields could be considered to be for appellee's own benefit because he was raising show cattle; however, again without the promise to be given the interest in the farm, appellee may not have decided to raise cattle. From the above, it is clear that there was sufficient evidence presented from which the trial court could instruct the jury and allow the jury to consider the issue of whether the doctrine of part performance applied to take the agreement out of the statute of frauds. Accordingly, appellants' third and fifth assignments of error are overruled.

. . . .

Judgment affirmed.

Jasmin v. Alberico

Supreme Court of Vermont, 1977.
135 Vt. 287, 376 A.2d 32.

■ BARNEY, CHIEF JUSTICE.

In this case an action of ejectment became an action for specific performance. Title to premises now occupied by the defendants, the Albericos, is recorded in the name of the plaintiff, Phyllis Jasmin, and her deceased husband. She sought to evict the defendants as tenants at will. They resisted her action and brought a counterclaim for specific performance, alleging an agreement between the parties to convey title to the Albericos upon payment of $2,000.00.

The trial court heard the matter and denied the action for ejectment. Under the counterclaim, judgment was given for specific performance of the claimed agreement upon payment of $2,000.00. The matter is now here.

The plaintiff's basic challenge to the decision below centers on the lack of legal support for the result. It is her position that specific performance is not an available remedy in this situation. We must agree and accordingly reverse.

This decision is required even with full acceptance of the facts as found below. They disclose that the defendant, John Alberico, and plaintiff's deceased husband, Arthur Jasmin, were life-long friends. Arthur Jasmin was a successful businessman. In 1969, the house, the subject of the present controversy, became available at a modest price. John Alberico attempted to buy it. Financing was refused by the bank involved, even though Arthur Jasmin was willing to co-sign a $2,000.00 note to cover the down payment.

When this occurred, Arthur purchased the house, which he proposed to deed to John whenever John repaid the $2,000.00 down payment. In the meantime the Albericos were to make the mortgage payments, including taxes, credit life insurance on the life of Arthur Jasmin, and water rent.

The Albericos moved in and worked, with the help of Arthur Jasmin, to make it liveable.

The arrangement was known to friends and relatives of both the Jasmins and the Albericos, but was never the subject of a writing. When Arthur Jasmin died, the mortgage was paid off by the proceeds of the insurance policy. Subsequently, John Alberico sought to pay to the plaintiff $2,000.00 and obtain a deed, but he was put off, and finally refused. The Albericos continued to pay the same payments to Mrs. Jasmin after Mr. Jasmin's death until August of 1972, although not always timely. Finally, this ejectment action was brought.

Given a contractual obligation dealing with that classically unique [form of property], land, specific performance follows almost as a matter of course. * * * However, there are grounds for denying specific performance, even in the presence of a written contract, in that the granting of this particular kind of relief may produce an unsupportably inequitable result. * * *

Where, as here, there is no such writing, the proponent of specific performance has a double burden. First, he has to establish an agreement enforceable in the face of the Statute of Frauds, 12 V.S.A. § 181. If that burden is met, his contract is still subject to the standards for specific enforcement. * * *.

The validation of an oral contract to convey real estate in spite of the prohibition against enforcement of the Statute of Frauds depends on the doctrine of part performance. The real issue is change of position by the one claiming relief in reliance on the oral agreement to such a measure that the parties cannot be restored to reasonable equivalence to their former condition. *Cooley v. Hatch*, 91 Vt. 128, 133, 99 A. 784 (1917). As that case states, it is a requirement that the reliance be something beyond injury adequately compensable in money, since even the payment of part or all of the alleged purchase price will not take the contract out of the operation of the Statute.

The performance advanced here, as set out in the findings of the lower court, took several forms. The Albericos paid mortgage payments, taxes, and water and sewer assessments from May, 1969, to Arthur Jasmin's death on January 3, 1971. Their monthly payments included the premium on the credit life insurance that discharged the mortgage effective January 3, 1971.

This, the lower court said, taken together with the defendant's indication to Mrs. Jasmin that they were prepared to pay the balance of $2,000.00, represented sufficient partial performance to take the case out of the Statute of Frauds. The rule of the case of *Cooley v. Hatch, supra,* 91 Vt. 128, 133, 99 A. 784 (1917) has recently been restated in *Troy v. Hanifin,* 132 Vt. 76, 82, 315 A.2d 875 (1974); money payments on the purchase are not enough to give the oral agreement enforceable status, even coupled with possession, in the face of the Statute of Frauds. That rule applies here.

Although the acts were not the performance called for under the claimed agreement, the defendants did make improvements to the property such as repairing a back porch, having gas piped to the house, making electrical and plumbing repairs and doing some landscaping. Besides these improvements, two stoves were brought in for heating purposes. Under *Hunt v. Spaulding,* 108 Vt. 309, 312, 187 A. 379 (1936), substantial improvements by one in possession may take the oral contract out of the Statute. But the trial court did not assign this evidence for that purpose, and we think quite rightly. The Hunt case requires that the improvements be such that the parties making them cannot be restored to their former situation. This was not so in this case, the activities being indistinguishable from those of a tenant responsible for maintenance of leased premises. They simply do not meet the test of a substantial and irretrievable change of position set out in our case law.
* * *

The judgment order in this case cannot stand, and the case must be returned to the lower court for consideration of the issues raised in the original complaint. Judgment reversed and cause remanded.

NOTES

Gleason v. Gleason and *Jasmin v. Alberico* apply the same rule known as the "doctrine of past performance", but the different facts lead to different results. Restate, in your own words, what allowed Walter Gleason to be awarded a half-interest in the land on which he worked, but did not allow the Albericos title to the property in which they resided.

2. COMPENSATION FOR EXPENDITURES IN RELIANCE ON ORAL AGREEMENT

Boone v. Coe

Court of Appeals of Kentucky, 1913.
153 Ky. 233, 154 S.W. 900.

■ CLAY, C.

Plaintiffs, W.H. Boone and J.T. Coe, brought this action against defendant, J.F. Coe, to recover certain damages, alleged to have resulted from defendant's breach of a parol contract of lease for one year to commence at a future date. It appears from the petition that the defendant was the owner of a large and valuable farm in Ford county, Tex. Plaintiffs were farmers, and were living with their families in Monroe county, Ky. In the fall of 1909 defendant made a verbal contract with plaintiffs, whereby he rented to them his farm in Texas for a period of 12 months, to commence from the date of plaintiffs' arrival at defendant's farm.

Defendant agreed that if plaintiffs would leave their said homes and businesses in Kentucky, and with their families, horses, and wagons, move to defendant's farm in Texas, and take charge of, manage, and cultivate same in wheat, corn and cotton for the 12 months next following plaintiffs' arrival at said farm, the defendant would have a dwelling completed on said farm and ready for occupancy upon their arrival, which dwelling plaintiffs would occupy as a residence during the period of said tenancy. Defendant also agreed that he would furnish necessary material at a convenient place on said farm out of which to erect a good and commodious stock and grain barn, to be used by plaintiffs.

The petition further alleges that plaintiffs were to cultivate certain portions of the farm, and were to receive certain portions of the crops raised, and that plaintiffs, in conformity with their said agreement, did move from Kentucky to the farm in Texas, and carried with them their families, wagons, horses, and camping outfit, and in going to Texas they traveled for a period of 55 days. It is also charged that defendant broke his contract, in that he failed to have ready and completed on the farm a dwelling house in which plaintiffs and their families could move, and also failed to furnish the necessary material for the erection of a suitable barn; that on December 6th defendant refused to permit plaintiffs to occupy the house and premises, and failed and refused to permit them to cultivate the land or any part thereof; that on the ___ day of December, 1909, they started for their home in Kentucky, and arrived there after traveling for a period of 4 days.

It is charged that plaintiffs spent in going to Texas, in cash, the sum of $150; that the loss of time to plaintiffs and their teams in making the trip to Texas was reasonably worth $8 a day for a period of 55 days, or the sum of $440; that the loss of time to them and their teams during the period they remained in Texas was $8 a day for 22 days, or $176; that they paid out in actual cash for transportation for themselves, families, and teams from Texas to Kentucky the sum of $211.80; that the loss of time to them and their teams in making the last-named trip was reasonably worth the sum of $100; that in abandoning and giving up their homes and businesses in Kentucky they had been damaged in the sum of $150, making a total damage of $1387.80, for which judgment was asked.

Defendant's demurrer to the petition was sustained and the petition dismissed. Plaintiffs appeal.

. . .

The statute of frauds (section 470, subsecs. 6 and 7, Kentucky Statutes) provides as follows: "No action shall be brought to charge any person: 6. Upon any contract for the sale of real estate, or any lease thereof, for longer term than one year; nor 7. Upon any agreement which is not to be performed within one year from the making thereof, unless the promise, contract, agreement, representation, assurance, or ratification, or some memorandum or note thereof, be in writing, and signed by the party to be charged therewith, or by his authorized agent; but the consideration need not be expressed in the writing; it may be proved when necessary, or disproved by parol or other evidence." A parol lease of land for one year, to commence at a future date, is within the statute. * * *

The question sharply presented is: May plaintiffs recover for expenses incurred and time lost on the faith of a contract that is unenforceable under the statute of frauds?

. . .

'[I]t would leave but little, if anything, of the statute of frauds to hold that a party might be mulcted in damages for refusing to execute in writing a verbal agreement which, unless in writing, is invalid under the statute of frauds.' *Chase v. Fitz*, 132 Mass. 361; *Lawrence v. Chase*, 54 Me. 196." It is the general rule that damages cannot be recovered, for violation of a contract within the statute of frauds.

. . . .

To this general rule there are certain well-recognized exceptions. Thus, . . . it has been held that, where services have been rendered during the life of another, on the promise that the person rendering the service should receive at the death of the person served a legacy, and the contract so made is within the statute of frauds, a reasonable compensation may be recovered for the services actually rendered. It has also been held that the vendee of land under a parol contract is entitled to recover any portion of the purchase money he may have paid, and is also entitled to compensation for improvements. * * *

And under a contract for personal services within the statute an action may be maintained on a quantum meruit. * * * The doctrine of these cases proceeds upon the theory that the defendant has actually received some benefits from the acts of part performance; and the law therefore implies a promise to pay. In 29 Am. & Eng. Ency. 836, the rule is thus stated: "Although part performance by one of the parties to a contract within the statute of frauds will not, at law, entitle such party to recover upon the contract itself, he may nevertheless recover for money paid by him, or property delivered, or services rendered in accordance with and upon the faith of the contract. The law will raise an implied promise on the part of the other party to pay for what has been done in the way of part performance. But this right of recovery is not absolute. The plaintiff is entitled to compensation only under such circumstances as would warrant a recovery in case there was no express contract; and hence it must appear that the defendant has actually received, or will receive, some benefit from the acts of part performance. It is immaterial that the plaintiff may have suffered a loss because he is unable to enforce his contract."

. . . .

In the case under consideration the plaintiffs merely sustained a loss. Defendant received no benefit. Had he received a benefit, the law would imply an obligation to pay therefor. Having received no benefit, no obligation to pay is implied. The statute says that the contract of defendant made with plaintiffs is unenforceable. Defendant therefore had the legal right to decline to carry it out. To require him to pay plaintiffs for losses and expenses incurred on the faith of the contract, without any benefit accruing to him, would, in effect, uphold a contract upon which the statute expressly declares no action shall be brought. The statute was enacted for the purpose of preventing frauds and perjuries. That it is a valuable statute is shown by the fact that similar statutes are in force in practically all, if not all, of the states of the Union. Being a valuable statute, the purpose of the lawmakers in its enactment should not be defeated by permitting recoveries in cases to which its provisions were intended to apply.

. . .

Restatement (Second) of Contracts § 139

McIntosh v. Murphy
Supreme Court of Hawaii, 1970.
52 Haw. 29, 469 P.2d 177.

■ LEVINSON, JUSTICE.

This case involves an oral employment contract which allegedly violates the provision of the Statute of Frauds requiring 'any agreement that is not to be performed within one year from the making thereof' to be in writing in order to be enforceable. * * * In this action the plaintiff-employee Dick McIntosh seeks to recover damages from his employer, George Murphy and Murphy Motors, Ltd., for the breach of an alleged one-year oral employment contract.

While the facts are in sharp conflict, it appears that defendant George Murphy was in southern California during March, 1964 interviewing prospective management personnel for his Chevrolet-Oldsmobile dealerships in Hawaii. He interviewed the plaintiff twice during that time. The position of sales manager for one of the dealerships was fully discussed but no contract was entered into. In April, 1964 the plaintiff received a call from the general manager of Murphy Motors informing him of possible employment within thirty days if he was still available. The plaintiff indicated his continued interest and informed the manager that he would be available. Later in April, the plaintiff sent Murphy a telegram to the effect that he would arrive in Honolulu on Sunday, April 26, 1964. Murphy then telephoned McIntosh on Saturday, April 25, 1964 to notify him that the job of assistant sales manager was open and work would begin on the following Monday, April 27, 1964. At that time McIntosh expressed surprise at the change in job title from sales manager to assistant sales manager but reconfirmed the fact that he was arriving in Honolulu the next day, Sunday. McIntosh arrived on Sunday, April 26, 1964 and began work on the following day, Monday, April 27, 1964.

As a consequence of his decision to work for Murphy, McIntosh moved some of his belongings from the mainland to Hawaii, sold other possessions, leased an apartment in Honolulu and obviously forwent any other employment opportunities. In short, the plaintiff did all those things which were incidental to changing one's residence permanently from Los Angeles to Honolulu, a distance of approximately 2200 miles. McIntosh continued working for Murphy until July 16, 1964, approximately two and one-half months, at which time he was discharged on the grounds that he was unable to close deals with prospective customers and could not train the salesmen.

At the conclusion of the trial, the defense moved for a directed verdict arguing that the oral employment agreement was in violation of the Statute of Frauds, there being no written memorandum or note thereof. The trial court ruled that as a matter of law the contract did not come within the Statute, reasoning that Murphy bargained for acceptance by the actual commencement of performance by McIntosh, so that McIntosh was not bound by a contract until he came to work on Monday, April 27, 1964. Therefore, assuming that the contract was for a year's employment, it was performable within a year exactly to the day and no writing was required for it to be enforceable. Alternatively, the court ruled that if the agreement was made final by the telephone call between the parties on Saturday, April 25, 1964, then that part of the weekend which remained would not be counted in calculating the year, thus taking the contract out of the Statute of Frauds. With commendable candor the trial judge gave as the motivating force for the decision his desire to avoid a mechanical and unjust application of the Statute.[1]

The case went to the jury on the following questions: (1) whether the contract was for a year's duration or was performable on a trial basis, thus making it terminable at the will of either party; (2) whether the plaintiff was discharged for just cause; and (3) if he was not discharged for just cause, what damages were due the plaintiff. The jury returned a

---

[1] THE COURT: You make the law look ridiculous, because one day is Sunday and the man does not work on Sunday; the other day is Saturday; he is up in Fresno. He can't work down there. And he is down here Sunday night and shows up for work on Monday. To me that is a contract within a year. I don't want to make the law look ridiculous, Mr. Clause, because it is one day later, one day too much, and that one day is a Sunday, and a non-working day.

verdict for the plaintiff in the sum of $12,103.40. The defendants appeal to this court on four principal grounds, three of which we find to be without merit. The remaining ground of appeal is whether the plaintiff can maintain an action on the alleged oral employment contract in light of the prohibition of the Statute of Frauds making unenforceable an oral contract that is not to be performed within one year.

I.   TIME OF ACCEPTANCE OF THE EMPLOYMENT AGREEMENT

The defendants contend that the trial court erred in refusing to give an instruction to the jury that if the employment agreement was made more than one day before the plaintiff began performance, there could be no recovery by the plaintiff. The reason given was that a contract not to be performed within one year from its making is unenforceable if not in writing.

The defendants are correct in their argument that the time of acceptance of an offer is a question of fact for the jury to decide. But the trial court alternatively decided that even if the offer was accepted on the Saturday prior to the commencement of performance, the intervening Sunday and part of Saturday would not be counted in computing the year for the purposes of the Statute of Frauds. The judge stated that Sunday was a non-working day and only a fraction of Saturday was left which he would not count. In any event, there is no need to discuss the relative merits of either ruling since we base our decision in this case on the doctrine of equitable estoppel which was properly briefed and argued by both parties before this court, although not presented to the trial court.

II.   ENFORCEMENT BY VIRTUE OF ACTION IN RELIANCE ON THE ORAL CONTRACT

In determining whether a rule of law can be fashioned and applied to a situation where an oral contract admittedly violates a strict interpretation of the Statute of Frauds, it is necessary to review the Statute itself together with its historical and modern functions. The Statute of Frauds, which requires that certain contracts be in writing in order to be legally enforceable, had its inception in the days of Charles II of England. Hawaii's version of the Statute is substantially the same as the original English Statute.

The first English Statute was enacted almost 300 years ago to prevent 'many fraudulent practices, which are commonly endeavored to be upheld by perjury and subornation of perjury'. 29 Car. 2, c. 3 (1677). Certainly, there were compelling reasons in those days for such a law. At the time of enactment in England, the jury system was quite unreliable, rules of evidence were few, and the complaining party was disqualified as a witness so he could neither testify on direct-examination nor, more importantly, be cross-examined. * * * The aforementioned structural and evidentiary limitations on our system of justice no longer exist.

Retention of the Statute today has nevertheless been justified on at least three grounds: (1) the Statute still serves an evidentiary function thereby lessening the danger of perjured testimony (the original rationale); (2) the requirement of a writing has a cautionary effect which causes reflection by the parties on the importance of the agreement; and (3) the writing is an easy way to distinguish enforceable contracts from those which are not, thus channeling certain transactions into written form.[2]

In spite of whatever utility the Statute of Frauds may still have, its applicability has been drastically limited by judicial construction over the years in order to mitigate the harshness of a mechanical application.[3] Furthermore, learned writers continue to disparage the Statute regarding it as 'a statute for promoting fraud' and a 'legal anachronism.' . . .

It is appropriate for modern courts to cast aside the raiments of conceptualism which cloak the true policies underlying the reasoning behind the many decisions enforcing contracts that violate the Statute of Frauds. There is certainly no need to resort to legal rubrics or meticulous legal formulas when better explanations are available. The policy behind enforcing an oral agreement which violated the Statute of Frauds, as a policy of avoiding unconscionable injury, was well set out by the California Supreme Court. In *Monarco v. Lo Greco*, 35 Cal.2d 621, 623, 220 P.2d 737, 739 (1950), a case which involved an action to enforce an oral contract for the conveyance of land on the grounds of 20 years performance by the promisee, the court said:

> The doctrine of estoppel to assert the statute of frauds has been consistently applied by the courts of this state to prevent fraud that would result from refusal to enforce oral contracts in certain circumstances. Such fraud may inhere in the unconscionable injury that would result from denying enforcement of the contract after one party has been induced by the other seriously to change his position in reliance on the contract

See also Seymour v. Oelrichs, 156 Cal. 782, 106 P. 88 (1909) (an employment contract enforced).

In seeking to frame a workable test which is flexible enough to cover diverse factual situations and also provide some reviewable standards,

---

[2] Fuller, Consideration and Form, 41 Colum.L.Rev. 799, 800–03 (1941); Note: Statute of Frauds—The Doctrine of Equitable Estoppel and the Statute of Frauds, 66 Mich.L.Rev. 170 (1967).

[3] Thus a promise to pay the debt of another has been construed to encompass only promises made to a creditor which do not benefit the promisor (Restatement of Contracts § 184 (1932); 3 Williston, Contracts § 452 (Jaeger ed. 1960)); a promise in consideration of marriage has been interpreted to exclude mutual promises to marry (Restatement, supra § 192; 3 Williston, supra § 485); a promise not to be performed within one year means a promise not performable within one year (Restatement, supra § 198; 3 Williston, supra, § 495); a promise not to be performed within one year may be removed from the Statute of Frauds if one party has fully performed (Restatement, supra § 198; 3 Williston, supra § 504); and the Statute will not be applied where all promises involved are fully performed (Restatement, supra § 219; 3 Williston, supra § 528).

we find very persuasive section [139] of the Second Restatement of Contracts. That section specifically covers those situations where there has been reliance on an oral contract which falls within the Statute of Frauds. Section [139] states:

(1) A promise which the promisor should reasonably expect to induce action or forbearance on the part of the promisee or a third person and which does induce the action or forbearance is enforceable notwithstanding the Statute of Frauds if injustice can be avoided only by enforcement of the promise. The remedy granted for breach is to be limited as justice requires.

(2) In determining whether injustice can be avoided only by enforcement of the promise, the following circumstances are significant: (a) the availability and adequacy of other remedies, particularly cancellation and restitution; (b) the definite and substantial character of the action or forbearance in relation to the remedy sought; (c) the extent to which the action or forbearance corroborates evidence of the making and terms of the promise, or the making and terms are otherwise established by clear and convincing evidence; (d) the reasonableness of the action or forbearance; (e) the extent to which the action or forbearance was foreseeable by the promisor.

We think that the approach taken in the Restatement is the proper method of giving the trial court the necessary latitude to relieve a party of the hardships of the Statute of Frauds. Other courts have used similar approaches in dealing with oral employment contracts upon which an employee had seriously relied. * * * This is to be preferred over having the trial court bend over backwards to take the contract out of the Statute of Frauds. In the present case the trial court admitted just this inclination and forthrightly followed it.

There is no dispute that the action of the plaintiff in moving 2200 miles from Los Angeles to Hawaii was foreseeable by the defendant. In fact, it was required to perform his duties. Injustice can only be avoided by the enforcement of the contract and the granting of money damages. No other remedy is adequate. The plaintiff found himself residing in Hawaii without a job.

It is also clear that a contract of some kind did exist. The plaintiff performed the contract for two and one-half months receiving $3,484.60 for his services. The exact length of the contract, whether terminable at will as urged by the defendant, or for a year from the time when the plaintiff started working, was up to the jury to decide.

In sum, the trial court might have found that enforcement of the contract was warranted by virtue of the plaintiff's reliance on the defendant's promise. Naturally, each case turns on its own facts. Certainly there is considerable discretion for a court to implement the true policy behind the Statute of Frauds, which is to prevent fraud or any other type of unconscionable injury. We therefore affirm the judgment of the trial court on the ground that the plaintiff's reliance was such that injustice could only be avoided by enforcement of the contract.

Affirmed.

■ ABE, JUSTICE (dissenting).

The majority of the court has affirmed the judgment of the trial court; however, I respectfully dissent. . . .

As acknowledged by this court, the trial judge erred when as a matter of law he ruled that the alleged employment contract did not come within the Statute of Frauds; however, I cannot agree that this error was not prejudicial as this court intimates.

On this issue, the date that the alleged contract was entered into was all important and the date of acceptance of an offer by the plaintiff was a question of fact for the jury to decide. In other words, it was for the jury to determine when the alleged one-year employment contract was entered into and if the jury had found that the plaintiff had accepted the offer more than one day before plaintiff was to report to work, the contract would have come within the Statute of Frauds and would have been unenforceable. * * *

This court holds that though the alleged one-year employment contract came within the Statute of Frauds, nevertheless the judgment of the trial court is affirmed 'on the ground that the plaintiff's reliance was such that injustice could only be avoided by enforcement of the contract.'

. . .

Now assuming that the defendant had agreed to hire the plaintiff under a one-year employment contract and the contract came within the Statute of Frauds, I cannot agree, as intimated by this court, that we should circumvent the Statute of Frauds by the exercise of the equity powers of courts. As to statutory law, the sole function of the judiciary is to interpret the statute and the judiciary should not usurp legislative power and enter into the legislative field. *A. C. Chock, Ltd. v. Kaneshiro*, 51 Haw. 87, 93, 451 P.2d 809 (1969); *Miller v. Miller*, 41 Ohio Op. 233, 83 N.E.2d 254 (Ct.C.P.1948). Thus, if the Statute of Frauds is too harsh as intimated by this court, and it brings about undue hardship, it is for the legislature to amend or repeal the statute and not for this court to legislate.

■ KOBAYASHI, J., joins in this dissent.

NOTE

There are two different Restatement provisions on the effect of action taken in reliance on a promise that would otherwise be unenforceable under the Statute of Frauds.

RESTATEMENT (SECOND) OF CONTRACTS § 129 deals only with agreements for the sale of land, and it deals only with requests for specific performance. The principle of this provision is quite widely accepted.

RESTATEMENT (SECOND) OF CONTRACTS § 139 is a newer provision added in the Second Restatement. Note that unlike Section 129, it is not limited to oral agreements for the sale of land, but applies to any agreement that would fall within any part of the Statute of Frauds. Note also that, unlike Section 129, the remedy contemplated by Section 139 is not specific performance, but rather a flexible award of damages, for example, damages computed in accordance with the reliance interest. Note also that, unlike Section 129, Section 139 has a subsection suggesting various reasons that a court might or might not allow some remedy.

The two preceding cases, *Boone v. Coe* and *McIntosh v. Murphy* show different approaches to the problem, with *Boone* (the older case) denying any remedy and *McIntosh* (the more recent case) permitting recovery. A useful representation of the tension between the two positions is to be found in comparing the majority and dissent in *McIntosh v. Murphy*. Which position do you find more convincing?

CHAPTER SEVEN

REMEDIES—SELECTED ISSUES

> Humpty Dumpty sat on a wall.
> Humpty Dumpty had a great fall.
> All the king's horses and all the king's men
> Couldn't put Humpty together again.

A. INTRODUCTION

At the beginning of the course, when we examined *Hawkins v. McGee*, we saw that the general objective of an award of damages for breach of contract is to place the non-breaching party in the position she would have been in if the promise had been performed. Throughout our study of particular doctrines of contract law we have seen that problems can sometimes be resolved by devoting attention to the remedy sought.

For example, we have repeatedly seen that if a contractual arrangement goes awry—for almost any reason—a person who has conferred a benefit on the other party will ordinarily have a right to recover that benefit under the law of restitution. Sometimes the award of restitution is just a simpler way of computing recovery where the defendant fails to perform an enforceable contract, as in *Yurchak v. Jack Boiman Constr. Co.*, which we examined in Chapter 1.G. Sometimes restitution provides a means of recovery where it is unclear whether one could describe the defendants act as breach or promise or just unjust retention of benefit, as in *Kellum v. Browning's Adm'r*, which we examined in Chapter 2.B. But, restitution is also available in cases where the plaintiff could not recover on a theory of breach of contract. For example, in *Britton v. Turner*, which we examined in Chapter 2.C, even though it was the employee who broke the contract, he recovered restitution of the net benefit he had conferred on the employer. In *Gilton v. Chapman*, which we examined in Chapter 6.E, a buyer was granted restitution of the down payment even though the agreement was not enforceable because of the Statute of Frauds.

We have also seen a number of situations in which there was some reason to doubt whether full expectation damages should be available, but it did not seem fair to leave the plaintiff with no remedy because too much water had run over the dam. Not uncommonly, that sort of tension has been resolved by allowing an award of reliance damages, even though full expectation damages would not be allowed. That's what the Massachusetts court did in *Sullivan v. O'Connor*, which we examined in Chapter 1.F. You should recall that the *Sullivan* was essentially a modern replay of the "hairy hand case," *Hawkins v. McGee*. In the classic "promissory estoppel" scenario examined in Chapter 5, the plaintiff can recover reliance damages even though the promise was not supported by consideration. In *McIntosh v. Murphy*, Chapter 6.F, the plaintiff recovered reliance damages even though the defendant's promise was unenforceable under the Statute of Frauds.

As we examine other areas of contract law, we will see that pattern repeated: A rule that prevents full enforcement by an award of expectation damages will almost never prevent restitution of any net benefit conferred. And, quite often, we are left with hard issues about whether a party who cannot recover expectation damages should still be allowed to recover reliance damages.

In this chapter we examine different issues. Suppose we are in a setting where there is no doubt that the plaintiff is entitled to recover expectation damages, that is, a remedy designed to place the non-breaching party in the position she would have been in if the defendant had performed. How do we do that? There are, of course, evidentiary and computational issues. For example, in *Hawkins v. McGee* the court ruled that the patient was entitled to recover the difference between the value of the hand in the condition promised by the surgeon and the value of the hand as it actually was. Going from that general concept to a specific number is obviously pretty hard. Maybe one could introduce evidence of how much more the plaintiff could have earned each year if his hand had been as promised, and then compute the present value of the difference in earnings over his expected lifetime.

There may be situations where the computational problems are so severe that there simply is no solution. For example, in *Kenford Co, v. County of Erie*, 493 N.E.2d 234 (N.Y. 1986) a county entered into an agreement under which Dome Stadium, Inc. ("DSI") was to have the right for twenty years to operate a domed stadium that the county was to have constructed. There was no question in the case that the agreement was enforceable and that the county had breached. The problem was how to compute the damages. Theoretically, the answer is easy: DSI was entitled to an amount of money that would place it in the position it would have been in if the county had performed, that is, DSI was entitled to the present value of the profits that it would have earned over the twenty-year contract. But, like any other element of its case, DSI had to prove the amount of its damages. In the case itself, the Court concluded that the effort to provide that proof was just not sufficient to establish the amount of damages with the requisite degree of certainty. As the Court said,

> [W]e note that despite the massive quantity of expert proof submitted by DSI, the ultimate conclusions are still projections, and as employed in the present day commercial world, subject to adjustment and modification. We of course recognize that any projection cannot be absolute, nor is there any such requirement, but it is axiomatic that the degree of certainty is dependent upon known or unknown factors which form the basis of the ultimate conclusion. Here, the foundations upon which

the economic model was created undermine the certainty of the projections. DSI assumed that the facility was completed, available for use and successfully operated by it for 20 years, providing professional sporting events and other forms of entertainment, as well as hosting meetings, conventions and related commercial gatherings. At the time of the breach, there was only one other facility in this country to use as a basis of comparison, the Astrodome in Houston. Quite simply, the multitude of assumptions required to establish projections of profitability over the life of this contract require speculation and conjecture, making it beyond the capability of even the most sophisticated procedures to satisfy the legal requirements of proof with reasonable certainty.

The economic facts of life, the whim of the general public and the fickle nature of popular support for professional athletic endeavors must be given great weight in attempting to ascertain damages 20 years in the future. New York has long recognized the inherent uncertainties of predicting profits in the entertainment field in general * * * and, in this case, we are dealing, in large part, with a new facility furnishing entertainment for the public.

493 N.E.2d at 236.

It's hard to formulate any very helpful rules on the issue of the degree of certainty needed, but you should at least be aware of the general issue.

Cases like *Kenford Co, v. County of Erie* present hard evidentiary and computational problems, but the general concept of what we are trying to do is clear enough. In this chapter we will examine several settings in which hard questions are presented at the general conceptual level. That is, we are looking at situations where the plaintiff is entitled to expectation damages, but there are genuine conceptual (not just computational) problems in deciding what would be necessary to place the non-breaching party in the position she would have been in if the defendant had performed.

PROBLEM

A famous case, *Chicago Coliseum Club v. Dempsey*, 265 Ill.App. 542 (1932) illustrates the problem of certainty. A boxing promoter brought an action against boxer Jack Dempsey for breach of a contract to engage in a match with Harry Wills for the world's heavy-weight championship. The promoter's claim of loss of profits, which would have been derived from the match, was deemed purely speculative and not a proper element of damages. Hence, the trial court was held to have properly sustained the objection to the testimony of anticipated gross receipts, expenses, and net profits. Though successful in the claim of breach, the promoter was able to recover reliance damages only. Do you agree that this expectation is too uncertain? Had you been acting for the promoter, what other evidence might you have brought?

B.　LIQUIDATED DAMAGE CLAUSES

U.C.C. § 2–718(1)

Restatement (Second) of Contracts § 356

[handwritten margin note: Rule: a provision in the contract fixing damages will not be upheld if the amount is not a reasonable measure of the anticipated harm]

City of Rye v. Public Serv. Mut. Ins. Co.

Court of Appeals of New York, 1974.
34 N.Y.2d 470, 315 N.E.2d 458.

■ BREITEL, CHIEF JUDGE.

In this action to recover on a surety bond given to secure timely completion of some six buildings, the City of Rye, as obligee under the bond, seeks to recover the face amount of $100,000. The surety and the developers are defendants. Special Term denied the city's motion for summary judgment, and a divided Appellate Division affirmed the denial. . . .

The order of the Appellate Division denying plaintiff city's motion for summary judgment should be affirmed. The bond of $100,000 posted by the developers with the city to ensure completion of the remaining six 'peripheral' buildings by a date certain did not reflect a reasonable estimate of probable monetary harm or damages to the city, but a penalty

. . . .

The developers, under a plan approved by the City Planning Commission, had constructed six luxury co-operative apartment buildings and were to construct six more. In order to obtain certificates of occupancy for the six completed buildings the developers were required to post a bond with the city to ensure completion of the remaining six buildings. By letter agreement with the city in the fall of 1967, they agreed to post a $100,000 bond and to pay $200 per day for each day after April 1, 1971 that the six remaining buildings were not completed, up to the aggregate amount of the bond. More than 500 days have passed without the additional buildings having been completed within the time limit. The city seeks to recover the entire $100,000 amount of the bond.

. . . The sole issue, then, becomes whether the agreement exacted from the developers and the conditional bond supplied provide for a penalty or for liquidated damages. If the agreement provides for a penalty or forfeiture . . . it is unenforceable. Where, however, damages flowing from a breach are difficult to ascertain, a provision fixing the damages in advance will be upheld if the amount is a reasonable measure of the anticipated probable harm * * * If, on the other hand, the amount fixed is grossly disproportionate to the anticipated probable harm or if there were no anticipatable harm, the provision will not be enforced.

The harm which the city contends it would suffer by delay in construction is minimal, speculative, or simply not cognizable. The city urges that its inspectors and employees will be required to devote more time to the project than anticipated because it has taken extra years to complete. It also urges that it will lose tax revenues for the years the buildings are not completed. It contends, too, that it is harmed by a continuing violation of the height restrictions of its zoning ordinance. This is entailed because the 12 buildings in the entire complex vary in height between two and four stories; the ordinance sets a maximum average height of 30 feet for the complex; and the taller buildings, those higher than the allowable average, were built first. Only after all of the structures in the complex are built will the project comply with the average height requirement of the ordinance.

The most serious disappointments in expectation suffered by the city are not pecuniary in nature and therefore not measurable in monetary damages. The effect on increased inspectorial services or on tax revenue are not likely to be substantial and, in any event, are not developed in the record on summary judgment. There is nothing to show that either the sum of $200 per day or the aggregate amount of the bond bear any reasonable relationship to the pecuniary harm likely to be suffered or in fact suffered. . . .

Accordingly, the order of the Appellate Division should be affirmed . . . .

PROBLEM

The following problem involves a drafting exercise, which you can complete by yourself or in a group. Drafting requires you to think like a planner, rather than a litigator: a far more common role for contract-based lawyering. In completing this exercise, you might find it useful to think about what has been described as the "three P's" of drafting: "*Predict* what may happen; *Provide* for that contingency; and *Protect* your client with a remedy": Scott J. Burnham, DRAFTING AND ANALYZING CONTRACTS 2 (4th ed., 2016) (emphasis in original).

In a broader sense, a transactional lawyer needs to be considering how to keep things running smoothly, as well as contemplating what to do in the event of things breaking down. Issues you might think about are (1) understanding the commercial and/or broader profile of the contracting parties; (2) predicting the overall environment in which the parties' contract will operate; (3) understanding the desired outcomes, especially for your client; and (4) working out the parameters set by the relevant law. Drafting is about crafting the appropriate text once these issues are thought through.

So, imagine you a lawyer for a city in the same predicament as the City of Rye, as they negotiate with developers. The City is very concerned about the costs of delay. Draft a letter agreement for your client to present to the developers, that would address this concern, and be safely considered liquidated damages rather than a penalty.

Banta v. Stamford Motor Co.

Supreme Court of Errors of Connecticut, 1914.
89 Conn. 51, 92 A. 665.

On June 1, 1911, the defendant contracted with the plaintiff to build for him a gasoline power yacht for the purchase price, exclusive of machinery and equipment, of $5,500, the same to be paid in installments as the work of construction progressed. In the contract the defendant agreed to have the yacht complete and ready for delivery on or before September 1, 1911, save under exceptional conditions not present in this case. It was further agreed that for each day the boat was ready for delivery before that date the plaintiff should pay the defendant $5 per day in addition to the contract price, and that for each day of delay in delivery beyond that date the defendant should pay to the plaintiff $15. The boat was not completed and ready for delivery until November 25, 1911.

. . .

The boat was a pleasure craft, and was intended by the plaintiff for use by him in cruising in Chesapeake Bay during the months of October and November, and later for a pleasure trip in Florida waters. The defendant was aware of the plaintiff's purpose, and that he wanted the boat on the day of delivery in order that he might start South sufficiently early to carry out his plans. As a result of the delay in the completion of the boat, the plaintiff was unable to enjoy it as he had planned, and was compelled to give up his intended cruise in Chesapeake Bay. The rental value of such a boat is, and at the time of the execution of the contract was, $15 a day. The sum of $15 a day was a fair and reasonable one to be paid for delay in completion. The plaintiff did not rent another boat or incur any expense or make any disbursement occasioned by the delay in delivery. He had no intention of renting the boat, and would not have rented it, or obtained any revenue from it had it been delivered as agreed. The parties to the contract did not at any time discuss or calculate the amount of probable damage that would follow from failure to make delivery upon the date fixed in the contract.

■ PRENTICE, C. J. (after stating the facts as above).

The plaintiff sues to recover, as liquidated damages, the total of per diem sums stipulated in a contract for the construction of a pleasure boat to be paid by the defendant, the builder, in the event of delay in its completion as provided in the contract. The defendant contends that these sums, being in the nature of a penalty, and not, as the plaintiff asserts, of liquidated damages, are not recoverable. The defendant by his contract with the plaintiff agreed to pay these sums in the event named. He must abide by his bargain in this particular, unless his undertaking was one which the law will not permit to be enforced as involving the exaction of a penalty.

"As a general rule, parties are allowed to make such contracts as they please, including contracts to liquidate, and fix beforehand the amount to be paid as damages for a breach of such contracts; but the courts have always exercised a certain power of control over contracts to liquidate damages, so as to keep them in harmony with the fundamental general rule that compensation shall be commensurate with the extent of the injury. . . . When the nature of the engagement is such that, upon a breach of it, the amount of damages would be uncertain or difficult of proof, and the parties have beforehand expressly agreed upon the amount of damages, and that amount is not greatly disproportionate to the presumable loss, their expressed intent will be carried out." *New Britain v. New Britain Telephone Co.,* 74 Conn. 326, 332, 333, 50 Atl. 881, 884.

. . .[W]hen certain conditions coexist, the provision for the payment of a stipulated sum in the event of a breach of contract will be regarded and enforced as one for liquidated damages. These conditions . . . are: (1) The damages to be anticipated as resulting from the breach must be uncertain in amount or difficult to prove; (2) there must have been an intent on the part of the parties to liquidate them in advance; and (3) the amount stipulated must be a reasonable one—that is to say, not greatly disproportioned to the presumable loss or injury.

As to the second of these conditions, there cannot be any reasonable doubt that the intent of the provision under consideration was not to exact a penalty for nonperformance, but to determine in advance the fair amount to be paid as damages in the event of breach. This was a construction contract—one of a kind, therefore, which furnishes conditions peculiarly suitable for provisions liquidating damages, and which very commonly contains such provisions. * * * The provision in this contract undoubtedly was not understood as differing in purpose or character from those which so frequently enter into construction contracts, and are commonly understood as furnishing the agreed amount of damages.

That the first condition was satisfied is a self-demonstrating proposition. The situation was such that the loss or injury to be anticipated from a breach and the extent of it would inevitably lie in the field of uncertainty and be difficult to prove, and that an attempt to measure it in the terms of dollars and cents would be beset by even greater difficulties.

The defendant's contention, and the one upon which it chiefly relies, is that the third condition is necessarily wanting, since the plaintiff, in the absence of the provision in controversy, could recover nothing for delay in the completion and delivery of the yacht, for the reason that it was an article of luxury intended solely for the plaintiff's use for his personal pleasure and gratification, and no direct pecuniary loss through the hiring of a substitute or otherwise was shown. This claim came under our consideration in *Cook v. Packard Motor Car Co.*, 88 Conn. 590, 92 Atl. 413, recently decided, and was there overruled. . . . The situation there presented was in all respects analogous to the one before us, and the conclusion reached was that one who has been wrongfully deprived of the use of an article is not barred from the recovery of substantial damages therefor by reason of the fact that it was an article of luxury, and by him devoted solely to personal pleasure and gratification.

The plaintiff being in a position to recover substantial damages for the defendant's delay, the latter's only remaining hope lies in his ability to show that $15 a day was unreasonable in amount. The standard of measure here is not furnished by the plaintiff's actual loss or injury, as the event proved, but by loss or injury which might reasonably have been anticipated at the time the contract was made, or, as we said in *New Britain v. New Britain Telephone Co.*, 74 Conn. 326, 333, 50 Atl. 881, 884, "the presumable loss." It is the look forward, and not backward, that we are called upon to take, and the plaintiff is under no obligation to show actual damage suffered substantially commensurate with the $15 a day rate in order to support the provision as one in liquidation of damages.

The extent that the plaintiff might have been injured by delay in the completion of the yacht which he was desirous of using in the fall months for cruising in the Chesapeake and Florida waters, and the measure of it in money, both lie in a marked degree in the field of uncertainty. It is apparent that the date of delivery was not a matter of unconcern to the plaintiff. He was, as the contract shows, willing to pay $5 a day for earlier delivery. It is quite conceivable that time in the fall was a considerable factor in the execution of cherished plans. Possibly the prospect of having the yacht for fall use was the moving motive in ordering it at all. The defendant was informed of the plaintiff's purpose in using the boat. Presumably he, being a boat builder, was aware of the conditions of pleasure boat using. They mutually agreed upon the figure which was incorporated into the contract as the measure of damages for delay. They did not indeed formally sit down and canvass the situation, and figure out as best they could what would be a fair allowance for the probable damage which the plaintiff would suffer by delay in the yacht's delivery. That was unnecessary. The defendant was not dealing with a matter concerning which he was without knowledge. He signed the contract voluntarily, and by that signature signified his concurrence in the stipulation as to damages it contained. The situation was one peculiarly appropriate for some stipulation upon that subject. The parties made one which the trial court has found to be reasonable. We cannot say that it erred in reaching that conclusion. . . .

There is no error. In this opinion the other Judges concurred.

NOTE & QUESTION

In *Banta,* the damages clause was enforced. Another technique for the buyer would have been to offer $5 a day more for completion and delivery each day earlier than agreed delivery date. Would this be enforceable? What about if the buyer offered $15 more for each day early? Would this be a disguised penalty?

Pacheco v. Scoblionko
Supreme Judicial Court of Maine, 1987.
532 A.2d 1036.

■ SCOLNIK, JUSTICE.

The defendants, Eric and Diane Scoblionko, appeal from a judgment in a jury-waived trial in the Superior Court, Oxford County, requiring them to return to the plaintiff, Albert Pacheco, a camp tuition fee he paid for his son totaling $3,100.00, plus interest and costs. The Scoblionkos base their appeal on [the ground that] . . . there was an inadequate basis for the Superior Court's finding that a liquidated damages clause in the contract between them and Pacheco was an unenforceable penalty . . . . We affirm the judgment.

The facts in this case are as follows. Pacheco had sent his son to Camp Wekeela, a summer camp owned and operated by the Scoblionkos in Canton for several years. In 1985, Pacheco paid a full camp fee of $3,100.00 prior to February 1, 1985. This early payment allowed Pacheco to receive a discount on the regular camp fee, the amount of which is not specified in the record. The contract Pacheco signed in registering his son with the camp was on a pre-printed form. In one clause of the contract it was specified that if notice of a camper's withdrawal was received after May 1, 1985, the amount paid to the camp up to the time of the receipt of the notice would be retained by the camp.[1]

On June 14, Pacheco was informed that because his son, a high school student, had failed his final exam in Spanish, he would be required to attend summer school. That same day, Pacheco telephoned Eric Scoblionko, informing him that his son would be unable to attend camp and asking for the return of the fees paid to the camp. Scoblionko refused to refund any portion of the $3,100.00.

Pacheco then initiated this action in the Superior Court, seeking return of the deposit. After a jury-waived trial held on January 14, 1987, the court, concluding that the liquidated damages clause was an unenforceable penalty, entered judgment in plaintiff's favor for the full amount claimed. Defendants did not counterclaim for actual damages.

---

[1]   The contract provision reads:

The $500.00 deposit will be refunded if a request is received by the camp prior to February 1st, less a $25.00 administrative processing fee. If a refund request is received on or after February 1st and prior to May 1st, then no refund of the $500.00 deposit will be made. If a refund request is received on or after May 1st, the entire sum then paid to date shall be retained by the camp. The parties agree that any deposit so retained would constitute liquidated damages for cancellation of the contract.

By including in their camp contract language explicitly stating that the deposit was retainable as liquidated damages for cancellation of the contract, the Scoblionkos have made the validity of this provision as a liquidated damages clause the central question of the case. Indeed, they state in their brief that the issue of its validity, which the Superior Court decided adversely to them, is "at the heart of this case."

In order to be valid, a liquidated damages provision must meet two requirements: "[T]he damages caused by the breach are very difficult to estimate accurately and . . . the amount so fixed is a reasonable forecast of the amount necessary to justly compensate one party for the loss occasioned by the other's breach."

. . .

In these circumstances, the "liquidated damages" provision appears to be a penalty, "placed in the contract . . . for its *in terrorem* effect," *Dairy Farm Leasing,* 395 A.2d at 1140. The apparent intent of the clause is to deter parents from withdrawing their children from camp at a late date, without regard to any reasonable, good faith estimate of consequent damages. Accordingly, we conclude that the Superior Court did not commit error in determining that the liquidated damages clause was an unenforceable penalty.

PROBLEM

1.   As you did for the city in *City of Rye v. Public Serv. Mut. Ins. Co.,* draft a clause for the summer camp that would allow them to recover a pre-set amount for late withdrawals.

2.   Consider whether your clause would be a useful template to use for any summer camp proprietor, in their contracts sent to prospective families. If so, then you've just come up with what is commonly called "*boilerplate*". "Boilerplate" can be understood in two senses: first, as all-purpose language that can be placed in a variety of documents; or as fixed language that the proposing party may view as relatively non-negotiable. These two (overlapping) meanings stem from the metal plates of text or art that were distributed to newspapers and could not be edited. We will encounter this feature of contract again in our treatment of standard form contracts in Chapter 8.C and unconscionability in Chapter 11.E.

Fretwell v. Protection Alarm Co.

Supreme Court of Oklahoma, 1988.
1988 OK 84, 764 P.2d 149.

■ ALMA WILSON, JUSTICE.

As a result of a burglary in August, 1984, the Fretwells sued Protection Alarm Company, which installed and maintained a burglary alarm system in the Fretwells' residence. In a negligence action, the Fretwells claimed that the alarm company had failed to notify the police department of a cut in their telephone service, which is the line that carried the alarm signal; that they failed to use the house key supplied by the Fretwells to check the residence; and that they failed to call the list provided by the Fretwells of persons to be notified in the event of an alarm.

The testimony during the trial revealed that the alarm company had notified the police upon receiving the alarm signal at their monitoring station and had dispatched one of their employees to check the residence. Upon the employee's arrival, he was notified by the police officers on the scene that the residence was secure. He did not obtain the key to the residence to inspect the inside, nor did he inspect the premises and find that the line running from the residence to the alarm company had been cut, thereby prohibiting a second signal from being received. Apparently after the police and the employee left, one or more burglars entered the residence removing property valued at $91,379.93. The jury rendered a verdict in favor of the Fretwells for that amount.

The main contention of the alarm company on appeal is that the contract between Fretwell's, Inc. and the alarm company . . . limits the liability of the alarm company to fifty dollars. The two pertinent paragraphs in the contract provide:

> It is agreed that Protection is not an insurer; that the payments hereinabove named are based solely on the value of the services provided for herein; that, from the nature of the services to be rendered, it is impractical and extremely difficult to fix the actual damages, if any, which may proximately result from the failure of the alarm system to properly operate or the failure of Protection to perform any of its obligations hereunder; that in case of either of such failures and resulting loss to the Subscriber, the liability of Protection shall be limited to the sum of Fifty Dollars ($50.00) or the actual loss of the Subscriber, whichever of these two figures is the lesser, as liquidated damages, and not as a penalty, and this liability shall be exclusive. If Subscriber desires Protection to assume a greater liability or responsibility than that set forth herein to either Subscriber or Subscriber's insurance carrier by way of subrogation, an additional price must be quoted.

> In the event any person, not a party to this agreement, including Subscriber's insurance company, shall make any claim or file any lawsuit against Protection for any reason whatsoever, including but not limited to the installation, maintenance, operation or nonoperation of the alarm system, Subscriber agrees to indemnify, defend and hold Protection harmless from any and all claims and lawsuits including the payment of all damages, expenses, costs and attorneys fees whether these claims be based upon alleged intentional conduct, active or passive negligence, or strict or product liability, on the part of Protection, its agents, servants or employees.

The agreement in effect at the time of the burglary provided for a monthly payment of $46.00. Protection Alarm Company had furnished the alarm equipment and alarm service for the Fretwells' residence since 1974. The contract above was a renewal contract dated February 1, 1982, between Fretwells, Inc. and Protection Alarm Company, Inc., and subscribed by Edward Fretwell as president of Fretwells, Inc.

The dispositive issue in this case is the effect the contract has upon the damages allowed in the negligence action. To resolve this issue, [the following] question must be addressed: . . . (2) Is the clause of the contract enforceable which limits the damages to fifty dollars? . . .

The tort, alleged by plaintiffs . . . is one arising out of a contractual relationship, and as such bears a close resemblance to an action for pure breach of contract. *See General Motors Corp. v. Piskor,* 281 Md. 627, 381 A.2d 16, 22–23 (1977). A tort arising out of a contractual relationship exhibits characteristics of both tort and contract actions. *Piskor,* 381 A.2d at 23. In a contract action a breach occurs when a party fails to perform a duty arising under or imposed by agreement, whereas a tort is a violation of a duty imposed by law independent of contract. *Lewis v. Farmers Ins. Co., Inc.,* 681 P.2d 67, 69 (Okla.1983). "A common law duty to perform with care, skill, reasonable expediency, and faithfulness accompanies every contract." *Lewis,* 681 P.2d at 69.

It reasonably follows that since the contract established the duty, any lawful limitations in the contract may also limit the liability of the tortfeasor. . . .

We next examine whether the limitation of liability set by the burglar alarm agreement was enforceable. . . .

The Fretwells argue that the "liquidated damages" clause of the contract is unenforceable because it is either in the nature of a penalty, which is void by statute, 15 O.S. 1981, § 213, or is void based upon the facts and construction of 15 O.S. 1981, §§ 214, 215 which provide that when damages for breach of a contract are determined in anticipation of a breach, such determination is void unless from the nature of the case, it would be impracticable or extremely difficult to fix the actual damage. . . . The contract wording is, "[T]he liability of Protection shall be limited to the sum of Fifty Dollars ($50.00) or the actual loss of the Subscriber, whichever of these two figures is the lesser." The Supreme Court of Minnesota reached the same conclusion under a similar contract clause in *Morgan Co. v. Minnesota Mining & Mfg. Co.,* 310 Minn. 305, 246 N.W.2d 443 (1976). Quoting from *Wedner v. Fidelity Security Systems, Inc.,* 228 Pa.Super. 67, 307 A.2d 429 (1973), the Minnesota court affirmed a trial court grant of summary judgment which limited recovery of damages to $250, which was the amount recited in the contract as "liquidated damages." As the Pennsylvania court was equally divided, the case was affirmed. Judge Watkins . . . stated concerning the issue of limitation of damages:

Much reliance is placed upon the Restatement of Contracts § 339, but the appellant disregards Comment [g], which provides:

"An agreement limiting the amount of damages recoverable for breach is not an agreement to pay either liquidated damages or a penalty. Except in the case of certain public service contracts, the contracting parties can by agreement limit their liability in damages to a specified amount, either at the time of making their principal contract, or subsequently thereto. Such a contract, or subsequent thereto, does not purport to make an estimate of the harm caused by a breach, nor is its purpose to operate in terrorem to induce performance."

It can hardly be contended that the words "liability is and shall be limited" to the yearly service charge of $312 are anything but a limitation of liability and not really a liquidated damage clause. Surely, if the loss to the customer was $150, the expressed mutual assent was that recovery should be $150 and not $312.

The fact that the words "liquidated damages" were used in the contract has little bearing on the nature of the provision. It is well settled that in determining whether a particular clause calls for liquidated damages or for a penalty, the name given to the clause by the parties "is but of slight weight, and the controlling elements are the intention of the parties and the special circumstances of the case." *Laughlin v. Baltalden, Inc.,* 191 Pa.Super. 611, 617, 159 A.2d 26, 29 (1960). The same principle applies here. Nor can it be argued that the use of these words automatically creates an ambiguity to be resolved against the appellee as the drafter of the instrument. The meaning of the words is clear—the fixed limit of liability was $312. We are, therefore, not dealing with a liquidated damage problem. *Wedner,* 307 A.2d at 431.

. . .

Provisions limiting liability and the amount of damages under burglar alarm service agreements have been upheld in the majority of jurisdictions. * * * The alarm company is not an insurer against burglary as such systems can be disabled. The contract before this Court explicitly states that the alarm company is not an insurer and offers to increase the monthly payment if insurance is desired. We conclude that the contractual provision before this Court is neither unconscionable nor against public policy. Therefore, the damages to the Fretwells is limited to fifty dollars.

. . .

NOTES

U.C.C. § 2–715 provides, in part, for consequential damages for breaches of contracts involving the sale of goods, as you will read in Part D below. U.C.C. § 2–719, entitled "Contractual Modification or Limitation of Remedy," allows firms to curtail the remedies otherwise available, except in certain situations, such as when the limitation would be unconscionable. You will read about unconscionability in Chapter 11.E, but for present purposes note that the U.C.C. suggests that while limitation of consequential damages for personal injury is prima facie unconscionable, limitation of damages where the loss is commercial is not (U.C.C. § 2–719(3)).

C. COST OR VALUE

Groves v. John Wunder Co.

Supreme Court of Minnesota, 1939.
205 Minn. 163, 286 N.W. 235.

■ STONE, JUSTICE.

Action for breach of contract. Plaintiff got judgment for a little over $15,000. Sorely disappointed by that sum, he appeals.

In August, 1927, S. J. Groves & Sons Company, a corporation (hereinafter mentioned simply as Groves), owned a tract of 24 acres of Minneapolis suburban real estate. It was served or easily could be reached by railroad trackage. It is zoned as heavy industrial property. But for lack of development of the neighborhood its principal value thus far may have been in the deposit of sand and gravel which it carried. The Groves company had a plant on the premises for excavating and screening the gravel. Nearby defendant owned and was operating a similar plant.

In August, 1927, Groves and defendant made the involved contract. For the most part it was a lease from Groves, as lessor, to defendant, as lessee; its term seven years. Defendant agreed to remove the sand and gravel and to leave the property 'at a uniform grade, substantially the same as the grade now existing at the roadway . . . on said premises, and that in stripping the overburden . . . it will use said overburden for the purpose of maintaining and establishing said grade.'

Under the contract defendant got the Groves screening plant. The transfer thereof and the right to remove the sand and gravel made the consideration moving from Groves to defendant, except that defendant incidentally got rid of Groves as a competitor. On defendant's part it paid Groves $105,000. So that from the outset, on Groves' part the contract was executed except for defendant's right to continue using the property for the stated term. (Defendant had a right to renewal which it did not exercise.)

Defendant breached the contract deliberately. It removed from the premises only 'the richest and best of the gravel' and wholly failed, according to the findings, 'to perform and comply with the terms, conditions, and provisions of said lease . . . with respect to the condition in which the surface of the demised premises was required to be left.' Defendant surrendered the premises, not substantially at the grade required by the contract 'nor at any uniform grade.' Instead, the ground was 'broken, rugged, and uneven.' Plaintiff sues as assignee and successor in right of Groves.

As the contract was construed below, the finding is that to complete its performance 288,495 cubic yards of overburden would need to be excavated, taken from the premises, and deposited elsewhere. The reasonable cost of doing that was found to be upwards of $60,000. But, if defendant had left the premises at the uniform grade required by the lease, the reasonable value of the property on the determinative date would have been only $12,160. The judgment was for that sum, including interest, thereby nullifying plaintiff's claim that cost of completing the contract rather than difference in value of the land was the measure of damages. The gauge of damage adopted by the decision was the difference between the market value of plaintiff's land in the condition it was when the contract was made and what it would have been if defendant had performed. The one question for us arises upon plaintiff's assertion that he was entitled, not to that difference in value, but to the reasonable cost to him of doing the work called for by the contract which defendant left undone.

Defendant's breach of contract was wilful. There was nothing of good faith about it. Hence, that the decision below handsomely rewards bad faith and deliberate breach of contract is obvious. That is not allowable. Here the rule is well settled, and has been since *Elliott v. Caldwell*, 43 Minn. 357, 45 N.W. 845, 9 L.R.A. 52, that, where the contractor wilfully and fraudulently varies from the terms of a construction contract, he cannot sue thereon and have the benefit of the equitable doctrine of substantial performance. That is the rule generally. * * *

Jacob & Youngs, Inc. v. Kent, 230 N.Y. 239, 243, 244, 129 N.E. 889, 891, 23 A.L.R. 1429, is typical. It was a case of substantial performance of a building contract. (This case is distinctly the opposite.) Mr. Justice Cardozo, in the course of his opinion, stressed the distinguishing features. 'Nowhere,' he said, 'will change be tolerated, however, if it is so dominant or pervasive as in any real or substantial measure to frustrate the purpose of the contract.' Again, 'the willful transgressor must accept the penalty of his transgression.'

In reckoning damages for breach of a building or construction contract, the law aims to give the disappointed promisee, so far as money will do it, what he was promised. * * * It is so ruled by a long line of decisions in this state, beginning with *Carli v. Seymour, Sabin & Co.*, 26 Minn. 276, 3 N.W. 348, where the contract was for building a road. There was a breach. Plaintiff was held entitled to recover what it would cost to complete the grading as contemplated by the contract. * * *

Never before, so far as our decisions show, has it even been suggested that lack of value in the land furnished to the contractor who had bound himself to improve it any escape from the ordinary consequences of a breach of the contract.

A case presently as interesting as any of our own, is *Sassen v. Haegle*, 125 Minn. 441, 147 N.W. 445, 446, 52 L.R.A.,N.S., 1176. The defendant, lessee of a farm, had agreed to haul and spread manure. He removed it, but spread it elsewhere than on the leased farm. Plaintiff had a verdict, but a new trial was ordered for error in the charge as to the measure of damages. The point was thus discussed by Mr. Justice Holt [125 Minn. page 443, 147 N.W. page 446, 52 L.R.A.,N.S., 1176]: 'But it is also true that the landlord had a perfect right to stipulate as to the disposal of the manure or as to the way in which the farm should be worked, and the tenant cannot evade compliance by showing that the farm became more valuable or fertile by omitting the agreed work or doing other work. . . . The question is not whether plaintiff made a wise or foolish agreement. He had a right to have it performed as made, and the resulting damage, in case of failure, is the reasonable cost of performance. Whether such performance affects the value of the farm was no concern of defendant.'

Even in case of substantial performance in good faith, the resulting defects being remediable, it is error to instruct that the measure of damage is 'the difference in value between the house as it was and as it would have been if constructed according to contract.' The 'correct doctrine' is that the cost of remedying the defect is the 'proper' measure of damages. *Snider v. Peters Home Building Co.*, 139 Minn. 413, 414, 416, 167 N.W. 108.

Value of the land (as distinguished from the value of the intended product of the contract, which ordinarily will be equivalent to its reasonable cost) is no proper part of any measure of damages for wilful breach of a building contract. The reason is plain.

The summit from which to reckon damages from trespass to real estate is its actual value at the moment. The owner's only right is to be compensated for the deterioration in value caused by the tort. That is all he has lost. But not so if a contract to improve the same land has been breached by the contractor who refuses to do the work, especially where, as here, he has been paid in advance. The summit from which to reckon damages for that wrong is the hypothetical peak of accomplishment (not value) which would have been reached had the work been done as demanded by the contract.

The owner's right to improve his property is not trammeled by its small value. It is his right to erect thereon structures which will reduce its value. If that be the result, it can be of no aid to any contractor who declines performance. As said long ago in *Chamberlain v. Parker*, 45 N.Y.

569, 572: 'A man may do what he will with his own, * * * and if he chooses to erect a monument to his caprice or folly on his premises, and employs and pays another to do it, it does not lie with a defendant who has been so employed and paid for building it, to say that his own performance would not be beneficial to the plaintiff.' To the same effect is Restatement, Contracts, § 346, p. 576, Illustrations of Subsection (1), par. 4.

Suppose a contractor were suing the owner for breach of a grading contract such as this. Would any element of value, or lack of it, in the land have any relevance in reckoning damages? Of course not. The contractor would be compensated for what he had lost, i. e., his profit. Conversely, in such a case as this, the owner is entitled to compensation for what he has lost, that is, the work or structure which he has been promised, for which he has paid, and of which he has been deprived by the contractor's breach.

To diminish damages recoverable against him in proportion as there is presently small value in the land would favor the faithless contractor. It would also ignore and so defeat plaintiff's right to contract and build for the future. To justify such a course would require more of the prophetic vision than judges possess. This factor is important when the subject matter is trackage property in the margin of such an area of population and industry as that of the Twin Cities.

. . .

It is suggested that because of little or no value in his land the owner may be unconscionably enriched by such a reckoning. The answer is that there can be no unconscionable enrichment, no advantage upon which the law will frown, when the result is but to give one party to a contract only what the other has promised; particularly where, as here, the delinquent has had full payment for the promised performance.

It is said by the Restatement, Contracts, § 346, comment b: 'Sometimes defects in a completed structure cannot be physically remedied without tearing down and rebuilding, at a cost that would be imprudent and unreasonable. The law does not require damages to be measured by a method requiring such economic waste. If no such waste is involved, the cost of remedying the defect is the amount awarded as compensation for failure to render the promised performance.'

The 'economic waste' declaimed against by the decisions applying that rule has nothing to do with the value in money of the real estate, or even with the product of the contract. The waste avoided is only that which would come from wrecking a physical structure, completed, or nearly so, under the contract. The cases applying that rule go no further. * * * Absent such waste, as it is in this case, the rule of the Restatement, Contracts, § 346, is that 'the cost of remedying the defect is the amount awarded as compensation for failure to render the promised performance.' That means that defendants here are liable to plaintiff for the reasonable cost of doing what defendants promised to do and have wilfully declined to do. . . .

So ordered.

■ JULIUS J. OLSON, JUSTICE (dissenting) . . .

The involved lease provides that the granted premises were to be used by defendant 'for the purpose of removing the sand and gravel therefrom.' The cash consideration was $105,000, plus defendant's covenant to level and grade the premises to a specified base. There was no segregation or allocation of the cash consideration made applicable to any of the various items going into the deal, and the instrument does not suggest any sum as being representative of the cost of performance by defendant of the leveling and grading process. Nor is there any finding that the contractor 'wilfully and fraudulently' violated the terms of its contract. All that can be said is that defendant did nothing except to mine the sand and gravel purchased by it and deemed best suited to its own interest and advantage. No question of partial or substantial performance of its covenant is involved since it did nothing in that behalf. The sole question here is whether the rule adopted by the court respecting recoverable damages is wrong. The essential facts, not questioned, are that 'the fair and reasonable value as of the end of the term of said lease, May 1, 1934, of performing the said work necessary to put the premises in the condition in which they were required by the terms of said lease to be left, is the sum of $60,893.28,' and that if defendant 'had left said premises at a uniform grade as required by said lease, the fair and reasonable value of said premises on May 1, 1934, would have been the sum of $12,160.' In that sum, plus interest from May 1, 1934, plaintiff was awarded judgment, $15,053.58. His sole contention before the trial court and here is that upon these findings the court, as a matter of law, should have allowed him the cost of performance, $60,893.28, plus interest since date of the breach, May 1, 1934, amounting to more than $76,000.

Since there is no issue of fact we should limit our inquiry to the single legal problem presented: What amount in money will adequately compensate plaintiff for his loss caused by defendant's failure to render performance?

. . .

Another principle, of universal application, is that a party is entitled to have that for which he contracted, or its equivalent. What that equivalent is depends upon the circumstances of each case. If the effect of performance is such that the defective part 'may be remedied without the destruction of any substantial part of the benefit which the owner's property has received by reason of the contractor's work, the equivalent to which the owner is entitled is the cost of making the work conform to the contract.' 9 Am.Jur., Building and Construction Contracts, § 152. Here, however, defendant did nothing. As such plaintiff 'is entitled to be placed, in so far as this can be done by money, in the same position he would have occupied if the contract had been performed.' But 'his recovery is limited to the loss he has actually suffered by reason of the breach; he is not entitled to be placed in a better position than he would have been in if the contract had not been broken.' 15 Am.Jur., Damages, § 43. The measure of damages 'is not affected by the financial condition of the one entitled to the damages'; nor may there be included in the assessment of damages 'the motive of the defendant in breaking' his contract, compensatory damages alone being involved. In such a case the measure is 'the same whatever the cause of the breach, regardless of whether it was due to mistake, accident, or inability to perform or was wilful and malicious.' Id. § 48. Liability in damages has for its basis the value of the promised performance to the promisee, not what it would cost the promisor in completing performance. * * * Plaintiff as the injured party is entitled to have compensation for all injuries sustained by him due to defendant's default. But he is only entitled to recover 'actual pecuniary compensation,' and this is true 'whether the action is on contract or in tort,' there being here no circumstances warranting allowance of exemplary damages. 8 R.C.L. § 8, pp. 431, 432, and cases cited under notes 16, 17, and 18.

> 'Since one who has been injured by the breach of a contract or the commission of a tort is entitled to a just and adequate compensation for such injury and no more, it follows that his recovery must be limited to a fair compensation and indemnity for his injury and loss. And so in no case should the injured party be placed in a better position than he would be in had the wrong not been done, or the contract not been broken. The defendant may therefore show that, notwithstanding his default, the plaintiff has suffered no damages. And if any circumstances exist which mitigate the injury, they must be considered and taken into account.' 8 R.C.L. § 9, pp. 434–435, and cases under notes 9, 10, 11, and 12.

. . .

The theory upon which plaintiff relies for application of the cost of performance rule must have for its basis cases where the property or the improvement to be made is unique or personal instead of being of the kind ordinarily governed by market values. His action is one at law for damages, not for specific performance. As there was no affirmative showing of any peculiar fitness of this property to a unique or personal use, the rule to be applied is, I think, the one applied by the [trial] court. . . .

The principle for which I contend is not novel in construction contract cases. It is well stated in McCormick, Damages, § 168, pp. 648, 649, as follows: 'In whatever way the issue arises, the generally approved standards for measuring the owner's loss from defects in the work are two: First, in cases where the defect is one that can be repaired or cured without undue expense, so as to make the building conform to the agreed plan, then the owner recovers such amount as he has reasonably expended, or will reasonably have to spend, to remedy the defect. Second, if, on the other hand, the defect in material or construction is one that cannot be remedied without an expenditure for reconstruction disproportionate to the end to be attained, or without endangering unduly other parts of the building, then the damages will be measured not by the cost of remedying the defect, but by the difference between the value of the building as it is and what it would have been worth if it had been built in conformity with the contract.'

And the same thought was expressed by Mr. Justice Cardozo in *Jacob & Youngs, Inc. v. Kent*, 230 N.Y. 239, 244, 129 N.E. 889, 891, 23 A.L.R. 1429, 1433, thus: 'The owner is entitled to the money which will permit him to complete, unless the cost of completion is grossly and unfairly out of proportion to the good to be attained. When that is true, the measure is the difference in value.' * * * In 1 Restatement, Contracts, § 346 p. 576, Illustrations of Subsection (1), par. 3, reads: 'A contracts with B to sink an oil well on A's own land adjacent to the land of B, for development and exploration purposes. Other exploration wells prove that there is no oil in that region; and A breaks his promise to sink the well. B can get judgment for only nominal damages, not the cost of sinking the well.'

. . .

No one doubts that a party may contract for the doing of anything he may choose to have done (assuming what is no be done is not unlawful) 'although the thing to be produced had no marketable value.' 45 N.Y. page 572. In 1 Restatement, Contracts, § 346, pp. 576, 577, Illustrations of Subsection (1), par. 4, the same thought is thus stated: 'A contracts to construct a monumental fountain in B's yard for $5,000, but abandons the work after the foundation has been laid and $2800 has been paid by B. The contemplated fountain is so ugly that it would decrease the number of possible buyers of the place. The cost of completing the fountain would be $4000. B can get judgment for $1800, the cost of completion less the part of price unpaid.' But that is not what plaintiff's predecessor in interest contracted for. Such a provision might well have been made, but the parties did not. They could undoubtedly have provided for liquidated damages for nonperformance (2 Dunnell, Minn.Dig., 2d ed. & Supps., §§ 2536, 2537), or they might have determined in money what the value of performance was considered to be and thereby have contractually provided a measure for failure of performance.

The [majority] opinion also suggests that this property lies in an area where the owner might rightly look for future development, being in a so-called industrial zone, and that as such he should be privileged to so hold it. This he may of course do. But let us assume that on May 1, 1934, condemnation to acquire this area had so far progressed as to leave only the question of price (market value) undetermined; that the area had been graded in strict conformity with the contract but that the actual market value of the premises was only $12,160, as found by the court and acquiesced in by plaintiff, what would the measure of his damages be? Obviously, the limit of his recovery could be no more than the then market value of his property. In that sum he has been paid with interest and costs; and he still has the fee title to the premises, something he would not possess if there had been condemnation. In what manner has plaintiff been hurt beyond the damages awarded? As to him 'economic waste' is not apparent. Assume that defendant abandoned the entire project without taking a single yard of gravel therefrom but left the premises as they were when the lease was made, could plaintiff recover damages upon the basis here established? The trouble with the prevailing opinion is that here plaintiff's loss is not made the basis for the amount of his recovery but rather what it would cost the defendant. No case has been decided upon that basis until now.

. . .

I think the judgment should be affirmed.

■ HOLT, JUSTICE. I join in the foregoing dissent.

■ HILTON, J., being incapacitated by illness, took no part. LORING, J., took no part.

Peevyhouse v. Garland Coal & Mining Co.

Supreme Court of Oklahoma, 1962.
1962 OK 267, 382 P.2d 109.

■ JACKSON, JUSTICE.

In the trial court, plaintiffs Willie and Lucille Peevyhouse sued the defendant, Garland Coal and Mining Company, for damages for breach of contract. Judgment was for plaintiffs in an amount considerably less than was sued for. Plaintiffs appeal and defendant cross-appeals.

In the briefs on appeal, the parties present their argument and contentions under several propositions; however, they all stem from the basic question of whether the trial court properly instructed the jury on the measure of damages.

Briefly stated, the facts are as follows: plaintiffs owned a farm containing coal deposits, and in November, 1954, leased the premises to defendant for a period of five years for coal mining purposes. A 'stripmining' operation was contemplated in which the coal would be taken from pits on the surface of the ground, instead of from underground mine shafts. In addition to the usual covenants found in a coal mining lease, defendant specifically agreed to perform certain restorative and remedial work at the end of the lease period. It is unnecessary to set out the details of the work to be done, other than to say that it would involve the moving of many thousands of cubic yards of dirt, at a cost estimated by expert witnesses at about \$29,000.00. However, plaintiffs sued for only \$25,000.00.

During the trial, it was stipulated that all covenants and agreements in the lease contract had been fully carried out by both parties, except the remedial work mentioned above; defendant conceded that this work had not been done.

Plaintiffs introduced expert testimony as to the amount and nature of the work to be done, and its estimated cost. Over plaintiffs' objections, defendant thereafter introduced expert testimony as to the 'diminution in value' of plaintiffs' farm resulting from the failure of defendant to render performance as agreed in the contract—that is, the difference between the present value of the farm, and what its value would have been if defendant had done what it agreed to do.

At the conclusion of the trial, the court instructed the jury that it must return a verdict for plaintiffs, and left the amount of damages for jury determination. On the measure of damages, the court instructed the jury that it might consider the cost of performance of the work defendant agreed to do, 'together with all of the evidence offered on behalf of either party'.

It thus appears that the jury was at liberty to consider the 'diminution in value' of plaintiffs' farm as well as the cost of 'repair work' in determining the amount of damages.

It returned a verdict for plaintiffs for \$5000.00—only a fraction of the 'cost of performance', *but more than the total value of the farm even after the remedial work is done.*

On appeal, the issue is sharply drawn. Plaintiffs contend that the true measure of damages in this case is what it will cost plaintiffs to obtain performance of the work that was not done because of defendant's default. Defendant argues that the measure of damages is the cost of performance 'limited, however, to the total difference in the market value before and after the work was performed'.

It appears that this precise question has not heretofore been presented to this court. In *Ardizonne v. Archer*, 72 Okl. 70, 178 P. 263, this court held that the measure of damages for breach of a contract to drill an oil well was the reasonable cost of drilling the well, but here a slightly different factual situation exists. The drilling of an oil well will yield valuable geological information, even if no oil or gas is found, and of course if the well is a producer, the value of the premises increases. In the case before us, it is argued by defendant with some force that the performance of the remedial work defendant agreed to do will add at the most only a few hundred dollars to the value of plaintiffs' farm, and that the damages should be limited to that amount because that is all plaintiffs have lost.

Plaintiffs rely on *Groves v. John Wunder Co.,* 205 Minn. 163, 286 N.W. 235, 123 A.L.R. 502. In that case, the Minnesota court, in a substantially similar situation, adopted the 'cost of performance' rule as-opposed to the 'value' rule. The result was to authorize a jury to give plaintiff damages in the amount of $60,000, where the real estate concerned would have been worth only $12,160, even if the work contracted for had been done.

It may be observed that *Groves v. John Wunder Co.,* supra, is the only case which has come to our attention in which the cost of performance rule has been followed under circumstances where the cost of performance greatly exceeded the diminution in value resulting from the breach of contract. Incidentally, it appears that this case was decided by a plurality rather than a majority of the members of the court.

Defendant relies principally upon *Sandy Valley & E. R. Co., v. Hughes,* 175 Ky. 320, 194 S.W. 344; *Bigham v. Wabash-Pittsburg Terminal Ry. Co.,* 223 Pa. 106, 72 A. 318; and *Sweeney v. Lewis Const. Co.,* 66 Wash. 490, 119 P. 1108. These were all cases in which, under similar circumstances, the appellate courts followed the 'value' rule instead of the 'cost of performance' rule. Plaintiff points out that in the earliest of these cases (Bigham) the court cites as authority on the measure of damages an earlier Pennsylvania *tort* case, and that the other two cases follow the first, with no explanation as to why a measure of damages ordinarily followed in cases sounding in tort should be used in contract cases. Nevertheless, it is of some significance that three out of four appellate courts have followed the diminution in value rule under circumstances where, as here, the cost of performance greatly exceeds the diminution in value.

The explanation may be found in the fact that the situations presented are artificial ones. It is highly unlikely that the ordinary property owner would agree to pay $29,000 (or its equivalent) for the construction of 'improvements' upon his property that would increase its value only about ($300) three hundred dollars. The result is that we are called upon to apply principles of law theoretically based upon reason and reality to a situation which is basically unreasonable and unrealistic.

In *Groves v. John Wunder Co.,* supra, in arriving at its conclusions, the Minnesota court apparently considered the contract involved to be analogous to a building and construction contract, and cited authority for the proposition that the cost of performance or completion of the building as contracted is ordinarily the measure of damages in actions for damages for the breach of such a contract.

In an annotation following the Minnesota case beginning at 123 A.L.R. 515, the annotator places the three cases relied on by defendant (Sandy Valley, Bigham and Sweeney) under the classification of cases involving 'grading and excavation contracts'.

We do not think either analogy is strictly applicable to the case now before us. The primary purpose of the lease contract between plaintiffs and defendant was neither 'building and construction' nor 'grading and excavation'. It was merely to accomplish the economical recovery and marketing of coal from the premises, to the profit of all parties. The special provisions of the lease contract pertaining to remedial work were incidental to the main object involved.

Even in the case of contracts that are unquestionably building and construction contracts, the authorities are not in agreement as to the factors to be considered in determining whether the cost of performance rule or the value rule should be applied. The American Law Institute's Restatement of the Law, Contracts, Volume 1, Sections 346(1)(a)(i) and (ii) submits the proposition that the cost of performance is the proper measure of damages 'if this is possible and does not involve *unreasonable economic waste';* and that the diminution in value caused by the breach is the proper measure 'if construction and completion in accordance with the contract would involve *unreasonable economic waste'*. (Emphasis supplied.) In an explanatory comment immediately following the text, the Restatement makes it clear that the 'economic waste' referred to consists of the destruction of a substantially completed building or other structure. Of course no such destruction is involved in the case now before us.

On the other hand, in McCormick, Damages, Section 168, it is said with regard to building and construction contracts that '. . . in cases where the defect is one that can be repaired or cured without *undue expense'* the cost of performance is the proper measure of damages, but where '. . . the defect in material or construction is one that cannot be remedied without *an expenditure for reconstruction disproportionate to the end to be attained'* (emphasis supplied) the value rule should be followed. The same idea was expressed in *Jacob & Youngs, Inc. v. Kent*, 230 N.Y. 239, 129 N.E. 889, 23 A.L.R. 1429, as follows:

'The owner is entitled to the money which will permit him to complete, unless the cost of completion is grossly and unfairly out of proportion to the good to be attained. When that is true, the measure is the difference in value.'

It thus appears that the prime consideration in the Restatement was 'economic waste'; and that the prime consideration in McCormick, Damages, and in *Jacob & Youngs, Inc. v. Kent*, supra, was the relationship between the expense involved and the 'end to be attained'— in other words, the 'relative economic benefit'.

In view of the unrealistic fact situation in the instant case, and certain Oklahoma statutes . . . , we are of the opinion that the 'relative economic benefit' is a proper consideration here. This is in accord with the recent case of *Mann v. Clowser*, 190 Va. 887, 59 S.E.2d 78, where, in applying the cost rule, the Virginia court specifically noted that '. . . the defects are remediable from a practical standpoint and the costs *are not grossly disproportionate to the results to be obtained'* (Emphasis supplied).

23 O.S. 1961 §§ 96 and 97 provide as follows:

'§ 96. . . . Notwithstanding the provisions of this chapter, no person can recover a greater amount in damages for the breach of an obligation, than he would have gained by the full performance thereof on both sides . . . .

'§ 97. . . . Damages must, in all cases, be reasonable, and where an obligation of any kind appears to create a right to unconscionable and grossly oppressive damages, contrary to substantial justice no more than reasonable damages can be recovered.'

Although it is true that the above sections of the statute are applied most often in tort cases, they are by their own terms, and the decisions of this court, also applicable in actions for damages for breach of contract. It would seem that they are peculiarly applicable here where, under the 'cost of performance' rule, plaintiffs might recover an amount about nine times the total value of their farm. Such would seem to be 'unconscionable and grossly oppressive damages, contrary to substantial justice' within the meaning of the statute. Also, it can hardly be denied that if plaintiffs here are permitted to recover under the 'cost of performance' rule, they will receive a greater benefit from the breach than could be gained from full performance, contrary to the provisions of Sec. 96.

An analogy may be drawn between the cited sections, and the provisions of 15 O.S. 1961 §§ 214 and 215. These sections tend to render void any provisions of a contract which attempt to fix the amount of stipulated damages to be paid in case of a breach, except where it is impracticable or extremely difficult to determine the actual damages. This results in spite of the agreement of the parties, and the obvious and well known rationale is that insofar as they exceed the actual damages suffered, the stipulated damages amount to a penalty or forfeiture which the law does not favor.

23 O.S. 1961 §§ 96 and 97 have the same effect in the case now before us. *In spite of the agreement of the parties*, these sections limit the damages recoverable to a reasonable amount not 'contrary to substantial justice'; they prevent plaintiffs from recovering a 'greater amount in damages for the breach of an obligation' than they would have 'gained by the full performance thereof'.

We therefore hold that where, in a coal mining lease, lessee agrees to perform certain remedial work on the premises concerned at the end of the lease period, and thereafter the contract is fully performed by both parties except that the remedial work is not done, the measure of damages in an action by lessor against lessee for damages for breach of contract is ordinarily the reasonable cost of performance of the work; however, where the contract provision breached was merely incidental to the main purpose in view, and where the economic benefit which would result to lessor by full performance of the work is grossly disproportionate to the cost of performance, the damages which lessor may recover are limited to the diminution in value resulting to the premises because of the non-performance.

We believe the above holding is in conformity with the intention of the Legislature as expressed in the statutes mentioned, and in harmony with the better-reasoned cases from the other jurisdictions where analogous fact situations have been considered. It should be noted that the rule as stated does not interfere with the property owner's right to 'do what he will with his own' *Chamberlain v. Parker*, 45 N.Y. 569), or his right, if he chooses, to contract for 'improvements' which will actually have the effect of reducing his property's value. Where such result is in fact contemplated by the parties, and is a main or principal purpose of those contracting, it would seem that the measure of damages for breach would ordinarily be the cost of performance. . . .

. . .

We are of the opinion that the judgment of the trial court for plaintiffs should be, and it is hereby, modified and reduced to the sum of $300.00, and as so modified it is affirmed.

- WELCH, DAVISON, HALLEY, and JOHNSON, JJ., concur.

- WILLIAMS, C. J., BLACKBIRD, V. C. J., and IRWIN and BERRY, JJ., dissent.

- IRWIN, JUSTICE (dissenting).

By the specific provisions in the coal mining lease under consideration, the defendant agreed as follows:

'7b Lessee agrees to make fills in the pits dug on said premises on the property line in such manner that fences can be placed thereon and access had to opposite sides of the pits.

'7c Lessee agrees to smooth off the top of the spoil banks on the above premises.

'7d Lessee agrees to leave the creek crossing the above premises in such a condition that it will not interfere with the crossings to be made in pits as set out in 7b.

. . .

'7f Lessee further agrees to leave no shale or dirt on the high wall of said pits. . . .'

Following the expiration of the lease, plaintiffs made demand upon defendant that it carry out the provisions of the contract and to perform those covenants contained therein.

Defendant admits that it failed to perform its obligations that it agreed and contracted to perform under the lease contract and there is nothing in the record which indicates that defendant could not perform its obligations. Therefore, in my opinion defendant's breach of the contract was wilful and not in good faith.

Although the contract speaks for itself, there were several negotiations between the plaintiffs and defendant before the contract was executed. Defendant admitted in the trial of the action, that plaintiffs insisted that the above provisions be included in the contract and that they would not agree to the coal mining lease unless the above provisions were included.

In consideration for the lease contract, plaintiffs were to receive a certain amount as royalty for the coal produced and marketed and in addition thereto their land was to be restored as provided in the contract.

Defendant received as consideration for the contract, its proportionate share of the coal produced and marketed and in addition thereto, the *right to use* plaintiffs' land in the furtherance of its mining operations.

The cost for performing the contract in question could have been reasonably approximated when the contract was negotiated and executed and there are no conditions now existing which could not have been reasonably anticipated by the parties. Therefore, defendant had knowledge, when it prevailed upon the plaintiffs to execute the lease, that the cost of performance might be disproportionate to the value or benefits received by plaintiff for the performance.

Defendant has received its benefits under the contract and now urges, in substance, that plaintiffs' measure of damages for its failure to perform should be the economic value of performance to the plaintiffs and not the cost of performance.

If a peculiar set of facts should exist where the above rule should be applied as the proper measure of damages, (and in my judgment those facts do not exist in the instant case) before such rule should be applied, consideration should be given to the benefits received or contracted for by the party who asserts the application of the rule.

Defendant did not have the right to mine plaintiffs' coal or to use plaintiffs' property for its mining operations without the consent of plaintiffs. Defendant had knowledge of the benefits that it would receive under the contract and the approximate cost of performing the contract. With this knowledge, it must be presumed that defendant thought that it would be to its economic advantage to enter into the contract with plaintiffs and that it would reap benefits from the contract, or it would have not entered into the contract.

Therefore, if the value of the performance of a contract should be considered in determining the measure of damages for breach of a contract, the value of the benefits received under the contract by a party who breaches a contract should also be considered. However, in my judgment, to give consideration to either in the instant action, completely rescinds and holds for naught the solemnity of the contract before us and makes an entirely new contract for the parties.

. . .

'The law will not make a better contract for parties than they themselves have seen fit to enter into, or alter it for the benefit of one party and to the detriment of the others; the judicial function of a court of law is to enforce a contract as it is written.'

I am mindful of Title 23 O.S. 1961 § 96, which provides that no person can recover a greater amount in damages for the breach of an obligation than he could have gained by the full performance thereof on both sides, except in cases not applicable herein. However, in my judgment, the above statutory provision is not applicable here.

In my judgment, we should follow the case of *Groves v. John Wunder Company*, 205 Minn. 163, 286 N.W. 235, 123 A.L.R. 502, which defendant agrees 'that the fact situation is apparently similar to the one in the case at bar', and where the Supreme Court of Minnesota held:

'The owner's or employer's damages for such a breach (i. e. breach hypothesized in 2d syllabus) are to be measured, not in respect to the value of the land to be improved, but by the reasonable cost of doing that which the contractor promised to do and which he left undone.'

The hypothesized breach referred to states that where the contractor's breach of a contract is wilful, that is, in bad faith, he is not entitled to any benefit of the equitable doctrine of substantial performance.

In the instant action defendant has made no attempt to even substantially perform. The contract in question is not immoral, is not tainted with fraud, and was not entered into through mistake or accident and is not contrary to public policy. It is clear and unambiguous and the parties understood the terms thereof, and the approximate cost of fulfilling the obligations could have been approximately ascertained. There are no conditions existing now which could not have been reasonably anticipated when the contract was negotiated and executed. The defendant could have performed the contract if it desired. It has accepted and reaped the benefits of its contract and now urges that plaintiffs' benefits under the contract be denied. If plaintiffs' benefits are denied, such benefits would inure to the direct benefit of the defendant.

Therefore, in my opinion, the plaintiffs were entitled to specific performance of the contract and since defendant has failed to perform, the proper measure of damages should be the cost of performance. Any other measure of damage would be holding for naught the express provisions of the contract; would be taking from the plaintiffs the benefits of the contract and placing those benefits in defendant which has failed to perform its obligations; would be granting benefits to defendant without a resulting obligation; and would be completely rescinding the solemn obligation of the contract for the benefit of the defendant to the detriment of the plaintiffs by making an entirely new contract for the parties.

I therefore respectfully dissent to the opinion promulgated by a majority of my associates.

NOTES

1.   In both *Groves* and *Peevyhouse*, everyone agrees that the damages should be computed to give the landowner the monetary equivalent of the mining company's promise to do the restoration work. That is, in both cases the non-breaching party is entitled to expectation damages. The issue is how to determine what sum of money would accomplish that.

In *Groves* the evidence suggested that the cost of the work might have been as much as $60,000, but the value of the land if the work had been done would be only about $12,000. The appellate court ruled that the landowner was entitled to damages measured by the cost of doing the work, but remanded for additional evidence on exactly what that amount would have been.

In *Peevyhouse* the evidence suggested that the cost of the work might have been as much as $29,000, but the value of the land if the work had been done would increase by only about $300. The appellate court ruled that the landowner was not entitled to damages measured by the cost of doing the work, but only damages measured by the diminution in value of the land as a result of the mining company's failure to do the work.

Obviously the two cases are not consistent, indeed the later opinion, *Peevyhouse*, explicitly declines to follow *Groves*. But, this is not a situation where we simply have a change in the law. Everyone would concede that there may be some cases where the right way to measure expectation damages is by the cost of doing the work and other cases where the right way to measure expectation damages is by the diminution in value. The hard part is deciding what factors should determine the outcome.

2.   Both *Groves* and *Peevyhouse* involve unusual factual situations. In both case the cost of doing the work greatly exceeded the increase in value that would be produced by doing the work. That's unusual. In the usual case, one would expect that a landowner would decide to have work done only if the owner figured that doing the work would increase the value of the land by more than the cost of the work. Suppose, for example, that landowner owns unimproved land worth $600,000. The landowner is considering having a building built on the land. The cost of doing the work would be $300,000. If the landowner concludes that the value of the land after the building is built would only be $800,000, then the landowner would presumably decide not to have the building constructed. By contrast, if the landowner concludes that the value of the land after the building is built would be $1,100,000, then the landowner might decide to have the building constructed.

Thus in the usual case we don't have the problem presented in *Groves* and *Peevyhouse,* because the cost of doing the work will be less than the difference in value that would result from doing the work. So in dealing with the *Groves* and *Peevyhouse* situations, it's worth thinking a bit more about *why* it might have been the case that the cost of doing the work in those cases exceeded the difference in value.

3. One of the hypothetical situations discussed in the dissenting opinion in *Groves* is the "Ugly Fountain Hypo" described in section 346 of the First Restatement. Simplifying somewhat, suppose that Owner contracts with Builder to build an ugly fountain on Owner's land for an agreed contract price of $5000. Builder defaults. Owner learns that it will cost $6000 to get someone else to do the work. Owner (who has not paid anything to Builder) sues for $1000 damages, on the theory that the $1000 damages from Builder, plus the $5000 that Owner had expected to pay, will enable Owner to get the fountain, and do so for the agreed net price of $5000.

Builder seeks to defend by showing that the fountain would be so ugly that constructing it would actually decrease the value of the land by tens of thousands of dollars. Builder says "Owner hasn't suffered any harm by my breach. Indeed, Owner is better off. Doing the work would not increase the value of the land by more than the cost of doing the work. In that respect, the case is like *Groves* and *Peevyhouse*. In fact, doing the work would reduce the value of the land, so Owner is not entitled to any damages from me."

It seems pretty clear that Builder's argument should be rejected. The issue is *why.* Think about *why* Owner should win, and then think about how you would resolve *Groves* and *Peevyhouse* in a fashion consistent with your resolution of the Ugly Fountain hypo.

4. Another scenario discussed in both *Groves* and *Peevyhouse* is based on the case of *Jacob & Youngs v. Kent.* The actual case involves a somewhat different issue. We'll study it later on, in Chapter 10. For now, think of the scenario as follows: Builder contracts to build a house on land owned by Owner. The contract price is $77,000. The specifications and plans included as part of the contract calls for Builder to use Reading brand pipe. After all the work is finished, Owner discovers that Builder has used a different brand of pipe, Cohoes pipe. There's no dispute that it was a breach for Builder to use Cohoes pipe instead of Reading pipe. The issue is how to measure the recovery.

Because the agreement called for owner to make payments to Builder as the work was done, Owner has paid Builder all but $3500 of the agreed contract price. Builder sues for last $3500.

Owner resists saying that while it's true that Builder has a right to recover the remaining contract price ($3500), Owner is entitled to an offset for any damages that Owner has suffered from Builder's breach. The question is how to compute the damages that Owner is entitled to receive for that breach.

The damages, according to Owner, should be computed by determining how much it would *cost* the Owner to have the job completed in accordance with the contract. That means removing the Cohoes pipe and installing

Reading pipe. Owner proves that the cost of doing that work would be $15,000.

The damages, according to Builder, should be computed by determining how much difference in *value* there is between in the house with the wrong pipe (Cohoes) and the house with the correct pipe (Reading). Builder proves that there is no difference in value, whichever pipe was used. So, Builder says Owner is not entitled to any damages.

Note that here we have another situation, like *Groves* and *Peevyhouse,* where it's hard to decide whether damages should be computed by cost or value. You need to think not just about what the right result would be in the *Jacob & Youngs v. Kent* situation, but *why* that is the right result. Then, you need to think about how your reason for resolving the *Jacob & Youngs v. Kent* situation bears on the resolution of the *Groves* and *Peevyhouse* situations.

5.   Think about the evolving societal understandings—and laws—about environmental protection. Rachel Carson's influential book SILENT SPRING was not published until 1962, the same year of the *Peevyhouse* decision on appeal; the first Earth Day was in 1970. How would an appreciation for the natural environment factor into an assessment of "value" nowadays? It's worth noting, of course, that conservationist ideas were around at the time of *Peevyhouse,* although not yet mainstream: think of Henry David Thoreau, who published WALDEN in 1854, or John Muir, who helped establish Yosemite as a national park in 1890. What if Willie and Lucille were proto-environmentalists, as is possible? Think about the burden of proof. For further background, see Judith L. Maute, Peevyhouse v. Garland Coal & Mining Co. *Revisited: The Ballad of Willie and Lucille,* 89 Nw. U. L. Rev. 501 (1995).

PROBLEM

Young wants to borrow Rogers' 1993 Ford Explorer for one week. They sign an agreement under which Rogers agrees to let Young use the car for one week, and Young promises (a) to pay $100 in rent, and (b) to repair any damage that happens to the car while Young has it.

Young borrows car pursuant to the agreement, gets into a collision, and the car is seriously damaged.

Rogers sues Young. Rogers says the damages should be measured by the *cost* of repairing the car, which he proves would be $13,000. Young proves *value* of the car, even if fixed, is only $2000.

So, here is yet another situation, like *Groves* and *Peevyhouse,* where we have to decide whether damages should be computed by cost or value. You need to think not just about what the right result would be in the car rental situation, but *why* that is the right result. Then, you need to think about how your reason for resolving the car rental situation bears on the resolution of the *Groves* and *Peevyhouse* situations.

D. FORESEEABILITY AS A LIMIT ON CONSEQUENTIAL DAMAGES

U.C.C. §§ 2–713(1) & 2–715

Restatement (Second) of Contracts § 351

Hadley v. Baxendale
Court of Exchequer, England, 1854.
9 Exch. 341.

. . . At the trial before Crompton. J., at the last Gloucester Assizes, it appeared that the plaintiffs carried on an extensive business as millers at Gloucester; and that on the 11th of May, their mill was stopped by a breakage of the crank shaft by which the mill was worked. The steam-engine was manufactured by Messrs. Joyce & Co., the engineers, at Greenwich, and it became necessary to send the shaft as a pattern for a new one to Greenwich. The fracture was discovered on the 12th, and on the 13th the plaintiffs sent one of their servants to the office of the defendants, who are the well-known carriers trading under the name of Pickford & Co., for the purpose of having the shaft carried to Greenwich. The plaintiffs' servant told the clerk that the mill was stopped, and that the shaft must be sent immediately; and in answer to the inquiry when the shaft would be taken, the answer was, that if it was sent up by twelve o'clock any day, it would be delivered at Greenwich on the following day. On the following day the shaft was taken by the defendants, before noon, for the purpose of being conveyed to Greenwich, and the sum of 21. 4s. was paid for its carriage for the whole distance; at the same time the defendants' clerk was told that a special entry, if required, would be made to hasten its delivery. The delivery of the shaft at Greenwich was delayed by some neglect; and the consequence was, that the plaintiffs did not receive the new shaft for several days after they would otherwise have done, and the working of their mill was thereby delayed, and they thereby lost the profits they would otherwise have received.

On the part of the defendants, it was objected that these damages were too remote, and that the defendants were not liable with respect to them. The learned Judge left the case generally to the jury, who found a verdict with 251. damages beyond the amount paid into Court.

ALDERSON, B. We think that there ought to be a new trial in this case; but, in so doing we deem it to be expedient and necessary to state explicitly the rule which the Judge, at the next trial, ought, in our opinion, to direct the jury to be governed by when they estimate the damages.

. . .

Now we think the proper rule in such a case as the present is this:—Where two parties have made a contract which one of them has broken, the damages which the other party ought to receive in respect of such breach of contract should be such as may fairly and reasonably be considered either arising naturally, i.e., according to the usual course of things, from such breach of contract itself, or such as may reasonably be supposed to have been in the contemplation of both parties, at the time they made the contract, as the probable result of the breach of it.

Now, if the special circumstances under which the contract was actually made were communicated by the plaintiffs to the defendants, and thus known to both parties, the damages resulting from the breach of such a contract, which they would reasonably contemplate, would be the amount of injury, which would ordinarily follow from a breach of contract under these circumstances so known and communicated. But, on the other had, if these special circumstances were wholly unknown to the party breaking the contract, he, at the most, could only be supposed to have had in his contemplation the amount of injury which would arise generally, and in the great multitude of cases not affected by any special circumstances, from such breach of contract. For, had the special circumstances been known, the parties might have specially provided for the breach of contract by special terms as to the damages in that case; and of this advantage it would be very unjust to deprive them.

. . .

Now, in the present case, if we are to apply the principles above laid down, we find that the only circumstances here communicated by the plaintiffs to the defendants at the time the contract was made, were, that the article to be carried was the broken shaft of a mill, and that the plaintiffs were the millers of that mill. But how do these circumstances shew reasonably that the profits of the mill must be stopped by an unreasonable delay in the delivery of the broken shaft by the carrier to the third person? Suppose the plaintiffs had another shaft in their possession put up or putting up at the time, and that they only wished to send back their broken shaft to the engineer who made it; it is clear that this would be quite consistent with the above circumstances, and yet the unreasonable delay in the delivery would have no effect upon the intermediate profits of the mill. Or, again, suppose that, at the time of the delivery to the carrier, the machinery of the mill had been in other respects defective, then, also, the same results would follow.

Here it is true that the shaft was actually sent back to serve as a model for a new one, and that the want of a new one was the only cause of the stoppage of the mill, and that the loss of profits really arose from not sending down the new shaft in proper time, and that this arose from the delay in delivering the broken one to serve as a model. But, it is obvious that, in the great multitude of cases millers sending off broken shafts to third parties by a carrier under ordinary circumstances, such consequences would not, in all probability, have occurred; and these special circumstances were here never communicated by the plaintiffs to the defendants.

It follows, therefore, that the loss of profits here cannot reasonably be considered such a consequence of the breach of contract as could have been fairly and reasonably contemplated by both the parties when they made this contract. For such loss would neither have flowed naturally from the breach of this contract in the great multitude of such cases occurring under ordinary circumstances, nor were the special circumstances, which, perhaps, would have made it a reasonable and natural consequence of such breach of contract, communicated to or known by the defendants. The Judge ought, therefore, to have told the jury, that, upon the facts then before them, they ought not to take the loss of profits into consideration at all in estimating the damages. There must therefore be a new trial in this case.

NOTES

1.   There is a well-known problem in understanding this opinion. In the first paragraph of the excerpt above, it is stated that:

> The plaintiffs' servant told the clerk that the mill was stopped, and that the shaft must be sent immediately; and in answer to the inquiry when the shaft would be taken, the answer was, that if it was sent up by twelve o'clock any day, it would be delivered at Greenwich on the following day.

This remark, however, was not written by the judge that decided the case. Rather, it is part of the "headnote" written by the person who published the book containing reports of decisions of the English courts. Accordingly it is not an authoritative statement.

In the opinion itself Baron Alderson (one of the judges of the Court of Exchequer that heard the case) says:

> the only circumstances here communicated by the plaintiffs to the defendants at the time the contract was made, were, that the article to be carried was the broken shaft of a mill, and that the plaintiffs were the millers of that mill.

Those are the facts that the decision is based on. In other words, for purposes of understanding the case, you should assume that the carrier's clerk was not told that the mill would be shut down until the shaft was carried to the engineers.

2.   Recall one of the Cotton Futures Cases, *Bolin Farms v. American Cotton,* that we examined at the beginning of the course in Chapter 1.D. Why couldn't the farmers argue, on the basis of *Hadley v. Baxendale,* that no one could have foreseen that the price of cotton would go up so dramatically, and therefore they should not be liable for the unforeseeable damages?

3.   The general principle of *Hadley v. Baxendale* is uniformly accepted. There is however, quite a bit of confusion in the words used to express the

concept. A good deal of that confusion concerns the terms "general" and "special" damages.

One way of expressing the point would be to say that the first element of damages is the cost of getting a substitute for the performance that the defendant was supposed to provide. One could use the term "general" damages for that element. For example, U.C.C. § 2–713(1) says that if the seller fails to deliver, the buyer is entitled to "the difference between the market price . . . and the contract price." "Foreseeability" doesn't enter the equation on that subject, because it's pretty obvious that if the seller doesn't supply the goods, then the buyer is going to have to get them somewhere else.

A different potential element of damages would be **other harms that** befell the non-breaching party as a result of not receiving the promised performance. The term "consequential" damages is sometimes used for that element. So, in *Hadley*, one could say that there really weren't any significant "general damages"—after all the carrier did deliver the goods, and there's nothing to suggest that there were different prices for fast or slow delivery. The significant damage claim in *Hadley* was the claim for "consequential" damages. The shipper argued that because the carrier did not carry the goods quickly, other harm occurred—the mill was shut down for a longer period than expected. So, *Hadley* could be understood as meaning that foreseeability is a limitation on "consequential" damages. That's how the U.C.C. expresses it. Section 2–713 says that in addition to damages measured by the difference between market price and contract price, the non-beaching party may be able to recover "consequential damages" under § 2–715. But, § 2–715(2) says a buyer can recover as consequential damages "any loss resulting from . . . requirements and needs [of the buyer] *of which the seller at the time of contracting had reason to know . . . .*" Using the terms "general damages" and "consequential damages" in the sense just described, one would say that foreseeability is a limit on consequential damages, but not relevant to general damages.

Scholars differ on whether the terms "general" and "consequential" are helpful or confusing. The Restatement avoids any use of those terms. As a result, the Restatement rule formulates the *Hadley* foreseeability rule without using the phrase "consequential damages." The Restatement states the relevant rule as follows:

Restatement (Second) of Contracts § 351

Unforeseeability and Related Limitations on Damages

(1) Damages are not recoverable for loss that the party in breach did not have reason to foresee as a probable result of the breach when the contract was made.

(2) Loss may be foreseeable as a probable result of a breach because it follows from the breach

(a) in the ordinary course of events, or

(b)   as a result of special circumstances, beyond the ordinary course of events, that the party in breach had reason to know.

(3)   A court may limit damages for foreseeable loss by excluding recovery for loss of profits, by allowing recovery only for loss incurred in reliance, or otherwise if it concludes that in the circumstances justice so requires in order to avoid disproportionate compensation.

That formulation is a bit tricky. Subsection (1), read in isolation, seems to say that foreseeability is a relevant limit in all damage calculation. That would seem to imply that the farmers in the Cotton Futures Cases would have had a plausible argument that they should not be liable because the increase in the market price of cotton was so unexpected. But, that can't be right. Looking more carefully, we see that subsection (2) says that loss is "foreseeable" if either (a) it flows from the breach in the ordinary course of events, or (b) it flows from special circumstances of which the defendant had reason to know. Subsection (a) would cover the increased cost of getting a substitute—like the increased price of cotton in the Cotton Futures Cases. In effect, subsection 2(a) says that that loss is always "foreseeable." That's the same point that many cases and other scholars express by saying that foreseeability is not a limit on "general damages." Subsection 2(b) covers the cases where the foreseeability limit makes a real difference—the situations that that many cases and other scholars express by using the phrase "consequential damages."

4.   *Hadley* establishes that a defaulting party is not liable for consequential damages that were not foreseeable. Does that mean that a defaulting party is liable for consequential damages that were foreseeable?

Suppose that a farmer buys a tractor, the tractor is defective, and the farmer loses that year's crops as a result of inability to plow the fields with the new tractor. Assume that the defect in the tractor does amount to a breach of warranty, that is, a promise that the tractor will perform to a certain standard. Should the farmer have a right to recover, not only for the cost of repairing the tractor (or diminution in its value), but also for the lost value of that year's crops? Cases reach inconsistent results. *Compare Prutch v. Ford Motor Co.*, 618 P.2d 657 (Colo. 1980) (yes) *with Lamkins v. Int'l Harvester Co.*, 182 S.W.2d 203 (Ark. 1944) (no).

5.   The question of the extent to which consequential damages may be recovered became a significant issue in the 1980s in connection with the business of electronic funds transfers through the banking system. *Evra Corp. v. Swiss Bank Corp*, 673 F.2d 951 (7th Cir. 1982). A company had a long term contract to "charter," that is, rent, a ship from its owner. The contract was very favorable to the ship renter, because ship rental prices increased dramatically not long after the contract was signed. The contract required the ship renter to pay $27,000 per month in rent by the 26th day of each month. If the rent was not paid on time, the ship owner could cancel the deal. On the 25th of April, the ship renter went to its bank in Chicago and filled out the paperwork for the bank to transfer $27,000 to the ship owner in Switzerland by an electronic funds transfer. Something went wrong with the transfer, and the money did not get to the ship owner on time. The ship

owner cancelled the contract, and the ship renter had to renegotiate with the owner, agreeing to pay the current rent rather than the low contract rent. As a result, the ship rental contract ended up costing the ship renter more the $2 million extra.

The ship renter sued the banks saying that the banks had failed to carry out their agreement to make the electronic funds transfer and, as a result, the ship renter ended up having to pay $2 million more. The Seventh Circuit, in an opinion by the well-known judge Richard Posner, said the case was just like the old *Hadley v. Baxendale* situation. The court ruled that the banks were not liable for the $2 million in consequential damages, because the circumstances were not such as would place them on notice that such dire consequences would flow from a failure to compete an electronic funds transfer.

While the banks were undoubtedly happy about the result in that particular case, they became very worried about the reasoning. If the reason they won in *Evra* was that the loss was not foreseeable, would that mean that they would lose in a case where the loss was foreseeable? What if the ship renter in *Evra* had told the clerk at the bank "It's very important that the $27,000 get to the ship owner in Switzerland by tomorrow, otherwise we stand to lose millions." Would that mean that the bank would be liable because the consequential damages would have been foreseeable? Banks were not happy about that possibility. As a consequence, banks became strong supporters of an effort that had been started some years before to write a new statute dealing with electronic funds transfers. That statute is now Article 4A of the U.C.C. One of the major points established by Article 4A is that a bank is *not* liable for consequential damages from failure to complete an electronic funds transfer—a principle that does not depend on notions of foreseeability. See U.C.C. § 4A–305.

E. MITIGATION OF DAMAGES

Restatement (Second) of Contracts § 350

PROBLEMS

1.   The owner of three paintings enters into a contract with a painting conservator to restore the three paintings. The contract price is $1500 per painting, for a total of $4500. Assume that the restorer can prove that it would cost $1200 per painting to do the work, that is, he would have earned a profit of $300 per painting. Restorer does the work on the first painting. Then, without any contractual justification, the owner tells the restorer not to finish the work.

Nonetheless, the restorer does the restoration work on the second two paintings, as well as the work already done on the first painting.

Restorer sues Owner. How much should the restorer recover? $4500? $1500? $2100?

See *Clark v. Marsiglia*, 1 Denio 317 (N.Y. 1845).

2. Rockingham County in North Carolina was contemplating having a bridge built, but the issue was fairly controversial. At a time when advocates of the bridge project were in power, the county entered into a contract with Luten Bridge Co. for construction of the bridge. After Luten had done work worth about $19,000 the other side in the political controversy got control of the county. So, the county then told Luten to cease work. Nonetheless, Luten completed work—maybe because Luten thought that maybe the county would change its mind again. Anyway, Luten sued the county for the full cost of the job, about $183,000. Assume that there is no doubt that the county was breaking the contract when it told Luten to cease work. Should Luten get only the value of its work before the county said stop (about $19,000) or the full cost of the work ($183,000)?

See Rockingham County v. Luten Bridge Co., 35 F.2d 301 (4th Cir. 1929).

Parker v. Twentieth Century Fox Film Corp.

Supreme Court of California, 1970.
3 Cal.3d 176, 474 P.2d 689.

■ BURKE, JUSTICE.

Defendant Twentieth Century-Fox Film Corporation appeals from a summary judgment granting to plaintiff the recovery of agreed compensation under a written contract for her services as an actress in a motion picture. As will appear, we have concluded that the trial court correctly ruled in plaintiff's favor and that the judgment should be affirmed.

Plaintiff is well known as an actress,[a] and in the contract between plaintiff and defendant is sometimes referred to as the 'Artist.' Under the contract, dated August 6, 1965, plaintiff was to play the female lead in defendant's contemplated production of a motion picture entitled 'Bloomer Girl.' The contract provided that defendant would pay plaintiff a minimum 'guaranteed compensation' of '53,571.42 per week for 14 weeks commencing May 23, 1966, for a total of $750,000. Prior to May 1966 defendant decided not to produce the picture and by a letter dated April 4, 1966, it notified plaintiff of that decision and that it would not 'comply with our obligations to you under' the written contract.

By the same letter and with the professed purpose 'to avoid any damage to you,' defendant instead offered to employ plaintiff as the leading actress in another film tentatively entitled 'Big Country, Big Man' (hereinafter, 'Big Country'). The compensation offered was identical, as were 31 of the 34 numbered provisions or articles of the original contract.[1] Unlike 'Bloomer Girl,' however, which was to have

---

[a] [Otherwise known as Shirley MacLaine—Eds]

[1] Among the identical provisions was the following found in the last paragraph of Article 2 of the original contract: 'We (defendant) shall not be obligated to utilize your (plaintiff's) services in or in connection with the Photoplay hereunder, our sole obligation, subject to the

been a musical production, 'Big Country' was a dramatic 'western type' movie. 'Bloomer Girl' was to have been filmed in California; 'Big Country' was to be produced in Australia. Also, certain terms in the proffered contract varied from those of the original.[2] Plaintiff was given one week within which to accept; she did not and the offer lapsed. Plaintiff then commenced this action seeking recovery of the agreed guaranteed compensation.

The complaint sets forth two causes of action. The first is for money due under the contract; the second, based upon the same allegations as the first, is for damages resulting from defendant's breach of contract. Defendant in its answer admits the existence and validity of the contract, that plaintiff complied with all the conditions, covenants and promises and stood ready to complete the performance, and that defendant breached and 'anticipatorily repudiated' the contract. It denies, however, that any money is due to plaintiff either under the contract or as a result of its breach, and pleads as an affirmative defense to both causes of action plaintiff's allegedly deliberate failure to mitigate damages, asserting that she unreasonably refused to accept its offer of the leading role in 'Big Country.'

Plaintiff moved for summary judgment under Code of Civil Procedure section 437c, the motion was granted, and summary judgment for $750,000 plus interest was entered in plaintiff's favor. This appeal by defendant followed.

The familiar rules are that the matter to be determined by the trial court on a motion for summary judgment is whether facts have been

---

terms and conditions of this Agreement, being to pay you the guaranteed compensation herein provided for.'

[2]   Article 29 of the original contract specified that plaintiff approved the director already chosen for 'Bloomer Girl' and that in case he failed to act as director plaintiff was to have approval rights of any substitute director. Article 31 provided that plaintiff was to have the right of approval of the 'Bloomer Girl' dance director, and Article 32 gave her the right of approval of the screenplay.

Defendant's letter of April 4 to plaintiff, which contained both defendant's notice of breach of the 'Bloomer Girl' contract and offer of the lead in 'Big Country,' eliminated or impaired each of those rights. It read in part as follows: 'The terms and conditions of our offer of employment are identical to those set forth in the 'BLOOMER GIRL' Agreement, Articles 1 through 34 and Exhibit A to the Agreement, except as follows:

'1. Article 31 of said Agreement will not be included in any contract of employment regarding 'BIG COUNTRY, BIG MAN' as it is not a musical and it thus will not need a dance director.

'2. In the 'BLOOMER GIRL' agreement, in Articles 29 and 32, you were given certain director and screenplay approvals and you had preapproved certain matters. Since there simply is insufficient time to negotiate with you regarding your choice of director and regarding the screenplay and since you already expressed an interest in performing the role in 'BIG COUNTRY, BIG MAN,' we must exclude from our offer of employment in 'BIG COUNTRY, BIG MAN' any approval rights as are contained in said Articles 29 and 32; however, we shall consult with you respecting the director to be selected to direct the photoplay and will further consult with you with respect to the screenplay and any revisions or changes therein, provided, however, that if we fail to agree . . . the decision of . . . (defendant) with respect to the selection of a director and to revisions and changes in the said screenplay shall be binding upon the parties to said agreement.

presented which give rise to a triable factual issue. The court may not pass upon the issue itself. Summary judgment is proper only if the affidavits or declarations in support of the moving party would be sufficient to sustain a judgment in his favor and his opponent does not by affidavit show facts sufficient to present a triable issue of fact. . . .

As stated, defendant's sole defense to this action which resulted from its deliberate breach of contract is that in rejecting defendant's substitute offer of employment plaintiff unreasonably refused to mitigate damages.

The general rule is that the measure of recovery by a wrongfully discharged employee is the amount of salary agreed upon for the period of service, less the amount which the employer affirmatively proves the employee has earned or with reasonable effort might have earned from other employment. * * * However, before projected earnings from other employment opportunities not sought or accepted by the discharged employee can be applied in mitigation, the employer must show that the other employment was comparable, or substantially similar, to that of which the employee has been deprived; the employee's rejection of or failure to seek other available employment of a different or inferior kind may not be resorted to in order to mitigate damages. * * *

In the present case defendant has raised no issue of reasonableness of efforts by plaintiff to obtain other employment; the sole issue is whether plaintiff's refusal of defendant's substitute offer of 'Big Country' may be used in mitigation. Nor, if the 'Big Country' offer was of employment different or inferior when compared with the original 'Bloomer Girl' employment, is there an issue as to whether or not plaintiff acted reasonably in refusing the substitute offer. Despite defendant's arguments to the contrary, no case cited or which our research has discovered holds or suggests that reasonableness is an element of a wrongfully discharged employee's option to reject, or fail to seek, different or inferior employment lest the possible earnings therefrom be charged against him in mitigation of damages.

Applying the foregoing rules to the record in the present case, with all intendments in favor of the party opposing the summary judgment motion—here, defendant—it is clear that the trial court correctly ruled that plaintiff's failure to accept defendant's tendered substitute employment could not be applied in mitigation of damages because the offer of the 'Big Country' lead was of employment both different and inferior, and that no factual dispute was presented on that issue. The mere circumstance that 'Bloomer Girl' was to be a musical review calling upon plaintiff's talents as a dancer as well as an actress, and was to be produced in the City of Los Angeles, whereas 'Big Country' was a straight dramatic role in a 'Western Type' story taking place in an opal mine in Australia, demonstrates the difference in kind between the two employments; the female lead as a dramatic actress in a western style motion picture can by no stretch of imagination be considered the equivalent of or substantially similar to the lead in a song-and-dance production.

Additionally, the substitute 'Big Country' offer proposed to eliminate or impair the director and screenplay approvals accorded to plaintiff under the original 'Bloomer Girl' contract (see fn. 2, Ante), and thus constituted an offer of inferior employment. No expertise or judicial notice is required in order to hold that the deprivation or infringement of an employee's rights held under an original employment contract converts the available 'other employment' relied upon by the employer to mitigate damages, into inferior employment which the employee need not seek or accept. * * *

. . .

In view of the determination that defendant failed to present any facts showing the existence of a factual issue with respect to its sole defense—plaintiff's rejection of its substitute employment offer in mitigation of damages—we need not consider plaintiff's further contention that for various reasons, including the provisions of the original contract set forth in footnote 1, Ante, plaintiff was excused from attempting to mitigate damages.

The judgment is affirmed.

■ SULLIVAN, ACTING CHIEF JUSTICE (dissenting).

The basic question in this case is whether or not plaintiff acted reasonably in rejecting defendant's offer of alternate employment. The answer depends upon whether that offer (starring in 'Big Country, Big Man') was an offer of work that was substantially similar to her former employment (starring in 'Bloomer Girl') or of work that was of a different or inferior kind. To my mind this is a factual issue which the trial court should not have determined on a motion for summary judgment. The majority have not only repeated this error but have compounded it by applying the rules governing mitigation of damages in the employer-employee context in a misleading fashion. Accordingly, I respectfully dissent.

The familiar rule requiring a plaintiff in a tort or contract action to mitigate damages embodies notions of fairness and socially responsible behavior which are fundamental to our jurisprudence. Most broadly stated, it precludes the recovery of damages which, through the exercise of due diligence, could have been avoided. Thus, in essence, it is a rule requiring reasonable conduct in commercial affairs. This general principle governs the obligations of an employee after his employer has wrongfully repudiated or terminated the employment contract. Rather than permitting the employee simply to remain idle during the balance of the contract period, the law requires him to make a reasonable effort to secure other employment.[1] He is not obliged, however, to seek or accept

---

[1]   The issue is generally discussed in terms of a duty on the part of the employee to minimize loss. The practice is long-established and there is little reason to change despite Judge

any and all types of work which may be available. Only work which is in the same field and which is of the same quality need be accepted.[2]

Over the years the courts have employed various phrases to define the type of employment which the employee, upon his wrongful discharge, is under an obligation to accept. Thus in California alone it has been held that he must accept employment which is 'substantially similar' (*Lewis v. Protective Security Life Ins. Co.* (1962) 208 Cal.App.2d 582, 584, 25 Cal.Rptr. 213; * * *); 'comparable employment' (*Erler v. Five Points Motors, Inc.* (1967) 249 Cal.App.2d 560, 562, 57 Cal.Rptr. 516; * * *); employment 'in the same general line of the first employment' (*Rotter v. Stationers Corporation* (1960) 186 Cal.App.2d 170, 172, 8 Cal.Rptr. 690, 691); 'equivalent to his prior position' (*De Angeles v. Roos Bros., Inc.* (1966) 244 Cal.App.2d 434, 443, 52 Cal.Rptr. 783); 'employment in a similar capacity' (*Silva v. McCoy* (1968) 259 Cal.App.2d 256, 260, 66 Cal.Rptr. 364); employment which is 'not . . . of a different or inferior kind. . . .' (*Gonzales v. Internat. Assn. of Machinists* (1963) 213 Cal.App.2d 817, 822, 29 Cal.Rptr. 190, 193.)

For reasons which are unexplained, the majority cite several of these cases yet select from among the various judicial formulations which contain one particular phrase, 'Not of a different or inferior kind,' with which to analyze this case. I have discovered no historical or theoretical reason to adopt this phrase, which is simply a negative restatement of the affirmative standards set out in the above cases, as the exclusive standard. Indeed, its emergence is an example of the dubious phenomenon of the law responding not to rational judicial choice or changing social conditions, but to unrecognized changes in the language of opinions or legal treatises. However, the phrase is a serviceable one and my concern is not with its use as the standard but rather with what I consider its distortion.

The relevant language excuses acceptance only of employment which is of a different kind. * * * It has never been the law that the mere existence of differences between two jobs in the same field is sufficient, as a matter of law, to excuse an employee wrongfully discharged from one from accepting the other in order to mitigate damages. Such an approach would effectively eliminate any obligation of an employee to attempt to minimize damage arising from a wrongful discharge. The only

---

Cardozo's observation of its subtle inaccuracy. 'The servant is free to accept employment or reject it according to his uncensored pleasure. What is meant by the supposed duty is merely this: That if he unreasonably reject, he will not be heard to say that the loss of wages from then on shall be deemed the jural consequence of the earlier discharge. He has broken the chain of causation, and loss resulting to him thereafter is suffered through his own act.' (McClelland v. Climax Hosiery Mills (1930) 252 N.Y. 347, 359, 169 N.E. 605, 609, concurring opinion.)

   [2]   This qualification of the rule seems to reflect the simple and humane attitude that it is too severe to demand of a person that he attempt to find and perform work for which he has no training or experience. Many of the older cases hold that one need not accept work in an inferior rank or position nor work which is more menial or arduous. This suggests that the rule may have had its origin in the bourgeois fear of resubmergence in lower economic classes.

alternative job offer an employee would be required to accept would be an offer of his former job by his former employer.

Although the majority appear to hold that there was a difference 'in kind' between the employment offered plaintiff in 'Bloomer Girl' and that offered in 'Big Country' (opn. at p. 10), an examination of the opinion makes crystal clear that the majority merely point out differences between the two films (an obvious circumstance) and then apodictically assert that these constitute a difference in the kind of employment. The entire rationale of the majority boils down to this: that the 'mere circumstances' that 'Bloomer Girl' was to be a musical review while 'Big Country' was a straight drama 'demonstrates the difference in kind' since a female lead in a western is not 'the equivalent of or substantially similar to' a lead in a musical. This is merely attempting to prove the proposition by repeating it. It shows that the vehicles for the display of the star's talents are different but it does not prove that her employment as a star in such vehicles is of necessity different in kind and either inferior or superior.

I believe that the approach taken by the majority (a superficial listing of differences with no attempt to assess their significance) may subvert a valuable legal doctrine. The inquiry in cases such as this should not be whether differences between the two jobs exist (there will always be differences) but whether the differences which are present are substantial enough to constitute differences in the kind of employment or, alternatively, whether they render the substitute work employment of an inferior kind.

It seems to me that this inquiry involves, in the instant case at least, factual determinations which are improper on a motion for summary judgment. Resolving whether or not one job is substantially similar to another or whether, on the other hand, it is of a different or inferior kind, will often (as here) require a critical appraisal of the similarities and differences between them in light of the importance of these differences to the employee. This necessitates a weighing of the evidence, and it is precisely this undertaking which is forbidden on summary judgment. * * *

This is not to say that summary judgment would never be available in an action by an employee in which the employer raises the defense of failure to mitigate damages. No case has come to my attention, however, in which summary judgment has been granted on the issue of whether an employee was obliged to accept available alternate employment. Nevertheless, there may well be cases in which the substitute employment is so manifestly of a dissimilar or inferior sort, the declarations of the plaintiff so complete and those of the defendant so conclusionary and inadequate that no factual issues exist for which a trial is required. This, however, is not such a case.

. . .

I believe that the judgment should be reversed so that the issue of whether or not the offer of the lead role in 'Big Country, Big Man' was of employment comparable to that of the lead role in 'Bloomer Girl' may be determined at trial.

NOTES & QUESTIONS

1.	The judges in *Parker*, when describing the musical, Bloomer Girl, do not include any details about Amelia Bloomer, the suffragette, women's rights advocate, and abolitionist, whose name became associated with the style of dress—resembling Turkish pants—designed in the 1850s to relieve women from restrictive long skirts, hoops and petticoats. Does this link change your reading of "different or inferior"? See further Mary Ann Frug, *Re-reading Contracts: A Feminist Analysis of a Casebook*, 34 AM. U. L. REV. 1065 (1985).

2.	The principle in *Parker* is sometimes described as a "duty to mitigate" damages. The phrase "duty" is rather misleading. Read, with care, the footnote in Judge Sullivan's opinion, quoting from Judge Cardozo's accurate comment in *McClelland v. Climax Hosiery*.

3.	Consider the following variant of the facts in the *Parker* case:

Parker had a contract with 20th Century Fox to work on Bloomer Girl for $750,000. 20th Century Fox cancels Bloomer Girl, without any justification, and offers Parker no alternative role.

Another company (MGM) offers Parker $600,000 for a role in another musical, with the same production schedule. Parker declines. Parker does no other work for that period.

Parker sues 20th Century Fox for $750,000.

What result?

CHAPTER EIGHT

INTERPRETATION

It depends on what the meaning of the word 'is' is.

—Bill Clinton

A. "SUBJECTIVE" AND "OBJECTIVE" THEORIES OF CONTRACT

Embry v. Hargadine, McKittrick Dry Goods Co.
105 S.W. 777 (Mo. Ct. App. 1907).

■ GOODE, J.

. . . The appellant was an employee of the respondent company under a written contract to expire December 15, 1903, at a salary of $2,000 per annum. . . . It was his business to select samples for the traveling salesmen of the company, which is a wholesale dry goods concern, to use in selling goods to retail merchants. Appellant contends that on December 23, 1903, he was re-engaged by respondent, through its president, Thos. H. McKittrick, for another year at the same compensation and for the same duties stipulated in his previous written contract. On March 1, 1904, he was discharged, having been notified in February that, on account of the necessity of retrenching expenses, his services and that of some other employés would no longer be required. The respondent company contends that its president never re-employed appellant after the termination of his written contract, and hence that it had a right to discharge him when it chose. The point with which we are concerned requires an epitome of the testimony of appellant and the counter testimony of McKittrick, the president of the company, in reference to the alleged re-employment. Appellant testified: That several times prior to the termination of his written contract on December 15, 1903, he had endeavored to get an understanding with McKittrick for another year, but had been put off from time to time. That on December 23d, eight days after the expiration of said contract, he called on McKittrick, in the latter's office, and said to him that as appellant's written employment had lapsed eight days before, and as there were only a few days between then and the 1st of January in which to seek employment with other firms, if respondent wished to retain his services longer he must have a contract for another year, or he would quit respondent's service then and there. That he had been put off twice before and wanted an understanding or contract at once so that he could go ahead without worry. That McKittrick asked him how he was getting along in his department, and appellant said he was very busy, as they were in the height of the season getting men out—had about 110 salesmen on the line and others in preparation. That McKittrick then said: "Go ahead, you're all right. Get your men out, and don't let that worry you." That appellant took McKittrick at his word and worked until February 15th without any question in his mind. It was on February 15th that he was notified his services would be discontinued on March 1st. McKittrick denied this conversation as related by appellant, and said that, when accosted by the latter on December 23d, he (McKittrick) was working on his books in order to get out a report for a stockholders' meeting, and, when appellant said if he did not get a contract he would leave, that he (McKittrick) said: "Mr. Embry, I am just getting ready for the stockholders' meeting to-morrow. I have no time to take it up now. I have told you before I would not take it up until I had these matters out of the way. You will have to see me at a later time. I said: 'Go back upstairs and get your men out on the road.' I may have asked him one or two other questions relative to the department, I don't remember. The whole conversation did not take more than a minute."

. . . Appellant requested an instruction to the jury setting out, in substance, the conversation between him and McKittrick according to his version, and declaring that those facts, if found to be true, constituted a contract between the parties that defendant would pay plaintiff the sum of $2,000 for another year, provided the jury believed from the evidence that plaintiff commenced said work believing he was to have $2,000 for the year's work. This instruction was refused, but the court gave another embodying in substance appellant's version of the conversation, and declaring it made a contract "if you (the jury) find both parties thereby intended and did contract with each other for plaintiff's employment for one year from and including December 23, 1903, at a salary of $2,000 per annum." Embry swore that, on several occasions when he spoke to McKittrick about employment for the ensuing year, he asked for a renewal of his former contract, and that on December 23d, the date of the alleged renewal, he went into Mr. McKittrick's office and told him his contract had expired, and he wanted to renew it for a year, having always worked under year contracts. Neither the refused instruction nor the one given by the court embodied facts quite as strong as appellant's testimony, because neither referred to appellant's alleged statement to McKittrick that unless he was re-employed he would stop work for respondent then and there.

It is assigned for error that the court required the jury, in order to return a verdict for appellant, not only to find the conversation occurred as appellant swore, but that both parties intended by such conversation to contract with each other for plaintiff's employment for the year from December, 1903. . . . [T]o put the question more precisely: Did what was said constitute a contract of re-employment on the previous terms irrespective of the intention or purpose of McKittrick?

Judicial opinion and elementary treatises abound in statements of the rule that to constitute a contract there must be a meeting of the minds of the parties, and both must agree to the same thing in the same sense. Generally speaking, this may be true; but it is not literally or universally true. That is to say, the inner intention of parties to a conversation subsequently alleged to create a contract cannot either make a contract of what transpired, or prevent one from arising, if the words used were sufficient to constitute a contract. In so far as their intention is an influential element, it is only such intention as the words or acts of the parties indicate; not one secretly cherished which is inconsistent with those words or acts. The rule is thus stated by a text-writer, and many decisions are cited in support of his text: "The primary object of construction in contract law is to discover the intention of the parties. This intention in express contracts is, in the first instance, embodied in the words which the parties have used and is to be deduced therefrom. This rule applies to oral contracts, as well as to contracts in writing, and is the rule recognized by courts of equity." 2 Paige, Contracts, § 1104. . . . In *Brewington v. Mesker*, 51 Mo. App. 348, 356, it is said that the meeting of minds, which is essential to the formation of a contract, is not determined by the secret intention of the parties, but by their expressed intention, which may be wholly at variance with the former. . . . If the validity of such a contract depended upon secret intentions of the parties, then no oral contract of sale could be relied on with safety." . . . In 9 Cyc. 245, we find the following text: "The law imputes to a person an intention corresponding to the reasonable meaning of his words and acts. It judges his intention by his outward expressions and excludes all questions in regard to his unexpressed intention. If his words or acts, judged by a reasonable standard, manifest an intention to agree in regard to the matter in question, that agreement is established, and it is immaterial what may be the real, but unexpressed, state of his mind on the subject." . . . In view of those authorities, we hold that, though McKittrick may not have intended to employ Embry by what transpired between them according to the latter's testimony, yet if what McKittrick said would have been taken by a reasonable man to be an employment, and Embry so understood it, it constituted a valid contract of employment for the ensuing year.

The next question is whether or not the language used was of that character, namely, was such that Embry, as a reasonable man, might consider he was re-employed for the ensuing year on the previous terms, and act accordingly. We do not say that in every instance it would be for the court to pronounce on this question, because, peradventure, instances might arise in which there would be such an ambiguity in the language relied on to show an assent by the obligor to the proposal of the obligee that it would be for the jury to say whether a reasonable mind would take it to signify acceptance of the proposal. . . . The general rule is that it is for the court to construe the effect of writings relied on to make a contract, and also the effect of unambiguous oral words. * * * However, if the words are in dispute, the question of whether they were used or not is for the jury. . . .

With these rules of law in mind, let us recur to the conversation of December 23d between Embry and McKittrick as related by the former. Embry was demanding a renewal of his contract, saying he had been put off from time to time, and that he had only a few days before the end of the year in which to seek employment from other houses, and that he would quit then and there unless he was reemployed. McKittrick inquired how he was getting along with the department, and Embry said they, i.e., the employés of the department, were very busy getting out salesmen. Whereupon McKittrick said: "Go ahead, you are all right. Get your men out, and do not let that worry you." We think no reasonable man would construe that answer to Embry's demand that he be employed for another year, otherwise than as an assent to the demand, and that Embry had the right to rely on it as an assent. The natural inference is, though we do not find it testified to, that Embry was at work getting samples ready for the salesmen to use during the ensuing season. Now, when he was complaining of the worry and mental distress he was under because of his uncertainty about the future, and his urgent need, either of an immediate contract with respondent, or a refusal by it to make one, leaving him free to seek employment elsewhere, McKittrick must have answered as he did for the purpose of assuring appellant that any apprehension was needless, as appellant's services would be retained by the respondent. The answer was unambiguous, and we rule that if the conversation was according to appellant's version, and he understood he was employed, it constituted in law a valid contract of re-employment, and the court erred in making the formation of a contract depend on a finding that both parties intended to make one. It was only necessary that Embry, as a reasonable man, had a right to and did so understand. . . .

The judgment is reversed, and the cause remanded. All concur.

NOTES

1.   The *Embry* case is a nice illustration of why it's misleading to think of contract formation through the metaphor of "meeting of the minds", although you've encountered that phrase in many cases in these materials. No one thinks that the employer (McKittrick) thought that he was proposing to hire the employee (Embry) for another year. Embry might have thought that he was being hired for another year, but it's pretty clear that McKittrick did not think that. So, if the requirement of a "meeting of the minds" was dispositive, we'd conclude that no contract was formed. But, the result is the opposite—Embry could have a contract for another year's work even though McKittrick didn't mean to hire him. As in *Lucy v. Zehmer,* Chapter 1A, what counts is not what was going on inside the promisor's (McKittrick's) head, but what a reasonable person in the promisee's (Embry's) situation would have understood the promisor's words to mean.

2.   While the "objective" approach to contract formation and interpretation may help in some cases, there will be others where that's not the case. There is a famous old English case, *Raffles v. Wichelhaus*, 159 Eng.

Rep. 375 (Ex. 1864), that illustrates the problem. Buyer and Seller entered into a contract for the sale of the cotton that was to arrive in England from India on the ship *Peerless*. Unknown to either Buyer or Seller, there were two ships named *Peerless*, both carrying cotton from India to England. One arrived in October, one in December. As a result of the Civil War in the United States, the market price of cotton was swinging wildly. If the agreement had been interpreted as meaning the cotton on the ship that arrived in October, it would have been very favorable to one side, while if the agreement meant the December ship, it would have been very favorable to the other side. Construing the communications from the standpoint of the reasonable recipient wouldn't solve the problem because each party's understanding was entirely plausible. The court concluded that the misunderstanding prevented formation of a binding agreement. It was as if Seller said "I'll sell a horse" and Buyer said "I'll buy a cow."

B. WORKING WITH CONTRACT LANGUAGE AND OTHER AIDS TO INTERPRETATION

Frigaliment Importing Co. v. B.N.S. Int'l Sales Corp.

United States District Court for the Southern District of New York, 1960.
190 F Supp. 116.

■ FRIENDLY, CIRCUIT JUDGE.

The issue is, what is chicken? Plaintiff says 'chicken' means a young chicken, suitable for broiling and frying. Defendant says 'chicken' means any bird of that genus that meets contract specifications on weight and quality, including what it calls 'stewing chicken' and plaintiff pejoratively terms 'fowl'. Dictionaries give both meanings, as well as some others not relevant here. To support its, plaintiff sends a number of volleys over the net; defendant essays to return them and adds a few serves of its own. Assuming that both parties were acting in good faith, the case nicely illustrates Holmes' remark 'that the making of a contract depends not on the agreement of two minds in one intention, but on the agreement of two sets of external signs—not on the parties' having meant the same thing but on their having said the same thing.' The Path of the Law, in Collected Legal Papers, p. 178. I have concluded that plaintiff has not sustained its burden of persuasion that the contract used 'chicken' in the narrower sense.

The action is for breach of the warranty that goods sold shall correspond to the description, New York Personal Property Law, McKinney's Consol. Laws, c. 41, § 95. Two contracts are in suit. In the first, dated May 2, 1957, defendant, a New York sales corporation, confirmed the sale to plaintiff, a Swiss corporation, of

'US Fresh Frozen Chicken, Grade A, Government Inspected, Eviscerated 2 ½–3 lbs. and 1 ½–2 lbs. each all chicken individually wrapped in cryovac, packed in secured fiber cartons or wooden boxes, suitable for export

> 75,000 lbs. 2 ½–3 lbs.   @$33.00
>
> 25,000 lbs. 1 ½–2 lbs.   @$36.50

per 100 lbs. FAS New York

scheduled May 10, 1957 pursuant to instructions from Penson & Co., New York.'

The second contract, also dated May 2, 1957, was identical save that only 50,000 lbs. of the heavier 'chicken' were called for, the price of the smaller birds was $37 per 100 lbs., and shipment was scheduled for May 30. The initial shipment under the first contract was short but the balance was shipped on May 17. When the initial shipment arrived in Switzerland, plaintiff found, on May 28, that the 2 ½–3 lbs. birds were not young chicken suitable for broiling and frying but stewing chicken or 'fowl'; indeed, many of the cartons and bags plainly so indicated. Protests ensued. Nevertheless, shipment under the second contract was made on May 29, the 2 ½–3 lbs. birds again being stewing chicken. Defendant stopped the transportation of these at Rotterdam.

This action followed. Plaintiff says that, notwithstanding that its acceptance was in Switzerland, New York law control under the principle of *Rubin v. Irving Trust Co.*, 1953, 305 N.Y. 288, 305, 113 N.E.2d 424, 431; defendant does not dispute this, and relies on New York decisions. I shall follow the apparent agreement of the parties as to the applicable law.

Since the word 'chicken' standing alone is ambiguous, I turn first to see whether the contract itself offers any aid to its interpretation. Plaintiff says the 1 ½–2 lbs. birds necessarily had to be young chicken since the older birds do not come in that size, hence the 2 ½–3 lbs. birds must likewise be young. This is unpersuasive—a contract for 'apples' of two different sizes could be filled with different kinds of apples even though only one species came in both sizes. Defendant notes that the contract called not simply for chicken but for 'US Fresh Frozen Chicken, Grade A, Government Inspected.' It says the contract thereby incorporated by reference the Department of Agriculture's regulations, which favor its interpretation; I shall return to this after reviewing plaintiff's other contentions.

The first hinges on an exchange of cablegrams which preceded execution of the formal contracts. The negotiations leading up to the contracts were conducted in New York between defendant's secretary, Ernest R. Bauer, and a Mr. Stovicek, who was in New York for the Czechoslovak government at the World Trade Fair. A few days after meeting Bauer at the fair, Stovicek telephoned and inquired whether defendant would be interested in exporting poultry to Switzerland. Bauer then met with Stovicek, who showed him a cable from plaintiff dated April 26, 1957, announcing that they 'are buyer' of 25,000 lbs. of chicken

2 ½–3 lbs. weight, Cryovac packed, grade A Government inspected, at a price up to 33¢ per pound, for shipment on May 10, to be confirmed by the following morning, and were interested in further offerings. After testing the market for price, Bauer accepted, and Stovicek sent a confirmation that evening. Plaintiff stresses that, although these and subsequent cables between plaintiff and defendant, which laid the basis for the additional quantities under the first and for all of the second contract, were predominantly in German, they used the English word 'chicken'; it claims this was done because it understood 'chicken' meant young chicken whereas the German word, 'Huhn,' included both 'Brathuhn' (broilers) and 'Suppenhuhn' (stewing chicken), and that defendant, whose officers were thoroughly conversant with German, should have realized this. Whatever force this argument might otherwise have is largely drained away by Bauer's testimony that he asked Stovicek what kind of chickens were wanted, received the answer 'any kind of chickens,' and then, in German, asked whether the cable meant 'Huhn' and received an affirmative response. . . .

Plaintiff's next contention is that there was a definite trade usage that 'chicken' meant 'young chicken.' Defendant showed that it was only beginning in the poultry trade in 1957, thereby bringing itself within the principle that 'when one of the parties is not a member of the trade or other circle, his acceptance of the standard must be made to appear' by proving either that he had actual knowledge of the usage or that the usage is 'so generally known in the community that his actual individual knowledge of it may be inferred.' 9 Wigmore, Evidence (3d ed. § 1940) 2464. Here there was no proof of actual knowledge of the alleged usage; indeed, it is quite plain that defendant's belief was to the contrary. In order to meet the alternative requirement, the law of New York demands a showing that 'the usage is of so long continuance, so well established, so notorious, so universal and so reasonable in itself, as that the presumption is violent that the parties contracted with reference to it, and made it a part of their agreement.' *Walls v. Bailey*, 1872, 49 N.Y. 464, 472–473.

Plaintiff endeavored to establish such a usage by the testimony of three witnesses and certain other evidence. Strasser, resident buyer in New York for a large chain of Swiss cooperatives, testified that 'on chicken I would definitely understand a broiler.' However, the force of this testimony was considerably weakened by the fact that in his own transactions the witness, a careful businessman, protected himself by using 'broiler' when that was what he wanted and 'fowl' when he wished older birds. Indeed, there are some indications, dating back to a remark of Lord Mansfield, *Edie v. East India Co.*, 2 Burr. 1216, 1222 (1761), that no credit should be given 'witnesses to usage, who could not adduce instances in verification.' 7 Wigmore, Evidence (3d ed. 1940), § 1954; see *McDonald v. Acker, Merrall & Condit Co.*, 2d Dept.1920, 192 App.Div. 123, 126, 182 N.Y.S. 607. While Wigmore thinks this goes too far, a witness' consistent failure to rely on the alleged usage deprives his opinion testimony of much of its effect. Niesielowski, an officer of one of the companies that had furnished the stewing chicken to defendant, testified that 'chicken' meant 'the female species of the poultry industry. That could be a broiler, a fryer or a roaster', but not a stewing chicken; however, he also testified that upon receiving defendant's inquiry for 'chickens', he asked whether the desire was for 'fowl or frying chickens' and, in fact, supplied fowl, although taking the precaution of asking defendant, a day or two after plaintiff's acceptance of the contracts in suit, to change its confirmation of its order from 'chickens,' as defendant had originally prepared it, to 'stewing chickens.' Dates, an employee of Urner-Barry Company, which publishes a daily market report on the poultry trade, gave it as his view that the trade meaning of 'chicken' was 'broilers and fryers.' In addition to this opinion testimony, plaintiff relied on the fact that the Urner-Barry service, the Journal of Commerce, and Weinberg Bros. & Co. of Chicago, a large supplier of poultry, published quotations in a manner which, in one way or another, distinguish between 'chicken,' comprising broilers, fryers and certain other categories, and 'fowl,' which, Bauer acknowledged, included stewing chickens. This material would be impressive if there were nothing to the contrary. However, there was, as will now be seen.

Defendant's witness Weininger, who operates a chicken eviscerating plant in New Jersey, testified 'Chicken is everything except a goose, a duck, and a turkey. Everything is a chicken, but then you have to say, you have to specify which category you want or that you are talking about.' Its witness Fox said that in the trade 'chicken' would encompass all the various classifications. Sadina, who conducts a food inspection service, testified that he would consider any bird coming within the classes of 'chicken' in the Department of Agriculture's regulations to be a chicken. The specifications approved by the General Services Administration include fowl as well as broilers and fryers under the classification 'chickens.' Statistics of the Institute of American Poultry Industries use the phrases 'Young chickens' and 'Mature chickens,' under the general heading 'Total chickens.' and the Department of Agriculture's daily and weekly price reports avoid use of the word 'chicken' without specification.

Defendant advances several other points which it claims affirmatively support its construction. Primary among these is the regulation of the Department of Agriculture, 7 C.F.R. § 70.300–70.370, entitled, 'Grading and Inspection of Poultry and Edible Products Thereof.' and in particular 70.301 which recited:

"*Chickens*. The following are the various classes of chickens:

(a)   Broiler or fryer . . .

(b)   Roaster . . .

(c)   Capon . . .

(d) Stag . . .

(e) Hen or stewing chicken or fowl . . .

(f) Cock or old rooster . . .

Defendant argues, as previously noted, that the contract incorporated these regulations by reference. Plaintiff answers that the contract provision related simply to grade and Government inspection and did not incorporate the Government definition of 'chicken,' and also that the definition in the Regulations is ignored in the trade. However, the latter contention was contradicted by Weininger and Sadina; and there is force in defendant's argument that the contract made the regulations a dictionary, particularly since the reference to Government grading was already in plaintiff's initial cable to Stovicek.

Defendant makes a further argument based on the impossibility of its obtaining broilers and fryers at the 33¢ price offered by plaintiff for the 2 ½–3 lbs. birds. There is no substantial dispute that, in late April, 1957, the price for 2 ½–3 lbs. broilers was between 35 and 37¢ per pound, and that when defendant entered into the contracts, it was well aware of this and intended to fill them by supplying fowl in these weights. It claims that plaintiff must likewise have known the market since plaintiff had reserved shipping space on April 23, three days before plaintiff's cable to Stovicek, or, at least, that Stovicek was chargeable with such knowledge. It is scarcely an answer to say, as plaintiff does in its brief, that the 33¢ price offered by the 2 ½–3 lbs. 'chickens' was closer to the prevailing 35¢ price for broilers than to the 30¢ at which defendant procured fowl. Plaintiff must have expected defendant to make some profit—certainly it could not have expected defendant deliberately to incur a loss.

Finally, defendant relies on conduct by the plaintiff after the first shipment had been received. On May 28 plaintiff sent two cables complaining that the larger birds in the first shipment constituted 'fowl.' Defendant answered with a cable refusing to recognize plaintiff's objection and announcing 'We have today ready for shipment 50,000 lbs. chicken 2 ½–3 lbs. 25,000 lbs. broilers 1 ½–2 lbs.,' these being the goods procured for shipment under the second contract, and asked immediate answer 'whether we are to ship this merchandise to you and whether you will accept the merchandise.' After several other cable exchanges, plaintiff replied on May 29 'Confirm again that merchandise is to be shipped since resold by us if not enough pursuant to contract chickens are shipped the missing quantity is to be shipped within ten days stop we resold to our customers pursuant to your contract chickens grade A you have to deliver us said merchandise we again state that we shall make you fully responsible for all resulting costs.' Defendant argues that if plaintiff was sincere in thinking it was entitled to young chickens, plaintiff would not have allowed the shipment under the second contract to go forward, since the distinction between broilers and chickens drawn in defendant's cablegram must have made it clear that the larger birds would not be broilers. However, plaintiff answers that the cables show plaintiff was insisting on delivery of young chickens and that defendant shipped old ones at its peril. Defendant's point would be highly relevant on another disputed issue—whether if liability were established, the measure of damages should be the difference in market value of broilers and stewing chicken in New York or the larger difference in Europe, but I cannot give it weight on the issue of interpretation. Defendant points out also that plaintiff proceeded to deliver some of the larger birds in Europe, describing them as 'poulets'; defendant argues that it was only when plaintiff's customers complained about this that plaintiff developed the idea that 'chicken' meant 'young chicken.' There is little force in this in view of plaintiff's immediate and consistent protests.

When all the evidence is reviewed, it is clear that defendant believed it could comply with the contracts by delivering stewing chicken in the 2 ½–3 lbs. size. Defendant's subjective intent would not be significant if this did not coincide with an objective meaning of 'chicken.' Here it did coincide with one of the dictionary meanings, with the definition in the Department of Agriculture Regulations to which the contract made at least oblique reference, with at least some usage in the trade, with the realities of the market, and with what plaintiff's spokesman had said. Plaintiff asserts it to be equally plain that plaintiff's own subjective intent was to obtain broilers and fryers; the only evidence against this is the material as to market prices and this may not have been sufficiently brought home. In any event it is unnecessary to determine that issue. For plaintiff has the burden of showing that 'chicken' was used in the narrower rather than in the broader sense, and this it has not sustained.

This opinion constitutes the Court's findings of fact and conclusions of law. Judgment shall be entered dismissing the complaint with costs.

NOTES

1.   Note that Judge Friendly treats this as a case where there was a binding contract for the sale of "chickens." Thus the issue is whether the buyer can prevail in its argument that the agreement, properly interpreted, meant broilers. If so, then the buyer is entitled to damages measured by the difference in value between the broilers that the buyer was entitled to and the stewing chicken that were actually delivered. In the case itself, Judge Friendly concludes that the buyer has not succeeded in proving that the agreement meant broilers, so the buyer loses.

Judge Friendly assumes that there was a binding agreement for the sale of birds, but concludes that buyer can't prove that the agreement meant broilers rather than fowl. The case might have been approached in a different way. One might have thought of it as akin to *Raffles v. Wichelhaus*, noted at the end of the previous section. That is, one might have said that the seller reasonably believed that the buyer was offering to buy fowl, while the buyer reasonably believed that the seller was offering to sell broilers. Indeed, a year after the *Frigaliment* case, Judge Friendly suggested that it might have made more sense to treat the case that way, though the result would have been about the same. See *Dadourian Export Corp. v. United States*, 291 F.2d 178, 187 n. 4 (2d Cir. 1961) (Friendly, J., dissenting).

For our purposes, the important thing about the *Frigaliment* case is to consider quite carefully how Judge Friendly treated the various arguments about how the ambiguous word "chicken" in the agreement should be interpreted.

2. Though the *Frigaliment* case dealt with a sale of goods, governed by Article 2 of the U.C.C., the case arose before the enactment of the U.C.C. The approach to interpretation taken by Judge Friendly is, however, fully consistent with the relevant Article 2 rules, which categorize the following:

- Course of performance
- Course of dealing
- Usage of trade

Look carefully at what the U.C.C. says about how to interpret an agreement if there is any inconsistency among these three: U.C.C. § 1–303. This general section combines previous § 1–205 and § 2–208.

U.C.C. § 1–303. Course of Performance, Course of Dealing, and Usage of Trade

PROBLEM

In 2006, Panera Bread sued its landlord in a shopping center, contending that the landlord had breached a provision in the lease that Panera would be the only "sandwich" shop in the mall, by leasing to a Mexican restaurant (Qdoba) that sold burritos.

Is a burrito a sandwich? Both parties submitted evidence from chefs and other culinary experts. The New Webster Third International Dictionary states that a "sandwich" is "two thin pieces of bread, usually buttered, with a thin layer (as of meat, cheese, or savory mixture) spread between them."

Consider what you would advise Panera, had you been their lawyer. Does one apply the "ordinary meaning" or is the term sandwich ambiguous? What might "course of performance" add?

See *White City Shopping Ctr., LP, v. PR Restaurants*, LLC, 2006 WL 3292641 (Mass. Super. Ct.); and further Marjorie Florestal, *Is A Burrito A Sandwich? Exploring Race, Class, and Culture in Contracts*, 14 Mich. J. Race & L. 1 (2008).

C. "BATTLE OF THE FORMS"

1. INTRODUCTION

In this section, we will engage the text of U.C.C. § 2–207 in depth. The section is reproduced here:

U.C.C. § 2–207

Additional Terms in Acceptance or Confirmation.

(1) A definite and seasonable expression of acceptance or a written confirmation which is sent within a reasonable time operates as an acceptance even though it states terms additional to or different from those offered or agreed upon, unless acceptance is expressly made conditional on assent to the additional or different terms.

(2) The additional terms are to be construed as proposals for addition to the contract. Between merchants such terms become part of the contract unless:

(a) the offer expressly limits acceptance to the terms of the offer;

(b) they materially alter it; or

(c) notification of objection to them has already been given or is given within a reasonable time after notice of them is received.

(3) Conduct by both parties which recognizes the existence of a contract is sufficient to establish a contract for sale although the writings of the parties do not otherwise establish a contract. In such case the terms of the particular contract consist of those terms on which the writings of the parties agree, together with any supplementary terms incorporated under any other provisions of this Act.

In particular, in this section, we look at the effort made by the drafters of Article 2 of the U.C.C. to deal with a common problem: Seller and Buyer are planning on entering into a sales contract. The business people may negotiate over a few significant terms, such as the price, but the dollar amount of the transaction does not warrant the expenditure of money on lawyers to negotiate a full-blown sales contract. Each side has a standard form that its lawyers have prepared for such situations. Not surprisingly, the forms differ. The buyer's form, commonly called a "purchase order" has terms generally favorable to the buyer. The seller's form, commonly called an "invoice" has terms generally favorable to the seller. Is a contract formed by the exchange of the two forms if each form has its own provisions? If so, what are the terms of the contract? That's the set of problems referred to by the phrase "battle of the forms."

It is very important to consider very carefully two completely different settings in which this sort of "battle of the forms" problem might arise.

First, one side might want to get out of the deal before performance. The party who wants out of the deal looks carefully at the two forms, sees that they don't match, and concludes that no contract was formed. Accordingly, the party who wants out considers itself free to walk away from the deal. The problem in this setting is one of *contract formation*: Does the discrepancy between the two forms force us to conclude that no contract was formed?

Second, the parties might go ahead and do the deal without noticing the discrepancy between the forms. The seller ships the goods and the buyer pays. Then, some dispute arises. At that point, for the first time, the parties (or their lawyers) actually read the forms. They find that they differ. Not surprisingly, the buyer's form favors the buyer, while the seller's form favors the seller. It's pretty obvious that there was a contract for sale of goods. How else do we account for the facts that the seller shipped the goods to the buyer and the buyer paid the seller for them? The problem in this setting is one of *contract interpretation*: How do we decide what the terms of the contract are if the parties' forms said different things?

2. CONTRACT FORMATION

Cast your minds back to our discussion of the rules of contract formation, particular offer and acceptance, in Chapter 3 (e.g., *Ardente v. Horan* 266 A.2d 162). The contract formation problem that arises in the "Battle of the Forms" scenario is illustrated by the old case of *Poel v. Brunswick-Balke-Collender Co.*, 216 N.Y. 310 (N.Y. 1915). Poel, the prospective seller, and Brunswick company, the prospective buyer, had preliminary discussions about the sale of twelve tons of rubber for delivery the following year. On April 4, 1910, Poel (Seller) sent a form to Brunswick (Buyer) specifying that it would sell the rubber at a stated price and with stated delivery terms beginning in January 1911. In response, on April 6, 1910, Brunswick (Buyer) sent along a purchase order form, with the same price and delivery terms, but some additional language. Nothing more happened until the time for delivery came, in January 1911. At that point, Brunswick (Buyer) wrote to Poel (Seller) saying that they were not willing to go through with the deal. Apparently, a person of the suspicious name "Rogers" had acted on behalf of the Brunswick company, and the company contended that Rogers was not actually authorized to make contracts on its behalf.

Poel (Seller) sued Brunswick (Buyer) for failure to take the goods and pay the specified price. The court said that the outcome depended on whether there was a contract, and that, in turn, depended on an offer and acceptance analysis. The court treated the form sent by Poel (Seller) on April 4 as the offer. So, the outcome turned on whether the purchase order form sent along by Brunswick (Buyer) on April 6 counted as an acceptance. Though most of the terms in the April 6 form were the same as the terms in the April 4 form, the two forms were not exactly the same. In fact, there was no fight between the parties about the matters on which their two forms differed, but that did not matter to the outcome. Rather the court said that the difference prevented the buyer's April 6 form from operating as an acceptance of the seller's April 4 form:

> The letter of the defendant of April 6th did not accept this offer. If the intention of the defendant had been to accept the offer made in the plaintiffs' letter of April 4th, it would have been a simple matter for the defendant to have indorsed its acceptance upon the proposed contract which the plaintiffs' letter of April 4th had inclosed. Instead of adopting this simple and obvious method of indicating an intent to accept the contract proposed by the plaintiffs, the defendant submitted its own proposal and specified the terms and conditions upon which is should be accepted. The defendant's letter of April 6th was not an acceptance of this offer made by the plaintiffs in their letter of April 4th. It was a counter offer or proposition for a contract.

110 N.E. at 621. The approach taken in the *Poel* case has come to be known as the "mirror image rule," that is, a communication sent in response to an offer can constitute an acceptance only if it is a "mirror image" of the offer.

The drafters of Article 2 of the U.C.C. thought that the outcome in *Poel* was silly. Neither the buyer nor the seller had ever noticed that their forms were different. In the case itself, buyer had a genuine argument— that Rogers did not have authority to act on its behalf—but that argument had nothing to do with the fact that there were minor differences in the two forms. The Article 2 drafters would have said that the differences between the forms should not preclude the formation of a contract, so that the outcome of the case would turn on the real issue in dispute, whether Rogers was authorized to bind Brunswick.

Moreover, the fact that the parties used slightly different forms, and did not notice the discrepancies, is hardly surprising. In the excerpt from the *Poel* opinion quoted above, the court says that the "simple and obvious" way for the buyer to indicate assent to the seller's proposal would have been to "indorse . . . its acceptance upon the proposed contract which the plaintiffs' letter of April 4th had inclosed." Maybe if you are a lawyer that seems like the "simple and obvious" way to do it. But, if you are a business person, that might seem like the cumbersome way of doing it.

When a company of any size buys or sells goods, the relevant information needs to be communicated not only to the other side of the transaction, but to various internal departments. Consider the situation of the buyer in *Poel*. The important facts about the proposed deal need to be communicated to various internal departments such as (1) the purchasing department that keeps track of purchases, (2) the receiving department where the goods are to be sent, (3) the manufacturing department that will be using the goods, and (4) the accounting department that will be processing the payment. The "simple and obvious" way of getting the same information to each of those departments is to have a single form that gets filled out with duplicate carbon copies, and send various copies to the various different departments. Each department will know where the information that matters to it is located on the form and will know how to process it. Having the buyer "indorse . . . its acceptance upon the [seller's form]" would be likely to strike anyone inside the buyer's organization as an odd and cumbersome way of processing the transaction. Of course, the fact of assent needs to be communicated to the other side of the deal, but the fact that a sale has been made also needs to be communicated to various internal departments. It's much simpler to have the same form go to all the different internal departments.

So, the drafters of Article 2 of the U.C.C. wanted to reject the "mirror image" approach to contract formation represented by cases such as *Poel*. They did so by adopting Subsection (1) of Section 2–207, which reads as follows:

> A definite and seasonable expression of acceptance or a written confirmation which is sent within a reasonable time operates as an acceptance even though it states terms additional to or different from those offered or agreed upon, unless acceptance is expressly made conditional on assent to the additional or different terms.

The last clause ("unless acceptance is expressly made conditional on assent to the additional or different terms") proved to have other problems that we will examine shortly. Stripped of that, and making a few other simplifications, the rule of Subsection 1 would be as follows:

> A definite and seasonable expression of . . . [assent] . . . operates as an acceptance even though it states terms additional to or different from those offered or agreed upon . . . .

That's all that is needed to dispose of the offer and acceptance problem in the *Poel* case. The response sent by Brunswick (Buyer) on April 6, 1910 would amount to an expression of assent. Accordingly, it would operate as an acceptance, even though it stated other terms. That would permit us to conclude that a contract could be formed by the exchange of forms. Accordingly, on the actual facts, the case would turn on the point that the parties really were fighting about—whether Rogers had authority to bind Brunswick.

3. CONTRACT INTERPRETATION

A different and more difficult problem is presented in cases where parties exchange forms that do not mirror each other, but the parties do go ahead with the transaction. Suppose that thereafter a dispute arises. And, suppose that the subject matter of the dispute is one of those points on which the two parties' forms differed. The facts give us no choice but to say that the parties did form a contract. The hard issue is deciding what the terms of the contract are.

On the issue of contract interpretation, just like on the issue of contract formation, our starting point is an approach suggested by an old case, *Hobbs v. Massasoit Whip Co.,* 33 N.E. 495 (Mass. 1893), which—*mirabile dictu*—seems to have involved buggy whips! Hobbs (Seller) had shipped eel skins to Massasoit Whip (Buyer) on various occasions in the past. Buyer had always paid for them. So, apparently Hobbs thought there was nothing unusual about sending along another shipment, although the opinion does not indicate anything about what sort of discussions, if indeed there were any, the parties had before the shipment. Massasoit Whip kept the eels skins for several months. When Massasoit Whip refused to pay, Hobbs sued.

In one sense *Hobbs v. Massasoit Whip Co.* illustrates nothing more than a simple offer and acceptance issue, that is, that the buyer's act of retaining the goods can count as acceptance of the offer made by the seller in shipping the goods, at least where the parties have had such dealings in the past. We saw that point earlier in the course in connection with "acceptance by silence," or, as I suggested it was more properly termed, "acceptance by conduct."

Suppose, though, that the fight in *Hobbs* had not been about whether the buyer was obligated to a sales contract, but about the terms of the contract. Suppose, for example, that the seller thought that one of the terms of the contract was that disputes would be settled by arbitration, but the buyer thought that the contract meant that disputes would be settled by the ordinary process of litigation. Suppose that lots of forms went back and forth between seller and buyer in the process that preceded shipment, perhaps because it took several rounds for the parties to reach agreement on other matters, such as the price. Suppose further that each form was different from the immediately prior form. Applying the "mirror image" rule of the *Poel* case, a court in the nineteenth or early-twentieth century would presumably say that none of the *forms* could count as an acceptance of the immediately prior form. But, if the goods were sent by the seller and received by the buyer, and payment was made by the buyer and received by the seller, we would have to conclude that there was a contract for sale. So, what were the *terms* of the contract? Our old offer and acceptance concepts tell us that each form operated as a counter-offer rather than an acceptance. But, a contract was formed. How was the contract formed? It must have been that the offer made in the last *form* was accepted by the *act* of proceeding with the transaction. Accordingly, the *terms* of the contract would be whatever terms were set out in the last form that passed between the parties. That approach came to be known as the "last shot approach."

The drafters of Article 2 of the U.C.C. thought that the "last shot" approach to contract interpretation was just as silly as the "mirror image" approach to contract formation. So, in subsections (2) and (3) of Section 2–207 they attempted to set out a different approach to contract interpretation. The problem, however, has proven to be a good deal harder than the drafters probably first thought. There is an enormous body of case law and commentary discussing the twists and turns of Section 2–207. We will examine some aspects of the much-disputed problem in connection with the *Gardner Zemke* case below.

4. WARRANTIES UNDER U.C.C. ARTICLE 2

U.C.C. §§ 2–314, 2–315, 2–316, and 2–313

Many of the cases involving "battle of the forms" issue deal with warranties in the sale of goods. To understand the battle of the forms issue, we need to have a general understanding of the U.C.C. Article 2 provisions on warranties.

Suppose a builder orders an air-conditioning unit from a supplier for use in a construction project. By selling something that is called an "air conditioner" it's a fair inference that the seller is saying that it is a machine that will cool the air in the building. If it doesn't work at all, we would hardly expect the seller to be able to avoid any liability by saying "I never said that thing would cool air; besides, it makes a terrific paper weight." Merely from the fact that the thing sold is described as an "air conditioner," one can reasonably infer that the seller was promising ("warranting") that it would, more or less, work in the fashion that people reasonably assume that air conditioners work. That simple point is the heart of the Article 2 provision on the *implied warranty of merchantability*. Read U.C.C. § 2–314.

Suppose the builder goes to the supplier and asks for "an air conditioner that will cool a 50,000 square foot building to at least 65 degrees," and the supplier says "Oh, an Acme Model 2300 will do that just fine." Here the buyer is relying on the skill of the seller to select a unit that will meet the buyer's needs, so it is sensible to say that the seller warrants that the goods are suitable for the buyer's needs. That point is covered by the Article 2 *implied warranty of fitness for a particular purpose*. Read U.C.C. § 2–315.

Sellers of goods tend to find the Article 2 implied warranties somewhat worrisome. It's one thing to say that a thing sold as an air conditioner ought to cool air rather than just being a nice paperweight. It's another thing to say what does and does not count as being a "merchantable" air conditioner or being "suitable" for the buyer's expressed needs. Accordingly, sellers commonly do two things. First, they make "express warranties," that is, they say that the goods will be free from defects for a certain stated period of time, and say what they will do if the goods are defective. Read U.C.C. § 2–313. Second, they say that other than the stated express warranties, the seller disclaims any implied warranty of merchantability or fitness. Read U.C.C. § 2–316.

Many of the battle of the forms cases, such as the *Gardner Zemke* case below, involve the interpretation of forms in cases where the seller's form has a disclaimer of implied warranties.

Having mentioned warranties, it's worth noting some of the complex issues on the subject that we will not have time to examine in this course.

First, there is the matter of who makes the warranty. Article 2 speaks of a *seller* making a warranty to a buyer. That makes perfect sense in some situations, for example, where the manufacturer of an air conditioning unit sells it to a builder. But, in many cases the buyer of the goods has no direct dealings with the manufacturer of the goods. Instead, the buyer deals only with a retailer. Suppose you walk into Sears and buy a GE air conditioner. The air conditioner proves to be defective. Do you have rights against Sears, GE, or both?

Second, there is the matter of what liability a person making a warranty incurs. Suppose the GE air conditioner that you bought from Sears has a wiring defect, and that defect causes a fire. Assume that you do have an action for breach of warranty (against Sears and/or GE). Can you recover not only the money you spent on the air conditioner, but also damages for destruction of your house in the fire? Suppose that someone is injured or killed in the fire. Does the warranty liability extend to personal injury?

These matters are further complicated by the fact that—particularly in the personal injury cases—one might think of the injured party's potential cause of action as being based either in contract on a breach of warranty theory or in tort on a negligence or strict liability theory.

These complex issues have come to be regarded as the subject matter of an entire body of law, known as the law of products liability. Also, some of these issues are governed by a federal statute, the Magnuson-Moss Warranty Act, and regulations promulgated thereunder by the Federal Trade Commission.

And as a final note, the implied or default warranties, U.C.C. §§ 2–314 and 2–315, are very important examples of a gap-filling (or "default") rule that parties can contract around by prior agreement. Such default rules may not always represent "what the parties would have contracted for", but may be considered instead as opportunities for lawmakers to regulate behavior. When sellers contract around them, for example, they are forced to reveal information to consumers about the extent of their coverage. For exploration, see Ian Ayres & Robert Gertner, *Filling Gaps in Incomplete Contracts: An Economic Theory of Default Rules*, 99 Yale L. J. 87 (1989).

5. BATTLE OF THE FORMS AND CONTRACT INTERPRETATION

Gardner Zemke Co. v. Dunham Bush, Inc.

Supreme Court of New Mexico, 1993.
115 N.M. 260, 850 P.2d 319.

■ FRANCHINI, JUSTICE.

This case involves a contract for the sale of goods and accordingly the governing law is the Uniform Commercial Code—Sales, as adopted in New Mexico. . . . The case presents us with our first opportunity to consider a classic "battle of the forms" scenario arising under Section 2–207. Appellant Gardner Zemke challenges the trial court's judgment that a Customer's Acknowledgment (Acknowledgment) sent by appellee manufacturer Dunham Bush, in response to a Gardner Zemke Purchase Order (Order), operated as a counteroffer, thereby providing controlling warranty terms under the contract formed by the parties. We find merit in appellants' argument and remand for the trial court's reconsideration.

I.

Acting as the general contractor on a Department of Energy (DOE) project, Gardner Zemke issued its Order to Dunham Bush for air-conditioning equipment, known as chillers, to be used in connection with the project. The Order contained a one-year manufacturer's warranty provision and the requirement that the chillers comply with specifications attached to the Order. Dunham Bush responded with its preprinted Acknowledgment containing extensive warranty disclaimers, a statement that the terms of the Acknowledgment controlled the parties' agreement, and a provision deeming silence to be acquiescence to the terms of the Acknowledgment.

The parties did not address the discrepancies in the forms exchanged and proceeded with the transaction. Dunham Bush delivered the chillers, and Gardner Zemke paid for them. Gardner Zemke alleges that the chillers provided did not comply with their specifications and that they incurred additional costs to install the nonconforming goods. Approximately five or six months after start up of the chillers, a DOE representative notified Gardner Zemke of problems with two of the chillers. In a series of letters, Gardner Zemke requested on-site warranty repairs. Through its manufacturer's representative, Dunham Bush offered to send its mechanic to the job site to inspect the chillers and absorb the cost of the service call only if problems discovered were within any component parts it provided. Further, Dunham Bush required that prior to the service call a purchase order be issued from the DOE, to be executed by Dunham Bush for payment for their services in the event their mechanic discovered problems not caused by manufacturing defects. Gardner Zemke rejected the proposal on the basis that the DOE had a warranty still in effect for the goods and would not issue a separate purchase order for warranty repairs.

Ultimately, the DOE hired an independent contractor to repair the two chillers. The DOE paid $24,245.00 for the repairs and withheld $20,000.00 from its contract with Gardner Zemke. This breach of contract action then ensued, with Gardner Zemke alleging failure by Dunham Bush to provide equipment in accordance with the project plans and specifications and failure to provide warranty service.

II.

On cross-motions for summary judgment, the trial court granted partial summary judgment in favor of Dunham Bush, ruling that its Acknowledgment was a counteroffer to the Gardner Zemke Order and that the Acknowledgment's warranty limitations and disclaimers were controlling. Gardner Zemke filed an application for interlocutory appeal from the partial summary judgment in this Court, which was denied. A bench trial was held in December 1991, and the trial court again ruled the Acknowledgment was a counteroffer which Gardner Zemke accepted by silence and that under the warranty provisions of the Acknowledgment, Gardner Zemke was not entitled to damages.

On appeal, Gardner Zemke raises two issues: (1) the trial court erred as a matter of law in ruling that the Acknowledgment was a counteroffer; and (2) Gardner Zemke proved breach of contract and contract warranty, breach of code warranties, and damages.

III.

Karl N. Llewellyn, the principal draftsman of Article 2, described it as "[t]he heart of the Code." Karl N. Llewellyn, *Why We Need the Uniform Commercial Code,* 10 U.Fla.L.Rev. 367, 378 (1957). Section 2–207 is characterized by commentators as a "crucial section of Article 2" and an "iconoclastic Code section." *Bender's Uniform Commercial Code Service* (Vol. 3, Richard W. Duesenberg & Lawrence P. King, Sales & Bulk Transfers Under The Uniform Commercial Code) § 3.01 at 3–2 (1992). Recognizing its innovative purpose and complex structure Duesenberg and King further observe Section 2–207 "is one of the most important, subtle, and difficult in the entire Code, and well it may be said that the product as it finally reads is not altogether satisfactory." *Id.* § 3.02 at 3–13.

Relying on Section 2–207(1), Gardner Zemke argues that the trial court erred in concluding that the Dunham Bush Acknowledgment was a counteroffer rather than an acceptance. Gardner Zemke asserts that even though the Acknowledgment contained terms different from or in addition to the terms of their Order, it did not make acceptance expressly conditional on assent to the different or additional terms and therefore should operate as an acceptance rather than a counteroffer.

At common law, the "mirror image" rule applied to the formation of contracts, and the terms of the acceptance had to exactly imitate or "mirror" the terms of the offer. *Idaho Power Co. v. Westinghouse Elec. Corp.,* 596 F.2d 924, 926 (9th Cir.1979). If the accepting terms were different from or additional to those in the offer, the result was a counteroffer, not an acceptance. *Id.* * * *. Thus, from a common law perspective, the trial court's conclusion that the Dunham Bush Acknowledgment was a counteroffer was correct.

However, the drafters of the Code "intended to change the common law in an attempt to conform contract law to modern day business transactions." *Leonard Pevar Co. v. Evans Prods. Co.,* 524 F.Supp. 546, 551 (D.Del.1981). As Professors White and Summers explain:

> The rigidity of the common law rule ignored the modern realities of commerce. Where preprinted forms are used to structure deals, they rarely mirror each other, yet the parties usually assume they have a binding contract and act accordingly. Section 2–207 rejects the common law mirror image rule and converts many common law counteroffers into acceptances under 2–207(1).

James J. White & Robert S. Summers, HANDBOOK OF THE LAW UNDER THE UNIFORM COMMERCIAL CODE § 1–3 at 29–30 (3d ed. 1988) (footnotes omitted).

On its face, Section 2–207(1) provides that a document responding to an offer and purporting to be an acceptance will be an acceptance, despite the presence of additional and different terms. Where merchants exchange preprinted forms and the essential contract terms agree, a contract is formed under Section 2–207(1). Duesenberg & King, § 3.04 at 3–47 to –49. A responding document will fall outside of the provisions of Section 2–207(1) and convey a counteroffer, only when its terms differ radically from the offer, or when "acceptance is expressly made conditional on assent to the additional or different terms"—whether a contract is formed under Section 2–207(1) here turns on the meaning given this phrase.

Dunham Bush argues that the language in its Acknowledgment makes acceptance expressly conditional on assent to the additional or different terms set forth in the Acknowledgment. The face of the Acknowledgment states:

> IT IS UNDERSTOOD THAT OUR ACCEPTANCE OF THIS ORDER IS SUBJECT TO THE TERMS AND CONDITIONS ENUMERATED ON THE REVERSE SIDE HEREOF, IT BEING STRICTLY UNDERSTOOD THAT THESE TERMS AND CONDITIONS BECOME A PART OF THIS ORDER AND THE ACKNOWLEDGMENT THEREOF.

The following was among the terms and conditions on the reverse side of the Acknowledgment.

> Failure of the Buyer to object in writing within five (5) days of receipt thereof to Terms of Sale contained in the Seller's

acceptance and/or acknowledgment, or other communications, shall be deemed an acceptance of such Terms of Sale by Buyer.

In support of its contention that the above language falls within the "expressly conditional" provision of Section 2–207, Dunham Bush urges that we adopt the view taken by the First Circuit in *Roto-Lith, Ltd. V. F.P. Bartlett & Co.,* 297 F.2d 497 (1st Cir.1962). There, Roto-Lith sent an order for goods to Bartlett, which responded with an acknowledgment containing warranty disclaimers, a statement that the acknowledgment reflected the terms of the sale, and a provision that if the terms were unacceptable Roto-Lith should notify Bartlett at once. *Id.* at 498–99. Roto-Lith did not protest the terms of the acknowledgment and accepted and paid for the goods. The court held the Bartlett acknowledgment was a counteroffer that became binding on Roto-Lith with its acceptance of the goods, reasoning that "a response which states a condition materially altering the obligation solely to the disadvantage of the offeror" falls within the "expressly conditional" language of 2–207(1). *Id.* at 500.

Dunham Bush suggests that this Court has demonstrated alliance with the principles of *Roto-Lith* in *Fratello v. Socorro Electric Cooperative, Inc.,* 107 N.M. 378, 758 P.2d 792 (1988). *Fratello* involved the terms of a settlement agreement in which one party sent the other party a proposed stipulated order containing an additional term. In the context of the common law, we cited *Roto-Lith* in support of the proposition that the additional term made the proposed stipulation a counteroffer. *Fratello,* 107 N.M. at 381, 758 P.2d at 795.

We have never adopted *Roto-Lith* in the context of the Code and decline to do so now. While ostensibly interpreting Section 2–207(1), the First Circuit's analysis imposes the common law doctrine of offer and acceptance on language designed to avoid the common law result. *Roto-Lith* has been almost uniformly criticized by the courts and commentators as an aberration in Article 2 jurisprudence. *Leonard Pevar Co.,* 524 F.Supp. at 551 (and cases cited therein); Duesenberg & King, § 3.05[1] at 3–61 to –62; White & Summers, § 1–3 at 36–37.

Mindful of the purpose of Section 2–207 and the spirit of Article 2, we find the better approach suggested in *Dorton v. Collins & Aikman Corp.,* 453 F.2d 1161 (6th Cir.1972). In *Dorton,* the Sixth Circuit considered terms in acknowledgment forms sent by Collins & Aikman similar to the terms in the Dunham Bush Acknowledgment. The Collins & Aikman acknowledgments provided that acceptance of orders was subject to the terms and conditions of their form, together with at least seven methods in which a buyer might acquiesce to their terms, including receipt and retention of their form for ten days without objection. *Id.* at 1167–68.

Concentrating its analysis on the concept of the offeror's "assent," the Court reasoned that it was not enough to make acceptance expressly conditional on additional or different terms; instead, the expressly conditional nature of the acceptance must be predicated on the offeror's "assent" to those terms. *Id.* at 1168. The Court concluded that the "expressly conditional" provision of Section 2–207(1) "was intended to apply only to an acceptance which clearly reveals that the offeree is unwilling to proceed with the transaction unless he is assured of the offeror's assent to the additional or different terms therein." *Id.* This approach has been widely accepted. * * *.

We agree with the court in *Dorton* that the inquiry focuses on whether the offeree clearly and unequivocally communicated to the offeror that its willingness to enter into a bargain was conditioned on the offeror's "assent" to additional or different terms. An exchange of forms containing identical dickered terms, such as the identity, price, and quantity of goods, and conflicting undickered boilerplate provisions, such as warranty terms and a provision making the bargain subject to the terms and conditions of the offeree's document, however worded, will not propel the transaction into the "expressly conditional" language of Section 2–207(1) and confer the status of counteroffer on the responsive document.

While *Dorton* articulates a laudable rule, it fails to provide a means for the determination of when a responsive document becomes a counteroffer. We adopt the rule in *Dorton* and add that whether an acceptance is made expressly conditional on assent to different or additional terms is dependent on the commercial context of the transaction. Official Comment 2 to Section 2–207 suggests that "[u]nder this article a proposed deal which in commercial understanding has in fact been closed is recognized as a contract."² While the comment applies broadly and envisions recognition of contracts formed under a variety of circumstances, it guides us to application of the concept of "commercial understanding" to the question of formation. *See* 2 William D. Hawkland, *Uniform Commercial Code Series* § 2–207:02 at 160 (1992) ("The basic question is whether, in commercial understanding, the proposed deal has been closed.").

Discerning whether "commercial understanding" dictates the existence of a contract requires consideration of the objective manifestations of the parties' understanding of the bargain. It requires consideration of the parties' activities and interaction during the making of the bargain; and when available, relevant evidence of course of performance, Section 2–208; and course of dealing and usage of the trade, Section 1–205. The question guiding the inquiry should be whether the

---

² While we recognize that the Official Comments do not carry the force of law, they are a part of the official text of the Code adopted by our legislature and we do look to them for guidance. * * * As Professor Llewellyn explained, the Comments were:

> prepared, as was the Code itself, under the joint auspices of the Conference of Commissioners on Uniform State Laws and the American Law Institute. These comments are very useful in presenting something of the background and purposes of the sections, and of the way in which the details and policies build into a whole. In these aspects they greatly aid understanding and construction.

Karl N. Llewellyn, Why We Need the Uniform Commercial Code, 10 U.Fla.L.Rev. 367, 375 (1957).

offeror could reasonably believe that in the context of the commercial setting in which the parties were acting, a contract had been formed. This determination requires a very fact specific inquiry. *See* John E. Murray, Jr., *Section 2–207 Of The Uniform Commercial Code: Another Word About Incipient Unconscionability,* 39 U.Pitt.L.Rev., 597, 632–34 (1978) (discussing *Dorton* and identifying the commercial understanding of the reasonable buyer as the "critical inquiry").

Our analysis does not yield an iron clad rule conducive to perfunctory application. However, it does remain true to the spirit of Article 2, as it calls the trial court to consider the commercial setting of each transaction and the reasonable expectations and beliefs of the parties acting in that setting. *Id.* at 600; § 1–102(2)(b) (stating one purpose of the act is "to permit the continued expansion of commercial practices through custom, usage and agreement of the parties").

The trial court's treatment of this issue did not encompass the scope of the inquiry we envision. We will not attempt to make the factual determination necessary to characterize this transaction on the record before us. Not satisfied that the trial court adequately considered all of the relevant factors in determining that the Dunham Bush Acknowledgment functioned as a counteroffer, we remand for reconsideration of the question.

In the event the trial court concludes that the Dunham Bush Acknowledgment constituted an acceptance, it will face the question of which terms will control in the exchange of forms. In the interest of judicial economy, and because this determination is a question of law, we proceed with our analysis.

IV.

The Gardner Zemke Order provides that the "[m]anufacturer shall replace or repair all parts found to be defective during initial year of use at no additional cost." Because the Order does not include any warranty terms, Article 2 express and implied warranties arise by operation of law. Section 2–313 (express warranties), § 2–314 (implied warranty of merchantability), § 2–315 (implied warranty of fitness for a particular purpose). The Dunham Bush Acknowledgment contains the following warranty terms.

> WARRANTY: We agree that the apparatus manufactured by the Seller will be free from defects in material and workmanship for a period of one year under normal use and service and when properly installed: and our obligation under this agreement is limited solely to repair or replacement at our option, at our factories, of any part or parts thereof which shall within one year from date of original installation or 18 months from date of shipment from factory to the original purchaser, whichever date may first occur be returned to us with transportation charges prepaid which our examination shall

disclose to our satisfaction to have been defective. THIS AGREEMENT TO REPAIR OR REPLACE DEFECTIVE PARTS IS EXPRESSLY IN LIEU OF AND IS HEREBY DISCLAIMER OF ALL OTHER EXPRESS WARRANTIES, AND IS IN LIEU OF AND IN DISCLAIMER AND EXCLUSION OF ANY IMPLIED WARRANTIES OF MERCHANTABILITY AND FITNESS FOR A PARTICULAR PURPOSE, AS WELL AS ALL OTHER IMPLIED WARRANTIES, IN LAW OR EQUITY, AND OF ALL OTHER OBLIGATIONS OR LIABILITIES ON OUR PART. THERE ARE NO WARRANTIES WHICH EXTEND BEYOND THE DESCRIPTION HEREOF. . . . Our obligation to repair or replace shall not apply to any apparatus which shall have been repaired or altered outside our factory in any way. . . .

The one proposition on which most courts and commentators agree at this point in the construction of the statute is that Section 2–207(3) applies only if a contract is not found under Section 2–207(1). *Dorton,* 453 F.2d at 1166; Duesenberg & King, § 3.03[1] at 3–40; 2 Hawkland, § 2–207:04 at 178–79; White & Summers, § 1–3 at 35. However, there are courts that disagree even with this proposition. *See Westinghouse Elec. Corp. v. Nielsons, Inc.,* 647 F.Supp. 896 (D.Colo.1986) (dealing with different terms, finding a contract under 2–207(1) and proceeding to apply 2–207(2) and 2–207(3)).

The language of the statute makes it clear that "additional" terms are subject to the provisions of Section 2–207(2). However, a continuing controversy rages among courts and commentators concerning the treatment of "different" terms in a Section 2–207 analysis. While Section 2–207(1) refers to both "additional or different" terms, Section 2–207(2) refers only to "additional" terms. The omission of the word "different" from Section 2–207(2) gives rise to the questions of whether "different" terms are to be dealt with under the provisions of Section 2–207(2), and if not, how they are to be treated. That the terms in the Acknowledgment are "different" rather than "additional" guides the remainder of our inquiry and requires that we join the fray. Initially, we briefly survey the critical and judicial approaches to the problem posed by "different" terms.

One view is that, in spite of the omission, "different" terms are to be analyzed under Section 2–207(2). 2 Hawkland, § 2–207:03 at 168. The foundation for this position is found in Comment 3, which provides "[w]hether or not additional or different terms will become part of the agreement depends upon the provisions of Subsection (2)." Armed with this statement in Comment 3, proponents point to the ambiguity in the distinction between "different" and "additional" terms and argue that the distinction serves no clear purpose. *Steiner v. Mobile Oil Corp.,* 20 Cal.3d 90, 141 Cal.Rptr. 157, 165–66 n. 5, 569 P.2d 751, 759–60 n. 5 (1977); *Boese-Hilburn Co. v. Dean Machinery Co.,* 616 S.W.2d 520, 527 (Mo.Ct.App. 1981). Following this rationale in this case, and relying on the observation in Comment 4 that a clause negating implied warranties would "materially alter" the contract, the Dunham Bush warranty terms would not become a part of the contract, and the Gardner Zemke warranty provision, together with the Article 2 warranties would control. § 2–207(2)(b).

Another approach is suggested by Duesenberg and King who comment that the ambiguity found in the treatment of "different" and "additional" terms is more judicially created than statutorily supported. While conceding that Comment 3 "contributes to the confusion," they also admonish that "the Official Comments do not happen to be the statute." Duesenberg & King, § 3.05 at 3–52. Observing that "the drafters knew what they were doing, and that they did not sloppily fail to include the term 'different' when drafting subsection (2)," Duesenberg and King postulate that a "different" term in a responsive document operating as an acceptance can never become a part of the parties' contract under the plain language of the statute. *Id.* § 3.03[1] at 3–38.

The reasoning supporting this position is that once an offeror addresses a subject it implicitly objects to variance of that subject by the offeree, thereby preventing the "different" term from becoming a part of the contract by prior objection and obviating the need to refer to "different" terms in Section 2–207(2). *Id.* § 3.05[1] at 3–77; *Air Prods. & Chems. Inc. v. Fairbanks Morse, Inc.,* 58 Wis.2d 193, 206 N.W.2d 414, 423–25 (1973). Professor Summers lends support to this position. White & Summers, § 1–3 at 34. Although indulging a different analysis, following this view in the case before us creates a result identical to that flowing from application of the provisions of Section 2–207(2) as discussed above—the Dunham Bush warranty provisions fall out, and the stated Gardner Zemke and Article 2 warranty provisions apply.

Yet a third analysis arises from Comment 6, which in pertinent part states:

> Where clauses on confirming forms sent by both parties conflict each party must be assumed to object to a clause of the other conflicting with one on the confirmation sent by himself. As a result the requirement that there be notice of objection which is found in Subsection (2) is satisfied and the conflicting terms do not become a part of the contract. The contract then consists of the terms originally expressly agreed to, terms on which the confirmations agree, and terms supplied by this act, including Subsection (2).

The import of Comment 6 is that "different" terms cancel each other out and that existing applicable code provisions stand in their place. The obvious flaws in Comment 6 are the use of the words "confirming forms," suggesting the Comment applies only to variant confirmation forms and not variant offer and acceptance forms, and the reference to Subsection 2–207(2)—arguably dealing only with "additional" terms—in the context of "different" terms. Of course, Duesenberg and King remind us that

Comment 6 "is only a comment, and a poorly drawn one at that." Duesenberg & King, § 3.05[1] at 3–79.

The analysis arising from Comment 6, however, has found acceptance in numerous jurisdictions including the Tenth Circuit. *Daitom, Inc. v. Pennwalt Corp.,* 741 F.2d 1569, 1578–79 (10th Cir.1984). Following a discussion similar to the one we have just indulged, the court found this the preferable approach. *Id.* at 1579 * * *. Professor White also finds merit in this analysis. White & Summers, § 1–3 at 33–35. Application of this approach here cancels out the parties' conflicting warranty terms and allows the warranty provisions of Article 2 to control.

We are unable to find comfort or refuge in concluding that any one of the three paths drawn through the contours of Section 2–207 is more consistent with or true to the language of the statute. We do find that the analysis relying on Comment 6 is the most consistent with the purpose and spirit of the Code in general and Article 2 in particular. We are mindful that the overriding goal of Article 2 is to discern the bargain struck by the contracting parties. However, there are times where the conduct of the parties makes realizing that goal impossible. In such cases, we find guidance in the Code's commitment to fairness, Section 1–102(3); good faith, Sections 1–203 & –2–103(1)(b); and unconscionable conduct, Section 2–302.

While Section 2–207 was designed to avoid the common law result that gave the advantage to the party sending the last form, we cannot conclude that the statute was intended to shift that advantage to the party sending the first form. Such a result will generally follow from the first two analyses discussed. We adopt the third analysis as the most even-handed resolution of a difficult problem. We are also aware that under this analysis even though the conflicting terms cancel out, the Code may provide a term similar to one rejected. We agree with Professor White that "[a]t least a term so supplied has the merit of being a term that the draftsmen considered fair." White & Summers, § 1–3 at 35.

Due to our disposition of this case, we do not address the second issue raised by Gardner Zemke. On remand, should the trial court conclude a contract was formed under Section 2–207(1), the conflicting warranty provisions in the parties' forms will cancel out, and the warranty provisions of Article 2 will control.

IT IS SO ORDERED

NOTES

1. Recall the status of the U.C.C. as statute, when adopted by individual state legislatures. What is the status of the official comments as "official text"? See *Gardner Zemke* footnote. Do they enjoy persuasive or binding authority? Do they offer support on the theory that they aid in interpretation or construction, or that they help discern the intent of the legislature in adopting the statutory scheme? Or both?

2. Consider the meaning of "expressly made conditional" in U.C.C. § 2–207(1). See the treatment by the court in *Gardner Zemke* of the inquiry set out in *Dorton v. Collins & Aikman Corp.*, 453 F.2d 1161 (6th Cir. 1972). State, in your own words, what is required.

3. Consider the meaning of "materially alter" in U.C.C. § 2–207(2)(b). "Material" suggests an economically significant impact, or perhaps an alteration that would affect a party's decision whether to enter into the contract. Is this the approach of the Official Comments? Consider:

a. Examples of typical clauses which would normally "materially alter" the contract and so result in surprise or hardship if incorporated without express awareness by the other party are: a clause negating such standard warranties as that of merchantability or fitness for a particular purpose in circumstances in which either warranty normally attaches; . . . [or] a clause requiring that complaints be made in a time materially shorter than customary or reasonable. [Cmt 4].

b. Examples of clauses which involve no element of unreasonable surprise and which therefore are to be incorporated in the contract unless notice of objection is seasonably given are: . . . a clause fixing a reasonable time for complaints within customary limits, ...; a clause providing for interest on overdue invoices or fixing the seller's standard credit terms where they are within the range of trade practice and do not limit any credit bargained for; a clause limiting the right of rejection for defects which fall within the customary trade tolerances for acceptance "with adjustment" or otherwise limiting remedy in a reasonable manner (see Sections 2–718 and 2–719). [Cmt 5]

Consider, too, the role of industry practice.

4. Define the three approaches discussed in *Gardner Zemke*. What is a "Last Shot" approach. What is a "Knock Out" rule? (This latter phrase is a common reference to the rule adopted in *Gardner Zemke*.) Restate, in your own words, the policies that might support each.

PROBLEMS

1. Carpet Retailers, Inc purchases 12 carpets from Durable Carpet Mills, Inc., a manufacturing company. Carpet Retailers send their purchase order form, which contains an offer to purchase, and is silent on a warranty. Durable Carpet Mills returns a printed sales invoice, which states, after details on shipping and billing addresses, nature and price of order, and payment options, the following:

ANY AND ALL IMPLIED WARRANTIES OF MERCHANTABILITY ARE HEREBY DISCLAIMED. COMPLAINTS MUST BE MADE WITHIN 45 DAYS.

Durable Carpet Mills ships the 12 carpets. Five months later, in response to a customer complaint about the carpet showing severe wear and tear, Carpet Retailers learns that the carpets are made, not of the durable polyester carpet fiber that is standard in the industry, but a cheaper, inferior one. A dispute thus arises between Carpet Retailers and Durable Carpet Mills for breach of implied warranty.

What is the likely outcome under U.C.C. § 2–207?

2. Consider the same facts, in Question 1 above, but with an amendment to the Durable Carpet Mills' invoice. It now states:

> This invoice operates as an acceptance only if you agree to all terms hereof. Hence, the acceptance of your order is subject to all of the terms and conditions on the face and reverse side hereof, all of which are accepted by buyer; it supersedes buyer's order form, if any. It shall become a contract either (a) when signed and delivered by buyer to seller and accepted in writing by seller, or (b) at Seller's option, when buyer shall have given to seller specification of assortments, delivery dates, shipping instructions, or instructions to bill and hold as to all or any part of the merchandise herein described, or when buyer has received delivery of the whole or any part thereof, or when buyer has otherwise assented to the terms and conditions hereof.

On the reverse side, it states

ANY   AND   ALL   IMPLIED   WARRANTIES   OF
MERCHANTABILITY ARE HEREBY DISCLAIMED.

What is the likely outcome under § 2–207?

3. Consider the same facts, in Question 1 above, but with an amendment to Carpet Retailers' purchase order. While it remains an offer, silent on warranty, it includes the term "we object to any terms different from the terms in this purchase order."

Do Durable Carpet Mill's additional terms still operate?

4. Consider a different background to the agreement. In offering to purchase the 12 carpets, Carpet Retailers writes the following letter to Ms. Main, the head of sales at Durable Carpet Mills:

Dear Ms. Main,

> Re: Offer to purchase

> We were pleased to make your acquaintance at the recent trade fair in Atlanta. We are delighted to learn about the durability of your carpets, and expect our trusted customers to be equally happy. I enclose a shipping requisition for 12 carpets, with details below.

> [Following details on shipping information, billing information, nature and price of order, and payment options, the following sentence]:

> "Any disputes will be settled by arbitration."

Durable Carpet Mills returns a printed sales invoice, which states:

> The acceptance of your order is subject to all of the terms and conditions on the face and reverse side hereof, all of which are

accepted by buyer; it supersedes buyer's order form, if any. It shall become a contract either (a) when signed and delivered by buyer to seller and accepted in writing by seller, or (b) at Seller's option, when buyer shall have given to seller specification of assortments, delivery dates, shipping instructions, or instructions to bill and hold as to all or any part of the merchandise herein described, or when buyer has received delivery of the whole or any part thereof, or when buyer has otherwise assented to the terms and conditions hereof.

On the reverse side, it states, among other things:

SELLER REFUSES TO SUBMIT TO ARBITRATION.

Does § 2–207 resolve whether the contract does or does not call for arbitration?

6. BATTLE OF THE FORMS UNDER PROPOSED REVISION OF ARTICLE 2 AND CISG

During the 1990s and early 2000s, there were a series of related projects looking toward a comprehensive revision of Article 2 of the U.C.C. The projects, however, encountered significant difficulties in the effort to bridge deeply held divisions of opinion on major issues between various constituencies, such as sellers of goods and consumer representatives. The history of the projects is quite complex. After a decade or so of work on a comprehensive revision, the sponsors of the Code shifted direction, proposing a more modest set of amendments to the existing text of Article 2. The result of that more limited project was a proposed amendment, approved by the Code sponsors in 2003. These amendments also proved controversial. No state adopted the amendments. In 2011, the Code sponsors gave up and abandoned the proposed amendments.

On some issues, however, the proposed revised text is still somewhat useful in indicating how problems with the existing law might be resolved. The § 2–207 "battle of the forms" issues is a good example. The proposed amendment would have distinguished much more clearly than the existing law between issues of contract formation and issues of contract interpretation.

Proposed Revised 2–206 deals with contract formation. A new subsection (3) incorporates some of the language that was previously in subsection (1) of 2–207. Proposed Revised 2–206(3) would have read as follows:

(3) A definite and seasonable expression of acceptance in a record operates as an acceptance even if it contains terms additional to or different from the offer.

Note the key differences from the existing text of 2–207(1):

(1) A definite and seasonable expression of acceptance ~~or a written confirmation which is sent within a reasonable time~~ operates as an acceptance even though it states terms additional to or different from [the offer] ~~those offered or agreed upon, unless acceptance is expressly made conditional on assent to the additional or different terms.~~

The "proviso" of existing 2–207(1) ("unless acceptance is expressly made conditional on assent to the additional or different terms") would have been dropped altogether. The thought was any real issues that might have been addressed by the proviso could be handled as questions about whether a certain communication was or was not intended as "a definite and seasonable expression of [assent]."

On the contract interpretation issues that have proved so difficult under existing 2–207(2) & (3), the proposed revision would have taken the approach of saying that the effort made by current 2–207(2)—with all the messy issues about what constitutes "material alteration" etc.—is not worth the effort. Instead, the proposed revision would have adopted a much more open-textured approach to interpretation. The proposed revision would have essentially dropped both 2–207(2) & (3) (see excerpt at beginning of section) and stated:

> If (i) conduct by both parties recognizes the existence of a contract although their records do not otherwise establish a contract, (ii) a contract is fo rmed by an offer and acceptance, or (iii) a contract formed in any manner is confirmed by a record that contains terms additional to or different from those in the contract being confirmed, the terms of the contract, subject to Section 2–202, are:
>
> > (a) terms that appear in the records of both parties;
> >
> > (b) terms, whether in a record or not, to which both parties agree; and
> >
> > (c) terms supplied or incorporated under any provision of this Act.

Note that the key language in the proposed revision is in subsection (b), with the reference to "terms . . . to which both parties agree." The Comments to proposed revised 2–207 indicate that it contemplates a very fact specific inquiry into what does and does not constitute "agree."

The difficulties raised by the Battle of the Forms are also reflected in the Convention on the International Sale of Goods.

CISG, Article 19

[Refer to Statutory Supplement]

NOTES & QUESTIONS

1.   How does the text of CISG, art. 19 depart from that of UCC § 2–207?

2.   Just as for the U.C.C., there are different views on how CISG, art. 19 should be interpreted. One view holds that a solution has to be found in domestic law; another opinion applies the Last Shot approach; and a third follows the Knock Out rule.

3.   The UNIDROIT Principles, as well as the Principles of European Contract Law (PECL), which sets out a uniform approach in Europe, follow the Knock Out rule for conflicting standard terms: UNIDROIT, art. 2.22; PECL art. 2:209.

4.   For the position in Germany, in which both the Last Shot approach and the Knock Out rule have been applied, with reference to the general principle of good faith in the domestic law of obligations, see Kaia Wildner, *Art. 19 CISG: The German Approach to the Battle of the Forms in International Contract Law: The Decision of the Federal Supreme Court of Germany of 9 January 2002*, 20 PACE INT'L L. REV. 1 (2008). See also CISG, art. 7(1) (noting regard for good faith in international trade); UNIDROIT, art. 1.7.

D.   PAROL EVIDENCE RULE

1.   INTRODUCTION

Farmers Cooperative Ass'n v. Garrison
Supreme Court of Arkansas, 1970.
248 Ark. 948, 454 S.W.2d 644.

■ HOLT, JUSTICE.

This is an action by appellant to collect on two notes. Appellees, Randall Garrison and his wife, are in the poultry business. Julian Hendren is the general manager of appellant corporation, Farmers Cooperative Association, Inc., a chicken feed retailer. In the early part of 1967, Hendren, along with Kenneth Handy, a representative of Farmland Industries, Inc. (a regional supplier in which appellant has an ownership interest), approached appellees to solicit their participation in a layer-feeder program. This program was a joint project of Farmers Cooperative and Farmland Industries. On April 5, 1967, a 'Feeder Contract' was consummated between appellees and appellant.

The contract provided that appellant would sell to appellees, and appellees would purchase from appellant their entire requirements of mixed feed and concentrates at appellant's 'regular retail price or prices in effect on date of delivery * * *.' Appellant also agreed to furnish appellees with 21,000 layer hens together with sufficient financing for the program. In this contract the appellees agreed to execute a promissory note to appellant for $34,650.00, covering the price of the hens and 29,800 pounds of feed, which sum plus interest was payable on demand. Without limiting the right of appellant to demand payment in full or in part at any time, the contract specified that all indebtedness evidenced by appellees' note 'shall be paid in full on or before May 1, 1968.' Appellant also retained by this contract the sole option to make advances to appellees, not to exceed at any one time the original sum of the note. The final provision of this contract provided that the appellees have read and presently understand the agreements and that by signing the contract they agree to be bound by all of its terms. About a month later, or on May 9, 1967, both appellees executed to appellant a promissory note for $34,650.00. On August 2, 1967, appellee Randall Garrison executed a second note, payable on November 1, 1967, for the sum of $12,000.00.

Appellant brought suit against appellees on November 18, 1968, on the two promissory notes. The unpaid principal balances were then $34,603.93 on the initial note and $3,325.41 on the second note. Appellees answered and denied liability on the notes because of a partial failure of consideration. They asserted that it had been agreed upon between the parties that the notes would be repaid only from the proceeds of the egg production; that appellant would continue to refinance appellees with successive layer hens until such time as the egg proceeds paid the appellees' indebtedness in full; and that appellant breached the contract by refusing to so refinance. Appellees also counterclaimed for: (1) $35,155.02 loss of income because of the partial premature molt of their hens resulting from appellant's failure to promptly deliver feed; and (2) $5,299.99 as an overcharge on feed, in that appellant breached its agreement to supply feed at competitive market prices.

Both Hendren and Handy testified, each denying that they ever made any representations or promises to refinance appellees with successive layer hens or to sell feed at competitive market prices. Over the objections of appellant, appellee Randall Garrison testified, and adduced testimony from other farmers who had been approached regarding the layer-feeder program, that Hendren and Handy persuasively represented such refinancing provisions and competitive prices as a part of the program. Garrison and his brother, who was present during part of the negotiations leading to the contractual agreement, testified that Hendren and Handy specifically promised to refinance appellees if necessary and to furnish feed at competitive prices. . . .

By . . . instructions . . . given by the court, the existence of any agreements regarding refinancing and competitive market prices for feed was presented as questions of fact. Thus the issues of appellees' liability on the two notes and of appellant's liability on the counterclaims were submitted to the jury. The jury found that appellant was entitled to recover nothing on the note ($34,650.00) dated May 9, 1967; denied appellees' claim for damages for loss of income ($35,155.02) alleged to have resulted from a delay in the delivery of feed; awarded appellant $3,797.54 on the note dated August 2, 1967; and found that appellees were entitled to recover $5,299.99 on their counterclaim alleging overcharge in feed prices. Appellant moved for a judgment notwithstanding the verdict on the note dated May 9, 1967. The motion was denied. From the judgment on the verdict comes this appeal.

One of appellant's contentions for reversal is: 'Any testimony regarding prior or contemporaneous oral modification of the written feeder contract should not have been admitted into evidence under the doctrine of merger.' We must agree.

It is a general proposition of the common law that in the absence of fraud, accident or mistake, a written contract merges, and thereby extinguishes, all prior and contemporaneous negotiations, understandings and verbal agreements on the same subject. * * * This is simply the affirmative expression of the parol evidence rule. In analyzing the present case, it is helpful to refer initially to 3 Corbin on Contracts, § 573 (1960), which begins:

> "When two parties have made a contract and have expressed it in a writing to which they have both assented as the complete and accurate integration of that contract, evidence, whether parol or otherwise, of antecedent understandings and negotiations will not be admitted for the purpose of varying or contradicting the writing. This is in substance what is called the 'parol evidence rule,' a rule that scarcely deserves to be called a rule of evidence of any kind, * * *. The use of such a name for this rule has had unfortunate consequences, principally by distracting the attention from the real issues that are involved. These issues may be any one or more of the following: (1) Have the parties made a contract? (2) Is that contract void or voidable because of illegality, fraud, mistake, or any other reason? (3) Did the parties assent to a particular writing as the complete and accurate 'integration' of that contract?
>
> In determining these issues, or any one of them, there is no 'parol evidence rule' to be applied. On these issues, no relevant evidence, whether parol or otherwise, is excluded."

In the case at bar, it is not disputed that the parties made a contract; in fact, appellees not only admitted the existence of a contract and the alleged indebtedness, but based their defense and founded their counterclaims on an alleged breach thereof. Nor have appellees asserted that the contract is void or voidable on the basis of illegality, fraud, or mistake. However, appellees do in effect contend that the writing was not assented to as a complete 'integration' of the contract and further point

out that '(t)he record does not show that the court affirmatively found the feeder contract to have been integrated.' We cannot agree with appellees' contention. . . . [A]s we view the record, the evidence adduced by appellees concerning the alleged agreements of refinancing and competitive market prices did not go to prove that the written contract was not intended as a complete integration of prior negotiations; but rather it tended to show what purportedly was the parties' actual antecedent understanding which was in variance with the clearly expressed terms of the contract. Being of this latter nature, such evidence was introduced in violation of the parol evidence rule. * * * Appellees here, in effect, sought to impeach the written contract, urging that it did not express the true intent of the parties, rather than simply attempting to prove that the writing was not a complete integration of the parties' prior agreements. * * * In the case at bar, we do not construe the parol evidence to be of the effect that the parties did not assent to the writing as the complete integration of their contract.

The parol evidence rule is one of substantive law. In 4 Williston on Contracts, § 631 (1961), this proposition is explained as follows:

"The parol evidence rule * * * fixes the subject matter for interpretation, though not itself a rule of interpretation.

'It does not exclude evidence for any of the reasons ordinarily requiring exclusion, based on the probative value of such evidence or the policy of its admission. The rule as applied to contracts is simply that as a matter of substantive law, a certain act, the act of embodying the complete terms of an agreement in a writing (the 'integration'), becomes the contract of the parties. The point then is, not how the agreement is to be proved, because as a matter of law the writing is the agreement. Extrinsic evidence is excluded because it cannot serve to prove what the agreement was, this being determined as a matter of law to be the writing itself." . . .

. . . .

With these principles in mind, we are of the view that the written contract constitutes a complete integration. Therefore, appellees' proffered evidence of agreements, prior to and contemporaneous with the written contract, regarding the promised refinancing and assured competitive market prices for feed, should not have been admitted. The contract (dated April 5, 1967) clearly states that a note to be given later (the note was dated May 9, 1967) is to be payable on demand and must be paid in full on or before May 1, 1968. The contract is not silent on this point, and it is patently inconsistent with the clearly expressed terms therein to contend that credit was to be extended beyond the specified due date. . . .

. . . .

Reversed and remanded.

NOTES

1. In the chapter on the Statute of Frauds, we saw rules of contract law that turned on whether there was a writing. So too here. But, the Parol Evidence Rule issues we are now examining are entirely different from the Statute of Frauds issues considered earlier.

Suppose we have facts somewhat like those in the *Ardente v. Horan* case we studied in the chapter on contract formation:

T1	Buyer:	I'll buy for $225,000, if furniture included
T2	Seller:	I'll sell for $250,000, but no furniture
T3	Buyer:	Price OK, but want furniture
T4	Seller:	OK

If there is no writing, is the Seller's promise enforceable? What sort of writing might suffice for purposes of the Statute of Frauds? How about a few words scribbled on the back of a restaurant check?

2. Now suppose the same facts as in the preceding note, except that:

T5   Seller and Buyer sign comprehensive P&S Agreement.

First, suppose that the P&S Agreement contained a provision that explicitly said that the furniture was *not* included. Can Buyer introduce evidence that at T4 Seller had agreed that the furniture would be included? If not, why not. Could you explain the reason for your result, in language that a twelve year old child would understand? This seems like a silly question, but it's not. Being very clear about the reason for the result in this case is the key to understanding the "parol evidence rule."

Second, suppose that the P&S Agreement was silent on the question whether the furniture was included or not. Can Buyer introduce evidence that at T4 Seller had agreed that the furniture would be included? If not, why not?

2. OPERATION OF PAROL EVIDENCE RULE

It's easy to get confused about the "parol evidence rule." Part of the problem comes from taking the label "parol evidence rule" too seriously. Here, as in many situations, there is an important difference between the *name* of a rule and the *content* of that rule. Consider another setting. In labor law, one encounters the phrase "yellow dog contract." That term refers to an arrangement where an employer requires employees, as a condition of taking their jobs, to agree not to join a union. Since the 1930s, such agreements have been prohibited by a federal statute known as the Norris LaGuardia Act. Suppose that an employer did require employees to enter into such agreements, and then seeks to enforce the agreements. It would hardly be a plausible argument for the employer to say that "I didn't violate the Norris LaGuardia Act's prohibition of yellow dog contracts because I did not enter into any agreements with jaundiced canines." In that setting, it's obvious that the name "yellow dog contract" is not a useful guide to the meaning of the law that prohibits yellow dog contracts. The same is true, but less obvious, about the "parol evidence rule."

To get a better sense of how the rule known as the "parol evidence rule" operates, look at how it is stated in the Restatement (Second) of Contracts:

Restatement (Second) of Contracts, §§ 209, 213, 216

Section 209(1) Integrated Agreements "An integrated agreement is a writing or writings constituting a final expression of one or more terms of an agreement."

Section 213(1) Effect of Integrated Agreement on Prior Agreements (Parol Evidence Rule) "A binding integrated agreement discharges prior agreements to the extent that it is inconsistent with them."

Section 215 Contradiction of Integrated Terms "[W]here there is a binding agreement, either completely or partially integrated, evidence of prior or contemporaneous agreements or negotiations is not admissible in evidence to contradict a term of the writing."

Section 216(1) Consistent Additional Terms "Evidence of a consistent additional term is admissible to supplement an integrated agreement unless the court finds that the agreement was completely integrated."

Note that section 209(1) is just a definition of the term "integrated agreement." Section 211, as the title points out, is a statement of the rule known as the "parol evidence rule." Note that the rule is stated as a rule of substantive law, that is, the parties' act of signing an "integrated agreement" discharges any prior inconsistent agreements. Section 215 and 216 state the evidentiary consequences of the substantive rule stated in section 213(1): If any alleged prior agreement has been discharged by execution of the integrated agreement, there is no point in wasting time listening to evidence about the alleged prior agreement. (This brief summary does not address the difference between a "completely" integrated agreement and a "partially" integrated agreement. We'll consider those concepts anon.)

To get a clearer understanding, consider the following hypotheticals:

PROBLEMS

1.   Suppose we have facts somewhat like those in note 2 above except that the alleged deal about the furniture was in writing, that is:

T1   Buyer: I'll buy for $225,000, if furniture included

T2   Seller: I'll sell for $250,000, but no furniture

T3   Buyer: *Written statement:* Price OK, but want furniture

T4   Seller: OK

T5   Seller and Buyer sign comprehensive P&S agreement

Would you expect that a rule known as the "parol evidence rule" would apply to this hypo? What does the word "parol" mean? Here's a standard dictionary definition: "Parol . . . An oral utterance; word of mouth." *American Heritage Dictionary* (1978). Does the rule stated in section 213 of the Restatement apply to this case? *See* Restatement (Second) of Contracts § 213 & comment a.

2.   Would your answer to the previous question be different if the Buyer could produce extremely trust-worthy, reliable evidence that the Seller had agreed at T4 that the furniture would be included?

3.   Suppose that in a case similar to *Lucy v. Zehmer*, the writing signed at the bar that night had not just been some words scribbled on the back of a restaurant check. Instead suppose that someone at the bar happened to have with him a standard form of purchase and sale agreement for real estate commonly used by real estate broker in the area. Lucy and Zehmer filled it in and signed it.

The next day, when everyone had sobered up, Seller told Buyer that he would not go through with the deal. He explained that everything that happened the night before was just a bunch of drunks shooting off their mouths. Buyer, however, wanted to go through with the deal and sued.

At a pretrial conference trial, Seller's lawyer tells the judge that he plans to introduce evidence that would show that no reasonable person in the position of the Buyer could have understood what happened at the bar as a serious real estate transaction. Seller's lawyer tells the judge that he has five witnesses who are ready to testify about what happened at the bar that night. Buyer's lawyer contends that under the parol evidence rule, none of that evidence should be admitted.

How would you rule on the issue were you the trial judge? Note the language of Restatement (Second) of Contracts § 213(1) "A *binding* integrated agreement discharges prior agreements to the extent that it is inconsistent with them." *See* Restatement (Second) of Contracts § 214(a) & (b).

4.   Suppose that in a case similar to *Farmers Coop v. Garrison* the farmers had been illiterate. Suppose that when the written agreement was to be signed, they asked the Coop "Does the agreement say that we'll have to pay only out of the profits of the chicken operation?" Suppose that the Coop said yes—and that the Coop knew this was not true.

The Coop sues the farmers on the notes.

At a pretrial conference trial, the farmers' lawyer tells the judge that he plans to introduce evidence that would show that the Coop had lied about that matter. The Coop's lawyer contends that under the parol evidence rule, that evidence should not be admitted.

How would you rule on the issue were you the trial judge? See Restatement (Second) of Contracts § 214(d) & (e).

5.   Suppose that in a case similar to *Farmers Coop v. Garrison*, the agreement, signed in 1967, said nothing to the effect that the farmers would have to pay only out of the profits of the chicken operation.

The Coop sues the farmers on the notes.

At a pretrial conference trial, the farmers' lawyer tells the judge that he plans to introduce evidence that would show that in 1968, the Coop had promised the farmers that they would have to pay only out of the profits of the chicken operation. The Coop's lawyer contends that under the parol evidence rule, that evidence should not be admitted.

How would you rule on the issue were you the trial judge? What other issues might the Coop's lawyer raise?

3.   "COLLATERAL" AGREEMENTS; "COMPLETE" VERSUS "PARTIAL" INTEGRATION

PROBLEM

Here are the facts of a famous case, *Mitchell v. Lath*, 247 N.Y. 377 (1928), involving the parol evidence rule. Puzzle over how the Court should decide the case:

> In the fall of 1923 the Laths owned a farm. This they wished to sell. Across the road, on land belonging to Lieutenant-Governor Lunn, they had an ice house which they might remove. Mrs. Mitchill looked over the land with a view to its purchase. She found the ice house objectionable. Thereupon "the defendants orally promised and agreed, for and in consideration of the purchase of their farm by the plaintiff, to remove the said ice house in the spring of 1924." Relying upon this promise, she made a written contract to buy the property for $8,400, for cash and a mortgage and containing various provisions usual in such papers. Later receiving a deed, she entered into possession and has spent considerable sums in improving the property for use as a summer residence. The defendants have not fulfilled their promise as to the ice house and do not intend to do so. We are not dealing, however, with their moral delinquencies. The question before us is whether their oral agreement may be enforced.

Lee v. Joseph E. Seagram & Sons, Inc.
United States Court of Appeals, Second Circuit, 1977.
552 F.2d 447.

■ GURFEIN, CIRCUIT JUDGE.

This is an appeal by defendant Joseph E. Seagram & Sons, Inc. ("Seagram") from a judgment entered by the District Court, Hon. Charles H. Tenney, upon the verdict of a jury in the amount of $407,850 in favor of the plaintiffs on a claim asserting common law breach of an oral contract. . . . The plaintiffs are Harold S. Lee (now deceased) and his two sons, Lester and Eric ("the Lees"). Jurisdiction is based on diversity of citizenship. We affirm.

. . . The Lees owned a 50% interest in Capitol City Liquor Company, Inc. ("Capitol City"), a wholesale liquor distributorship located in Washington, D.C. The other 50% was owned by Harold's brother, Henry D. Lee, and his nephew, Arthur Lee. Seagram is a distiller of alcoholic beverages. Capitol City carried numerous Seagram brands and a large portion of its sales were generated by Seagram lines.

The Lees and the other owners of Capitol City wanted to sell their respective interests in the business and, in May 1970, Harold Lee, the father, discussed the possible sale of Capitol City with Jack Yogman ("Yogman"), then Executive Vice President of Seagram (and now President), whom he had known for many years. Lee offered to sell Capitol City to Seagram but conditioned the offer on Seagram's agreement to relocate Harold and his sons, the 50% owners of Capitol City, in a new distributorship of their own in a different city.

About a month later, another officer of Seagram, John Barth, an assistant to Yogman, visited the Lees and their co-owners in Washington and began negotiations for the purchase of the assets of Capitol City by Seagram on behalf of a new distributor, one Carter, who would take it over after the purchase. The purchase of the assets of Capitol City was consummated on September 30, 1970 pursuant to a written agreement. The promise to relocate the father and sons thereafter was not reduced to writing.

Harold Lee had served the Seagram organization for thirty-six years in positions of responsibility before he acquired the half interest in the Capitol City distributorship. . . . During this long period he enjoyed the friendship and confidence of the principals of Seagram.

The plaintiffs claimed a breach of the oral agreement to relocate Harold Lee's sons, alleging that Seagram had had opportunities to procure another distributorship for the Lees but had refused to do so. The Lees brought this action on January 18, 1972, fifteen months after the sale of the Capitol City distributorship to Seagram. They contended that they had performed their obligation by agreeing to the sale by Capitol City of its assets to Seagram, but that Seagram had failed to perform its obligation under the separate oral contract between the Lees and Seagram. The agreement which the trial court permitted the jury to find was "an oral agreement with defendant which provided that if they agreed to sell their interest in Capitol City, defendant in return, within a reasonable time, would provide the plaintiffs a Seagram distributorship whose price would require roughly an amount equal to the capital obtained by the plaintiffs for the sale of their interest in Capitol City, and which distributorship would be in a location acceptable to plaintiffs." No specific exception was taken to this portion of the charge. By its verdict for the plaintiffs, we must assume . . . that this is the agreement which the jury found was made before the sale of Capitol City was agreed upon.

Appellant . . . contends that . . . plaintiffs' proof of the alleged oral agreement is barred by the parol evidence rule . . . .

Judge Tenney, in a careful analysis of the application of the parol evidence rule, decided that the rule did not bar proof of the oral agreement. We agree.

The District Court . . . treated the issue as whether the written agreement for the sale of assets was an "integrated" agreement not only of all the mutual agreements concerning the sale of Capitol City assets, but also of all the mutual agreements of the parties. Finding the language of the sales agreement "somewhat ambiguous," the court decided that the determination of whether the parol evidence rule applies must await the taking of evidence on the issue of whether the sales agreement was intended to be a complete and accurate integration of all of the mutual promises of the parties.

Seagram did not avail itself of this invitation. It failed to call as witnesses any of the three persons who negotiated the sales agreement on behalf of Seagram regarding the intention of the parties to integrate all mutual promises or regarding the failure of the written agreement to contain an integration clause.

Appellant contends that, as a matter of law, the oral agreement was "part and parcel" of the subject-matter of the sales contract and that failure to include it in the written contract barred proof of its existence. *Mitchill v. Lath*, 247 N.Y. 377, 380, 160 N.E. 646 (1928). The position of appellant, fairly stated, is that the oral agreement was either an inducing cause for the sale or was a part of the consideration for the sale, and in either case, should have been contained in the written contract. In either case, it argues that the parol evidence rule bars its admission.

Appellees maintain, on the other hand, that the oral agreement was a collateral agreement and that, since it is not contradictory of any of the terms of the sales agreement, proof of it is not barred by the parol evidence rule. Because the case comes to us after a jury verdict we must assume that there actually was an oral contract, such as the court instructed the jury it could find. The question is whether the strong policy for avoiding fraudulent claims through application of the parol evidence rule nevertheless mandates reversal on the ground that the jury should not have been permitted to hear the evidence. * * *.

The District Court stated the cardinal issue to be whether the parties "intended" the written agreement for the sale of assets to be the complete and accurate integration of all the mutual promises of the parties. If the written contract was not a complete integration, the court held, then the parol evidence rule has no application. We assume that the District Court determined intention by objective standards. See 3 Corbin on Contracts §§ 573–574. The parol evidence rule is a rule of substantive law. *Fogelson v. Rackfay Constr. Co., supra*; *Higgs v. De Maziroff,* 263 N.Y. 473, 477, 189 N.E. 555 (1934); *Smith v. Bear*, 237 F.2d 79, 83 (2d Cir. 1956).

The law of New York is not rigid or categorical, but is in harmony with this approach. As Judge Fuld said in *Fogelson*:

"Decision in each case must, of course, turn upon the type of transaction involved, the scope of the written contract and the content of the oral agreement asserted."

300 N.Y. at 338, 90 N.E.2d at 883. And the Court of Appeals wrote in *Ball v. Grady*, 267 N.Y. 470, 472, 196 N.E. 402, 403 (1935):"In the end, the court must find the limits of the integration as best it may by reading the writing in the light of surrounding circumstances."

* * * Thus, certain oral collateral agreements, even though made contemporaneously, are not within the prohibition of the parol evidence rule "because (if) they are separate, independent, and complete contracts, although relating to the same subject. . . . (t)hey are allowed to be proved by parol, because they were made by parol, and no part thereof committed to writing." *Thomas v. Scutt*, 127 N.Y. 133, 140–41, 27 N.E. 961, 963 (1891).

. . . [T]he overarching question is whether, in the context of the particular setting, the oral agreement was one which the parties would ordinarily be expected to embody in the writing. * * * For example, integration is most easily inferred in the case of real estate contracts for the sale of land, e. g., *Mitchill v. Lath*, supra, 247 N.Y. 377, 160 N.E. 646, or leases * * *. In more complex situations, in which customary business practice may be more varied, an oral agreement can be treated as separate and independent of the written agreement even though the written contract contains a strong integration clause. *See Gem Corrugated Box Corp. v. National Kraft Container Corp.*, 427 F.2d 499, 503 (2d Cir. 1970).

Thus, as we see it, the issue is whether the oral promise to the plaintiffs, as individuals, would be an expectable term of the contract for the sale of assets by a corporation in which plaintiffs have only a 50% interest, considering as well the history of their relationship to Seagram.

Here, there are several reasons why it would not be expected that the oral agreement to give Harold Lee's sons another distributorship would be integrated into the sales contract. In the usual case, there is an identity of parties in both the claimed integrated instrument and in the oral agreement asserted. Here, although it would have been physically possible to insert a provision dealing with only the shareholders of a 50% interest, the transaction itself was a corporate sale of assets. Collateral agreements which survive the closing of a corporate deal, such as employment agreements for particular shareholders of the seller or consulting agreements, are often set forth in separate agreements. . . . It was expectable that such an agreement as one to obtain a new distributorship for certain persons, some of whom were not even parties to the contract, would not necessarily be integrated into an instrument for the sale of corporate assets. . . .

Similarly, it is significant that there was a close relationship of confidence and friendship over many years between two old men, Harold Lee and Yogman, whose authority to bind Seagram has not been questioned. It would not be surprising that a handshake for the benefit of Harold's sons would have been thought sufficient. In point, as well, is the circumstance that the negotiations concerning the provisions of the sales agreement were not conducted by Yogman but by three other Seagram representatives, headed by John Barth. The two transactions may not have been integrated in their minds when the contract was drafted.

Finally, the written agreement does not contain the customary integration clause, even though a good part of it (relating to warranties and negative covenants) is boilerplate. The omission may, of course, have been caused by mutual trust and confidence, but in any event, there is no such strong presumption of exclusion because of the existence of a detailed integration clause, as was relied upon by the Court of Appeals in *Fogelson*, supra, 300 N.Y. at 340, 90 N.E. 881.

Nor do we see any contradiction of the terms of the sales agreement. * * * The written agreement dealt with the sale of corporate assets, the oral agreement with the relocation of the Lees. Thus, the oral agreement does not vary or contradict the money consideration recited in the contract as flowing to the selling corporation. That is the only consideration recited, and it is still the only consideration to the corporation.

We affirm Judge Tenney's reception in evidence of the oral agreement and his denial of the motion under Rule 50(b) with respect to the parol evidence rule.

NOTES

1. Why do you think the court made a distinction between real estate agreements and complex business transactions, in relation to whether integration can be inferred?

2. A bit of information about corporate law helps to understand the reasoning in this case. The liquor distributorship was owned and operated by a corporation, Capitol City Liquor Company, Inc. ("Capitol City, Inc."), in which Harold Lee and other members of his family owned all of the stock. The acquisition by Seagram was structured as an asset acquisition, that is, the corporation, Capitol City, Inc., agreed to sell all of its assets to Seagram. The seller in that agreement is the corporation, Capitol City, Inc., not the shareholders.[a] As a matter of corporate law, however, before the corporation itself can enter into such an important contract, the corporation has to get the approval of its stockholders, that is, the Lee family.

---

[a] The deal might have been structured in a different way: The shareholders of Capitol City, Inc. might have sold all of their shares of stock to Seagram. In that case, the sellers would be the shareholders, rather than the corporation.

The agreement described in the opinion was the asset purchase agreement between Capitol City, Inc. and Seagram. The "side deal" was a promise allegedly made by Seagram to Harold Lee that the next time a liquor distributorship became available, it would go to the Lee children.

3.   The conclusion in *Lee v Seagram* was that the execution of the asset purchase agreement between Seagram and Capitol Cities, Inc. did not preclude the Lees from introducing evidence of the alleged agreement between Seagram and the Lees. Such conclusions can be expressed in several ways. First, one can describe the "side deal" as a "collateral" agreement. As the court notes, it's common in corporate acquisitions for the acquiring company to agree to employ some of the key employees of the acquired company for at least a period of time. In a carefully documented transaction, those employment agreements would be in writing, but the writings would be entirely separate from the agreement for acquisition of the company. One could describe the employment contracts as "collateral" to the acquisition agreement. Accordingly, if, as in *Lee v Seagram,* the employment agreements are not in writing, execution of the acquisition agreement would not discharge any such separate agreements. (Of course, the proponent of the separate agreement would have to prove that there really was such an agreement.)

Another way of expressing more or less the same point is to use the terms "complete integration" and "partial integration." Here's how the Restatement defines those terms:

Restatement (Second) of Contracts, §§ 210, 213

§ 210   Completely and Partially Integrated Agreements

(1)   A completely integrated agreement is an integrated agreement adopted by the parties as a complete and exclusive statement of the terms of the agreement.

(2)   A partially integrated agreement is an integrated agreement other than a completely integrated agreement.

One can make that a bit more understandable by altering the language a bit, as follows:

§ 210   Completely and Partially Integrated Agreements

(1)   A completely integrated agreement is an integrated agreement adopted by the parties as a complete and exclusive statement of the *[all of]* terms of the agreement.

(2)   A partially integrated agreement is an integrated agreement ~~other than a completely integrated agreement~~ [*adopted by the parties as a complete and exclusive statement of some but not all of the terms of the agreement.*]

Turning from definitions to rules of substantive law, one can state the effect of a "completely integrated" agreement and a "partially integrated" agreement as follows:

§ 213   Effect of Integrated Agreement on Prior Agreements (Parol Evidence Rule)

(1)   A binding integrated agreement discharges prior agreements to the extent that it is inconsistent with them.

(2)   A binding completely integrated agreement discharges prior agreements to the extent that they are within its scope.

This is saying more or less the same thing as was expressed in *Lee v Seagram* in the language of "collateral" agreements.

Notice that the same general set of issues could be expressed in either of two ways. First, there is the way the issues are described in the *Lee v. Seagram* opinion itself. One could say there are only two categories: (1) issues involving the deal in the main agreement, and (2) entirely different issues, such as the alleged separate promise in *Lee v Seagram* to set the children up with a new distributorship. The execution of an integrated agreement covering the main deal discharges any inconsistent understanding about the matters within the scope of the main deal, but has no effect on matters concerning the alleged separate promise.

Second, there is the way the issues are described in the Restatement. One could say that there are three categories: (1) issues involving the deal in the written agreement and covered by the agreement, (2) issues related to the deal in the written agreement but not covered by the agreement, and (3) entirely different issues. The execution of an integrated agreement obviously has no impact on issues in the third category. For issues in the first two categories, one could say that a "completely integrated" agreement discharges issues in the first category and in the second category, but that a "partially integrated agreement" discharges issues in the first category but not in the second category.

It doesn't make a great deal of difference how one expresses the point. If you understand the way the issue is addressed in *Lee v. Seagram,* but find the Restatement's more complicated concepts confusing, don't worry about it.

4.   HOW DO WE DECIDE WHETHER AN AGREEMENT IS "INTEGRATED"

We have seen that the rule known as the "parol evidence rule" comes into play only if we have an "integrated" agreement, that is, the parties have reduced their understanding to a comprehensive writing that is a complete and final expression of the parties' agreement. The three cases that follow deal with the issue of *whether* the parties have adopted an integration of their understanding. First, consider who decides that question, judge or jury? Although the issue seems to be one of fact—did the parties intend that the writing was to be a complete and exclusive statement of their agreement—it is well settled that this issue is decided by the judge, not the jury. Thus, Restatement § 209(2) says that "whether there is an integrated agreement is to be determined *by the court* as a question preliminary to determination of a question of interpretation or to application of the parol evidence rule." (emphasis added)

A more difficult question, on which different jurisdictions differ, is how the judge is to decide whether the written agreement should be treated as an integrated agreement. As you read these cases, look very carefully at this issue. Suppose that you are a trial judge in a jury trial in a case presenting facts identical to those in these cases, and suppose that you are in the jurisdiction which decided each of the following cases. In a pre-trial conference, or at a side bar at trial, one side makes an offer of proof of the alleged side deal. You, as trial judge, have to decide whether to allow the jury to hear the evidence of the alleged side deal. That depends on whether the written agreement should be treated as an integrated agreement. But, how are you as the judge to decide whether the written agreement should be treated as an integrated agreement? Are you as judge supposed to consider evidence? If so, there will need to be a preliminary hearing to present evidence on this question. If you as the judge decide that the written agreement is not to be treated as an integrated agreement, then the evidence of the alleged side deal can be presented to the jury.

Gianni v. R. Russel & Co.

Supreme Court of Pennsylvania, 1924.
281 Pa. 320, 126 A 791.

■ SCHAFFER, J.

Plaintiff had been a tenant of a room in an office building in Pittsburgh wherein he conducted a store, selling tobacco, fruit, candy and soft drinks. Defendant acquired the entire property in which the storeroom was located, and its agent negotiated with plaintiff for a further leasing of the room. A lease for three years was signed. It contained a provision that the lessee should 'use the premises only for the sale of fruit, candy, soda water,' etc., with the further stipulation that 'it is expressly understood that the tenant is not allowed to sell tobacco in any form, under penalty of instant forfeiture of this lease.' The document was prepared following a discussion about renting the room between the parties and after an agreement to lease had been reached. It was signed after it had been left in plaintiff's hands and admittedly had been read over to him by two persons, one of whom was his daughter.

Plaintiff sets up that in the course of his dealings with defendant's agent it was agreed that, in consideration of his promises not to sell tobacco and to pay an increased rent, and for entering into the agreement as a whole, he should have the exclusive right to sell soft drinks in the building. No such stipulation is contained in the written lease. Shortly after it was signed defendant demised the adjoining room in the building to a drug company without restricting the latter's right to sell soda water and soft drinks. Alleging that this was in violation of the contract which defendant had made with him, and that the sale of these beverages by the drug company had greatly reduced his receipts and profits, plaintiff brought this action for damages for breach of the alleged oral contract, and was permitted to recover. Defendant has appealed.

Plaintiff's evidence was to the effect that the oral agreement had been made at least two days, possibly longer, before the signing of the instrument, and that it was repeated at the time he signed; that, relying upon it, he executed the lease. Plaintiff called one witness who said he heard defendant's agent say to plaintiff at a time admittedly several days before the execution of the lease that he would have the exclusive right to sell soda water and soft drinks, to which the latter replied if that was the case he accepted the tenancy. Plaintiff produced no witness who was present when the contract was executed to corroborate his statement as to what then occurred. Defendant's agent denied that any such agreement was made, either preliminary to or at the time of the execution of the lease.

Appellee's counsel argues this is not a case in which an endeavor is being made to reform a written instrument because of something omitted as a result of fraud, accident, or mistake, but is one involving the breach of an independent oral agreement which does not belong in the writing at all and is not germane to its provisions. We are unable to reach this conclusion.

> 'Where parties, without any fraud or mistake, have deliberately put their engagements in writing, the law declares the writing to be not only the best, but the only evidence of their agreement.' * * *

> 'All preliminary negotiations, conversations and verbal agreements are merged in and superseded by the subsequent written contract, * * * and 'unless fraud, accident, or mistake be averred, the writing constitutes the agreement between the parties, and its terms cannot be added to nor subtracted from by parol evidence." *Union Storage Co. v. Speck*, 194 Pa. 126, 133, 45 A. 48, 49 * * *.

The writing must be the entire contract between the parties if parol evidence is to be excluded, and to determine whether it is or not the writing will be looked at, and if it appears to be a contract complete within itself, 'couched in such terms as import a complete legal obligation without any uncertainty as to the object or extent of the engagement, it is conclusively presumed that the whole engagement of the parties, and the extent and manner of their undertaking, were reduced to writing.' *Seitz v. Brewers' Refrigerating Machine Co.*, 141 U. S. 510, 517, 12 S. Ct. 46, 48 (35 L. Ed. 837).

When does the oral agreement come within the field embraced by the written one? This can be answered by comparing the two, and determining whether parties, situated as were the ones to the contract, would naturally and normally include the one in the other if it were made. If they relate to the same subject-matter, and are so interrelated that both would be executed at the same time and in the same contract, the scope of the subsidiary agreement must be taken to be covered by the writing. This question must be determined by the court.

In the case at bar the written contract stipulated for the very sort of thing which plaintiff claims has no place in it. It covers the use to which the storeroom was to be put by plaintiff and what he was and what he was not to sell therein. He was 'to use the premises only for the sale of fruit, candy, soda water,' etc., and was not 'allowed to sell tobacco in any form.' Plaintiff claims his agreement not to sell tobacco was part of the consideration for the exclusive right to sell soft drinks. Since his promise to refrain was included in the writing, it would be the natural thing to have included the promise of exclusive rights. Nothing can be imagined more pertinent to these provisions which were included than the one appellee avers.

In cases of this kind, where the cause of action rests entirely on an alleged oral understanding concerning a subject which is dealt with in a written contract it is presumed that the writing was intended to set forth the entire agreement as to that particular subject.

> 'In deciding upon this intent [as to whether a certain subject was intended to be embodied by the writing], the chief and most satisfactory index . . . is found in the circumstance whether or not the particular element of the alleged extrinsic negotiation is dealt with at all in the writing. If it is mentioned, covered, or dealt with in the writing, then presumably the writing was meant to represent all of the transaction on that element, if it is not, then probably the writing was not intended to embody that element of the negotiation.' Wigmore on Evidence (2d Ed.) vol. 5, p. 309.

As the written lease is the complete contract of the parties, and since it embraces the field of the alleged oral contract, evidence of the latter is inadmissible under the parol evidence rule. . . .

We have stated on several occasions recently that we propose to stand for the integrity of written contracts. * * * We reiterate our position in this regard.

The judgment of the court below is reversed, and is here entered for defendant.

Masterson v. Sine

Supreme Court of California, 1968.
68 Cal.2d 222, 436 P.2d 561.

■ Traynor, Chief Justice.

Dallas Masterson and his wife Rebecca owned a ranch as tenants in common. On February 25, 1958, they conveyed it to Medora and Lu Sine by a grant deed 'Reserving unto the Grantors herein an option to purchase the above described property on or before February 25, 1968' for the 'same consideration as being paid heretofore plus their depreciation value of any improvements Grantees may add to the property from and after two and a half years from this date.' Medora is Dallas' sister and Lu's wife. Since the conveyance Dallas has been adjudged bankrupt. His trustee in bankruptcy and Rebecca brought this declaratory relief action to establish their right to enforce the option.

The case was tried without a jury. Over defendants' objection the trial court admitted extrinsic evidence that by 'the same consideration as being paid heretofore' both the grantors and the grantees meant the sum of $50,000 and by 'depreciation value of any improvements' they meant the depreciation value of improvements to be computed by deducting from the total amount of any capital expenditures made by defendants grantees the amount of depreciation allowable to them under United States income tax regulations as of the time of the exercise of the option.

The court also determined that the parol evidence rule precluded admission of extrinsic evidence offered by defendants to show that the parties wanted the property kept in the Masterson family and that the option was therefore personal to the grantors and could not be exercised by the trustee in bankruptcy.

Defendants appeal. They contend that the option provision is too uncertain to be enforced and that extrinsic evidence as to its meaning should not have been admitted. The trial court properly refused to frustrate the obviously declared intention of the grantors to reserve an option to repurchase by an overly meticulous insistence on completeness and clarity of written expression. * * * It properly admitted extrinsic evidence to explain the language of the deed * * * to the end that the consideration for the option would appear with sufficient certainty to permit specific enforcement * * * The trial court erred, however, in excluding the extrinsic evidence that the option was personal to the grantors and therefore nonassignable.

When the parties to a written contract have agreed to it as an 'integration'—a complete and final embodiment of the terms of an agreement—parol evidence cannot be used to add to or vary its terms. * * * When only part of the agreement is integrated, the same rule applies to that part, but parol evidence may be used to prove elements of the agreement not reduced to writing. * * *

The crucial issue in determining whether there has been an integration is whether the parties intended their writing to serve as the exclusive embodiment of their agreement. The instrument itself may help to resolve that issue. It may state, for example, that 'there are no previous understandings or agreements not contained in the writing,' and thus express the parties' 'intention to nullify antecedent understandings or agreements.' (See 3 Corbin, Contracts (1960) § 578, p. 411.) Any such collateral agreement itself must be examined, however, to determine whether the parties intended the subjects of negotiation it deals with to be included in, excluded from, or otherwise affected by the writing. Circumstances at the time of the writing may also aid in the determination of such integration. * * *

California cases have stated that whether there was an integration is to be determined solely from the face of the instrument * * * and that the question for the court is whether it 'appears to be a complete . . . agreement . . . .' * * * Neither of these strict formulations of the rule, however, has been consistently applied. The requirement that the writing must appear incomplete on its face has been repudiated in many cases where parol evidence was admitted 'to prove the existence of a separate oral agreement as to any matter on which the document is silent and which is not inconsistent with its terms'—even though the instrument appeared to state a complete agreement. * * * Even under the rule that the writing alone is to be consulted, it was found necessary to examine the alleged collateral agreement before concluding that proof of it was precluded by the writing alone. (See 3 Corbin, Contracts (1960) § 582, pp. 444—446.) It is therefore evident that 'The conception of a writing as wholly and intrinsically self-determinative of the parties' intent to make it a sole memorial of one or seven or twenty-seven subjects of negotiation is an impossible one.' (9 Wigmore, Evidence (3d ed. 1940) § 2431, p. 103.) For example, a promissory note given by a debtor to his creditor may integrate all their present contractual rights and obligations, or it may be only a minor part of an underlying executory contract that would never be discovered by examining the face of the note.

In formulating the rule governing parol evidence, several policies must be accommodated. One policy is based on the assumption that written evidence is more accurate than human memory. * * * This policy, however, can be adequately served by excluding parol evidence of agreements that directly contradict the writing. Another policy is based on the fear that fraud or unintentional invention by witnesses interested in the outcome of the litigation will mislead the finder of facts. * * * McCormick has suggested that the party urging the spoken as against the written word is most often the economic underdog, threatened by severe hardship if the writing is enforced. In his view the parol evidence rule arose to allow the court to control the tendency of the jury to find through sympathy and without a dispassionate assessment of the probability of fraud or faulty memory that the parties made an oral agreement collateral to the written contract, or that preliminary tentative agreements were not abandoned when omitted from the writing. (See McCormick, Evidence (1954) § 210.) He recognizes, however, that if this theory were adopted in disregard of all other considerations, it would lead to the exclusion of testimony concerning oral agreements whenever there is a writing and thereby often defeat the true intent of the parties. See McCormick, op. cit. supra, § 216, p. 441.)

Evidence of oral collateral agreements should be excluded only when the fact finder is likely to be misled. The rule must therefore be based on the credibility of the evidence. One such standard, adopted by section 240(1)(b) of the Restatement of Contracts, permits proof of a collateral agreement if it 'is such an agreement as might *naturally* be made as a separate agreement by parties situated as were the parties to the written contract.' (Italics added; see McCormick, Evidence (1954) § 216, p. 441; see also 3 Corbin, Contracts (1960) § 583, p. 475, § 594, pp. 568—569; 4 Williston, Contracts (3d ed. 1961) § 638, pp. 1039–1045.) The draftsmen of the Uniform Commercial Code would exclude the evidence in still fewer instances: 'If the additional terms are such that, if agreed upon, they would *certainly* have been included in the document in the view of the court, then evidence of their alleged making must be kept from the trier of fact.' (Com. 3, § 2–202, italics added.)

The option clause in the deed in the present case does not explicitly provide that it contains the complete agreement, and the deed is silent on the question of assignability. Moreover, the difficulty of accommodating the formalized structure of a deed to the insertion of collateral agreements makes it less likely that all the terms of such an agreement were included. * * * The statement of the reservation of the option might well have been placed in the recorded deed solely to preserve the grantors' rights against any possible future purchasers and this function could well be served without any mention of the parties' agreement that the option was personal. There is nothing in the record to indicate that the parties to this family transaction, through experience in land transactions or otherwise, had any warning of the disadvantages of failing to put the whole agreement in the deed. This case is one, therefore, in which it can be said that a collateral agreement such as that alleged 'might naturally be made as a separate agreement.' A fortiori, the case is not one in which the parties 'would certainly' have included the collateral agreement in the deed. * * *

It is contended, however, that an option agreement is ordinarily presumed to be assignable if it contains no provisions forbidding its transfer or indicating that its performance involves elements personal to the parties. * * * The fact that there is a written memorandum, however, does not necessarily preclude parol evidence rebutting a term that the law would otherwise presume.

. . .

In the present case defendants offered evidence that the parties agreed that the option was not assignable in order to keep the property in the Masterson family. The trial court erred in excluding that evidence.

The judgment is reversed.

■ PETERS, TOBRINER, MOSK, and SULLIVAN, JJ., concur.

DISSENTING OPINION

■ BURKE, JUSTICE.

I dissent. The majority opinion:

(1) Undermines the parol evidence rule as we have known it in this state since at least 1872 by declaring that parol evidence should have been admitted by the trial court to show that a written option, absolute and unrestricted in form, was intended to be limited and nonassignable;

(2) Renders suspect instruments of conveyance absolute on their face;

(3) Materially lessens the reliance which may be placed upon written instruments affecting the title to real estate; and

(4) Opens the door, albeit unintentionally to a new technique for the defrauding of creditors.

The opinion permits defendants to establish by parol testimony that their grant to their brother (and brother-in-law) of a written option, absolute in terms, was nevertheless agreed to be nonassignable by the grantee (now a bankrupt), and that therefore the right to exercise it did not pass, by operation of the bankruptcy laws, to the trustee for the benefit of the grantee's creditors.

And how was this to be shown? By the proffered testimony of the bankrupt optionee himself! Thereby one of his assets (the option to purchase defendants' California ranch) would be withheld from the trustee in bankruptcy and from the bankrupt's creditors. Understandably the trial court, as required by the parol evidence rule, did not allow the bankrupt by parol to so contradict the unqualified language of the written option.

The court properly admitted parol evidence to explain the intended meaning of the 'same consideration' and 'depreciation value' phrases of the written option to purchase defendants' land, as the intended meaning of those phrases was not clear. However, there was nothing ambiguous about the *granting* language of the option and not the slightest suggestion in the document that the option was to be nonassignable. Thus, to permit such words of limitation to be added by parol is to *contradict* the absolute nature of the grant, and to directly violate the parol evidence rule.

Just as it is unnecessary to state in a deed to 'lot X' that the house located thereon goes with the land, it is likewise unnecessary to add to 'I grant an option to Jones' the words *'and his assigns'* for the option to be assignable. As hereinafter emphasized in more detail, California statutes expressly declare that it is assignable, and only if I add language in writing showing my intent to withhold or restrict the right of assignment may the grant be so limited. Thus, to seek to restrict the grant by parol is to *contradict* the written document in violation of the parol evidence rule.

The majority opinion arrives at its holding via a series of false premises which are not supported either in the record of this case or in such California authorities as are offered.

The parol evidence rule is set forth in clear and definite language in the statutes of this state. (Civ.Code, § 1625; Code Civ.Proc., § 1856.) It 'is not a rule of evidence but is one of substantive law. . . . The rule as applied to contracts is simply that as a matter of substantive law, a certain act, the act of embodying the complete terms of an agreement in a writing (the 'integration'), becomes the contract of the parties.' * * * The rule is based upon the sound principle that the parties to a written instrument, after committing their agreement to or evidencing it by the writing, are not permitted to add to, vary or *contradict* the terms of the writing by parol evidence. As aptly expressed by the author of the present majority opinion, speaking for the court in *Parsons v. Bristol Development Co.* (1965) 62 Cal.2d 861, 865(2), 44 Cal.Rptr. 767, 402 P.2d 839, * * *, such evidence is 'admissible to interpret the instrument, but *not* to give it a meaning to which it is not reasonably susceptible.' (Italics added.) Or, as stated by the same author, concurring in *Laux v. Freed* (1960) 53 Cal.2d 512, 527, 2 Cal.Rptr. 265, 273, 348 P.2d 873, 881, 'extrinsic evidence is not admissible to 'add to, *detract* from, or vary its terms." (Italics added.)

. . .

The right of an optionee to transfer his option to purchase property is accordingly one of the basic rights which accompanies the option unless limited under the language of the option itself. To allow an optionor to resort to parol evidence to support his assertion that the written option is not transferable is to authorize him to limit the option by attempting to restrict and reclaim rights with which he has already parted. A clearer violation of two substantive and basic rules of law—the parol evidence rule and the right of free transferability of property—would be difficult to conceive. . . .

This new rule, not hitherto recognized in California, provides that proof of a claimed collateral oral agreement is admissible if it is such an agreement as might *naturally* have been made a separate agreement by the parties under the particular circumstances. I submit that this approach opens the door to uncertainty and confusion. Who can know what its limits are? Certainly I do not. For example, in its application to this case who could be expected to divine as 'natural' a separate oral agreement between the parties that the assignment, absolute and unrestricted on its face, was intended by the parties to be limited to the Masterson family?

Or, assume that one gives to his relative a promissory note and that the payee of the note goes bankrupt. By operation of law the note becomes an asset of the bankruptcy. The trustee attempts to enforce it. Would the relatives be permitted to testify that by a separate oral agreement made at the time of the execution of the note it was understood that should the payee fail in his business the maker would be excused from payment of the note, or that, as here, it was intended that the benefits of the note would be *personal* to the payee? I doubt that trial judges should be burdened with the task of conjuring whether it would have been 'natural under those circumstances for such a separate agreement to have been made by the parties. Yet, under the application of the proposed rule, this is the task the trial judge would have, and in essence the situation presented in the instant case is no different.

. . .

In an effort to provide justification for applying the newly pronounced 'natural' rule to the circumstances of the present case, the majority opinion next attempts to account for the silence of the writing in this case concerning assignability of the option, by asserting that 'the difficulty of accommodating the formalized structure of a deed to the insertion of collateral agreements makes it less likely that all the terms of such an agreement were included.' What difficulty would have been involved here, to add the words 'this option is nonassignable'? The asserted 'formalized structure of a deed' is no formidable barrier. The Legislature has set forth the requirements in simple language in section 1092 of the Civil Code. It is this: 'I, A B, grant to C D all that real property situated in (naming county), State of California * * * described as follows: (describing it).' To this the grantor desiring to reserve an option to repurchase need only so state, as was done here. It is a matter of common knowledge that collateral agreements (such as the option clause here involved, or such as deed restrictions) are frequently included in deeds, without difficulty of any nature.

. . . [T]he majority assert that 'There is *nothing* in the record to indicate that the parties to this family transaction, through experience in land transactions or otherwise, had any warning of the disadvantages of failing to put the whole agreement in the deed.' (Italics added.) The facts of this case, however, do not support such claim of naivete. The grantor husband (the bankrupt businessman) testified that as none of the parties were attorneys 'we wanted to contact my attorney . . . which we did. . . . The wording in the option was obtained from (the attorney). . . . I told him what my discussion was with the Sines (defendant grantees) and he wanted . . . a little time to compose it . . . . And, then this (the wording provided by the attorney) was taken to the title company at the time Mr. and Mrs. Sine and I went in to *complete* the transaction.' (Italics added.) The witness was an experienced businessman who thus demonstrated awareness of the wisdom of seeking legal guidance and advice in this business transaction, and who did so. Wherein lies the family transaction postulated by the majority?

. . .

Comment hardly seems necessary on the convenience to a bankrupt of such a device to defeat his creditors. He need only produce parol testimony that any options (or other property, for that matter) which he holds are subject to an oral 'collateral agreement' with family members (or with friends) that the property is nontransferable 'in order to keep the property in the family' on in the friendly group. In the present case the value of the ranch which the bankrupt and his wife held an option to purchase has doubtless increased substantially during the years since they acquired the option. The initiation of this litigation by the trustee in bankruptcy to establish his right to enforce the option indicates his belief that there is substantial value to be gained for the creditors from this asset of the bankrupt. Yet the majority opinion permits defeat of the trustee and of the creditors through the device of an asserted collateral oral agreement that the option was 'personal' to the bankrupt and nonassignable 'in order to keep the property in the family'! . . .

I would hold that the trial court ruled correctly on the proffered parol evidence, and would affirm the judgment.

■ McComb, J., concurs.

Notes

Some background information helps to understand the *Masterson v. Sine* facts. Dallas Masterson and his wife had conveyed the property to Medora Sine (Dallas' sister) and her husband. The deed contained the option that is the focus of the dispute, that is, the grantees (Sines) promised to convey the property back to the grantors (Mastersons). Dallas Masterson became bankrupt. The trustee in bankruptcy searched for assets to distribute to Dallas' creditors. Think about the option. If, as seems likely, the property is now worth much more than at the time of the conveyance from the Mastersons to the Sines, then that option is itself a valuable asset. Suppose, for example that the original price was $50,000 and that the property is now worth $200,000. The trustee in bankruptcy might exercise the option, pay $50,000 for the property and then sell it to someone else for $200,000. That would mean there would be $150,000 more to distribute to the creditors. Ordinarily a deed conveying any interest in property—such as the option involved in the case—would mean that the interest runs to the grantee or anyone else to whom the grantee assigns the interest, whether voluntarily or by operation of law. (As a matter of bankruptcy law, the trustee in bankruptcy succeeds, by operation of law, to any interest in property held by the bankrupt). The Sines contended (and, of course, the Masterson did not dispute) that there was a side deal that the option could only be exercised by the Mastersons themselves, not by anyone to whom their interest was assigned. Hence the issue in the case of whether that alleged side deal survived the execution of the deed.

Moore v. Pennsylvania Castle Energy Corp.

United States Court of Appeals, Eleventh Circuit, 1996.
89 F.3d 791.

■ ANDERSON, CIRCUIT JUDGE.

In this diversity case involving Alabama law, Pennsylvania Castle Energy Corporation ("Penn Castle") appeals from a final judgment entered in the district court upon a jury verdict in favor of plaintiff Gladys Moore. The issue raised by Penn Castle on appeal concerns the introduction of parol evidence to vary the terms of a written agreement, which Penn Castle claims is complete and unambiguous. . . .

Because we conclude that the district court erred in admitting the parol evidence, we reverse the judgment entered in favor of Moore. . . .

I.   FACTS

Moore owns the surface rights to several hundred acres of land in Tuscaloosa County, Alabama; however, she does not own the subsurface minerals and mineral rights. In 1907, Moore's predecessor-in-interest conveyed by severance deed the title to all minerals in the land, along with certain rights to use the surface land in the extraction of the minerals. Penn Castle is the lessee of the subsurface mineral estate and all rights appurtenant thereto. Penn Castle acquired this leasehold interest by assignment from TRW, Inc. ("TRW") in 1990.

Under Alabama law and the terms of the severance deed, TRW had the right to enter and to make reasonable use of Moore's land to explore, develop, and produce subsurface minerals, including coalbed methane gas. * * * Notwithstanding this right of reasonable surface use, Penn Castle presented evidence that producers in the Alabama coalbed methane industry often negotiate "surface access and surface damage agreements" with surface estate owners. The purpose of such agreements is to avoid litigation by compensating surface estate owners for any damage that might be caused by the use of the surface property in the extraction of minerals.

In 1983, TRW became interested in drilling several wells on Moore's property, and in entering a surface access and surface damage agreement with Moore. As negotiations progressed during the spring of 1983, TRW representatives met with Moore and spoke to her by telephone several times. During this period, TRW sent Moore a map of her property, which indicated the locations of six proposed gas well drill sites. On August 2, 1983, Moore and her son Gene Moore met with several TRW representatives at Moore's house, with the map spread across a table. According to the trial testimony of Moore and her son, she and the TRW representatives reached an oral agreement after three hours of negotiation. The parties orally agreed to the following terms: (1) TRW would never drill more than six gas wells on Moore's property; (2) TRW would drill these gas wells in accordance with the six drill sites indicated on the map; and (3) TRW would never drill a gas well in a fifty-acre field on the Moore property (the "Field"). These three oral understandings were not reduced to writing that day.

On the next day, a TRW representative came to Moore's house and dropped off a proposed written contract. In this proposal, TRW promised to pay Moore $10,000 in exchange for a "perpetual easement with the right to construct six (6) drill sites for drilling and production of coalbed methane gas, construction of necessary access roads, installation of power lines and gathering systems and other coalbed methane gas recovery activity. . . ." The $10,000 was to constitute "full and complete payment for any and all damages to and/or loss of trees and vegetation, easements and drill sites for six (6) coalbed methane gas wells." The locations of two of the six drill sites were specified in the written proposal. With respect to the four remaining drill sites contemplated, the written proposal provided as follows:

> It is agreed and understood that TRW will discuss with Surface Owner the easement and drill site locations for the remaining four (4) coalbed methane gas wells of which TRW has the final decision for location. Each of the four (4) drill sites will not exceed one (1) acre and the associated easement for the four (4) drill sites will not exceed three (3) net acres. Should additional easement be required, TRW will remunerate Surface Owner at the rate of Six Hundred Dollars ($600.00) per net acre.

Moore expressed disagreement about the last sentence of the above-quoted paragraph, and it was changed to read: "Should additional easement be required, TRW will remunerate Surface Owner at a rate to be negotiated per net acre."

On August 5, 1983, Moore and her son met with the TRW representatives again. After making and initialing a correction to a description of the location of "Well Site 1" in paragraph two, Moore signed the proposed contract (hereinafter, the "written agreement"). The written agreement includes the modified language in paragraph two, and an attached "Exhibit A," referred to in paragraph two, which more specifically describes the locations of the two drill sites and associated easements. The written agreement does not incorporate or otherwise refer to the map, nor does it mention TRW's oral promise never to drill more than six wells. The written agreement also does not mention the oral promise not to drill in the Field. To the contrary, the written agreement states that "TRW has the final decision for location" with respect to the four remaining drill sites contemplated by the written agreement. Nevertheless, Moore and her son testified that at the August 5, 1983, meeting, TRW representatives repeated the oral assurances that TRW would drill its gas wells only in accordance with the drill sites indicated on the map, and that it would never drill in the Field. After hearing these oral assurances, Moore signed the written agreement.

Between December of 1983 and August of 1984, TRW and Moore executed three supplemental letter agreements, each of which described an additional drill site on Moore's property (for a total of five). Although none of the supplemental letter agreements mentioned the map or the oral promise not to drill on the Field, all five of the drill sites chosen by TRW roughly corresponded to the sites on the map, and TRW did not drill on the Field. TRW completed its drilling on the Moore property in late 1984, apparently without having chosen a sixth drill site.

In 1990, TRW assigned its lease to the defendant, Penn Castle. Beginning in October of 1992, a representative of Penn Castle contacted Moore in an effort to negotiate additional drill sites. However, Moore and her son told Penn Castle that they were not amenable to additional wells. Several subsequent attempts to negotiate additional drill sites failed. Unable to reach a compromise, Penn Castle began constructing an access road and drill pad in the middle of the Field on December 26, 1992.

II. PROCEDURAL HISTORY

On August 24, 1993, Moore filed this action against Penn Castle in Alabama state court, stating claims for breach of oral contract and trespass. Penn Castle removed the case to federal court based on diversity of citizenship. *See* 28 U.S.C. § 1332. The case proceeded to trial.

During the trial, the district court admitted evidence of the oral conversations between Moore and TRW over Penn Castle's objection that such negotiations were merged into the written agreement. Penn Castle similarly objected to the admission of the map into evidence, but the district court overruled the objection. . . .

III. DISCUSSION

We address only one issue on appeal: whether the district court erred in permitting Moore to present evidence of her alleged oral agreement with TRW.[2] Under Alabama law, once the parties to a contract have reduced their agreement to writing, all prior statements, promises, and negotiations are merged into the resulting written document. *See Guilford v. Spartan Food Systems, Inc.,* 372 So.2d 7 (Ala.1979) (noting that it is presumed at law that "all prior negotiations are merged into the written contract, which purports to cover the entire transaction"). In the absence of fraud, mistake, or illegality, parol evidence is not admissible to explain, contradict, vary, add to, or subtract from the express terms of a complete and unambiguous written agreement. *See Lake*

---

[2]   This issue is dispositive: Moore's entire case depends upon the oral promises allegedly made by TRW. Moore does not argue that Penn Castle breached any term of the written agreement. In addition, Moore offered no evidence, and makes no argument, that Penn Castle's use of her land was unreasonable, and thus not within the common-law right of reasonable use. Similarly, Moore's trespass claim also depends entirely on the alleged oral promises. Moore's only argument in support of her trespass claim is that the breach of the oral agreement automatically resulted in a trespass to her property.

Martin/Alabama Power Licensee Assoc., Inc. v. Alabama Power Co., Inc., 601 So.2d 942, 945 (Ala.1992).

Moore . . . contends that the written document does not reflect the complete agreement of the parties, and that extrinsic evidence of their "true agreement" is therefore admissible. . . .

. . .

Moore's second argument in support of the district court's admission of the parol evidence is that the parties did not intend the written instrument to embody their complete agreement. "The parol evidence rule is based upon the idea that a completely integrated writing, executed by the parties, contains all of the stipulations, engagements, and promises that the parties intended to make, and that all of the previous negotiations, conversations, and parol agreements are merged into the terms of the instrument." *Quimby v. Memorial Parks, Inc.,* 667 So.2d 1353, 1357 (Ala.1995) (quoting *Alfa Mutual Ins. Co. v. Northington,* 561 So.2d 1041, 1044 (Ala.1990)). In light of its purpose, "[t]he parol evidence rule . . . does not apply to every contract of which there exists written evidence, but applies only when the parties to an agreement reduce it to writing, and agree or intend that the writing shall be their complete agreement." *Hibbett Sporting Goods, Inc. v. Biernbaum,* 375 So.2d 431, 434 (Ala.1979) * * *. Accordingly, prior negotiations and oral conversations merge into a resulting written instrument only if that instrument was actually intended to contain the parties' entire agreement. *See Hibbett,* 375 So.2d at 436 . . .

"(1) The agreement must in form be a collateral one; (2) it must not contradict express or implied provisions of the written contract; (3) it must be one that parties would not ordinarily be expected to embody in the writing. . . ."

Id. at 353 (quoting *Mitchill v. Lath,* 247 N.Y. 377, 160 N.E. 646, 647 (1928) * * *.

Examining the written agreement itself, as well as the surrounding circumstances, we conclude that the written instrument was intended to be a complete integration of the parties' agreement. Therefore, the alleged oral agreement between Moore and TRW merged into the written document as a matter of law. Several considerations persuade us to reach this conclusion.

First, we note that the written agreement itself is a formal document that appears to embody all the terms of the parties' agreement with respect to the six wells, as opposed to an informal memorandum not purporting to be complete. *Cf. I.H.M. v. Central Bank of Montgomery,* 340 So.2d 30, 33 (Ala.1976) (parol evidence held admissible because document at issue was intended only as an informal, preliminary memorandum of agreement).[3] Also, Moore studied the written document

---

[3]   Moore points out that the written document does not contain an integration, or merger, clause, which states that the written document expresses the complete agreement of the parties

and insisted upon certain changes before she agreed to sign it, which indicates that she recognized the importance of the written document in governing the parties' relationship. Moore's conduct also indicates that she had the opportunity to require TRW to put its alleged oral promises in writing.

Second, with respect to TRW's alleged oral promises relating to the location of the wells, we note that the written agreement directly addresses that same subject. The written agreement specifically describes the location of two wells, and provides that "TRW has the final decision for location" of the remaining four wells. The alleged oral agreement that TRW would drill its wells only in accordance with the sites indicated on the map, and that TRW would never drill in the Field, is inconsistent with this language. If the parties wished to confine TRW to the drill sites shown on the map, then presumably they would have described all six sites (rather than just two) in the written agreement, and they would not have left the location of four of the sites to TRW's absolute discretion.

Third, we find that TRW's alleged oral promise never to drill more than six wells on the Moore property is not collateral to the written agreement, and therefore that this promise also merged into the written agreement. The purpose of the written agreement was to define the parties' rights and obligations with respect to TRW's contemplated extraction of methane gas from the Moore property. Accordingly, any forfeiture of TRW's common-law right to drill more than six wells would reasonably be expected to appear in the written document. Although Moore agreed to accept $10,000 as full payment for any damage which might be occasioned by TRW's construction and operation of six coalbed methane gas wells, nowhere in the written agreement does TRW trade away its common-law right to drill additional wells, if drilling such additional wells is reasonably necessary to extract the methane gas. We conclude that the parol evidence rule bars the admission of TRW's alleged oral promise never to drill more than six wells.

. . .

---

and that all prior negotiations are merged into the written document. Basically, an integration clause "is a portion of a particular contract that restates the rationale of the parol evidence rule within the terms of the contract." *Environmental Systems, Inc. v. Rexham Corp.,* 624 So.2d 1379, 1383 (Ala.1993). The presence or absence of an integration clause may be a significant, although not a conclusive, factor in ascertaining whether the parties intended the written instrument to be a complete integration. *See, e.g., Chandler v. Lamar County Bd. of Educ.,* 528 So.2d 309, 313 (Ala.1988) (citing the absence of an integration clause as one reason for the court to examine parol evidence); *Colafrancesco v. Crown Pontiac-GMC, Inc.,* 485 So.2d 1131, 1133 (Ala.1986) (citing the presence of a merger clause as a reason to exclude parol evidence). *See also* II Farnsworth on Contracts § 7.3, at 204–07 (1990). Stated differently, the absence of a merger clause does not preclude a finding that a written contract constitutes an integration of the parties' entire agreement. *See, e.g., Jake C. Byers, Inc. v. J.B.C. Investments,* 834 S.W.2d 806, 813 (Mo.App.1992) ("The existence of a merger clause may be a strong indication the writing is intended to be complete, but its existence is not necessarily determinative. More important, the absence of a merger clause is likewise not determinative; the writing still may be complete on its face.") . . .

IV. CONCLUSION

Without the parol evidence admitted by the district court, Moore's breach of contract and trespass claims fail as a matter of Alabama law. Accordingly, the judgment of the district court that was entered upon the jury verdict in favor of Moore is REVERSED. We REMAND the case to the district court for judgment to be entered for Penn Castle.

NOTES & QUESTIONS

1.   Compare the statements of law in the three cases, above. Do you think the legal differences have a practical impact? Come up with your own hypothetical set of facts where you would prefer to be located in California, under *Masterson v. Sine*, rather than in Pennsylvania, under *Gianni v. R. Russel & Co.*

2.   By giving an account of the history of the parol evidence rule, one commentator has suggested that adherence to it tends to place a greater burden on the weaker party, often with gendered results: Hila Keren, *Textual Harassment: A New Historicist Reappraisal of the Parol Evidence Rule with Gender in Mind*, 13 Am. U. J. Gender Soc. Pol'y & L. 251, 255–56 (2005). How do you think such a burden might be created, in a general sense?

3.   Consider footnote 2 in *Moore v. Penn Castle*. Are you surprised that the presence of an integration clause does not have a more conclusive effect? Are you surprised that the absence of an integration clause does not have a more conclusive effect? Are these issues—of absence and presence— equivalent?

E. PLAIN MEANING RULE

In all of the case in the preceding section, one party attempted to prove that even though the parties had signed a written agreement, there was some prior "side agreement" that survived execution of the writing. In this section we consider a different, but related problem. Let's assume that we have concluded that the writing is a complete expression of the parties' contract. But suppose that some dispute arises about the meaning of that agreement. What evidence can one introduce to explain the meaning of the written agreement?

No one disputes that if the written agreement is ambiguous on a certain matter, then we can consider extrinsic evidence to explain the meaning of the written agreement. The problem comes when one party contends that the written agreement really means "such and such," while the other party says that the written agreement is clear, and doesn't mean that. Can the proponent of the interpretive issue offer evidence about the parties' prior dealings in the effort to prove the interpretation that party puts forth? Or, should we say that the writing itself settles the interpretation question, so that no extrinsic evidence should be admitted?

Lawyers, including judges, are often not very careful with the language they use to describe these issues. You are going to be among the best lawyers in the country, which means that you will learn to use language precisely, whether or not other lawyers and judges do so. Accordingly:

We shall use the phrase "*parol evidence rule*" when we are asking whether extrinsic evidence can be admitted in support of a party's contention that there is a promise that is not included in the written agreement.

We shall use the phrase "*plain meaning rule*" when we are asking whether extrinsic evidence can be admitted in support of a party's contention that although the writing does set out all of the parties' promises, some of those written promises cannot be properly interpreted without considering extrinsic evidence, such as evidence of the parties' prior discussions.

As we shall see, the cases on interpretation show a divergence of approach that is very much analogous to the divergence in the "parol evidence rule" cases. Thus, as we will see, the *Dennison v. Harden* case on the admissibility of evidence on interpretation takes a fairly rigid approach, very much like the *Gianni v. Russel* case on the "parol evidence rule." The *Pacific Gas & Electric Co.* case takes a very expansive view of the admissibility of evidence on interpretation, much like the *Masterson v. Sine* case on the "parol evidence rule."

Dennison v. Harden

Supreme Court of Washington, Department 1, 1947.
29 Wash.2d 243, 186 P.2d 908.

■ HILL, JUSTICE.

On May 12, 1943, the appellant and his wife and the respondents entered into an executory real estate contract whereby the respondents agreed to sell, and the appellant and his wife agreed to purchase, for twelve thousand dollars,

'the following described lot, tract, or parcel of land situated in King County, State of Washington, to-wit:

'TL–17 that portion of NE ¼ OF SE ¼, LY N of Ethel O. Peck Rd Less S 96' of W. 417.39' Thereof, Sec. 8 Twp 22 Range 4.

'Purchase price to include property and fruit trees, all tools, tractor, truck, fertilizer, etc., fruit trees, berry bushes, and crops in ground.

'With the appurtenances thereto belonging.'

One thousand dollars was paid on the execution of the contract, and the balance was to be paid in installments of fifty dollars a month.

. . .

Appellant urges that there was a warranty that there were 276 Pacific Gold peach trees, that being the number of trees in the so-called 'commercial orchard.' Appellant expressly disclaims any fraud on the part of the respondents, but insists that there was a breach of the warranty in that the trees were of a scrub or worthless variety, and asks damages therefor. The evidence sustaining this claim of express warranty was that the respondents had represented, on two or three occasions during the preliminary negotiations, that there were 276 Pacific Gold peach trees in the commercial orchard, and had agreed to and did furnish documents from the nursery company which had supplied the trees substantiating the fact that they were Pacific Gold peach trees. These documents were offered and refused as exhibits.

The trial court ultimately became convinced that the parol evidence rule was applicable, and that the evidence which had been received and the exhibits which had been offered, varied and added to the terms of the written contract between the parties. It therefore granted a motion to strike the evidence which had already been admitted, and a judgment of dismissal necessarily followed.

We will not restate or discuss that familiar rule and the reasons for it. * * * It is to be noted that, as cited in *Farley v. Letterman*, 87 Wash. 641, 152 P. 515, 516:

> 'By 'parol' in connection with the present principle is properly meant, not merely oral utterances, but also informal writings, i.e., writings (letters, memoranda, etc.) other than the single and final written memorial. . . .' I Greenleaf on Evidence, 16th Ed., 449, note to § 305g.

Appellant urges four reasons why the evidence concerning the warranty was admissible:

1. It went in without objection. → rejected

The parol evidence rule is not a rule of evidence; it is a rule of substantive law, and testimony falling within the inhibitions of the rule does not become admissible merely because it is not objected to: *Andersonian Inv. Co. v. Wade*, 108 Wash. 373, 184 P. 327. * * *.

2. It was within an exception to the rule permitting parol and extrinsic evidence to 'clarify and properly identify the subject matter of the contract.' → rejected

We assume that the recognized exception to the parol evidence rule that appellant has in mind is that parol evidence is admissible to explain an ambiguity. Appellant argues that because the contract said 'fruit trees' and did not identify the kind, other evidence should have been admitted for that purpose. Appellant states in his reply brief:

> 'The very fact that under the terms of the contract as written by the respondents, the subject-matter is shrouded in

mystery and confusion, demands the admission of parol or extrinsic evidence to clarify this patent ambiguity.'

No question is raised here concerning the meaning of 'etc.,' which is the only word that might call for clarification. We see nothing shrouded in mystery and confusion about 'property and fruit trees' or 'fruit trees, berry bushes, and crops in ground.' The purchaser knew exactly what trees he was getting; the contract called for fruit trees, and he got fruit trees. There would be no patent ambiguity clarified by permitting appellant to add, after 'fruit trees,' the words 'of which 276 are Pacific Gold peach trees.'

. . .[Court's discussion of third and fourth arguments is omitted— mostly because it's hopelessly confused!]

Finding no merit in any of the four arguments advanced by the appellant as to why the evidence stricken by the trial court should have been received, we are of the opinion that the trial court was correct, and the judgment of dismissal which necessarily followed that opinion is affirmed.

Pacific Gas & Elec. Co. v. G. W. Thomas Drayage & Rigging Co.

Supreme Court of California, 1968.
69 Cal.2d 33, 442 P.2d 641.

■ TRAYNOR, CHIEF JUSTICE.

Defendant appeals from a judgment for plaintiff in an action for damages for injury to property under an indemnity clause of a contract.

In 1960 defendant entered into a contract with plaintiff to furnish the labor and equipment necessary to remove and replace the upper metal cover of plaintiff's steam turbine. Defendant agreed to perform the work 'at (its) own risk and expense' and to 'indemnify' plaintiff 'against all loss, damage, expense and liability resulting from . . . injury to property, arising out of or in any way connected with the performance of this contract.' Defendant also agreed to procure not less than $50,000 insurance to cover liability for injury to property. Plaintiff was to be an additional named insured, but the policy was to contain a cross-liability clause extending the coverage to plaintiff's property.

During the work the cover fell and injured the exposed rotor of the turbine. Plaintiff brought this action to recover $25,144.51, the amount it subsequently spent on repairs. During the trial it dismissed a count based on negligence and thereafter secured judgment on the theory that the indemnity provision covered injury to all property regardless of ownership.

Defendant offered to prove by admissions of plaintiff's agents, by defendant's conduct under similar contracts entered into with plaintiff, and by other proof that in the indemnity clause the parties meant to cover injury to property of third parties only and not to plaintiff's property. Although the trial court observed that the language used was 'the classic language for a third party indemnity provision' and that 'one could very easily conclude that . . . its whole intendment is to indemnify third parties,' it nevertheless held that the 'plain language' of the agreement also required defendant to indemnify plaintiff for injuries to plaintiff's property. Having determined that the contract had a plain meaning, the court refused to admit any extrinsic evidence that would contradict its interpretation.

When a court interprets a contract on this basis, it determines the meaning of the instrument in accordance with the 'extrinsic evidence of the judge's own linguistic education and experience.' (3 Corbin on Contracts (1960 ed.) (1964 Supp. § 579, p. 225, fn. 56).) The exclusion of testimony that might contradict the linguistic background of the judge reflects a judicial belief in the possibility of perfect verbal expression. (9 Wigmore on Evidence (3d ed. 1940) § 2461, p. 187.) This belief is a remnant of a primitive faith in the inherent potency[2] and inherent meaning of words.[3]

The test of admissibility of extrinsic evidence to explain the meaning of a written instrument is not whether it appears to the court to be plain and unambiguous on its face, but whether the offered evidence is relevant to prove a meaning to which the language of the instrument is reasonably susceptible. * * *

A rule that would limit the determination of the meaning of a written instrument to its four-corners merely because it seems to the court to be clear and unambiguous, would either deny the relevance of the intention of the parties or presuppose a degree of verbal precision and stability our language has not attained.

Some courts have expressed the opinion that contractual obligations are created by the mere use of certain words, whether or not there was any intention to incur such obligations.[4] Under this view, contractual obligations flow, not from the intention of the parties but from the fact

---

[2]   E.g., 'The elaborate system of taboo and verbal prohibitions in primitive groups; the ancient Egyptian myth of Khern, the apotheosis of the word, and of Thoth, the Scribe of Truth, the Giver of Words and Script, the Master of Incantations; the avoidance of the name of God in Brahmanism, Judaism and Islam; totemistic and protective names in mediaeval Turkish and Finno-Ugrian languages; the misplaced verbal scruples of the 'Pre cieuses'; the Swedish peasant custom of curing sick cattle smitten by witchcraft, by making them swallow a page torn out of the psalter and put in dough.' from Ullman, The Principles of Semantics (1963 ed.) 43. (See also Ogden and Richards, The Meaning of Meaning (rev. ed. 1956) pp. 24–47.)

[3]   "Rerum enim vocabula immutabilia sunt, homines mutabilia," (Words are unchangeable, men changeable) from Dig. XXXIII, 10, 7, § 2, de sup. leg. as quoted in 9 Wigmore on Evidence, op. cit. supra, § 2461, p. 187.

[4]   'A contract has, strictly speaking, nothing to do with the personal, or individual, intent of the parties. A contract is an obligation attached by the mere force of law to certain acts of the parties, usually words, which ordinarily accompany and represent a known intent.' *Hotchkiss v. National City Bank of New York* (S.D.N.Y.1911) 200 F. 287, 293. * * *

that they used certain magic words. Evidence of the parties' intention therefore becomes irrelevant.

In this state, however, the intention of the parties as expressed in the contract is the source of contractual rights and duties.[5] A court must ascertain and give effect to this intention by determining what the parties meant by the words they used. Accordingly, the exclusion of relevant, extrinsic evidence to explain the meaning of a written instrument could be justified only if it were feasible to determine the meaning the parties gave to the words from the instrument alone.

If words had absolute and constant referents, it might be possible to discover contractual intention in the words themselves and in the manner in which they were arranged. Words, however, do not have absolute and constant referents. 'A word is a symbol of thought but has no arbitrary and fixed meaning like a symbol of algebra or chemistry.' (*Pearson v. State Social Welfare Board* (1960) 54 Cal.2d 184, 195, 5 Cal.Rptr. 553, 559, 353 P.2d 33, 39.) The meaning of particular words or groups of words varies with the 'verbal context and surrounding circumstances and purposes in view of the linguistic education and experience of their users and their hearers or readers (not excluding judges). . . . A word has no meaning apart from these factors; much less does it have an objective meaning, one true meaning.' (Corbin, The Interpretation of Words and the Parol Evidence Rule (1965) 50 Cornell L.Q. 161, 187.) Accordingly, the meaning of a writing 'can only be found by interpretation in the light of all the circumstances that reveal the sense in which the writer used the words. The exclusion of parol evidence regarding such circumstances merely because the words do not appear ambiguous to the reader can easily lead to the attribution to a written instrument of a meaning that was never intended. . . .

Although extrinsic evidence is not admissible to add to, detract from, or vary the terms of a written contract, these terms must first be determined before it can be decided whether or not extrinsic evidence is being offered for a prohibited purpose. The fact that the terms of an instrument appear clear to a judge does not preclude the possibility that the parties chose the language of the instrument to express different terms. That possibility is not limited to contracts whose terms have acquired a particular meaning by trade usage,[6] but exists whenever the

---

[5] 'A contract must be so interpreted as to give effect to the mutual intention of the parties as it existed at the time of contracting, so far as the same is ascertainable and lawful.' * * *

[6] Extrinsic evidence of trade usage or custom has been admitted to show that the term 'United Kingdom' in a motion picture distribution contract included Ireland (*Ermolieff v. R.K.O. Radio Pictures* (1942) 19 Cal.2d 543, 549–552, 122 P.2d 3); that the word 'ton' in a lease meant a long ton or 2,240 pounds and not the statutory ton of 2,000 pounds (*Higgins v. Cal. Petroleum Co.* (1898) 120 Cal. 629, 630–632, 52 P. 1080); that the word 'stubble' in a lease included not only stumps left in the ground but everything 'left on the ground after the harvest time' (*Callahan v. Stanley* (1881) 57 Cal. 476, 477–479); [and] that the term 'north' in a contract dividing mining claims indicated a boundary line running along the 'magnetic and not the true meridian' (*Jenny Lind Co. v. Bower & Co.* (1858) 11 Cal. 194, 197–199) . . .

parties' understanding of the words used may have differed from the judge's understanding.

Accordingly, rational interpretation requires at least a preliminary consideration of all credible evidence offered to prove the intention of the parties.[7] * * * Such evidence includes testimony as to the 'circumstances surrounding the making of the agreement . . . including the object, nature and subject matter of the writing' so that the court can 'place itself in the same situation in which the parties found themselves at the time of contracting.' * * * If the court decides, after considering this evidence, that the language of a contract, in the light of all the circumstances, is 'fairly susceptible of either one of the two interpretations contended for . . . .' * * * extrinsic evidence relevant to prove either of such meanings is admissible.[8]

In the present case the court erroneously refused to consider extrinsic evidence offered to show that the indemnity clause in the contract was not intended to cover injuries to plaintiff's property. Although that evidence was not necessary to show that the indemnity clause was reasonably susceptible of the meaning contended for by defendant, it was nevertheless relevant and admissible on that issue. Moreover, since that clause was reasonably susceptible of that meaning, the offered evidence was also admissible to prove that the clause had that meaning and did not cover injuries to plaintiff's property.[9] Accordingly, the judgment must be reversed. . . .

---

[7]   When objection is made to any particular item of evidence offered to prove the intention of the parties, the trial court may not yet be in a position to determine whether in the light of all of the offered evidence, the item objected to will turn out to be admissible as tending to prove a meaning of which the language of the instrument is reasonably susceptible or inadmissible as tending to prove a meaning of which the language is not reasonably susceptible. In such case the court may admit the evidence conditionally by either reserving its ruling on the objection or by admitting the evidence subject to a motion to strike. (See Evid.Code, § 403.)

[8]   Extrinsic evidence has often been admitted in such cases on the stated ground that the contract was ambiguous (*e.g., Universal Sales Corp. v. Cal. Press Mfg. Co., supra,* 20 Cal.2d 751, 761, 128 P.2d 665). This statement of the rule is harmless if it is kept in mind that the ambiguity may be exposed by extrinsic evidence that reveals more than one possible meaning.

[9]   The court's exclusion of extrinsic evidence in this case would be error even under a rule that excluded such evidence when the instrument appeared to the court to be clear and unambiguous on its face. The controversy centers on the meaning of the word 'indemnify' and the phrase 'all loss, damage, expense and liability.' The trial court's recognition of the language as typical of a third party indemnity clause and the double sense in which the word 'indemnify' is used in statutes and defined in dictionaries demonstrate the existence of an ambiguity [citing examples].

Plaintiff's assertion that the use of the word 'all' to modify 'loss, damage, expense and liability' dictates an all inclusive interpretation is not persuasive. If the word 'indemnify' encompasses only third-party claims, the word 'all' simply refers to all such claims. The use of the words 'loss,' 'damage,' and 'expense' in addition to the word 'liability' is likewise inconclusive. These words do not imply an agreement to reimburse for injury to an indemnitee's property since they are commonly inserted in third-party indemnity clauses, to enable an indemnitee who settles a claim to recover from his indemnitor without proving his liability. (* * * Civ.Code, § 2778, provides: '1. Upon an indemnity against liability . . . the person indemnified is entitled to recover upon becoming liable; 2. Upon an indemnity against claims, or demands, or damages, or costs . . . the person indemnified is not entitled to recover without payment thereof.')

The provision that defendant perform the work 'at his own risk and expense' and the provisions relating to insurance are equally inconclusive. By agreeing to work at its own risk

NOTES

The different approaches to interpretation represented above can be categorized (in rather simplified terms) as a formalist position by Justice Hill in *Dennison* and a contextualist approach by Chief Justice Traynor in *Pacific Gas*. We will encounter below a third, middle, approach. In your evaluation of each approach, consider doing so from two standpoints: the *ex ante* and *ex post* perspectives.

The *ex post* perspective is backward looking: its focus is "after the event" when considering the transaction between the parties. It emphasizes the dispute-settlement functions of the courts. It may thus seek to ensure that the breaching party does not escape liability because of a formal technicality.

The *ex ante* perspective is forward looking: its focus is "before the event". It may consider future parties who have not yet contracted, and focus on what incentives they have to transact, and how they should be encouraged to go about it. Such an approach may emphasize the deterrent or hortatory functions of the law.

Consider how each case holds up under each view.

As an additional exercise in revision, you can apply the same categories of analysis to *Chomicky v. Buttolph* and *Radke v. Brenon* in Chapter 6.C. Do you think differently about the two cases from an *ex post* or *ex ante* perspective? Think about other areas under study in which the different approaches bring clarity to the stakes of the law.

Eskimo Pie Corp. v. Whitelawn Dairies, Inc.

United States District Court for the Southern District of New York, 1968.
284 F. Supp 987.

■ MANSFIELD, DISTRICT JUDGE.

. . . This decision deals principally with the procedure to be followed by the parties in obtaining rulings with respect to certain evidence to be offered at trial.

The actions arise out of written contracts between Eskimo Pie Corporation ('Eskimo' herein), Whitelawn Dairies, Inc. ('Whitelawn' herein) and Supermarket Advisory Sales, Inc. ('SAS' herein) (Whitelawn and SAS are collectively referred to herein as 'Whitelawn-SAS') entered into on or about December 30, 1960, and modified in various respects in 1961 and 1962. These contracts are referred to by the parties as the 'Package Deal.' All parties agree that the Package Deal is an integrated agreement setting forth in several writings all of the essential terms agreed upon by Eskimo and Whitelawn-SAS. Under the terms of the Package Deal Eskimo granted to Whitelawn, an ice cream manufacturer,

---

defendant may have released plaintiff from liability for any injuries to defendant's property arising out of the contract's performance, but this provision did not necessarily make defendant an insurer against injuries to plaintiff's property. Defendant's agreement to procure liability insurance to cover damages to plaintiff's property does not indicate whether the insurance was to cover all injuries or only injuries caused by defendant's negligence.

the right to manufacture certain ice cream products bearing 'Eskimo' wrappers and labels and to SAS the right to purchase such Eskimo-branded products from Eskimo or an Eskimo-authorized manufacturer for sale in the New York City Metropolitan Area as follows:

> 'During the term of this Agreement (SAS) shall have the *non-exclusive* right to purchase the Eskimo stock and stickless products listed in Exhibit A hereto, which may be amended from time to time by addition or deletion, from Eskimo or from a manufacturer authorized by Eskimo to manufacture such products within the New York City metropolitan area . . .' (emphasis supplied).

The present lawsuits were instituted after Eskimo, beginning sometime in 1962 and 1963, sold its Eskimo-branded products to others in the New York City Metropolitan Area, and entered into agreements with M. H. Renken Dairy Co. ('Renken' herein) to manufacture, and with Food Enterprises, Inc. ('Food Enterprises' herein) to sell, such products, and assisted Harry L. Darnstaedt and Imperial Ice Cream Novelties, Inc. ('Imperial' herein) in selling such products in the New York City Metropolitan Area. This led to a deterioration in the relationship between the parties to the Package Deal; a purported termination by Whitelawn and SAS of purchases and sales thereunder; and mutual claims of breach of contract, since Whitelawn and SAS appear to have refused to accept and pay for certain products.

. . .

A threshold question, which appears to be central to the entire dispute between the parties, arises out of the meaning of the word 'non-exclusive' as used in the above quotation from the Package Deal, and the proposal of Whitelawn-SAS to offer parol evidence with respect to its meaning. Whitelawn and SAS contend that the word 'non-exclusive' as used in the Package Deal meant that Eskimo would have the right to continue existing licenses granted by it to others in the New York City Metropolitan Area and to grant new licenses to national companies . . . but not to grant licenses to so-called 'independent' companies unless required to do so by order of a court or governmental agency, and that Eskimo itself was not to compete with Whitelawn and SAS in the sale of Eskimo-branded ice cream products. Eskimo denies such contentions as to the meaning of the word 'non-exclusive' and asserts that it plainly meant that Eskimo was granting a bare non-exclusive right to Whitelawn and SAS to manufacture and sell Eskimo products, while retaining the unfettered right to license others as it saw fit to manufacture and sell Eskimo-branded ice cream products.

Whitelawn-SAS proposes, upon the jury trial of the issues of liability raised by the two lawsuits, to introduce not only the written agreements constituting the Package Deal, but also parol and extrinsic evidence as to what the parties understood and intended the term 'non-exclusive' to mean, including earlier drafts of the Package Deal, correspondence and conversations between the parties leading up to its execution, and subsequent conduct of the parties, including a letter written by Darnstaedt on February 12, 1963 stating that the parties 'had a gentlemen's agreement that Eskimo would not solicit any stick franchises in New York City except any of the national companies that Eskimo is serving around the country.' More specifically, Whitelawn-SAS would offer testimony of its lawyers and others who negotiated the Package Deal on its behalf to the effect that earlier drafts, including one submitted by an Eskimo official named Gunn (now deceased) contained a clause which would have obligated Eskimo not to license or franchise the Eskimo mark, or sell Eskimo-branded ice cream products, to anyone in the New York City Metropolitan Area other than existing licensees or national dairy organizations, unless Eskimo should be required to do so by court or governmental order; that thereafter Eskimo refused to sign an agreement containing the express clause because of a fear expressed by Eskimo's counsel that the proposed clause might violate the federal antitrust laws; and that accordingly, after a series of conferences, the proposed clause was deleted on the understanding that its meaning would be deemed incorporated into the word 'non-exclusive' used in the above quoted license to Whitelawn-SAS.

Although Eskimo, if such parol evidence were admitted at the trial, would offer testimony of its officials contradicting that of the Whitelawn-SAS negotiators, it argues that such evidence is barred by the parol evidence rule, and seeks preliminary rulings before trial is commenced.

. . .

The question of whether parol evidence should be admitted at trial is one of law to be determined and ruled upon by the Court. See James, Civil Procedure § 7.10, at 267 (1965); Weiner, The Civil Jury Trial and the Law-Fact Distinction, 54 Calif.L.Rev. 1867, 1870 n. 12 (1966). Normally such rulings are made when the evidence is offered during trial, with the party offering the evidence, should objection be sustained, preserving his rights through an offer of proof out of the jury's presence. In this case, however, Eskimo asserts that since the parol evidence to be offered is extensive (both parties agreeing that if the evidence is admitted several witnesses will be required to testify for at least a few days), Eskimo would be forced to engage in multiple and continuous objections to, and/or motions to strike, testimony as to each of the numerous conversations between the negotiators, and proof of each item of correspondence, drafts, etc., with the result that even if the evidence should ultimately be excluded, Eskimo would be unduly prejudiced before the jury. This argument has much merit and is supported by those who follow the practice in such cases of holding a preliminary hearing for the purpose of ruling on the admissibility of such evidence. Wigmore on Evidence § 1808 at 275–76 (3d ed.). Whitelawn-SAS contends, however, that since the parol evidence should be admitted at trial, a preliminary hearing would result in needless waste and expense occasioned by duplication in testimony and proof. In view of these opposing contentions, consideration by the Court at this time of the applicable evidentiary principles seems appropriate.

. . .

Whitelawn-SAS argues that parol evidence should be admitted on the ground that the term 'non-exclusive' is ambiguous, and that even if it in fact lacks ambiguity such evidence may be received to show that the parties gave the term special or particular meaning not to be gathered from the language by a reasonably intelligent person having knowledge of the custom, usage and surrounding circumstances. In support of their position, Whitelawn-SAS relies principally on § 2–202 of the Uniform Commercial Code ('UCC' herein), Corbin on Contracts §§ 535, 536, 542, 543, 579 and decisions of the late respected Judge Frank, *e.g., United States v. Lenox Metal Manufacturing Co.*, 225 F.2d 302 (2d Cir. 1955); *R. H. Johnson & Co. v. SEC,* 198 F.2d 690, 696 (2d Cir.), cert. denied, 344 U.S. 855, 73 S.Ct. 94, 97 L.Ed. 664 (1952).

Section 2–202 of New York's U.C.C. provides:

> 'Terms with respect to which the confirmatory memoranda of the parties agree or which are otherwise set forth in a writing intended by the parties as a final expression of their agreement with respect to such terms as are included therein may not be contradicted by evidence of any prior agreement or of a contemporaneous oral agreement but may be explained or supplemented
>
> (a) by course of dealing or usage of trade (Section 1–205) or by course of performance (Section 2–208)'

. . .

Since the Package Deal predated the effective date of the U.C.C., and since the U.C.C. was not intended to have retroactive effect, § 2–202 does not apply and the Court must look to prior law. . . .

In any event, even if § 2–202 of the U.C.C. were applicable to the written contract here at issue, much of the proof which Whitelawn-SAS would offer to show what the parties intended the word 'non-exclusive' to mean would not be admissible. Section 2–202 limits the parties, in explaining the meaning of language in a written integrated contract, to proof of a 'course of dealing,' 'usage of the trade,' and a 'course of performance.' None of these terms encompass testimony or other proof as to the subjective intent of the parties. The term 'course of dealing' as defined in § 1–205(1)[b] refers to 'previous conduct between the parties' indicating a common basis for interpreting expressions used by them. In short, proof of such conduct is limited to objective facts as distinguished from oral statements of agreement. Likewise the term 'usage of trade' is defined in § 1–205(2) as

---

[b] Fn Ed: Now § 1–303—for revised formulation, see Chapter 8.B.

'any practice or method of dealing having such regularity of observance in a place, vocation or trade as to justify an expectation that it will be observed with respect to the transaction in question. The existence and scope of such a usage are to be proved as facts. If it is established that such a usage is embodied in a written trade code or similar writing the interpretation of the writing is for the court.'

The comments of the drafters as well as those of independent commentators make it clear that 'usage of the trade' refers to evidence of generalized industry practice or similar recognized custom, as distinguished from particular conversations or correspondence between the parties with respect to the terms of the agreement. * * * The same general conclusions must be reached with respect to proof of a 'course of performance.'

As previously noted, the admissibility of parol evidence in this case is governed by the law of New York as it existed prior to the effective date of § 2–202, and therefore this Court must first determine what New York law is on this question before embarking upon any expedition into unchartered territory which might permit consideration of advanced schools of semantic thought that have been espoused by Judge Frank and Professor Corbin, see, generally, Farnsworth, 'Meaning' in the Law of Contracts, 76 Yale L.J. 939 (1967), but which have not obtained widespread judicial acceptance. As a learned member of the Second Circuit Court of Appeals, Judge Kaufman, has said:

'The proper function of this Court is to ascertain what New York law is, and not to speculate about what it will be, or in Learned Hand's felicitous phrase, 'to embrace the exhilarating opportunity of anticipating a doctrine which may be in the womb of time, but whose birth is distant.' Spector Motor Service v. Walsh, 139 F.2d 809, 823 (2nd Cir. 1943) (dissent), vacated, 323 U.S. 101, 65 S.Ct. 152, 89 L.Ed. 101 (1944). It is certainly not our function to apply the rule we think better or wiser.' (Hausman v. Buckley, 299 F.2d 696, 704, 93 A.L.R.2d 1340 (2d Cir.), cert. denied, 369 U.S. 885, 82 S.Ct. 1157, 8 L.Ed.2d 286 (1962))

In this instance, ascertainment of New York law on the issue does not require 'prolonged celebration.' The courts of New York have never subscribed to the view that, in the absence of ambiguity, evidence as to the subjective intent of the parties may be substituted for the plain meaning that would otherwise be ascribed to the language of a written agreement by a reasonably intelligent person having knowledge of the surrounding circumstances, customs and usages. On the contrary, prior New York law adhered to time-honored objective standards to determine the meaning of language found in writings which represent as did the Package Deal here the final and complete integrated agreement reached by the parties. * * * The cardinal principles forming the cornerstone of those standards are (1) that the meaning to be attributed to the language of such an instrument is that which a reasonably intelligent person acquainted with general usage, custom and the surrounding circumstances would attribute to it; and (2) that in the absence of ambiguity parol evidence will not be admitted to determine the meaning that is to be attributed to such language. * * *

> 'The question is as to the fair and reasonable meaning that may be given to the writing sued on. Written words may have more than one meaning. 'The letter killeth but the spirit giveth life.' 2 Cor. 3:6. 'Form should not prevail over substance and a sensible meaning of words should be sought.' *Atwater & Co. v. Panama R.R. Co.,* 246 N.Y. 519, 524, 159 N.E. 418, 419. But plain meanings may not be changed by parol, and the courts will not make a new contract for the parties under the guise of interpreting the writing. 'The fact that the parties intended their words to bear a certain meaning, would be immaterial were it not for the fact that the words either normally or locally might properly bear such meaning.' Williston on Contracts, § 613.' *Heller v. Pope*, 250 N.Y. 132, 164 N.E. 881 (1928) (Pound, J.)

Thus the oral statements of the parties as to what they intended unambiguous language in an integrated document to mean are excluded by the parol evidence rule, because the very purpose and essence of the rule is to avoid fraud that might be perpetrated if testimony as to subjective intent could be substituted for the plain meaning, objectively interpreted in the light of surrounding circumstances, customs and usage. The effect of admitting such testimony in the absence of some showing of ambiguity would be to permit a party to substitute his view of his obligations for those clearly stated. Where—as in the present case—some of the negotiators of the written agreement have died or are unavailable, the door could be opened to fraud. Accordingly, the view of the New York courts has been that an objective standard is essential to maintain confidence in the written integrated agreement as the medium for conducting commercial relations.

The first question to be determined in the present case, therefore, is whether the term 'non-exclusive' as used in the Package Deal is ambiguous, which must be decided by the Court. * * * An 'ambiguous' word or phrase is one capable of more than one meaning when viewed objectively by a reasonably intelligent person who has examined the context of the entire integrated agreement and who is cognizant of the customs, practices, usages and terminology as generally understood in the particular trade or business. * * * In the absence of proof that the term 'non-exclusive' could possibly have the meaning, among others, attributed to it by Whitelawn-SAS, parol evidence must be excluded.

Applying the foregoing principles, the word 'non-exclusive' when used—as was the case here—in an integrated license agreement drafted by legal counsel, has an established legal meaning that is usually accepted in the absence of a qualifying context, custom, usage or similar surrounding circumstance. The term has repeatedly been defined as meaning that the licensee is granted a bare right to use the trademark or patent being licensed without any right to exclude others, including other licensees taking from the grantor, from utilizing the mark or invention involved. * * * Ellis, Patent Licenses § 387 (1958). As Ellis points out:

> 'If a non-exclusive license is given there is by the very nature of the license an understanding that licenses may be granted to others. The number of licensees may run into hundreds . . . There is no implied agreement by the licensor that he will not grant licenses at lower royalties or that he will sue infringers. Both these two classes of persons constitute competition and the licensee by accepting a non-exclusive license has agreed to accept competition. If it is more severe than he had anticipated that is his fault for not having contracted against such competition.'

Despite the meaning thus usually ascribed by the law to the term 'non-exclusive' Whitelawn-SAS urge that here the legal draftsmen intended it to have a contrary meaning, i.e., that subject to certain detailed and specific exceptions (The Borden Company, National Dairy Products Corporation, existing licensees and existing written commitments to others), and except to the extent that Eskimo might be required to deviate therefrom by court or governmental order, the term meant 'exclusive.' In a business world not noted for its economy of language (the Package Deal covers 70 typewritten pages, including amendments) no business reason, custom or usage is advanced for attaching such an elaborate and paradoxical meaning to the term 'non-exclusive,' when legal counsel negotiating for both sides could easily have spelled out such specifics in comprehensible terms. Whitelawn-SAS's assertion that the term was used to conceal a detailed secret 'gentlemen's agreement' that was feared by Eskimo to violate the antitrust laws hardly comports with the word's having a secondary meaning as a matter of generalized trade usage or custom. On the contrary, such evidence would indicate that the term, despite the definite and plain meaning usually attributed to it, was being used to express a particular, subjective meaning initially conceived by the parties solely for the purpose at hand, and not because the term would be recognized by others as having such a special meaning. Unless the language is meaningless on its face (e.g. 'abracadabra') or ambiguous, however, the test for admission of parol evidence is not a secret code meaning given to it by the parties but whether it might objectively be recognized by a reasonably intelligent person acquainted with applicable customs, usages and the surrounding circumstances as having such a special meaning. For instance, would an executive in the ice cream business, who was not privy to the secret oral 'gentlemen's agreement,' recognize the term 'non-exclusive' in this context and setting as granting an 'exclusive' right, subject to certain exceptions or as having a meaning other than that usually attributed to it? If so, parol evidence would be admissible. If the law were otherwise, not only the term 'non-exclusive' but every apparently clear term in a written agreement, such as a specific purchase price (e.g., '$10,000') could be changed by secret oral agreement to mean something different (e.g., '$25,000').

Nevertheless, although the term 'non-exclusive' as used in the Package Deal does not on its face appear to be ambiguous, Whitelawn-SAS will be afforded the opportunity to offer proof showing that the term is ambiguous, and Eskimo the opportunity to rebut such proof. In accordance with the principles hereinabove outlined, proof on the issue of ambiguity may encompass the terms of the Package Deal itself, the surrounding circumstances, common usage and custom as to the meaning attributed to it, and subsequent conduct of the parties under the Package Deal, but evidence of the subjective understanding of the parties as to the meaning attributed by them to the term 'non-exclusive' will not be received.

Since the issue of ambiguity must be determined by the Court before ruling on the admission of parol evidence and since Eskimo might suffer prejudice if such rulings were made in the jury's presence, the proof with respect to ambiguity will be received at a preliminary hearing by the Court. Upon conclusion of the preliminary hearing, the Court will rule upon the issue of ambiguity, and the admissibility of the evidence at trial will be governed accordingly. Thereupon, . . . the Court will hold a separate jury trial of the issue of liability, to be followed by trial before the same jury of the damage issues. . . .

So ordered.

F. IMPLICATION OF TERMS: GOOD FAITH PERFORMANCE

Restatement (Second) of Contracts § 205; U.C.C. § 1–304

PROBLEM

Baker Co has filed suit against Holding Co seeking damages in the amount of $250,000 as compensation for expenditures that Baker incurred, primarily for fees of accountants and attorneys, in connection with failed negotiations looking toward a possible acquisition by Baker Co of a wholly owned subsidiary of Holding Co, called SubCo.

In substance the facts alleged in the complaint are as follows: Holding Co was approached by Able Co concerning the possibility of an acquisition of SubCo by Able. Able indicated that it was willing to pay $150 million, in cash, for SubCo. Holding Company was interested in selling SubCo, and was particularly interested in the Able deal because of the fact that Able was talking about an acquisition for cash rather than a deal in which the buyer paid with stock, but Holding Co thought that Able would probably be willing to pay a good deal more than $150 million.

After receiving the proposal from Able, Holding Company approached Baker Co, indicated that SubCo might be available for sale, and asked whether Baker was interested. Holding Co knew that Baker had done other such acquisitions, and that Baker always did acquisitions for stock, not cash. Baker said that it might be interested, but would need to conduct an investigation of the operations and financial condition of SubCo. Holding Co told Baker that it would make available to Baker whatever information Baker reasonably needed. Baker hired the accountants and attorneys to conduct the investigations, incurring the $250,000 expenses for which it seeks compensation in the suit. After the investigation was completed, Baker sent a written offer to Holding Co, offering to buy SubCo from Holding Co for a package of Baker stock that it valued at about $175 million.

Holding Co immediately took the Baker offer to Able and told Able that unless Able raised its bid, Holding Co would sell SubCo to Baker. A few days later, Able offered $170 million, in cash. Holding Co accepted, and notified Baker that its offer was rejected. SubCo was then sold to Able.

Baker's complaint alleges that Holding Co never had any intention of giving serious consideration to any offer from Baker and that Holding Co sought out Baker's offer solely for the purpose of using it in an effort to induce Able to raise its bid.

Holding Co filed a motion to dismiss the lawsuit. Baker responds by arguing that its case is supported by the rule in § 205 of the RESTATEMENT (SECOND) OF CONTRACTS. What result?

Wood v. Lucy, Lady Duff Gordon

Court of Appeals of New York, 1917.
222 N.Y. 88, 118 N.E. 214.

[Review the *Wood v. Lucy, Lady Duff Gordon* opinion, which appears in Chapter 4.D on Consideration, at page 158.]

NOTES

Suppose that Lucy had not broken her promise to place endorsements only through Wood. Suppose that the arrangement did not generate as much revenue for Lucy as she had expected. Suppose that Lucy believes that Wood has not tried very hard to market her endorsements. Could Lucy sue Wood? How would the court decide whether Wood's performance was or was not consistent with the contract. Recall Judge Cardozo's observation that although Wood "does not promise in so many words that he will use reasonable efforts to place the defendant's endorsements and market her designs. We think, however, that such a promise is fairly to be implied."

Bloor v. Falstaff Brewing Corp.

United States Court of Appeals, Second Circuit, 1979.
601 F.2d 609.

■ FRIENDLY, CIRCUIT JUDGE.

This action, wherein federal jurisdiction is predicated on diversity of citizenship, 28 U.S.C. § 1332, was brought in the District Court for the Southern District of New York, by James Bloor, Reorganization Trustee of Balco Properties Corporation, formerly named P. Ballantine & Sons (Ballantine), a venerable and once successful brewery based in Newark, N. J. He sought to recover from Falstaff Brewing Corporation (Falstaff) for breach of a contract dated March 31, 1972, wherein Falstaff bought the Ballantine brewing labels, trademarks, accounts receivable, distribution systems and other property except the brewery. The price was $4,000,000 plus a royalty of fifty cents on each barrel of the Ballantine brands sold between April 1, 1972 and March 31, 1978. Although other issues were tried, the appeals concern only two provisions of the contract. These are:

> 8.   Certain Other Covenants of Buyer. (a) After the Closing Date the (Buyer) will use its best efforts to promote and maintain a high volume of sales under the Proprietary Rights.

> 2(a)(v)   (The Buyer will pay a royalty of $.50 per barrel for a period of 6 years), provided, however, that if during the Royalty Period the Buyer substantially discontinues the distribution of beer under the brand name "Ballantine" (except as the result of a restraining order in effect for 30 days issued by a court of competent jurisdiction at the request of a governmental authority), it will pay to the Seller a cash sum equal to the years and fraction thereof remaining in the Royalty Period times $1,100,000, payable in equal monthly installments on the first day of each month commencing with the first month following the month in which such discontinuation occurs . . . .

Bloor claimed that Falstaff had breached the best efforts clause, 8(a), and indeed that its default amounted to the substantial discontinuance that would trigger the liquidated damage clause, 2(a)(v). In an opinion that interestingly traces the history of beer back to Domesday Book and beyond, Judge Brieant upheld the first claim and awarded damages but dismissed the second. Falstaff appeals from the former ruling, Bloor from the latter. Both sides also dispute the court's measurement of damages for breach of the best efforts clause.

We shall assume familiarity with Judge Brieant's excellent opinion, 454 F.Supp. 258 (S.D.N.Y.1978), from which we have drawn heavily, and will state only the essentials. Ballantine had been a family owned business, producing low-priced beers primarily for the northeast market, particularly New York, New Jersey, Connecticut and Pennsylvania. Its sales began to decline in 1961, and it lost money from 1965 on. On June

1, 1969, Investors Funding Corporation (IFC), a real estate conglomerate with no experience in brewing, acquired substantially all the stock of Ballantine for $16,290,000. IFC increased advertising expenditures, leveling off in 1971 at $1 million a year. This and other promotional practices, some of dubious legality, led to steady growth in Ballantine's sales despite the increased activities in the northeast of the "nationals"[1] which have greatly augmented their market shares at the expense of smaller brewers. However, this was a profitless prosperity; there was no month in which Ballantine had earnings and the total loss was $15,500,000 for the 33 months of IFC ownership.

After its acquisition of Ballantine, Falstaff continued the $1 million a year advertising program, IFC's pricing policies, and also its policy of serving smaller accounts not solely through sales to independent distributors, the usual practice in the industry, but by use of its own warehouses and trucks the only change being a shift of the retail distribution system from Newark to North Bergen, N.J., when brewing was concentrated at Falstaff's Rhode Island brewery. However, sales declined and Falstaff claims to have lost $22 million in its Ballantine brand operations from March 31, 1972 to June 1975. Its other activities were also performing indifferently, although with no such losses as were being incurred in the sale of Ballantine products, and it was facing inability to meet payrolls and other debts. In March and April 1975 control of Falstaff passed to Paul Kalmanovitz, a businessman with 40 years experience in the brewing industry. After having first advanced $3 million to enable Falstaff to meet its payrolls and other pressing debts, he later supplied an additional $10 million and made loan guarantees, in return for which he received convertible preferred shares in an amount that endowed him with 35% of the voting power and became the beneficiary of a voting trust that gave him control of the board of directors.

Mr. Kalmanovitz determined to concentrate on making beer and cutting sales costs. He decreased advertising, with the result that the Ballantine advertising budget shrank from $1 million to $115,000 a year. In late 1975 he closed four of Falstaff's six retail distribution centers, including the North Bergen, N.J. depot, which was ultimately replaced by two distributors servicing substantially fewer accounts. He also discontinued various illegal practices that had been used in selling Ballantine products.[3] What happened in terms of sales volume is shown in plaintiff's exhibit 114 J . . . . With 1974 as a base, Ballantine declined 29.72% in 1975 and 45.81% in 1976 as compared with a 1975 gain of

---

[1]   Miller's, Schlitz, Anheuser-Busch, Coors and Pabst.

[3]   There were two kinds of illegal practices, the testimony on both of which is, unsurprisingly, rather vague. Certain "national accounts", i. e. large draught beer buyers, were gotten or retained by "black bagging", the trade term for commercial bribery. On a smaller scale, sales to taverns were facilitated by the salesman's offering a free round for the house of Ballantine if it was available ("retention"), or the customer's choice ("solicitation"). Both practices seem to have been indulged in by many brewers, including Falstaff before Kalmanovitz took control.

2.24% and a 1976 loss of 13.08% for all brewers excluding the top 15. Other comparisons are similarly devastating, at least for 1976. Despite the decline in the sale of its own labels as well as Ballantine's, Falstaff, however, made a substantial financial recovery. In 1976 it had net income of $8.7 million and its year-end working capital had increased from $8.6 million to $20.2 million and its cash and certificates of deposit from $2.2 million to $12.1 million. . . .

Seizing upon remarks made by the judge during the trial that Falstaff's financial standing in 1975 and thereafter "is probably not relevant" and a footnote in the opinion, 454 F.Supp. at 267 n. 7, appellate counsel for Falstaff contend that the judge read the best efforts clause as requiring Falstaff to maintain Ballantine's volume by any sales methods having a good prospect of increasing or maintaining sales or, at least, to continue lawful methods in use at the time of purchase, no matter what losses they would cause. Starting from this premise, counsel reason that the judge's conclusion was at odds with New York law, stipulated by the contract to be controlling, as last expressed by the Court of Appeals in *Feld v. Henry S. Levy & Sons, Inc.*, 37 N.Y.2d 466, 373 N.Y.S.2d 102, 335 N.E.2d 320 (1975). The court was there dealing with a contract whereby defendant agreed to sell and plaintiff to purchase all bread crumbs produced by defendant at a certain factory. During the term of the agreement defendant ceased producing bread crumbs because production with existing facilities was "very uneconomical", and the plaintiff sued for breach. The case was governed by § 2–306 of the Uniform Commercial Code which provides:

§ 2–306. Output, Requirements and Exclusive Dealings

(1) A term which measures the quantity by the output of the seller or the requirements of the buyer means such actual output or requirements as may occur in good faith, except that no quantity unreasonably disproportionate to any stated estimate or in the absence of a stated estimate to any normal or otherwise comparable prior output or requirements may be tendered or demanded.

(2) A lawful agreement by either the seller or the buyer for exclusive dealing in the kind of goods concerned imposes unless otherwise agreed an obligation by the seller to use best efforts to supply the goods and by the buyer to use best efforts to promote their sale.

Affirming the denial of cross-motions for summary judgment, the court said that, absent a cancellation on six months' notice for which the contract provided:

defendant was expected to continue to perform in good faith and could cease production of the bread crumbs, a single facet of its operation, only in good faith. Obviously, a bankruptcy or genuine imperiling of the very existence of its entire business caused by the production of the crumbs would warrant cessation of production of that item; the yield of less profit from its sale than expected would not. Since bread crumbs were but a part of defendant's enterprise and since there was a contractual right of cancellation, good faith required continued production until cancellation, even if there be no profit. In circumstances such as these and without more, defendant would be justified, in good faith, in ceasing production of the single item prior to cancellation only if its losses from continuance would be more than trivial, which, overall, is a question of fact.

37 N.Y.2d 471–72, 373 N.Y.S.2d 106, 335 N.E.2d 323. Falstaff argues from this that it was not bound to do anything to market Ballantine products that would cause "more than trivial" losses.

We do not think the judge imposed on Falstaff a standard as demanding as its appellate counsel argues that he did. . . . [H]e did not in fact proceed on the basis that the best efforts clause required Falstaff to bankrupt itself in promoting Ballantine products or even to sell those products at a substantial loss. He relied rather on the fact that Falstaff's obligation to "use its best efforts to promote and maintain a high volume of sales" of Ballantine products was not fulfilled by a policy summarized by Mr. Kalmanovitz as being:

> We sell beer and you pay for it. . . . We sell beer, F.O.B. the brewery. You come and get it.

however sensible such a policy may have been with respect to Falstaff's other products. Once the peril of insolvency had been averted, the drastic percentage reductions in Ballantine sales as related to any possible basis of comparison, . . . required Falstaff at least to explore whether steps not involving substantial losses could have been taken to stop or at least lessen the rate of decline. The judge found that, instead of doing this, Falstaff had engaged in a number of misfeasances and nonfeasances which could have accounted in substantial measure for the catastrophic drop in Ballantine sales shown in the chart, see 454 F.Supp. at 267–72. These included the closing of the North Bergen depot which had serviced "Mom and Pop" stores and bars in the New York metropolitan area; Falstaff's choices of distributors for Ballantine products in the New Jersey and particularly the New York areas, where the chosen distributor was the owner of a competing brand; its failure to take advantage of a proffer from Guinness-Harp Corporation to distribute Ballantine products in New York City through its Metrobeer Division; Falstaff's incentive to put more effort into sales of its own brands which sold at higher prices despite identity of the ingredients and were free from the $.50 a barrel royalty burden; its failure to treat Ballantine products evenhandedly with Falstaff's; its discontinuing the practice of setting goals for salesmen; and the general Kalmanovitz policy of stressing profit at the expense of volume. In the court's judgment, these misfeasances and nonfeasances warranted a conclusion that, even taking account of Falstaff's right to give reasonable consideration to its own interests, Falstaff had breached its duty to use best efforts as stated in the *Van Valkenburgh* decision, *supra*, 30 N.Y.2d at 46, 330 N.Y.S.2d at 334, 281 N.E.2d at 145.

Falstaff levels a barrage on these findings. The only attack which merits discussion is its criticism of the judge's conclusion that Falstaff did not treat its Ballantine brands evenhandedly with those under the Falstaff name. We agree that the subsidiary findings "that Falstaff but not Ballantine had been advertised extensively in Texas and Missouri" and that "(i)n these same areas Falstaff, although a 'premium' beer, was sold for extended periods below the price of Ballantine," while literally true, did not warrant the inference drawn from them. Texas was Falstaff territory and, with advertising on a cooperative basis, it was natural that advertising expenditures on Falstaff would exceed those on Ballantine. The lower price for Falstaff was a particular promotion of a bicentennial can in Texas, intended to meet a particular competitor.

However, we do not regard this error as undermining the judge's ultimate conclusion of breach of the best efforts clause. While that clause clearly required Falstaff to treat the Ballantine brands as well as its own, it does not follow that it required no more. With respect to its own brands, management was entirely free to exercise its business judgment as to how to maximize profit even if this meant serious loss in volume. Because of the obligation it had assumed under the sales contract, its situation with respect to the Ballantine brands was quite different. The royalty of $.50 a barrel on sales was an essential part of the purchase price. Even without the best efforts clause Falstaff would have been bound to make a good faith effort to see that substantial sales of Ballantine products were made, unless it discontinued under clause 2(a)(v) with consequent liability for liquidated damages. *Cf. Wood v. Duff-Gordon*, 222 N.Y. 88, 118 N.E. 214 (1917) (Cardozo, J.). Clause 8 imposed an added obligation to use "best efforts to promote and maintain a *high* volume of sales . . . ." (emphasis supplied). Although we agree that even this did not require Falstaff to spend itself into bankruptcy to promote the sales of Ballantine products, it did prevent the application to them of Kalmanovitz' philosophy of emphasizing profit *uber alles* without fair consideration of the effect on Ballantine volume. Plaintiff was not obliged to show just what steps Falstaff could reasonably have taken to maintain a high volume for Ballantine products. It was sufficient to show that Falstaff simply didn't care about Ballantine's volume and was content to allow this to plummet so long as that course was best for Falstaff's overall profit picture, an inference which the judge permissibly drew. The burden then shifted to Falstaff to prove there was nothing significant it could have done to promote Ballantine sales that would not have been financially disastrous.

Having correctly concluded that Falstaff had breached its best efforts covenant, the judge was faced with a difficult problem in computing what the royalties on the lost sales would have been. There is no need to rehearse the many decisions that, in a situation like this, certainty is not required; "[t]he plaintiff need only show a 'stable foundation for a reasonable estimate of royalties he would have earned had defendant not breached' ". *Contemporary Mission, Inc. v. Famous Music Corp.*, 557 F.2d 918, 926 (2 Cir. 1977), *quoting Freund v. Washington Square Press, Inc.*, 34 N.Y.2d 379, 383, 357 N.Y.S.2d 857, 861, 314 N.E.2d 419, 421 (1974). After carefully considering other possible bases, the court arrived at the seemingly sensible conclusion that the most nearly accurate comparison was with the combined sales of Rheingold and Schaefer beers, both, like Ballantine, being "price" beers sold primarily in the northeast, and computed what Ballantine sales would have been if its brands had suffered only the same decline as a composite of Rheingold and Schaefer.

. . .

We can dispose quite briefly of the portion of the plaintiff's cross-appeal which claims error in the rejection of his contention that Falstaff's actions triggered the liquidated damage clause. One branch of this puts heavy weight on the word "distribution"; the claim is that the closing of the North Bergen center and Mr. Kalmanovitz' general come-and-get-it philosophy was, without more, a substantial discontinuance of "distribution". On this basis plaintiff would be entitled to invoke the liquidated damage clause even if Falstaff's new methods had succeeded in checking the decline in Ballantine sales. . . . [T]he term "distribution", as used in the brewing industry, does not require distribution by the brewer's own trucks and employees. The norm rather is distribution through independent wholesalers. Falstaff's default under the best efforts clause was not in returning to that method simpliciter but in its failure to see to it that wholesale distribution approached in effectiveness what retail distribution had done.

Plaintiff contends more generally that permitting a decline of 63.12% In Ballantine sales from 1974 to 1977 was the equivalent of quitting the game. However, as Judge Brieant correctly pointed out, a large part of this drop was attributable "to the general decline of the market share of the smaller brewers" as against the "nationals", 454 F.Supp. at 266, and even the 518,899 barrels sold in 1977 were not a negligible amount of beer.

The judgment is affirmed. . . .

NOTES

1.   The facts of *Bloor* are a bit confusing. Some further information appears in the District Court's opinion. In 1969, IFC bought all the shares of Ballantine Corp. In 1972, Ballantine Corp sold its assets to Falstaff, under the contract that is in dispute in the case. The corporation "Ballantine Corp." continued to exist, with its principal asset now being the rights under the contract with Falstaff. IFC is the shareholder of Ballantine Corp. Hence the

case is Ballantine Corp (through its reorganization trustee, Bloor) versus Falstaff. Once the case is resolved, that will determine what assets Ballantine Corp has. Then in the reorganization, it will be sorted out how those rights get divided up between the shareholder of Ballantine Corp (IFC) and other claimants, such as, presumably, creditors of Ballantine Corp.

2. U.C.C. § 2–306, removes indefiniteness and lack of mutuality in variable quantity (output and requirements) contracts by reading in a good faith standard (§ 2–306(1)) and in exclusive dealing contracts by reading in a best efforts standard (§ 2–306(2)).

PROBLEM

Buster Douglas, a professional boxer, argued that his promoter breached the covenant of good faith in their promotion agreement by attempting to influence the outcome of his heavyweight title fight with Mike Tyson. In the agreement, the promoter received the "sole and exclusive right to secure and arrange all professional boxing bouts" for Douglas, but reserved his right to promote other heavyweights. He represented Tyson separately. During the fight, Douglas was knocked down by Tyson in the ninth round; when he got up, his promoter yelled at the referee for giving him too much time to recover. When Douglas ultimately won, his promoter petitioned the world boxing commission to invalidate the fight.

Should Douglas' claim succeed? See *Don King Productions, Inc. v. Douglas*, 742 F. Supp. 741 (S.D. N.Y. 1990), on reargument, 742 F. Supp. 786 (S.D. N.Y. 1990).

Fortune v. National Cash Register Co.

Supreme Judicial Court of Massachusetts, Norfolk, 1977.
373 Mass. 96, 364 N.E.2d 1251.

Orville E. Fortune (Fortune), a former salesman of The National Cash Register Company (NCR), brought suit to recover certain commissions allegedly due as a result of a sale of cash registers to First National Stores Inc. (First National) in 1968. . . . Judgment on a jury verdict for Fortune was reversed by the Appeals Court, Fortune v. National Cash Register Co., 349 N.E.2d 350 (1976), and this court granted leave to obtain further appellate review. We affirm the judgment of the Superior Court. We hold, for the reasons stated herein, there was no error in submitting the issue of "bad faith" termination of an employment at will contract to the jury.

Fortune was employed by NCR under a written "salesman's contract" which was terminable at will, without cause, by either party on written notice. The contract provided that Fortune would receive a weekly salary in a fixed amount plus a bonus for sales made within the "territory" (i. e., customer accounts or stores) assigned to him for "coverage or supervision," whether the sale was made by him or someone else. The amount of the bonus was determined on the basis of "bonus credits," which were computed as a percentage of the price of products sold. Fortune would be paid a percentage of the applicable bonus credit as follows: (1) 75% if the territory was assigned to him at the date of the order, (2) 25% if the territory was assigned to him at the date of delivery and installation, or (3) 100% if the territory was assigned to him at both times. The contract further provided that the "bonus interest" would terminate if shipment of the order was not made within eighteen months from the date of the order unless (1) the territory was assigned to him for coverage at the date of delivery and installation, or (2) special engineering was required to fulfill the contract. In addition, NCR reserved the right to sell products in the salesman's territory without paying a bonus. However, this right could be exercised only on written notice.

In 1968, Fortune's territory included First National. This account had been part of his territory for the preceding six years; he had been successful in obtaining several orders from First National, including a million dollar order in 1963. Sometime in late 1967, or early 1968, NCR introduced a new model cash register, Class 5. Fortune corresponded with First National in an effort to sell the machine. He also helped to arrange for a demonstration of the Class 5 to executives of First National on October 4, 1968. NCR had a team of men also working on this sale.

On November 27, 1968, NCR's manager of chain and department stores, and the Boston branch manager, both part of NCR's team, wrote to First National regarding the Class 5. The letter covered a number of subjects, including price protection, trade-ins, and trade-in protection against obsolescence. While NCR normally offered price protection for only an eighteen-month term, apparently the size of the proposed order from First National caused NCR to extend its price protection terms for either a two-year or four-year period. On November 29, 1968, First National signed an order for 2,008 Class 5 machines to be delivered over a four-year period at a purchase price of approximately $5,000,000. Although Fortune did not participate in the negotiation of the terms of the order, his name appeared on the order form in the space entitled "salesman credited." The amount of the bonus credit as shown on the order was $92,079.99.

On January 6, 1969, the first working day of the new year, Fortune found an envelope on his desk at work. It contained a termination notice addressed to his home dated December 2, 1968. Shortly after receiving the notice, Fortune spoke to the Boston branch manager with whom he was friendly. The manager told him, "You are through," but, after considering some of the details necessary for the smooth operation of the First National order, told him to "stay on," and to "(k)eep on doing what you are doing right now." Fortune remained with the company in a position entitled "sales support." In this capacity, he coordinated and expedited delivery of the machines to First National under the November 29 order as well as servicing other accounts.

Commencing in May or June, Fortune began to receive some bonus commissions on the First National order. Having received only 75% of the applicable bonus due on the machines which had been delivered and installed, Fortune spoke with his manager about receiving the full amount of the commission. Fortune was told "to forget about it." Sixty-one years old at that time, and with a son in college, Fortune concluded that it "was a good idea to forget it for the time being."

NCR did pay a systems and installations person the remaining 25% of the bonus commissions due from the First National order although contrary to its usual policy of paying only salesmen a bonus. NCR, by its letter of November 27, 1968, had promised the services of a systems and installations person; the letter had claimed that the services of this person, Bernie Martin (Martin), would have a forecasted cost to NCR of over $45,000. As promised, NCR did transfer Martin to the First National account shortly after the order was placed.

Approximately eighteen months after receiving the termination notice, Fortune, who had worked for NCR for almost twenty-five years, was asked to retire. When he refused, he was fired in June of 1970. Fortune did not receive any bonus payments on machines which were delivered to First National after this date.

. . . [T]he case was sent to the jury for special verdicts on two questions:

"1. Did the Defendant act in bad faith . . . when it decided to terminate the Plaintiff's contract as a salesman by letter dated December 2, 1968, delivered on January 6, 1969?

"2. Did the Defendant act in bad faith . . . when the Defendant let the Plaintiff go on June 5, 1970?"

The jury answered both questions affirmatively, and judgment entered in the sum of $45,649.62.

The central issue on appeal is whether this "bad faith" termination constituted a breach of the employment at will contract. Traditionally, an employment contract which is "at will" may be terminated by either side without reason. *See Fenton v. Federal St. Bldg. Trust*, 310 Mass. 609, 612, 39 N.E.2d 414 (1942); * * * 9 S. Williston, Contracts § 1017 (3d ed. 1967); Restatement (Second) of Agency § 442 (1958). Although the employment at will rule has been almost uniformly criticised, see Blades, Employment at Will vs. Individual Freedom: On Limiting the Abusive Exercise of Employer Power, 67 Colum.L.Rev. 1404 (1967); Blumrosen, Workers' Rights Against Employers and Unions: Justice Francis A Judge for Our Season, 24 Rutgers L.Rev. 480 (1970), it has been widely followed.

The contract at issue is a classic terminable at will employment contract. It is clear that the contract itself reserved to the parties an explicit power to terminate the contract without cause on written notice. It is also clear that under the express terms of the contract Fortune has received all the bonus commissions to which he is entitled. Thus, NCR claims that it did not breach the contract, and that it has no further liability to Fortune. According to a literal reading of the contract, NCR is correct.

However, Fortune argues that, in spite of the literal wording of the contract, he is entitled to a jury determination on NCR's motives in terminating his services under the contract and in finally discharging him. We agree. We hold that NCR's written contract contains an implied covenant of good faith and fair dealing, and a termination not made in good faith constitutes a breach of the contract.

We do not question the general principles that an employer is entitled to be motivated by and to serve its own legitimate business interests; that an employer must have wide latitude in deciding whom it will employ in the face of the uncertainties of the business world; and that an employer needs flexibility in the face of changing circumstances. We recognize the employer's need for a large amount of control over its work force. However, we believe that where, as here, commissions are to be paid for work performed by the employee, the employer's decision to terminate its at will employee should be made in good faith. NCR's right to make decisions in its own interest is not, in our view, unduly hampered by a requirement of adherence to this standard.

On occasion some courts have avoided the rigidity of the "at will" rule by fashioning a remedy in tort. We believe, however, that in this case there is remedy on the express contract. In so holding we are merely recognizing the general requirement in this Commonwealth that parties to contracts and commercial transactions must act in good faith toward one another. Good faith and fair dealing between parties are pervasive requirements in our law; it can be said fairly, that parties to contracts or commercial transactions are bound by this standard. See G.L. c. 106, § 1–203 (good faith in contracts under Uniform Commercial Code); G.L. c. 93B, § 4(3)(c) (good faith in motor vehicle franchise termination).

A requirement of good faith has been assumed or implied in a variety of contract cases. * * * *Kerrigan v. Boston,* 361 Mass. 24, 33, 278 N.E.2d 387 (1972) (collective bargaining contract). *Murach v. Massachusetts Bonding & Ins. Co.,* 339 Mass. 184, 187, 158 N.E.2d 338 (1959) (insurance contract insurer must exercise discretionary power to settle claims in good faith). * * * *Clark v. State St. Trust Co.,* 270 Mass. 140, 153, 169 N.E. 897 (1930) (secondary agreement to a stock option agreement). *Elliott v. Kazajian,* 255 Mass. 459, 462, 152 N.E. 351 (1926) (broker's commission). *Chandler, Gardner & Williams, Inc. v. Reynolds,* 250 Mass. 309, 314, 145 N.E. 476 (1924) (contracts to be performed to the satisfaction of the other party).

The requirement of good faith was reaffirmed in *RLM Assocs. v. Carter Mfg. Corp.,* 356 Mass. 718, 248 N.E.2d 646 (1969). In that case the plaintiff (RLM), a manufacturer's representative of the defendant (Carter), was entitled to a commission on all of Carter's sales within a specified territory. Either party could terminate this arrangement on thirty days' notice. Carter cancelled the agreement shortly before being awarded a contract discovered and brought to Carter's attention by RLM. Because "(t)he evidence permitted the conclusion that Carter's termination of the arrangement was in part based upon a desire to avoid paying a commission to RLM" (ibid.), we held that the question of bad faith was properly placed before the jury. The present case differs from RLM Assocs., in that Fortune was credited with the sale to First National but was fired immediately thereafter. NCR seeks to avoid the thrust of RLM Assocs. by arguing that bad faith is not an issue where it has been careful to protect a portion of Fortune's bonus commission under the contract. We disagree. The fact that the discharge was after a portion of the bonus vested still creates a question for the jury on the defendant's motive in terminating the employment.

Recent decisions in other jurisdictions lend support to the proposition that good faith is implied in contracts terminable at will. In a recent employment at will case, *Monge v. Beebe Rubber Co.*, 114 N.H. 130, 133, 316 A.2d 549, 552 (1974), the plaintiff alleged that her oral contract of employment had been terminated because she refused to date her foreman. The New Hampshire Supreme Court held that "(i)n all employment contracts, whether at will or for a definite term, the employer's interest in running his business as he sees fit must be balanced against the interest of the employee in maintaining his employment, and the public's interest in maintaining a proper balance between the two. . . . We hold that a termination by the employer of a contract of employment at will which is motivated by bad faith or malice . . . constitutes a breach of the employment contract. . . . Such a rule affords the employee a certain stability of employment and does not interfere with the employer's normal exercise of his right to discharge, which is necessary to permit him to operate his business efficiently and profitably."

We believe that the holding in the *Monge* case merely extends to employment contracts the rule that " 'in *every* contract there is an implied covenant that neither party shall do anything which will have the effect of destroying or injuring the right of the other party to receive the fruits of the contract, which means that in *every* contract there exists an implied covenant of good faith and fair dealing' (emphasis supplied). * * *

In the instant case, we need not pronounce our adherence to so broad a policy nor need we speculate as to whether the good faith requirement is implicit in every contract for employment at will. It is clear, however, that, on the facts before us, a finding is warranted that a breach of the contract occurred. Where the principal seeks to deprive the agent of all compensation by terminating the contractual relationship when the agent is on the brink of successfully completing the sale, the principal has acted in bad faith and the ensuing transaction between the principal and the buyer is to be regarded as having been accomplished by the agent. Restatement (Second) of Agency § 454, and Comment a (1958).

The same result obtains where the principal attempts to deprive the agent of any portion of a commission due the agent. Courts have often applied this rule to prevent overreaching by employers and the forfeiture by employees of benefits almost earned by the rendering of substantial services. *See, e.g., RLM Assocs. v. Carter Mfg. Corp.*, 356 Mass. 718, 248 N.E.2d 646 (1969) * * * . In our view, the Appeals Court erroneously focused only on literal compliance with payment provisions of the contract and failed to consider the issue of bad faith termination. Restatement (Second) of Agency § 454, and Comment a (1958).

NCR argues that there was no evidence of bad faith in this case; therefore, the trial judge was required to direct a verdict in any event. We think that the evidence and the reasonable inferences to be drawn therefrom support a jury verdict that the termination of Fortune's twenty-five years of employment as a salesman with NCR the next business day after NCR obtained a $5,000,000 order from First National was motivated by a desire to pay Fortune as little of the bonus credit as it could. The fact that Fortune was willing to work under these circumstances does not constitute a waiver or estoppel; it only shows that NCR had him "at their mercy." *Commonwealth v. DeCotis*, 366 Mass. 234, 243, 316 N.E.2d 748 (1974).

NCR also contends that Fortune cannot complain of his firing in June, 1970, as his employment contract clearly indicated that bonus credits would be paid only for an eighteen-month period following the date of the order. As we have said, the jury could have found that Fortune was stripped of his "salesman" designation in order to disqualify him for the remaining 25% of the commissions due on cash registers delivered prior to the date of his first termination. Similarly, the jury could have found that Fortune was fired so that NCR would avoid paying him any commissions on cash registers delivered after June, 1970.

Conversely, the jury could have found that Fortune was assigned by NCR to the First National account; that all he did in this case was arrange for a demonstration of the product; that he neither participated in obtaining the order nor did he assist NCR in closing the order; and that nevertheless NCR credited him with the sale. This, however, did not obligate the trial judge to direct a verdict. Where evidence is conflicting, the rule is clear: "If upon any reasonable view of the evidence there is found any combination of circumstances from which a rational inference may be drawn in favor of the plaintiff, then there was no error in the denial of the motion, even if there may be other and different circumstances disclosed in the evidence which, if accepted as true by the jury, would support a conclusion adverse to the plaintiff." *Howes v. Kelman*, 326 Mass. 696, 696–697, 96 N.E.2d 394, 395 (1951).

We think that NCR's conduct in June, 1970 permitted the jury to find bad faith.

. . .

NOTES

1. Attempts have been made to provide examples or principles for defining good faith (see, e.g., RESTATEMENT (SECOND) § 205 cmt a.— emphasizing "faithfulness to an agreed common purpose and consistency with the justified expectations of the other party"; RESTATEMENT (SECOND) § 205 cmt b.—countering "evasion of the spirit of the bargain, lack of diligence and slacking off, willful rendering of imperfect performance, abuse of power to specify terms, and interference with or failure to cooperate in the other party's performance". Yet disagreement on what constitutes good faith continues. See, e.g., Todd D. Rakoff, *Good Faith in Contract Performance: Market Street Associates Partnership v. Frey*, 120 HARV. L. REV. 1187 (2007) (questioning Judge Posner's conclusion that intentional trickery is the "dispositive" standard for violating the duty of good faith performance).

2. Non-legal sanctions for unfair dealing include, for example, a refusal to deal with a party in the future, or heavy reputational costs. What conclusions should we draw from this observed fact? Should law be more or less flexible as a result? Consider Stewart Macaulay, *Non-Contractual Relations in Business: A Preliminary Study*, 28 Am. Soc. Rev. 55 (1963).

3. The duty of good faith applies to the performance of the agreed terms in the contract. It does not usually apply to the parties' negotiations prior to reaching agreement. As we have seen, the issue of pre-contractual liability stemming from failed negotiations is classically analyzed through the lens of offer and acceptance, and as a consequence, is not typically recognized by U.S. courts. Recall *Reprosystem v. SCM Corp.*, 727 F.2d 257 (1984) in Chapter 3.A., and consider specifically note 5 on page 94. Thus, the broad freedom enjoyed by the parties prior to the formation is subject to only occasional exceptions, for example, if an aggrieved party has a claim in restitution for a benefit conferred during negotiations, has been harmed by a misrepresentation (see Chapter 11.B) or has relied on a specific promise (see Chapter 5.D). Parties may agree to abide by a duty to negotiate though a 'letter of intent' or 'agreement to agree' or other stipulation as to their relationship. However, the circumstances in which courts will find and enforce a duty to negotiate vary depending on the jurisdiction. (For the particular issue of indefiniteness, see Chapter 11.A). In this respect, the U.S. common law stands in contrast with many civil law jurisdictions, where the mere act of entering negotiations can create a binding obligation to continue negotiating in good faith, under general principles of contract (e.g. in Germany) or tort (e.g. in France) law: E. Allan Farnsworth, *Precontractual Liability and Preliminary Agreements: Fair Dealing and Failed Negotiations*, 87 Colum. L. Rev. 217, 239–241 (1987).

4. Indeed, in many international and comparative settings, the principle of good faith occupies a much more prominent role. Consider the UNIDROIT Principles, for example, art. 1.7(1) (establishing requirement of good faith and fair dealing in international trade) and arts. 2.1.15(1) and 2.1.15(3) (liability for negotiations or termination of negotiations in bad faith). Such expansive treatment is very different from U.S. law. What might be the advantages of having a more prominent signal to commercial parties

of such a standard? Do you think this would lead to more certainty and predictability in the law? Consider K. N. Llewellyn, *The Standardization of Commercial Contracts in English and Continental Law*, 52 HARV. L. REV. 700, 703 (1939), who suggested that the Anglo-American use of "covert" fairness-seeking tools may result in "unnecessary confusion and unpredictability, together with inadequate remedy, and evil persisting that calls for remedy. Covert tools are never reliable tools." Or regardless, is this an area where we might think that certainty may not be an unqualified good, as it is in other parts of the law?

CHAPTER NINE

EXPRESS CONDITIONS

> Dese are de conditions dat prevail
>
> —Jimmy Durante

A. EXPRESS CONDITIONS—GENERAL CONCEPT

Restatement (Second) of Contracts § 224

Condition Defined

A condition is an event, not certain to occur, which must occur, unless its non-occurrence is excused, before performance under a contract becomes due.

Comment:

a. *"Condition" limited to event.* "Condition" is used in this Restatement to denote an event which qualifies a duty under a contract. . . . It is recognized that "condition" is used with a wide variety of other meanings in legal discourse. . . . Sometimes it is used to refer to a term (§ 5) in an agreement that makes an event a condition, or more broadly to refer to any term in an agreement (e.g., "standard conditions of sale"). For the sake of precision, "condition" is not used here in these other senses.

Illustration:

1. A contracts to sell and B to buy goods pursuant to a writing which provides, under the heading "Conditions of Sale," that "the obligations of the parties are conditional on B obtaining from X Bank by June 30 a letter of credit" on stated terms. The quoted language is a term of the agreement (§ 5), not a condition. The event referred to by the term, obtaining the letter of credit by June 30, is a condition.

Luttinger v. Rosen

Supreme Court of Connecticut, 1972.
164 Conn. 45, 316 A.2d 757.

■ LOISELLE, ASSOCIATE JUSTICE.

The plaintiffs contracted to purchase for $85,000 premises in the city of Stamford owned by the defendants and paid a deposit of $8500. The contract was 'subject to and conditional upon the buyers obtaining first mortgage financing on said premises from a bank or other lending institution in an amount of $45,000 for a term of not less than twenty (20) years and at an interest rate which does not exceed 8 ½ per cent per annum.' The plaintiffs agreed to use due diligence in attempting to obtain such financing. The parties further agreed that if the plaintiffs were unsuccessful in obtaining financing as provided in the contract, and notified the seller within a specific time, all sums paid on the contract would be refunded and the contract terminated without further obligation of either party.

In applying for a mortgage which would satisfy the contingency clause in the contract, the plaintiffs relied on their attorney who applied at a New Haven lending institution for a $45,000 loan at 8 ¼ percent per annum interest over a period of twenty-five years. The plaintiffs' attorney knew that this lending institution was the only one which at that time would lend as much as $45,000 on a mortgage for a single-family dwelling. A mortgage commitment was obtained for $45,000 with 'interest at the prevailing rate at the time of closing but not less that 8 ¾%.' Since this commitment failed to meet the contract requirement, timely notice was given to the defendants and demand was made for the return of the down payment. . . . [O]n the defendants' refusal to return the deposit an action was brought. From a judgment rendered in favor of the plaintiffs the defendants have appealed.

The defendants claim that the plaintiffs did not use due diligence in seeking a mortgage within the terms specified in the contract. The unattacked findings by the court establish that the plaintiffs' attorney was fully informed as to the conditions and terms of mortgages being granted by various banks and lending institutions in and out of the area and that the application was made to the only bank which might satisfy the mortgage conditions of the contingency clause at that time. These findings adequately support the court's conclusion that due diligence was used in seeking mortgage financing in accordance with the contract provisions. *Brauer v. Freccia*, 159 Conn. 289, 293, 268 A.2d 645. The defendants assert that notwithstanding the plaintiffs' reliance on their counsel's knowledge of lending practices, applications should have been made to other lending institutions. This claim is not well taken. The law does not require the performance of a futile act. * * *

The remaining assignment of error briefed by the defendants is that the court erred in concluding that the mortgage contingency clause of the contract, a condition precedent, was not met and, therefore, the plaintiffs were entitled to recover their deposit. 'A condition precedent is a fact or event which the parties intend must exist or take place before there is a right to performance.' *Lach v. Cahill*, 138 Conn. 418, 421, 85 A.2d 481, 482. If the condition precedent is not fulfilled the contract is not enforceable. *Lach v. Cahill, supra; Bialeck v. Hartford*, 135 Conn. 551, 556, 66 A.2d 610. In this case the language of the contract is unambiguous and clearly indicates that the parties intended that the purchase of the defendants' premises be conditioned on the obtaining by the plaintiffs of a mortgage as specified in the contract. From the subordinate facts found the court could reasonably conclude that since the plaintiffs were unable to obtain a $45,000 mortgage at no more than 8 ½ percent per annum interest 'from a bank or other lending institution' the condition precedent to performance of the contract was not met and the plaintiffs were entitled to the refund of their deposit. . . .

There is no error.

NOTES

The *Luttinger* case uses the phrase "condition precedent." That's a common, but somewhat silly, bit of lawyer jargon. First, we should note the odd pronunciation. One would think that "precedent" would be pronounced "pres'-uh-dent" as in descriptions of prior judicial decisions. In this context, however, lawyers pronounce it "pre-see'-dent." We have no idea why.

Passing pronunciation, one might ask why not just use the simple term "condition" rather than the fancy one "condition precedent," and how a condition *precedent* is different from some other kind of condition. The usual response would be that it's useful to distinguish *conditions precedent* from *conditions subsequent*. Theoretically, the difference is a matter of timing. A condition precedent is an event that must occur before performance of a promise comes due. A condition subsequent is an event that, if it does occur, discharges the obligation to perform a promise. (Remember the deadline for the P&S agreement in McCarthy v. Tobin, 429 Mass. 84, 706 N.E.2d 629 (1999) back in Chapter 3?) But, nothing of any substance turns on that distinction. We only care about whether performance of a promise is due at some particular moment. If performance of a promise is subject to a condition precedent, and that condition has not occurred, then performance is not due. If performance of a promise is subject to a condition subsequent, and that condition has occurred, then performance is no longer due. So what?

If any of you plan to practice law before, say, the middle of the twentieth century, the distinction might be relevant as a matter of civil procedure. The old pleading rule was that a complaint had to specifically plead and prove the occurrence of all conditions precedent. By contrast, a complaint did not have to plead the non-occurrence of conditions subsequent. That difference in pleading rules, however, is rejected in the Federal Rules of Civil Procedure, and state procedural rules modeled on them. FRCP 9(c) says that one does not have to specifically plead the occurrence of conditions. Rather it's good enough to "aver generally that all conditions precedent have been performed or have occurred."

Modern contract law does not use the terms "precedent" and "subsequent." See Restatement (Second) of Contracts § 224, comment e. But, lawyers still like fancy talk, so you'll often hear the phrase "condition precedent" with its odd pronunciation. Actually, we've always thought that if you hear a lawyer on the other side using that term, it's a good sign for you, since the opposing lawyer is basically saying "I don't really know what I'm talking about, but it does sound cool."

B. INTERPRETATION TO AVOID FORFEITURE

Peacock Constr. Co. v. Modern Air Conditioning, Inc.

Supreme Court of Florida, 1977.
353 So.2d 840.

■ BOYD, ACTING CHIEF JUSTICE.

We issued an order allowing certiorari in these two causes because the decisions in them of the District Court of Appeal, Second District, conflict with the decision in *Edward J. Gerrits, Inc. v. Astor Electric Service, Inc.*, 328 So.2d 522 (Fla.3d DCA 1976). The two causes have been consolidated for all appellate purposes in this Court because they involve the same issue. That issue is whether the plaintiffs, Modern Air Conditioning and Overly Manufacturing, were entitled to summary judgments against Peacock Construction Company in actions for breaches of identical contractual provisions.

Peacock Construction was the builder of a condominium project. Modern Air Conditioning subcontracted with Peacock to do the heating and air conditioning work and Overly Manufacturing subcontracted with Peacock to do the "rooftop swimming pool" work. Both written subcontracts provided that Peacock would make final payment to the subcontractors,

> "within 30 days after the completion of the work included in this sub-contract, written acceptance by the Architect and full payment therefor by the Owner."

Modern Air Conditioning and Overly Manufacturing completed the work specified in their contracts and requested final payment. When Peacock refused to make the final payments the two subcontractors separately brought actions in the Lee County Circuit Court for breach of contract. In both actions it was established that no deficiencies had been found in the completed work. But Peacock established that it had not received from the owner[4] full payment for the subcontractors' work. And it defended on the basis that such payment was a condition which, by express term of the final payment provision, had to be fulfilled before it was obligated to perform under the contract. On motions by the plaintiffs, the trial judges granted summary judgments in their favor. The orders of judgment implicitly interpreted the contract not to require payment by the owner as a condition precedent to Peacock's duty to perform.

The Second District Court of Appeal affirmed the lower court's judgment in the appeal brought by Modern Air Conditioning. In so doing it adopted the view of the majority of jurisdictions in this country that provisions of the kind disputed here do not set conditions precedent but rather constitute absolute promises to pay, fixing payment by the owner

---

[4]   The owner, a corporation, had entered proceedings in bankruptcy.

as a reasonable time for when payment to the subcontractor is to be made. When the judgment in the Overly Manufacturing case reached the Second District Court, Modern Air Conditioning had been decided and the judgment, therefore, was affirmed on the authority of the latter decision. These two decisions plainly conflict with *Gerrits*, *supra*.

In *Gerrits*, the Court had summarily ordered judgment for the plaintiff/subcontractor against the defendant/general contractor on a contractual provision for payment to the subcontractor which read,

> "The money to be paid in current funds and at such times as the General Contractor receives it from the Owner." Id. at 523.

In its review of the judgment, the Third District Court of Appeal referred to the fundamental rule of interpretation of contracts that it be done in accordance with the intention of the parties. Since the defendant had introduced below the issue of intention, a material issue, and since the issue was one that could be resolved through a factual determination by the jury, the Third District reversed the summary judgment and remanded for trial.

Peacock urges us to adopt *Gerrits* as the controlling law in this State. It concedes that the Second District's decisions are backed by the weight of authority. But it argues that they are incorrect because the issue of intention is a factual one which should be resolved after the parties have had an opportunity to present evidence on it. Peacock urges, therefore, that the causes be remanded for trial. If there is produced no evidence that the parties intended there be condition precedents, only then, says Peacock, should the judge, by way of a directed verdict for the subcontractors, be allowed to take the issue of intention from the jury.

The contractual provisions in dispute here are susceptible to two interpretations. They may be interpreted as setting a condition precedent or as fixing a reasonable time for payment. The provision disputed in Gerrits is susceptible to the same two interpretations. The questions presented by the conflict between these decisions, then, are whether ambiguous contractual provisions of the kind disputed here may be interpreted only by the factfinder, usually the jury, or if they should be interpreted as a matter of law by the court, and if so what interpretation they should be given.

Although it must be admitted that the meaning of language is a factual question, the general rule is that interpretation of a document is a question of law rather than of fact. 4 Williston on Contracts, 3rd Ed., § 616. If an issue of contract interpretation concerns the intention of parties, that intention may be determined from the written contract, as a matter of law, when the nature of the transaction lends itself to judicial interpretation. A number of courts, with whom we agree, have recognized that contracts between small subcontractors and general contractors on large construction projects are such transactions. * * * The reason is that the relationship between the parties is a common one and usually their intent will not differ from transaction to transaction, although it may be differently expressed.

That intent in most cases is that payment by the owner to the general contractor is not a condition precedent to the general contractor's duty to pay the subcontractors. This is because small subcontractors, who must have payment for their work in order to remain in business, will not ordinarily assume the risk of the owner's failure to pay the general contractor. And this is the reason for the majority view in this country, which we now join.

Our decision to require judicial interpretation of ambiguous provisions for final payment in subcontracts in favor of subcontractors should not be regarded as anti-general contractor. It is simply a recognition that this is the fairest way to deal with the problem. There is nothing in this opinion, however, to prevent parties to these contracts from shifting the risk of payment failure by the owner to the subcontractor. But in order to make such a shift the contract must unambiguously express that intention. And the burden of clear expression is on the general contractor.

The decisions of the Second District Court of Appeal to affirm the summary judgments were correct. We adopt, therefore, these two decisions as the controlling law in Florida and we overrule *Gerrits*, to the extent it is inconsistent with this opinion.

The orders allowing certiorari in these two causes are discharged. It is so ordered.

NOTES & QUESTIONS

1. The *Peacock* case is another example of the common arrangement in construction where the owner enters into a contract with the general contractor, and then the general contractor enters into separate contracts with subcontractors. *Peacock* was an action by a subcontractor against the general contractor. The disputed term, saying that the general would pay the sub "within 30 days after . . . payment therefor by the Owner" was a term of the agreement between the general and the sub. If that term had been interpreted as creating a condition to the general's duty to perform its promise to pay, then the result would have been that the sub risks not getting paid for the work if the owner doesn't pay the general. If, as was the result in the case, that term is not interpreted as creating a condition, then the sub is entitled to payment from the general, and the general is the one who takes all of the risk of the owner's insolvency.

2. Suppose Lawyer enters into a contract with Client under which Lawyer agrees to bring a lawsuit on behalf of Client, and Client agrees to pay Lawyer one-third of any amount that Client is awarded in the lawsuit. Suppose that Lawyer does an excellent job representing Client, and Lawyer spends a great deal of time on the case. Nonetheless, the court rules against

Client. Is Lawyer entitled to any compensation from Client, perhaps at an hourly rate?

3.   Sometimes an agreement will provide that A will do work for B, and B will pay "if satisfied" with the work. There's no question that the agreement makes B's satisfaction a condition of B's duty to perform the promise to pay. There is, however, room for dispute about how the "satisfaction" term should be interpreted. Does it mean that B doesn't have to pay if—for any reason—B just says "I'm not satisfied"? Or, does it mean that B is obligated to pay if a reasonable person in B's situation would have been satisfied?

One can describe fairly easy polar cases: If A promises to paint a portrait of B, and the agreement says that B will only pay if B is "satisfied" with the portrait, then there's not much room for second guessing an assertion by B that he is not satisfied. In a job where personal taste is so significant, it's hard to say that B's statement that "I'm not satisfied" was unreasonable. Moreover, the artist in that case went into the transaction with eyes wide open, realizing there was a risk that if B didn't like the portrait A would not get paid.

By contrast suppose that A is a house painter, and A enters into an agreement under which A will paint B's house, and B will pay a certain amount, provided that the work is satisfactorily completed. In that case, one might say that we can look to the general standards of house painters' work to decide what is and is not satisfactory completion. Accordingly, we'd say that A is entitled to payment if a reasonable person in B's situation would have been satisfied with the work.

C. DISTINGUISHING PROMISES FROM CONDITIONS

Merritt Hill Vineyards Inc. v. Windy Heights Vineyard, Inc.

Court of Appeals of New York, 1984.
61 N.Y.S.2d 106, 460 N.E.2d 1077.

■ KAYE, JUDGE.

In a contract for the sale of a controlling stock interest in a vineyard, the seller's undertaking to produce a title insurance policy and mortgage confirmation at closing constituted a condition and not a promise, the breach of which excused the buyer's performance and entitled it to the return of its deposit, but not to consequential damages. On the buyer's motion for summary judgment seeking recovery of both the deposit and consequential damages, the Appellate Division 94 A.D.2d 947, 463 N.Y.S.2d 960, correctly awarded summary judgment to the buyer for its deposit and to the seller dismissing the cause of action for consequential damages, even though the seller had not sought this relief by cross appeal.

In September, 1981, plaintiff, Merritt Hill Vineyards, entered into a written agreement with defendants, Windy Heights Vineyard and its sole shareholder Leon Taylor, to purchase a majority stock interest in respondents' Yates County vineyard, and tendered a $15,000 deposit. The agreement provides that "[i]f the sale contemplated hereby does not close, Taylor shall retain the deposit as liquidated damages unless Taylor or Windy Heights failed to satisfy the conditions specified in Section 3 thereof." Section 3, in turn, lists several "conditions precedent" to which the obligation of purchaser to pay the purchase price and to complete the purchase is subject. Among the conditions are that, by the time of the closing, Windy Heights shall have obtained a title insurance policy in a form satisfactory to Merritt Hill, and Windy Heights and Merritt Hill shall have received confirmation from the Farmers Home Administration that certain mortgages on the vineyard are in effect and that the proposed sale does not constitute a default.

In April, 1982, at the closing, plaintiff discovered that neither the policy nor the confirmation had been issued. Plaintiff thereupon refused to close and demanded return of its deposit. When defendants did not return the deposit, plaintiff instituted this action, asserting two causes of action, one for return of the deposit, and one for approximately $26,000 in consequential damages allegedly suffered as a result of defendants' failure to perform.

Special Term denied plaintiff's motion for summary judgment on both causes of action. The Appellate Division unanimously reversed Special Term's order, granted plaintiff's motion for summary judgment as to the cause of action for return of the deposit, and upon searching the record pursuant to CPLR 3212 (subd. [b]), granted summary judgment in favor of defendants, dismissing plaintiff's second cause of action for consequential damages. Both plaintiff and defendants appealed from that decision. . . .

. . .

On the merits, plaintiff's right to return of its deposit or to consequential damages depends upon whether the undertaking to produce the policy and mortgage confirmation is a promise or a condition.

A promise is "a manifestation of intention to act or refrain from acting in a specified way, so made as to justify a promisee in understanding that a commitment has been made." (Restatement, Contracts 2d, § 2, subd. [1].) A *condition,* by comparison, is "an event, not certain to occur, which must occur, unless its non-occurrence is excused, before performance under a contract becomes due." (Restatement, Contracts 2d, § 224.) Here, the contract requirements of a title insurance policy and mortgage confirmation are expressed as conditions of plaintiff's performance rather than as promises by defendants. The requirements are contained in a section of the agreement entitled "Conditions Precedent to Purchaser's Obligation to Close," which provides that plaintiff's obligation to pay the purchase price and complete the purchase of the vineyard is "subject to" fulfillment of those requirements. No words of promise are employed.* Defendants' agreement to sell the stock of the vineyard, not those conditions, was the promise by defendants for which plaintiff's promise to pay the purchase price was exchanged.

Defendants' failure to fulfill the conditions of section 3 entitles plaintiff to a return of its deposit but not to consequential damages. While a contracting party's failure to fulfill a condition excuses performance by the other party whose performance is so conditioned, it is not, without an independent promise to perform the condition, a breach of contract subjecting the nonfulfilling party to liability for damages (Restatement, Contracts 2d, § 225, subds. [1], [3]; 3A Corbin, Contracts, § 663; 5 Williston, Contracts [Jaeger—3d ed.], § 665). This is in accord with the parties' expressed intent, for section 1 of their agreement provides that if defendants fail to satisfy the conditions of section 3 plaintiff's deposit will be returned. It does not provide for payment of damages.

On the merits of this case the Appellate Division thus correctly determined that plaintiff was entitled to the return of its deposit but not to consequential damages.

Accordingly, the order of the Appellate Division should be affirmed.

PROBLEM

Dressmaker & Customer agree that:

> Customer will pay $4000;
>
> Dressmaker will make a dress conforming to certain design specifications; and
>
> "Dress is to be finished by 17 May."

What are the consequences if the dress is not finished by 17 May?

Imagine various reasons that the parties might have included the term about completion by May 17, and consider how various versions of the facts might bear on the interpretation of that term.

---

* Plaintiff contends that the failure to produce the policy and confirmation is also a breach of section 5, entitled "Representations, Warranties and Agreements." A provision may be both a condition and a promise, if the parties additionally promise to perform a condition as part of their bargain. Such a promise is not present here. The only provision of section 5 conceivably relevant is that "Windy Heights has good and marketable title to the Property and all other properties and assets . . . as of December 31, 1980". But this is quite different from the conditions of section 3 that a title insurance policy and mortgage confirmation be produced at the closing, which took place in April, 1982. Both the complaint and plaintiff's affidavits are premised on nonperformance of section 3 of the agreement, not section 5.

CHAPTER TEN

CONSTRUCTIVE CONDITIONS OF EXCHANGE

> You first, my dear Gaston
> After you, my dear Alphonse
>
> —Frederick Burr Opper

A. CONSTRUCTIVE CONDITIONS OF EXCHANGE— GENERAL CONCEPT

Restatement (Second) of Contracts §§ 237 & 238

Consider a simple contract for sale of real estate. Seller promises to convey the real estate on a certain date. Buyer promises to pay a certain sum of money. Each party's promise is supported by consideration, in the form of the return promise. That is, the consideration for the Seller's promise to convey the real estate is the Buyer's promise to pay the agreed price. The consideration for the Buyer's promise to pay the price is the Seller's promise to convey the real estate.

Now, suppose that the date for the closing comes, and the Seller is unwilling or unable to convey. It seems pretty obvious that if the Seller doesn't convey the real estate, then the Buyer is not obligated to pay the price. That is, neither party is obligated to perform its promise unless the other side is going to perform its promise.

Somewhat surprisingly, English law apparently had trouble working through this fairly simple point. Maybe the problem was confusion between consideration concepts, which were developing in the sixteenth and seventeenth centuries, and the notion that each party's duty to perform depends on the other sides' performance. Note that the consideration for the seller's promise to convey is not the buyer's *payment* but the buyer's *promise to pay*. That's why both sides are contractually obligated at the moment that the agreement is executed. The difference between the consideration point and the performance point may have been what led to an odd result in the old English case of *Nichols v. Raynbred*, 80 Eng. Rep. 238 (K.B. 1615). There was an agreement for sale of a cow. The seller sued the buyer for the price, and the Court said that "the plaintiff [seller] need not aver delivery of the cow, because it is promise for promise." Taken literally, that would seem to mean that the seller could win an action for the price even if the seller did not deliver the cow. The buyer's right would presumably be to bring another law suit, suing the seller for breach of the promise to deliver, and thereby get back the money that the seller won in the first law suit. That's pretty silly. The law on this problem was straightened out by Lord Mansfield in the well-known case of *Kingston v. Preston*:

Kingston v. Preston
Court of King's Bench, 1773.
99 Eng. Rep. 437.[a]

[The owner of a silk business made an agreement with a person who was serving as his apprentice. The deal was that the apprentice would work for about a year, and then the business owner would transfer the business to him. The apprentice couldn't afford to pay the full purchase price. The seller was willing to accept payment in installments over a period of time, but the seller was not willing to accept merely the apprentice's promise to pay. Accordingly, the agreement provided that the apprentice would get someone else, more financially responsible, to give the seller a guaranty of the buyer's promise to pay.

When the time for the seller to convey the business came, the buyer had not gotten the guaranty called for by the agreement, so the seller—not surprisingly—refused to convey the business. Drawing on the odd notions derived from *Nichols v. Raynbred*, the buyer sued the seller. The buyer's argument was that the seller's promise to convey was enforceable because it was supported by consideration—the return promise of the buyer to pay and the promise of the buyer to get a guaranty. The buyer argued that the seller was not justified in refusing to convey the business. If the seller was unhappy about not getting the guaranty, let the seller sue. Lord Mansfield rejected that argument, ruling that (to put it in modern language) it was a "constructive condition" of the seller's duty to perform its promise to convey that the buyer have performed the promise to get a guaranty. Here's how Lord Mansfield explained the idea:]

In delivering the judgment of the Court, Lord Mansfield expressed himself to the following effect:

There are three kinds of covenants:

1.   Such as are called mutual and independent, where either party may recover damages from the other, for the injury he may have received by a breach of the covenants in his favour, and where it is no excuse for the defendant, to allege a breach of the covenants on the part of the plaintiff.

2.   There are covenants which are conditions and dependant, in which the performance of one depends on the prior performance of another, and, therefore, till this prior condition is performed, the other party is not liable to an action on his covenant.

---

[a]   The excerpt from report printed here is from the version commonly used. It actually appears as part of the argument of counsel in another case, *Jones v. Barkley*, 99 Eng. Rep. 434 (K.B. 1781).

3.   There is also a third sort of covenants, which are mutual conditions to be performed at the same time; and, in these, if one party was ready, and offered, to perform his part, and the other neglected, or refused, to perform his, he who was ready, and offered, has fulfilled his engagement, and may maintain an action for the default of the other; though it is not certain that either is obliged to do the first act.

His Lordship then proceeded to say, that the dependence, or independence, of covenants, was to be collected from the evident sense and meaning of the parties, and, that, however transposed they might be in the deed, their precedency must depend on the order of time in which the intent of the transaction requires their performance. That, in the case before the Court, it would be the greatest injustice if the plaintiff should prevail: the essence of the agreement was that the defendant should not trust to the personal security of the plaintiff, but, before he delivered up his stock and business, should have good security for the payment of the money. The giving such security, therefore, must necessarily be a condition precedent.

Judgment was accordingly given for the defendant, because the part to be performed by the plaintiff was clearly a condition precedent.

NOTES

Though it's hard to follow, Lord Mansfield's decision in *Kingston v. Preston* is a nice illustration of how an extremely capable judge changes the law. Mansfield says that where we have an agreement in which the parties exchange promises, there are three possible treatments of the effect on one party's failure to perform on the other party's duty to perform. First, there is the category that Mansfield called "independent" promises. In that category of case, the failure of one party to perform is not an excuse for the other party's failure to perform. As we will see, that's a rare category today. But, at the time of Mansfield's decision in *Kingston v. Preston*, that category was the whole ball of wax. That's the significance of the old case of *Nichols v. Raynbred*.

Lord Mansfield might have said "*Nichols v. Raynbred* was wrong and we decline to follow it." That, however, would have been a bold move in a system of case law built on the concept of *stare decisis*. Instead, Mansfield cleverly got around *Nichols v. Raynbred* by saying that it illustrated only one category. Then Mansfield proceeded to, in essence, invent the other category (or categories) of "dependent" promises, in which the failure of one party to perform does excuse the other party from a duty to perform. In the case itself, he ruled that the apprentice's promise to get the guaranty and the master's promise to convey the business were "dependent," so that the apprentice's failure to perform the promise to get the guaranty did excuse the master's failure to perform the promise to convey.

Mansfield's second and third categories are different only with respect to the time for performance of the dependent promises. In his second category, the agreement indicates that one party is to perform before the other party performs. That would be called "dependent sequential" in more modern terminology. In his third category, the agreement indicates that the promises are to be performed at the same time. That would be called "dependent simultaneous" in more modern terminology. We will look at the timing question shortly.

NOTE ON TERMINOLOGY: "DEPENDENT" AND "INDEPENDENT" PROMISES

Restatement (Second) of Contracts §§ 231 & 232

Contracts law scholars disagree on whether the terms "dependent" and "independent" are or are not useful is describing the problem of the effect on one side's failure to perform on the other side's duty to perform. The Restatement takes the position that those terms are not helpful. *See* RESTATEMENT (SECOND) OF CONTRACTS § 231, Reporter's Note (The Restatement "avoids as misleading . . . any classification of promises as either 'dependent' or 'independent.'"). But, the terminology is commonly used, so we think it may be just as well for us to become familiar with it.

Instead of using the terms "dependent" and "independent," the Restatement speaks of "performances to be exchanged under an exchange of promises." See RESTATEMENT (SECOND) OF CONTRACTS § 231. That's essentially the same notion that is captured by the phrase "dependent promises." Take the situation in *Kingston v. Preston*. Cases and common lawyer jargon would express the outcome in Kingston by saying that Mansfield ruled that that the apprentice's promise to get the guaranty and the master's promise to convey the business were "dependent," so that the apprentice's failure to perform the promise to get the guaranty did excuse the master's failure to perform the promise to convey. The Restatement would express the same point by saying that in the agreement the apprentice and the master exchanged promises, but it was understood that the *performance* of those promises was also to be exchanged, that is, the agreement called for "performances to be exchanged under an exchange of promises."

RESTATEMENT (SECOND) OF CONTRACTS §§ 231 & 232 state rules for deciding whether an agreement should be interpreted as providing for "performances to be exchanged under an exchange of promises"

> Performances are to be exchanged under an exchange of promises if each promise is at least part of the consideration for the other and the performance of each promise is to be exchanged at least in part for the performance of the other.

> Where the consideration given by each party to a contract consists in whole or in part of promises, all the performances to be rendered by each party taken collectively are treated as performances to be exchanged under an exchange of promises, unless a contrary intention is clearly manifested.

That's going to be the case in virtually all agreements. Take the agreement for sale of real estate. The consideration for the seller's promise to convey is the buyer's promise to pay, and the seller's performance (actually conveying) is to be exchanged for the buyer's performance (actually paying).

The category of "independent promises"—or agreements that do not involve "performances to be exchanged under an exchange of promises" to use the Restatement's terminology—is pretty rare. We consider it in the next section.

B. INDEPENDENT PROMISES

Orkin Exterminating Co. v. Harris

Supreme Court of Georgia, 1968.
224 Ga. 759, 164 S.E.2d 727.

■ GRICE, JUSTICE.

A suit seeking injunctive relief against alleged violation of restrictive covenants as to employment produced this appeal. Orkin Exterminating Company, Inc., filed the action against its former employee, Billy Harris, in the Superior Court of Baldwin County. Upon conclusion of a hearing the trial court entered an order vacating a restraining order previously granted and denying the employer's prayer for interlocutory injunction. Enumerated as error are the entry of this order, and also the refusal to pass upon and grant the employer's motion for judgment on the pleadings.

At the hearing it appeared without dispute that the parties entered into a written contract of employment dated December 31, 1964, which, among other matters, prohibited the employee for a period of two years immediately following its termination 'for any reason whatsoever,' directly or indirectly, for himself or on behalf of any other person or company, from calling upon or soliciting customers of Orkin and from engaging in the same business in a designated area of this State. It also appeared without contradiction that the employee, during the prohibited time and within the prohibited area, made such solicitations and engaged in the same business.

The same contract provisions in issue here have been upheld as reasonable restraint of trade and therefore enforceable by this court in the following cases: *Orkin Exterminating Company, Inc., of South Georgia v. Mills*, 218 Ga. 340, 127 S.E.2d 796; *Thomas v. Orkin Termite Company, Inc.*, 222 Ga. 207, 149 S.E.2d 85; *Orkin Exterminating Company, Inc. v. Gill*, 222 Ga. 760, 152 S.E.2d 411; and *Rider v. Orkin Exterminating Company, Inc.*, 224 Ga. 145, 160 S.E.2d 381. The *Mills* and *Gill* cases, *supra*, involved, as here, denial of temporary injunctions and were reversed by this court.

In the case at bar the employee seeks to excuse his admitted violation of the covenants as to solicitation and competition upon the ground that the evidence showed the employer had breached the contract. He claims (1) that he was not paid certain compensation due him and therefore there was a failure of consideration for the covenants now in question; (2) that the employer sought to have him agree to a new contract provision as to compensation and upon his refusal, wrongfully terminated his employment; and (3) that the employer had failed to instruct him on the secret methods and means of pest control referred to in the contract and thereby made a material misrepresentation as to the benefits accruing to him under the contract.

This contention is not meritorious.

We regard the *Gill* case, 222 Ga. 760, 152 S.E.2d 411, supra, as controlling. There the employee defended upon the ground that the employer had discharged him, in violation of the terms of the contract, and thereby failed to do equity. The trial court based its denial of injunction upon that defense. However, upon review, this court's opinion stressed the contract language that "These covenants (restrictive) on the part of the employee shall be construed as an agreement independent of any other provision in this agreement, and the existence of any claim or cause of action of the employee against the company whether predicated on this agreement or otherwise, shall not constitute a defense to the enforcement by the Company of said covenants.' (Emphasis supplied.)' The contract in the case at bar contains this same provision.

The *Gill* opinion stated that the case was controlled by *Mansfield v. B. & W. Gas, Inc.*, 222 Ga. 259(2), 149 S.E.2d 482, which said that under a comparable contract '. . . whether the employee voluntarily terminated the contract or was involuntarily discharged would be of no consequence, for the covenant restricting the right of the individual to work for a competitor would not be contingent on the manner of termination but 'regardless of who was at fault' would be valid and enforceable.' This court then held that under the *Mansfield* decision the trial judge 'was bound as a matter of law to grant the temporary injunction, and it was error not to do so.'

The ruling thus made in the *Gill* case, and its supporting *Mansfield* decision, that the covenants in the contract are independent, compels the conclusion that the contentions relied upon by the employee here are not maintainable. See also the *Rider* case, 224 Ga. 145, 160 S.E.2d 381, supra, especially in connection with the contention as to failure of consideration.

We therefore hold that the evidence demanded the injunctive relief sought, and that its denial was error.

. . .

All the Justices concur.

NOTES

Like the equitable remedy of specific performance (recall Chapter 1.C), the injunction is an extraordinary remedy that compels a party to do (or, in this case, not do) something. An interlocutory injunction aims to preserve the status quo until judgment can be made.

C. DEPENDENT PROMISES—TIMING ISSUES

1. SEQUENTIAL OR SIMULTANEOUS

Stewart v. Newbury

Court of Appeals of New York, 1917.
220 N.Y. 379, 115 N.E. 984.

■ CRANE, J.

The defendants are partners in the pipe fitting business under the name of Newbury Manufacturing Company. The plaintiff is a contractor and builder residing at Tuxedo, N.Y.

The parties had the following correspondence about the erection for the defendants of a concrete mill building at Monroe, N.Y.:

Alexander Stewart,
Contractor and Builder,
Tuxedo, N. Y.

July 18, 1911.

Newbury Mfg. Company

Monroe, N. Y.

Gentlemen:

With reference to the proposed work on the new foundry building I had hoped to be able to get up and see you this afternoon, but find that impossible and am, in consequence, sending you these prices, which I trust you will find satisfactory.

I will agree to do all excavation work required at sixty-five ($.65) cents per cubic yard.

I will put in the concrete work, furnishing labor and forms only, at two and 05–100 ($2.05) dollars per cubic yard.

I will furnish labor to put in reinforcing at four ($4.00) dollars per ton.

I will furnish labor only to set all window and door frames, window sash and doors, including the setting of hardware for one hundred twelve ($112) dollars. As alternative I would be willing to do any or all of the above work for cost plus 10 per cent., furnishing you with first class mechanics and giving the work considerable of my personal time.

Hoping to hear favorably from you in this regard, I am,

Respectfully yours,

[Signed] Alexander Stewart.

The Newbury Mfg. Co.,
Steam Fittings, Grey Iron Castings,
Skylight Opening Apparatus,
Monroe, N. Y.

July 22, 1911.

Alexander Stewart

Tuxedo Park, N. Y.

Dear Sir:

Confirming the telephone conversation of this morning we accept your bid of July the 18th to do the concrete work on our new building. We trust that you will be able to get at this the early part of next week.

Yours truly,

The Newbury Mfg. Co.,

H. A. Newbury.

Nothing was said in writing about the time or manner of payment. The plaintiff, however, claims that after sending his letter, and before receiving that of the defendant, he had a telephone communication with Mr. Newbury and said: 'I will expect my payments in the usual manner,' and Newbury said, 'All right, we have got the money to pay for the building.' This conversation over the telephone was denied by the defendants. The custom, the plaintiff testified, was to pay 85 per cent every 30 days or at the end of each month, 15 per cent being retained till the work was completed.

In July the plaintiff commenced work and continued until September 29th, at which time he had progressed with the construction as far as the first floor. He then sent a bill for the work done up to that date for $896.35. The defendants refused to pay the bill and work was discontinued. The plaintiff claims that the defendants refused to permit him to perform the rest of his contract, they insisting that the work already done was not in accordance with the specifications. The defendants claimed upon the trial that the plaintiff voluntarily abandoned the work after their refusal to pay his bill.

On October 5, 1911, the defendants wrote the plaintiff a letter containing the following:

'Notwithstanding you promised to let us know on Monday whether you would complete the job or throw up the contract, you have not up to this time advised us of your intention. . . . Under the circumstances, we are compelled to accept your action as being an abandonment of your contract and of every effort upon your part to complete your work on our building. As you know, the bill which you sent us and which we declined to pay is not correct, either in items or amount, nor is there anything due you under our contract as we understand it until you have completed your work on our building.'

To this letter the plaintiff replied the following day. In it he makes no reference to the telephone communication agreeing, as he testified, to make 'the usual payments,' but does say this:

'There is nothing in our agreement which says that I shall wait until the job is completed before any payment is due, nor can this be reasonably implied. . . . As to having given you positive date as to when I should let you know what I proposed doing, I did not do so; on the contrary, I told you that I would not tell you positively what I would do until I had visited the job, and I promised that I would do this at my earliest convenience and up to the present time I have been unable to get up there.'

The defendant Herbert Newbury testified that the plaintiff 'ran away and left the whole thing.' And the defendant F. A. Newbury testified that he was told by Mr. Stewart's man that Stewart was going to abandon the job; that he thereupon telephoned Mr. Stewart, who replied that he would let him know about it the next day, but did not.

In this action, which is brought to recover the amount of the bill presented, as the agreed price and $95.68 damages for breach of contract, the plaintiff had a verdict for the amount stated in the bill, but not for the other damages claimed, and the judgment entered thereon has been affirmed by the Appellate Division.

The appeal to us is upon exceptions to the judge's charge. The court charged the jury as follows:

'Plaintiff says that he was excused from completely performing the contract by the defendants' unreasonable failure to pay him for the work he had done during the months of August and September. Was it understood that the payments were to be made monthly? If it was not so understood, the defendants' only obligation was to make payments at reasonable periods, in view of the character of the work, the amount of work being done, and the value of it. In other words, if there was no agreement between the parties respecting the payments, the defendants' obligation was to make payments at reasonable times. But whether there was such an agreement or not, you may consider whether it was reasonable or unreasonable for him to exact a payment at that time and in that amount.'

The court further said, in reply to a request to charge:

'I will say in that connection, if there was no agreement respecting the time of payment, and if there was no custom that was understood by both parties, and with respect to which they made the contract, then the plaintiff was entitled to payments at reasonable times.'

The defendants' counsel thereupon made the following request, which was refused:

'I ask your honor to instruct the jury that, if the circumstances existed as your honor stated in your last instruction, then the plaintiff was not entitled to any payment until the contract was completed.'

The jury was plainly told that if there were no agreement as to payments, yet the plaintiff would be entitled to part payment at reasonable times as the work progressed, and if such payments were refused he could abandon the work and recover the amount due for the work performed.

This is not the law. Counsel for the plaintiff omits to call our attention to any authority sustaining such a proposition and our search reveals none. In fact, the law is very well settled to the contrary. This was an entire contract. *Ming v. Corbin*, 142 N. Y. 334, 340, 341, 37 N. E. 105. Where a contract is made to perform work and no agreement is made as to payment, the work must be substantially performed before payment can be demanded. * * *

. . .

The judgment should be reversed, and a new trial ordered; costs to abide the event.

PROBLEMS

1.   Employee signs a one-year employment contract with Employer. The contract provides that the employment is to begin on Feb. 1, and that the salary will be $90,000 per year. Employee shows up for work on Feb. 1 and says "Pay me the $90,000 and I'll start working." Is Employer obligated to do so? What if Employee said "Pay me one month's salary and I'll start working."

2.   Suppose the same facts, but employee begins work without receiving any advance payment. Employee works for one month, and then comes to the office expecting to collect the paycheck. The office is closed, and there is a note on the door saying that the Employer has gone bankrupt. What are Employee's rights?

3.   Buyer and Seller sign an agreement for sale of real estate for $625,000. At the time fixed for the closing, Buyer says to Seller: "I won't be able to get the $625,000 until next week, but I insist that you give me a deed for the property now." Is Seller obligated to deliver the deed?

4.   Buyer and Seller sign an agreement for sale of real estate for $625,000. At the time fixed for the closing, Seller says to Buyer: "I won't be able to deed the property until next week, but I insist that you pay me the $625,000 now." Is Buyer obligated to pay the money?

2. BREACH BY ANTICIPATORY REPUDIATION

Hochster v. De La Tour

Queen's Bench, 1853.
118 Eng. Rep. 922.

On the trial before Erle, J., at the London sittings in last Easter Term, it appeared that plaintiff was a courier, who in April, 1852, was engaged by defendant to accompany him on a tour, to commence on 1st June, 1852, on the terms mentioned in the declaration. On the 11th May, 1852, defendant wrote to plaintiff that he had changed his mind, and declined his services. He refused to make him any compensation. The action was commenced on 22d May. The plaintiff, between the commencement of the action and the 1st of June, obtained an engagement with Lord Ashburton, on equally good terms, but not commencing till July 4th. The defendant's counsel objected that there could be no breach of the contract before the 1st of June. The learned judge was of a contrary opinion, but reserved leave to enter a nonsuit on this objection. The other questions were left to the jury, who found for the plaintiff.

. . .

■ LORD CAMPBELL, C.J., now delivered the judgment of the Court.

On this motion in arrest of judgment, the question arises, Whether, if there be an agreement between A and B, whereby B engages to employ A on and from a future day for a given period of time, to travel with him into a foreign country as a courier, and to start with him in that capacity on that day, A being to receive a monthly salary during the continuance of such service, B may, before the day, refuse to perform the agreement and break and renounce it, so as to entitle A before the day to commence an action against B to recover damages for breach of the agreement; A having been ready and willing to perform it, til it was broken and renounced by B. The defendant's counsel very powerfully contended that, if the plaintiff was not contented to dissolve the contract and to abandon all remedy upon it, he was bound to remain ready and willing to perform it till the day when the actual employment as courier in the service of the defendant was to begin; and that there could be no breach of the agreement before that day to give a right of action. But it cannot be laid down as a universal rule that, whereby agreement an act is to be done on a future day, no action can be brought for a breach of the agreement till the day for doing the act has arrived. If a man promises to marry a woman on a future day, and before that day marries another woman, he is instantly liable to an action for breach of promise of marriage.

If a man contracts to execute a lease on and from a future day for a certain term, and before that day executes a lease to another for the same term, he may be immediately sued for breaking the contract. So, if a man contracts to sell and deliver specific goods on a future day, and before the day he sells and delivers them to another, he is immediately liable to an action at the suit of the person with whom he first contracted to sell and deliver them. One reason alleged in support of such an action is, that the defendant has, before the day, rendered it impossible for him to perform the contract at the day, but this does not necessarily follow; for prior to the day fixed for doing the act, the first wife may have died, a surrender of the lease executed might be obtained, and the defendant might have repurchased the goods so as to be in a situation to sell and deliver them to the plaintiff. Another reason may be that, where there is a contract to do an act on a future day, there is a relation constituted between the parties in the meantime by the contract, and that they impliedly promise that in the meantime neither will do anything to the prejudice of the other inconsistent with that relation. As for example, a man and woman engaged to marry are affianced to one another during the period between the time of engagement and the celebration of marriage. In this very case of traveller and courier, from the day of hiring till the day when the employment was to begin, they were engaged to each other; and it seems to be a breach of an implied contract if either of them renounces the engagement. . . .

The declaration in the present case, in alleging a breach, states a great deal more than a passing intention on the part of the defendant which he may repent of, and could only be proved by evidence that he had utterly renounced the contract, or done some act which rendered it impossible for him to perform it. If the plaintiff has no remedy for breach of the contract unless he treats the contract as in force, and acts upon it down to June 1st, 1852, it follows that, till then, he must enter into no employment which will interfere with his promise "to start with the defendant on such travels on the day and year," and that he must then be properly equipped in all respects as a courier for a three months' tour on the continent of Europe. But it is surely much more rational, and more for the benefit of both parties, that, after the renunciation of the agreement by the defendant, the plaintiff should be at liberty to consider himself absolved from any future performance of it, retaining his right to sue for any damage he has suffered from the breach of it. Thus, instead of remaining idle and laying out money in preparations which must be useless, he is at liberty to seek service under another employer, which would go in mitigation of the damages to which he would otherwise be entitled for a breach of the contract. It seems strange that the defendant, after renouncing the contract, and absolutely declaring that he will never act under it, should be permitted to object that faith is given to his assertion, and that an opportunity is not left to him of changing his mind.

If the plaintiff is barred of any remedy by entering into an engagement inconsistent with starting as a courier with the defendant on the 1st June, he is prejudiced by putting faith in the defendant's assertion; and it would be more consistent with principle, if the defendant were precluded from saying that he had not broken the contract when he declared that he entirely renounced it.

Suppose that the defendant, at the time of his renunciation, had embarked on a voyage for Australia, so as to render it physically impossible for him to employ the plaintiff as a courier on the continent of Europe in the months of June, July and August, 1852; according to decided cases, the action might have been brought before the 1st June; but the renunciation may have been founded on other facts, to be given in evidence, which would equally have rendered the defendant's performance of the contract impossible. The man who wrongfully renounces a contract into which he has deliberately entered cannot justly complain if he is immediately sued for a compensation in damages by the man whom he has injured; and it seems reasonable to allow an option to the injured party, either to sue immediately, or to wait till the time when the act was to be done, still holding it as prospectively binding for the exercise of this option, which may be advantageous to the innocent party, and cannot be prejudicial to the wrong-doer. An argument against the action before the 1st of June is urged from the difficulty of calculating the damages; but this argument is equally strong against an action before the 1st of September, when the three months would expire. In either case, the jury in assessing the damages would be justified in looking to all that happened, or was likely to happen, to increase or mitigate the loss of the plaintiff down to the day of trial. We do not find any decision contrary to the view we are taking of this case. . . .

. . .

Upon the whole, we think that the declaration in this case is sufficient. . . .

NOTES

1. In one sense, the issue in *Hochster* is fairly trivial. The employment agreement was made in April. The employment was to begin June 1. The employer repudiated on May 11. The employee brought suit on May 22. The precise issue in the case is whether the employee could bring suit on May 22, or should have waited until June 1. If he had waited until June 1 to sue, there'd have been no issue. Performance would have been due from the employer, the employer would have breached, and therefore the employee would be discharged from his obligation to perform and could sue. Who cares whether the suit can be brought on May 22 or not until June 1?

2. Implicit in *Hochster*, however, is an issue of more significance. The facts indicate that, before June 1, Hochster was offered another similar job by Lord Ashburton. Suppose Hochster got that offer from Lord Ashburton on May 18, but Lord Ashburton said he was leaving on May 25 and needed an immediate response. What is Hochster to do?

Suppose that the offer from Ashburton had been for similar work, but at a lower salary than the De La Tour agreement. Suppose that Hochster decides that he needs to work, and so he takes the job with Ashburton. He comes to us to ask whether, if he takes the job with Ashburton, he can still sue De La Tour for the difference in salary. Before the decision in the case, we'd have to worry a bit. If Hochster sued De La Tour, maybe De La Tour would argue that Hochster was not entitled to anything, because Hochster was the one who broke the agreement. After all, De La Tour might say, Hochster was not able to begin work for De La Tour on June 1, because Hochster was off traveling with Ashburton.

That's an issue worth worrying about, unlike the question whether the lawsuit can be brought on May 22 or only on June 1. The effect of the *Hochster* decision was to establish the principle known as *breach by anticipatory repudiation*. The concept is pretty simple. It just means that if, before the time for performance comes due, a party clearly says that he will not perform, then the other side can treat the statement that "I will not perform" just as if the time for performance had come due and performance was not rendered.

3.   Note that the *Hochster* principle of breach by anticipatory repudiation deals only with the timing issue. There was no question that De La Tour's planned action of not paying Hochster would have been a very serious breach that would, in a qualitative sense, justify Hochster's refusal to perform. One can, however, imagine situations that present both the timing issue involved in *Hochster* and a qualitative issue.

> Suppose that on May 11, De La Tour told Hochster that he was going to take the trip as planned, and told Hochster that Hochster would be required to wear livery when on the job. Hochster thinks that the agreement that they entered into in April does not require him to wear livery.
>
> On May 18, Hochster gets an offer from someone else for similar work at the same salary, but the substitute job does not require him to wear livery.

Suppose Hochster comes to us for advice. We have two different issues. The timing issue is fairly simple. Under the *Hochster* case we can analyze the situation as if the time for performance had come due, and De La Tour insisted that Hochster wear livery.

But, there is a much harder qualitative issue. Assuming that it is a breach for De La Tour to insist that Hochster wear livery. Is that breach *so serious* that it would justify Hochster in saying "Deal's off—I'm not going to work for you"?

One can imagine various things that might be a breach of promise by the employer, but would not justify the employee in calling off the deal. Suppose, for example, that the Hochster says that the agreement, properly construed, entitles him to a holiday on Guy Fawkes Day, but De La Tour insists that he will have to work that day. Even if Hochster is right, one might say that he is entitled to damages for not receiving the day off on Guy Fawkes Day, but that the breach by De La Tour is not so serious that it would justify Hochster in quitting. That's a hard issue. We'll examine it anon. The point now is only to see that the *Hochster* case deals only with the timing issue; not the qualitative issue.

3. DEMAND FOR ASSURANCE OF PERFORMANCE

U.C.C. § 2–609

Restatement (Second) of Contracts § 251

Suppose we have facts akin to Hochster, that is, in April, Hochster and Count De la Tour enter into an employment agreement under which Hochster will be employed by De La Tour for one-year on a trip that De La Tour is planning to begin on June 1. On May 11, articles appear in the newspaper indicating the De La Tour has been involved in a scandal and may well be indicted soon. On May 18, Hochster gets an offer from Lord Ashburton for an alternate job, but at a slightly lower salary. Lord Ashburton says he is leaving on May 25 and needs an immediate response.

What is Hochster to do? Suppose he takes the job with Ashburton, but then De La Tour is not indicted and goes on the planned trip. Hochster will then be the one who breached. Not only would Hochster have no right to sue De La Tour for the lower pay, but Hochster might well be sued by De La Tour if it cost De La Tour more to get someone else to work as his courier.

Suppose Hochster turns down the offer from Ashburton, but then on May 25, De La Tour is indicted and does not take the trip. Sure, Hochster has an action against De La Tour for breach, but that means suing. In the meantime, Hochster will be kicking himself for not having taken the job with Ashburton.

What Hochster wants is some way of knowing—after reading the newspaper articles on May 11 but before he has to decide whether to take the offer from Ashburton—whether De La Tour will or will not perform when the time for performance comes due on June 1.

In the setting of contracts for the sale of goods, U.C.C. Section 2–609 tries to provide some help to someone in Hochster's position. If one side has "reasonable grounds for insecurity" then he can "demand adequate assurance of due performance" from the other side. If the other side does not provide such assurances, the party who made the demand can treat the failure to provide assurances as a repudiation. That is, the failure to provide adequate assurances is equivalent to a statement that one will not perform.

The concept of Section 2–609 makes perfect sense in theory, but its application presents some very difficult factual issues. What would count as circumstances that give rise to "*reasonable* grounds for insecurity"? Suppose one does have reasonable grounds for insecurity, what would count as "*adequate* assurances"? In our hypo, suppose that Hochster writes to De La Tour saying that as a result of the newspaper articles, he is concerned about whether De La Tour will be making the trip. De La Tour writes back "The newspaper articles are rubbish. I'm an honorable man. There won't be any trouble about the planned tour." Is that "adequate assurance"?

The idea that one can demand assurance of performance was something of an innovation when it appeared as Section 2–609 of Article 2 of the U.C.C. It is far from clear whether a similar right would be recognized in contracts not governed by U.C.C. Article 2. Section 251 of the RESTATEMENT (SECOND) OF CONTRACTS states a rule analogous to U.C.C. § 2–609, but it is far from clear whether that principle would be recognized by all courts.

D. DEPENDENT PROMISES—QUALITATIVE ISSUES: SUBSTANTIAL PERFORMANCE AND MATERIAL BREACH

1. SUBSTANTIAL PERFORMANCE

Jacob & Youngs v. Kent
Court of Appeals of New York, 1921.
230 N.Y. 239, 129 N.E. 889.

■ CARDOZO, J.

The plaintiff built a country residence for the defendant at a cost of upwards of $77,000, and now sues to recover a balance of $3,483.46, remaining unpaid. The work of construction ceased in June, 1914, and the defendant then began to occupy the dwelling. There was no complaint of defective performance until March, 1915. One of the specifications for the plumbing work provides that

> 'All wrought-iron pipe must be well galvanized, lap welded pipe of the grade known as 'standard pipe' of Reading manufacture.'

The defendant learned in March, 1915, that some of the pipe, instead of being made in Reading, was the product of other factories. The plaintiff was accordingly directed by the architect to do the work anew. The plumbing was then encased within the walls except in a few places where it had to be exposed. Obedience to the order meant more than the substitution of other pipe. It meant the demolition at great expense of substantial parts of the completed structure. The plaintiff left the work untouched, and asked for a certificate that the final payment was due. Refusal of the certificate was followed by this suit.

The evidence sustains a finding that the omission of the prescribed brand of pipe was neither fraudulent nor willful. It was the result of the oversight and inattention of the plaintiff's subcontractor. Reading pipe is distinguished from Cohoes pipe and other brands only by the name of the manufacturer stamped upon it at intervals of between six and seven feet. Even the defendant's architect, though he inspected the pipe upon arrival, failed to notice the discrepancy. The plaintiff tried to show that the brands installed, though made by other manufacturers, were the same in quality, in appearance, in market value, and in cost as the brand stated in the contract—that they were, indeed, the same thing, though manufactured in another place. The evidence was excluded, and a verdict directed for the defendant. The Appellate Division reversed, and granted a new trial.

We think the evidence, if admitted, would have supplied some basis for the inference that the defect was insignificant in its relation to the project. The courts never say that one who makes a contract fills the measure of his duty by less than full performance. They do say, however, that an omission, both trivial and innocent, will sometimes be atoned for by allowance of the resulting damage, and will not always be the breach of a condition to be followed by a forfeiture. *Spence v. Ham*, 163 N. Y. 220, 57 N. E. 412, 51 L. R. A. 238; * * * The distinction is akin to that between dependent and independent promises, or between promises and conditions. Anson on Contracts (Corbin's Ed.) § 367; 2 Williston on Contracts, § 842. Some promises are so plainly independent that they can never by fair construction be conditions of one another. * * * Others are so plainly dependent that they must always be conditions. Others, though dependent and thus conditions when there is departure in point of substance, will be viewed as independent and collateral when the departure is insignificant. * * * Considerations partly of justice and partly of presumable intention are to tell us whether this or that promise shall be placed in one class or in another. The simple and the uniform will call for different remedies from the multifarious and the intricate. The margin of departure within the range of normal expectation upon a sale of common chattels will vary from the margin to be expected upon a contract for the construction of a mansion or a 'skyscraper.' There will be harshness sometimes and oppression in the implication of a condition when the thing upon which labor has been expended is incapable of surrender because united to the land, and equity and reason in the implication of a like condition when the subject-matter, if defective, is in shape to be returned. From the conclusion that promises may not be treated as dependent to the extent of their uttermost minutiae without a sacrifice of justice, the progress is a short one to the conclusion that they may not be so treated without a perversion of intention. Intention not otherwise revealed may be presumed to hold in contemplation the reasonable and probable. If something else is in view, it must not be left to implication. There will be no assumption of a purpose to visit venial faults with oppressive retribution.

Those who think more of symmetry and logic in the development of legal rules than of practical adaptation to the attainment of a just result will be troubled by a classification where the lines of division are so wavering and blurred. Something, doubtless, may be said on the score of consistency and certainty in favor of a stricter standard. The courts have balanced such considerations against those of equity and fairness, and found the latter to be the weightier. The decisions in this state commit us to the liberal view, which is making its way, nowadays, in jurisdictions slow to welcome it. * * * Where the line is to be drawn between the important and the trivial cannot be settled by a formula. 'In the nature of the case precise boundaries are impossible.' 2 Williston on Contracts, § 841. The same omission may take on one aspect or another according to its setting. Substitution of equivalents may not have the same significance in fields of art on the one side and in those of mere utility on the other. Nowhere will change be tolerated, however, if it is so dominant or pervasive as in any real or substantial measure to frustrate the purpose of the contract. * * * There is no general license to install whatever, in the builder's judgment, may be regarded as 'just as good.' *Easthampton L. & C. Co., Ltd., v. Worthington*, 186 N. Y. 407, 412, 79 N. E. 323. The question is one of degree, to be answered, if there is doubt, by the triers of the facts * * * and, if the inferences are certain, by the judges of the law * * *. We must weigh the purpose to be served, the desire to be gratified, the excuse for deviation from the letter, the cruelty of enforced adherence. Then only can we tell whether literal fulfillment is to be implied by law as a condition. This is not to say that the parties are not free by apt and certain words to effectuate a purpose that performance of every term shall be a condition of recovery. That question is not here. This is merely to say that the law will be slow to impute the purpose, in the silence of the parties, where the significance of the default is grievously out of proportion to the oppression of the forfeiture. The willful transgressor must accept the penalty of his transgression. * * * For him there is no occasion to mitigate the rigor of implied conditions. The transgressor whose default is unintentional and trivial may hope for mercy if he will offer atonement for his wrong. *Spence v. Ham, supra.*

In the circumstances of this case, we think the measure of the allowance is not the cost of replacement, which would be great, but the difference in value, which would be either nominal or nothing. Some of the exposed sections might perhaps have been replaced at moderate expense. The defendant did not limit his demand to them, but treated the plumbing as a unit to be corrected from cellar to roof. In point of fact, the plaintiff never reached the stage at which evidence of the extent of the allowance became necessary. The trial court had excluded evidence that the defect was unsubstantial, and in view of that ruling there was no occasion for the plaintiff to go farther with an offer of proof. We think, however, that the offer, if it had been made, would not of necessity have been defective because directed to difference in value. It is true that in most cases the cost of replacement is the measure. Spence v. Ham, supra. The owner is entitled to the money which will permit him to complete, unless the cost of completion is grossly and unfairly out of proportion to the good to be attained. When that is true, the measure is the difference in value. Specifications call, let us say, for a foundation built of granite quarried in Vermont. On the completion of the building, the owner learns that through the blunder of a subcontractor part of the foundation has been built of granite of the same quality quarried in New Hampshire. The measure of allowance is not the cost of reconstruction. 'There may be omissions of that which could not afterwards be supplied exactly as called for by the contract without taking down the building to its foundations, and at the same time the omission may not affect the value of the building for use or otherwise, except so slightly as to be hardly appreciable.' *Handy v. Bliss*, 204 Mass. 513, 519, 90 N. E. 864, 134 Am. St. Rep. 673. * * * The rule that gives a remedy in cases of substantial performance with compensation for defects of trivial or inappreciable importance has been developed by the courts as an instrument of justice. The measure of the allowance must be shaped to the same end.

The order should be affirmed, and judgment absolute directed in favor of the plaintiff upon the stipulation, with costs in all courts.

■ McLAUGHLIN, J.

I dissent. The plaintiff did not perform its contract. Its failure to do so was either intentional or due to gross neglect which, under the uncontradicted facts, amounted to the same thing, nor did it make any proof of the cost of compliance, where compliance was possible.

Under its contract it obligated itself to use in the plumbing only pipe (between 2,000 and 2,500 feet) made by the Reading Manufacturing Company. The first pipe delivered was about 1,000 feet and the plaintiff's superintendent then called the attention of the foreman of the subcontractor, who was doing the plumbing, to the fact that the specifications annexed to the contract required all pipe used in the plumbing to be of the Reading Manufacturing Company. They then examined it for the purpose of ascertaining whether this delivery was of that manufacture and found it was. Thereafter, as pipe was required in the progress of the work, the foreman of the subcontractor would leave word at its shop that he wanted a specified number of feet of pipe, without in any way indicating of what manufacture. Pipe would thereafter be delivered and installed in the building, without any examination whatever. Indeed, no examination, so far as appears, was made by the plaintiff, the subcontractor, defendant's architect, or any one else, of any of the pipe except the first delivery, until after the building had been completed. Plaintiff's architect then refused to give the certificate of completion, upon which the final payment depended, because all of the pipe used in the plumbing was not of the kind called for by the contract. After such refusal, the subcontractor removed the covering or insulation from about 900 feet of pipe which was exposed in the basement, cellar, and attic, and all but 70 feet was found to have been manufactured, not by the Reading Company, but by other manufacturers, some by the Cohoes Rolling Mill Company, some by the National Steel Works, some by the South Chester Tubing Company, and some which bore no manufacturer's mark at all. The balance of the pipe had been so installed in the building that an inspection of it could not be had without demolishing, in part at least, the building itself.

I am of the opinion the trial court was right in directing a verdict for the defendant. The plaintiff agreed that all the pipe used should be of the Reading Manufacturing Company. Only about two-fifths of it, so far as appears, was of that kind. If more were used, then the burden of proving that fact was upon the plaintiff, which it could easily have done, since it knew where the pipe was obtained. The question of substantial performance of a contract of the character of the one under consideration depends in no small degree upon the good faith of the contractor. If the plaintiff had intended to, and had, complied with the terms of the contract except as to minor omissions, due to inadvertence, then he might be allowed to recover the contract price, less the amount necessary to fully compensate the defendant for damages caused by such omissions. * * * But that is not this case. It installed between 2,000 and 2,500 feet of pipe, of which only 1,000 feet at most complied with the contract. No explanation was given why pipe called for by the contract was not used, nor that any effort made to show what it would cost to remove the pipe of other manufacturers and install that of the Reading Manufacturing Company. The defendant had a right to contract for what he wanted. He had a right before making payment to get what the contract called for. It is no answer to this suggestion to say that the pipe put in was just as good as that made by the Reading Manufacturing Company, or that the difference in value between such pipe and the pipe made by the Reading Manufacturing Company would be either 'nominal or nothing.' Defendant contracted for pipe made by the Reading Manufacturing Company. What his reason was for requiring this kind of pipe is of no importance. He wanted that and was entitled to it. It may have been a mere whim on his part, but even so, he had a right to this kind of pipe, regardless of whether some other kind, according to the opinion of the contractor or experts, would have been 'just as good, better, or done just as well.' He agreed to pay only upon condition that the pipe installed were made by that company and he ought not to be compelled to pay unless that condition be performed. * * * *Smith v. Brady*, 17 N. Y. 173, * * * The rule, therefore, of substantial performance, with damages for unsubstantial omissions, has no application.

What was said by this court in *Smith v. Brady, supra,* is quite applicable here:

> 'I suppose it will be conceded that every one has a right to build his house, his cottage or his store after such a model and in such style as shall best accord with his notions of utility or be most agreeable to his fancy. The specifications of the contract become the law between the parties until voluntarily changed. If the owner prefers a plain and simple Doric column, and has so provided in the agreement, the contractor has no right to put in its place the more costly and elegant Corinthian. If the owner,

having regard to strength and durability, has contracted for walls of specified materials to be laid in a particular manner, or for a given number of joists and beams, the builder has no right to substitute his own judgment or that of others. Having departed from the agreement, if performance has not been waived by the other party, the law will not allow him to allege that he has made as good a building as the one he engaged to erect. He can demand payment only upon and according to the terms of his contract, and if the conditions on which payment is due have not been performed, then the right to demand it does not exist. To hold a different doctrine would be simply to make another contract, and would be giving to parties an encouragement to violate their engagements, which the just policy of the law does not permit.' (17 N. Y. 186, 72 Am. Dec. 422).

I am of the opinion the trial court did not err in ruling on the admission of evidence or in directing a verdict for the defendant.

For the foregoing reasons I think the judgment of the Appellate Division should be reversed and the judgment of the Trial Term affirmed.

■ HISCOCK, C. J., and HOGAN and CRANE, JJ., concur with CARDOZO, J.

■ POUND and ANDREWS, JJ., concur with MCLAUGHLIN, J.

NOTES

1.   Suppose the Owner had paid the full $77,000 contract price. Then Owner learns that Builder used wrong pipe—Cohoes instead of Reading. Suppose Owner sues Builder for damages. How would we compute the damages? Would the damages be measured by the difference between the value of the house with Reading pipe and the value of the house with Cohoes pipe? Or, would the damages be measured by the cost of ripping out the Cohoes pipe and installing Reading pipe? Recall two case that we examined in Chapter 7 in connection with computation of expectation damages: *Groves v. John Wunder Co.* and *Peevyhouse v. Garland Coal & Mining Co.*

2.   It's important to realize that the issue in *Jacob & Youngs v. Kent* is not (1) whether *Owner* is entitled to damages from Builder, or (2) how we would compute the damages. Rather, admitting that Owner is entitled to offset any damages he can prove against any claim of the Builder for payment, the issue is whether the *Builder* has any right to sue Owner for Owner's failure to complete performance of the promise to pay. Recall the *Kingston v. Preston* concept that it is a constructive condition of each party's duty to perform that the other party has performed. Owner in *Jacob & Youngs* says "Builder did not perform, so I'm not obligated to perform."

Note that in the case itself, the agreement called for progress payments and all but about $3400 of the total contract price of $77,000 had been paid. Suppose that the contract had *not* called for progress payments. Suppose instead that Builder finished the job, albeit using the wrong pipe, and then sued Owner for the $77,000 contract price. What result under the approaches suggested by the majority and dissent in the case?

3.   Suppose that the agreement did not call for progress payments. Suppose that the Builder has done about one-half of the work. Builder then stops work. That might happen for various reasons, e.g., the Builder dies, the Builder has taken on too much work on other jobs, or the Builder & Owner had a fight. Is Builder entitled to any recovery from Owner? What would the theory of Builder case be? Can Builder enforce Owner's promise to pay?

Plante v. Jacobs

Supreme Court of Wisconsin, 1960.
10 Wis.2d 567, 103 N.W.2d 296.

■ HALLOWS, JUSTICE.

The defendants argue the plaintiff cannot recover any amount because he has failed to substantially perform the contract. The plaintiff conceded he failed to furnish the kitchen cabinets, gutters and downspouts, sidewalk, closet clothes poles, and entrance seat amounting to $1,601.95. This amount was allowed to the defendants. The defendants claim some 20 other items of incomplete or faulty performance by the plaintiff and no substantial performance because the cost of completing the house in strict compliance with the plans and specifications would amount to 25 or 30 per cent of the contract price. The defendants especially stress the misplacing of the wall between the living room and the kitchen, which narrowed the living room in excess of one foot. The cost of tearing down this wall and rebuilding it would be approximately $4,000. The record is not clear why and when this wall was misplaced, but the wall is completely built and the house decorated and the defendants are living therein. Real estate experts testified that the smaller width of the living room would not affect the market price of the house.

The defendants rely on *Manitowoc Steam Boiler Works v. Manitowoc Glue Co.*, 1903, 120 Wis. 1, 97 N.W. 515, for the proposition there can be no recovery on the contract as distinguished from *quantum meruit* unless there is substantial performance. This is undoubtedly the correct rule at common law. For recovery on *quantum meruit, see Valentine v. Patrick Warren Construction Co.*, 1953, 263 Wis. 143, 56 N.W.2d 860. The question here is whether there has been substantial performance. The test of what amounts to substantial performance seems to be whether the performance meets the essential purpose of the contract. In the *Manitowoc* case the contract called for a boiler having a capacity of 150 per cent of the existing boiler. The court held there was no substantial performance because the boiler furnished had a capacity of only 82 per cent of the old boiler and only approximately one-half of the boiler capacity contemplated by the contract. In *Houlahan v. Clark*, 1901, 110 Wis. 43, 85 N.W. 676, the contract provided the plaintiff was to drive pilings in the lake and place a boat house thereon parallel and in line with a neighbor's dock. This was not done and the contractor so positioned the boat house that it was practically useless to the owner. *Manthey v. Stock*, 1907, 133 Wis. 107, 113 N.W. 443, involved a contract to paint a house and to do a good job, including the removal of the old paint where necessary. The plaintiff did not remove the old paint, and blistering and roughness of the new paint resulted. The court held that the plaintiff failed to show substantial performance. The defendants also cite *Manning v. School District No. 6*, 1905, 124 Wis. 84, 102 N.W. 356. However, this case involved a contract to install a heating and ventilating plant in the school building which would meet certain tests which the heating apparatus failed to do. The heating plant was practically a total failure to accomplish the purposes of the contract. *See also Nees v. Weaver*, 1936, 222 Wis. 492, 269 N.W. 266, 107 A.L.R. 1405 (roof on a garage).

Substantial performance as applied to construction of a house does not mean that every detail must be in strict compliance with the specifications and the plans. Something less than perfection is the test of [substantial] performance unless all details are made the essence of the contract. This was not done here. There may be situations in which features or details of construction of special or of great personal importance, which if not performed, would prevent a finding of substantial performance of the contract. In this case the plan was a stock floor plan. No detailed construction of the house was shown on the plan. There were no blueprints. The specifications were standard printed forms with some modifications and additions written in by the parties. Many of the problems that arose during the construction had to be solved on the basis of practical experience. No mathematical rule relating to the percentage of the price, of cost of completion or of completeness can be laid down to determine substantial performance of a building contract. Although the defendants received a house with which they are dissatisfied in many respects, the trial court was not in error in finding the contract was substantially performed.

The next question is what is the amount of recovery when the plaintiff has substantially, but incompletely, performed. For substantial performance the plaintiff should recover the contract price less the damages caused the defendant by the incomplete performance. Both parties agree. *Venzke v. Magdanz*, 1943, 243 Wis. 155, 9 N.W.2d 604, states the correct rule for damages due to faulty construction amounting to such incomplete performance, which is the difference between the value of the house as it stands with faulty and incomplete construction and the value of the house if it had been constructed in strict accordance with the plans and specifications. This is the diminished-value rule. The cost of replacement or repair is not the measure of such damage, but is an element to take into consideration in arriving at value under some circumstances. The cost of replacement or the cost to make whole the omissions may equal or be less than the difference in value in some cases and, likewise, the cost to rectify a defect may greatly exceed the added value to the structure as corrected. The defendants argue that under the *Venzke* rule their damages are $10,000. The plaintiff on review argues the defendants' damages are only $650. Both parties agree the trial court applied the wrong rule to the facts.

The trial court applied the cost-of-repair or replacement rule as to several items, relying on *Stern v. Schlafer*, 1943, 244 Wis. 183, 11 N.W.2d 640, 12 N.W.2d 678, wherein it was stated that when there are a number of small items of defect or omission which can be remedied without the reconstruction of a substantial part of the building or a great sacrifice of work or material already wrought in the building, the reasonable cost of correcting the defect should be allowed. However, in *Mohs v. Quarton*, 1950, 257 Wis. 544, 44 N.W.2d 580, the court held when the separation of defects would lead to confusion, the rule of diminished value could apply to all defects.

In this case no such confusion arises in separating the defects. The trial court disallowed certain claimed defects because they were not proven. This finding was not against the great weight and clear preponderance of the evidence and will not be disturbed on appeal. Of the remaining defects claimed by the defendants, the court allowed the cost of replacement or repair except as to the misplacement of the living-room wall. Whether a defect should fall under the cost-of-replacement rule or be considered under the diminished-value rule depends upon the nature and magnitude of the defect. This court has not allowed items of such magnitude under the cost-of-repair rule as the trial court did. Viewing the construction of the house as a whole and its cost we cannot say, however, that the trial court was in error in allowing the cost of repairing the plaster cracks in the ceilings, the cost of mud jacking and repairing the patio floor, and the cost of reconstructing the non-weight-bearing and nonstructural patio wall. Such reconstruction did not involve an unreasonable economic waste.

The item of misplacing the living room wall under the facts of this case was clearly under the diminished-value rule. There is no evidence that defendants requested or demanded the replacement of the wall in the place called for by the specifications during the course of construction. To tear down the wall now and rebuild it in its proper place would involve a substantial destruction of the work, if not all of it, which was put into the wall and would cause additional damage to other parts of the house and require replastering and redecorating the walls and ceilings of at least two rooms. Such economic waste is unreasonable and unjustified. The rule of diminished value contemplates the wall is not going to be moved. Expert witnesses for both parties, testifying as to the value of the house, agreed that the misplacement of the wall had no effect on the market price. The trial court properly found that the defendants suffered no legal damage, although the defendants' particular desire for specified room size was not satisfied. For a discussion of these rules of damages for defective or unfinished construction and their application see Restatement, 1 Contracts, pp. 572–573, sec. 346(1)(a) and illustrations.

On review the plaintiff raises two questions: Whether he should have been allowed compensation for the disallowed extras, and whether the cost of reconstructing the patio wall was proper. The trial court was not in error in disallowing the claimed extras. None of them was agreed to in writing as provided by the contract, and the evidence is conflicting whether some were in fact extras or that the defendants waived the applicable requirements of the contract. The plaintiff had the burden of proof on these items. The second question raised by the plaintiff has already been disposed of in considering the cost-of-replacement rule.

It would unduly prolong this opinion to detail and discuss all the disputed items of defects of workmanship or omissions. We have reviewed the entire record and considered the points of law raised and believe the findings are supported by the great weight and clear preponderance of the evidence and the law properly applied to the facts.

Judgment affirmed.

2. MATERIAL BREACH

Restatement (Second) of Contracts § 241

PROBLEM

Suppose that we have a construction agreement of the sort involved in *Jacob & Youngs v. Kent*. The agreement calls the Owner to make progress payments to the Builder on last day each month

Builder has submitted bill for $20,000 for this month's work, due November 30.

Owner discovers that Builder has used Cohoes instead of Reading pipe:

1/3 of pipe has been installed and the walls around it have been finished

1/3 of the pipe has been installed, but is still exposed

1/3 the pipe has been purchased by Builder and delivered to the job site, but has not yet been installed

Owner calls us and asks "Do I have to make the Nov 30 payment?"

Suppose Owner refuses to make the Nov 30 payment unless Builder replaces all the pipe. Builder calls us and asks "Do I have to replace all the pipe?"

Note that in *Jacob & Youngs v. Kent*, the issue came up only after the house had been built. If the problem had been presented to lawyers, they would have thought about what arguments they might make to a court, or whether the litigate or settle. In this problem, the issue arises during the course of the work. The lawyer has to tell the client what to do. That's a decision that has to be made before any lawsuits are filed, but it will have a big impact on what lawsuits might be filed and the stakes in any such suits.

The following case illustrates the problem.

K & G Constr. Co. v. Harris

Court of Appeals of Maryland, 1960.
223 Md. 305, 164 A.2d 451.

■ PRESCOTT, JUDGE.

Feeling aggrieved by the action of the trial judge of the Circuit Court for Prince George's County, sitting without a jury, in finding a judgment against it in favor of a subcontractor, the appellant, the general contractor on a construction project, appealed.

The principal question presented is: Does a contractor, damaged by a subcontractor's failure to perform a portion of his work in a workmanlike manner, have a right, under the circumstances of this case, to withhold, in partial satisfaction of said damages, an installment payment, which, under the terms of the contract, was due the subcontractor, unless the negligent performance of his work excused its payment?

The appeal is presented on a case stated . . . as follows:

"... K & G Construction Company, Inc. (hereinafter called Contractor) . . . was owner and general contractor of a housing subdivision project being constructed (herein called Project). Harris and Brooks (hereinafter called Subcontractor) . . . entered into a contract with Contractor to do excavating and earth-moving work on the Project. Pertinent parts of the contract are set forth below:

" 'Section 3. The Subcontractor agrees to complete the several portions and the whole of the work herein sublet by the time or times following:

" '(a)　　Without delay, as called for by the Contractor.

" '(b)　　It is expressly agreed that time is of the essence of this contract, and that the Contractor will have the right to terminate this contract and employ a substitute to perform the work in the event of delay on the part of Subcontractor, and Subcontractor agrees to indemnify the Contractor for any loss sustained thereby, provided, however, that nothing in this paragraph shall be construed to deprive Contractor of any rights or remedies it would otherwise have as to damage for delay.

" 'Section 4. (b)　　Progress payments will be made each month during the performance of the work. Subcontractor will submit to Contractor, by the 25th of each month, a requisition for work performed during the preceding month. Contractor will pay these requisitions, less a retainer equal to ten per cent

(10%), by the 10th of the months in which such requisitions are received.

" '(c) No payments will be made under this contract until the insurance requirements of Sec. 9 hereof have been complied with.

" 'Section 5. The Contractor agrees—

" '(1)   That no claim for services rendered or materials furnished by the Contractor to the Subcontractor shall be valid unless written notice thereof is given by the Contractor to the Subcontractor during the first ten days of the calendar month following that in which the claim originated. . . .

" 'Section 8. . . . All work shall be performed in a workmanlike manner, and in accordance with the best practices.

"Section 9.   Subcontractor agrees to carry, during the progress of the work, . . . liability insurance against . . . property damage, in such amounts and with such companies as may be satisfactory to Contractor and shall provide Contractor with certificates showing the same to be in force.'

"While in the course of his employment by the Subcontractor on the Project, a bulldozer operator drove his machine too close to Contractor's house while grading the yard, causing the immediate collapse of a wall and other damage to the house. The resulting damage to contractor's house was $3,400.00. Subcontractor had complied with the insurance provision (Sec. 9) of the aforesaid contract. Subcontractor reported said damages to their liability insurance carrier. The Subcontractor and its insurance carrier refused to repair damage or compensate Contractor for damage to the house, claiming that there was no liability on the part of the Subcontractor.

"Contractor gave no written notice to Subcontractor for any services rendered or materials furnished by the Contractor to the Subcontractor. . . .

"Contractor was generally satisfied with Subcontractor's work and progress as required under Sections 3 and 8 of the contract until September 12, 1958, with the exception of the bulldozer accident of August 9, 1958.

"Subcontractor performed work under the contract during July, 1958, for which it submitted a requisition by the 25th of July, as required by the contract, for work done prior to the 25th of July, payable under the terms of the contract by Contractor on or before August 10, 1958. Contractor was current as to payments due under all preceding monthly requisitions from

Subcontractor. The aforesaid bulldozer accident damaging Contractor's house occurred on August 9, 1958. Contractor refused to pay Subcontractor's requisition due on August 10, 1958, because the bulldozer damage to Contractor's house had not been repaired or paid for. Subcontractor continued to work on the project until the 12th of September, 1958, at which time they discontinued working on the project because of Contractor's refusal to pay the said work requisition and notified Contractor by registered letters of their position and willingness to return to the job, but only upon payment. At that time, September 12, 1958, the value of the work completed by Subcontractor on the project for which they had not been paid was $1,484.50.

"Contractor later requested Subcontractor to return and complete work on the Project which Subcontractor refused to do because of nonpayment of work requisitions of July 25 and thereafter. Contractor's house was not repaired by Subcontractor nor compensation paid for the damage.

"It was stipulated that Subcontractor had completed work on the Project under the contract for which they had not been paid in the amount of $1,484.50 and that if they had completed the remaining work to be done under the contract, they would have made a profit of $1,340.00 on the remaining uncompleted portion of the contract. It was further stipulated that it cost the Contractor $450.00 above the contract price to have another excavating contractor complete the remaining work required under the contract. It was the opinion of the Court that if judgment were in favor of the Subcontractor, it should be for the total amount of $2,824.50.

". . . Contractor filed suit against the Subcontractor in two counts: (1), for the aforesaid bulldozer damage to Contractor's house, alleging negligence of the Subcontractor's bulldozer operator, and (2) for the $450.00 costs above the contract price in having another excavating subcontractor complete the uncompleted work in the contract. Subcontractor filed a counter-claim for recovery of work of the value of $1,484.50 for which they had not received payment and for loss of anticipated profits on uncompleted portion of work in the amount of $1,340.00. By agreement of the parties, the first count of Contractor's claim, i.e., for aforesaid bulldozer damage to Contractor's house, was submitted to jury who found in favor of Contractor in the amount of $3,400.00. Following the finding by the jury, the second count of the Contractor's claim and the counter-claims of the Subcontractor, by agreement of the parties, were submitted to the Court for determination, without jury. All of the facts recited herein above were stipulated to by the parties to the Court. Circuit Court Judge Fletcher found for counter-plaintiff Subcontractor in the amount of $2,824.50 from which Contractor has entered this appeal."

The $3,400 judgment has been paid.

It is immediately apparent that our decision turns upon the respective rights and liabilities of the parties under that portion of their contract whereby the subcontractor agreed to do the excavating and earth-moving work in 'a workmanlike manner, and in accordance with the best practices,' with time being of the essence of the contract, and the contractor agreed to make progress payments therefor on the 10th day of the months following the performance of the work by the subcontractor.[3] The subcontractor contends, of course, that when the contractor failed to make the payment due on August 10, 1958, he breached his contract and thereby released him (the subcontractor) from any further obligation to perform. The contractor, on the other hand, argues that the failure of the subcontractor to perform his work in a workmanlike manner constituted a material breach of the contract, which justified his refusal to make the August 10 payment; and, as there was no breach on his part, the subcontractor had no right to cease performance on September 12, and his refusal to continue work on the project constituted another breach, which rendered him liable to the contractor for damages. The vital question, more tersely stated, remains: Did the contractor have a right, under the circumstances, to refuse to make the progress payment due on August 10, 1958?

The answer involves interesting and important principles of contract law. Promises and counter-promises made by the respective parties to a contract have certain relations to one another, which determine many of the rights and liabilities of the parties. Broadly speaking, they are (1) independent of each other, or (2) mutually dependent, one upon the other. They are independent of each other if the parties intend that *performance* by each of them is in no way conditioned upon *performance* by the other. 5 Page, The Law of Contracts, ¶ 2971. In other words, the parties exchange promises for promises, not the *performance* of promises for the *performance* of promises. 3 Williston, Contracts (Rev. Ed.), ¶ 813, n. 6. A failure to perform an independent promise does not excuse non-performance on the part of the adversary party, but each is required to perform his promise, and, if one does not perform, he is liable to the adversary party for such non-performance. (Of course, if litigation ensues questions of set-off or recoupment frequently arise.) Promises are mutually dependent if the parties intend *performance* by one to be conditioned upon *performance* by the other, and, if they be mutually dependent, they may be (a) precedent, i. e., a promise that is to be performed before a corresponding promise on the part of the adversary

---

[3] The statement of the case does not show the exact terms concerning the remuneration to be paid the subcontractor. It does not disclose whether he was to be paid a total lump sum, by the cubic yard, by the day, or in some other manner. It does state that the excavation finally cost the contractor $450 more than the 'contract price.'

party is to be performed, (b) subsequent, i. e., a corresponding promise that is not to be performed until the other party to the contract has performed a precedent covenant, or (c) concurrent, i. e., promises that are to be performed at the same time by each of the parties, who are respectively bound to perform each. Page, op. cit., ¶¶ 2941, 2951, 2961.

. . .

In the early days, it was settled law that covenants and mutual promises in a contract were *prima facie* independent, and that they were to be so construed in the absence of language in the contract clearly showing that they were intended to be dependent. * * *. In the case of *Kingston v. Preston*, 2 Doug. 689, decided in 1774, Lord Mansfield, contrary to three centuries of opposing precedents, changed the rule, and decided that performance of one covenant might be dependent on prior performance of another, although the contract contained no express condition to that effect. * * * The modern rule, which seems to be of almost universal application, is that there is a presumption that mutual promises in a contract are dependent and are to be so regarded, whenever possible. Page, op. cit., ¶ 2946; Restatement, Contracts, ¶ 266. Cf. Williston, op. cit., ¶ 812.

. . .

Considering the presumption that promises and counter-promises are dependent and the statement of the case, we have no hesitation in holding that the promise and counter-promise under consideration here were mutually dependent, that is to say, the parties intended performance by one to be conditioned on performance by the other; and the subcontractor's promise was, by the explicit wording of the contract, precedent to the promise of payment, monthly, by the contractor. In *Shapiro Engineering Corp. v. Francis O. Day Co.*, 215 Md. 373, 380, 137 A.2d 695, we stated that it is the general rule that where a total price for work is fixed by a contract, the work is not rendered divisible by progress payments. It would, indeed present an unusual situation if we were to hold that a building contractor, who has obtained someone to do work for him and has agreed to pay each month for the work performed in the previous month, has to continue the monthly payments, irrespective of the degree of skill and care displayed in the performance of work, and his only recourse is by way of suit for ill-performance. If this were the law, it is conceivable, in fact, probable, that many contractors would become insolvent before they were able to complete their contracts. As was stated by the Court in *Measures Brothers Ltd. v. Measures*, 2 Ch. 248: 'Covenants are to be construed as dependent or independent according to the intention of the parties and the good sense of the case.'

We hold that when the subcontractor's employee negligently damaged the contractor's wall, this constituted a breach of the subcontractor's promise to perform his work in a 'workmanlike manner, and in accordance with the best practices.' * * * And there can be little doubt that the breach was material: the damage to the wall amounted to

more than double the payment due on August 10. *Speed v. Bailey*, 153 Md. 655, 661, 662, 139 A. 534. 3A Corbin, Contracts, § 708, says: 'The failure of a contractor's [in our case, the subcontractor's] performance to constitute 'substantial' performance may justify the owner [in our case, the contractor] in refusing to make a progress payment . . . If the refusal to pay an installment is justified on the owner's [contractor's] part, the contractor [subcontractor] is not justified in abandoning work by reason of that refusal. His abandonment of the work will itself be a wrongful repudiation that goes to the essence, even if the defects in performance did not.' See also Restatement, Contracts, § 274 * * * Professor Corbin, in § 954, states further: 'The unexcused failure of a contractor to render a promised performance when it is due is always a breach of contract . . . . Such failure may be of such great importance as to constitute what has been called herein a 'total' breach. . . . For a failure of performance constituting such a 'total' breach, an action for remedies that are appropriate thereto is at once maintainable. Yet the injured party is not required to bring such action. He has the option of treating the non-performance as a 'partial' breach only . . . .' In permitting the subcontractor to proceed with work on the project after August 9, the contractor, obviously, treated the breach by the subcontractor as a partial one. As the promises were mutually dependent and the subcontractor had made a material breach in his performance, this justified the contractor in refusing to make the August 10 payment; hence, as the contractor was not in default, the subcontractor again breached the contract when he, on September 12, discontinued work on the project, which rendered him liable (by the express terms of the contract) to the contractor for his increased cost in having the excavating done-a stipulated amount of $450. . . .

NOTES

1.   Suppose the General Contractor had been your client. The General Contractor calls you after the Subcontractor (and its insurer) have failed to pay damages for the bulldozer accident. The general asks you: "Should I let the Subcontractor continue the work? Or, if I fire the Subcontractor and get somebody else to do the work, what legal risks will I face?"

2.   Look carefully at the opinion to see how the court decided whether the Sub's failure to perform in a workmanlike manner (and failure to pay damages for the bulldozer accident) was or was not a "material breach."

3.   Look carefully at how the Restatement describes how one should decide whether a breach is a "material breach." RESTATEMENT (SECOND) OF CONTRACTS § 241.

3. TIMING ISSUES IN SUBSTANTIAL PERFORMANCE AND MATERIAL BREACH CASES: "TIME IS OF THE ESSENCE"

Restatement (Second) of Contracts § 242

Suppose that a real estate sales agreement provides that the closing is to take place on November 1, that is, on November 1 the seller is to deliver a deed, thereby performing the promise to convey marketable title, and the buyer is to pay the money, thereby performing its promise to pay. Suppose that in the title examination process, seller learns that there is a minor problem—there was an old mortgage on the property and although the mortgage was presumably paid off long ago, a formal discharge was never recorded. Seller looks in its files and finds that it does have a mortgage discharge—apparently someone just forgot to record it.

If the seller did not have, and could not obtain, the mortgage discharge, the seller would certainly not be able to perform its promise to convey marketable title. That is, conveying the land only subject to the mortgage would be a serious breach of the seller's promise to convey marketable title. Qualitatively, that breach would discharge the buyer's duty to pay.

In our case, however, the seller will be able to convey marketable title, once the mortgage discharge is recorded. Suppose, however, that it won't be possible for the seller to do that until a few days after the November 1 date that the agreement set for the closing. What rights does the buyer have?

One possibility is for the buyer to say that the failure to convey on Nov 1 is a breach, but the buyer will not treat that as so serious a matter as to warrant calling off the deal, so long as (1) the seller "cures" within a reasonable time and (2) the seller pays damages, if any, for any harm the buyer suffers. For example, if the closing has to be put off until Nov 8, maybe the buyer will have to pay a bit more in rent, or whatever.

But, suppose that the buyer wants to say—for whatever reason—"either convey on November 1, or the deal is off." Does the buyer have the right to do that, or does the seller have the right to "cure" the breach? As a general rule, the seller would have the right to cure, *see* RESTATEMENT (SECOND) OF CONTRACTS § 242, so long as the seller is able to cure within a reasonable time and so long as there is nothing unusual about the arrangement that would justify a conclusion that the difference between November 1 and November 8 was terribly important.

But, suppose the agreement contained a provision reading as follows:

"It is agreed by the parties that time is of the essence in this agreement."

What, you say you can't read that? OK. Let's print it in somewhat more legible fashion.

"It is agreed by the parties that time is of the essence in this agreement."

OK, now it's legible, but is it any more comprehensible? What in the world does it mean to say that "time is of the essence." Consider the following case:

Sun Bank of Miami v. Lester

District Court of Appeal of Florida, Third District, 1981.
404 So.2d 141.

■ BARKDULL, JUDGE.

Defendant, Sun Bank of Miami, brings this appeal from a final judgment entered in the Dade County Circuit Court in favor of the plaintiff, Lester. Plaintiff has cross-appealed, urging that there was an inadequate award of attorney fees.

Plaintiff, a licensed real estate salesperson, contracted for the purchase of a condominium unit. At the time of signing, on January 17, 1979, an initial $7,000.00 deposit was made. The contract called for an additional deposit by May 1, 1979. The contract read, in part, as follows:

"17. DEFAULTS. If the Buyer shall fail to do promptly any of the things required of him herein within the time allowed therefor, this agreement may, at the option of the Seller, be deemed terminated and all of the Buyer's payments made hereunder shall be deemed and considered as liquidated and agreed upon damages and all obligations and duties of the parties hereto shall thereupon terminate; provided, that if the default consists of an act or omission other than the failure to close when specified or failure to pay monies when required, the Buyer shall have ten (10) days from time of notification of default within which to cure the same. It is agreed by the parties that the apartment and its appurtenances are a part of a large development and that the exact amount of damages suffered by the Seller upon the default hereunder by the Buyer is incapable of practical ascertainment. The Escrow Agent upon being notified by the Seller in writing that the Buyer has defaulted shall forthwith pay to the Seller all of the deposits and interest thereon and the Escrow Agent shall have no duty or obligation to make an independent investigation, determination or confirmation of the alleged default. Buyer agrees that Seller's sole liability and obligation to Buyer in the event Seller fails to complete construction or otherwise fail to close this transaction is the return of the Buyer's deposits together with interest thereon. No action of specific performance of this agreement shall lie in favor of either party. Time is of the essence in this agreement. In the event that Seller is required to institute or defend any action by or against the Buyer by reason of Buyer's breach of any covenants herein, Seller shall be entitled to recover reasonable attorneys' fees and costs."

When the additional deposit had not been paid, the defendant's agent notified the plaintiff by telephone that the initial deposit was being returned. The plaintiff's offer to pay the additional deposit forthwith was refused. A May 3, 1979 check for the additional deposit, accompanied by a May 9 transmittal letter, was received by the defendant on May 16. However, the defendant refused to reinstate the contract and the plaintiff then brought the present action for specific performance and declaratory relief. The defendant answered and counterclaimed for attorney fees. After both parties moved for summary judgments, the trial court granted the plaintiff's motion, reserving its ruling on the questions of damages, costs, and attorney fees. Following a non-jury trial, the summary judgment was incorporated into a final judgment, awarding the plaintiff $6,500.00 in attorney fees and granting specific performance.

The appellant contends it was error to hold that as a matter of law the plaintiff was entitled to cure her default and enforce the contract, despite her waiver of notice and her non-performance. First of all, the May 1st deadline for the additional deposit was crucial because this was a "time is of the essence" contract. Secondly, the plaintiff should not have been permitted to cure her default because the default resulted from her own negligence, and the lack of pre-termination notice is inapplicable because the contract specifically waived notice of intention to terminate. The appellant also contends specific performance was improper, because the contract waived the specific performance remedy. *See: Dillard Homes, Inc. v. Carroll*, 152 So.2d 738 (Fla. 3d DCA 1963). Further, the appellant contends that the award of a $6,500.00 attorney fee to the plaintiff was excessive where no facts were presented to support such an award.

We reverse. The contract made time of the essence; it clearly indicated that no notice would be given if a default was occasioned by the "failure to pay monies when required". The provision waiving specific performance as a remedy was valid. *Dillard Homes, Inc. v. Carroll, supra; Black v. Frank,* 176 So.2d 113 (Fla. 1st DCA 1965). The buyer admittedly failed to make the additional deposit as required, by May 1, 1979. The seller declared a default; the buyer's attempt to cure the default by her actions came too late. * * *

The appellee relies principally upon the cases of *Lance v. Martinez-Arango*, 251 So.2d 707 (Fla. 3d DCA 1971), and *Blanton Lake Properties, Inc. v. WWW, Ltd.*, 301 So.2d 485 (Fla. 2d DCA 1974). The first case is distinguishable because the buyer tendered the payment before any default was declared and, also, the seller attempted to forfeit the buyer's deposit, whereas in the instant case the deposit was returned. In the second case, the subsequent payment was tendered on time but there was a scrivener's error in the check: the numbers stated $332,000.00 but the words were for Three Hundred Thirty-Two Dollars. Upon being put on notice, the maker of the check attempted to correct the scrivener's error within three days. On the facts, this case is not similar to the one sub judice.

Therefore, the summary judgment and final judgment in favor of the buyer are reversed. The award of attorney's fees to the buyer is reversed, and the cause is remanded to the trial court to consider the award and the amount of attorney's fees, if any, to the seller on its counterclaim.

Reversed and remanded, with directions.

■ FERGUSON, JUDGE (dissenting).

I dissent on the grounds that under the facts of this case, a strict enforcement of the provisions of paragraph 17 of the sales agreement unreasonably and unjustly penalizes Lester.

This case involves a pre-construction purchase of a condominium unit which is governed by Florida Condominium Law, Chapter 718, Florida Statutes (1979). The purchase price of the condominium unit was $126,000.00 and by the time of the trial it is undisputed that the same unit had a value of $225,000.00. By a mortgage rider attached to and made part of the sales agreement, the developers were to select the mortgage lender and give written notification to the buyer for the purpose of executing all applicable documents necessary to secure financing. At the time of default, the developer had yet to notify buyer that a mortgage lender had been selected. By the terms of the sales agreement, the completion of construction and closing date was estimated to be February, 1980, nine months after the subject deposit was due. No part of the deposit was available for use by the developer as § 718.202, Florida Statutes (1979) requires that the entire deposit be maintained in an interest bearing escrow account until closing with a member of the Florida Bar as escrow agent.

It is clear that under the facts of this case, seller has suffered no damages by buyer's two day delay in tendering the balance of deposit due. To the contrary, seller has the potential of recognizing large profits by refusing the prompt tender of buyer's late payment. Here the majority's rigid enforcement[1] of the "time is of the essence" clause will result in enforcing an excessive penalty in the unjust forfeiture of Lester's right to purchase the condominium. See 3A Corbin, Contracts, § 715 (1960); Restatement, Contracts (2d), § 267, Comment d (such stock phrases as "time is of the essence" do not necessarily have this effect although they are to be considered along with other circumstances).

---

[1] While I agree that a default has technically occurred, *see, e. g., Richards v. Hasty*, 158 Fla. 459, 28 So.2d 876 (1947) (vendor must communicate intent to declare default), I would preclude enforcement of the contractual provision on the grounds of equity. See 3A Corbin, Contracts, infra.

Finding no material breach under the circumstances of this case, and that the forfeiture would be inequitable, I would not enforce the "time is of the essence" provision of the contract.

NOTES

The Restatement suggests that the inclusion of the magic words "time is of the essence" does not necessarily settle the issue:

> d. *Effect of agreement.* The agreement of the parties often contains a provision for the time of performance or tender. It may simply provide for performance on a stated date. In that event, a material breach on that date entitles the injured party to withhold his performance and gives him a claim for damages for delay, but it does not of itself discharge the other party's remaining duties. Only if the circumstances, viewed as of the time of the breach, indicate that performance or tender on that day is of genuine importance are the injured party's remaining duties discharged immediately, with no period of time during which they are merely suspended. It is, of course, open to the parties to make performance or tender by a stated date a condition by their agreement, in which event, absent excuse . . . delay beyond that date results in discharge . . . . Such stock phrases as "time is of the essence" do not necessarily have this effect, although under Subsection (c) they are to be considered along with other circumstances in determining the effect of delay.

RESTATEMENT (SECOND) OF CONTRACTS § 242, comment d. Sounds good, and maybe the approach suggested by the dissenting judge in the Sun Bank case would be a more common result. But, tell that to the buyer in the case who lost out on the deal to buy a condo worth $225,000 for a price of $126,000. Suppose the buyer had been represented by an attorney. The attorney had briefly reviewed the agreement and either (1) didn't notice, or understand, the phrase "time is of the essence," or, (2) figured that such clauses "do not necessarily have th[e] effect" of settling the question and so did not advise the buyer that closing on the agreed date was important. Would you want to represent that attorney in a malpractice action after the buyer lost the case?

4. "DIVISIBILITY"

Suppose that Builder agrees to build a building for Owner. The agreement sets a price of $300,000 for the work, but does not provide for progress payments. The price set in the agreement is very favorable to the builder—the fair market value of the work would only be $200,000. Builder finishes half the job, then dies. Owner gets someone else to finish the job for $100,000. Can Builder's estate sue to enforce Owner's promise to pay? Can Builder's estate sue in restitution?

Suppose that Builder agrees to build two identical buildings for Owner. The agreement sets a total price of $300,000 for the work, but does not provide for progress payments. The price set in the agreement is very favorable to the builder—the fair market value of the work would only be $200,000. Builder finishes one of the buildings, but has not even begun work on the other. Then, Builder dies. Owner gets someone else to finish the job for $100,000. Can Builder's estate sue to enforce Owner's promise to pay? Can Builder's estate Builder sue in restitution? Does this arrangement involve one contract or two?

Consider the following case:

Gill v. Johnstown Lumber Co.

Supreme Court of Pennsylvania, 1892.
151 Pa. 534, 25 A. 120.

■ HEYDRICK, J.

The single question in this cause is whether the contract upon which the plaintiff sued is entire or severable. If it is entire, it is conceded that the learned court below properly directed a verdict for the defendant; if severable, it is not denied that the cause ought to have been submitted to the jury. The criterion by which it is to be determined to which class any particular contract shall be assigned is thus stated in Parsons on Contracts, 29–31: 'If the part to be performed by one party consists of several and distinct items, and the price to be paid by the other is apportioned to each item to be performed, or is left to be implied by law, such a contract will generally be held to be severable. . . . But if the consideration to be paid is single and entire, the contract must be held to be entire, although the subject of the contract may consist of several distinct and wholly independent items.' The rule thus laid down was . . . applied in *Ritchie v. Atkinson*, 10 East, 295, a case not unlike the present. There the master and freighter of a vessel of 400 tons mutually agreed that the ship should proceed to St. Petersburgh, and there load from the freighter's factors a complete cargo of hemp and iron, and deliver the same to the freighter at London on being paid freight, for hemp £5 per ton, for iron 5s. per ton, and certain other charges, one half to be paid on delivery and the other at three months. The vessel proceeded to St. Petersburgh, and when about half loaded was compelled by the imminence of a Russian embargo upon British vessels to leave, and returning to London delivered to the freighter so much of the stipulated cargo as had been taken on board. The freighter, conceiving that the contract was entire, and the delivery of a complete cargo a condition precedent to a recovery of any compensation, refused to pay at the stipulated rate for so much as was delivered. Lord ELLENBOROUGH said: 'The delivery of the cargo is in its nature divisible, and therefore I think it is not a condition precedent; but the plaintiff is entitled to recover freight in proportion to the extent of such delivery; leaving the defendant to his remedy in damages for the short delivery.'

Applying the test of an apportionable or apportioned consideration to the contract in question, it will be seen at once that it is severable. The work undertaken to be done by the plaintiff consisted of several items, viz., driving logs, first, of oak, and, second, of various other kinds of timber, from points upon Stony creek and its tributaries above Johnstown to the defendant's boom at Johnstown, and also driving cross-ties from some undesignated point or points, presumably understood by the parties, to Bethel, in Somerset county, and to some other point or points below Bethel. For this work the consideration to be paid was not an entire sum, but was apportioned among the several items at the rate of $1 per 1,000 feet for the oak logs; 75 cents per 1,000 feet for all other logs; 3 cents each for cross-ties driven to Bethel; and 5 cents each for cross-ties driven to points below Bethel. But while the contract is severable, and the plaintiff entitled to compensation at the stipulated rate for all logs and ties delivered at the specified points, there is neither reason nor authority for the claim for compensation in respect to logs that were swept by the flood to and through the defendant's boom, whether they had been driven part of the way by plaintiff, or remained untouched by him at the coming of the flood. In respect to each particular log the contract in this case is like a contract of common carriage, which is dependent upon the delivery of the goods at the designated place, and, if by *casus* the delivery is prevented, the carrier cannot recover *pro tanto* for freight for part of the route over which the goods were taken. Whart. Cont. § 714. Indeed, this is but an application of the rule already stated. The consideration to be paid for driving each log is an entire sum per 1,000 feet for the whole distance, and is not apportioned to parts of the drive. The judgment is reversed, and a *venire facias de novo* is awarded.

CHAPTER ELEVEN

GROUNDS FOR REFUSING TO ENFORCE AGREEMENTS

No Fair!

A. INDEFINITENESS

At the beginning of Chapter 7, on Remedies, we noted briefly the general problem that the plaintiff must be able to prove the amount of damages with sufficient certainty to warrant an award. We noted the case of *Kenford Co, v. County of Erie*, 493 N.E.2d 234 (N.Y. 1986), where the court ruled that no damages were recoverable because the amount of damages was too uncertain. In that setting, we were dealing with situations where there was no question that the parties had entered into an otherwise enforceable agreement, but the plaintiff had problems proving the amount of damages suffered as a consequence of the defendant's breach. There is a different, but related problem.

Suppose that two parties sign a formal agreement which, though it specifies the parties' rights and duties in other respects very clearly, leaves some matters very uncertain. Recall that what it means to say that an agreement is legally enforceable is that we will grant the non-breaching party damages that will place her in the position that she would have been in if the other side had performed. Suppose that the matters left uncertain in the agreement make it difficult to figure out where the non-breaching party would have been if the other side had performed. We might have to conclude that, even though the parties clearly expressed an intention to be contractually bound by executing the agreement, the agreement is just too indefinite to be enforced.

A classic example of the problem is provided by *Sun Printing & Pub. Ass'n v. Remington Paper & Power Co.*, 139 N.E. 470 (N.Y. 1923). A newspaper publisher entered into an agreement with a paper company under which the paper company promised to sell certain amounts of paper over a 16 month period. The agreement specified a set price for the first four months, but then said that:

> For the balance of the period of this agreement the price of the paper and length of terms for which such price shall apply shall be agreed upon by and between the parties hereto fifteen days prior to the expiration of each period for which the price and length of term thereof have been previously agreed upon, said price in no event to be higher than the contract price for news print charged by the Canadian Export Paper Company to

the large consumers, the seller to receive the benefit of any differentials in freight rates.

The parties were unable to come to an agreement on the price for the last twelve months, and the newspaper company sued when the paper company refused to supply paper. The New York Court of Appeals, in an opinion by Judge Cardozo, ruled that the agreement was too indefinite to enforce. True, it set a maximum as the price charged by the Canadian Export Paper Co., but it didn't specify how many months were covered. One might say that the price should be determined month by month, or one might say that the price for the full twelve month period was the price charged by the Canadian Export Paper Co in the first month of that twelve month period. A strong dissenting opinion by Judge Crane took the opposite view, noting that "We have reason to believe that the parties supposed they were making a binding contract; that they had fixed the terms by which one was required to take and the other to deliver; that the Canadian Export Paper Company price was to be the highest that could be charged in any event. These things being so, the court should be very reluctant to permit a defendant to avoid its contract."

Many commentators think that the majority opinion in *Sun Printing* imposed too rigorous a requirement of definiteness. In the specific setting of sale of goods, the result in *Sun Printing* would probably be different today under Article 2 of the U.C.C. Section 2–305 states that an agreement for sale of goods is enforceable even though the price is not set: "The parties if they so intend can conclude a contract for sale even though the price is not settled. In such a case the price is a reasonable price . . . ." *Cf.* U.C.C. § 2–201, cmt 1 (a memorandum can suffice for Statute of Frauds purposes even though the writing does "not contain all the material terms of the contract . . . . The only term which must appear is the quantity term which need not be accurately stated but recovery is limited to the amount stated. The price, time and place of payment or delivery, the general quality of the goods, or any particular warranties may all be omitted.")

The issue of definiteness has been particularly problematic in connection with preliminary agreements in corporate acquisitions. Suppose that Acquiring Company is considering buying Target Company. There are many details to be worked out before the parties can definitely commit to the transaction. Often the parties will sign a document entitled something like "letter of intent" indicating that they do intend to move forward with the transaction. If the deal breaks down, one side might contend that by signing the "letter of intent" the parties undertook contractual obligations to each other. One possibility is that the "letter of intent" can be interpreted as an agreement for the sale of the company. The notion would be that although the parties expected some details to be worked out later on, they had already reached a binding agreement on the basic elements of the transaction. Often, however, the "letter of intent" leaves so many issues open that it cannot be interpreted as a binding agreement for sale of the company. Another possibility is that although the "letter of intent" was not an agreement for sale of the company, it was an agreement in which each side made a promise to negotiate in good faith in the effort to reach an agreement for sale of the company.[a] Then, one party might sue alleging that the other side broke its promise to negotiate in good faith. Such cases present problems about the requirement of definiteness. Is an agreement to negotiate in good faith sufficiently definite to be enforced? At one time, most courts would probably have said no. In recent years, however, there have been some decisions ruling that the parties did contractually agree to negotiate in good faith and that, at least in some circumstances, a court could conclude that one party's conduct was not consistent with that promise.

B. MISREPRESENTATION

Restatement (Second) of Contracts §§ 164, 162, 161

Suppose that Seller has a house for sale. Seller knows that the basement floods with every rainstorm, but is worried that if potential buyers know that they will be unwilling to buy, or will pay less than Seller hopes to get for the house. Suppose that a prospective buyer asks Seller "Does the basement flood?" Seller lies, and says no. Relying on Seller's representation that the basement does not flood, Buyer agrees to buy the house. It's pretty easy to see that Seller has committed a "no no." Seller is a bad person, and it's not surprising that Seller may suffer some legal consequences.

Suppose, however, that the prospective buyer never asks whether the basement floods, and Seller doesn't volunteer that information. Buyer agrees to buy the house. Is Seller's failure to disclose a "no no"? Does Seller face any legal risks if Seller fails to disclose?

Take another scenario. Seller has a house for sale. Buyer asks "Is there any termite damage?" Seller, honestly believing that there is no termite damage says "No, there is no termite damage." As it turns out, Seller was wrong about that. The house had in fact suffered serious termite damage. Seller said something that was not true, though Seller did that innocently. Is Seller's misstatement a "no no"? Does Seller face any legal risks as a consequence of the innocent misrepresentation?

There are at least two obstacles to clarity in discussing such cases.

First, there is a tendency to use the word "fraud" in describing the seller's conduct in at least some variants. It's a very good idea to force yourself into the habit of avoiding that word. As Prosser noted, in such

---

[a]   As we saw in Chapter 8, the law does not itself impose a duty to negotiate in good faith. If the parties have entered into a contract, they have a duty to *perform* in good faith, but that's different from saying that they have a duty to *negotiate* in good faith when they have not yet reached an agreement.

matters "there has been no little confusion . . . which has been increased by the indiscriminate use of the word 'fraud,' a term so vague that it requires definition in nearly every case." William Prosser, Law of Torts (4th ed. 1971) at 684. Often the word "fraud" is just used as a vague pejorative. A better way of discussing the problems would be to ask what legal consequences flow from a *misrepresentation* of a fact, or from *non-disclosure* of a fact.

Second, there is the old problem of forgetting to ask the fundamental question "Who sued whom for what?" Consider the following cases:

Lively v. Garnick

Court of Appeals of Georgia, 1982.
160 Ga.App. 591, 287 S.E.2d 553.

On June 27, 1974, plaintiff-appellees entered into a contract with defendant-appellants to purchase a house which, at the time of the execution of the contract, was partially built. Appellants were to complete construction of the house in accordance with certain stipulations set forth in the contract for sale of realty. At the time scheduled for the closing of the sale some of the special stipulations had not been met. However, both parties were desirous of closing the transaction and it was agreed that the sum of $1,000 would be held in escrow and paid to appellants upon completion of the improvements in accordance with the special stipulations of the sales contract. This agreement was incorporated into the closing statement and the sale was consummated.

Subsequently appellees instituted the instant action to recover damages and predicated their claim upon appellant's alleged fraud and deceit in connection with the representations and promises made at the closing and also with respect to certain alleged latent defects in the construction of the house discovered after the sale. Appellants' answer to the complaint denied the material allegations thereof and the case proceeded to trial. Final judgment was entered against appellants on a jury verdict in appellees' favor. Appellants appeal, enumerating as error several of the trial court's evidentiary rulings but the primary contention being that the evidence adduced at trial did not, as a matter of law, support a finding of fraud.

It is important at the outset to establish as the premise for resolving the issue of the general grounds that the action against appellants was not based upon negligent construction, breach of warranty or breach of contract. Appellees alleged that they were defrauded by appellants' failure to disclose certain defects in the property they were purchasing. * * * Fraud, unlike negligence, breach of warranty or breach of contract, is premised upon the "actual moral guilt" of the defrauding party. *Dundee Land Co. v. Simmons*, 204 Ga. 248, 249(1), 49 S.E.2d 488 (1949). "Mere concealment of [a material fact], unless done in such a manner as to deceive and mislead, will not support an action. In all cases of deceit, knowledge of the falsehood constitutes an essential element." Code Ann. § 105–302. "The element of intention to deceive is as necessary in an action based on concealment as one based on wilful misrepresentation. [Cit.] An action for fraud and deceit must [be based upon a] representation (or . . . concealment) [which] was made with the intention and purpose of deceiving the opposite party ([Cit.]), and for the purpose of injuring him. [Cit.]" *Camp Realty Co. v. Jennings*, 77 Ga.App. 149, 151, 47 S.E.2d 917 (1948). "In all cases of deceit, knowledge of the falsehood constitutes an essential element." *Cooley v. King & Co.*, 113 Ga. 1163(2), 39 S.E. 486 (1901). " 'In order to recover in an action of deceit, it is indispensable that the *scienter* be . . . proved.' " *Leatherwood v. Boomershine Motors*, 53 Ga.App. 592, 593, 186 S.E. 897 (1936).

Having thus established the applicable principles of law in the light of which the evidence in the instant case is to be viewed, we turn to the question of whether appellees proved that they were defrauded by appellants' concealment of latent defects in the construction of the house. "[I]n cases of passive concealment by the seller of defective realty, we find there to be an exception to the rule of caveat emptor . . . That exception places upon the seller a duty to disclose in situations where he or she has special knowledge not apparent to the buyer and is aware that the buyer is acting under a misapprehension as to facts which would be important to the buyer and would probably affect [his] decision. [Cits.]" *Wilhite v. Mays*, 140 Ga.App. 816, 818, 232 S.E.2d 141 (1976). This means, of course, that the buyer must prove that the vendor's concealment of the defect was an act of fraud and deceit, including evidence that the defect "could [not] have been discovered by the buyer by the exercise of due diligence . . . [and that the] seller was . . . aware of the problems and did not disclose them . . ." *Wilhite v. Mays*, 239 Ga. 31, 32, 235 S.E.2d 532 (1977).

Most of the alleged defects in the house, such as smeared grout on the tile, nails showing in the baseboard and mismatched trim on the exterior, were "discoverable by the purchasers' exercise of reasonable diligence to investigate and inspect" and cannot serve as the basis for holding appellants liable in fraud for "concealing" them. *P. B. R. Enterprises v. Perren*, 243 Ga. 280, 283, 253 S.E.2d 765 (1979). These defects would in all probability support a finding of negligent construction, breach of warranty or breach of contract, but not fraud. There is, however, evidence in the instant case which indisputably demonstrates that the house purchased by appellees contained defects which were not discoverable until after they had moved into it. Indeed, the evidence demonstrates that there were defects in the original construction of the house, such as a faulty air conditioner, a sagging carport roof and leaky chimney, which could not have become apparent until some time after it was occupied as a dwelling. We have carefully and thoroughly reviewed the transcript to discover if there was any evidence whatsoever from which a jury could find that appellants knew at the time they sold the house that it was "defective" in the ways which ultimately became apparent to appellees. We find no such evidence of appellants' "moral guilt" with regard to these defects in the house. The most the evidence shows is that appellants were negligent builders or in breach of warranty or of contract. While it is clear that the house contained defects which were likely the result of negligent construction or failure to conform to contract or warranty specifications, there is no evidence that at the time appellants sold the house they had "special knowledge" of these defects and yet concealed them from appellees. Compare, e.g., *Wilhite v. Mays*, 239 Ga. 31, 235 S.E.2d 532, supra; *Holman v. Ruesken*, 246 Ga. 557, 272 S.E.2d 292 (1980).

Appellees urge that the jury was entitled to infer from the fact that appellants built the house that appellants had actual knowledge that it would prove defective. It is clear, however, that in a fraudulent concealment action the allegedly defrauded party must prove that the alleged defrauder had *actual*, not merely constructive, knowledge of the fact concealed. * * * Obviously this is true because if there is no actual knowledge of the defect on the part of the silent party there can be no concealment of it with the *intent* and for the purpose of deceiving the opposite party. An assertion that one "should have known" of a defect alleges "at most a constructive knowledge". *Whaley*, 110 Ga.App. at 230, 138 S.E.2d 196, supra. There must be some evidence of the silent party's actual knowledge that the defect exists at the time of the sale from which his "moral guilt" in concealing it can be inferred. * * * *Windsor Forest Inc. v. Rocker*, 115 Ga.App. 317, 154 S.E.2d 627 (1967) (laying brickwork in freezing weather with knowledge that it would result in "bad bonding"); *Batey v. Stone*, 127 Ga.App. 81, 192 S.E.2d 528 (1972) (aware of defective waterproofing which was actively concealed); *Thibadeau Co. v. McMillan*, 132 Ga.App. 842, 209 S.E.2d 236 (1974) (builder aware of defective mortar); *Allred v. Dobbs*, 137 Ga.App. 227, 223 S.E.2d 265 (1976) (seller-builder aware of termite infestation and had actively concealed it). But to hold that evidence merely that a builder constructed a house which subsequently develops defects presents a jury question as to his "moral guilt" for fraud without some evidence that he had actual knowledge of the defect at the time of sale would mean that the legal theories of res ipsa loquitur or strict liability are applicable to a suit for the tort of fraud and deceit. In our opinion a builder may negligently construct a house or be in breach of his contract or of warranty and yet be free of the moral guilt of fraud. Accordingly we hold that it is not a "reasonable or logical" inference from the mere fact that a builder-seller has constructed a house subsequently discovered to be "defective" that he *knowingly concealed* those defects and thereby deceived and defrauded the purchaser. * * *

The evidence in the instant case demonstrates that the house sold by appellants contained "defects" which subsequent to the sale became apparent to appellees. However, there is likewise no evidence that these defects were apparent to appellants at any time before they were discovered by appellees. There is no evidence whatsoever that appellants actively pursued a known course of "defective" construction with knowledge of that fact or made any effort to actively conceal defects known to them nor any other evidence from which it could be inferred that appellants defrauded the appellees in the sale of the house. See e.g., *Jim Walter Corp. v. Ward*, 150 Ga.App. 484, 490(4), 258 S.E.2d 159 (1979), revd on the grounds, 245 Ga. 355, 265 S.E.2d 7 (1980). Absent some evidence of appellants' "moral guilt" in effectuating the sale with actual knowledge of the house's defects, a recovery and judgment predicated upon appellants' fraud and deceit cannot stand. *Windjammer Associates v. Hodge*, 246 Ga. 85, 269 S.E.2d 1, supra. It was error to deny appellants' motion for judgment n. o. v. as to these latent defects in the house.

Appellees' complaint, as amended alleged that they had been defrauded by appellants' failure to disclose that the house was situated so close to the boundary lines as to violate applicable protective covenants and zoning ordinances and, in fact, encroached upon drainage and utility easements. Again, it is important to note that appellees alleged that this failure to disclose was an act of fraudulent concealment and, therefore, it was incumbent upon them to prove that appellants had actual knowledge of the defect at the time of the sale. Our review of the transcript reveals no evidence that appellants had actual knowledge at the time of the sale that the house was in violation of the covenants and encroached upon the easement. The most that the evidence shows is that appellants had "constructive notice" of the covenants and easement through a recorded plat. [B]ut to make out the charge of fraud against [them] it would be necessary to go further and show . . . that [they] had actual notice, and there is no proof adduced in this case that [they] had ever seen [the plat], or that [they] had examined the record and therefore knew that [the house was in violation of the easement and covenants] at the time" they sold the house to appellees. *Baker v. Moore*, 182 Ga. 131, 137, 184 S.E. 729 (1935). Surely it was a grievous omission on the part of appellants to fail to check the records and it is possible that appellees had a breach of warranty claim against appellants but the action is not based in negligence or in contract but in fraud. It was error to fail to grant appellants' motion for judgment n. o. v. Compare *Fenley v. Moody*, 104 Ga. 790, 30 S.E. 1002 (1898); *Patterson v. Correll*, 92 Ga.App. 214, 88 S.E.2d 327 (1955).

Appellees also allege that they were fraudulently induced by appellants to consummate the sale by appellants' promises that the house would be completed in accordance with the special stipulations of the sales contract and that such promises were made with an intention not to perform. The general rule is that actionable fraud cannot be predicated upon promises to perform some act in the future. * * * Nor does actionable fraud result from a mere failure to perform promises made. *Pantone v. Pantone*, 203 Ga. 347, 46 S.E.2d 498 (1948). "[o]therwise any breach of a contract would amount to fraud." *Ga. Real Estate Comm. v. James*, 152 Ga.App. 193, 195, 262 S.E.2d 531 (1979). However, appellees attempt to place the promises made here within the ambit of appellate decisions which make an exception to the general rule and hold that fraud may be predicated on a promise as to future events made with a present intention not to perform (*Hill v. Delta Air Lines*, 143 Ga.App. 103, 105, 237 S.E.2d 597 (1977)) or where the promisor knows that the future event will not take place. See *Hayes v. Hallmark Apts.*, 232 Ga. 307, 308, 207 S.E.2d 197 (1974); *Hill v. Stewart*, 93 Ga.App. 792, 796, 92 S.E.2d 829 (1956).

The evidence in the instant case reveals that in spite of the fact that the house had not been completed, the appellees were at least as anxious as appellants to close the sale. All parties agreed that $1,000 was to be held in escrow and would not be disbursed to appellants until the house was completed in accordance with the special stipulations of the contract. Even construing the evidence most strongly in favor of appellees, it appears that appellants or their employees went to appellees' house "many times" and completed the vast majority of the improvements pursuant to the agreement at closing. Mr. Garnick did testify that certain problems arose in connection with maintenance and equipment installed in the house; however, these were not improvements that appellants agreed to complete at the closing. If the evidence shows anything, it shows a mere breach of contract. There is no evidence that appellants did not intend to comply with the terms of the special stipulations at the time the promises were made at the closing. Compare *Four Oaks Properties v. Carusi*, 156 Ga.App. 422(1), 274 S.E.2d 783 (1980); *McCravy v. McCravy*, 244 Ga. 336, 337–338, 260 S.E.2d 52 (1979). As the evidence was insufficient to establish fraud predicated on promises prospective in nature, the trial court should have granted appellees' motion for directed verdict as to appellees' claim based upon the special stipulations. *Pantone v. Pantone*, supra. Therefore, the denial of the motion for judgment n. o. v. as to these claims was also error.

For the reasons discussed supra, it was error to fail to grant appellants' motion for judgment n. o. v. Remaining enumerations of error are therefore moot and need not be addressed.

Judgment reversed.

Swinton v. Whitinsville Savings Bank

Supreme Judicial Court of Massachusetts, Middlesex, 1942.
311 Mass. 677, 42 N.E.2d 808.

The declaration alleges that on or about September 12, 1938, the defendant sold the plaintiff a house in Newton to be occupied by the plaintiff and his family as a dwelling; that at the time of the sale the house 'was infested with termites, an insect that is most dangerous and destructive to buildings'; that the defendant knew the house was so infested; that the plaintiff could not readily observe this condition upon inspection; that 'knowing the internal destruction that these insects were creating in said house', the defendant falsely and fraudulently concealed from the plaintiff its true condition; that the plaintiff at the time of his purchase had no knowledge of the termites, exercised due care thereafter, and learned of them about August 30, 1940; and that, because of the destruction that was being done and the dangerous condition that was being created by the termites, the plaintiff was put to great expense for repairs and for the installation of termite control in order to prevent the loss and destruction of said house.

There is no allegation of any false statement or representation, or of the uttering of a half truth which may be tantamount to a falsehood. There is no intimation that the defendant by any means prevented the plaintiff from acquiring information as to the condition of the house. There is nothing to show any fiduciary relation between the parties, or that the plaintiff stood in a position of confidence toward or dependence upon the defendant. So far as appears the parties made a business deal at arm's length. The charge is concealment and nothing more; and it is concealment in the simple sense of mere failure to reveal, with nothing to show any peculiar duty to speak. The characterization of the concealment as false and fraudulent of course adds nothing in the absence of further allegations of fact. * * *

If this defendant is liable on this declaration every seller is liable who fails to disclose any nonapparent defect known to him in the subject of the sale which materially reduces its value and which the buyer fails to discover. Similarly it would seem that every buyer would be liable who fails to disclose any nonapparent virtue known to him in the subject of the purchase which materially enhances its value and of which the seller is ignorant. * * * The law has not yet, we believe, reached the point of imposing upon the frailties of human nature a standard so idealistic as this. That the particular case here stated by the plaintiff possesses a certain appeal to the moral sense is scarcely to be denied. Probably the reason is to be found in the facts that the infestation of buildings by termites has not been common in Massachusetts and constitutes a concealed risk against which buyers are off their guard. But the law cannot provide special rules for termites and can hardly attempt to determine liability according to the varying probabilities of the existence and discovery of different possible defects in the subjects of trade. The rule of nonliability for bare nondisclosure has been stated and followed by this court in *Matthews v. Bliss*, 22 Pick. 48, 52, 53; *Potts v. Chapin*, 133 Mass. 276; Van *Houten v. Morse*, 162 Mass. 414, 38 N.E. 705, 26 L.R.A. 430, 44 Am.St.Rep. 373; *Phinney v. Friedman*, 224 Mass. 531, 533, 113 N.E. 285; *Windram Mfg. Co. v. Boston Blacking Co.*, 239 Mass. 123, 126, 131 N.E. 454, 17 A.L.R. 669; *Wellington v. Rugg*, 243 Mass. 30, 35, 36, 136 N.E. 831, and *Brockton Olympia Realty Co. v. Lee*, 266 Mass. 550,

561, 165 N.E. 873. It is adopted in the American Law Institute's Restatement of Torts, § 551. See Williston on Contracts, Rev.Ed., §§ 1497, 1498, 1499.

The order sustaining the demurrer is affirmed, and judgment is to be entered for the defendant.

Bates v. Cashman

Supreme Judicial Court of Massachusetts, Essex, 1918.
230 Mass. 167, 119 N.E. 663.

This is a suit to recover for the breach of a written contract to buy the stocks and bonds of the Newburyport Cordage Company. The securities were the means by which to convey control of land with a factory and machinery. There is no controversy that the contract was made. The defendant contends that he was induced to sign it by such false representations by the plaintiff as release him from obligation to perform. The case was referred to a master. It is reserved upon his report with exceptions thereto and the pleadings. There is no report of evidence.

It has been found that during the negotiations preceding the contract the plaintiff represented that a right of way, which was a substantial factor of value in the real estate, was owned by the Newburyport Cordage Company and could not be interfered with. This representation was untrue. The plaintiff did not know that it was untrue. The defendant relied upon it and would not have signed the contract if he had known that it was false. A person seasonably may rescind a contract to which he has been induced to become a party in reliance upon false though innocent misrepresentations respecting a cognizable material fact made as of his own knowledge by the other party to the contract. The fraud in such a representation consists in stating as a fact that which is not known positively to be a fact. It is no excuse for making such a statement as of one's own knowledge that it was believed to be true or that the true state of affairs had been forgotten. It is fraud to state a fact as true of one's own knowledge when he has no such knowledge.

. . .

C. MISTAKE

When I make a mistake, it's a beaut!

—*Fiorello La Guardia*

Restatement (Second) of Contracts §§ 151–158

1. INTRODUCTION: DIFFERENT TYPES OF MISTAKE CASES

There are some situations in life where the last thing you want to hear is "Ooops!" Maybe Law is one of those. In any event, the impact of mistake on contract law can be a rather confusing subject. As a starting place, it's useful to distinguish a variety of rather different types of cases in which mistake affects contracts. The great scholar of the law of restitution, George Palmer, laid out a very useful typology of different types of "mistake" scenarios:

> Mistake is so varied that time spent in an attempt to establish an exhaustive scheme of classification would not be well spent. In the area of agreements, nonetheless, there are four principal categories that deserve special consideration. The first is *misunderstanding* between the parties as to a term of an apparent agreement. This statement is merely descriptive of the states of mind attributed to the parties; it is not a legal concept or the expression of legal consequences. As a useful legal category, misunderstanding raises the question whether formation of a contract was prevented. The second is *mistake in expression or integration,* which occurs when parties reach an agreement that they intend to put in writing, but through error the writing fails to express the agreement accurately. The third is *mistake in underlying assumptions,* which usually occurs when an agreement is reached and is expressed correctly, but one or both parties make a false assumption concerning some matter relevant to the decision to enter into the contract. The last is *mistake in performance,* typified by a performance rendered in the belief that it is due under an actual or supposed contract when in fact it is not due.

2 George E. Palmer, The Law of Restitution § 11.2 at 482 (1978)

Let's consider simple examples of each of these types of cases.

Misunderstanding

Suppose that Buyer and Seller agree on the sale of a cow named Rose for $12,500. Unknown to either Buyer or Seller, there are actually two cows named Rose. Buyer reasonably thought that the subject of the sale was the brown cow named Rose. Seller reasonably thought that the subject of the sale was the black cow named Rose. Neither party knew that the other was thinking of a different cow. For some reason, it makes a great deal of difference to both parties whether the subject of the sale is the brown cow or the black cow.

Is there a binding contract between the parties for the sale of a cow? Recall *Raffles v. Wichelhaus*, described in Chapter 8A.

Mistake in expression or integration

Suppose that Buyer and Seller agree on the sale of a cow for $12,500. Both parties were thinking about the same cow, a valuable brown cow, and both parties thought that cow's name was Rose. They signed an agreement providing for the sale of the cow named "Rose."

As it turns out, the cow both parties were thinking about was not named Rose, rather, she was named "Petunia." Seller does own a cow

[handwritten margin note: may reform the writing to make the original contract — court allows to fix]

named Rose, but she is an old cow, of undistinguished blood line, and worth only a couple hundred dollars.

Seller says "Tough luck, Buyer. I'm keeping the valuable cow (Petunia) and you have to take the old cow (Rose) and pay me $12,500 for her."

What relief is necessary to fix the problem that Buyer faces? Is Seller entitled to receive $12,500 for the old cow?

Mistake in performance

Cattle Rancher and Butcher agree on the sale of a cow for 55¢ per pound. The cow is weighed, and turns out to weigh 1420 lb. The calculation is made (1420 × $0.55), but someone goofs in the multiplication, producing the result of $891, instead of the correct figure of $781. Buyer pays Seller $891. Then, Buyer discovers the mistake and sues Seller for return of the excess $110.

Should Buyer win? What theory? Does it matter who did the erroneous calculation? Does it matter whether the error was big or small?

In connection with this hypo, go back and look at the case of *Bank of Naperville v. Catalano*, at the beginning of Chapter 2.

[handwritten margin note: restitution seller needs to pay the $110 back]

Mistake in underlying assumption

Seller, a cattle breeder, learns that one of its cows, named Rose, is infertile. If she could breed, she would be worth about $20,000 due to her distinguished bloodline. Infertile, she is worth only her value as meat, about 55¢ per pound. Seller agrees to sell her to Amour Meatpacking Co., a company in the business of slaughtering cows and selling them for meat. The price is 55¢ per pound, and she weighs 1420 lb, so the agreed price is $781. Just before delivery, Seller realizes that Rose is, in fact, pregnant. Since she is worth $20,000 as a breeding cow, Seller refuses to deliver her to Amour Meatpacking Co.

Amour Meatpacking Co. sues Seller for $19,219, on the grounds that if Seller had performed, Amour would have gotten a cow worth $20,000 for a payment of $781.

What result? The issue here is akin to that in *Sherwood v. Walker*, below, the actual saga of Rose 2d of Aberlone.

2. MUTUAL MISTAKE IN UNDERLYING ASSUMPTION

Sherwood v. Walker
Supreme Court of Michigan, 1887.
66 Mich. 568, 33 N.W. 919.

■ MORSE, J.

[Plaintiff, Sherwood, agreed to buy a cow from Defendant, Hiram Walker & Sons. Defendant refused to deliver the cow, for the reasons noted in the opinion below, and Sherwood sued to enforce the agreement.

The procedure was actually a bit more complex, but that's not significant for our purposes.]

... The defendants reside at Detroit, but are in business at Walkerville, Ontario, and have a farm at Greenfield, in Wayne county, upon which were some blooded cattle supposed to be barren as breeders. The Walkers are importers and breeders of polled Angus cattle. The plaintiff is a banker living at Plymouth, in Wayne county. He called upon the defendants at Walkerville for the purchase of some of their stock, but found none there that suited him. Meeting one of the defendants afterwards, he was informed that they had a few head upon their Greenfield farm. He was asked to go out and look at them, with the statement at the time that they were probably barren, and would not breed. May 5, 1886, plaintiff went out to Greenfield, and saw the cattle. A few days thereafter, he called upon one of the defendants with the view of purchasing a cow, known as "Rose 2d of Aberlone." After considerable talk, it was agreed that defendants would telephone Sherwood at his home in Plymouth in reference to the price. The second morning after this talk he was called up by telephone, and the terms of the sale were finally agreed upon. He was to pay five and one-half cents per pound, live weight, fifty pounds shrinkage. He was asked how he intended to take the cow home, and replied that he might ship her from King's cattle-yard. He requested defendants to confirm the sale in writing, which they did by sending him the following letter:

WALKERVILLE, May 15, 1886.

T.C. Sherwood, President, etc

DEAR SIR: We confirm sale to you of the cow Rose 2d of Aberlone, lot 56 of our catalogue, at five and half cents per pound, less fifty pounds shrink. We inclose herewith order on Mr. Graham for the cow. You might leave check with him, or mail to us here, as you prefer.

Yours, truly,

HIRAM WALKER & SONS

The order upon Graham inclosed in the letter read as follows:

WALKERVILLE, May 15, 1886.

George Graham:

You will please deliver at King's cattle-yard to Mr. T.C. Sherwood, Plymouth, the cow Rose 2d of Aberlone, lot 56 of our catalogue. Send halter with the cow, and have her weighed.

Yours truly,

HIRAM WALKER & SONS.

On the twenty-first of the same month the plaintiff went to defendants' farm at Greenfield, and presented the order and letter to

Graham, who informed him that the defendants had instructed him not to deliver the cow. Soon after, the plaintiff tendered to Hiram Walker, one of the defendants, $80,[b] and demanded the cow. Walker refused to take the money or deliver the cow. The plaintiff then instituted this suit. . . . The defendants . . . introduced evidence tending to show that at the time of the alleged sale it was believed by both the plaintiff and themselves that the cow was barren and would not breed; that she cost $850, and if not barren would be worth from $750 to $1,000; that after the date of the letter, and the order to Graham, the defendants were informed by said Graham that in his judgment the cow was with calf, and therefore they instructed him not to deliver her to plaintiff, and on the twentieth of May, 1886, telegraphed plaintiff what Graham thought about the cow being with calf, and that consequently they could not sell her. The cow had a calf in the month of October following. On the nineteenth of May, the plaintiff wrote Graham as follows:

> PLYMOUTH, May 19, 1886.
>
> Mr. George Graham, Greenfield
>
> DEAR SIR: I have bought Rose or Lucy from Mr. Walker, and will be there for her Friday morning, nine or ten o'clock. Do not water her in the morning."
>
> Yours, etc.,
>
> T.C. SHERWOOD.

Plaintiff explained the mention of the two cows in this letter by testifying that, when he wrote this letter, the order and letter of defendants was at his home, and, writing in a hurry, and being uncertain as to the name of the cow, and not wishing his cow watered, he thought it would do no harm to name them both, as his bill of sale would show which one he had purchased. Plaintiff also testified that he asked defendants to give him a price on the balance of their herd at Greenfield, as a friend thought of buying some, and received a letter dated May 17, 1886, in which they named the price of five cattle, including Lucy, at $90, and Rose 2d at $80. When he received the letter he called defendants up by telephone, and asked them why they put Rose 2d in the list, as he had already purchased her. They replied that they knew he had, but thought it would make no difference if plaintiff and his friend concluded to take the whole herd.

The foregoing is the substance of all the testimony in the case.

. . . .

It appears from the record that both parties supposed this cow was barren and would not breed, and she was sold by the pound for an insignificant sum as compared with her real value if a breeder. She was evidently sold and purchased on the relation of her value for beef, unless the plaintiff had learned of her true condition, and concealed such

---

b   [The cow weighed about 1400 lbs, so the price, at 5.5¢ per pound, was about $80.]

knowledge from the defendants. Before the plaintiff secured the possession of the animal, the defendants learned that she was with calf, and therefore of great value, and undertook to rescind the sale by refusing to deliver her. The question arises whether they had a right to do so. The circuit judge ruled that this fact did not avoid the sale and it made no difference whether she was barren or not. I am of the opinion that the court erred in this holding. I know that this is a close question, and the dividing line between the adjudicated cases is not easily discerned. But it must be considered as well settled that a party who has given an apparent consent to a contract of sale may refuse to execute it, or he may avoid it after it has been completed, if the assent was founded, or the contract made, upon the mistake of a material fact,—such as the subject-matter of the sale, the price, or some collateral fact materially inducing the agreement; and this can be done when the mistake is mutual. * * *

> rule
> ↓
> limited to this case

If there is a difference or misapprehension as to the substance of the thing bargained for; if the thing actually delivered or received is different in substance from the thing bargained for, and intended to be sold,—then there is no contract; but if it be only a difference in some quality or accident, even though the mistake may have been the actuating motive to the purchaser or seller, or both of them, yet the contract remains binding. "The difficulty in every case is to determine whether the mistake or misapprehension is as to the substance of the whole contract, going, as it were, to the root of the matter, or only to some point, even though a material point, an error as to which does not affect the substance of the whole consideration." *Kennedy v. Panama, etc., Mail Co.*, L.R. 2 Q.B. 580, 587. It has been held, in accordance with the principles above stated, that where a horse is bought under the belief that he is sound, and both vendor and vendee honestly believe him to be sound, the purchaser must stand by his bargain, and pay the full price, unless there was a warranty.

It seems to me, however, in the case made by this record, that the mistake or misapprehension of the parties went to the whole substance of the agreement. If the cow was a breeder, she was worth at least $750; if barren, she was worth not over $80. The parties would not have made the contract of sale except upon the understanding and belief that she was incapable of breeding, and of no use as a cow. It is true she is now the identical animal that they thought her to be when the contract was made; there is no mistake as to the identity of the creature. Yet the mistake was not of the mere quality of the animal, but went to the very nature of the thing. A barren cow is substantially a different creature than a breeding one. There is as much difference between them for all purposes of use as there is between an ox and a cow that is capable of breeding and giving milk. If the mutual mistake had simply related to the fact whether she was with calf or not for one season, then it might have been a good sale, but the mistake affected the character of the animal for all time, and for its present and ultimate use. She was not in fact the animal, or the kind of animal, the defendants intended to sell or the plaintiff to buy. She was not a barren cow, and, if this fact had been known, there would have been no contract. The mistake affected the substance of the whole consideration, and it must be considered that there was no contract to sell or sale of the cow as she actually was. The thing sold and bought had in fact no existence. She was sold as a beef creature would be sold; she is in fact a breeding cow, and a valuable one. The court should have instructed the jury that if they found that the cow was sold, or contracted to be sold, upon the understanding of both parties that she was barren, and useless for the purpose of breeding, and that in fact she was not barren, but capable of breeding, then the defendants had a right to rescind, and to refuse to deliver, and the verdict should be in their favor.

The judgment of the court below must be reversed, and a new trial granted, with costs of this court to defendants.

■ CAMPBELL, C.J., and CHAMPLIN, J., concurred.

■ SHERWOOD, J., (dissenting.) I do not concur in the opinion given by my brethren in this case. . . .

As has already been stated by my brethren, the record shows that the plaintiff is a banker and farmer as well, carrying on a farm, and raising the best breeds of stock, and lived in Plymouth, in the county of Wayne, 23 miles from Detroit; that the defendants lived in Detroit, and were also dealers in stock of the higher grades; that they had a farm at Walkerville, in Canada, and also one in Greenfield in said county of Wayne, and upon these farms the defendants kept their stock. The Greenfield farm was about 15 miles from the plaintiff's. In the spring of 1886 the plaintiff, learning that the defendants had some "polled Angus cattle" for sale, was desirous of purchasing some of that breed, and meeting the defendants, or some of them, at Walkerville, inquired about them, and was informed that they had none at Walkerville, "but had a few head left on their farm in Greenfield, and asked the plaintiff to go and see them, stating that in all probability they were sterile and would not breed." In accordance with said request, the plaintiff, on the fifth day of May, went out and looked at the defendants' cattle at Greenfield, and found one called "Rose, Second," which he wished to purchase, and the terms were finally agreed upon at five and a half cents per pound, live weight, 50 pounds to be deducted for shrinkage. The sale was in writing, and the defendants gave an order to the plaintiff directing the man in charge of the Greenfield farm to deliver the cow to plaintiff. This was done on the fifteenth of May. On the twenty-first of May plaintiff went to get his cow, and the defendants refused to let him have her; claiming at the time that the man in charge at the farm thought the cow was with calf, and, if such was the case, they would not sell her for the price agreed upon. The record further shows that the defendants, when they sold the cow, believed the cow was not with calf, and barren; that from what the plaintiff had been told by defendants (for it does not appear he had any other knowledge or facts from which he could form an opinion) he believed the cow was farrow, but still thought she could be made to breed. The foregoing shows the entire interview and treaty between the parties as to the sterility and qualities of the cow sold to the plaintiff. The cow had a calf in the month of October.

There is no question but that the defendants sold the cow representing her of the breed and quality they believed the cow to be, and that the purchaser so understood it. And the buyer purchased her believing her to be of the breed represented by the sellers, and possessing all the qualities stated, and even more. He believed she would breed. There is no pretense that the plaintiff bought the cow for beef, and there is nothing in the record indicating that he would have bought her at all only that he thought she might be made to breed. Under the foregoing facts,—and these are all that are contained in the record material to the contract,—it is held that because it turned out that the plaintiff was more correct in his judgment as to one quality of the cow than the defendants, and a quality, too, which could not by any possibility be positively known at the time by either party to exist, the contract may be annulled by the defendants at their pleasure. I know of no law, and have not been referred to any, which will justify any such holding, and I think the circuit judge was right in his construction of the contract between the parties.

It is claimed that a mutual mistake of a material fact was made by the parties when the contract of sale was made. There was no warranty in the case of the quality of the animal. When a mistaken fact is relied upon as ground for rescinding, such fact must not only exist at the time the contract is made, but must have been known to one or both of the parties. Where there is no warranty, there can be no mistake of fact when no such fact exists, or, if in existence, neither party knew of it, or could know of it; and that is precisely this case. If the owner of a Hambletonian horse had speeded him, and was only able to make him go a mile in three minutes, and should sell him to another, believing that was his greatest speed, for $300, when the purchaser believed he could go much faster, and made the purchase for that sum, and a few days thereafter, under more favorable circumstances, the horse was driven a mile in 2 min. 16 sec., and was found to be worth $20,000, I hardly think it would be held, either at law or in equity, by any one, that the seller in such case could rescind the contract. The same legal principles apply in each case.

In this case neither party knew the actual quality and condition of this cow at the time of the sale. The defendants say, or rather said, to the plaintiff, "they had a few head left on their farm in Greenfield, and asked plaintiff to go and see them, stating to plaintiff that in all probability they were sterile and would not breed." Plaintiff did go as requested, and found there these cows, including the one purchased, with a bull. The cow had been exposed, but neither knew she was with calf or whether she would breed. The defendants thought she would not, but the plaintiff says that he thought she could be made to breed, but believed she was not with calf. The defendants sold the cow for what they believed her to be, and the plaintiff bought her as he believed she was, after the statements made by the defendants. No conditions whatever were attached to the terms of sale by either party. It was in fact as absolute as it could well be made, and I know of no precedent as authority by which this court can alter the contract thus made by these parties in writing,—interpolate in it a condition by which, if the defendants should be mistaken in their belief that the cow was barren, she could be returned to them and their contract should be annulled. It is not the duty of courts to destroy contracts when called upon to enforce them, after they have been legally made. There was no mistake of any material fact by either of the parties in the case as would license the vendors to rescind. There was no difference between the parties, nor misapprehension, as to the substance of the thing bargained for, which was a cow supposed to be barren by one party, and believed not to be by the other. As to the quality of the animal, subsequently developed, both parties were equally ignorant, and as to this each party took his chances. If this were not the law, there would be no safety in purchasing this kind of stock.

I entirely agree with my brethren that the right to rescind occurs whenever "the thing actually delivered or received is different in substance from the thing bargained for, and intended to be sold; but if it be only a difference in some quality or accident, even though the misapprehension may have been the actuating motive" of the parties in making the contract, yet it will remain binding. In this case the cow sold was the one delivered. What might or might not happen to her after the sale formed no element in the contract. . . .

. . .

NOTES & QUESTIONS

Sherwood v. Walker is perhaps the classic "mistake" case in contract law. Indeed, Rose is the subject of a lengthy somewhat humorous poem by Brainerd Currie, a well-respected mid-twentieth century law professor.[c] The facts of the case provide a good basis for thinking through what circumstances should and should not warrant a conclusion that an agreement should not be enforced because it was entered into on the basis of a serious mistake.

The analysis used in *Sherwood* is, however, fairly problematic. Both the majority and dissenting opinions seem to say that the decision should be based on the distinction between a mistake as to the subject matter of the agreement and a mere mistake as to an attribute of the subject matter. That is, if the parties thought they were dealing with a cow, but instead Rose was a horse, that would be a mistake as to subject matter that would warrant a

---

[c] Brainerd Currie, Rose of Aberlone (Being an Entry for an Index), 10 Student Lawyer Journal 4–8 (1965) available at:

http://scholarship.law.duke.edu/cgi/viewcontent.cgi?article=5665&context=faculty_scholarship.

conclusion that the agreement should not be enforced. By contrast if they knew they were dealing with a cow that would breed, but were mistaken about whether she was pregnant that season, that would be a mistake as to an attribute that would not warrant relief from the agreement.

Commentators pretty uniformly have concluded that the supposed distinction between "substance" and "attribute" is not very useful. In the facts of the case itself, how in the world is one supposed to decide whether the capacity to breed is merely an attribute of a cow or whether a cow that cannot breed a different thing than a cow that can breed?

Appellees contend . . . that in this case the parties were mistaken as to the very nature of the character of the consideration and claim that the pervasive and essential quality of this mistake renders rescission appropriate. They cite in support of that view *Sherwood v. Walker,* 66 Mich. 568, 33 N.W. 919 (1887), the famous "barren cow" case. . . .

As the parties suggest, the foregoing precedent arguably distinguishes mistakes affecting the essence of the consideration from those which go to its quality or value, affording relief on a per se basis for the former but not the latter. * * *

However, the distinctions which may be drawn from *Sherwood* . . . do not provide a satisfactory analysis of the nature of a mistake sufficient to invalidate a contract. Often, a mistake relates to an underlying factual assumption which, when discovered, directly affects value, but simultaneously and materially affects the essence of the contractual consideration. It is disingenuous to label such a mistake collateral. . . .

Appellant and appellee both mistakenly believed that the property which was the subject of their land contract would generate income as rental property. The fact that it could not be used for human habitation deprived the property of its income-earning potential and rendered it less valuable. However, this mistake, while directly and dramatically affecting the property's value, cannot accurately be characterized as collateral because it also affects the very essence of the consideration. "The thing sold and bought [income generating rental property] had in fact no existence". *Sherwood v. Walker,* 66 Mich. 578, 33 N.W. 919.

We find that the inexact and confusing distinction between contractual mistakes running to value and those touching the substance of the consideration serves only as an impediment to a clear and helpful analysis for the equitable resolution of cases in which mistake is alleged and proven. Accordingly, the holding of . . . *Sherwood* with respect to the material or collateral nature of a mistake [is] limited to the facts of [that] case.

Instead, we think the better-reasoned approach is a case-by-case analysis whereby rescission is indicated when the mistaken belief relates to a basic assumption of the parties upon which the contract is made, and which materially affects the agreed performances of the parties. * * *Rescission is not available, however, to relieve a party who has assumed the risk of loss in connection with the mistake.* * *

like the cases Cotton above

331 N.W.2d at 209–210.

1.   A note on terminology. "Rescission" is a term used by lawyers, courts and business people in many different senses. For example, parties to a contract can mutually agree to rescind their contract to discharge their contractual duties. Rescission, in this context, refers to an equitable remedy invalidating the contract. When a mistake warrants relief, we can say the contract is "voidable" (as distinguished from void). See Rest. 2d § 153 below.

2.   What are the appropriate remedies due to mutual mistake? Think about the restitution remedy provided (for different reasons) in *Yurchak Jack Boiman Construction Co* in Chapter 1.D. Think about reliance. Some scholars have argued that, in order to prevent giving a windfall to one party, the remedy should rather split the difference, meaning that each party shares the loss equally: Gideon Parchomovsky, Peter Siegelman & Steve Thel, *Equal Wrongs and Half Rights*, 82 N.Y.U. L. Rev. 738 (2007). Do you think this would be an improvement in the law?

3.   The distinction drawn in *Sherwood* is reflected in many systems of private law:

> "In France, an error warrants relief if it is in substance (*substance*), in Italy, if it is "essential" (*essenziale*), in Germany, if it is in a characteristic "regarded in commercial dealings as essential" (*die im Verkehr als wesentlich angesehen werden*). . . . Most modern jurists have not found the word "substance" helpful in describing when relief should be given. Yet they have had difficulties formulating any alternative rule to describe when relief should be given".

James A. Gordley, *Mistake in Contract Formation*, 52 AM. J. COMP. L. 433, 434 (2004). Gordley instead asks us to reflect on why we generally award the expectation interest, rather than the reliance interest, as damages in contract law. The answer to that—including that a contract often serves to lock in a favorable bargain—helps to explain why certain mistakes do not warrant relief.

4.   So, how should we decide whether the mistake does or does not warrant relief from the obligation to perform the contract? What should the result be in the following cases?[d]

---

[d]   We've printed only the facts so you can puzzle through what the analysis and result should be. Of course, you could look up the cases, but then you would get no educational value out of the exercise. Your choice.

Smith v. Zimbalist

District Court of Appeal, Second District, Division 1, California, 1935.
2 Cal.App.2d 324, 38 P.2d 170.

■ HOUSER, JUSTICE.

From the "findings of fact" made pursuant to the trial of the action, it appears that plaintiff, who was of the age of 86 years, although not a dealer in violins, had been a collector of rare violins for many years; "that defendant was a violinist of great prominence, internationally known, and himself the owner and collector of rare and old violins made by the old masters"; that at the suggestion of a third person, and without the knowledge by plaintiff of defendant's intention in the matter, defendant visited plaintiff at the home of the latter and there asked plaintiff if he might see plaintiff's collection of old violins; that in the course of such visit and inspection, "plaintiff showed a part of his collection to defendant; that defendant picked up one violin and asked plaintiff what he would take for the violin, calling it a 'Stradivarius'; that plaintiff did not offer his violins, or any of them, for sale, but on account of his age, after he had been asked what he would take for them, said he would not charge as much as a regular dealer, but that he would sell it for $5,000; that thereafter defendant picked up another violin, calling it a 'Guarnerius', and asked plaintiff what he would take for that violin, and plaintiff said if defendant took both violins, he could have them for $8,000; that the defendant said 'all right', thereupon stating his financial condition and asking if he could pay $2,000 cash and the balance in monthly payments of $1,000." Thereupon a memorandum was signed by defendant as follows:

"I hereby acknowledge receipt of one violin by Joseph Guarnerius and one violin by Stradivarius dated 1717 purchased by me from George Smith for the total sum of Eight Thousand Dollars toward which purchase price I have paid Two Thousand Dollars the balance I agree to pay at the rate of one thousand dollars on the fifteenth day of each month until paid in full."

In addition thereto, a "bill of sale" in the following language was signed by plaintiff:

"This certifies that I have on this date sold to Mr. Efrem Zimbalist one Joseph Guarnerius violin and one Stradivarius violin dated 1717, for the full price of $8,000.00 on which has been paid $2,000.00.

"The balance of $6,000.00 to be paid $1,000.00 fifteenth of each month until paid in full, I agree that Mr. Zimbalist shall have the right to exchange these for any others in my collection should he so desire."

That at the time said transaction was consummated each of the parties thereto "fully believed that said violins were made one by *argument based on warranty*

↓

Zimbalist identified a specific type of violin on the memo + bill of sale

Antonius Stradivarius and one by Josef Guarnerius"; that preceding the closing of said transaction "plaintiff made no representations and warranties as to said violins, or either of them, as to who their makers were, but believed them to have been made one by Antonius Stradivarius and one by Josef Guarnerius in the early part of the eighteenth century; that plaintiff did not fraudulently make any representations or warranties to defendant at the time of said purchase"; that there was "a preponderance of evidence to the effect that said violins are not Stradivarius or Guarnerius violins, nor made by either Antonius Stradivarius or Josef Guarnerius, but were in fact made as imitations thereof, and were not worth more than $300.00."

The action which is the foundation of the instant appeal was brought by plaintiff against defendant to recover judgment for the unpaid balance of the purchase price of the two violins.

As is shown by the conclusions of law reached by the trial court from such facts, the theory upon which the case was decided was that the transaction in question was the result of "a mutual mistake on the part of plaintiff and defendant," and consequently that plaintiff was not entitled to recover judgment. From a judgment rendered in favor of defendant, plaintiff has appealed to this court.

not enforceable

Wood v. Boynton

Supreme Court of Wisconsin, 1885.
64 Wis. 265, 25 N.W. 42.

■ TAYLOR, J.

trial court's judgement is affirmed

↓

inadequacy of price is not enough to make it fraud

↓

also no mistake about the identity of the item being sold

This action was brought in the circuit court for Milwaukee county to recover the possession of an uncut diamond of the alleged value of $1,000. The case was tried in the circuit court, and after hearing all the evidence in the case, the learned circuit judge directed the jury to find a verdict for the defendants. The plaintiff excepted to such instruction, and, after a verdict was rendered for the defendants, moved for a new trial upon the minutes of the judge. The motion was denied, and the plaintiff duly excepted, and after judgment was entered in favor of the defendants, appealed to this court. The defendants are partners in the jewelry business. On the trial it appeared that on and before the twenty-eighth of December, 1883, the plaintiff was the owner of and in the possession of a small stone of the nature and value of which she was ignorant; that on that day she sold it to one of the defendants for the sum of one dollar. Afterwards it was ascertained that the stone was a rough diamond, and of the value of about $700. After hearing this fact the plaintiff tendered the defendants the one dollar, and ten cents as interest, and demanded a return of the stone to her. The defendants refused to deliver it, and therefore she commenced this action.

The plaintiff testified to the circumstances attending the sale of the stone to Mr. Samuel B. Boynton, as follows: "The first time Boynton saw that stone he was talking about buying the topaz, or whatever it is, in September or October. I went into the store to get a little pin mended, and I had it in a small box,—the pin,—a small ear-ring; . . . this stone, and a broken sleeve-button were in the box. Mr. Boynton turned to give me a check for my pin. I thought I would ask him what the stone was, and I took it out of the box and asked him to please tell me what that was. He took it in his hand and seemed some time looking at it. I told him I had been told it was a topaz, and he said it might be. He says, 'I would buy this; would you sell it?' I told him I did not know but what I would. What would it be worth? And he said he did not know; he would give me a dollar and keep it as a specimen, and I told him I would not sell it; and it was certainly pretty to look at. He asked me where I found it, and I told him in Eagle. He asked about how far out, and I said right in the village, and I went out. Afterwards, and about the twenty-eighth of December, I needed money pretty badly, and thought every dollar would help, and I took it back to Mr. Boynton and told him I had brought back the topaz, and he says, 'Well, yes; what did I offer you for it?' and I says, 'One dollar;' and he stepped to the change drawer and gave me the dollar, and I went out." In another part of her testimony she says: "Before I sold the stone I had no knowledge whatever that it was a diamond. I told him that I had been advised that it was probably a topaz, and he said probably it was. The stone was about the size of a canary bird's egg, nearly the shape of an egg,—worn pointed at one end; it was nearly straw color,—a little darker." She also testified that before this action was commenced she tendered the defendants $1.10, and demanded the return of the stone, which they refused. This is substantially all the evidence of what took place at and before the sale to the defendants, as testified to by the plaintiff herself. She produced no other witness on that point.

The evidence on the part of the defendant is not very different from the version given by the plaintiff . . . . Mr. Samuel B. Boynton, the defendant to whom the stone was sold, testified that at the time he bought this stone, he had never seen an uncut diamond; had seen cut diamonds, but they are quite different from the uncut ones; "he had no idea this was a diamond, and it never entered his brain at the time." Considerable evidence was given as to what took place after the sale and purchase, but that evidence has very little if any bearing, upon the main point in the case. . . .

. . .

We can find nothing in the evidence from which it could be justly inferred that Mr. Boynton, at the time he offered the plaintiff one dollar for the stone, had any knowledge of the real value of the stone, or that he entertained even a belief that the stone was a diamond. . . .

PROBLEM

From the *Antiques Roadshow* webpage:

Bogie's Autograph

A few years ago I went to the local estate sales to hunt for treasures. I came across an old chest full of books, and bought one for $1 that had watercolor pictures and lots of autographs. I had it appraised and found out it had Humphrey Bogart's autograph. It was valued at $1,500 to $5,000. My husband used to say, "You're wasting your time going to estate sales." Now before I leave he tells me, "Happy hunting, Sweetheart!"

- Karen, Turlock, California http://www.pbs.org/wgbh/pages /roadshow/stories/submission177.html

Could the seller of the book recover it from Karen upon discovering that it had Bogie's autograph? Would it matter if Karen realized it had Bogie's autograph in it before she bought the book at the estate sale?

3. UNILATERAL MISTAKE IN UNDERLYING ASSUMPTION

Restatement (Second) of Contracts § 153

Go back and review *Drennan v. Star Paving*, which we studied in Chapter Five. Recall that in that case Star Paving, a paving subcontractor, submitted a mistakenly low bid to Drennan, a general contractor. Drennan, in turn, submitted its bid to the owner, computing the total on the basis of Star's mistakenly low bid. Thus, under ordinary offer and acceptance principles, Star could have simply revoked its bid before acceptance by Drennan. That would be the case whatever the reason that Star didn't want to do the work for the amount of its bid, mistake or simple change of mind. As we saw in the case itself, however, the California Supreme Court ruled that in those circumstances an exception should be crafted to the usual offer and acceptance principles, so that Star did not have the usual privilege to revoke its bid.

Suppose the facts had been slightly different. Suppose that Drennan had accepted Star's bid before Star attempted to revoke, but after Drennan had entered into the contract with the owner on the basis of Star's mistakenly low bid. Then, under ordinary offer and acceptance principles, Star would have been contractually bound to Drennan to do the work for the low bid price. Could Star obtain relief from that contractual obligation on the grounds that it entered into the agreement on the basis of a mistake? Look at the last paragraph of the Drennan opinion, where Justice Traynor discusses that issue, rejecting a mistake argument by Star.

Now, consider a variant, where the error is made not by the subcontractor but by the general contractor. Suppose that there had been no mistake in the bid submitted by Star or any of the other subcontractors. But, suppose that Drennan, the general contractor, makes a computational error in adding up the amount of all the subs' bids, and, as a result, submits a mistakenly low bid to the school district. The school district opens the bids and notifies Drennan that its bid is accepted. The next day, Drennan realizes its mistake. Is Drennan bound to do the work for the school district for the mistakenly low price? That's the issue of "unilateral mistake" involved in the next case. → *respondent*

Boise Junior College Dist. v. Mattefs Constr. Co.

appellant

Supreme Court of Idaho, 1969.
92 Idaho 757, 450 P.2d 604.

■ SPEAR, JUSTICE.

The issue presented is whether, under the circumstances of this case, a contractor is entitled to the equitable relief of rescission when it has submitted a bid which contains a material clerical mistake. We conclude that such relief is available.

Mattefs Construction Company (hereinafter termed respondent) was one of ten bidders on a construction contract to be let by Boise Junior College District (hereinafter referred to as appellant). Along with its bid respondent submitted the customary bid bond containing a promise to pay the difference between its bid and the next higher bid actually accepted if respondent refused to enter into a contract with appellant. Contract specifications also provided that the bid could not be withdrawn for 45 days after it was opened.

The architect's estimate of costs on the building project was $150,000, but when the bids were opened seven of them ran in excess of $155,000 while three of them were less than $150,000. Fulton Construction Company bid $134,896. The respondent bid $141,048. The third bid by Cain and Hardy, Inc., was $148,915. When Fulton refused to sign a contract it was tendered to respondent who likewise refused to sign it. Ultimately the contract was awarded to Cain and Hardy, Inc., the third lowest bidder and appellant proceeded to attempt collection on respondent's bid bond.

One who errs in preparing a bid for a public works contract is entitled to the equitable relief of rescission if he can establish the following condition: (1) the mistake is material; (2) enforcement of a contract pursuant to the terms of the erroneous bid would be unconscionable; (3) the mistake did not result from violation of a positive legal duty or from culpable negligence; (4) the party to whom the bid is submitted will not be prejudiced except by the loss of his bargain; and (5) prompt notice of the error is given. These principles are established by substantial authority, * * * That appellant recognizes these principles is evident, because it has raised questions as to the existence of each one of these elements by its assignments of error. Therefore, we shall consider each of these conditions necessary for equitable relief, in the context of the objections raised.

I

Appellant contends that the trial court erred in determining that omission of the glass bid was a material mistake. The trial court found:

'This was the second largest sub bid item in the whole contract, only the mechanical sub bid being larger. It amounted to about 14% of the contract and was thus a material item.'

Thus, the issue is whether, as a matter of law, a 14% error in bid is a material error. We have no difficulty in reaching the conclusion that omission of an item representing 14% of the total bid submitted is substantial and material. Appellant cites a number of cases wherein courts have directly or indirectly determined that material error was not involved, in spite of mistakes which ranged up to 50%, i.e., * * * However, we are persuaded we should adopt a rule which is not so harsh and turn instead to authority such as *Elsinore Union Elementary School Dist. v. Kastorff,* 54 Cal.2d 380, 6 Cal.Rptr. 1, 353 P.2d 713 (1960), in which the court stated:

'Plaintiff suggests that in any event the amount of the plumbing bid omitted from the total was immaterial. The bid as submitted was in the sum of $89,994, and whether the sum for the omitted plumbing was $6,500 or $9,285 (the two sub bids), the omission of such a sum is plainly material to the total. *In Lemoge (Lemoge Electric v. County of San Mateo* (1956), *supra,* 46 Cal.2d 659, 661–662, 297 P.2d 638) the error which it was declared would have entitled plaintiff to rescind was the listing of the cost of certain materials as $104.52, rather than $10,452, in a total bid of $172,421. Thus the percentage of error here was larger than in Lemoge, and was plainly material.'

II

An error in the computation of a bid may be material, representing a large percentage of the total bid submitted, and yet requiring compliance with the bid may not be unconscionable. Thus, omission of a $25,000 item in a $100,000 bid would be material, but if the $100,000 bid included $50,000 in profit, no hardship would be created by requiring the contractor to comply with the terms of his bid.

This does not represent the case at bar. Here the record reveals that if respondent were forced to comply with the terms of its bid it would lose at least $10,000. Respondent's costs, including the omitted item, would be roughly $151,000 while the total amount of its bid was only $141,000. Enforcement of the bid is deemed unconscionable as working a substantial hardship on the bidder where it appears he would incur a substantial pecuniary loss. * * * This is particularly so where, as here, no injury is caused by withdrawal of the bid. (See sec. IV, *infra.*)

III

One who seeks equitable relief from error must establish that such error does not result from violation of a positive legal duty or from culpable negligence.

'[This] generally means carelessness or lack of good faith in calculation which violates a positive duty in making up a bid, so as to amount to gross negligence, or wilful negligence, when it takes on a sinister meaning and will furnish cause, if established, for holding a mistake of the offending bidder to be one not remediable in equity. *It is thus distinguished from a clerical or inadvertent error in handling items of a bid either through setting them down or transcription.'* (emphasis added) Annot., 52 A.L.R.2d 792, 794.

In several of its assignments appellant contends that the trial court erred in not finding that respondent was negligent to the point of being grossly negligent. Respondent's superintendent, who actually made the mistake, testified as follows:

'Q   what did you do relating to glass and glazing?

'A   I was putting this bid together. When I come to the glass section, I had a question of this bid. That is when I called Intermountain Glass to verify that their bid covered everything in this section.

'Q   What did you do after you verified it? What did you do with that bid?

'A   Well, I called them and got the information I needed so that I was satisfied in my mind that the bid really covered everything, but I had been working on the phone and the minute I hung up from talking to the man at Intermountain I had to answer another call before I could get that figure down and take another bid.

'Q   This was all during the lunch hour?

'A   Yes. I continued with my work sheet. This is when I made the mark that included another figure and just left the glass out.

'Q   Can you show what you did with reference to the bracket?

'A   Well, I had put just a little bracket to show what was included in the next two items, so that anyone coming in who was unfamiliar with it would immediately know it was included here, which it definitely shows that it is. Why I did that, I'll never know, with that other bracket with another figure that would indicate that it was included.'

. . .

On the basis of these facts the trial court concluded:

'There was no willful or even negligent act by plaintiff's agents which prevented knowledge of the error from reaching Mr. Mattefs prior to the opening. In preparing the bid Mattefs Construction Company proceeded in the usual way and under the same last minute pressures that are experienced by all general contractors bidding on bids of this kind. Under the evidence I concluded that it was using ordinary care in its methods of bid preparation; that is, the same care that other contractors in the area use in making bids of the kind here involved. There was no evidence of any gross negligence or fraudulent or willful intent to omit this item for the purpose of obtaining any advantage in the bidding.'

It is appellant's contention that the trial court erred in making these findings. It has long been the rule of this court that:

'Where the findings of the trial court are supported by substantial and competent, though conflicting, evidence, such findings will not be disturbed on appeal.'

Riley v. Larson, 91 Idaho 831 (1967) . . . Additionally, the trial judge is the arbiter of conflicting evidence; his determination of the weight, credibility, inference and implications thereof is not to be supplanted by this court's impressions or conclusions from the written record. * * * Also findings of fact shall not be set aside unless clearly erroneous. I.R.C.P. 52(a).

Thus, the finding of the trial court that the mistake of respondent was not due to the required type of negligence must be affirmed. As was held in the *Kemper* case:

'The type of error here involved is one which will sometimes occur in the conduct of reasonable and cautious businessmen, and, under all the circumstances, we cannot say as a matter of law that it constituted a neglect of legal duty such as would bar the right to equitable relief.' *M. F. Const. Co. v. City of Los Angeles*, 235 P.2d 7, at p. 11 (Cal. 1951).

IV

It is well settled by the authorities that a bid may not be withdrawn if such withdrawal would work a substantial hardship on the offeree. Many situations can be hypothesized where such a hardship would result. However, none appears here, nor has appellant attempted to prove any hardship. Appellant expected to pay $150,000 for the work it solicited. Its actual cost will be $149,000. It complains because it cannot have the work done for $141,000. Thus, appellant's injury consists of a failure to save $9,000 on its construction rather than saving $1,000. . . .

The most appellant can argue is that its damage is presumed by the requirement of a bid bond and that release of a bid bond and that release of a bidder whenever he makes a mistake will impair the purposes for which a bid bond is required. First of all, as previously pointed out, not all mistakes entitle a bidder to equitable rescission, and second, withdrawal of a bid under proper circumstances will not destroy the irrevocability of bids.

'There is a difference between mere mechanical or clerical errors made in tabulating or transcribing figures and errors of judgment, as, for example, underestimating the cost of labor or materials. The distinction between the two types of error is recognized in the cases allowing rescission and in the procedures provided by the state and federal governments for relieving contractors from mistakes in bids on public work. (* * *) Generally, relief is refused for error in judgment and allowed only for clerical or mathematical mistakes. (* * *) Where a person is denied relief because of an error in judgment, the agreement which is enforced is the one he intended to make, whereas if he is denied relief from a clerical error, he is forced to perform an agreement he had no intention of making. The statement in the bid form in the present case can be given effect by interpreting it as relating to errors of judgment as distinguished from clerical mistakes.' *M. F. Kemper Const. Co., supra*, at page 11.

The proper purpose of a provision against withdrawal of a bid was fully explained by the Maryland Court of Appeals, quoting from *Geremia v. Boyarsky*, 107 Conn. 387, 140 A. 749 (1928):

"It is objected that the rule should be different where, as here, there is a proviso forbidding the withdrawal of bids. To be sure, this puts a bidder on notice that there is a certain finality about bidding for a government contract. But this by no means should enable a governmental agency to take an unconscionable advantage of its special status as a government body. * * * The proper effect of the requirement that bids remain unrevoked is to assure the State that a bidder will be relieved of his obligation only when it is legally justifiable. That means that the State is in the same position as any acceptor when there is a question of rectifying an error. * * * Of course, it is obvious, as the State contends, that the system of public bidding, developed by experience and usual in public contracts, should not be broken down by lightly permitting bidders to withdraw because of change of mind. Such a course would be unfair to other straight-forward bidders, as well as disruptive of public business. But it can hardly be a substantial impairment of such system to grant the relief—which would clearly be given as between private citizens—in a case where a bona fide mistake is proven and was known to the State before acceptance or any loss to it." *City of Baltimore v. De Luca-Davis Construction Co.*, 124 A.2d at p. 565.

V

The final element of the right to equitable relief raised by appellant is actually an adjunct of the previous question of whether the offeree will be damaged by withdrawal of the bid. The requirement of prompt notice is separately stated here because appellant earnestly argues that it was not given such prompt notice. This contention is not supported by the evidence.

. . . Relief from mistaken bids is consistently allowed where the acceptor has actual notice of the error prior to its attempted acceptance and the other elements necessary for equitable relief are present. *M. F. Kemper Const. Co.,* 235 P.2d at page 10. We see no reason to deviate from this rule where, as here, the party opposing the grant of equitable relief can show no damage other than loss of benefit of an inequitable bargain. We conclude that appellant's position is no better here than it was when similar arguments were presented to the U.S. Supreme Court nearly 70 years ago. In quoting from the circuit court opinion, the court held:

> "If the defendants (appellants) are correct in their contention there is absolutely no redress for a bidder for public work, no matter how aggravated or palpable his blunder. The moment his proposal is opened by the executive board he is held as in a grasp of steel. There is no remedy, no escape. If, through an error of his clerk, he has agreed to do work worth $1,000,000 for $10, he must be held to the strict letter of his contract, while equity stands by with folded hands and sees him driven into bankruptcy. The defendants' (appellants') position admits of no compromise, no exception, no middle ground." *Moffett, Hodgkins & Clarke Co. v. City of Rochester,* 178 U.S. 373, 386, 20 S.Ct. 957, 961, 44 L.Ed. 1108 (1900).

This reasoning is equally applicable to the cause at bar.

Judgment affirmed. Costs to respondent.

D. IMPRACTICABILITY (IMPOSSIBILITY) AND FRUSTRATION

1. IMPRACTICABILITY (IMPOSSIBILITY)

Restatement (Second) of Contracts §§ 261, 262, 263

Taylor v. Caldwell
Court of Queen's Bench, 1863.
122 Eng. Rep. 309.

■ BLACKBURN, J.

In this case the plaintiffs and defendants had, on May 27th, 1861, entered into a contract by which the defendants agreed to let the plaintiffs have the use of The Surrey Gardens and Music Hall on four days then to come, viz., June 17th, July 15th, August 5th, and August 19th, for the purpose of giving a series of four grand concerts, and day and night fetes, at the Gardens and Hall on those days respectively; and the plaintiffs agreed to take the Gardens and Hall on those days, and pay £100 for each day.

The parties inaccurately call this a "letting," and the money to be paid, a "rent"; but the whole agreement is such as to show that the defendants were to retain the possession of the Hall and Gardens so that there was to be no demise of them, and that the contract was merely to give the plaintiffs the use of them on those days. Nothing, however, in our opinion, depends on this. The agreement then proceeds to set out various stipulations between the parties as to what each was to supply for these concerts and entertainments, and as to the manner in which they should be carried on. The effect of the whole is to show that the existence of the Music Hall in the Surrey Gardens in a state fit for a concert was essential for the fulfilment of the contract, such entertainments as the parties contemplated in their agreement could not be given without it.

After the making of the agreement, and before the first day on which a concert was to be given, the Hall was destroyed by fire. This destruction, we must take it on the evidence, was without the fault of either party, and was so complete that in consequence the concerts could not be given as intended. And the question we have to decide is whether, under these circumstances, the loss which the plaintiffs have sustained is to fall upon the defendants. The parties when framing their agreement evidently had not present to their minds the possibility of such a disaster, and have made no express stipulation with reference to it, so that the answer to the question must depend upon the general rules of law applicable to such a contract.

There seems no doubt that where there is a positive contract to do a thing, not in itself unlawful, the contractor must perform it or pay damages for not doing it, although in consequence of unforseen accidents the performance of his contract has become unexpectedly burdensome or even impossible. The law is so laid down in 1 Roll.Abr. 450, Condition (G), and in the note (2) to *Walton v. Waterhouse* (2 Wms.Saund. 421a, 6th Ed.) and is recognized as the general rule by all the judges in the much discussed case of *Hall v. Wright* (E.B. & E. 746). But this rule is only applicable when the contract is positive and absolute, and not subject to any condition either express or implied; and there are authorities which, as we think, establish the principle that where, from the nature of the contract, it appears that the parties must from the beginning have known that it could not be fulfilled unless when the time for the fulfilment of the contract arrived some particular specified thing continued to exist, so that, when entering into the contract, they must have contemplated such continuing existence as the foundation of what was to be done; there, in the absence of any express or implied warranty that the thing shall exist, the contract is not to be construed as a positive contract, but as subject to an implied condition that the parties shall be excused in case, before breach, performance becomes impossible from the perishing of the thing without default of the contractor.

There seems little doubt that this implication tends to further the great object of making the legal construction such as to fulfill the intention of those who entered into the contract. For in the course of affairs men in making such contracts in general would, if it were brought to their minds, say that there should be such a condition.

. . .

. . . In the present case, looking at the whole contract, we find that the parties contracted on the basis of the continued existence of the Music Hall at the time when the concerts were to be given, that being essential to their performance.

We think, therefore, that the Music Hall having ceased to exist, without fault of either party, both parties are excused, the plaintiffs from taking the gardens and paying the money, the defendants from performing their promise to give the use of the Hall and Gardens and other things.

NOTES

1. The *Taylor* opinion states the result—that the burning of the hall discharges the parties' contractual obligations—by using the concept of "condition." As the court puts it, the contract should be treated "as subject to an implied condition that the parties shall be excused in case, before breach, performance becomes impossible from the perishing of the thing without default of the contractor." But the concept of condition is really just a way of stating the issue: should the burning of the hall excuse the parties' duties or not. It doesn't really help us decide whether that should be the result or not. Judge Skelly Wright noted this point in a later impossibility case by recalling a famous remark by Oliver Wendell Holmes, "You can give any conclusion a logical form. You can always imply a condition in a contract. But why do you imply it? It is because of some belief as to the practice of the community or of a class, or because of some opinion as to policy . . . ." Holmes, *The Path of the Law*, 10 Harv. L. Rev. 457, 466 (1897), *quoted in Transatlantic Financing Corp. v. United States*, 363 F.2d 312 (D.C. Cir. 1966)(Skelly Wright, J.)

The doctrine derived from *Taylor v. Caldwell* is often described by the phrase "impossibility." That's a somewhat misleading description, because it makes the issue seem too simple. Suppose we ask "Is the hall owner obligated to make the hall available once it burned down?" That seems like an easy question. Once the hall has burned down, it's "impossible" for the owner to make it available. But remember—what it means to say that a promise is legally enforceable is that the promisor must either perform or pay damages. So, if the hall owner is contractually obligated, then the owner either has to make the hall available or pay damages. The fact that the hall has burned down means that the owner won't perform, but it hardly makes it "impossible" for the owner to pay damages. That's the issue: is the owner excused from the obligation to pay damages?

More recently, the issue involved in *Taylor* has come to be known as "impracticability." A classic modern decision is Judge Skelly Wright's opinion in *Transatlantic Financing Corp. v. United States*, 363 F.2d 312 (D.C. Cir. 1966). A shipping company agreed to carry a cargo of wheat from the United States to Iran for a fixed price of about $300,000. After the agreement was made, the Suez Canal was closed as a result of the 1956 war. As a consequence, the ship had to take a longer route, around the Cape of Good Hope. The issue in the case was whether the outbreak of the war and closing of the canal should be treated as the kind of supervening event that discharged the shipping company's contractual obligation to transport the cargo for the agreed price. Obviously it was possible to take the longer route, so the court phrased the issue as one of "impracticability" rather than "impossibility." As Judge Skelly Wright put it:

> The doctrine of impossibility of performance has gradually been freed from the earlier fictional and unrealistic strictures of such tests as the 'implied term' and the parties' 'contemplation.' . . . It is now recognized that "A thing is impossible in legal contemplation when it is not practicable; and a thing is impracticable when it can only be done at an excessive and unreasonable cost." *Mineral Park land Co. v. Howard*, 172 Cal. 289, 293, 156 P. 458, 460, L.R.A. 1916F, 1 (1916). . . . The doctrine ultimately represents the ever-shifting line, drawn by courts hopefully responsive to commercial practices and mores, at which the community's interest in having contracts enforced according to their terms is outweighed by the commercial senselessness of requiring performance

In the case itself, the court concluded that the closing of the Suez Canal did not excuse the shipping company's contractual duty to do the job for the agreed price, even though it ended up costing the shipping company more to do so. That's hardly a surprising result. One of the main functions of fixed price contracts is to set the price for goods or work in advance. Recall the cotton futures case that we read in Chapter One, *Bolin Farms v. American Cotton Shippers Ass'n*. The farmers were surprised, and very upset, that conditions had changed so dramatically that they had to sell cotton for 30¢ per pound even though the market price had shot up to 80¢ per pound. As Judge Owens put it: "The defendants, naturally, don't want to sell cotton because the price has gone up and if I were one of those defendants I would feel the same way. I would be sick as an old hound dog who ate a rotten skunk, but unfortunately—well, not unfortunately—fortunately we all abide by contracts and that (is) the foundation of which all of the business that you have heard about here today is done." So, while modern courts are more likely to speak of "impracticability" than "impossibility," it's still pretty unlikely that contractual duties will be excused by unforeseen events, and it's still pretty hard to formulate any very helpful general rules on the subject.

2.   There are a few recurring settings in which the rules on impracticability have become fairly well settled. One is where a certain person has agreed to do certain work, where it really matters who does the work, and then that person dies. Suppose, for example, that Artist promises to paint a portrait of Jones. Artist dies before performance. It's fairly well-settled that the duty to perform is discharged. Note again that the phrase "impossibility" is a bit misleading here. The question is not whether the dead artist is supposed to paint the portrait. Rather, the question is whether the artist's estate is liable to Jones for any damages that Jones suffers, for example, if it costs Jones more to get someone else to paint the portrait. The usual conclusion is that artist's death does excuse the contractual duty, so the estate is not liable for damages. RESTATEMENT (SECOND) OF CONTRACTS § 262.

By contrast, in settings where personal taste and special abilities are not so significant, the death of the promisor does not discharge contractual duties. Suppose that Smith, a house painter, contracts to paint Jones' house for $10,000. Smith dies, and it ends up costing Jones $12,000 to get someone else to do the job. Jones sues Smith's estate for the $2000 damage that Jones suffered as a result of the fact that Smith did not do the job as promised. In this sort of case, it's quite settled that Smith's death does not discharge the contractual duty, so Smith's estate would be liable for damages for breach.

3.   Another setting where the rules have become fairly well-settled involves construction contracts. Suppose Acme agrees to redo the kitchen of Smith's house. Then, the house burns down. The destruction of the house would routinely be held to discharge Acme's duty. Thus, Acme would not be liable for breach of contract—even if the contract price was quite favorable to Smith. RESTATEMENT (SECOND) OF CONTRACTS § 263. By contrast, suppose that Acme agrees to build a house for Smith. After doing part of the work, the structure burns. In that case, the destruction of the partially completed structure would not discharge Acme's duty. Thus, Acme would be liable for breach of contract if Acme does not redo the work. The difference is between a promise to do work on an existing building, and a promise to build a building. Note that in this setting, it's so common to have fire insurance that the rules on discharge really just determine who should buy the insurance.

PROBLEM

Consider the following facts. Alexandra lives in Staten Island, New York, and has contracted for a honeymoon safari expedition to East Africa, with a Manhattan-based travel agency. The contract provides for a refund only if notice of cancellation is received before Sept. 14, 2001. Notice the dates. She cancelled on Sept. 27, 2001.

Alexandra comes to you to ask your legal opinion on whether she can be excused for the late cancellation based on the travel and communication difficulties in New York City after the terrorist attack on the World Trade Center on Sept. 11, 2001. The city had been placed in virtual lockdown, and a state of emergency had been declared. She is now reluctant to travel abroad. Imagine it is early 2002, and no statute of limitations issues apply.

What would you advise her? See *Bush v. ProTravel International, Inc.,* 746 N.Y.S. 2d 790 (Civ. Ct. 2002).

2. FRUSTRATION

Restatement (Second) of Contracts § 265

Krell v. Henry
Court of Appeal, 1902.
2 K.B. 740.

[Plaintiff Krell owned a flat on Pall Mall in London. The flat was along the parade route for the planned coronation of Albert Edward ("Bertie"), son of Queen Victoria, as King Edward VII. The coronation parade was expected to be a great social event, since there had not been a coronation in England since Queen Victoria assumed the throne more than sixty years earlier. Defendant Henry agreed to hire Krell's room for days of the coronation parade for £75. Alas, "Bertie" came down with appendicitis, and the coronation parade was cancelled. Needless to say, Henry did not take the rooms to watch ordinary traffic pass by. Krell sued Henry for the agreed price.]

■ VAUGHAN WILLIAMS L.J.: read the following written judgment.

The real question in this case is the extent of the application in English law of the principle of the Roman law which has been adopted and acted on in many English decisions, and notably in the case of *Taylor v. Caldwell.* . . . Whatever may have been the limits of the Roman law, . . . the English law applies the principle not only to cases where the performance of the contract becomes impossible by the cessation of existence of the thing which is the subject-matter of the contract, but also to cases where the event which renders the contract incapable of performance is the cessation or non-existence of an express condition or state of things, going to the root of the contract, and essential to its performance.

It is said, on the one side, that the specified thing, state of things, or condition the continued existence of which is necessary for the fulfilment of the contract, so that the parties entering into the contract must have contemplated the continued existence of that thing, condition, or state of things as the foundation of what was to be done under the contract, is limited to things which are either the subject-matter of the contract or a condition or state of things, present or anticipated, which is expressly mentioned in the contract. But, on the other side, it is said that the condition or state of things need not be expressly specified, but that it is sufficient if that condition or state of things clearly appears by extrinsic evidence to have been assumed by the parties to be the foundation or basis of the contract, and the event which causes the impossibility is of such a character that it cannot reasonably be supposed to have been in the contemplation of the contracting parties when the contract was made. In such a case the contracting parties will not be held bound by the general words which, though large enough to include, were not used with reference to a possibility of a particular event rendering performance of the contract impossible.

I do not think that the principle of the civil law as introduced into the English law is limited to cases in which the event causing the impossibility of performance is the destruction or non-existence of some thing which is the subject-matter of the contract or of some condition or state of things expressly specified as a condition of it. I think that you first have to ascertain, not necessarily from the terms of the contract, but, if required, from necessary inferences, drawn from surrounding circumstances recognised by both contracting parties, what is the substance of the contract, and then to ask the question whether that substantial contract needs for its foundation the assumption of the existence of a particular state of things. If it does, this will limit the operation of the general words, and in such case, if the contract becomes impossible of performance by reason of the non-existence of the state of things assumed by both contracting parties as the foundation of the contract, there will be no breach of the contract thus limited.

Now what are the facts of the present case? The contract is contained in two letters of June 20 which passed between the defendant and the plaintiff's agent, Mr. Cecil Bisgood. These letters do not mention the coronation, but speak merely of the taking of Mr. Krell's chambers, or, rather, of the use of them, in the daytime of June 26 and 27, for the sum of £75, £25 then paid, balance £50 to be paid on the 24th. But the affidavits, which by agreement between the parties are to be taken as stating the facts of the case, shew that the plaintiff exhibited on his premises, third floor, 56A, Pall Mall, an announcement to the effect that windows to view the Royal coronation procession were to be let, and that the defendant was induced by that announcement to apply to the housekeeper on the premises, who said that the owner was willing to let the suite of rooms for the purpose of seeing the Royal procession for both days, but not nights, of June 26 and 27.

In my judgment the use of the rooms was let and taken for the purpose of seeing the Royal procession. It was not a demise of the rooms, or even an agreement to let and take the rooms. It is a licence to use rooms for a particular purpose and none other. And in my judgment the taking place of those processions on the days proclaimed along the proclaimed route, which passed 56A, Pall Mall, was regarded by both contracting parties as the foundation of the contract; and I think that it cannot reasonably be supposed to have been in the contemplation of the contracting parties, when the contract was made, that the coronation would not be held on the proclaimed days, or the processions not take place on those days along the proclaimed route; and I think that the words imposing on the defendant the obligation to accept and pay for the use of the rooms for the named days, although general and unconditional, were not used with reference to the possibility of the particular contingency which afterwards occurred.

It was suggested in the course of the argument that if the occurrence, on the proclaimed days, of the coronation and the procession in this case were the foundation of the contract, and if the general words are thereby limited or qualified, so that in the event of the non-occurrence of the coronation and procession along the proclaimed route they would discharge both parties from further performance of the contract, it would follow that if a cabman was engaged to take some one to Epsom on Derby Day at a suitable enhanced price for such a journey, say £10, both parties to the contract would be discharged in the contingency of the race at Epsom for some reason becoming impossible; but I do not think this follows, for I do not think that in the cab case the happening of the race would be the foundation of the contract. No doubt the purpose of the engager would be to go to see the Derby, and the price would be proportionately high; but the cab had no special qualifications for the purpose which led to the selection of the cab for this particular occasion. Any other cab would have done as well. Moreover, I think that, under the cab contract, the hirer, even if the race went off, could have said, "Drive me to Epsom; I will pay you the agreed sum; you have nothing to do with the purpose for which I hired the cab," and that if the cabman refused he would have been guilty of a breach of contract, there being nothing to qualify his promise to drive the hirer to Epsom on a particular day. Whereas in the case of the coronation, there is not merely the purpose of the hirer to see the coronation procession, but it is the coronation procession and the relative position of the rooms which is the basis of the contract as much for the lessor as the hirer; and I think that if the King, before the coronation day and after the contract, had died, the hirer could not have insisted on having the rooms on the days named. It could not in the cab case be reasonably said that seeing the Derby race was the foundation of the contract, as it was of the licence in this case. Whereas in the present case, where the rooms were offered and taken, by reason of their peculiar suitability from the position of the rooms for a view of the coronation procession, surely the view of the coronation procession was the foundation of the contract, which is a very different thing from the purpose of the man who engaged the cab—namely, to see the race— being held to be the foundation of the contract.

Each case must be judged by its own circumstances. In each case one must ask oneself, first, what, having regard to all the circumstances, was the foundation of the contract? Secondly, was the performance of the contract prevented? Thirdly, was the event which prevented the performance of the contract of such a character that it cannot reasonably be said to have been in the contemplation of the parties at the date of the contract? If all these questions are answered in the affirmative (as I think they should be in this case), I think both parties are discharged from further performance of the contract. . . .

. . .

NOTES

1.   *Krell v. Henry* involves the flip side of the impracticability issue that we saw in *Taylor v. Caldwell*. If the coronation parade had been held, but the house on Pall Mall burned down the day before, we'd have a case just like *Taylor*. The parade viewer might have to pay someone else a good deal more for a last-minute hire of rooms to watch the parade, but under *Taylor v. Caldwell*, the owner's promise to let the parade viewer use the rooms would be discharged by impossibility/impracticability as a consequence of the destruction of the house. In the *Krell v. Henry* case itself, the house is still there, but the parade has been cancelled. So, it's the renter who seeks to be excused from his contractual duty to pay the agreed price for the use of the rooms.

If we think of the agreements in general terms, both *Taylor v. Caldwell* and *Krell v. Henry* involved agreements between a Seller (of the use of property, etc.) and a Buyer. In *Taylor v. Caldwell,* the Seller says "My duty to perform my promise to *sell* the use of the property to Buyer (or pay damages) should be excused because circumstances changed radically when the building burned down." In *Krell v. Henry,* the Buyer says "My duty to perform my promise to *buy* the use of the property from Seller (or pay damages) should be excused because circumstances changed radically when the coronation parade was cancelled." Though the two situations involve similar issues, different terminology is commonly used to describe them. In *Krell v. Henry*, it doesn't seem apt to say that the buyer's performance has become "impossible" or even "impracticable." Henry could rent the rooms, have a nice party, and watch the ordinary traffic go by. But, the whole point of renting the rooms was to watch the parade, and there isn't going to be a parade. So, the issue is commonly described as involving the concept of "frustration of purpose," that is, should Henry's contractual duty to pay for the rooms be discharged when the purpose of the arrangement was frustrated by an unexpected turn of events.

2.   Justice Vaughan Williams (uncle of the composer Ralph Vaughan Williams) says that the case is very different from the example, discussed in arguments of the case, of a person who refused to pay the agreed high price for a cab to Epsom when the races were cancelled. It's very hard to see why Justice Vaughan Williams though the two cases were different. The leading Contracts scholar Arthur Corbin expressed considerable skepticism at the purported distinction:

> Would the hirer (or the cabman) be discharged from duty in case the race became impossible? The Lord Justice thought not, because he thought that the holding of the race was not the "foundation of the contract." The cab "had no special qualifications for the purpose . . . any other cab would have done as well." The present writer can not perceive any important distinction. It is true

that another cab would have done as well, if the hirer could get one. Some of the other rooms facing on Pall Mall might have done even better than those hired. The rooms had the peculiar merit of affording a view of the street, but were not movable; the cab had the peculiar merit of being available on Derby day, and was movable. In both cases the hirer had a known special purpose, a purpose that enabled the other party to charge a "suitably enhanced price." In both cases a supervening event, for which neither party was at fault, frustrated the purpose of the hirer—the purpose that had inflated the value of the use of the property hired. In neither case did the event make impossible any performance that was promised.

Corbin on Contracts, vol. 6, at 456–66 n.10 (1962).

3.   As with the similar concept of impracticability, though one can state the abstract principle that in some situations a party may be relieved from a contractual duty by frustration of purpose, one should not expect that a frustration argument will often succeed. So, for example, RESTATEMENT (SECOND) OF CONTRACTS § 265 states the general rule that sometimes frustration will excuse a failure to perform, but it does so in terms that aren't really very helpful in distinguishing the unusual cases where the frustration excuse might succeed from the routine case where a party is obligated to perform even though she regrets having made the agreement.

It's not difficult to see why the frustration argument will rarely succeed. Suppose Buyer, a resident of Massachusetts, agrees to buy a house in California because Buyer has gotten a job in California. After she signs the sales contract for the house in California, the company that was going to hire her goes bankrupt, the job falls through, and she decides to stay in Massachusetts. Buyer wants out of the deal to buy the house in California, because, from her perspective, the whole reason for the deal was the assumption that she would be moving to California. Seller may well have known that as well. Is Buyer relieved from her contractual obligation to buy (or pay damages)? Clearly not. The whole point of contracts is to bind parties to deals, and that really only matters when one side regrets having made the deal. An obvious reason that someone might regret a deal is that she agreed to buy something and then finds that, as a result of an unforeseen change of circumstances, she no longer needs it. That's not an excuse for non-performance; it's why people sue to enforce contracts.

4.   Note the similarity between the issues of impracticability or frustration, on the one hand, and the issues of mistake in basic assumption, on the other hand. In the preceding section we saw how hard it is to decide whether a party should be relieved from the consequences of a contract entered into on the basis of mistake. As we saw in that context, the difficulty can be seen, in part, as a tension between the unjust enrichment principle and the basic contract principle that parties are held to their bargains. We see the same tension in the impracticability and frustration cases. Indeed, the difference between the two doctrines may be solely a matter of timing. Consider the situation in *Taylor v. Caldwell*. After the time that the parties entered into the agreement, the hall burned down. So, the issue would be

described as a matter of impracticability. Suppose, however, that at the time the parties entered into the agreement, the hall had just burned down, but neither party to the agreement was aware of that fact. We might view this as still an impracticability issue, the difference being only that it's a case of impracticability existing at the time of the agreement. Or, we might view it as a mistake case: the parties entered into an agreement on the basis of a mutual mistake that the hall was still in existence. There really isn't much difference between the two ways of describing the problem. Under either description, the problem is whether the unknown event should relieve a party from the obligation to perform. So perhaps we should think of the impracticability and frustration doctrines as analogous to the mistake in basic assumption doctrine—all represent the notion that, in extreme cases, we might be unwilling to enforce agreements that turn out to be quite disadvantageous to one side as a result of something unforeseen, but we should not expect such excuse arguments to work very often.

3. REMEDIAL ISSUES IN IMPRACTICABILITY AND FRUSTRATION CASES

Restatement (Second) of Contracts § 272

Thus far we have considered impracticability and frustration cases without specific attention to remedial matters. That is, we have asked simply whether the promise should or should not be enforceable. In many other settings, however, we have seen that a simple binary way of framing the question is overly simplistic. Rather, following the lead of Lon Fuller's pathbreaking article, L. Fuller & W. Perdue, *The Reliance Interest in Contract Damages I & II*, 46 Y<small>ALE</small> L.J. 52, 373 (1936, 1937), we have seen that sometimes tensions about whether a promise should or should not be enforceable can be mediated by adjusting the remedy that we are prepared to grant.

For example, we started our study of contract law with *Hawkins v. McGee* (1929), holding that a doctor's promise about the outcome of an operation could be contractually enforceable. As we saw in *Hawkins*, the assumption at the time of that case was that if the promise was enforceable, then the patient was entitled to recover damages measured by how much better off he would have been if the promise had been performed. Later, we saw in *Sullivan v. O'Connor* (1973) that at least some modern courts have taken the view that a doctor's promise about the outcome of an operation might be enforceable, but the remedy should be limited to recovery of reliance damages rather than expectation damages.

We have seen the same pattern in other areas. Recall cases involving oral promises for which the Statute of Frauds requires a writing. No one doubts that if someone seeks expectation damages for breach of an oral promise within the Statute of Frauds, the effort will fail. What it means to say that a promise is "unenforceable" if not in writing is that we will not grant expectation damages for breach of the promise. Suppose, however, that a prospective buyer of land has made a down payment on an oral agreement for sale. The buyer will not be able to get expectation damages (or specific performance), but the fact that the promise is not fully enforceable would not preclude an action by the prospective buyer seeking only restitution of the amount of the down payment. We saw that in *Gilton v. Chapman* in Chapter 6. Now suppose that prospective buyer has not paid money to the prospective seller, but the prospective buyer has incurred other expenses in reliance on a promise that is unenforceable under the Statute of Frauds. Should the prospective buyer be able to recover what we would, in modern terminology, describe as reliance damages? In Chapter 6, we saw that at one time the usual answer was no, *Boone v. Coe* (1913), but today many courts would allow recovery of reliance damages, *McIntosh v. Murphy* (1970).

Similar issues might be presented in any case where, for reasons of the sort considered in this Chapter, we conclude that an agreement should not be enforceable, for reasons of indefiniteness, misrepresentation, mistake, impracticability, frustration, or the like. Those issues are often presented in impracticability and frustration cases, simply because it is fairly likely that the parties may have begun performance before the event that prevents completion of the deal.

Consider *Krell v. Henry*. In that case the court concluded that the agreement to hire the rooms was unenforceable by reason of frustration when the coronation procession was cancelled. That certainly means that the owner of the rooms could not recover what we would now term "expectation damages," that is, the £75 that Henry had promised to pay Krell for use of the rooms. If we adjust the amounts for inflation, we see the significance of that point. According to one set of conversion statistics we examined, £75 in 1902 is the equivalent of over $10,000 in 2016! So the promise to pay that sum for the use of the rooms really was a classic example of someone promising to pay a very high sum of money because that person had some special reason for wanting the promised performance.

What about restitution in such a situation? As it happens, Henry had paid Krell £25 of the £75, so the action by Krell against Henry was for the remaining £50. That's the claim that was denied in the case itself. Originally, Henry filed a counter-claim seeking the return of the £25 that he had paid. In the case itself, however, Henry dropped that counter-claim. There were, however, other cases arising out of similar facts. In one of them, *Chandler v. Webster*, 1 K.B. 493 (1904), the English court refused to allow restitution of the amount of the down payment. Perhaps the notion was that denying both expectation and restitution would, in many such cases, amount to a rough sort of "split the difference" justice. For example, on the *Krell v. Henry* facts, the result was that Henry lost the £25 he had already paid, but Krell lost the £50 he had not yet received.

American decisions, however, were generally more favorable towards restitution recovery under agreements that become unenforceable by reason of impracticability or frustration. A leading case is *Butterfield v. Byron*, 27 N.E. 667 (Mass. 1891). Owner entered into an agreement with Builder. After part of the work was done, the building was destroyed by fire. The first question was whether this should be treated as a promise by Builder to build a structure—in which case the fire would not discharge Builder's obligation to build—or a promise to do work on Owner's building—in which case the fire would discharge Builder's obligation to complete. In the case, itself, the Massachusetts court ruled that it should be treated as a promise to do work on the owner's building, so that the fire did discharge the parties' contractual duties under the concept of impracticability (impossibility). The next question was whether Builder was entitled to recovery for the work that had been done before the fire. In modern terminology, we'd phrase the question as whether Builder was entitled to restitution of the value of the work done. The approach taken in the English coronation cases would suggest no recovery for the builder, but the Massachusetts court did allow recovery. That approach has been generally followed in other American cases. By the mid-twentieth century, England changed position and followed the American approach. *Chandler v. Webster* was overruled in *Fibrosa Spolka Akcyjna v. Fairbain Lawson Combe Barbour, Ltd.*, [1943] A.C. 32. The Restatement recognizes the rule that restitution is available for benefits conferred under agreements that have become unenforceable by reason of impracticability or frustration. RESTATEMENT (SECOND) OF CONTRACTS § 272(1).

Now, what about reliance recovery? One approach to the issue, that we have seen before in connection with Statute of Frauds cases, is to expand the concept of "benefit" so that the problem can be fit within the principle that restitution of benefits conferred is available when an agreement becomes unenforceable by reason of impracticability (impossibility) or frustration. That approach is illustrated by a delightful old Massachusetts case, *Angus v. Scully*, 57 N.E. 674 (Mass. 1900). Angus agreed to move a building owned by Scully from a lot on Third St. in Cambridge to a lot on First St. When the building had been moved half way, it was destroyed by fire—not as a result of any neglect by the mover or owner. Angus was allowed to recover from Scully for the reasonable value of the work done before the building burned. In modern terminology, one might say that a "benefit" accrued to Scully with each inch that the building was moved toward its planned destination.

In other cases, however, it would be hard, even with a very expansive concept of "benefit" to fit the problem into any notion of restitution. The facts of the first impossibility case we examined—*Taylor v. Caldwell*—provide a good illustration. You will recall that was the case in which it was held that the burning of the music hall discharged the parties' obligations under a contract to hire the hall. The opinion as printed earlier in this Chapter does not say anything about what sum the plaintiff sought to recover. Certainly if the plaintiff had sued for profits that he would have made from the concerts if the hall had not burned, plaintiff would have lost. Saying that parties' obligations under the agreement were discharged by impracticability (impossibility) certainly means that neither side can recover expectation damages from the other. If one looks at the original report of the decision, however, one sees from the reporter's headnote that the plaintiff was not seeking lost profits. Rather, the plaintiff sought compensation for wasted expenditures: "the plaintiffs lost divers moneys paid by them for printing advertisements of and in advertising the concerts, and also lost divers sums expended and expenses incurred by them in preparing for the concerts." In modern terminology, plaintiff sought reliance damages, not expectation damages. Of course, at the time that the case was decided, those concepts had not yet evolved or become part of the working concepts of contract law and contract damages. After all, *Taylor v. Caldwell* was decided in 1863 and Lon Fuller's article, *The Reliance Interest in Contract Damages,* was published in 1936. If the same facts were to occur today, it would not be all that surprising to see a court hand down a decision to the effect that the burning of the hall means plaintiff cannot recover expectation damages, but might recover reliance damages. See RESTATEMENT (SECOND) OF CONTRACTS § 272(2). There are some cases leaning in that direction, but the matter would have to be described as still an open issue.

E. UNCONSCIONABILITY

U.C.C. § 2–302

Restatement (Second) of Contracts § 208

Campbell Soup Co. v. Wentz

United States Court of Appeals, Third Circuit, 1948.
172 F.2d 80.

While this would be a case for specific performance it is not b/c the contract is so one-sided & thus unconscionable

■ GOODRICH, CIRCUIT JUDGE.

These are appeals from judgments of the District Court denying equitable relief to the buyer under a contract for the sale of carrots. The defendants in No. 9648 are the contract sellers. The defendant in No. 9649 is the second purchaser of part of the carrots which are the subject matter of the contract.

The transactions which raise the issues may be briefly summarized. On June 21, 1947, Campbell Soup Company (Campbell), a New Jersey corporation, entered into a written contract with George B. Wentz and Harry T. Wentz, who are Pennsylvania farmers, for delivery by the Wentzes to Campbell of all the Chantenay red cored carrots to be grown on fifteen acres of the Wentz farm during the 1947 season. . . . Where the contract was entered into does not appear. The contract provides, however, for delivery of the carrots at the Campbell plant in Camden, New Jersey. The prices specified in the contract ranged from $23 to $30 per ton according to the time of delivery. The contract price for January, 1948 was $30 a ton.

The Wentzes harvested approximately 100 tons of carrots from the fifteen acres covered by the contract. Early in January, 1948, they told a Campbell representative that they would not deliver their carrots at the contract price. The market price at that time was at least $90 per ton, and Chantenay red cored carrots were virtually unobtainable. The Wentzes then sold approximately 62 tons of their carrots to the defendant Lojeski, a neighboring farmer. Lojeski resold about 58 tons on the open market, approximately half to Campbell and the balance to other purchasers.

On January 9, 1948, Campbell, suspecting that Lojeski was selling it 'contract carrots,' refused to purchase any more, and instituted these suits against the Wentz brothers and Lojeski to enjoin further sale of the contract carrots to others, and to compel specific performance of the contract. The trial court denied equitable relief.[1] We agree with the result reached, but on a different ground from that relied upon by the District Court.

. . . A party may have specific performance of a contract for the sale of chattels if the legal remedy is inadequate. Inadequacy of the legal remedy is necessarily a matter to be determined by an examination of the facts in each particular instance.

We think that on the question of adequacy of the legal remedy the case is one appropriate for specific performance. It was expressly found that at the time of the trial it was 'virtually impossible to obtain Chantenay carrots in the open market.' This Chantenay carrot is one which the plaintiff uses in large quantities, furnishing the seed to the growers with whom it makes contracts. It was not claimed that in nutritive value it is any better than other types of carrots. Its blunt shape makes it easier to handle in processing. And its color and texture differ from other varieties. The color is brighter than other carrots. The trial court found that the plaintiff failed to establish what proportion of its carrots is used for the production of soup stock and what proportion is used as identifiable physical ingredients in its soups. We do not think lack of proof on that point is material. It did appear that the plaintiff uses carrots in fifteen of its twenty-one soups. It also appeared that it uses these Chantenay carrots diced in some of them and that the appearance is uniform. The preservation of uniformity in appearance in a food article

[1] The issue is preserved on appeal by an arrangement under which Campbell received all the carrots held by the Wentzes and Lojeski, paying a stipulated market price of $90 per ton, $30 to the defendants, and the balance into the registry of the District Court pending the outcome of these appeals.

marketed throughout the country and sold under the manufacturer's name is a matter of considerable commercial significance and one which is properly considered in determining whether a substitute ingredient is just as good as the original.

The trial court concluded that the plaintiff had failed to establish that the carrots, 'judged by objective standards,' are unique goods. This we think is not a pure fact conclusion like a finding that Chantenay carrots are of uniform color. It is either a conclusion of law or of mixed fact and law and we are bound to exercise our independent judgment upon it. That the test for specific performance is not necessarily 'objective' is shown by the many cases in which equity has given it to enforce contracts for articles—family heirlooms and the like—the value of which was personal to the plaintiff.

Judged by the general standards applicable to determining the adequacy of the legal remedy we think that on this point the case is a proper one for equitable relief. There is considerable authority, old and new, showing liberality in the granting of an equitable remedy. We see no reason why a court should be reluctant to grant specific relief when it can be given without supervision of the court or other time-consuming processes against one who has deliberately broken his agreement. Here the goods of the special type contracted for were unavailable on the open market, the plaintiff had contracted for them long ahead in anticipation of its needs, and had built up a general reputation for its products as part of which reputation uniform appearance was important. We think if this were all that was involved in the case specific performance should have been granted.

The reason that we shall affirm instead of reversing with an order for specific performance is found in the contract itself. We think it is too hard a bargain and too one-sided an agreement to entitle the plaintiff to relief in a court of conscience. For each individual grower the agreement is made by filling in names and quantity and price on a printed form furnished by the buyer. This form has quite obviously been drawn by skilful draftsmen with the buyer's interests in mind.

Paragraph 2 provides for the manner of delivery. Carrots are to have their stalks cut off and be in clean sanitary bags or other containers approved by Campbell. This paragraph concludes with a statement that Campbell's determination of conformance with specifications shall be conclusive.

The defendants attack this provision as unconscionable. We do not think that it is, standing by itself. We think that the provision is comparable to the promise to perform to the satisfaction of another and that Campbell would be held liable if it refused carrots which did in fact conform to the specifications.

The next paragraph allows Campbell to refuse carrots in excess of twelve tons to the acre. The next contains a covenant by the grower that

One-sided

he will not sell carrots to anyone else except the carrots rejected by Campbell nor will he permit anyone else to grow carrots on his land. Paragraph 10 provides liquidated damages to the extent of $50 per acre for any breach by the grower. There is no provision for liquidated or any other damages for breach of contract by Campbell.

The provision of the contract which we think is the hardest is paragraph 9, set out in the margin.[11] It will be noted that Campbell is excused from accepting carrots under certain circumstances. But even under such circumstances the grower, while he cannot say Campbell is liable for failure to take the carrots, is not permitted to sell them elsewhere unless Campbell agrees. This is the kind of provision which the late Francis H. Bohlen would call 'carrying a good joke too far.' What the grower may do with his product under the circumstances set out is not clear. He has covenanted not to store it anywhere except on his own farm and also not to sell to anybody else.

We are not suggesting that the contract is illegal. Nor are we suggesting any excuse for the grower in this case who has deliberately broken an agreement entered into with Campbell. We do think, however, that a party who has offered and succeeded in getting an agreement as tough as this one is, should not come to a chancellor and ask court help in the enforcement of its terms. That equity does not enforce unconscionable bargains is too well established to require elaborate citation.[12] . . .

[T]he sum total of its provisions drives too hard a bargain for a court of conscience to assist. . . .

Williams v. Walker-Thomas Furniture Co.

United States Court of Appeals, District of Columbia Circuit, 1965.
350 F.2d 445.

■ Before BAZELON, CHIEF JUDGE, and DANAHER and WRIGHT, CIRCUIT JUDGES.

■ J. SKELLY WRIGHT, CIRCUIT JUDGE.

Appellee, Walker-Thomas Furniture Company, operates a retail furniture store in the District of Columbia. During the period from 1957 to 1962 each appellant in these cases purchased a number of household

---

[11] 'Grower shall not be obligated to deliver any Carrots which he is unable to harvest or deliver, nor shall Campbell be obligated to receive or pay for any Carrots which it is unable to inspect, grade, receive, handle, use or pack at or ship in processed form from its plants in Camden (1) because of any circumstance beyond the control of Grower or Campbell, as the case may be, or (2) because of any labor disturbance, work stoppage, slow-down, or strike involving any of Campbell's employees. Campbell shall not be liable for any delay in receiving Carrots due to any of the above contingencies. During periods when Campbell is unable to receive Grower's Carrots, Grower may with Campbell's written consent, dispose of his Carrots elsewhere. Grower may not, however, sell or otherwise dispose of any Carrots which he is unable to deliver to Campbell.'

[12] 4 Pomeroy, Equity Jurisprudence § 1405a (5th ed. 1941); 5 Williston, Contracts § 1425 (Rev. ed. 1937).

items from Walker-Thomas, for which payment was to be made in installments. The terms of each purchase were contained in a printed form contract which set forth the value of the purchased item and purported to lease the item to appellant for a stipulated monthly rent payment. The contract then provided, in substance, that title would remain in Walker-Thomas until the total of all the monthly payments made equaled the stated value of the item, at which time appellants could take title. In the event of a default in the payment of any monthly installment, Walker-Thomas could repossess the item.

The contract further provided that 'the amount of each periodical installment payment to be made by (purchaser) to the Company under this present lease shall be inclusive of and not in addition to the amount of each installment payment to be made by (purchaser) under such prior leases, bills or accounts; and all payments now and hereafter made by (purchaser) shall be credited pro rata on all outstanding leases, bills and accounts due the Company by (purchaser) at the time each such payment is made.' The effect of this rather obscure provision was to keep a balance due on every item purchased until the balance due on all items, whenever purchased, was liquidated. As a result, the debt incurred at the time of purchase of each item was secured by the right to repossess all the items previously purchased by the same purchaser, and each new item purchased automatically became subject to a security interest arising out of the previous dealings.

On May 12, 1962, appellant Thorne purchased an item described as a Daveno, three tables, and two lamps, having total stated value of $391.10. Shortly thereafter, he defaulted on his monthly payments and appellee sought to replevy all the items purchased since the first transaction in 1958. Similarly, on April 17, 1962, appellant Williams bought a stereo set of stated value of $514.95.[1] She too defaulted shortly thereafter, and appellee sought to replevy all the items purchased since December, 1957. The Court of General Sessions granted judgment for appellee. The District of Columbia Court of Appeals affirmed, and we granted appellants' motion for leave to appeal to this court.

Appellants' principal contention, rejected by both the trial and the appellate courts below, is that these contracts, or at least some of them, are unconscionable and, hence, not enforceable. In its opinion in Williams v. Walker-Thomas Furniture Company, 198 A.2d 914, 916 (1964), the District of Columbia Court of Appeals explained its rejection of this contention as follows:

> 'Appellant's second argument presents a more serious question. The record reveals that prior to the last purchase appellant had reduced the balance in her account to $164. The last purchase, a stereo set, raised the balance due to $678.

---

[1]   At the time of this purchase her account showed a balance of $164 still owing from her prior purchases. The total of all the purchases made over the years in question came to $1,800. The total payments amounted to $1,400.

Significantly, at the time of this and the preceding purchases, appellee was aware of appellant's financial position. The reverse side of the stereo contract listed the name of appellant's social worker and her $218 monthly stipend from the government. Nevertheless, with full knowledge that appellant had to feed, clothe and support both herself and seven children on this amount, appellee sold her a $514 stereo set.

'We cannot condemn too strongly appellee's conduct. It raises serious questions of sharp practice and irresponsible business dealings. A review of the legislation in the District of Columbia affecting retail sales and the pertinent decisions of the highest court in this jurisdiction disclose, however, no ground upon which this court can declare the contracts in question contrary to public policy. We note that were the Maryland Retail Installment Sales Act, Art. 83 §§ 128–153, or its equivalent, in force in the District of Columbia, we could grant appellant appropriate relief. We think Congress should consider corrective legislation to protect the public from such exploitive contracts as were utilized in the case at bar.'

We do not agree that the court lacked the power to refuse enforcement to contracts found to be unconscionable. In other jurisdictions, it has been held as a matter of common law that unconscionable contracts are not enforceable.[2] While no decision of this court so holding has been found, the notion that an unconscionable bargain should not be given full enforcement is by no means novel. In *Scott v. United States*, 79 U.S. (12 Wall.) 443, 445, 20 L.Ed. 438 (1870), the Supreme Court stated:

'If a contract be unreasonable and unconscionable, but not void for fraud, a court of law will give to the party who sues for its breach damages, not according to its letter, but only such as he is equitably entitled to.'

Since we have never adopted or rejected such a rule, the question here presented is actually one of first impression.

Congress has recently enacted the Uniform Commercial Code, which specifically provides that the court may refuse to enforce a contract which it finds to be unconscionable at the time it was made. 28 D.C.CODE § 2–302 (Supp. IV 1965). The enactment of this section, which occurred subsequent to the contracts here in suit, does not mean that the common law of the District of Columbia was otherwise at the time of enactment, nor does it preclude the court from adopting a similar rule in the exercise of its powers to develop the common law for the District of Columbia. In fact, in view of the absence of prior authority on the point, we consider

---

[2]   *Campbell Soup Co. v. Wentz*, 3 Cir., 172 F.2d 80 (1948); *Indianapolis Morris Plan Corporation v. Sparks*, 132 Ind.App. 145, 172 N.E.2d 899 (1961); *Henningsen v. Bloomfield Motors, Inc.*, 32 N.J. 358, 161 A.2d 69, 84–96, 75 A.L.R.2d 1 (1960). *Cf.* 1 Corbin, Contracts § 128 (1963)

the congressional adoption of § 2–302 persuasive authority for following the rationale of the cases from which the section is explicitly derived. Accordingly, we hold that where the element of unconscionability is present at the time a contract is made, the contract should not be enforced.

Unconscionability has generally been recognized to include an absence of meaningful choice on the part of one of the parties together with contract terms which are unreasonably favorable to the other party.[6] Whether a meaningful choice is present in a particular case can only be determined by consideration of all the circumstances surrounding the transaction. In many cases the meaningfulness of the choice is negated by a gross inequality of bargaining power.[7] The manner in which the contract was entered is also relevant to this consideration. Did each party to the contract, considering his obvious education or lack of it, have a reasonable opportunity to understand the terms of the contract, or were the important terms hidden in a maze of fine print and minimized by deceptive sales practices? Ordinarily, one who signs an agreement without full knowledge of its terms might be held to assume the risk that he has entered a one-sided bargain. But when a party of little bargaining power, and hence little real choice, signs a commercially unreasonable contract with little or no knowledge of its terms, it is hardly likely that his consent, or even an objective manifestation of his consent, was ever given to all the terms. In such a case the usual rule that the terms of the agreement are not to be questioned should be abandoned and the court should consider whether the terms of the contract are so unfair that enforcement should be withheld.

In determining reasonableness or fairness, the primary concern must be with the terms of the contract considered in light of the circumstances existing when the contract was made. The test is not simple, nor can it be mechanically applied. The terms are to be considered 'in the light of the general commercial background and the commercial needs of the particular trade or case.' Comment, Uniform Commercial Code § 2–307. Corbin suggests the test as being whether the terms are 'so extreme as to appear unconscionable according to the mores and business practices of the time and place.' 1 Corbin, op. cit.[12] We think this

---

[6]   See *Henningsen v. Bloomfield Motors, Inc., supra; Campbell Soup Co. v. Wentz, supra.*

[7]   See *Henningsen v. Bloomfield Motors, Inc., supra*, and authorities there cited. Inquiry into the relative bargaining power of the two parties is not an inquiry wholly divorced from the general question of unconscionability, since a one-sided bargain is itself evidence of the inequality of the bargaining parties. This fact was vaguely recognized in the common law doctrine of intrinsic fraud, that is, fraud which can be presumed from the grossly unfair nature of the terms of the contract. See the oft-quoted statement of Lord Hardwicke in Earl of Chesterfield v. Janssen, 28 Eng. Rep. 82, 100 (1751): '(Fraud) may be apparent from the intrinsic nature and subject of the bargain itself; such as no man in his senses and not under delusion would make.' . . .

[12]   See *Henningsen v. Bloomfield Motors, Inc., supra; Mandel v. Liebman*, 303 N.Y. 88, 100 N.E.2d 149 (1951). The traditional test as stated in *Greer v. Tweed*, supra, 13 Abb.Pr.,N.S., at 429, is 'such as no man in his senses and not under delusion would make on the one hand, and as no honest or fair man would accept, on the other.'

formulation correctly states the test to be applied in those cases where no meaningful choice was exercised upon entering the contract.

Because the trial court and the appellate court did not feel that enforcement could be refused, no findings were made on the possible unconscionability of the contracts in these cases. Since the record is not sufficient for our deciding the issue as a matter of law, the cases must be remanded to the trial court for further proceedings.

So ordered.

■ DANAHER, CIRCUIT JUDGE (dissenting).

The District of Columbia Court of Appeals obviously was as unhappy about the situation here presented as any of us can possibly be. Its opinion in the Williams case, quoted in the majority text, concludes: 'We think Congress should consider corrective legislation to protect the public from such exploitive contracts as were utilized in the case at bar.'

My view is thus summed up by an able court which made no finding that there had actually been sharp practice. Rather the appellant seems to have known precisely where she stood.

There are many aspects of public policy here involved. What is a luxury to some may seem an outright necessity to others. Is public oversight to be required of the expenditures of relief funds? A washing machine, e.g., in the hands of a relief client might become a fruitful source of income. Many relief clients may well need credit, and certain business establishments will take long chances on the sale of items, expecting their pricing policies will afford a degree of protection commensurate with the risk. Perhaps a remedy when necessary will be found within the provisions of the 'Loan Shark' law, D.C.CODE §§ 26–601 et seq. (1961).

I mention such matters only to emphasize the desirability of a cautious approach to any such problem, particularly since the law for so long has allowed parties such great latitude in making their own contracts. I dare say there must annually be thousands upon thousands of installment credit transactions in this jurisdiction, and one can only speculate as to the effect the decision in these cases will have.

I join the District of Columbia Court of Appeals in its disposition of the issues.

Brower v. Gateway 2000, Inc.

Supreme Court, Appellate Division, New York, 1998.
246 A.D.2d 246, 676 N.Y.S.2d 569.

■ MILONAS, J.

Appellants are among the many consumers who purchased computers and software products from defendant Gateway 2000 through a direct-sales system, by mail or telephone order. As of July 3, 1995, it was Gateway's practice to include with the materials shipped to the purchaser along with the merchandise a copy of its "Standard Terms and Conditions Agreement" and any relevant warranties for the products in the shipment. The Agreement begins with a "NOTE TO CUSTOMER," which provides, in slightly larger print than the remainder of the document, in a box that spans the width of the page: "This document contains Gateway 2000's Standard Terms and Conditions. By keeping your Gateway 2000 computer system beyond thirty (30) days after the date of delivery, you accept these Terms and Conditions." The document consists of 16 paragraphs, and, as is relevant to this appeal, paragraph 10 of the agreement, entitled "DISPUTE RESOLUTION," reads as follows:

> Any dispute or controversy arising out of or relating to this Agreement or its interpretation shall be settled exclusively and finally by arbitration. The arbitration shall be conducted in accordance with the Rules of Conciliation and Arbitration of the International Chamber of Commerce. The arbitration shall be conducted in Chicago, Illinois, U.S.A. before a sole arbitrator. Any award rendered in any such arbitration proceeding shall be final and binding on each of the parties, and judgment may be entered thereon in a court of competent jurisdiction.

Plaintiffs commenced this action on behalf of themselves and others similarly situated for compensatory and punitive damages, alleging deceptive sales practices in seven causes of action, including breach of warranty, breach of contract, fraud and unfair trade practices. In particular, the allegations focused on Gateway's representations and advertising that promised "service when you need it," including around-the-clock free technical support, free software technical support and certain on-site services. According to plaintiffs, not only were they unable to avail themselves of this offer because it was virtually impossible to get through to a technician, but also Gateway continued to advertise this claim notwithstanding numerous complaints and reports about the problem.

. . . Gateway moved to dismiss the complaint based on the arbitration clause in the Agreement. Appellants argued that the arbitration clause is invalid under UCC 2–207, unconscionable under UCC 2–302 and an unenforceable contract of adhesion. Specifically, they claimed that the provision was obscure; that a customer could not reasonably be expected to appreciate or investigate its meaning and effect; that the International Chamber of Commerce ("ICC") was not a forum commonly used for consumer matters; and that because ICC headquarters were in France, it was particularly difficult to locate the organization and its rules. To illustrate just how inaccessible the forum was, appellants advised the court that the ICC was not registered with the Secretary of State, that efforts to locate and contact the ICC had been unsuccessful and that apparently the only way to attempt to contact the

ICC was through the United States Council for International Business, with which the ICC maintained some sort of relationship.

In support of their arguments, appellants submitted a copy of the ICC's Rules of Conciliation and Arbitration and contended that the cost of ICC arbitration was prohibitive, particularly given the amount of the typical consumer claim involved. For example, a claim of less than $50,000 required advance fees of $4,000 (more than the cost of most Gateway products), of which the $2000 registration fee was nonrefundable even if the consumer prevailed at the arbitration. Consumers would also incur travel expenses disproportionate to the damages sought, which appellants' counsel estimated would not exceed $1,000 per customer in this action, as well as bear the cost of Gateway's legal fees if the consumer did not prevail at the arbitration; in this respect, the ICC rules follow the "loser pays" rule used in England. Also, although Chicago was designated as the site of the actual arbitration, all correspondence must be sent to ICC headquarters in France.

The [trial] court dismissed the complaint as to appellants based on the arbitration clause in the Agreements delivered with their computers. We agree with the court's decision and reasoning in all respects but for the issue of the unconscionability of the designation of the ICC as the arbitration body.

First, the court properly rejected appellants' argument that the arbitration clause was invalid under UCC 2–207. Appellants claim that when they placed their order they did not bargain for, much less accept, arbitration of any dispute, and therefore the arbitration clause in the agreement that accompanied the merchandise shipment was a "material alteration" of a preexisting oral agreement. Under UCC 2–207(2), such a material alteration constitutes "proposals for addition to the contract" that become part of the contract only upon appellants' express acceptance. However, as the court correctly concluded, the clause was not a "material alteration" of an oral agreement, but, rather, simply one provision of the sole contract that existed between the parties. That contract, the court explained, was formed and acceptance was manifested not when the order was placed but only with the retention of the merchandise beyond the 30 days specified in the Agreement enclosed in the shipment of merchandise. Accordingly, the contract was outside the scope of UCC 2–207.

In reaching its conclusion, the [trial] court took note of the litigation in Federal courts on this very issue, and, indeed, on this very arbitration clause. In *Hill v. Gateway 2000, Inc.*, 105 F.3d 1147, *cert. denied* 522 U.S. 808, 118 S.Ct. 47, 139 L.Ed.2d 13, plaintiffs in a class action contested the identical Gateway contract in dispute before us, including the enforceability of the arbitration clause. As that court framed the issue, the "[t]erms inside Gateway's box stand or fall together. If they constitute the parties contract because the Hills had an opportunity to return the computer after reading them, then all must be enforced" (*id.* at 1148).

The court then concluded that the contract was not formed with the placement of a telephone order or with the delivery of the goods. Instead, an enforceable contract was formed only with the consumer's decision to retain the merchandise beyond the 30-day period specified in the agreement. Thus, the agreement as a whole, including the arbitration clause, was enforceable.

This conclusion was in keeping with the same court's decision in *ProCD, Inc. v. Zeidenberg,* 86 F.3d 1447, where it found that detailed terms enclosed within the packaging of particular computer software purchased in a retail outlet constituted the contract between the vendor and the consumer who retained the product. In that case, the Seventh Circuit held that UCC 2–207 did not apply and indeed was "irrelevant" to such transactions, noting that the section is generally invoked where multiple agreements have been exchanged between the parties in a classic "battle of the forms," whereas *ProCD* (as well as *Hill* and this case) involves but a single form (*id.* at 1452).

The *Hill* decision, in its examination of the formation of the contract, takes note of the realities of conducting business in today's world. Transactions involving "cash now, terms later" have become commonplace, enabling the consumer to make purchases of sophisticated merchandise such as computers over the phone or by mail—and even by computer. Indeed, the concept of "[p]ayment preceding the revelation of full terms" is particularly common in certain industries, such as air transportation and insurance (*id.* at 1149; *ProCD v. Zeidenberg, supra,* at 1451).

Second, with respect to appellants' claim that the arbitration clause is unenforceable as a contract of adhesion, in that it involved no choice or negotiation on the part of the consumer but was a "take it or leave it" proposition * * *, we find that this argument, too, was properly rejected by the [trial] court. Although the parties clearly do not possess equal bargaining power, this factor alone does not invalidate the contract as one of adhesion. As the [trial] court observed, with the ability to make the purchase elsewhere and the express option to return the goods, the consumer is not in a "take it or leave it" position at all; if any term of the agreement is unacceptable to the consumer, he or she can easily buy a competitor's product instead—either from a retailer or directly from the manufacturer—and reject Gateway's agreement by returning the merchandise (*see, e.g., Carnival Cruise Lines v. Shute,* 499 U.S. 585, 593–594, 111 S.Ct. 1522, 1527–1528, 113 L.Ed.2d 622; * * *). The consumer has 30 days to make that decision. Within that time, the consumer can inspect the goods and examine and seek clarification of the terms of the agreement; until those 30 days have elapsed, the consumer has the unqualified right to return the merchandise, because the goods or terms are unsatisfactory or for no reason at all.

While returning the goods to avoid the formation of the contract entails affirmative action on the part of the consumer, and even some expense, this may be seen as a trade-off for the convenience and savings for which the consumer presumably opted when he or she chose to make a purchase of such consequence by phone or mail as an alternative to on-site retail shopping. That a consumer does not read the agreement or thereafter claims he or she failed to understand or appreciate some term therein does not invalidate the contract any more than such claim would undo a contract formed under other circumstances. . . .

Finally, we turn to appellants' argument that the [trial] court should have declared the contract unenforceable, pursuant to UCC 2–302, on the ground that the arbitration clause is unconscionable due to the unduly burdensome procedure and cost for the individual consumer. The [trial] court found that while a class-action lawsuit, such as the one herein, may be a less costly alternative to the arbitration (which is generally less costly than litigation), that does not alter the binding effect of the valid arbitration clause contained in the agreement * * *

As a general matter, under New York law, unconscionability requires a showing that a contract is "both procedurally and substantively unconscionable when made" (*Gillman v. Chase Manhattan Bank,* 73 N.Y.2d 1, 10, 537 N.Y.S.2d 787, 534 N.E.2d 824). That is, there must be "some showing of 'an absence of meaningful choice on the part of one of the parties together with contract terms which are unreasonably favorable to the other party' [citation omitted]" (*Matter of State of New York v. Avco Financial Service,* 50 N.Y.2d 383, 389, 429 N.Y.S.2d 181, 406 N.E.2d 1075). The *Avco* court took pains to note, however, that the purpose of this doctrine is not to redress the inequality between the parties but simply to ensure that the more powerful party cannot "surprise" the other party with some overly oppressive term (*id.,* at 389, 429 N.Y.S.2d 181, 406 N.E.2d 1075).

As to the procedural element, a court will look to the contract formation process to determine if in fact one party lacked any meaningful choice in entering into the contract, taking into consideration such factors as the setting of the transaction, the experience and education of the party claiming unconscionability, whether the contract contained "fine print," whether the seller used "high-pressured tactics" and any disparity in the parties' bargaining power (*Gillman v Chase Manhattan Bank, supra,* at 11, 537 N.Y.S.2d 787, 534 N.E.2d 824). None of these factors supports appellants' claim here. Any purchaser has 30 days within which to thoroughly examine the contents of their shipment, including the terms of the Agreement, and seek clarification of any term therein (*e.g., Matter of Ball, supra,* at 161, 665 N.Y.S.2d 444). The Agreement itself, which is entitled in large print "STANDARD TERMS AND CONDITIONS AGREEMENT," consists of only three pages and 16 paragraphs, all of which appear in the same size print. Moreover, despite appellants' claims to the contrary, the arbitration clause is in no way "hidden" or "tucked away" within a complex document of inordinate length, nor is the option of returning the merchandise, to avoid the contract, somehow a "precarious" one. We also reject appellants' insinuation that, by using the word "standard," Gateway deliberately meant to convey to the consumer that the terms were standard within the industry, when the document clearly purports to be no more than *Gateway*'s "standard terms and conditions."

With respect to the substantive element, which entails an examination of the substance of the agreement in order to determine whether the terms unreasonably favor one party (*Gillman v. Chase Manhattan Bank, supra,* 73 N.Y.2d, at 12, 537 N.Y.S.2d 787, 534 N.E.2d 824), we do not find that the possible inconvenience of the chosen site (Chicago) alone rises to the level of unconscionability. We do find, however, that the excessive cost factor that is necessarily entailed in arbitrating before the ICC is unreasonable and surely serves to deter the individual consumer from invoking the process * * *. Barred from resorting to the courts by the arbitration clause in the first instance, the designation of a financially prohibitive forum effectively bars consumers from this forum as well; consumers are thus left with no forum at all in which to resolve a dispute. . . .

While it is true that, under New York law, unconscionability is generally predicated on the presence of both the procedural and substantive elements, the substantive element alone may be sufficient to render the terms of the provision at issue unenforceable * * * Excessive fees, such as those incurred under the ICC procedure, have been grounds for finding an arbitration provision unenforceable or commercially unreasonable.

In . . . *Filias* [*v Gateway 2000*, Inc. N.D.Ill., January 15, 1998], the Federal District Court stated that it was "inclined to agree" with the argument that selection of the ICC rendered the clause unconscionable, but concluded that the issue was moot because Gateway had agreed to arbitrate before the American Arbitration Association ("AAA")

As noted, however, appellants complain that the AAA fees are also excessive and thus in no way have they accepted defendant's offer (*see,* UCC 2–209); because they make the same claim as to the AAA as they did with respect to the ICC, the issue of unconscionability is not rendered moot, as defendant suggests. We cannot determine on this record whether the AAA process and costs would be so "egregiously oppressive" that they, too, would be unconscionable (*Avildsen v. Prystay,* 171 A.D.2d 13, 14, 574 N.Y.S.2d 535, *appeal dismissed,* 79 N.Y.2d 841, 580 N.Y.S.2d 193, 588 N.E.2d 91). Thus, we modify the order on appeal to the extent of finding that portion of the arbitration provision requiring arbitration before the ICC to be unconscionable and remand to Supreme Court so that the parties have the opportunity to seek appropriate substitution of an arbitrator pursuant to the Federal Arbitration Act (9 U.S.C. § 1 et seq.), which provides for such court designation of an arbitrator upon application of either party, where, for whatever reason, one is not otherwise designated (9 U.S.C. § 5). . . .

Order, Supreme Court, New York County (Beatrice Shainswit, J.), entered October 21, 1997, modified, on the law and the facts, to the extent of vacating that portion of the arbitration agreement as requires arbitration before the International Chamber of Commerce, with leave to the parties to seek appointment of an arbitrator pursuant to 9 U.S.C. § 5 and remanding the matter for that purpose, and otherwise affirmed, without costs.

All concur.

NOTES & QUESTIONS

1.   From the *Brower v. Gateway 2000* judgment, identify and restate, in your own words:

   a)   why the Battle of the Forms argument did not succeed;

   b)   what the contract of adhesion argument consisted of;

   c)   what was found to be unconscionable in the agreement.

2.   The term "contracts of adhesion", underlines the take-it-or-leave-it quality of form contracts, which can prevent parties from negotiating their own terms: Friedrich Kessler, *Contracts of Adhesion—Some Thoughts about Freedom of Contract* 43 COLUM. L. REV. 629 (1943). Recall Chapter 3, and think about how contracts are formed through the manifestation of mutual assent. How might standard form contracts, involving a take-it-or-leave it step, and perhaps also a "repeat-player" drafter on one side, and a novice party, whose principal obligation is the payment of money, on the other, challenge such principles? See further Todd D. Rakoff, *Contracts of Adhesion: An Essay in Reconstruction*, 96 Harv. L. Rev. 1173 (1983). Think back to the differentiated treatment of competing standard form agreements in the Battle of the Forms scenario under U.C.C. § 2–207.

3.   Consider your own experience with "shrinkwrap" or "clickwrap" or "browsewrap" agreements. Did you read the terms? Did you understand them, if you did? If you have been a party to a "browsewrap" agreement, do you think it was more rational to spend the time reading the terms, or instead more rational to save time by simply clicking "I agree". Do you think contract law is a good model for policing these agreements? Consider Omri Ben-Shahar, *The Myth of the 'Opportunity to Read' in Contract Law*, 5 EUR. REV. OF CONT. L. 1 (2009) (proposing market devices such as ratings and labeling to counteract the potential for unfair trade practices produced by the lack of consumer reading of boilerplate). Consider how the new "internet of things" provides an even greater diminishment of the opportunity to read, when consumers are now able to purchase goods (or licenses) in fully automated transactions through devices with digital tracking technology and other intermediaries.

4.   The dissent in *Williams v. Walker-Thomas Furniture Company* favored "corrective legislation" over a doctrinal resolution. We have already examined efforts by the Federal Trade Commission ("FTC") to regulate deceptive advertising (in Chapter 3.B.) Congress and individual state legislatures have enacted a number of other consumer protection statutes

since the late 1960s, which require certain disclosures by commercial parties or which declare certain practices unlawful. The most recent federal effort in consumer protection is the creation of the Consumer Financial Protection Bureau, established by Congress in 2010 as a response to the financial crisis of 2007. See further www.consumerfinance.gov.

5.   Think about the reasons you might be party to a mandatory arbitration clause, in your credit card, student loan, phone, internet, or computer or software agreement, or with your health-care provider. How might this agreement have made the price of the good (governed by the U.C.C.) or the service less expensive? In other words, what would be the cost savings of arbitration, and how would these be passed on to the consumer?

6.   In this respect, are consumer contracts different from, for example, employment contracts? For an example of the latter, consider *Rent-A-Center, West, Inc. v. Jackson*, 561 U.S. 63, 130 S.Ct. 2772 (2010), where a former employee filed an employment discrimination suit, and the employer moved to compel arbitration. On appeal, the Supreme Court held that the dispute was for the arbitrator to resolve, since the claim of unconscionability was not levied at the arbitration clause specifically, but at the contract as a whole. Compare the contemporary use of arbitration clauses in dealings with consumers and employees with their historical deployment in contracts between commercial enterprises. Then consider the following consumer contract:

AT&T Mobility LLC v. Concepcion

Supreme Court of the United States.
563 U.S. 333 (2011).

■ JUSTICE SCALIA delivered the opinion of the Court.

Section 2 of the Federal Arbitration Act (FAA) makes agreements to arbitrate "valid, irrevocable, and enforceable, save upon such grounds as exist at law or in equity for the revocation of any contract." 9 U.S.C. § 2. We consider whether the FAA prohibits States from conditioning the enforceability of certain arbitration agreements on the availability of classwide arbitration procedures.

In February 2002, Vincent and Liza Concepcion entered into an agreement for the sale and servicing of cellular telephones with AT & T Mobility LCC (AT & T). The contract provided for arbitration of all disputes between the parties, but required that claims be brought in the parties' "individual capacity, and not as a plaintiff or class member in any purported class or representative proceeding." . . . The Concepcions purchased AT & T service, which was advertised as including the provision of free phones; they were not charged for the phones, but they were charged $30.22 in sales tax based on the phones' retail value. In March 2006, the Concepcions filed a complaint against AT & T in the United States District Court for the Southern District of California. The complaint was later consolidated with a putative class action alleging, among other things, that AT & T had engaged in false advertising and fraud by charging sales tax on phones it advertised as free.

In March 2008, AT & T moved to compel arbitration under the terms of its contract with the Concepcions. The Concepcions opposed the motion, contending that the arbitration agreement was unconscionable and unlawfully exculpatory under California law because it disallowed classwide procedures. The District Court denied AT & T's motion. . . .[R]elying on the California Supreme Court's decision in *Discover Bank v. Superior Court*, 36 Cal.4th 148, 30 Cal.Rptr.3d 76, 113 P.3d 1100 (2005), the court found that the arbitration provision was unconscionable because AT & T had not shown that bilateral arbitration adequately substituted for the deterrent effects of class actions. * * *

The Ninth Circuit affirmed, also finding the provision unconscionable under California law as announced in *Discover Bank*. . . .

Under California law, courts may refuse to enforce any contract found "to have been unconscionable at the time it was made," or may "limit the application of any unconscionable clause." Cal. Civ.Code Ann. § 1670.5(a) (West 1985). A finding of unconscionability requires "a 'procedural' and a 'substantive' element, the former focusing on 'oppression' or 'surprise' due to unequal bargaining power, the latter on 'overly harsh' or 'one-sided' results." * * *

In *Discover Bank*, the California Supreme Court applied this framework to class-action waivers in arbitration agreements and held as follows:

> "[W]hen the waiver is found in a consumer contract of adhesion in a setting in which disputes between the contracting parties predictably involve small amounts of damages, and when it is alleged that the party with the superior bargaining power has carried out a scheme to deliberately cheat large numbers of consumers out of individually small sums of money, then . . . the waiver becomes in practice the exemption of the party 'from responsibility for [its] own fraud, or willful injury to the person or property of another.' Under these circumstances, such waivers are unconscionable under California law and should not be enforced." Id., at 162, 30 Cal.Rptr.3d 76, 113 P.3d, at 1110 (quoting Cal. Civ.Code Ann. § 1668).

. . .

The overarching purpose of the FAA . . . is to ensure the enforcement of arbitration agreements according to their terms so as to facilitate streamlined proceedings. Requiring the availability of classwide arbitration interferes with fundamental attributes of arbitration and thus creates a scheme inconsistent with the FAA. . . . California's *Discover Bank* rule similarly interferes with arbitration. Although the rule does not require classwide arbitration, it allows any party to a consumer contract to demand it ex post. The rule is limited to adhesion contracts, * * * but the times in which consumer contracts were anything other than adhesive are long past. * * * *Hill v. Gateway 2000, Inc.*, 105 F.3d 1147, 1149 (C.A.7 1997). The rule also requires that damages be predictably small, and that the consumer allege a scheme to cheat consumers. . . . The former requirement, however, is toothless and malleable (the Ninth Circuit has held that damages of $4000 are sufficiently small . . .) and the latter has no limiting effect, as all that is required is an allegation. . . .

The dissent claims that class proceedings are necessary to prosecute small-dollar claims that might otherwise slip through the legal system. . . . But States cannot require a procedure that is inconsistent with the FAA, even if it is desirable for unrelated reasons. . . . Because it "stands as an obstacle to the accomplishment and execution of the full purposes and objectives of Congress," *Hines v. Davidowitz*, 312 U.S. 52, 67, 61 S.Ct. 399, 85 L.Ed. 581 (1941), California's *Discover Bank* rule is preempted by the FAA. The judgment of the Ninth Circuit is reversed, and the case is remanded for further proceedings consistent with this opinion.

It is so ordered.

■ JUSTICE BREYER, with whom JUSTICE GINSBURG, JUSTICE SOTOMAYOR, and JUSTICE KAGAN join, dissenting.

. . . The *Discover Bank* rule does not create a "blanket policy in California against class action waivers in the consumer context." *Provencher v. Dell, Inc.*, 409 F.Supp.2d 1196, 1201 (C.D.Cal.2006). Instead, it represents the "application of a more general [unconscionability] principle." *Gentry v. Superior Ct.*, 42 Cal.4th 443, 457, 64 Cal.Rptr.3d 773, 165 P.3d 556, 564 (2007). Courts applying California law have enforced class-action waivers where they satisfy general unconscionability standards. * * * And even when they fail, the parties remain free to devise other dispute mechanisms, including informal mechanisms, that, in context, will not prove unconscionable. . . .

Further, even though contract defenses, e.g., duress and unconscionability, slow down the dispute resolution process, federal arbitration law normally leaves such matters to the States. *Rent-A-Center, West, Inc. v. Jackson*, 561 U.S.___, ___, 130 S.Ct. 2772, 2775 (2010) (arbitration agreements "may be invalidated by 'generally applicable contract defenses'" (quoting *Doctor's Associates, Inc. v. Casarotto*, 517 U.S. 681, 687, 116 S.Ct. 1652, 134 L.Ed.2d 902 (1996))). A provision in a contract of adhesion (for example, requiring a consumer to decide very quickly whether to pursue a claim) might increase the speed and efficiency of arbitrating a dispute, but the State can forbid it. See, e.g., *Hayes v. Oakridge Home*, 122 Ohio St.3d 63, 67, 2009—Ohio—2054, ¶ 19, 908 N.E.2d 408, 412 ("Unconscionability is a ground for revocation of an arbitration agreement"); *In re Poly-America, L. P.*, 262 S.W.3d 337, 348 (Tex.2008) ("Unconscionable contracts, however—whether relating to arbitration or not—are unenforceable under Texas law"). . . .

Because California applies the same legal principles to address the unconscionability of class arbitration waivers as it does to address the unconscionability of any other contractual provision, the merits of class proceedings should not factor into our decision. If California had applied its law of duress to void an arbitration agreement, would it matter if the procedures in the coerced agreement were efficient?

Regardless, the majority highlights the disadvantages of class arbitrations, as it sees them. * * * (referring to the "greatly increase[d] risks to defendants"; the "chance of a devastating loss" pressuring defendants "into settling questionable claims"). But class proceedings have countervailing advantages. In general agreements that forbid the consolidation of claims can lead small-dollar claimants to abandon their claims rather than to litigate. . . . What rational lawyer would have signed on to represent the Concepcions in litigation for the possibility of fees stemming from a $30.22 claim? . . .

With respect, I dissent.

NOTES

1.   Preemption means that federal law prevails over state law: U.S. Const. art. VI, cl. 2 ("the Supremacy Clause") (federal law is the supreme law of the land). Contract law is state law, but state courts must now be wary of holding unconscionable arbitration clauses that, for example, might generally be said to unduly restrict the statute of limitations, or select inconvenient forums for arbitration or impose excessive confidentiality or inadequate discovery, or, as here, prohibit individuals to form a classwide arbitration. State courts thus continue to evaluate the unconscionability of arbitration clauses on a case by case basis: e.g., *Saleemi v. Doctor's Associates, Inc.,* 176 Wash.2d 368, 292 P.3d 108 (2013) (suggesting that *Concepcion* would preclude only a "rule classifying most collective-arbitration waivers in consumer contracts as unenforceable"). The Supreme Court has continued, however, to resist the use of unconscionability doctrine to limit mandatory arbitration, and its application to the question of arbitration has been regarded as "somewhat anomalous": Charles L. Knapp, *Unconscionability in American Contract Law: A Twenty-first Century Survey,* in CONTRACT LAW: TRANSATLANTIC PERSPECTIVES 309, 325 (L. DiMatteo, Q. Zhou, S. Saintier, & K. Rowley, eds., 2014) (nevertheless endorsing the doctrine's counterweight effect against the rise of mandatory arbitration).

2.   Recall our discussion of the relevance of trade usage in Chapter 8.B. Consider U.C.C. § 1–303, comment 5.

The policies of the Uniform Commercial Code controlling explicit unconscionable contracts and clauses (Sections 1–304, 2–302) apply to implicit clauses that rest on usage of trade and carry forward the policy underlying the ancient requirement that a custom or usage must be "reasonable." However, the emphasis is shifted. The very fact of commercial acceptance makes out a prima facie case that the usage is reasonable, and the burden is no longer on the usage to establish itself as being reasonable. But the anciently established policing of usage by the courts is continued to the extent necessary to cope with the situation arising if an unconscionable or dishonest practice should become standard.

Does this shift in emphasis, observed in the context of interpretation, suggest that mandatory arbitration clauses, if used throughout a particular industry, should become ever more acceptable? Consider the proposal that the reverse should be true, such that the more widespread the use of mandatory arbitration clauses (and other clauses that fall within the category of what Radin calls "mass-market boilerplate rights deletion schemes"), the more likely should a court find the waiver of any background legal rights invalid: MARGARET JANE RADIN, BOILERPLATE: THE FINE PRINT, VANISHING RIGHTS, AND THE RULE OF LAW 178–186 (2013).

CHAPTER TWELVE

RIGHTS OF THIRD PARTIES

It ain't what you takin'
It's who you takin' it from

—Omar Little, The Wire

A. THIRD PARTY BENEFICIARIES

Restatement (Second) of Contracts §§ 302, 304, 315

Lawrence v. Fox

Court of Appeals of New York, 1859.
20 N.Y. 268.

APPEAL from the Superior Court of the city of Buffalo. On the trial before Mr. Justice MASTEN, it appeared by the evidence of a bystander, that one Holly, in November, 1857, at the request of [Fox], loaned and advanced to [Fox] $300, stating at the time that he [Holly] owed that sum to [Lawrence] for money borrowed from him and had agreed to pay it to [Lawrence] the then next day; that the defendant [Fox] in consideration thereof, at the time of receiving the money, promised to pay it to the plaintiff [Lawrence] the then next day. . . . [Fox] moved for a nonsuit, upon [several] grounds, viz.: . . . that the agreement by [Fox] with Holly to pay [Lawrence] was void for want of consideration, and that there was no privity between [Lawrence] and [Fox]. The court overruled the motion, and . . . the jury . . . found a verdict for the plaintiff [Lawrence] for the amount of the loan and interest, $344.66, upon which judgment was entered; from which [Fox] appealed to the Superior Court, at general term, where the judgment was affirmed, and [Fox] appealed to this court.

■ H. GRAY, J.

The fact that the money advanced by Holly to [Fox] was a loan to him for a day, and that it thereby became the property of [Fox], seemed to impress [Fox's] counsel with the idea that because [Fox's] promise was not a trust fund placed by [Lawrence] in [Fox's] hands, out of which he was to realize money as from the sale of a chattel or the collection of a debt, the promise although made for the benefit of [Lawrence] could not enure to his benefit. The hay which [Moon] delivered to [Cleaveland] was not to be paid to Farley, but the debt incurred by Cleaveland for the purchase of the hay, like the debt incurred by the defendant for money borrowed, was what was to be paid. That case . . . puts to rest the objection that the defendant's promise was void for want of consideration.

The report of [*Farley v. Cleaveland*] shows that the promise was not only made to Moon but to the plaintiff Farley. In this case the promise was made to Holly and not expressly to [Lawrence]; and this difference between the two cases presents the question . . . as to the want of privity between the plaintiff and defendant. As early as 1806 it was announced by the Supreme Court of this State, upon what was then regarded as the settled law of England, "That where one person makes a promise to another for the benefit of a third person, that third person may maintain an action upon it." *Schermerhorn v. Vanderheyden* (1 John. R., 140), has often been re-asserted by our courts and never departed from. . . .

. . .

This question was subsequently . . . the subject of consideration by the Supreme Court, when it was held, that in declaring upon a promise, made to the debtor by a third party to pay the creditor of the debtor, founded upon a consideration advanced by the debtor, it was unnecessary to aver a promise to the creditor; for the reason that upon proof of a promise made to the debtor to pay the creditor, a promise to the creditor would be implied. . . . In *Hall v. Marston* [1822, 17 Mass. 575] the court say: "It seems to have been well settled that if A promises B for a valuable consideration to pay C, the latter may maintain assumpsit for the money;" and in *Brewer v. Dyer*, the recovery was upheld, as the court said, "upon the principle of law long recognized and clearly established, that when one person, for a valuable consideration, engages with another, by a simple contract, to do some act for the benefit of a third, the latter, who would enjoy the benefit of the act, may maintain an action for the breach of such engagement; that it does not rest upon the ground of any actual or supposed relationship between the parties as some of the earlier cases would seem to indicate, but upon the broader and more satisfactory basis, that the law operating on the act of the parties creates the duty, establishes a privity, and implies the promise and obligation on which the action is founded." . . .

But it is urged that because the defendant was not in any sense a trustee of the property of Holly for the benefit of the plaintiff, the law will not imply a promise. I agree that many of the cases where a promise was implied were cases of trusts, created for the benefit of the promiser. . . . *Felton v. Dickinson* (10 Mass., 189, 190), and others . . . are of that class; but concede them all to have been cases of trusts, and it proves nothing against the application of the rule to this case. The duty of the trustee to pay the *cestuis que trust*, according to the terms of the trust, implies his promise to the latter to do so. In this case the defendant, upon ample consideration received from Holly, promised Holly to pay his debt to the plaintiff; the consideration received and the promise to Holly made it as plainly his duty to pay the plaintiff as if the money had been remitted to him for that purpose, and as well implied a promise to do so as if he had been made a trustee of property to be converted into cash with which to pay. The fact that a breach of the duty imposed in the one case may be visited, and justly, with more serious consequences than in the other, by no means disproves the payment to be a duty in both. The principle illustrated by the example so frequently quoted (which concisely states the case in hand) "that a promise made to one for the benefit of another, he for whose benefit it is made may bring an action for its breach," has been applied to trust cases, not because it was exclusively applicable to those cases, but because it was a principle of law, and as such applicable to those cases.

It was also insisted that Holly could have discharged the defendant from his promise, though it was intended by both parties for the benefit of the plaintiff, and therefore the plaintiff was not entitled to maintain this suit for the recovery of a demand over which he had no control. It is enough that the plaintiff did not release the defendant from his promise, and whether he could or not is a question not now necessarily involved; but if it was, I think it would be found difficult to maintain the right of Holly to discharge a judgment recovered by the plaintiff upon confession or otherwise, for the breach of the defendant's promise; and if he could not, how could he discharge the suit before judgment, or the promise before suit, made as it was for the plaintiff's benefit and in accordance with legal presumption accepted by him (*Berley v. Taylor*, 5 Hill, 577–584, et seq.), until his dissent was shown. . . .

The judgment should be affirmed.

■ JOHNSON, CH. J., DENIO, SELDEN, ALLEN and STRONG, JS., concurred. JOHNSON, CH, J., and DENIO, J., were of opinion that the promise was to be regarded as made to the plaintiff through the medium of his agent, whose action he could ratify when it came to his knowledge, though taken without his being privy thereto.

■ COMSTOCK, J. (Dissenting.)

The plaintiff had nothing to do with the promise on which he brought this action. It was not made to him, nor did the consideration proceed from him. If he can maintain the suit, it is because an anomaly has found its way into the law on this subject. In general, there must be privity of contract. The party who sues upon a promise must be the promisee, or he must have some legal interest in the undertaking. In this case, it is plain that Holly, who loaned the money to the defendant, and to whom the promise in question was made, could at any time have claimed that it should be performed to himself personally. He had lent the money to the defendant, and at the same time directed the latter to pay the sum to the plaintiff. This direction he could countermand, and if he had done so, manifestly the defendant's promise to pay according to the direction would have ceased to exist. The plaintiff would receive a benefit by a complete execution of the arrangement, but the arrangement itself was between other parties, and was under their exclusive control. If the defendant had paid the money to Holly, his debt would have been discharged thereby. So Holly might have released the demand or assigned it to another person, or the parties might have annulled the promise now in question, and designated some other creditor of Holly as the party to whom the money should be paid. It has never been claimed, that in a case thus situated, the right of a third person to sue upon the promise rested on any sound principle of law. We are to inquire whether the rule has been so established by positive authority.

The cases which have sometimes been supposed to have a bearing on this question, are quite numerous. In some of them, the dicta of judges, delivered upon very slight consideration, have been referred to as the decisions of the courts. Thus, in *Schermerhorn v. Vanderheyden* (1 John., 140), the court is reported as saying, "We are of opinion, that where one person makes a promise to another, for the benefit of a third person, that third person may maintain an action on such promise." This remark was made on the authority of *Dalton v. Poole* (Vent., 318, 332), decided in England nearly two hundred years ago. It was, however, but a mere remark, as the case was determined against the plaintiff on another ground. Yet this decision has often been referred to as authority for similar observations in later cases.

. . .

The cases in which some trust was involved are also frequently referred to as authority for the doctrine now in question, but they do not sustain it. If A delivers money or property to B, which the latter accepts upon a trust for the benefit of C, the latter can enforce the trust by an appropriate action for that purpose. (*Berly v. Taylor*, 5 Hill, 577.) If the trust be of money, I think the beneficiary may assent to it and bring the action for money had and received to his use. If it be of something else than money, the trustee must account for it according to the terms of the trust, and upon principles of equity. There is some authority even for saying that an express promise founded on the possession of a trust fund may be enforced by an action at law in the name of the beneficiary, although it was made to the creator of the trust. Thus, in Comyn's Digest (Action on the case upon Assumpsit, B. 15), it is laid down that if a man promise a pig of lead to A, and his executor give lead to make a pig to B, who assumes to deliver it to A, an assumpsit lies by A against him. The case of The *Delaware and Hudson Canal Company v. The Westchester County Bank* (4 Denio, 97), involved a trust because the defendants had received from a third party a bill of exchange under an agreement that they would endeavor to collect it, and would pay over the proceeds when collected to the plaintiffs. A fund received under such an agreement does not belong to the person who receives it. He must account for it specifically; and perhaps there is no gross violation of principle in permitting the equitable owner of it to sue upon an express promise to pay it over. Having a specific interest in the thing, the undertaking to account for it may be regarded as in some sense made with him through the author of the trust. But further than this we cannot go without violating plain rules of law. In the case before us there was nothing in the nature of a trust or agency. The defendant borrowed the money of

Holly and received it as his own. The plaintiff had no right in the fund, legal or equitable. The promise to repay the money created an obligation in favor of the lender to whom it was made and not in favor of any one else.

The judgment of the court below should therefore be reversed, and a new trial granted.

■ GROVER, J., also dissented.

Judgment affirmed.

NOTES & QUESTIONS

1.   Define, in your own words, the notion of "privity".

2.   Recall the case of *Newman & Snell's State Bank v. Hunter* that we studied in Chapter 4.D. at p. 156. In that case, Husband owed money to Bank, and Wife promised to pay that debt. In a sense, *Lawrence v. Fox* involves a similar fact pattern: Holly owed money to Lawrence, and Fox promised to pay that debt. If the cases involved similar fact patterns, why were the legal issues different?

3.   The majority opinion in *Lawrence v. Fox* refers to *Farley v Cleaveland*. But note that there is a significant difference. In *Farley v. Cleaveland*, Moon owed money to Farley, and Cleaveland promised to pay the debt. But Cleaveland made the promise not only to Moon, but also to the plaintiff Farley. So, *Farley v. Cleavelend* did not present the question, involved in *Lawrence v. Fox*, of whether someone other than the promisee can sue on the promise.

4.   A trust, in this situation, would be observed if Holly had handed an envelope with $300 cash to Fox and said "Take this money and use it to pay Lawrence the $300 I owe him", which Fox agreed to do. Fox would then be a trustee, owing fiduciary duties to Lawrence as beneficiary. How are the facts in *Lawrence v. Fox* different?

5.   We have encountered over a dozen cases nineteenth century cases in these materials on contract law. Such cases, like *Lawrence v. Fox*, warrant our analysis, not only because of the substantive changes to the law that they signal, but also because of their style of analysis. Think about how the majority in *Lawrence v. Fox* brings about the change in the law, and how the dissent casts its disapproval. The dissent here was a powerful one: it was not until the twentieth century that the claims of third party beneficiaries advanced. Was the dissent's reasoning based on law or policy?

6.   In respect of history and policy, too, do you think the idea that "a contracting party [shouldn't have to] meet in litigation a person with whom he [or she] had not chosen to do business" is now outdated (as expressed in *Chaote, Hall & Stewart v. SCA Services, Inc.*, 378 Mass. 535, 392 N.E.2d 1045 (1979) per Kaplan, J)? Is this notion better suited to a "simple, neighbourly society . . . long vanquished"? (*Id.*) Consider the updated rule, flowing (eventually) from the *Fox* majority, which is "calculated to accord with the probable intentions of the contracting parties and to respond to the reasonable reliance of the third party [beneficiary]": *Id.* If we have sympathy

for a third party who is a creditor, like Lawrence, what about for a third party who might be expecting a gift? See below.

Seaver v. Ransom

Court of Appeals of New York, 1918.
224 N.Y. 233, 120 N.E. 639.

■ POUND, J.

Judge Beman and his wife were advanced in years. Mrs. Beman was about to die. She had a small estate, consisting of a house and lot in Malone and little else. Judge Beman drew his wife's will according to her instructions. It gave $1,000 to plaintiff, $500 to one sister, plaintiff's mother, and $100 each to another sister and her son, the use of the house to her husband for life, and remainder to the American Society for the Prevention of Cruelty to Animals. She named her husband as residuary legatee and executor. Plaintiff was her niece, 34 years old, in ill health, sometimes a member of the Beman household. When the will was read to Mrs. Beman, she said that it was not as she wanted it. She wanted to leave the house to plaintiff. She had no other objection to the will, but her strength was waning, and, although the judge offered to write another will for her, she said she was afraid she would not hold out long enough to enable her to sign it. So the judge said, if she would sign the will, he would leave plaintiff enough in his will to make up the difference. He avouched the promise by his uplifted hand with all solemnity and his wife then executed the will. When he came to die, it was found that his will made no provision for the plaintiff.

This action was brought, and plaintiff recovered judgment in the trial court, on the theory that Beman had obtained property from his wife and induced her to execute the will in the form prepared by him by his promise to give plaintiff $6,000, the value of the house, and that thereby equity impressed his property with a trust in favor of plaintiff. Where a legatee promises the testator that he will use property given him by the will for a particular purpose, a trust arises. * * * Beman received nothing under his wife's will but the use of the house in Malone for life. Equity compels the application of property thus obtained to the purpose of the testator, but equity cannot so impress a trust, except on property obtained by the promise. Beman was bound by his promise, but no property was bound by it; no trust in plaintiff's favor can be spelled out.[a]

An action on the contract for damages, or to make the executors trustees for performance, stands on different ground. * * * The Appellate Division properly passed to the consideration of the question whether the judgment could stand upon the promise made to the wife, upon a valid

---

[a]   [The point here is that if Judge Beman had received property from his wife's will, that property could be impressed with a trust. But in the case itself, by the time the dispute arose, Judge Beman held no property that he had received from Mrs. Beman's will. He had only a life estate in the house. So the case turns on whether Seaver can enforce the promise that Judge Beman made to Mrs. Beman.] Ed. fn.

consideration, for the sole benefit of plaintiff. The judgment of the trial court was affirmed by a return to the general doctrine laid down in the great case of *Lawrence v. Fox*, 20 N. Y. 268, which has since been limited as herein indicated.

Contracts for the benefit of third persons have been the prolific source of judicial and academic discussion. * * * The general rule, both in law and equity * * * was that privity between a plaintiff and a defendant is necessary to the maintenance of an action on the contract. The consideration must be furnished by the party to whom the promise was made. The contract cannot be enforced against the third party, and therefore it cannot be enforced by him. On the other hand, the right of the beneficiary to sue on a contract made expressly for his benefit has been fully recognized in many American jurisdictions, either by judicial decision or by legislation, and is said to be 'the prevailing rule in this country.' *Hendrick v. Lindsay*, 93 U. S. 143, 23 L. Ed. 855 * * *. It has been said that 'the establishment of this doctrine has been gradual, and is a victory of practical utility over theory, of equity over technical subtlety.' Brantly on Contracts (2d Ed.) p. 253. The reasons for this view are that it is just and practical to permit the person for whose benefit the contract is made to enforce it against one whose duty it is to pay. Other jurisdictions still adhere to the present English rule (7 Halsbury's Laws of England, 342, 343; Jenks' Digest of English Civil Law, § 229) that a contract cannot be enforced by or against a person who is not a party (*Exchange Bank v. Rice*, 107 Mass. 37, 9 Am. Rep. 1). * * *

In New York the right of the beneficiary to sue on contracts made for his benefit is not clearly or simply defined. It is at present confined: First. To cases where there is a pecuniary obligation running from the promisee to the beneficiary, 'a legal right founded upon some obligation of the promisee in the third party to adopt and claim the promise as made for his benefit.' *Farley v. Cleveland*, 4 Cow. 432, 15 Am. Dec. 387; *Lawrence v. Fox, supra*, *Vrooman v. Turner*, 69 N. Y. 280, 25 Am. Rep. 195 * * * Secondly. To cases where the contract is made for the benefit of the wife * * * affianced wife * * * or child * * * of a party to the contract. The close relationship cases go back to the early King's Bench case (1677), long since repudiated in England, of *Dutton v. Poole*, 2 Lev. 211 (s. c., 1 Ventris, 318, 332). See *Schemerhorn v. Vanderheyden*, 1 Johns. 139, 3 Am. Dec. 304. The natural and moral duty of the husband or parent to provide for the future of wife or child sustains the action on the contract made for their benefit. 'This is the farthest the cases in this state have gone,' says Cullen, J., in the marriage settlement case of *Borland v. Welch*, 162 N. Y. 104, 110, 56 N. E. 556.

The right of the third party is also upheld in, thirdly, the public contract cases * * * where the municipality seeks to protect its inhabitants by covenants for their benefit; and, fourthly, the cases where, at the request of a party to the contract, the promise runs directly to the beneficiary although he does not furnish the consideration * * * It may be safely said that a general rule sustaining recovery at the suit of the third party would include but few classes of cases not included in these groups, either categorically or in principle.

The desire of the childless aunt to make provision for a beloved and favorite niece differs imperceptibly in law or in equity from the moral duty of the parent to make testamentary provision for a child. The contract was made for the plaintiff's benefit. She alone is substantially damaged by its breach. The representatives of the wife's estate have no interest in enforcing it specifically. It is said in *Buchanan v. Tilden* that the common law imposes moral and legal obligations upon the husband and the parent not measured by the necessaries of life. It was, however, the love and affection or the moral sense of the husband and the parent that imposed such obligations in the cases cited, rather than any common-law duty of husband and parent to wife and child. If plaintiff had been a child of Mrs. Beman, legal obligation would have required no testamentary provision for her, yet the child could have enforced a covenant in her favor identical with the covenant of Judge Beman in this case. * * * The constraining power of conscience is not regulated by the degree of relationship alone. The dependent or faithful niece may have a stronger claim than the affluent or unworthy son. No sensible theory of moral obligation denies arbitrarily to the former what would be conceded to the latter. We might consistently either refuse or allow the claim of both, but I cannot reconcile a decision in favor of the wife in *Buchanan v. Tilden*, based on the moral obligations arising out of near relationship, with a decision against the niece here on the ground that the relationship is too remote for equity's ken. No controlling authority depends upon so absolute a rule. . . . . Kellogg, P. J., writing for the court below well said:

> 'The doctrine of Lawrence v. Fox is progressive, not retrograde. The course of the late decisions is to enlarge, not to limit, the effect of that case.'

The court in that leading case attempted to adopt the general doctrine that any third person, for whose direct benefit a contract was intended, could sue on it. . . . Finch, J., in *Gifford v. Corrigan*, 117 N. Y. 257, 262, 22 N. E. 756, 6 L. R. A. 610, 15 Am. St. Rep. 508, says that the case rests upon that broad proposition; Edward T. Bartlett, J., in *Pond v. New Rochelle Water Co.*, 183 N. Y. 330, 337, 76 N. E. 211, 213 (1 L. R. A. [N. S.] 958, 5 Ann. Cas. 504), calls it 'the general principle'; but Vrooman v. Turner, supra, confined its application to the facts on which it was decided. 'In every case in which an action has been sustained,' says Allen, J., 'there has been a debt or duty owing by the promisee to the party claiming to sue upon the promise.' 69 N. Y. 285, 25 Am. Rep. 195. As late as *Townsend v. Rackham*, 143 N. Y. 516, 523, 38 N. E. 731, 733, we find Peckham, J., saying that, 'to maintain the action by the third person, there must be this liability to him on the part of the promisee.' Buchanan v. Tilden went further than any case since Lawrence v. Fox in a desire to do justice rather than to apply with technical accuracy strict rules calling for a legal or equitable obligation. . . .

But, on principle, a sound conclusion may be reached. If Mrs. Beman had left her husband the house on condition that he pay the plaintiff $6,000, and he had accepted the devise, he would have become personally liable to pay the legacy, and plaintiff could have recovered in an action at law against him, whatever the value of the house. *Gridley v. Gridley*, 24 N. Y. 130 * * *. That would be because the testatrix had in substance bequeathed the promise to plaintiff, and not because close relationship or moral obligation sustained the contract. The distinction between an implied promise to a testator for the benefit of a third party to pay a legacy and an unqualified promise on a valuable consideration to make provision for the third party by will is discernible, but not obvious. The tendency of American authority is to sustain the gift in all such cases and to permit the donee beneficiary to recover on the contract. *Matter of Edmundson's Estate* (1918, Pa.) 103 Atl. 277, 259 Pa. 429. The equities are with the plaintiff, and they may be enforced in this action, whether it be regarded as an action for damages or an action for specific performance to convert the defendants into trustees for plaintiff's benefit under the agreement.

The judgment should be affirmed, with costs.

■ HOGAN, CARDOZO, and CRANE, JJ., concur.

■ HISCOCK, C. J., and COLLIN and ANDREWS, JJ., dissent.

NOTE

Recall the case of *Schnell v. Nell* that we studied in Chapter 4.C. at p. 149. In that case, Wife wanted money to go to Nell, and Husband promised to pay that money. In a sense, *Seaver v. Ransom* involves a similar fact pattern: Wife (Mrs. Beman) wanted money to go to Seaver, and husband (Judge Beman) promised to pay that money. If the cases involved similar fact patterns, why were the legal issues different?

NOTE ON RESTATEMENT TERMINOLOGY FOR THIRD PARTY BENEFICIARY CASES

The RESTATEMENT (FIRST) OF CONTRACTS (1932) used the terms "creditor beneficiary" and "donee beneficiary" to describe the principles involved in *Lawrence v. Fox* and *Seaver v. Ransom*.

In *Lawrence v Fox*, the third party who sued (Lawrence) was a creditor of the promisee (Holly). Though the promisor (Fox) made the promise only to the promisee (Holly), the third party was allowed to sue because the third party was a creditor of the promisee, and it made sense to allow the third party to sue because that was how the promisee wanted to pay the debt to the third party. As the FIRST RESTATEMENT put it, the plaintiff in such a case is a "creditor beneficiary" because "performance of the promise will satisfy . . . a duty of the promisee to the beneficiary." RESTATEMENT (FIRST) OF

CONTRACTS § 133(1)(b). One who fell within the category of "creditor beneficiary" was permitted to sue to enforce the promise. RESTATEMENT (FIRST) OF CONTRACTS § 136(1)(a).

In *Seaver v. Ransom,* the third party who sued (Seaver) wasn't a creditor of the promisee (Mrs. Beman), but the promisee wanted the third party to have the benefit of the promise, as a form of gift from the promisee. Though the promisor (Mr. Beman) made the promise only to the promisee (Mrs. Beman), the third party (Seaver) was allowed to sue because Mrs. Beman wanted to make a present to Seaver. As the First Restatement put it, the plaintiff in such a case is a "donee beneficiary" because "the purpose of the promisee in obtaining the promise . . . is to make a gift to the beneficiary." RESTATEMENT (FIRST) OF CONTRACTS § 133(1)(a). One who fell within the category of "donee beneficiary" was permitted to sue to enforce the promise. RESTATEMENT (FIRST) OF CONTRACTS § 135(a).

The First Restatement used the term "incidental beneficiary" to describe someone who would benefit from performance of a promise made to someone else, but who did not fall within the categories of "creditor beneficiary" or "donee beneficiary." RESTATEMENT (FIRST) OF CONTRACTS § 133(1)(c) (1932). An incidental beneficiary was not entitled to sue to enforce the promise. RESTATEMENT (FIRST) OF CONTRACTS § 147 (1932).

The RESTATEMENT (SECOND) OF CONTRACTS (1981) uses slightly different terminology, though does not make major substantive changes. The Second Restatement uses the terms "intended beneficiary" and "incidental beneficiary" in describing parties other than the actual promisee. An "intended beneficiary" is permitted to sue; an "incidental beneficiary" is not permitted to sue. RESTATEMENT (SECOND) OF CONTRACTS §§ 304, 315. The Second Restatement's term "intended beneficiary" covers more or less the same categories as the First Restatement's terms "creditor beneficiary" and "donee beneficiary." As RESTATEMENT (SECOND) OF CONTRACTS § 302 puts it, one is an "intended beneficiary" if

> recognition of a right to performance in the beneficiary is appropriate to effectuate the intention of the parties and either
>
> > (a) the performance of the promise will satisfy an obligation of the promisee to pay money to the beneficiary; or
> >
> > (b) the circumstances indicate that the promisee intends to give the beneficiary the benefit of the promised performance.

H. R. Moch Co. v. Rensselaer Water Co.

Court of Appeals of New York, 1928.
247 N.Y. 160, 159 N.E. 896.

■ CARDOZO, C. J.

The defendant, a waterworks company[,] made a contract with the city of Rensselaer for the supply of water during a term of years. Water was to be furnished to the city for sewer flushing and street sprinkling; for service to schools and public buildings; and for service at fire hydrants, the latter service at the rate of $42.50 a year for each hydrant. Water was to be furnished to private takers within the city at their homes and factories and other industries at reasonable rates, not exceeding a stated schedule. While this contract was in force, a building caught fire. The flames, spreading to the plaintiff's warehouse near by, destroyed it and its contents. The defendant, according to the complaint, was promptly notified of the fire, 'but omitted and neglected after such notice, to supply or furnish sufficient or adequate quantity of water, with adequate pressure to stay, suppress, or extinguish the fire before it reached the warehouse of the plaintiff, although the pressure and supply which the defendant was equipped to supply and furnish, and had agreed by said contract to supply and furnish, was adequate and sufficient to prevent the spread of the fire to and the destruction of the plaintiff's warehouse and its contents.' By reason of the failure of the defendant to 'fulfill the provisions of the contract between it and the city of Rensselaer,' the plaintiff is said to have suffered damage, for which judgment is demanded. A motion, in the nature of a demurrer, to dismiss the complaint, was denied at Special Term. The Appellate Division reversed by a divided court.

. . . The complaint, we are told, is to be viewed as stating: (1) A cause of action for breach of contract within *Lawrence v. Fox*, 20 N. Y. 268; (2) a cause of action for a common-law tort, within *MacPherson v. Buick Motor Co.,* 217 N. Y. 382, 111 N. E. 1050, L. R. A. 1916F, 696, Ann. Cas. 1916C, 440; or (3) a cause of action for the breach of a statutory duty. These several grounds of liability will be considered in succession.

(1) We think the action is not maintainable as one for breach of contract.

No legal duty rests upon a city to supply its inhabitants with protection against fire. *Springfield Fire & Marine Ins. Co. v. Village of Keeseville*, 148 N. Y. 46, 42 N. E. 405, 30 L. R. A. 660, 51 Am. St. Rep. 667. That being so, a member of the public may not maintain an action under *Lawrence v. Fox* against one contracting with the city to furnish water at the hydrants, unless an intention appears that the promisor is to be answerable to individual members of the public as well as to the city for any loss ensuing from the failure to fulfill the promise. No such intention is discernible here. On the contrary, the contract is significantly divided into two branches: One a promise to the city for the benefit of the city in its corporate capacity, in which branch is included the service at the hydrants; and the other a promise to the city for the benefit of private takers, in which branch is included the service at their homes and factories. In a broad sense it is true that every city contract, not improvident or wasteful, is for the benefit of the public. More than this, however, must be shown to give a right of action to a member of the public not formally a party. The benefit, as it is sometimes said, must be one that is not merely incidental and secondary. . . It must be primary and immediate in such a sense and to such a degree as to bespeak the assumption of a duty to make reparation directly to the individual members of the public if the benefit is lost. The field of obligation would be expanded beyond reasonable limits if less than this were to be demanded as a condition of liability. A promisor undertakes to supply fuel for heating a public building. He is not liable for breach of contract to a visitor who finds the building without fuel, and thus contracts a cold. The list of illustrations can be indefinitely extended. The carrier of the mails under contract with the government is not answerable to the merchant who has lost the benefit of a bargain through negligent delay. The householder is without a remedy against manufacturers of hose and engines, though prompt performance of their contracts would have stayed the ravages of fire. 'The law does not spread its protection so far.' *Robins Dry Dock & Repair Co. v. Flint*, 275 U. S. 303, 48 S. Ct. 134, 72 L. Ed. 290.

So with the case at hand. By the vast preponderance of authority, a contract between a city and a water company to furnish water at the city hydrants has in view a benefit to the public that is incidental rather than immediate, an assumption of duty to the city and not to its inhabitants. . . . Such with few exceptions has been the ruling in other jurisdictions. . . . . An intention to assume an obligation of indefinite extension to every member of the public is seen to be the more improbable when we recall the crushing burden that the obligation would impose. * * *. The consequences invited would bear no reasonable proportion to those attached by law to defaults not greatly different. A wrongdoer who by negligence sets fire to a building is liable in damages to the owner where the fire has its origin, but not to other owners who are injured when it spreads. The rule in our state is settled to that effect, whether wisely or unwisely. * * * If the plaintiff is to prevail, one who negligently omits to supply sufficient pressure to extinguish a fire started by another assumes an obligation to pay the ensuing damage, though the whole city is laid low. A promisor will not be deemed to have had in mind the assumption of a risk so overwhelming for any trivial reward.

The cases that have applied the rule of Lawrence v. Fox to contracts made by a city for the benefit of the public are not at war with this conclusion. Through them all there runs as a unifying principle the presence of an intention to compensate the individual members of the public in the event of a default. For example, in Pond v. New Rochelle Water Co., 183 N. Y. 330, 76 N. E. 211, 1 L. R. A. (N. S.) 958, 5 Ann. Cas. 504, the contract with the city fixed a schedule of rates to be supplied, not to public buildings, but to private takers at their homes. In . . . Rigney v. New York Cent. & H. R. R. Co., 217 N. Y. 31, 111 N. E. 226, covenants were made by contractors upon public works, not merely to indemnify the city, but to assume its liabilities. These and like cases come within the third group stated in the comprehensive opinion in Seaver v. Ransom, 224 N. Y. 233, 238, 120 N. E. 639, 2 L. R. A. 1187. The municipality was contracting in behalf of its inhabitants by covenants intended to be enforced by any of them severally as occasion should arise.

(2) We think the action is not maintainable as one for a common-law tort.

'It is ancient learning that one who assumes to act, even though gratuitously, may thereby become subject to the duty of acting carefully, if he acts at all.' *Glanzer v. Shepard*, 233 N. Y. 236, 239, 135 N. E. 275, 276 (23 A. L. R. 1425); * * *. The plaintiff would bring its case within the orbit of that principle. The hand once set to a task may not always be withdrawn with impunity though liability would fail if it had never been applied at all. A time-honored formula often phrases the distinction as one between misfeasance and nonfeasance. Incomplete the formula is, and so at times misleading. Given a relation involving in its existence a duty of care irrespective of a contract, a tort may result as well from acts of omission as of commission in the fulfillment of the duty thus recognized by law. Pollock, Torts (12th Ed.) p. 555; *Kelly v. Metropolitan Ry. Co.*, [1895] 1 Q. B. 944. What we need to know is not so much the conduct to be avoided when the relation and its attendant duty are established as existing. What we need to know is the conduct that engenders the relation. It is here that the formula, however incomplete, has its value and significance. If conduct has gone forward to such a stage that in action would commonly result, not negatively merely in withholding a benefit, but positively or actively in working an injury, there exists a relation out of which arises a duty to go forward. Bohlen, Studies in the Law of Torts, p. 87. So the surgeon who operates without pay is liable, though his negligence is in the omission to sterilize his instruments (*cf. Glanzer v. Shepard, supra*); the engineer, though his fault is in the failure to shut off steam (*Kelly v. Metropolitan Ry. Co., supra; cf. Pittsfield Cottonwear Mfg. Co. v. Pittsfield Shoe Co.*, 71 N. H. 522, 529, 533, 53 A. 807, 60 L. R. A. 116); the maker of automobiles, at the suit of some one other than the buyer, though his negligence is merely in inadequate inspection (*MacPherson v. Buick Motor Co.*, 217 N. Y. 382, 111 N. E. 1050, L. R. A. 1916F, 696, Ann. Cas. 1916C, 440). The query always is whether the putative wrongdoer has advanced to such a point as to have launched a force or instrument of harm, or has stopped where inaction is at most a refusal to become an instrument for good. . . .

The plaintiff would have us hold that the defendant, when once it entered upon the performance of its contract with the city, was brought into such a relation with every one who might potentially be benefited through the supply of water at the hydrants as to give to negligent performance, without reasonable notice of a refusal to continue, the quality of a tort. . . . We are satisfied that liability would be unduly and indeed indefinitely extended by this enlargement of the zone of duty. The dealer in coal who is to supply fuel for a shop must then answer to the customers if fuel is lacking. The manufacturer of goods, who enters upon the performance of his contract, must answer, in that view, not only to the buyer, but to those who to his knowledge are looking to the buyer for their own sources of supply. Every one making a promise having the quality of a contract will be under a duty to the promisee by virtue of the promise, but under another duty, apart from contract, to an indefinite number of potential beneficiaries when performance has begun. The assumption of one relation will mean the involuntary assumption of a series of new relations, inescapably hooked together. Again we may say in the words of the Supreme Court of the United States, 'The law does not spread its protection so far.' *Robins Dry Dock & Repair Co. v. Flint, supra* . . . What we are dealing with at this time is a mere negligent omission, unaccompanied by malice or other aggravating elements. The failure in such circumstances to furnish an adequate supply of water is at most the denial of a benefit. It is not the commission of a wrong.

(3)   We think the action is not maintainable as one for the breach of a statutory duty.

The defendant, a public service corporation, is subject to the provisions of the Transportation Corporations Act. The duty imposed upon it by that act is in substance to furnish water, upon demand by the inhabitants, at reasonable rates, through suitable connections at office, factory, or dwelling, and to furnish water at like rates through hydrants or in public buildings upon demand by the city, all according to its capacity. Transportation Corporations Law (Consol. Laws, c. 63) § 81 * * * We find nothing in these requirements to enlarge the zone of liability where an inhabitant of the city suffers indirect or incidental damage through deficient pressure at the hydrants. The breach of duty in any case is to the one to whom service is denied at the time and at the place where service to such one is due. The denial, though wrongful, is unavailing without more to give a cause of action to another. . . . If the defendant may not be held for a tort at common law, we find no adequate reason for a holding that it may be held under the statute.

The judgment should be affirmed, with costs.

■ POUND, CRANE, ANDREWS, LEHMAN, and KELLOGG, JJ., concur. O'BRIEN, J., not sitting.

NOTES & QUESTIONS

1.   Would the promisee in *Moch v. Rensselaer Water* (that is, the city), have reason for concern if citizens were allowed to sue to enforce the promise that the water company made to the city? What might those concerns be?

2.   Compare with the earlier cases. Would the promisee Holly have had concerns in *Lawrence v. Fox*? What about the promisee Mrs. Beman in *Seaver v. Ransom*?

3.   Now consider this hypo. Suppose that a coach's agreement with a sports team includes a promise to coach competently. If the coach does not do so, all kinds of people will be upset—T-shirt vendors, for example, might be very interested in whether the coach is performing the contract. Allowing

the third party to sue in that case would obviously be problematic from the standpoint of the promisee, the team. In that case, it is relatively straightforward to see that the team would want to decide whether to sue the coach or take any other action, and would not want the coach to waste time defending lawsuits by disappointed fans or vendors.

4.   Let's now compare other "strangers" to the contract: this time, not third party beneficiaries, but assignees.

B. ASSIGNMENT OF RIGHTS

Restatement (Second) of Contracts § 317

U.C.C. § 2–210(2)

Crane Ice Cream Co. v. Terminal Freezing & Heating Co.

Court of Appeals of Maryland, 1925.
147 Md. 588, 128 A. 280.

■ PARKE, J.

The appellee and one W. C. Frederick entered into a contract for the delivery of ice by the appellee to Frederick, and, before the expiration of the contract, Frederick executed an assignment of the contract to the appellant; and on the refusal of the appellee to deliver ice to the assignee it brought an action on the contract against the appellee to recover damages for the alleged breach. . . .

Terminal Freezing & Heating Company, appellee, was a corporation engaged in the manufacture and sale of ice at wholesale within the state of Maryland, and William C. Frederick made and sold ice cream in Baltimore. . . . The original contract between these two parties was made on April 2, 1917, and ran until April 2, 1920. The contract was modified on June 3, 1918, by the increase of the original contract price of ice from $2.75 a ton to $3.25, and before its expiration the contract was renewed by the parties for another three years so that the contract was continued until April 2, 1923, without change, save as to the higher agreed cost of the ice delivered.

The contract imposed upon the appellee the liability to sell and deliver to Frederick such quantities of ice as he might use in his business as an ice cream manufacturer to the extent of 250 tons per week, at and for the price of $3.25 a ton of 2,000 pounds on the loading platform of Frederick. The contractual rights of the appellee were (a) to be paid on every Tuesday during the continuation of the contract, for all ice purchased by Frederick during the week ending at midnight upon the next preceding Saturday; (b) to require Frederick not to buy or accept any ice from any other source than the appellee, except in excess of the weekly maximum of 250 tons; (c) to annul the contract upon any violation of the agreement by Frederick; and (d) to sustain no liability for any breach of contract growing out of causes beyond its control. The converse of these rights and liabilities of the appellee were the correlative liabilities and rights of Frederick under the contract.

There was a further provision that the contract in its entirety should continue in force from term to term, unless either party thereto gave to the other party at least 60 days' notice in writing before the expiration of the term of the intention to end the contract. The contract did not expressly permit or inhibit an assignment, but neither did it contain any word, such as assigns, to indicate that the parties contemplated an assignment by either.

Before the first year of the second term of the contract had expired Frederick, without the consent or knowledge of the appellee, executed and delivered to the appellant, for a valuable consideration, a written assignment dated February 15, 1921, of the modified agreement between him and the appellee. The attempted transfer of the contract was a part of the transaction between Frederick and the appellant whereby the appellant acquired by purchase the plant, equipment, rights, and credits, choses in action, "good will, trade, custom, patronage, rights, contracts," and other assets of Frederick's ice cream business, which had been established and conducted by him in Baltimore. The purchaser took full possession and continued the former business carried on by Frederick. It was then and is now a corporation "engaged in the ice cream business upon a large and extensive scale in the city of Philadelphia, as well as in the city of Baltimore, and state of Maryland," and had a large capitalization, ample resources, and credit to meet any of its obligations "and all and singular the terms and provisions" of the contract; and it was prepared to pay cash for all ice deliverable under the contract.

As soon as the appellee learned of this purported assignment and the absorption of the business of Frederick by the appellant, it notified Frederick that the contract was at an end, and declined to deliver any ice to the appellant. Until the day of the assignment the obligations of both original parties had been fully performed and discharged.

It may be stated as a general rule that a contract cannot be enforced by or against a person who is not a party to it, but there are circumstances under which either of the contracting parties may substitute another for himself in the rights and duties of the contract without obtaining the consent of the other party to the contract. The inquiry here is if the facts bring the case within the scope of the general rule, and the answer must be found from a consideration in detail of the relation of the parties concerned, the subject-matter of the contract, its terms, and the circumstances of its formation.

The basic facts upon which the question for solution depends must be sought in the effect of the attempted assignment of this executory bilateral contract on both the rights and the liabilities of the contracting parties, as every bilateral contract includes both rights and duties on each side while both sides remain executory. I Williston on Contracts, § 407. If the assignment of rights and the assignment of duties by Frederick are separated, they fall into these two divisions: (1) The rights of the assignor were (a) to take no ice, if the assignor used none in his business, but, if he did (b) to require the appellee to deliver, on the loading platform of the assignor, all the ice he might need in his business to the extent of 250 tons a week, and (c) to buy any ice he might need in excess of the weekly 250 tons from any other person; and (2) the liabilities of the assignor were (a) to pay to the appellee on every Tuesday during the continuance of the contract the stipulated price for all ice purchased and weighed by the assignor during the week ending at midnight upon the next preceding Saturday, and (b) not directly or indirectly, during the existence of this agreement, to buy or accept any ice from any other person, firm, or corporation than the said the Terminal Freezing & Heating Company, except such amounts as might be in excess of the weekly limit of 250 tons.

Whether the attempted assignment of these rights, or the attempted delegation of these duties must fail because the rights or duties are of too personal a character, is a question of construction to be resolved from the nature of the contract and the express or presumed intention of the parties. Williston on Contracts, § 431.

The contract was made by a corporation with an individual, William C. Frederick, an ice cream manufacturer, with whom the corporation had dealt for 3 years, before it executed a renewal contract for a second like period. The character, credit, and resources of Frederick had been tried and tested by the appellee before it renewed the contract. Not only had his ability to pay as agreed been established, but his fidelity to his obligation not to buy or accept any ice from any other source up to 250 tons a week had been ascertained. In addition, the appellee had not asked in the beginning, nor on entering into the second period of the contract, for Frederick to undertake to buy a specific quantity of ice or even to take any. Frederick simply engaged himself during a definite term to accept and pay for such quantities of ice as he might use in his business to the extent of 250 tons a week. If he used no ice in his business, he was under no obligation to pay for a pound. In any week, the quantity could vary from zero to 250 tons, and its weekly fluctuation, throughout the life of the contract, could irregularly range between these limits. The weekly payment might be nothing or as much as $812.50; and for every week a credit was extended to the eighth day from the beginning of every week's delivery. From the time of the beginning of every weekly delivery of the ice to the date of the payment therefor the title to the ice was in the purchaser, and the seller had no security for its payment except in the integrity and solvency of Frederick. The performances, therefore, were not concurrent, but the performance of the nonassigning party to the contract was to precede the payments by the assignor.

When it is also considered that the ice was to be supplied and paid for, according to its weight on the loading platform of Frederick, at an unvarying price without any reference either to the quantity used, or to the fluctuations in the cost of production or to market changes in the selling price, throughout 3 years, the conclusion is inevitable that the inducement for the appellee to enter into the original contract and into the renewal lay outside the bare terms of the contract, but was implicit in them, and was the appellee's reliance upon its knowledge of an average quantity of ice consumed, and probably to be needed, in the usual course of Frederick's business, at all times throughout the year, and its confidence in the stability of his enterprise, in his competency in commercial affairs, in his probity, personal judgment, and in his continuing financial responsibility. The contract itself emphasized the personal equation by specifying that the ice was to be bought for "use in his business as an ice cream manufacturer," and was to be paid for according to its weight "on the loading platform of the said W. C. Frederick."

When Frederick went out of business as an ice cream manufacturer, and turned over his plant and everything constituting his business to the appellant, it was no longer his business, or his loading platform, or subject to his care, control, or maintenance, but it was the business of a stranger, whose skill, competency, and requirements of ice were altogether different from those of Frederick. The assignor had his simple plant in Baltimore. The assignee, in its purchase, simply added another unit to its ice cream business which it had been, and is now, carrying on "upon a large and extensive scale in the city of Philadelphia and state of Pennsylvania, as well as in the city of Baltimore and state of Maryland." The appellee knew that Frederick could not carry on his business without ice wherewith to manufacture ice cream at his plant for his trade. It also was familiar with the quantities of ice he would require, from time to time, in his business at his plant in Baltimore, and it consequently could make its other commitments for ice with this knowledge as a basis.

The appellant, on the other hand, might wholly supply its increased trade acquired in the purchase of Frederick's business with its ice cream produced upon a large and extensive scale by its manufactory in Philadelphia, which would result in no ice being bought by the assignee of the appellee, and so the appellee would be deprived of the benefit of its contract by the introduction of a different personal relation or element which was never contemplated by the original contracting parties. Again, should the price of ice be relatively high in Philadelphia in comparison with the stipulated price, the assignee could run its business in Baltimore and furnish its patrons, or a portion of them, in Philadelphia with its product from the weekly maximum consumption of 250 tons of ice throughout the year. There can be no denial that the uniform delivery of the maximum quantity of 250 tons a week would be a consequence not within the normal scope of the contract, and would impose a greater liability on the appellee than was anticipated. 7 Halsbury's Laws of England, § 1015, p. 501.

Moreover, the contract here to supply ice was undefined except as indicated from time to time by the personal requirements of Frederick in his specified business. The quantities of ice to be supplied to Frederick to answer his weekly requirements must be very different from, and would not be the measure of the quantities needed by his assignee, and, manifestly, to impose on the seller the obligation to obey the demands of the substituted assignee is to set up a new measure of ice to be supplied, and so a new term in the agreement that the appellee never bound itself to perform. Up to 250 tons of ice a week Frederick engaged not to buy or accept any ice from any other party than the appellee. After Frederick had sold away his business, this covenant could not bind the assignee of his business, and, even if it continued to bind Frederick, his refraining from not buying ice elsewhere was not a contemplated consideration for selling ice to any one except Frederick himself. *Kemp v. Baerselman*, [1906] 2 K. B. 604, 608, 609. It was argued that Frederick was entitled to the weekly maximum of 250 tons, and that he might have expanded his business so as to require this weekly limit of ice, and that therefore the burdens of the contract might have been as onerous to the appellee, if Frederick had continued in business, as they could become under the purporting assignment by reason of the increased requirements of the larger business of the assignee. The unsoundness of this argument is that the law accords to every man freedom of choice in the party with whom he deals and the terms of his dealing. He cannot be forced to do a thing which he did not agree to do because it is like and no more burdensome than something which he did contract to do.

Under all the circumstances of the case, it is clear that the rights and duties of the contract under consideration were of so personal a character that the rights of Frederick cannot be assigned nor his duties be delegated without defeating the intention of the parties to the original contract. When Frederick went out of the business of making ice cream, he made it impossible for him to complete his performance of the contract, and his personal action and qualifications upon which the appellee relied were eliminated from a contract which presupposed their continuance. Frederick not only attempted an assignment, but his course is a repudiation of the obligations of the contract. He is not even alleged to be ready to pay for any ice which might be delivered after the date of the purporting assignment, but the allegations of the declaration simply aver that the assignee alone had undertaken to perform the further contractual obligations of the assignor. Frederick, however, cannot be heard to say that he has not repudiated a contract, whose contemplated performance his own act has made it impossible for him to fulfill. *Eastern Advertising Co. v. McGaw*, 89 Md. 86, 88, 42 A. 923.

While a party to a contract may as a general rule assign all his beneficial rights, except where a personal relation is involved, his liability under the contract is not assignable inter vivos, because any one who is bound to any performance whatever or who owes money cannot by any act of his own, or by any act in agreement with any other person than his creditor or the one to whom his performance is due, cast off his own liability and substitute another's liability. If this were not true, obligors could free themselves of their obligations by the simple expedient of assigning them. A further ground for the rule is that, not only is a party entitled to know to whom he must look for the satisfaction of his rights under the contract, but in the familiar words of Lord Denman in *Humble v. Hunter*, 12 Q. B. 317, "you have a right to the benefit you contemplate from the character, credit, and substance of the person with whom you contract." For these reasons it has been uniformly held that a man cannot assign his liabilities under a contract, but one who is bound so as to bear an unescapable liability may delegate the performance of his obligation to another, if the liability be of such a nature that its performance by another will be substantially the same thing as performance by the promisor himself. In such circumstances the performance of the third party is the act of the promisor, who remains liable under the contract and answerable in damages if the performance be not in strict fulfillment of the contract. * * *.

However, the analysis of the facts on this appeal leaves no room for doubt that the case at bar falls into the category of those assignments where an attempt is made both to transfer the rights and to delegate the duties of the assignor under an executory bilateral contract whose terms and the circumstances make plain that the personal qualification and action of the assignor, with respect to both his benefits and burdens under the contract, were essential inducements in the formation of the contract, and, further, that the assignment was a repudiation of any future liability of the assignor. The attempted assignment before us altered the conditions and obligations of the undertaking. The appellee would here be obliged not only to perform the subsequent stipulations of the contract for the benefit of a stranger and in conformity with his will, but also to accept the performance of the stranger in place of that of the assignor with whom it contracted, and upon whose personal integrity, capacity, and management in the course of a particular business he must be assumed to have relied by reason of the very nature of the provisions of the contract and of the circumstances of the contracting parties. The nature and stipulations of the contract prevent it being implied that the nonassigning party had assented to such an assignment of rights and delegation of liabilities. The authorities are clear, on the facts at bar, that the appellant could not enforce the contract against the appellee. . . .

Judgment affirmed, with costs to the appellee.

NOTES & QUESTIONS

1. The first step toward clarity in treating issues of the sort involved in the *Crane Ice Cream Co.* case is precision in use of language. Regrettably,

lawyers and judges are often not precise. You will, for example, often hear discussions about whether someone "can assign the contract." That's always a terribly sloppy way of stating the question. One must distinguish two different sets of issues: (1) assignment of rights and (2) delegation of duties. Assume that a contract between A and B gives A certain rights and imposes on A certain duties. One set of questions is whether A can assign its rights to X, or, to be even more precise, what is the effect on B's duties if A attempts to assign its rights to X. Another set of questions is whether A can delegate its duties to X, or, to be more precise, what is the effect on B's duties if A attempts to delegate its duties of performance to X.

The *Crane Ice Cream Co.* deals principally with the assignment of rights issue. Under the agreement between Frederick and Terminal Freezing, Frederick had the right to receive from Terminal Freezing all of Frederick's requirements of ice, up to 250 tons per week, at a set price. Frederick attempted to transfer that right to Crane. The court held that the attempt to transfer that right was ineffective, that is, Terminal Freezing was not obligated to perform for Crane.

There might have been a delegation of duties issue in *Crane Ice Cream Co.* Note that the agreement between Frederick and Terminal Freezing provided that Frederick would pay for the ice delivered during the week on the following Tuesday, that is, Terminal Freezing was selling the ice to Frederick on short term credit. The delegation of duties issue would be what effect it would have on Terminal Freezing's obligations if Terminal Freezing learned that the payment was to be made not by Frederick but by Crane. As it happens, that issue was not really significant in the case, because the facts indicate that Crane was not insisting on receiving the ice on credit. Rather, Crane "was prepared to pay cash for all ice deliverable under the contract." We'll examine delegation of duties issues in the next section.

2.   Does it matter to Terminal Freezing whether it has to perform to Frederick or to Frederick's assignee Crane? Note that in the case itself, Terminal Freezing's promise was not to deliver a set quantity of ice, but to deliver all the ice that Frederick might require, up to 250 tons per week. Is there a significant difference between an obligation to deliver all the ice that Frederick might require, up to 250 tons per week, and an obligation to deliver all of the ice that Crane might require, up to 250 tons per week?

3.   "Requirements" contracts of the sort involved in *Crane Ice Cream Co.* present various legal issues. An old issue is whether Terminal Freezing's promise was enforceable at all, or whether Terminal Freezing might have been able to get out of its promise by arguing that it didn't really receive anything in exchange for that promise. The argument would be that Frederick's promise didn't really amount to anything real because Frederick didn't really promise to order any ice—only to order whatever amount Frederick wanted. Long ago, that would have presented some messy issues under the concept of consideration. A person in Terminal Freezing's position might have argued that its promise (even to Frederick) was not enforceable because not supported by "consideration." We explored some similar problems in Chapter 4.D.

The "consideration" problem is now pretty much resolved. All we need to do is to say that there really is some content to Frederick's promise to order its requirement of ice from Terminal Freezing. Article 2 of the U.C.C. does that by saying that a promise to supply the "requirements" of the buyer means "such actual . . . requirements as may occur in good faith, except that no quantity unreasonably disproportionate . . . to any normal or otherwise comparable prior . . . requirements may be . . . demanded." U.C.C. § 2–306(a). The idea is that by putting limits on the discretion of the buyer under a requirements agreement, we can provide sufficient content to the buyer's promise to provide consideration for the seller's promise. We saw a similar technique in *Wood v. Lucy, Lady Duff Gordon* in Chapter 4.D.

The resolution of the consideration issue might have an impact on the assignment issue in the *Crane Ice Cream Co.* itself. If Terminal Freezing's promise is not a promise to deliver whatever amount Frederick asks for, but rather is a promise to deliver an amount roughly proportionate to the amount that Frederick had been ordering in the past, then it's possible that one could say that Terminal Freezing is not really hurt if it must perform that promise to Crane instead of to Frederick. One could imagine arguments on both sides. Consider U.C.C. § 2–210(2) (which, like the wording of the Second Restatement § 317, does not allow an assignment, unless otherwise agreed, which would "materially change the duty of the other party, or increase materially the burden or risk imposed on him by his contract, or impair materially his chance of obtaining return performance"). The Official Comments to this section suggests that the good faith standard removes most of the "personal discretion" element.

The important point is to see that resolution of the assignment issue in *Crane Ice Cream Co.* turns on an assessment of the extent to which Terminal Freezing's position might be impaired if it has to perform for Crane instead of for Frederick.

4. Repudiation in *Crane*. U.C.C. 2–210(6) suggests that an assignment can be treated as "creating reasonable grounds for insecurity", which may allow that party to "demand assurances" from the assignee. Recall U.C.C. § 2–609 in Chapter 10.C. This issue is taken up in *Sally Beauty Co. v. Nexxus Products, Co,* below.

C. DELEGATION OF DUTIES

U.C.C. § 2–210(1)

Restatement (Second) of Contracts § 318

British Waggon Co. v. Lea & Co.

Court of Queen's Bench, 1880.
LR 5 Q.B.D. 149.

■ COCKBURN, C.J.

This was an action brought by the plaintiffs to recover rent for the hire of certain railway waggons, alleged to be payable by the defendants to the plaintiffs, or one of them, under the following circumstances:—

By an agreement in writing of the 10th of February, 1874, the Parkgate Waggon Company let to the defendants, who are coal merchants, fifty railway waggons for a term of seven years, at a yearly rent of 600l. a year, payable by equal quarterly payments. By a second agreement of the 13th of June, 1874, the company in like manner let to the defendants fifty other waggons, at a yearly rent of 625l., payable quarterly like the former.

Each of these agreements contained the following clause:

> "The owners, their executors, or administrators, will at all times during the said term, except as herein provided, keep the said waggons in good and substantial repair and working order, and, on receiving notice from the tenant of any want of repairs, and the number or numbers of the waggons requiring to be repaired, and the place or places where it or they then is or are, will, with all reasonable despatch, cause the same to be repaired and put into good working order."

On the 24th of October, 1874, the Parkgate Company passed a resolution, under the 129th section of the Companies Act, 1862, for the voluntary winding up of the company. Liquidators were appointed, and by an order of the Chancery Division of the High Court of Justice, it was ordered that the winding-up of the company should be continued under the supervision of the Court.

By an indenture of the 1st of April, 1878, the Parkgate Company assigned and transferred, and the liquidators confirmed to the British Company and their assigns, among other things, all sums of money, whether payable by way of rent, hire, interest, penalty, or damage, then due, or thereafter to become due, to the Parkgate Company, by virtue of the two contracts with the defendants, together with the benefit of the two contracts, and all the interest of the Parkgate Company and the said liquidators therein; the British Company, on the other hand covenanting with the Parkgate Company "to observe and perform such of the stipulations, conditions, provisions, and agreements contained in the said contracts as, according to the terms thereof were stipulated to be observed and performed by the Parkgate Company." On the execution of this assignment the British Company took over from the Parkgate Company the repairing stations, which had previously been used by the Parkgate Company for the repair of the waggons let to the defendants, and also the staff of workmen employed by the latter company in executing such repairs. It is expressly found that the British Company have ever since been ready and willing to execute, and have, with all due diligence, executed all necessary repairs to the said waggons. This, however, they have done under a special agreement come to between the parties since the present dispute has arisen, without prejudice to their respective rights.

In this state of things the defendants asserted their right to treat the contract as at an end, on the ground that the Parkgate Company had incapacitated themselves from performing the contract, first, by going into voluntary liquidation, secondly, by assigning the contracts, and giving up the repairing stations to the British Company, between whom and the defendants there was no privity of contract, and whose services, in substitution for those to be performed by the Parkgate Company under the contract, they the defendants were not bound to accept. The Parkgate Company not acquiescing in this view, it was agreed that the facts should be stated in a special case for the opinion of this Court, the use of the waggons by the defendants being in the meanwhile continued at a rate agreed on between the parties, without prejudice to either, with reference to their respective rights.

The first ground taken by the defendants is in our opinion altogether untenable in the present state of things, whatever it may be when the affairs of the company shall have been wound up, and the company itself shall have been dissolved under the 111th section of the Act. Pending the winding-up, the company is by the effect of §§ 95 and 131 kept alive, the liquidator having power to carry on the business, "so far as may be necessary for the beneficial winding-up of the company," which the continued letting of these waggons, and the receipt of the rent payable in respect of them, would, we presume, be.

What would be the position of the parties on the dissolution of the company it is unnecessary for the present purpose to consider.

The main contention on the part of the defendants, however, was that, as the Parkgate Company had, by assigning the contracts, and by making over their repairing stations to the British Company, incapacitated themselves to fulfil their obligation to keep the waggons in repair, that company had no right, as between themselves and the defendants, to substitute a third party to do the work they had engaged to perform, nor were the defendants bound to accept the party so substituted as the one to whom they were to look for performance of the contract; the contract was therefore at all end.

The authority principally relied on in support of this contention was the case of *Robson v. Drummond*, 2 B. & Ad. 303, approved of by this Court in *Humble v. Hunter*, 12 Q. B. 310. In *Robson v. Drummond* a carriage having been hired by the defendant of one Sharp, a coachmaker, for five years, at a yearly rent, payable in advance each year, the carriage to be kept in repair and painted once a year by the maker—Robson being then a partner in the business, but unknown to the defendant—on Sharp retiring from the business after three years had expired, and making over all interest in the business and property in the goods to Robson, it was held, that the defendant could not be sued on the contract—by Lord Tenterden on the ground that "the defendant might have been induced to enter into the contract by reason of the personal confidence which he reposed in Sharp, and therefore might have agreed to pay money in advance, for which reason the defendant had a right to object to its being performed by any other person;" and by Littledale and Parke, JJ., on the additional ground that the defendant had a right to the personal services of Sharp, and to the benefit of his judgment and taste, to the end of the contract.

. . . We entirely concur in the principle on which the decision in *Robson v. Drummond* rests, namely, that where a person contracts with another to do work or perform service, and it can be inferred that the person employed has been selected with reference to his individual skill, competency, or other personal qualification, the inability or unwillingness of the party so employed to execute the work or perform the service is a sufficient answer to any demand by a stranger to the original contract of the performance of it by the other party, and entitles the latter to treat the contract as at an end, notwithstanding that the person tendered to take the place of the contracting party may be equally well qualified to do the service. Personal performance is in such a case of the essence of the contract, which, consequently, cannot in its absence be enforced against an unwilling party. But this principle appears to us inapplicable in the present instance, inasmuch as we cannot suppose that in stipulating for the repair of these waggons by the company—a rough description of work which ordinary workmen conversant with the business would be perfectly able to execute—the defendants attached any importance to whether the repairs were done by the company, or by any one with whom the company might enter into a subsidiary contract to do the work. All that the hirers, the defendants, cared for in this stipulation was that the waggons should be kept in repair; it was indifferent to them by whom the repairs should be done. Thus if, without going into liquidation, or assigning these contracts, the company had entered into a contract with any competent party to do the repairs, and so had procured them to be done, we cannot think that this would have been a departure from the terms of the contract to keep the waggons in repair. While fully acquiescing in the general principle just referred to, we must take care not to push it beyond reasonable limits. And we cannot but think that, in applying the principle, the Court of Queen's Bench in *Robson v.*

Drummond went to the utmost length to which it can be carried, as it is difficult to see how in repairing a carriage when necessary, or painting it once a year, preference would be given to one coachmaker over another. Much work is contracted for, which it is known can only be executed by means of subcontracts; much is contracted for as to which it is indifferent to the party for whom it is to be done, whether it is done by the immediate party to the contract, or by someone on his behalf. . . .

In the view we take of the case, therefore, the repair of the waggons, undertaken and done by the British Company under their contract with the Parkgate Company, is a sufficient performance by the latter of their engagement to repair under their contract with the defendants. Consequently, so long as the Parkgate Company continues to exist, and, through the British Company, continues to fulfil its obligation to keep the waggons in repair, the defendants cannot, in our opinion, be heard to say that the former company is not entitled to the performance of the contract by them, on the ground that the company have incapacitated themselves from performing their obligations under it, or that, by transferring the performance thereof to others, they have absolved the defendants from further performance on their part. . . .

We are therefore of opinion that our judgment must be for the plaintiffs for the amount claimed.

Sally Beauty Co. v. Nexxus Products Co.

United States Court of Appeals, Seventh Circuit, 1986.
801 F.2d 1001.

■ CUDAHY, CIRCUIT JUDGE.

Nexxus Products Company ("Nexxus") entered into a contract with Best Barber & Beauty Supply Company, Inc. ("Best"), under which Best would be the exclusive distributor of Nexxus hair care products to barbers and hair stylists throughout most of Texas. When Best was acquired by and merged into Sally Beauty Company, Inc. ("Sally Beauty"), Nexxus cancelled the agreement. Sally Beauty is a wholly-owned subsidiary of Alberto-Culver Company ("Alberto-Culver"), a major manufacturer of hair care products and a competitor of Nexxus'. Sally Beauty claims that Nexxus breached the contract by cancelling; Nexxus asserts by way of defense that the contract was not assignable or, in the alternative, not assignable to Sally Beauty. The district court granted Nexxus' motion for summary judgment, ruling that the contract was one for personal services and therefore not assignable. We affirm on a different theory—that this contract could not be assigned to the wholly—owned subsidiary of a direct competitor under section 2–210 of the Uniform Commercial Code.

I.

Only the basic facts are undisputed and they are as follows. Prior to its merger with Sally Beauty, Best was a Texas corporation in the business of distributing beauty and hair care products to retail stores, barber shops and beauty salons throughout Texas. Between March and July 1979, Mark Reichek, Best's president, negotiated with Stephen Redding, Nexxus' vice-president, over a possible distribution agreement between Best and Nexxus. Nexxus, founded in 1979, is a California corporation that formulates and markets hair care products. Nexxus does not market its products to retail stores, preferring to sell them to independent distributors for resale to barbers and beauticians. On August 2, 1979, Nexxus executed a distributorship agreement with Best, in the form of a July 24, 1979 letter from Reichek, for Best, to Redding, for Nexxus:

Dear Steve:

It was a pleasure meeting with you and discussing the distribution of Nexus Products. The line is very exciting and we feel we can do a substantial job with it—especially as the exclusive distributor in Texas (except El Paso).

If I understand the pricing structure correctly, we would pay $1.50 for an item that retails for $5.00 (less 50%, less 40% off retail), and Nexus will pay the freight charges regardless of order size. This approach to pricing will enable us to price the items in the line in such a way that they will be attractive and profitable to the salons.

Your offer of assistance in promoting the line seems to be designed to simplify the introduction of Nexus Products into the Texas market. It indicates a sincere desire on your part to assist your distributors. By your agreeing to underwrite the cost of training and maintaining a qualified technician in our territory, we should be able to introduce the line from a position of strength. I am sure you will let us know at least 90 days in advance should you want to change this arrangement.

By offering to provide us with the support necessary to conduct an annual seminar (ie. mailers, guest artisit [sic]) at your expense, we should be able to reenforce our position with Nexus users and introduce the product line to new customers in a professional manner.

To satisfy your requirement of assured payment for merchandise received, each of our purchase orders will be accompanied by a Letter of Credit that will become negotiable when we receive the merchandise. I am sure you will agree that this arrangement is fairest for everybody concerned.

While we feel confident that we can do an outstanding job with the Nexus line and that the volume we generate will adequately compensate you for your continued support, it is usually best to have an understanding should we no longer be distributing Nexus Products—either by our desire or your request. Based on our discussions, cancellation or termination of Best Barber & Beauty Supply Co., Inc. as a distributor can only take place on the anniversary date of our original appointment as a distributor—and then only with 120 days prior notice. If Nexus terminates us, Nexus will buy back all of our inventory at cost and will pay the freight charges on the returned merchandise.

Steve, we feel that the Nexus line is exciting and very promotable. With the program outlined in this letter, we feel it can be mutually profitable and look forward to a long and successful business relationship. If you agree that this letter contains the details of our understanding regarding the distribution of Nexus Products, please sign the acknowledgment below and return one copy of this letter to me.

Very truly yours,

/s/ Mark E. Reichek

President

Acknowledged /s/ Stephen Redding

Date 8/2/79

In July 1981 Sally Beauty acquired Best in a stock purchase transaction and Best was merged into Sally Beauty, which succeeded to Best's rights and interests in all of Best's contracts. Sally Beauty, a Delaware corporation with its principal place of business in Texas, is a wholly-owned subsidiary of Alberto-Culver. Sally Beauty, like Best, is a distributor of hair care and beauty products to retail stores and hair styling salons. Alberto-Culver is a major manufacturer of hair care products and, thus, is a direct competitor of Nexxus in the hair care market.

Shortly after the merger, Redding met with Michael Renzulli, president of Sally Beauty, to discuss the Nexxus distribution agreement. After the meeting, Redding wrote Renzulli a letter stating that Nexxus would not allow Sally Beauty, a wholly-owned subsidiary of a direct competitor, to distribute Nexxus products:

As we discussed in New Orleans, we have great reservations about allowing our NEXXUS Products to be distributed by a company which is, in essence, a direct competitor. We appreciate your argument of autonomy for your business, but the fact remains that you are totally owned by Alberto-Culver.

Since we see no way of justifying this conflict, we cannot allow our products to be distributed by Sally Beauty Company.

In August 1983 Sally Beauty commenced this action . . .

II.

Sally Beauty's breach of contract claim alleges that by acquiring Best, Sally Beauty succeeded to all of Best's rights and obligations under the distribution agreement. It further alleges that Nexxus breached the agreement by failing to give Sally Beauty 120 days notice prior to terminating the agreement and by terminating it on other than an anniversary date of its formation. Nexxus, in its motion for summary judgment, argued that the distribution agreement it entered into with Best was a contract for personal services, based upon a relationship of personal trust and confidence between Reichek and the Redding family. As such, the contract could not be assigned to Sally without Nexxus' consent.

In opposing this motion Sally Beauty argued that the contract was freely assignable because (1) it was between two corporations, not two individuals and (2) the character of the performance would not be altered by the substitution of Sally Beauty for Best. It also argued that "the Distribution Agreement is nothing more than a simple, non-exclusive contract for the distribution of goods, the successful performance of which is in no way dependent upon any particular personality, individual skill or confidential relationship."

In ruling on this motion, the district court framed the issue before it as "whether the contract at issue here between Best and Nexxus was of a personal nature such that it was not assignable without Nexxus' consent." It ruled:

> The court is convinced, based upon the nature of the contract and the circumstances surrounding its formation, that the contract at issue here was of such a nature that it was not assignable without Nexxus's consent. First, the very nature of the contract itself suggests its personal character. A distribution agreement is a contract whereby a manufacturer gives another party the right to distribute its products. It is clearly a contract for the performance of a service. In the court's view, the mere selection by a manufacturer of a party to distribute its goods presupposes a reliance and confidence by the manufacturer on the integrity and abilities of the other party. . . . In addition, . . . Stephen Redding, Nexxus's vice-president, travelled to Texas and met with Best's president personally for several days before making the decision to award the Texas distributorship to Best. Best itself had been in the hair care business for 40 years and its president Mark Reichek had extensive experience in the industry. It is reasonable to conclude that Stephen Redding and Nexxus would want its distributor to be experienced and knowledgeable in the hair care field and that the selection of Best was based upon personal factors such as these.

The district court also rejected the contention that the character of performance would not be altered by a substitution of Sally Beauty for

Best: "Unlike Best, Sally Beauty is a subsidiary of one of Nexxus' direct competitors. This is a significant distinction and in the court's view, it raises serious questions regarding Sally Beauty's ability to perform the distribution agreement in the same manner as Best."

We cannot affirm this summary judgment on the grounds relied on by the district court. Under Fed.R.Civ.P. 56(c) summary judgment may be granted only where there is no genuine issue as to any material fact and the moving party is entitled to judgment as a matter of law. . . . Although it might be "reasonable to conclude" that Best and Nexxus had based their agreement on "a relationship of personal trust and confidence," and that Reichek's participation was considered essential to Best's performance, this is a finding of fact. *See Phillips v. Oil, Inc.,* 104 S.W.2d 576, 579 (Tex.Civ.App.1937, writ ref'd n.r.e.) (question whether contract was entered into because of parties' "personal confidence and trust" is for the determination of trier of fact). Since the parties submitted conflicting affidavits on this question,[3] the district court erred in relying on Nexxus' view as representing undisputed fact in ruling on this summary judgment motion. *See Cedillo v. Local 1, International Association of Bridge & Structural Iron Workers,* 603 F.2d 7, 11 (7th Cir.1979) ("questions of motive and intent are particularly inappropriate for summary adjudication").[4]

We may affirm this summary judgment, however, on a different ground if it finds support in the record. *United States v. Winthrop Towers,* 628 F.2d 1028, 1037 (7th Cir.1980). Sally Beauty contends that the distribution agreement is freely assignable because it is governed by the provisions of the Uniform Commercial Code (the "UCC" or the "Code"), as adopted in Texas. We agree with Sally that the provisions of the UCC govern this contract and for that reason hold that the assignment of the contract by Best to Sally Beauty was barred by the UCC rules on

---

[3] Reichek stated the following in an affidavit submitted in support of Sally Beauty's Memorandum in Opposition to Nexxus' Motion for Summary Judgment:

At no time prior to the execution of the Distribution Agreement did Steve Redding tell me that he was relying upon my personal peculiar tastes and ability in making his decision to award a Nexxus distributorship to Best. Moreover, I never understood that Steve Redding was relying upon my skill and ability in particular in choosing Best as a distributor.

I never considered the Distribution Agreement to be a personal service contract between me and Nexxus or Stephen Redding. I always considered the Distribution Agreement to be between Best and Nexxus as expressly provided in the Distribution Agreement which was written by my brother and me. At all times I conducted business with Nexxus on behalf of Best and not on my own behalf. In that connection, when I sent correspondence to Nexxus, I invariably signed it as president of Best.

Neither Stephen Redding nor any other Nexxus employee ever told me that Nexxus was relying on my personal financial integrity in executing the Distribution Agreement or in shipping Nexxus products to Best. . . .

Affidavit of Mark Reichek, ¶¶ 19–21, Appellant's Appendix at 189–190.

[4] It is also possible to read the district court's decision as ruling that all distribution agreements are as a matter of law personal services contracts and therefore nonassignable. For the reasons explained *infra,* we do not believe that this is an accurate statement of the law.

delegation of performance, UCC § 2–210(1), Tex.Bus & Com.Code Ann. § 2–210(a) (Vernon 1968).

III.

The UCC codifies the law of contracts applicable to "transactions in goods." UCC § 2–102, Tex.Bus. & Com.Code Ann. § 2–102 (Vernon 1968). Texas applies the "dominant factor" test to determine whether the UCC applies to a given contract or transaction: was the essence of or dominant factor in the formation of the contract the provision of goods or services? *Montgomery Ward & Co., Inc. v. Dalton,* 665 S.W.2d 507, 511 (Tex.App.1984) (contract for repair of roof predominantly involves services); *Garcia v. Rutledge,* 649 S.W.2d 307, 310 (Tex.App.1982) (contract for repair of truck predominantly a contract for services); *Potts v. W.Q. Richards Memorial Hospital,* 558 S.W.2d 939, 946 (Tex.Civ.App.1977) (essence of hospital stay is the furnishing of services); *Freeman v. Shannon Construction, Inc.,* 560 S.W.2d 732, 738 (Tex.Civ.App.1977) (sale of bulk cement in construction contract outweighed by predominant service of building structure). No Texas case addresses whether a distribution agreement is a contract for the sale of goods, but the rule in the majority of jurisdictions is that distributorships (both exclusive and non-exclusive) are to be treated as sale of goods contracts under the UCC. *See Kirby v. Chrysler Corp.,* 554 F.Supp. 743 (D.Md.1982) (automobile dealership) (applying Maryland law); *Quality Performance Lines v. Yoho Automotive, Inc.,* 609 P.2d 1340 (Utah 1980) (automotive parts distribution contract); *Meuse-Rhine-Ijssel Cattle Breeders of Canada, Ltd. v. Y Tex Corp.,* 590 P.2d 1300 (Wyo.1979) (cattle semen exclusive dealing contract); *Corenswet v. Amana Refrigeration, Inc.,* 594 F.2d 129 (5th Cir.), *cert. denied,* 444 U.S. 938, 100 S.Ct. 288, 62 L.Ed.2d 198 (1979) (exclusive refrigerator distributorship) (applying Iowa law); *Leibel v. Raynor Manufacturing Co.,* 571 S.W.2d 640 (Ky.App.1978) (exclusive garage door distributorship); *Warrick Beverage Corp. v. Miller Brewing Co.,* 170 Ind.App. 114, 352 N.E.2d 496 (1976) (exclusive beer distribution contract); *Ashland Oil, Inc. v. Donahue,* 159 W.Va. 463, 223 S.E.2d 433 (1976) (gas station dealership); *Aaron E. Levine & Co. v. Calkraft Paper Co.,* 429 F.Supp. 1039 (E.D.Mich.1976) (paper products distributorship) (applying Michigan law); *Artman v. International Harvester Co.,* 355 F.Supp. 482 (W.D.Pa.1973) (truck distribution franchise) (Pennsylvania law). *See also Zapatha v. Dairy-Mart, Inc.,* 381 Mass. 284, 408 N.E.2d 1370 (1980) (dicta); * * * *But see Vigano v. Wylain, Inc.,* 633 F.2d 522 (8th Cir.1980) (federal court bound to apply Missouri rule that UCC does not cover distribution agreements).

Several of these courts note that "a distributorship agreement is more involved than a typical sales contract," *Quality Performance Lines,* 609 P.2d at 1342, but apply the UCC nonetheless because the sales aspect in such a contract is predominant. *See Corenswet,* 594 F.2d at 134 ("Although most distributorship agreements, like franchise agreements, are more than sales contracts, the courts have not hesitated to apply the

Uniform Commercial Code to cases involving such agreements.");
Zapatha, 408 N.E.2d at 1374–75 n. 8 (courts have applied UCC to
distribution agreements because the sales aspect is predominant). This
is true of the contract at issue here (as embodied in the July 24, 1979
letter from Reichek to Redding). Most of the agreed-to terms deal with
Nexxus' sale of its hair care products to Best. We are confident that a
Texas court would find the sales aspect of this contract dominant and
apply the majority rule that such a distributorship is a contract for
"goods" under the UCC.

IV.

The fact that this contract is considered a contract for the sale of
goods and not for the provision of a service does not, as Sally Beauty
suggests, mean that it is freely assignable in all circumstances. The
delegation of performance under a sales contract (whether in conjunction
with an assignment of rights, as here, or not) is governed by UCC section
2–210(1), Tex.Bus. & Com.Code § 2–210(a) (Vernon 1968). The UCC
recognizes that in many cases an obligor will find it convenient or even
necessary to relieve himself of the duty of performance under a contract,
see Official Comment 1, UCC § 2–210 ("[T]his section recognizes both
delegation of performance and assignability as normal and permissible
incidents of a contract for the sale of goods."). The Code therefore
sanctions delegation except where the delegated performance would be
unsatisfactory to the obligee: "A party may perform his duty through a
delegate unless otherwise agreed to or unless the other party has a
substantial interest in having his original promisor perform or control
the acts required by the contract." UCC § 2–210(1), Tex.Bus. & Com.Code
Ann. § 2–210(a) (Vernon 1968). Consideration is given to balancing the
policies of free alienability of commercial contracts and protecting the
obligee from having to accept a bargain he did not contract for.

We are concerned here with the delegation of Best's duty of
performance under the distribution agreement, as Nexxus terminated
the agreement because it did not wish to accept Sally Beauty's
substituted performance. Only one Texas case has construed section 2–
210 in the context of a party's delegation of performance under an
executory contract. In *McKinnie v. Milford,* 597 S.W.2d 953
(Tex.Civ.App.1980, writ ref'd, n.r.e.), the court held that nothing in the
Texas Business and Commercial Code prevented the seller of a horse
from delegating to the buyer a pre-existing contractual duty to make the
horse available to a third party for breeding. "[I]t is clear that Milford
[the third party] had no particular interest in not allowing Stewart [the
seller] to delegate the duties required by the contract. Milford was only
interested in getting his two breedings per year, and such performance
could only be obtained from McKinnie [the buyer] after he bought the
horse from Stewart." *Id.* at 957. In *McKinnie,* the Texas court recognized
and applied the UCC rule that bars delegation of duties if there is some

reason why the non-assigning party would find performance by a delegate a substantially different thing than what he had bargained for.

In the exclusive distribution agreement before us, Nexxus had contracted for Best's "best efforts" in promoting the sale of Nexxus products in Texas. UCC § 2–306(2), Tex.Bus. & Com.Code Ann. § 2–306(b) (Vernon 1968), states that "[a] lawful agreement by either buyer or seller for exclusive dealing in the kind of goods concerned imposes unless otherwise agreed an obligation by the seller to use best efforts to supply the goods and by the buyer to use best efforts to promote their sale." This implied promise on Best's part was the consideration for Nexxus' promise to refrain from supplying any other distributors within Best's exclusive area. *See* Official Comment 5, UCC § 2–306. It was this contractual undertaking which Nexxus refused to see performed by Sally.

In ruling on Nexxus' motion for summary judgment, the district court noted: "Unlike Best, Sally Beauty is a subsidiary of one of Nexxus' direct competitors. This is a significant distinction and in the court's view, it raises serious questions regarding Sally Beauty's ability to perform the distribution agreement in the same manner as Best." * * * In *Berliner Foods Corp. v. Pillsbury Co.,* 633 F.Supp. 557 (D.Md.1986), the court stated the same reservation more strongly on similar facts. Berliner was an exclusive distributor of Haagen-Dazs ice cream when it was sold to Breyer's, manufacturer of a competing ice cream line. Pillsbury Co., manufacturer of Haagen-Dazs, terminated the distributorship and Berliner sued. The court noted, while weighing the factors for and against a preliminary injunction, that "it defies common sense to require a manufacturer to leave the distribution of its products to a distributor under the control of a competitor or potential competitor." *Id.* at 559–60.[7] We agree with these assessments and hold that Sally Beauty's position as a wholly-owned subsidiary of Alberto-Culver is sufficient to bar the delegation of Best's duties under the agreement.

We do not believe that our holding will work the mischief with our national economy that the appellants predict. We hold merely that the duty of performance under an exclusive distributorship may not be delegated to a competitor in the market place—or the wholly-owned subsidiary of a competitor—without the obligee's consent. We believe that such a rule is consonant with the policies behind section 2–210, which is concerned with preserving the bargain the obligee has struck. Nexxus should not be required to accept the "best efforts" of Sally Beauty when those efforts are subject to the control of Alberto-Culver. It is entirely reasonable that Nexxus should conclude that this performance would be a different thing than what it had bargained for. At oral argument, Sally Beauty argued that the case should go to trial to allow

---

[7] The effort by the dissent to distinguish *Berliner* merely because the court there apparently assumed in passing that distributorship agreements were a species of personal service contracts must fail. The *Berliner* court emphasizes that the sale of a distributorship to a competitor of the supplier is by itself a wholly sufficient reason to terminate the distributorship.

it to demonstrate that it could and would perform the contract as impartially as Best. It stressed that Sally Beauty is a "multi-line" distributor, which means that it distributes many brands and is not just a conduit for Alberto-Culver products. But we do not think that this creates a material question of fact in this case.[8] When performance of personal services is delegated, the trier merely determines that it is a personal services contract. If so, the duty is *per se* nondelegable. There is no inquiry into whether the delegate is as skilled or worthy of trust and confidence as the original obligor: the delegate was not bargained for and the obligee need not consent to the substitution.[9] And so here . . . The risk of an unfavorable outcome is not one which the law can force Nexxus to take. Nexxus has a substantial interest in not seeing this contract performed by Sally Beauty, which is sufficient to bar the delegation under section 2–210, Tex. Bus. Com. Code Ann. § 2–210 (Vernon 1968). Because Nexxus should not be forced to accept performance of the distributorship agreement by Sally, we hold that the contract was not assignable without Nexxus' consent.[10]

The judgment of the district court is Affirmed.

■ POSNER, CIRCUIT JUDGE, dissenting.

My brethren have decided, with no better foundation than judicial intuition about what businessmen consider reasonable, that the Uniform Commercial Code gives a supplier an absolute right to cancel an exclusive-dealing contract if the dealer is acquired, directly or indirectly, by a competitor of the supplier. I interpret the Code differently.

Nexxus makes products for the hair and sells them through distributors to hair salons and barbershops. It gave a contract to Best, cancellable on any anniversary of the contract with 120 days' notice, to be its exclusive distributor in Texas. Two years later Best was acquired by and merged into Sally Beauty, a distributor of beauty supplies and wholly owned subsidiary of Alberto-Culver. Alberto-Culver makes "hair care" products, too, though they mostly are cheaper than Nexxus's, and are sold to the public primarily through grocery stores and drugstores. My brethren conclude that because there is at least a loose competitive

---

[8] We do not address here the situation in which the assignee is not completely under the control of a competitor. If the assignee were only a partially-owned subsidiary, there presumably would have to be fact-finding about the degree of control the competitor-parent had over the subsidiary's business decisions.

[9] Of course, the obligee makes such an assessment of the prospective delegate. If it thinks the delegated performance will be as satisfactory, it is of course free to consent to the delegation. Thus, the dissent is mistaken in its suggestion that we find it improper—a "conflict of interest"— for one competitor to distribute another competitor's products. Rather, we believe only that it is commercially reasonable that the supplier in those circumstances have consented to such a state of affairs. To borrow the dissent's example, Isuzu allows General Motors to distribute its cars because it considers this arrangement attractive.

Nor is distrust of one's competitors a trait unique to lawyers (as opposed to ordinary businessmen), as the dissent may be understood to suggest.

[10] This disposition makes it unnecessary to address Nexxus' argument that Sally Beauty breached the distribution agreement by not giving Nexxus 120 days' notice of the Best-Sally Beauty merger.

relationship between Nexxus and Alberto-Culver, Sally Beauty cannot—as a matter of law, cannot, for there has been no trial on the issue—provide its "best efforts" in the distribution of Nexxus products. Since a commitment to provide best efforts is read into every exclusive-dealing contract by section 2–306(2) of the Uniform Commercial Code, the contract has been broken and Nexxus can repudiate it. Alternatively, Nexxus had "a substantial interest in having his original promisor perform or control the acts required by the contract," and therefore the delegation of the promisor's (Best's) duties to Sally Beauty was improper under section 2–210(1).

My brethren's conclusion that these provisions of the Uniform Commercial Code entitled Nexxus to cancel the contract does not leap out from the language of the provisions or of the contract; so one would expect, but does not find, a canvass of the relevant case law. My brethren cite only one case in support of their conclusion: a district court case from Maryland, *Berliner Foods Corp. v. Pillsbury Co.,* 633 F.Supp. 557 (D.Md.1986), which, since it treated the contract at issue there as one for personal services, *id.* at 559 (a characterization my brethren properly reject for the contract between Nexxus and Best), is not helpful. *Berliner* is the latest in a long line of cases that make the propriety of delegating the performance of a distribution contract depend on whether or not the contract calls for the distributor's personal (unique, irreplaceable, distinctive, and therefore nondelegable) services. See, e.g., *Bancroft v. Scribner,* 72 Fed. 988 (9th Cir.1896); *Detroit Postage Stamp Service Co. v. Schermack,* 179 Mich. 266, 146 N.W. 144 (1914); *W.H. Barbor Agency Co. v. Co-Op. Barrel Co.,* 133 Minn. 207, 158 N.W. 38 (1916); *Paige v. Faure,* 229 N.Y. 114, 127 N.E. 898 (1920). By rejecting that characterization here, my brethren have sawn off the only limb on which they might have sat comfortably.

A slightly better case for them * * * is *Wetherell Bros. Co. v. United States Steel Co.,* 200 F.2d 761, 763 (1st Cir.1952), which held that an exclusive sales agent's duties were nondelegable. The agent, a Massachusetts corporation, had agreed to use its "best endeavors" to promote the sale of the defendant's steel in the New England area. The corporation was liquidated and its assets sold to a Pennsylvania corporation that was not shown to be qualified to conduct business in Massachusetts, the largest state in New England. On these facts the defendant was entitled to treat the liquidation and sale as a termination of the contract. The *Wetherell* decision has been understood to depend on its facts. See *Jennings v. Foremost Dairies, Inc.,* 37 Misc.2d 328, 235 N.Y.S.2d 566, 574 (1962); 4 Corbin on Contracts, 1971 Pocket Part § 865, at p. 128. The facts of the present case are critically different. So far as appears, the same people who distributed Nexxus's products for Best (except for Best's president) continued to do so for Sally Beauty. Best was acquired, and continues, as a going concern; the corporation was dissolved, but the business wasn't. Whether there was a delegation of performance in any sense may be doubted. Cf *Rossetti v. City of New Britain,* 163 Conn. 283, 303 A.2d 714, 718–19 (1972). The general rule is that a change of corporate form—including a merger—does not in and of itself affect contractual rights and obligations. *United States Shoe Corp. v. Hackett,* 793 F.2d 161, 163–64 (7th Cir.1986).

The fact that Best's president has quit cannot be decisive on the issue whether the merger resulted in a delegation of performance. The contract between Nexxus and Best was not a personal-services contract conditioned on a particular individual's remaining with Best. Compare *Jennings v. Foremost Dairies, Inc., supra,* 235 N.Y.S.2d at 574. If Best had not been acquired, but its president had left anyway, as of course he might have done, Nexxus could not have repudiated the contract.

No case adopts the per se rule that my brethren announce. The cases ask whether, as a matter of fact, a change in business form is likely to impair performance of the contract. *Wetherell* asked this. . . . *Green v. Camlin,* 229 S.C. 129, 92 S.E.2d 125, 127 (1956), has some broad language which my brethren might have cited; but since the contract in that case forbade assignment it is not an apt precedent.

My brethren find this a simple case—as simple (it seems) as if a lawyer had undertaken to represent the party opposing his client. But notions of conflict of interest are not the same in law and in business, and judges can go astray by assuming that the legal-services industry is the pattern for the entire economy. The lawyerization of America has not reached that point. Sally Beauty, though a wholly owned subsidiary of Alberto-Culver, distributes "hair care" supplies made by many different companies, which so far as appears compete with Alberto-Culver as vigorously as Nexxus does. Steel companies both make fabricated steel and sell raw steel to competing fabricators. General Motors sells cars manufactured by a competitor, Isuzu. What in law would be considered a fatal conflict of interest is in business a commonplace and legitimate practice. The lawyer is a fiduciary of his client; Best was not a fiduciary of Nexxus.

Selling your competitor's products, or supplying inputs to your competitor, sometimes creates problems under antitrust or regulatory law—but only when the supplier or distributor has monopoly or market power and uses it to restrict a competitor's access to an essential input or to the market for the competitor's output, as in *Otter Tail Power Co. v. United States,* 410 U.S. 366, 93 S.Ct. 1022, 35 L.Ed.2d 359 (1973), or *FTC v. Brown Shoe Co.,* 384 U.S. 316, 86 S.Ct. 1501, 16 L.Ed.2d 587 (1966), or *United Air Lines, Inc. v. CAB,* 766 F.2d 1107, 1114–15 (7th Cir.1985). * * * There is no suggestion that Alberto-Culver has a monopoly of "hair care" products or Sally Beauty a monopoly of distributing such products, or that Alberto-Culver would ever have ordered Sally Beauty to stop carrying Nexxus products. Far from complaining about being squeezed out of the market by the acquisition, Nexxus is complaining in effect about Sally Beauty's refusal to boycott it!

How likely is it that the acquisition of Best could hurt Nexxus? Not very. Suppose Alberto-Culver had ordered Sally Beauty to go slow in pushing Nexxus products, in the hope that sales of Alberto-Culver "hair care" products would rise. Even if they did, since the market is competitive Alberto-Culver would not reap monopoly profits. Moreover, what guarantee has Alberto-Culver that consumers would be diverted from Nexxus to it, rather than to products closer in price and quality to Nexxus products? In any event, any trivial gain in profits to Alberto-Culver would be offset by the loss of goodwill to Sally Beauty; and a cost to Sally Beauty is a cost to Alberto-Culver, its parent. Remember that Sally Beauty carries beauty supplies made by other competitors of Alberto-Culver; Best alone carries "hair care" products manufactured by Revlon, Clairol, Bristol-Myers, and L'Oreal, as well as Alberto-Culver. Will these powerful competitors continue to distribute their products through Sally Beauty if Sally Beauty displays favoritism for Alberto-Culver products? Would not such a display be a commercial disaster for Sally Beauty, and hence for its parent, Alberto-Culver? Is it really credible that Alberto-Culver would sacrifice Sally Beauty in a vain effort to monopolize the "hair care" market, in violation of section 2 of the Sherman Act? Is not the ratio of the profits that Alberto-Culver obtains from Sally Beauty to the profits it obtains from the manufacture of "hair care" products at least a relevant consideration?

Another relevant consideration is that the contract between Nexxus and Best was for a short term. Could Alberto-Culver destroy Nexxus by failing to push its products with maximum vigor in Texas for a year? In the unlikely event that it could and did, it would be liable in damages to Nexxus for breach of the implied best-efforts term of the distribution contract. Finally, it is obvious that Sally Beauty does not have a bottleneck position in the distribution of "hair care" products, such that by refusing to promote Nexxus products vigorously it could stifle the distribution of those products in Texas; for Nexxus has found alternative distribution that it prefers—otherwise it wouldn't have repudiated the contract with Best when Best was acquired by Sally Beauty.

Not all businessmen are consistent and successful profit maximizers, so the probability that Alberto-Culver would instruct Sally Beauty to cease to push Nexxus products vigorously in Texas cannot be reckoned at zero. On this record, however, it is slight. And there is no principle of law that if something happens that trivially reduces the probability that a dealer will use his best efforts, the supplier can cancel the contract. Suppose there had been no merger, but the only child of Best's president had gone to work for Alberto-Culver as a chemist. Could Nexxus have canceled the contract, fearing that Best (perhaps unconsciously) would favor Alberto-Culver products over Nexxus products? That would be an absurd ground for cancellation, and so is Nexxus's actual ground. At most, so far as the record shows, Nexxus may have had grounds for "insecurity" regarding the performance by Sally Beauty of its obligation to use its best efforts to promote Nexxus products, but if so its remedy was not to cancel the contract but to demand assurances of due performance. See UCC § 2–609; Official Comment 5 to § 2–306. No such demand was made. An anticipatory repudiation by conduct requires conduct that makes the repudiating party unable to perform. Farnsworth, Contracts 636 (1982). The merger did not do this. At least there is no evidence it did. The judgment should be reversed and the case remanded for a trial on whether the merger so altered the conditions of performance that Nexxus is entitled to declare the contract broken.

PROBLEM

In considering delegation of duties issues, it's important to try to separate various different issues. To facilitate that task, let's start with a very simple form of agreement: Bank lends money to Rogers, and Rogers promises to repay the money to Bank.

Suppose Rogers attempts to delegate his duties to Young. Think carefully about various different legal issues:

First, there is the question whether the delegate (Young) has made a promise (to Rogers) that the delegate will perform Rogers' promise to Bank. That would be described as an issue of "assumption," that is, did Young assume Rogers' obligation.

Second, if we conclude that the answer to the first question is that Young did assume Rogers' obligation to Bank, we might ask whether Bank can sue to enforce Young's promise (made to Rogers) to perform Rogers' promise. That's a third party beneficiary issue, though, as it turns out, it's a fairly simple one.

Third, we can consider whether Bank has, by explicit agreement or by conduct, agreed to release Rogers. That would be described as an issue of "novation."

Fourth, there is the question whether Bank is obliged to accept performance from the delegate. That's the actual "delegation of duties" issue considered in *British Waggon Co v. Lea & Co.* and *Sally Beauty Co. v. Nexxus Products Co.* In connection with that issue, suppose that Bank learns that Rogers has arranged to have the promise (to repay) performed by Young. What can Bank do if Bank is unhappy about that?

CHAPTER THIRTEEN

PROPER SCOPE OF CONTRACT LAW

> Never promise more than you can perform
>
> —Publilius (Publius) Syrus

In re Baby M
Supreme Court of New Jersey, 1988.
109 N.J. 396, 537 A.2d 1227.

In this matter the Court is asked to determine the validity of a contract that purports to provide a new way of bringing children into a family. For a fee of $10,000, a woman agrees to be artificially inseminated with the semen of another woman's husband; she is to conceive a child, carry it to term, and after its birth surrender it to the natural father and his wife. The intent of the contract is that the child's natural mother will thereafter be forever separated from her child. The wife is to adopt the child, and she and the natural father are to be regarded as its parents for all purposes. The contract providing for this is called a "surrogacy contract," the natural mother inappropriately called the "surrogate mother."

We invalidate the surrogacy contract because it conflicts with the law and public policy of this State. While we recognize the depth of the yearning of infertile couples to have their own children, we find the payment of money to a "surrogate" mother illegal, perhaps criminal, and potentially degrading to women. Although in this case we grant custody to the natural father, the evidence having clearly proved such custody to be in the best interests of the infant, we void both the termination of the surrogate mother's parental rights and the adoption of the child by the wife/stepparent. We thus restore the "surrogate" as the mother of the child. We remand the issue of the natural mother's visitation rights to the trial court, since that issue was not reached below and the record before us is not sufficient to permit us to decide it *de novo*.

We find no offense to our present laws where a woman voluntarily and without payment agrees to act as a "surrogate" mother, provided that she is not subject to a binding agreement to surrender her child. Moreover, our holding today does not preclude the Legislature from altering the current statutory scheme, within constitutional limits, so as to permit surrogacy contracts. Under current law, however, the surrogacy agreement before us is illegal and invalid.

I.

FACTS

In February 1985, William Stern and Mary Beth Whitehead entered into a surrogacy contract. It recited that Stern's wife, Elizabeth, was infertile, that they wanted a child, and that Mrs. Whitehead was willing to provide that child as the mother with Mr. Stern as the father.

The contract provided that through artificial insemination using Mr. Stern's sperm, Mrs. Whitehead would become pregnant, carry the child to term, bear it, deliver it to the Sterns, and thereafter do whatever was necessary to terminate her maternal rights so that Mrs. Stern could thereafter adopt the child. Mrs. Whitehead's husband, Richard,[1] was also a party to the contract; Mrs. Stern was not. Mr. Whitehead promised to do all acts necessary to rebut the presumption of paternity under the Parentage Act. *N.J.S.A.* 9:17–43a(1), –44a. Although Mrs. Stern was not a party to the surrogacy agreement, the contract gave her sole custody of the child in the event of Mr. Stern's death. Mrs. Stern's status as a nonparty to the surrogate parenting agreement presumably was to avoid the application of the baby-selling statute to this arrangement. *N.J.S.A.* 9:3–54.

Mr. Stern, on his part, agreed to attempt the artificial insemination and to pay Mrs. Whitehead $10,000 after the child's birth, on its delivery to him. In a separate contract, Mr. Stern agreed to pay $7,500 to the Infertility Center of New York ("ICNY"). The Center's advertising campaigns solicit surrogate mothers and encourage infertile couples to consider surrogacy. ICNY arranged for the surrogacy contract by bringing the parties together, explaining the process to them, furnishing the contractual form, and providing legal counsel.

The history of the parties' involvement in this arrangement suggests their good faith. William and Elizabeth Stern were married in July 1974, having met at the University of Michigan, where both were Ph.D. candidates. Due to financial considerations and Mrs. Stern's pursuit of a medical degree and residency, they decided to defer starting a family until 1981. Before then, however, Mrs. Stern learned that she might have multiple sclerosis and that the disease in some cases renders pregnancy a serious health risk. Her anxiety appears to have exceeded the actual risk, which current medical authorities assess as minimal. Nonetheless that anxiety was evidently quite real, Mrs. Stern fearing that pregnancy might precipitate blindness, paraplegia, or other forms of debilitation. Based on the perceived risk, the Sterns decided to forego having their own children. The decision had special significance for Mr. Stern. Most

---

[1] Subsequent to the trial court proceedings, Mr. and Mrs. Whitehead were divorced, and soon thereafter Mrs. Whitehead remarried. Nevertheless, in the course of this opinion we will make reference almost exclusively to the facts as they existed at the time of trial, the facts on which the decision we now review was reached. We note moreover that Mr. Whitehead remains a party to this dispute. For these reasons, we continue to refer to appellants as Mr. and Mrs. Whitehead.

of his family had been destroyed in the Holocaust. As the family's only survivor, he very much wanted to continue his bloodline.

Initially the Sterns considered adoption, but were discouraged by the substantial delay apparently involved and by the potential problem they saw arising from their age and their differing religious backgrounds. They were most eager for some other means to start a family.

The paths of Mrs. Whitehead and the Sterns to surrogacy were similar. Both responded to advertising by ICNY. The Sterns' response, following their inquiries into adoption, was the result of their long-standing decision to have a child. Mrs. Whitehead's response apparently resulted from her sympathy with family members and others who could have no children (she stated that she wanted to give another couple the "gift of life"); she also wanted the $10,000 to help her family.

Both parties, undoubtedly because of their own self-interest, were less sensitive to the implications of the transaction than they might otherwise have been. Mrs. Whitehead, for instance, appears not to have been concerned about whether the Sterns would make good parents for her child; the Sterns, on their part, while conscious of the obvious possibility that surrendering the child might cause grief to Mrs. Whitehead, overcame their qualms because of their desire for a child. At any rate, both the Sterns and Mrs. Whitehead were committed to the arrangement; both thought it right and constructive.

Mrs. Whitehead had reached her decision concerning surrogacy before the Sterns, and had actually been involved as a potential surrogate mother with another couple. After numerous unsuccessful artificial inseminations, that effort was abandoned. Thereafter, the Sterns learned of the Infertility Center, the possibilities of surrogacy, and of Mary Beth Whitehead. The two couples met to discuss the surrogacy arrangement and decided to go forward. On February 6, 1985, Mr. Stern and Mr. and Mrs. Whitehead executed the surrogate parenting agreement. After several artificial inseminations over a period of months, Mrs. Whitehead became pregnant. The pregnancy was uneventful and on March 27, 1986, Baby M was born.

Not wishing anyone at the hospital to be aware of the surrogacy arrangement, Mr. and Mrs. Whitehead appeared to all as the proud parents of a healthy female child. Her birth certificate indicated her name to be Sara Elizabeth Whitehead and her father to be Richard Whitehead. In accordance with Mrs. Whitehead's request, the Sterns visited the hospital unobtrusively to see the newborn child.

Mrs. Whitehead realized, almost from the moment of birth, that she could not part with this child. She had felt a bond with it even during pregnancy. Some indication of the attachment was conveyed to the Sterns at the hospital when they told Mrs. Whitehead what they were going to name the baby. She apparently broke into tears and indicated that she did not know if she could give up the child. She talked about how the baby looked like her other daughter, and made it clear that she was experiencing great difficulty with the decision.

Nonetheless, Mrs. Whitehead was, for the moment, true to her word. Despite powerful inclinations to the contrary, she turned her child over to the Sterns on March 30 at the Whiteheads' home.

The Sterns were thrilled with their new child. They had planned extensively for its arrival, far beyond the practical furnishing of a room for her. It was a time of joyful celebration—not just for them but for their friends as well. The Sterns looked forward to raising their daughter, whom they named Melissa. While aware by then that Mrs. Whitehead was undergoing an emotional crisis, they were as yet not cognizant of the depth of that crisis and its implications for their newly-enlarged family.

Later in the evening of March 30, Mrs. Whitehead became deeply disturbed, disconsolate, stricken with unbearable sadness. She had to have her child. She could not eat, sleep, or concentrate on anything other than her need for her baby. The next day she went to the Sterns' home and told them how much she was suffering.

The depth of Mrs. Whitehead's despair surprised and frightened the Sterns. She told them that she could not live without her baby, that she must have her, even if only for one week, that thereafter she would surrender her child. The Sterns, concerned that Mrs. Whitehead might indeed commit suicide, not wanting under any circumstances to risk that, and in any event believing that Mrs. Whitehead would keep her word, turned the child over to her. It was not until four months later, after a series of attempts to regain possession of the child, that Melissa was returned to the Sterns, having been forcibly removed from the home where she was then living with Mr. and Mrs. Whitehead, the home in Florida owned by Mary Beth Whitehead's parents.

The struggle over Baby M began when it became apparent that Mrs. Whitehead could not return the child to Mr. Stern. Due to Mrs. Whitehead's refusal to relinquish the baby, Mr. Stern filed a complaint seeking enforcement of the surrogacy contract. He alleged, accurately, that Mrs. Whitehead had not only refused to comply with the surrogacy contract but had threatened to flee from New Jersey with the child in order to avoid even the possibility of his obtaining custody. The court papers asserted that if Mrs. Whitehead were to be given notice of the application for an order requiring her to relinquish custody, she would, prior to the hearing, leave the state with the baby. And that is precisely what she did. After the order was entered, *ex parte,* the process server, aided by the police, in the presence of the Sterns, entered Mrs. Whitehead's home to execute the order. Mr. Whitehead fled with the child, who had been handed to him through a window while those who came to enforce the order were thrown off balance by a dispute over the child's current name.

The Whiteheads immediately fled to Florida with Baby M. They stayed initially with Mrs. Whitehead's parents, where one of Mrs. Whitehead's children had been living. For the next three months, the Whiteheads and Melissa lived at roughly twenty different hotels, motels, and homes in order to avoid apprehension. From time to time Mrs. Whitehead would call Mr. Stern to discuss the matter; the conversations, recorded by Mr. Stern on advice of counsel, show an escalating dispute about rights, morality, and power, accompanied by threats of Mrs. Whitehead to kill herself, to kill the child, and falsely to accuse Mr. Stern of sexually molesting Mrs. Whitehead's other daughter.

Eventually the Sterns discovered where the Whiteheads were staying, commenced supplementary proceedings in Florida, and obtained an order requiring the Whiteheads to turn over the child. Police in Florida enforced the order, forcibly removing the child from her grandparents' home. She was soon thereafter brought to New Jersey and turned over to the Sterns. The prior order of the court, issued *ex parte,* awarding custody of the child to the Sterns *pendente lite,* was reaffirmed by the trial court after consideration of the certified representations of the parties (both represented by counsel) concerning the unusual sequence of events that had unfolded. Pending final judgment, Mrs. Whitehead was awarded limited visitation with Baby M.

The Sterns' complaint, in addition to seeking possession and ultimately custody of the child, sought enforcement of the surrogacy contract. Pursuant to the contract, it asked that the child be permanently placed in their custody, that Mrs. Whitehead's parental rights be terminated, and that Mrs. Stern be allowed to adopt the child, *i.e.,* that, for all purposes, Melissa become the Sterns' child.

The trial took thirty-two days over a period of more than two months. . . . [T]he bulk of the testimony was devoted to determining the parenting arrangement most compatible with the child's best interests. Soon after the conclusion of the trial, the trial court announced its opinion from the bench. 217 *N.J.Super.* 313, 525 *A.*2d 1128 (1987). It held that the surrogacy contract was valid; ordered that Mrs. Whitehead's parental rights be terminated and that sole custody of the child be granted to Mr. Stern; and, after hearing brief testimony from Mrs. Stern, immediately entered an order allowing the adoption of Melissa by Mrs. Stern, all in accordance with the surrogacy contract. Pending the outcome of the appeal, we granted a continuation of visitation to Mrs. Whitehead, although slightly more limited than the visitation allowed during the trial.

Although clearly expressing its view that the surrogacy contract was valid, the trial court devoted the major portion of its opinion to the question of the baby's best interests. The inconsistency is apparent. The surrogacy contract calls for the surrender of the child to the Sterns, permanent and sole custody in the Sterns, and termination of Mrs. Whitehead's parental rights, all without qualification, all regardless of any evaluation of the best interests of the child. As a matter of fact the contract recites (even before the child was conceived) that it is in the best interests of the child to be placed with Mr. Stern. In effect, the trial court awarded custody to Mr. Stern, the natural father, based on the same kind of evidence and analysis as might be expected had no surrogacy contract existed. Its rationalization, however, was that while the surrogacy contract was valid, specific performance would not be granted unless that remedy was in the best interests of the child. The factual issues confronted and decided by the trial court were the same as if Mr. Stern and Mrs. Whitehead had had the child out of wedlock, intended or unintended, and then disagreed about custody. The trial court's awareness of the irrelevance of the contract in the court's determination of custody is suggested by its remark that beyond the question of the child's best interests, "[a]ll other concerns raised by counsel constitute commentary." * * *.

On the question of best interests—and we agree, but for different reasons, that custody was the critical issue—the court's analysis of the testimony was perceptive, demonstrating both its understanding of the case and its considerable experience in these matters. We agree substantially with both its analysis and conclusions on the matter of custody.

The court's review and analysis of the surrogacy contract, however, is not at all in accord with ours. The trial court concluded that the various statutes governing this matter, including those concerning adoption, termination of parental rights, and payment of money in connection with adoptions, do not apply to surrogacy contracts. * * * It reasoned that because the Legislature did not have surrogacy contracts in mind when it passed those laws, those laws were therefore irrelevant. * * * Thus, assuming it was writing on a clean slate, the trial court analyzed the interests involved and the power of the court to accommodate them. It then held that surrogacy contracts are valid and should be enforced * * * and furthermore that Mr. Stern's rights under the surrogacy contract were constitutionally protected. * * *.

Mrs. Whitehead appealed. This Court granted direct certification. * * * The briefs of the parties on appeal were joined by numerous briefs filed by *amici* expressing various interests and views on surrogacy and on this case. We have found many of them helpful in resolving the issues before us. . . .

II.
INVALIDITY AND UNENFORCEABILITY OF SURROGACY CONTRACT

We have concluded that this surrogacy contract is invalid. Our conclusion has two bases: direct conflict with existing statutes and conflict with the public policies of this State, as expressed in its statutory and decisional law.

One of the surrogacy contract's basic purposes, to achieve the adoption of a child through private placement, though permitted in New Jersey "is very much disfavored." *Sees v. Baber,* 74 *N.J.* 201, 217, 377 *A.*2d 628 (1977). Its use of money for this purpose—and we have no doubt whatsoever that the money is being paid to obtain an adoption and not, as the Sterns argue, for the personal services of Mary Beth Whitehead— is illegal and perhaps criminal. *N.J.S.A.* 9:3–54. In addition to the inducement of money, there is the coercion of contract: the natural mother's irrevocable agreement, prior to birth, even prior to conception, to surrender the child to the adoptive couple. Such an agreement is totally unenforceable in private placement adoption. *Sees,* 74 *N.J.* at 212–14, 377 *A.*2d 628. Even where the adoption is through an approved agency, the formal agreement to surrender occurs only *after* birth (as we read *N.J.S.A.* 9:2–16 and –17, and similar statutes), and then, by regulation, only after the birth mother has been offered counseling. *N.J.A.C.* 10:121A–5.4(c). Integral to these invalid provisions of the surrogacy contract is the related agreement, equally invalid, on the part of the natural mother to cooperate with, and not to contest, proceedings to terminate her parental rights, as well as her contractual concession, in aid of the adoption, that the child's best interests would be served by awarding custody to the natural father and his wife—all of this before she has even conceived, and, in some cases, before she has the slightest idea of what the natural father and adoptive mother are like.

The foregoing provisions not only directly conflict with New Jersey statutes, but also offend long-established State policies. These critical terms, which are at the heart of the contract, are invalid and unenforceable; the conclusion therefore follows, without more, that the entire contract is unenforceable.

A. Conflict with Statutory Provisions

The surrogacy contract conflicts with: (1) laws prohibiting the use of money in connection with adoptions; (2) laws requiring proof of parental unfitness or abandonment before termination of parental rights is ordered or an adoption is granted; and (3) laws that make surrender of custody and consent to adoption revocable in private placement adoptions.

(1) Our law prohibits paying or accepting money in connection with any placement of a child for adoption. *N.J.S.A.* 9:3–54a. Violation is a high misdemeanor. *N.J.S.A.* 9:3–54c. Excepted are fees of an approved agency (which must be a non-profit entity, *N.J.S.A.* 9:3–38a) and certain expenses in connection with childbirth. *N.J.S.A.* 9:3–54b.[4]

---

[4]   *N.J.S.A.* 9:3–54 reads as follows:

a. No person, firm, partnership, corporation, association or agency shall make, offer to make or assist or participate in any placement for adoption and in connection therewith

    (1) Pay, give or agree to give any money or any valuable consideration, or assume or discharge any financial obligation; or

Considerable care was taken in this case to structure the surrogacy arrangement so as not to violate this prohibition. The arrangement was structured as follows: the adopting parent, Mrs. Stern, was not a party to the surrogacy contract; the money paid to Mrs. Whitehead was stated to be for her services—not for the adoption; the sole purpose of the contract was stated as being that "of giving a child to William Stern, its natural and biological father"; the money was purported to be "compensation for services and expenses and in no way . . . a fee for termination of parental rights or a payment in exchange for consent to surrender a child for adoption"; the fee to the Infertility Center ($7,500) was stated to be for legal representation, advice, administrative work, and other "services." Nevertheless, it seems clear that the money was paid and accepted in connection with an adoption.

The Infertility Center's major role was first as a "finder" of the surrogate mother whose child was to be adopted, and second as the arranger of all proceedings that led to the adoption. Its role as adoption finder is demonstrated by the provision requiring Mr. Stern to pay another $7,500 if he uses Mary Beth Whitehead again as a surrogate, and by ICNY's agreement to "coordinate arrangements for the adoption of the child by the wife." The surrogacy agreement requires Mrs. Whitehead to surrender Baby M for the purposes of adoption. The agreement notes that Mr. *and Mrs.* Stern wanted to have a child, and provides that the child be "placed" with Mrs. Stern in the event Mr. Stern dies before the child is born. The payment of the $10,000 occurs only on surrender of custody of the child and "completion of the duties and obligations" of Mrs. Whitehead, including termination of her parental rights to facilitate adoption by Mrs. Stern. As for the contention that the Sterns are paying only for services and not for an adoption, we need note only that they would pay nothing in the event the child died before the fourth month of pregnancy, and only $1,000 if the child were stillborn, even though the "services" had been fully rendered. Additionally, one of Mrs. Whitehead's estimated costs, to be assumed by Mr. Stern, was an "Adoption Fee," presumably for Mrs. Whitehead's incidental costs in connection with the adoption.

Mr. Stern knew he was paying for the adoption of a child; Mrs. Whitehead knew she was accepting money so that a child might be adopted; the Infertility Center knew that it was being paid for assisting in the adoption of a child. The actions of all three worked to frustrate the

---

(2) Take, receive, accept or agree to accept any money or any valuable consideration.

b. The prohibition of subsection a. shall not apply to the fees or services of any approved agency in connection with a placement for adoption, nor shall such prohibition apply to the payment or reimbursement of medical, hospital or other similar expenses incurred in connection with the birth or any illness of the child, or to the acceptance of such reimbursement by a parent of the child.

c. Any person, firm, partnership, corporation, association or agency violating this section shall be guilty of a high misdemeanor.

goals of the statute. It strains credulity to claim that these arrangements, touted by those in the surrogacy business as an attractive alternative to the usual route leading to an adoption, really amount to something other than a private placement adoption for money.

The prohibition of our statute is strong. Violation constitutes a high misdemeanor, *N.J.S.A.* 9:3–54c, a third-degree crime, *N.J.S.A.* 2C:43–1b, carrying a penalty of three to five years imprisonment. *N.J.S.A.* 2C:43–6a(3). The evils inherent in baby-bartering are loathsome for a myriad of reasons. The child is sold without regard for whether the purchasers will be suitable parents. N. Baker, *Baby Selling: The Scandal of Black Market Adoption* 7 (1978). The natural mother does not receive the benefit of counseling and guidance to assist her in making a decision that may affect her for a lifetime. In fact, the monetary incentive to sell her child may, depending on her financial circumstances, make her decision less voluntary. *Id.* at 44. Furthermore, the adoptive parents[5] may not be fully informed of the natural parents' medical history.

Baby-selling potentially results in the exploitation of all parties involved. *Ibid.* Conversely, adoption statutes seek to further humanitarian goals, foremost among them the best interests of the child. H. Witmer, E. Herzog, E. Weinstein, & M. Sullivan, *Independent Adoptions: A Follow-Up Study* 32 (1967). The negative consequences of baby-buying are potentially present in the surrogacy context, especially the potential for placing and adopting a child without regard to the interest of the child or the natural mother.

(2) The termination of Mrs. Whitehead's parental rights, called for by the surrogacy contract and actually ordered by the court, 217 *N.J.Super.* at 399–400, 525 *A.*2d 1128, fails to comply with the stringent requirements of New Jersey law. Our law, recognizing the finality of any termination of parental rights, provides for such termination only where there has been a voluntary surrender of a child to an approved agency or to the Division of Youth and Family Services ("DYFS"), accompanied by a formal document acknowledging termination of parental rights, *N.J.S.A.* 9:2–16, –17; *N.J.S.A.* 9:3–41; *N.J.S.A.* 30:4C–23, or where there has been a showing of parental abandonment or unfitness. . . . That showing is required in every context in which termination of parental rights is sought, be it an action by an approved agency, an action by DYFS, or a private placement adoption proceeding, even where the petitioning adoptive parent is, as here, a stepparent. While the statutes make certain procedural allowances when stepparents are involved, *N.J.S.A.* 9:3–48a(2), –48a(4), –48c(4), the substantive requirement for terminating the natural parents' rights is not relaxed one iota. * * * It is clear that a "best interests" determination is never sufficient to terminate parental rights; the statutory criteria must be proved.

---

[5] Of course, here there are no "adoptive parents," but rather the natural father and his wife, the only adoptive parent. As noted, however, many of the dangers of using money in connection with adoption may exist in surrogacy situations

In this case a termination of parental rights was obtained not by proving the statutory prerequisites but by claiming the benefit of contractual provisions. From all that has been stated above, it is clear that a contractual agreement to abandon one's parental rights, or not to contest a termination action, will not be enforced in our courts. The Legislature would not have so carefully, so consistently, and so substantially restricted termination of parental rights if it had intended to allow termination to be achieved by one short sentence in a contract.

Since the termination was invalid, it follows, . . . that adoption of Melissa by Mrs. Stern could not properly be granted.

(3)   The provision in the surrogacy contract stating that Mary Beth Whitehead agrees to "surrender custody . . . and terminate all parental rights" contains no clause giving her a right to rescind. It is intended to be an irrevocable consent to surrender the child for adoption—in other words, an irrevocable commitment by Mrs. Whitehead to turn Baby M over to the Sterns and thereafter to allow termination of her parental rights. The trial court required a "best interests" showing as a condition to granting specific performance of the surrogacy contract. 217 *N.J.Super.* at 399–400, 525 *A.2d* 1128. Having decided the "best interests" issue in favor of the Sterns, that court's order included, among other things, specific performance of this agreement to surrender custody and terminate all parental rights.

Mrs. Whitehead, shortly after the child's birth, had attempted to revoke her consent and surrender by refusing, after the Sterns had allowed her to have the child "just for one week," to return Baby M to them. The trial court's award of specific performance therefore reflects its view that the consent to surrender the child was irrevocable. We accept the trial court's construction of the contract; indeed it appears quite clear that this was the parties' intent. Such a provision, however, making irrevocable the natural mother's consent to surrender custody of her child in a private placement adoption, clearly conflicts with New Jersey law.

Our analysis commences with the statute providing for surrender of custody to an approved agency and termination of parental rights on the suit of that agency. The two basic provisions of the statute are *N.J.S.A.* 9:2–14 and 9:2–16. The former provides explicitly that

> [e]xcept as otherwise provided by law or by order or judgment of a court of competent jurisdiction or by testamentary disposition, no surrender of the custody of a child shall be valid in this state unless made to an approved agency pursuant to the provisions of this act. . . .

There is no exception "provided by law," and it is not clear that there could be any "order or judgment of a court of competent jurisdiction" validating a surrender of custody as a basis for adoption when that surrender was not in conformance with the statute. Requirements for a voluntary surrender to an approved agency are set forth in *N.J.S.A.* 9:2–16. This section allows an approved agency to take a voluntary surrender of custody from the parent of a child but provides stringent requirements as a condition to its validity. The surrender must be in writing, must be in such form as is required for the recording of a deed, and, pursuant to *N.J.S.A.* 9:2–17, must

> be such as to declare that the person executing the same desires to relinquish the custody of the child, acknowledge the termination of parental rights as to such custody in favor of the approved agency, and acknowledge full understanding of the effect of such surrender as provided by this act.

If the foregoing requirements are met, the consent, the voluntary surrender of custody

> shall be valid whether or not the person giving same is a minor and shall be irrevocable except at the discretion of the approved agency taking such surrender or upon order or judgment of a court of competent jurisdiction, setting aside such surrender upon proof of fraud, duress, or misrepresentation. [*N.J.S.A.* 9:2–16.] . . .

The statute speaks of such surrender as constituting "relinquishment of such person's parental rights in or guardianship or custody of the child *named therein* and consent by such person to adoption of the child." *Ibid.* (emphasis supplied). We emphasize "named therein," for we construe the statute to allow a surrender only after the birth of the child. The formal consent to surrender enables the approved agency to terminate parental rights. . . .

It is clear that the Legislature so carefully circumscribed all aspects of a consent to surrender custody—its form and substance, its manner of execution, and the agency or agencies to which it may be made—in order to provide the basis for irrevocability. It seems most unlikely that the Legislature intended that a consent not complying with these requirements would also be irrevocable, especially where, as here, that consent falls radically short of compliance. Not only do the form and substance of the consent in the surrogacy contract fail to meet statutory requirements, but the surrender of custody is made to a private party. It is not made, as the statute requires, either to an approved agency or to DYFS.

These strict prerequisites to irrevocability constitute a recognition of the most serious consequences that flow from such consents: termination of parental rights, the permanent separation of parent from child, and the ultimate adoption of the child. *See Sees v. Baber, supra,* 74 *N.J.* at 217, 377 *A.2d* 628. Because of those consequences, the Legislature severely limited the circumstances under which such consent would be irrevocable. The legislative goal is furthered by regulations requiring approved agencies, prior to accepting irrevocable consents, to provide advice and counseling to women, making it more likely that they fully understand and appreciate the consequences of their acts. *N.J.A.C.* 10:121A–5.4(c). . . .

The provision in the surrogacy contract whereby the mother irrevocably agrees to surrender custody of her child and to terminate her parental rights conflicts with the settled interpretation of New Jersey statutory law. There is only one irrevocable consent, and that is the one explicitly provided for by statute: a consent to surrender of custody and a placement with an approved agency or with DYFS. The provision in the surrogacy contract, agreed to before conception, requiring the natural mother to surrender custody of the child without any right of revocation is one more indication of the essential nature of this transaction: the creation of a contractual system of termination and adoption designed to circumvent our statutes.

B.   Public Policy Considerations

The surrogacy contract's invalidity, resulting from its direct conflict with the above statutory provisions, is further underlined when its goals and means are measured against New Jersey's public policy. The contract's basic premise, that the natural parents can decide in advance of birth which one is to have custody of the child, bears no relationship to the settled law that the child's best interests shall determine custody. * * * The fact that the trial court remedied that aspect of the contract through the "best interests" phase does not make the contractual provision any less offensive to the public policy of this State.

The surrogacy contract guarantees permanent separation of the child from one of its natural parents. Our policy, however, has long been that to the extent possible, children should remain with and be brought up by both of their natural parents. That was the first stated purpose of the previous adoption act, *L.*1953, *c.* 264, § 1, codified at *N.J.S.A.* 9:3–17 (repealed): "it is necessary and desirable (a) to protect the child from unnecessary separation from his natural parents. . . ." While not so stated in the present adoption law, this purpose remains part of the public policy of this State. * * * This is not simply some theoretical ideal that in practice has no meaning. The impact of failure to follow that policy is nowhere better shown than in the results of this surrogacy contract. A child, instead of starting off its life with as much peace and security as possible, finds itself immediately in a tug-of-war between contending mother and father.[9]

---

[9]   And the impact on the natural parents, Mr. Stern and Mrs. Whitehead, is severe and dramatic. The depth of their conflict about Baby M, about custody, visitation, about the goodness or badness of each of them, comes through in their telephone conversations, in which each tried to persuade the other to give up the child. The potential adverse consequences of surrogacy are poignantly captured here—Mrs. Whitehead threatening to kill herself and the baby, Mr. Stern begging her not to, each blaming the other. The dashed hopes of the Sterns, the agony of Mrs. Whitehead, their suffering, their hatred—all were caused by the unraveling of this arrangement.

The surrogacy contract violates the policy of this State that the rights of natural parents are equal concerning their child, the father's right no greater than the mother's. "The parent and child relationship extends equally to every child and to every parent, regardless of the marital status of the parents." *N.J.S.A.* 9:17–40. As the Assembly Judiciary Committee noted in its statement to the bill, this section establishes "the principle that regardless of the marital status of the parents, all children *and all parents* have equal rights with respect to each other." *Statement to Senate No. 888,* Assembly Judiciary, Law, Public Safety and Defense Committee (1983) (emphasis supplied). The whole purpose and effect of the surrogacy contract was to give the father the exclusive right to the child by destroying the rights of the mother.

The policies expressed in our comprehensive laws governing consent to the surrender of a child . . . stand in stark contrast to the surrogacy contract and what it implies. Here there is no counseling, independent or otherwise, of the natural mother, no evaluation, no warning.

The only legal advice Mary Beth Whitehead received regarding the surrogacy contract was provided in connection with the contract that she previously entered into with another couple. Mrs. Whitehead's lawyer was referred to her by the Infertility Center, with which he had an agreement to act as counsel for surrogate candidates. His services consisted of spending one hour going through the contract with the Whiteheads, section by section, and answering their questions. Mrs. Whitehead received no further legal advice prior to signing the contract with the Sterns.

Mrs. Whitehead was examined and psychologically evaluated, but if it was for her benefit, the record does not disclose that fact. The Sterns regarded the evaluation as important, particularly in connection with the question of whether she would change her mind. Yet they never asked to see it, and were content with the assumption that the Infertility Center had made an evaluation and had concluded that there was no danger that the surrogate mother would change her mind. From Mrs. Whitehead's point of view, all that she learned from the evaluation was that "she had passed." It is apparent that the profit motive got the better of the Infertility Center. Although the evaluation was made, it was not put to any use, and understandably so, for the psychologist warned that Mrs. Whitehead demonstrated certain traits that might make surrender of the child difficult and that there should be further inquiry into this issue in connection with her surrogacy. To inquire further, however, might have jeopardized the Infertility Center's fee. The record indicates that neither Mrs. Whitehead nor the Sterns were ever told of this fact, a fact that might have ended their surrogacy arrangement.

Under the contract, the natural mother is irrevocably committed before she knows the strength of her bond with her child. She never makes a totally voluntary, informed decision, for quite clearly any decision prior to the baby's birth is, in the most important sense, uninformed, and any decision after that, compelled by a pre-existing contractual commitment, the threat of a lawsuit, and the inducement of a $10,000 payment, is less than totally voluntary. Her interests are of little concern to those who controlled this transaction.

Although the interest of the natural father and adoptive mother is certainly the predominant interest, realistically the *only* interest served, even they are left with less than what public policy requires. They know little about the natural mother, her genetic makeup, and her psychological and medical history. Moreover, not even a superficial attempt is made to determine their awareness of their responsibilities as parents.

Worst of all, however, is the contract's total disregard of the best interests of the child. There is not the slightest suggestion that any inquiry will be made at any time to determine the fitness of the Sterns as custodial parents, of Mrs. Stern as an adoptive parent, their superiority to Mrs. Whitehead, or the effect on the child of not living with her natural mother.

This is the sale of a child, or, at the very least, the sale of a mother's right to her child, the only mitigating factor being that one of the purchasers is the father. Almost every evil that prompted the prohibition on the payment of money in connection with adoptions exists here.

The differences between an adoption and a surrogacy contract should be noted, since it is asserted that the use of money in connection with surrogacy does not pose the risks found where money buys an adoption. Katz, "Surrogate Motherhood and the Baby-Selling Laws," 20 *Colum.J.L. & Soc.Probs.* 1 (1986).

First, and perhaps most important, all parties concede that it is unlikely that surrogacy will survive without money. Despite the alleged selfless motivation of surrogate mothers, if there is no payment, there will be no surrogates, or very few. That conclusion contrasts with adoption; for obvious reasons, there remains a steady supply, albeit insufficient, despite the prohibitions against payment. The adoption itself, relieving the natural mother of the financial burden of supporting an infant, is in some sense the equivalent of payment.

Second, the use of money in adoptions does not *produce* the problem-conception occurs, and usually the birth itself, before illicit funds are offered. With surrogacy, the "problem," if one views it as such, consisting of the purchase of a woman's procreative capacity, at the risk of her life, is caused by and originates with the offer of money.

Third, with the law prohibiting the use of money in connection with adoptions, the built-in financial pressure of the unwanted pregnancy and the consequent support obligation do not lead the mother to the highest paying, ill-suited, adoptive parents. She is just as well-off surrendering the child to an approved agency. In surrogacy, the highest bidders will presumably become the adoptive parents regardless of suitability, so long as payment of money is permitted.

Fourth, the mother's consent to surrender her child in adoptions is revocable, even after surrender of the child, unless it be to an approved agency, where by regulation there are protections against an ill-advised surrender. In surrogacy, consent occurs so early that no amount of advice would satisfy the potential mother's need, yet the consent is irrevocable.

The main difference, that the unwanted pregnancy is unintended while the situation of the surrogate mother is voluntary and intended, is really not significant. Initially, it produces stronger reactions of sympathy for the mother whose pregnancy was unwanted than for the surrogate mother, who "went into this with her eyes wide open." On reflection, however, it appears that the essential evil is the same, taking advantage of a woman's circumstances (the unwanted pregnancy or the need for money) in order to take away her child, the difference being one of degree.

In the scheme contemplated by the surrogacy contract in this case, a middle man, propelled by profit, promotes the sale. Whatever idealism may have motivated any of the participants, the profit motive predominates, permeates, and ultimately governs the transaction. The demand for children is great and the supply small. The availability of contraception, abortion, and the greater willingness of single mothers to bring up their children has led to a shortage of babies offered for adoption. *See* N. Baker, *Baby Selling: The Scandal of Black Market Adoption, supra; Adoption and Foster Care, 1975: Hearings on Baby Selling Before the Subcomm. On Children and Youth of the Senate Comm. on Labor and Public Welfare,* 94th Cong.1st Sess. 6 (1975) (Statement of Joseph H. Reid, Executive Director, Child Welfare League of America, Inc.). The situation is ripe for the entry of the middleman who will bring some equilibrium into the market by increasing the supply through the use of money.

Intimated, but disputed, is the assertion that surrogacy will be used for the benefit of the rich at the expense of the poor. *See, e.g.,* Radin, "Market Inalienability," 100 *Harv.L.Rev.* 1849, 1930 (1987). In response it is noted that the Sterns are not rich and the Whiteheads not poor. Nevertheless, it is clear to us that it is unlikely that surrogate mothers will be as proportionately numerous among those women in the top twenty percent income bracket as among those in the bottom twenty percent. *Ibid.* Put differently, we doubt that infertile couples in the low-income bracket will find upper income surrogates.

In any event, even in this case one should not pretend that disparate wealth does not play a part simply because the contrast is not the dramatic "rich versus poor." At the time of trial, the Whiteheads' net assets were probably negative—Mrs. Whitehead's own sister was foreclosing on a second mortgage. Their income derived from Mr. Whitehead's labors. Mrs. Whitehead is a homemaker, having previously held part-time jobs. The Sterns are both professionals, she a medical doctor, he a biochemist. Their combined income when both were working was about $89,500 a year and their assets sufficient to pay for the surrogacy contract arrangements.

The point is made that Mrs. Whitehead *agreed* to the surrogacy arrangement, supposedly fully understanding the consequences. Putting aside the issue of how compelling her need for money may have been, and how significant her understanding of the consequences, we suggest that her consent is irrelevant. There are, in a civilized society, some things that money cannot buy. In America, we decided long ago that merely because conduct purchased by money was "voluntary" did not mean that it was good or beyond regulation and prohibition. *West Coast Hotel Co. v. Parrish,* 300 *U.S.* 379, 57 *S.Ct.* 578, 81 *L.Ed.* 703 (1937). Employers can no longer buy labor at the lowest price they can bargain for, even though that labor is "voluntary," 29 *U.S.C.* § 206 (1982), or buy women's labor for less money than paid to men for the same job, 29 *U.S.C.* § 206(d), or purchase the agreement of children to perform oppressive labor, 29 *U.S.C.* § 212, or purchase the agreement of workers to subject themselves to unsafe or unhealthful working conditions, 29 *U.S.C.* §§ 651 to 678. (Occupational Safety and Health Act of 1970). There are, in short, values that society deems more important than granting to wealth whatever it can buy, be it labor, love, or life. Whether this principle recommends prohibition of surrogacy, which presumably sometimes results in great satisfaction to all of the parties, is not for us to say. We note here only that, under existing law, the fact that Mrs. Whitehead "agreed" to the arrangement is not dispositive.

The long-term effects of surrogacy contracts are not known, but feared—the impact on the child who learns her life was bought, that she is the offspring of someone who gave birth to her only to obtain money; the impact on the natural mother as the full weight of her isolation is felt along with the full reality of the sale of her body and her child; the impact on the natural father and adoptive mother once they realize the consequences of their conduct. Literature in related areas suggests these are substantial considerations, although, given the newness of surrogacy, there is little information. * * *

The surrogacy contract is based on, principles that are directly contrary to the objectives of our laws.[10] It guarantees the separation of a

---

[10] We note the argument of the Sterns that the sperm donor section of our Parentage Act, *N.J.S.A.* 9:17–38 to –59, implies a legislative policy that would lead to approval of this surrogacy contract. Where a married woman is artificially inseminated by another with her husband's consent, the Parentage Act creates a parent-child relationship between the husband and the resulting child. *N.J.S.A.* 9:17–44. The Parentage Act's silence, however, with respect to surrogacy, rather than supporting, defeats any contention that surrogacy should receive treatment parallel to the sperm donor artificial insemination situation. In the latter case the statute expressly transfers parental rights from the biological father, *i.e.,* the sperm donor, to the mother's husband. *Ibid.* Our Legislature could not possibly have intended any other arrangement to have the consequence of transferring parental rights without legislative authorization when it had concluded that legislation was necessary to accomplish that result in the sperm donor artificial insemination context.

child from its mother; it looks to adoption regardless of suitability; it totally ignores the child; it takes the child from the mother regardless of her wishes and her maternal fitness; and it does all of this, it accomplishes all of its goals, through the use of money.

Beyond that is the potential degradation of some women that may result from this arrangement. In many cases, of course, surrogacy may bring satisfaction, not only to the infertile couple, but to the surrogate mother herself. The fact, however, that many women may not perceive surrogacy negatively but rather see it as an opportunity does not diminish its potential for devastation to other women.

In sum, the harmful consequences of this surrogacy arrangement appear to us all too palpable. In New Jersey the surrogate mother's agreement to sell her child is void.[11] Its irrevocability infects the entire contract, as does the money that purports to buy it.

This sperm donor provision suggests an argument not raised by the parties, namely, that the attempted creation of a parent-child relationship through the surrogacy contract has been preempted by the Legislature. The Legislature has explicitly recognized the parent-child relationship between a child and its natural parents, married and unmarried, *N.J.S.A.* 9:17–38 to –59, between adoptive parents and their adopted child, *N.J.S.A.* 9:3–37 to –56, and between a husband and his wife's child pursuant to the sperm donor provision, *N.J.S.A.* 9:17–44. It has not recognized any others—specifically, it has never legally equated the stepparent-stepchild relationship with the parent-child relationship, and certainly it has never recognized any concept of adoption by contract. It can be contended with some force that the Legislature's statutory coverage of the creation of the parent-child relationship evinces an intent to reserve to itself the power to define what is and is not a parent-child relationship. We need not, and do not, decide this question, however.

[11] Michigan courts have also found that these arrangements conflict with various aspects of their law. *See Doe v. Kelley,* 106 *Mich.App.* 169, 307 *N.W.*2d 438 (1981), *cert.* den., 459 *U.S.* 1183, 103 *S.Ct.* 834, 74 *L.Ed.*2d 1027 (1983) (application of sections of Michigan Adoption Law prohibiting the exchange of money to surrogacy is constitutional); * * * Most recently, a Michigan trial court in a matter similar to the case at bar held that surrogacy contracts are void as contrary to public policy and therefore are unenforceable. The court expressed concern for the potential exploitation of children resulting from surrogacy arrangements that involve the payment of money. The court also concluded that insofar as the surrogacy contract may be characterized as one for personal services, the thirteenth amendment should bar specific performance. * * *

The Supreme Court of Kentucky has taken a somewhat different approach to surrogate arrangements. In *Surrogate Parenting Assocs. v. Commonwealth ex. rel. Armstrong,* 704 *S.W.*2d 209 (Ky.1986), the court held that the "fundamental differences" between surrogate arrangements and baby-selling placed the surrogate parenting agreement beyond the reach of Kentucky's baby-selling statute.... Concomitant with this pro-surrogacy conclusion, however, the court held that a "surrogate" mother has the right to void the contract if she changes her mind during pregnancy or immediately after birth. * * * The court relied on statutes providing that consent to adoption or to the termination of parental rights prior to five days after the birth of the child is invalid, and concluded that consent before conception must also be unenforceable. * * *

The adoption phase of an uncontested surrogacy arrangement was analyzed in *Matter of Adoption of Baby Girl, L.J.,* 132 *Misc.*2d 972, 505 *N.Y.S.*2d 813 (Sur.1986). Although the court expressed strong moral and ethical reservations about surrogacy arrangements, it approved the adoption because it was in the best interests of the child. * * * The court went on to find that surrogate parenting agreements are not void, but are voidable if they are not in accordance with the state's adoption statutes. * * * The court then upheld the payment of money in connection with the surrogacy arrangement on the ground that the New York Legislature did not contemplate surrogacy when the baby-selling statute was passed. * * * Despite the court's ethical and moral problems

III.

TERMINATION

We have already noted that under our laws termination of parental rights cannot be based on contract, but may be granted only on proof of the statutory requirements. . . . Nothing in this record justifies a finding that would allow a court to terminate Mary Beth Whitehead's parental rights under the statutory standard. It is not simply that obviously there was no "intentional abandonment or very substantial neglect of parental duties without a reasonable expectation of reversal of that conduct in the future," *N.J.S.A.* 9:3–48c(1), quite the contrary, but furthermore that the trial court never found Mrs. Whitehead an unfit mother and indeed affirmatively stated that Mary Beth Whitehead had been a good mother to her other children. . . . . We therefore conclude that the natural mother is entitled to retain her rights as a mother.

IV.

CONSTITUTIONAL ISSUES

Both parties argue that the Constitutions—state and federal—mandate approval of their basic claims. The source of their constitutional arguments is essentially the same: the right of privacy, the right to procreate, the right to the companionship of one's child, those rights flowing either directly from the fourteenth amendment or by its incorporation of the Bill of Rights, or from the ninth amendment, or through the penumbra surrounding all of the Bill of Rights. They are the rights of personal intimacy, of marriage, of sex, of family, of procreation. Whatever their source, it is clear that they are fundamental rights protected by both the federal and state Constitutions. * * * *Griswold v. Connecticut,* 381 *U.S.* 479, 85 *S.Ct.* 1678, 14 *L.Ed.*2d 510 (1965); *Skinner v. Oklahoma,* 316 *U.S.* 535, 62 *S.Ct.* 1110, 86 *L.Ed.* 1655 (1942); *Meyer v. Nebraska,* 262 *U.S.* 390, 43 *S.Ct.* 625, 67 *L.Ed.* 1042 (1923). The right asserted by the Sterns is the right of procreation; that asserted by Mary Beth Whitehead is the right to the companionship of her child. We find that the right of procreation does not extend as far as claimed by the Sterns. As for the right asserted by Mrs. Whitehead, since we uphold it on other grounds (*i.e.,* we have restored her as mother and recognized her

with surrogate arrangements, it concluded that the Legislature was the appropriate forum to address the legality of surrogacy arrangements. * * *

In contrast to the law in the United States, the law in the United Kingdom concerning surrogate parenting is fairly well-settled. Parliament passed the Surrogacy Arrangements Act, 1985, ch. 49, which made initiating or taking part in any negotiations with a view to making or arranging a surrogacy contract a criminal offense. The criminal sanction, however, does not apply to the "surrogate" mother or to the natural father, but rather applies to other persons engaged in arranging surrogacy contracts on a commercial basis. Since 1978, English courts have held surrogacy agreements unenforceable as against public policy, such agreements being deemed arrangements for the purchase and sale of children. *A. v. C.,* [1985] *F.L.R.* 445, 449 (Fam. & C.A.1978). It should be noted, however, that certain surrogacy arrangements, *i.e.,* those arranged without brokers and revocable by the natural mother, are not prohibited under current law in the United Kingdom.

right, limited by the child's best interests, to her companionship), we need not decide that constitutional issue . . .

V.

CUSTODY

Having decided that the surrogacy contract is illegal and unenforceable, we now must decide the custody question without regard to the provisions of the surrogacy contract that would give Mr. Stern sole and permanent custody. . . . With the surrogacy contract disposed of, the legal framework becomes a dispute between two couples over the custody of a child produced by the artificial insemination of one couple's wife by the other's husband. Under the Parentage Act the claims of the natural father and the natural mother are entitled to equal weight, *i.e.,* one is not preferred over the other solely because he or she is the father or the mother. *N.J.S.A.* 9:17–40.[17] The applicable rule given these circumstances is clear: the child's best interests determine custody.

. . . The issue here is which life would be *better* for Baby M, one with primary custody in the Whiteheads or one with primary custody in the Sterns. The circumstances of this custody dispute are unusual and they have provoked some unusual contentions. The Whiteheads claim that even if the child's best interests would be served by our awarding custody to the Sterns, we should not do so, since that will encourage surrogacy contracts—contracts claimed by the Whiteheads, and we agree, to be violative of important legislatively-stated public policies. Their position is that in order that surrogacy contracts be deterred, custody should remain in the surrogate mother unless she is unfit, regardless of the best interests of the child. We disagree. Our declaration that this surrogacy contract is unenforceable and illegal is sufficient to deter similar

---

[17] At common law the rights of women were so fragile that the husband generally had the paramount right to the custody of children upon separation or divorce. *State v. Baird,* 21 *N.J.Eq.* 384, 388 (E. & A. 1869). In 1860 a statute concerning separation provided that children "within the age of seven years" be placed with the mother "unless said mother shall be of such character and habits as to render her an improper guardian." *L.*1860, *c.* 167. The inequities of the common-law rule and the 1860 statute were redressed by an 1871 statute, providing that "the rights of both parents, in the absence of misconduct, shall be held to be equal." *L.*1871, *c.* 48, § 6 (currently codified at *N.J.S.A.* 9:2–4). Under this statute the father's superior right to the children was abolished and the mother's right to custody of children of tender years was also eliminated. Under the 1871 statute, "the happiness and welfare of the children" were to determine custody, *L.*1871, *c.* 48, § 6, a rule that remains law to this day. *N.J.S.A.* 9:2–4.

    Despite this statute, however, the "tender years" doctrine persisted. * * * This presumption persisted primarily because of the prevailing view that a young child's best interests necessitated a mother's care. Both the development of case law and the Parentage Act, *N.J.S.A.* 9:17–40, however, provide for equality in custody claims. In *Beck v. Beck,* 86 *N.J.* 480, 488, 432 *A.2d* 63 (1981), we stated that it would be inappropriate "to establish a presumption . . . in favor of any particular custody determination," as any such presumption may "serve as a disincentive for the meticulous fact-finding required in custody cases." This does not mean that a mother who has had custody of her child for three, four, or five months does not have a particularly strong claim arising out of the unquestionable bond that exists at that point between the child and its mother; in other words, equality does not mean that all of the considerations underlying the "tender years" doctrine have been abolished.

agreements. We need not sacrifice the child's interests in order to make that point sharper. * * *

The Whiteheads also contend that the award of custody to the Sterns *pendente lite* was erroneous and that the error should not be allowed to affect the final custody decision. As noted above, at the very commencement of this action the court issued an *ex parte* order requiring Mrs. Whitehead to turn over the baby to the Sterns; Mrs. Whitehead did not comply but rather took the child to Florida. Thereafter, a similar order was enforced by the Florida authorities resulting in the transfer of possession of Baby M to the Sterns. The Sterns retained custody of the child throughout the litigation. The Whiteheads' point, assuming the *pendente* award of custody *was* erroneous, is that most of the factors arguing for awarding permanent custody to the Sterns resulted from that initial *pendente lite* order. Some of Mrs. Whitehead's alleged character failings, as testified to by experts and concurred in by the trial court, were demonstrated by her actions brought on by the custody crisis. For instance, in order to demonstrate her impulsiveness, those experts stressed the Whiteheads' flight to Florida with Baby M; to show her willingness to use her children for her own aims, they noted the telephone threats to kill Baby M and to accuse Mr. Stern of sexual abuse of her daughter; in order to show Mrs. Whitehead's manipulativeness, they pointed to her threat to kill herself; and in order to show her unsettled family life, they noted the innumerable moves from one hotel or motel to another in Florida. Furthermore, the argument continues, one of the most important factors, whether mentioned or not, in favor of custody in the Sterns is their continuing custody during the litigation, now having lasted for one-and-a-half years. The Whiteheads' conclusion is that had the trial court not given initial custody to the Sterns during the litigation, Mrs. Whitehead not only would have demonstrated her perfectly acceptable personality—the general tenor of the opinion of experts was that her personality problems surfaced primarily in crises—but would also have been able to prove better her parental skills along with an even stronger bond than may now exist between her and Baby M. Had she not been limited to custody for four months, she could have proved all of these things much more persuasively through almost two years of custody.

The argument has considerable force. It is of course possible that the trial court was wrong in its initial award of custody. It is also possible that such error, if that is what it was, may have affected the outcome. We disagree with the premise, however, that in determining custody a court should decide what the child's best interests *would be* if some hypothetical state of facts had existed. Rather, we must look to what those best interests *are, today,* even if some of the facts may have resulted in part from legal error. The child's interests come first: we will not punish it for judicial errors, assuming any were made. . .

Our custody conclusion is based on strongly persuasive testimony contrasting both the family life of the Whiteheads and the Sterns and the personalities and characters of the individuals. The stability of the Whitehead family life was doubtful at the time of trial. Their finances were in serious trouble (foreclosure by Mrs. Whitehead's sister on a second mortgage was in process). Mr. Whitehead's employment, though relatively steady, was always at risk because of his alcoholism, a condition that he seems not to have been able to confront effectively. Mrs. Whitehead had not worked for quite some time, her last two employments having been part-time. One of the Whiteheads' positive attributes was their ability to bring up two children, and apparently well, even in so vulnerable a household. Yet substantial question was raised even about that aspect of their home life. The expert testimony contained criticism of Mrs. Whitehead's handling of her son's educational difficulties. Certain of the experts noted that Mrs. Whitehead perceived herself as omnipotent and omniscient concerning her children. She knew what they were thinking, what they wanted, and she spoke for them. As to Melissa, Mrs. Whitehead expressed the view that she alone knew what that child's cries and sounds meant. Her inconsistent stories about various things engendered grave doubts about her ability to explain honestly and sensitively to Baby M—and at the right time—the nature of her origin. Although faith in professional counseling is not a *sine qua non* of parenting, several experts believed that Mrs. Whitehead's contempt for professional help, especially professional psychological help, coincided with her feelings of omnipotence in a way that could be devastating to a child who most likely will need such help. In short, while love and affection there would be, Baby M's life with the Whiteheads promised to be too closely controlled by Mrs. Whitehead. The prospects for wholesome, independent psychological growth and development would be at serious risk.

The Sterns have no other children, but all indications are that their household and their personalities promise a much more likely foundation for Melissa to grow and thrive. There *is* a track record of sorts—during the one-and-a-half years of custody Baby M has done very well, and the relationship between both Mr. and Mrs. Stern and the baby has become very strong. The household is stable, and likely to remain so. Their finances are more than adequate, their circle of friends supportive, and their marriage happy. Most important, they are loving, giving, nurturing, and open-minded people. They have demonstrated the wish and ability to nurture and protect Melissa, yet at the same time to encourage her independence. Their lack of experience is more than made up for by a willingness to learn and to listen, a willingness that is enhanced by their professional training, especially Mrs. Stern's experience as a pediatrician. They are honest; they can recognize error, deal with it, and learn from it. They will try to determine rationally the best way to cope with problems in their relationship with Melissa. When the time comes to tell her about her origins, they will probably have found a means of doing so that accords with the best interests of Baby M. All in all, Melissa's future appears solid, happy, and promising with them.

Based on all of this we have concluded, independent of the trial court's identical conclusion, that Melissa's best interests call for custody in the Sterns. Our above-mentioned disagreements with the trial court do not, as we have noted, in any way diminish our concurrence with its conclusions. We feel, however, that those disagreements are important enough to be stated. They are disagreements about the evaluation of conduct. They also may provide some insight about the potential consequences of surrogacy.

It seems to us that given her predicament, Mrs. Whitehead was rather harshly judged—both by the trial court and by some of the experts. She was guilty of a breach of contract, and indeed, she did break a very important promise, but we think it is expecting something well beyond normal human capabilities to suggest that this mother should have parted with her newly born infant without a struggle. Other than survival, what stronger force is there? We do not know of, and cannot conceive of, any other case where a perfectly fit mother was expected to surrender her newly born infant, perhaps forever, and was then told she was a bad mother because she did not. We know of no authority suggesting that the moral quality of her act in those circumstances should be judged by referring to a contract made before she became pregnant. We do not countenance, and would never countenance, violating a court order as Mrs. Whitehead did, even a court order that is wrong; but her resistance to an order that she surrender her infant, possibly forever, merits a measure of understanding. We do not find it so clear that her efforts to keep her infant, when measured against the Sterns' efforts to take her away, make one, rather than the other, the wrongdoer. The Sterns suffered, but so did she. And if we go beyond suffering to an evaluation of the human stakes involved in the struggle, how much weight should be given to her nine months of pregnancy, the labor of childbirth, the risk to her life, compared to the payment of money, the anticipation of a child and the donation of sperm? . . .

VI.

VISITATION

The trial court's decision to terminate Mrs. Whitehead's parental rights precluded it from making any determination on visitation. * * * Our reversal of the trial court's order, however, requires delineation of Mrs. Whitehead's rights to visitation. It is apparent to us that this factually sensitive issue, which was never addressed below, should not be determined *de novo* by this Court. We therefore remand the visitation issue to the trial court for an abbreviated hearing and determination . . . In all of this, the trial court should recall the touchstones of visitation: that it is desirable for the child to have contact with both parents; that besides the child's interests, the parents' interests also must be considered; but that when all is said and done, the best interests of the child are paramount. . . .

CONCLUSION

This case affords some insight into a new reproductive arrangement: the artificial insemination of a surrogate mother. The unfortunate events that have unfolded illustrate that its unregulated use can bring suffering to all involved. Potential victims include the surrogate mother and her family, the natural father and his wife, and most importantly, the child. Although surrogacy has apparently provided positive results for some infertile couples, it can also, as this case demonstrates, cause suffering to participants, here essentially innocent and well-intended.

We have found that our present laws do not permit the surrogacy contract used in this case. Nowhere, however, do we find any legal prohibition against surrogacy when the surrogate mother volunteers, without any payment, to act as a surrogate and is given the right to change her mind and to assert her parental rights. Moreover, the Legislature remains free to deal with this most sensitive issue as it sees fit, subject only to constitutional constraints.

If the Legislature decides to address surrogacy, consideration of this case will highlight many of its potential harms. We do not underestimate the difficulties of legislating on this subject. In addition to the inevitable confrontation with the ethical and moral issues involved, there is the question of the wisdom and effectiveness of regulating a matter so private, yet of such public interest. Legislative consideration of surrogacy may also provide the opportunity to begin to focus on the overall implications of the new reproductive biotechnology—*in vitro* fortilization, preservation of sperm and eggs, embryo implantation and the like. The problem is how to enjoy the benefits of the technology—especially for infertile couples—while minimizing the risk of abuse. The problem can be addressed only when society decides what its values and objectives are in this troubling, yet promising, area.

The judgment is affirmed in part, reversed in part, and remanded for further proceedings consistent with this opinion.

NOTES

1. Contracts that contemplate performance of an illegal act are an easy case of contracts that should be void because they are against the public policy of the state. But courts have broad power to find other contracts void for public policy. Nonetheless, most hesitate to do so. More usual is a common law court first requiring a statute or other authoritative legal directive that explicitly supports a finding that a feature of a contract would violate public policy. Consider how this makes public policy arguments jurisdiction-dependent.

2. Surrogacy is treated very differently in different U.S. states, not to mention across the world. In many cases, the legislatures have dealt with the issues; in others, courts must act without legislative guidance:

In approximately one-third of the [U.S.] states, legislatures have enacted statutes addressing surrogacy, the majority of which fall into one of three categories. First, some states have legislatively prohibited all surrogacy contracts, declaring their terms unenforceable and, in some instances, imposing criminal penalties for those who attempt to enter into or assist in creating such a contract. See, e.g., D.C.Code §§ 16–401(4)(A)–(B),–402(a) . . . ; Mich. Comp. Laws Ann. §§ 722.851–.863 . . . . A second category of states prohibit only certain types of surrogacy contracts—typically those involving a traditional surrogacy [in which the woman who carries the fetus provides her own egg]. See, e.g., Ky.Rev.Stat. Ann. § 199.590(4) . . . ; N.D. Cent.Code §§ 14–18–05, –08 . . . Finally, states in the third category authorize both traditional and gestational surrogacy [the latter in which the surrogate carries the fetus but does not provide the egg] contracts, subject to regulation and specified limitations. See, e.g., N.H.Rev.Stat. Ann. §§ 168–B:1 to –B:32 (. . . subject to certain conditions, including a traditional surrogate's right to revoke the agreement within seventy-two hours of birth); Va.Code Ann. §§ 20–156 to 20–165 (. . . providing a multi-step process for judicial pre-approval of such contracts); Wash. Rev.Code Ann. §§ 26.26.210–.260 (. . . prohibiting compensation beyond reasonable expenses and agreements involving a surrogate who is "an unemancipated minor female or a female diagnosed as having an intellectual disability, a mental illness, or developmental disability").: *In re Baby*, 447 S.W.3d 807, 819–20 (Tenn. 2014).

3. Consider how the result in *Baby M* might impact on various nontraditional families, including same-sex couples, whose right to marry, for example, is now constitutionally guaranteed: *Obergefell v. Hodges*, 576 U.S. ___ (2015). For a survey of developments, see J. Herbie Difonzo & Ruth C. Stern, *The Children of Baby M.*, 39 Cap. U. L. Rev. 345, 411 (2011) (suggesting that the ruling is outdated). Consider too, that the cultural attitudes towards childbearing change over time: and that the greater the social and personal value placed on being a parent, the greater the stigma and blow of childlessness might be: see further Carol Sanger, *Developing Markets in Babymaking: In the matter of Baby M,* in CONTRACTS STORIES 127, 134 (D. Baird ed., 2007).

4. Think about the role that the intermediaries played in setting up the surrogacy arrangement between Mary Beth Whitehead and the Sterns. Sanger, mentioned in note 2, suggests that the public policy objections in *Baby M* are really directed at the brokers. Do you agree?

5. This final topic allows us to return to the basis of contracts and ask why our legal system enforces them. Think about the selection of cases and doctrine in this book. Do you find (1) consent to be the most convincing basis, along with (2) free will and the liberty to bind oneself? What does *Baby M* add to that justification?

Consider other bases, such as (3) the promise as a morally binding act; (4) the reliance formed by the promisee; (5) the economic functions of a liberal capitalist society; or (6) the goal of efficiency. What about (7) the relationship

between (or among) the parties, or (8) broader relations with the community, or (9) the allocation of risks more generally? Do these bases complement each other? Are they in tension?

Now that you have an overview of contracts (and possibly, after this semester, the private law subjects of torts and property, and perhaps also the public law subject of constitutional law), how would you rank these bases, as a reflection of contract law? Or do you find, conversely, that the operation of contract law in discrete areas—employment agreements, consumer credit, consumer sales, house purchases, construction agreements, insurance agreements, shipping contracts, government contracts, donative promises, matrimonial agreements, surrogacy arrangements—is too diverse to represent any single basis?

INDEX

References are to Pages